A GUIDE TO FORENSIC
DNA PROFILING

A GUIDE TO FORENSIC
DNA PROFILING

Editors

Allan Jamieson
Scott Bader

The Forensic Institute, Glasgow, UK

WILEY

Library of Congress Cataloging-in-Publication Data

Names: Jamieson, Allan, editor. | Bader, Scott, editor.
Title: A guide to forensic DNA profiling / edited by Allan Jamieson, Scott
    Bader.
Description: Hoboken : Wiley, 2016. | Includes bibliographical references and
    index.
Identifiers: LCCN 2015040516 (print) | LCCN 2015040674 (ebook) | ISBN
    9781118751527 (hardback) | ISBN 9781118751503 (pdf) | ISBN 9781118751510
    (epub)
Subjects: LCSH: DNA fingerprinting.
Classification: LCC RA1057.55.G85 2016 (print) | LCC RA1057.55 (ebook) | DDC
    614/.1–dc23
LC record available at http://lccn.loc.gov/2015040516

A catalogue record for this book is available from the British Library.

Cover Image: Bart Sadowski/Getty

Typeset in 9.5/11.5 pt Times by SPi Global, Chennai, India
Printed and bound in Singapore by Markono Print Media Pte Ltd.

This book is printed on acid-free paper responsibly manufactured from sustainable forestry, in which as least two
trees are planted for each one used for paper production.

Contents

Contributors

Jeppe D. Andersen *University of Copenhagen, Copenhagen, Denmark*
Chapter 25: Single Nucleotide Polymorphism

Scott Bader *The Forensic Institute, Glasgow, UK*
Chapter 1: Introduction to Forensic Genetics

Jack Ballantyne *University of Central Florida and National Center for Forensic Science, Orlando, FL, USA*
Chapter 18: Y-Chromosome Short Tandem Repeats

Claus Børsting *University of Copenhagen, Copenhagen, Denmark*
Chapter 25: Single Nucleotide Polymorphism

John S. Buckleton *Institute of Environmental Science and Research Ltd., Auckland, New Zealand*
Chapter 33: DNA Databases and Evidentiary Issues

Bruce Budowle *University of North Texas Health Science Center, Fort Worth, TX, USA*
Chapter 30: Microbial Forensics

Christophe Champod *University of Lausanne, Institut de Police Scientifique, Lausanne, Switzerland*
Chapter 7: Identification and Individualization

Michael D. Coble *The Armed Forces DNA Identification Laboratory, Rockville, MD, USA*
Chapter 26: Mini-STRs

Christopher A. Flood *Federal Defenders of New York, Inc., New York, NY, USA*
Chapter 42: Legal Issues with Forensic DNA in the USA

Tony Frudakis *DNAPrint Genomics, Inc., Sarasota, FL, USA*
Chapter 27: Phenotype

Jason R. Gilder *Forensic Bioinformatics, Fairborn, OH, USA*
Chapter 16: Degraded Samples

Peter Gill *Norwegian Institute of Public Health, Oslo, Norway*
University of Oslo, Oslo, Norway
Chapter 19: Expert Systems in DNA Interpretation

Eleanor Alison May Graham	*Northumbria University, Newcastle upon Tyne, UK* Chapter 2: DNA: An Overview
Peter R. Gunn	*University of Technology Sydney, Broadway, New South Wales, Australia* Chapter 5: Biological Stains
Hinda Haned	*Netherlands Forensic Institute, The Hague, The Netherlands* Chapter 19: Expert Systems in DNA Interpretation
Erin K. Hanson	*University of Central Florida and National Center for Forensic Science, Orlando, FL, USA* Chapter 18: Y-Chromosome Short Tandem Repeats
Sally-Ann Harbison	*Institute of Environmental Science and Research Ltd., Auckland, New Zealand* Chapter 6: Sources of DNA
Hiroshi Ikegaya	*Kyoto Prefectural University of Medicine, Kyoto, Japan* Chapter 29: Geographical Identification by Viral Genotyping
Allan Jamieson	*The Forensic Institute, Glasgow, UK* Chapter 4: Introduction to Forensic DNA Profiling – The Electropherogram (epg) Chapter 9: Laboratory Accreditation Chapter 14: Interpretation of Mixtures; Graphical Chapter 43: Issues in Forensic DNA Chapter 44: Future Technologies and Challenges
Rebecca S. Just	*The Armed Forces DNA Identification Laboratory, Rockville, MD, USA* Chapter 26: Mini-STRs
Yoshinao Katsumata	*National Institute of Police Science, Tokyo, Japan* *Nagoya Isen, Nagoya, Japan* Chapter 29: Geographical Identification by Viral Genotyping
Jonathan J. Koehler	*Northwestern University School of Law, Chicago, IL, USA* Chapter 34: Communicating Probabilistic Forensic Evidence in Court
Dan E. Krane	*Wright State University, Dayton, OH, USA* Chapter 15: DNA Mixture Interpretation
Georgina E. Meakin	*University College London, London, UK* Chapter 8: Transfer
Ronald Meester	*VU University Amsterdam, Amsterdam, The Netherlands* Chapter 24: Familial Searching Chapter 32: DNA Databases – The Significance of Unique Hits and the Database Controversy

Terry Melton

Mitotyping Technologies, State College, PA, USA
Chapter 28: Mitochondrial DNA: Profiling

Andre A. Moenssens

University of Missouri at Kansas City, Kansas City, MO, USA
University of Richmond, Richmond, VA, USA
Chapter 37: Ethical Rules of Expert Behavior
Chapter 39: Direct Examination of Experts
Chapter 40: Cross-Examination of Experts

Niels Morling

University of Copenhagen, Copenhagen, Denmark
Chapter 25: Single Nucleotide Polymorphism

Robert I. O'Brien

National Forensic Science Technology Center (NFSTC), Largo, FL, USA
Chapter 12: Quantitation

Vania Pereira

University of Copenhagen, Copenhagen, Denmark
Chapter 25: Single Nucleotide Polymorphism

Burkhard Rolf

Eurofins Medigenomix Forensik GmbH, Ebersberg, Germany
Chapter 20: Paternity Testing

Campbell A. Ruddock

Oklahoma City Police Department, Forensic DNA unit, Oklahoma City, OK, USA
Chapter 10: Validation
Chapter 11: Extraction
Chapter 13: Amplification

Pekka J. Saukko

University of Turku, Turku, Finland
Chapter 29: Geographical Identification by Viral Genotyping

Klaas Slooten

VU University Amsterdam, Amsterdam, The Netherlands
Netherlands Forensic Institute, The Hague, The Netherlands
Chapter 24: Familial Searching

Takehiko Takatori

National Institute of Police Science, Tokyo, Japan
Chapter 29: Geographical Identification by Viral Genotyping

William C. Thompson

University of California, Irvine, CA, USA
Chapter 21: Observer Effects

Simon J. Walsh

Australian Federal Police, Canberra, ACT, Australia
Chapter 3: DNA
Chapter 17: Ceiling Principle: DNA
Chapter 22: Databases
Chapter 33: DNA Databases and Evidentiary Issues

Tony Ward

University of Hull, Hull, UK
Chapter 38: Verbal Scales: A Legal Perspective

Lucy M.I. Webster

Science and Advice for Scottish Agriculture, Edinburgh, UK
Chapter 31: Wildlife Crime

Bruce S. Weir

University of Washington, Seattle, WA, USA
Chapter 23: Missing Persons and Paternity: DNA

Rhonda M. Wheate

The Forensic Institute, Glasgow, UK
Chapter 35: Report Writing for Courts
Chapter 36: Discovery of Expert Findings
Chapter 41: DNA in the UK Courts

Peter Wiegand

University Hospital of Ulm, Ulm, Germany
Chapter 20: Paternity Testing

Phillip C. Williamson

University of North Texas Health Science Center, Fort Worth, TX, USA
Chapter 30: Microbial Forensics

Foreword

My contact with Professor Jamieson and Dr Bader (or Allan and Scott as I now know them and shall refer to them) began in the seminal trial of Sean Hoey (in relation to the Omagh Bombing) in Northern Ireland in 2007. This was the first serious challenge in the United Kingdom to the use of low copy number (LCN) DNA profiling, the first form of what has become more generally known as low template DNA profiling. Although Mr Hoey was primarily acquitted as a result of reservations surrounding the way in which key exhibits were seized, stored, and examined, the learned trial judge, the Honorable Mr Justice Weir, raised concerns in relation to the reliability of interpreting LCN DNA. Such concerns were no doubt borne out of the points we advanced on behalf of Mr Hoey, which were in turn borne out of the concerns of those from The Forensic Institute. From the outset, The Forensic Institute expressed the strongest of reservations as to the reliability of interpreting such minute amounts of DNA found on the relevant exhibits (none of which were from the Omagh incident as it happens).

These concerns caused a seismic response in scientific and legal circles, which continues to this day. Toward the end of 2014, I had the pleasure of working with Allan and Scott in a murder trial at the Old Bailey. They were instructed on behalf of the defense to comment upon the reliability and interpretability of low template DNA recovered from a murder scene. In this recent case, part of the argument focused upon the reliability of the methods employed by the prosecution to quantify the probative value of such low amounts of DNA. One of the methods employed involved the use of software, which was said to overcome the complex nature of the results; another was the "counting method." Following the cross-examination of one of the prosecution's lead forensic scientists the Crown withdrew the DNA evidence in the case.

There is no doubt that for lawyers, DNA profiling can present a daunting challenge. This is not only in understanding the science involved, but also in knowing how best to present the results in a way that can be easily understood. I am indebted to Allan and Scott for guiding our legal teams through the morass of graphs, statistics, and terminology, enabling us to be able to properly represent our clients on the most serious of allegations. I am optimistic that the clarity of their approach and the appreciation of the needs of the non-specialist will be reflected in the content of this book.

I am also delighted to learn that this will be one of the few books that brings together the scientific and legal aspects of DNA profiling in such a comprehensive approach. That is not an easy task; but I know that the Editors had assistance from Professor Andre Moenssens of the *Wiley Encyclopedia of Forensic Science* where many of the articles in this book originate.

Needless to say I write this having not read all of the articles in this work, but I am confident that if the skills I have taken advantage of in our casework are taken into the production of this work then it will provide a valuable resource for both lawyers and experts alike in the continuing quest to tackle the increasingly complex issues involved in forensic DNA profiling.

A lawyer writing a preface for a book written by scientists? Progress indeed.

Kieran Vaughan QC
Garden Court Chambers

Preface

Forensic DNA profiling has revolutionized forensic science. However, from relatively simple beginnings using what would now be regarded as huge amounts of sample (e.g., bloodstain), not only has the underlying technology changed (i.e., RFLP to STRs and SNPs) but the complexity of the interpretation of the analytical results has increased in the quest to get more information from smaller, and more complex, samples.

Most of these developments are published and debated in the scientific literature, although some are guarded for ostensibly commercial reasons, or sometimes it seems simply to avoid showing one's hand to the other side in an adversarial legal system. Much of the scientific and statistical debate remains active and there is no settled position. Indeed, it could be contended that in many of these arguments each side has a rational and reasoned position, simply different to their opponents.

This book does not seek to provide or claim to have the final answer on any of these, because for many issues there is none. In recognition of the state of flux within parts of the discipline we have not sought to provide only our view, or indeed the view of any author, as the final word and, therefore, no article can be taken to represent the view of anyone other than the authors of the article at the time of writing. Views in some articles may contradict views in others; that is a reflection of the state of the art and is common in science.

Although some articles in this work were created specifically with this book in mind, the vast majority of articles are from the *Wiley Encyclopedia of Forensic Science*.[1] The consequence of this is that there is inevitably some duplication of information. However, because we intend that each article can stand alone, we consider that such duplication, as exists, simply adds to the utility of the book.

Forensic science operates, by definition, within a legal context. This creates several problems in creating a volume like this one. Different jurisdictions may have different legal requirements of the expert, and even the experts may have local practices that differ from other localities nationally or internationally. Even within the United States and United Kingdom, depending on the level of court, there are widely differing expectations and standards for the admissibility of scientific evidence (e.g., Frye, Daubert, or none). We cannot expect to cover all of the variances and so the articles, other than where specifically addressing jurisdictional issues, should be taken as informing on the generality of practices.

The dichotomy between legal and scientific standards is perhaps best illustrated in the NAS report of 2009;

> "The bottom line is simple: In a number of forensic science disciplines, forensic science professionals have yet to establish either the validity of their approach or the accuracy of their conclusions, and the courts have been utterly ineffective in addressing this problem. For a variety of reasons – including the rules governing the admissibility of forensic evidence, the applicable standards governing appellate review of trial court decisions, the limitations of the adversary process, and the common lack of scientific expertise among judges and lawyers who must try to comprehend and evaluate forensic evidence – the legal system is ill-equipped to correct the problems of the forensic science community."

For those reasons, and others (e.g., availability of other evidence), we would caution (as have others) against using any court decision as validation or invalidation of any scientific test. It is not unknown for different courts

---

[1] www.wileyonlinelibrary.com/ref/efs

within the same jurisdiction to rule both ways on the same science; for example, the use of low template DNA in New York City.

Thus, this volume sets out to provide a comprehensive introduction to the scientific, statistical, and legal issues within the context of forensic DNA profiling. The rate of development of the field is so great that almost any publication will be out of date within a very short time. However, the information provided here will provide a solid foundation from which future developments can be understood and evaluated.

Allan Jamieson
Scott Bader
July 2015

Glossary

accreditation	recognition of procedural management at an institution
allele	one of alternative forms of a genetic marker, component/DNA type
amplification	increase in amount of sample DNA created by PCR process
amylase	enzyme of saliva, and to lesser extent some other body fluids
AP	Acid Phosphatase, detected by presumptive test for seminal fluid
base pair	building block unit of DNA
baseline	the experimental zero value on the x-axis of analytical results
bin	part of the epg showing known allelic sizes
body fluid	usually refers to any biological material from which DNA can be obtained
buccal	derived from mouth cavity
cell	smallest living structure of biological organism
chromosome	structure containing DNA including many genes, inherited as a single unit from cell to cell and generation to generation
coancestry coefficient	a measure of the relatedness of two people
Daubert	legal standard for admissibility of expert evidence in some US states
degraded DNA	partially destroyed DNA, usually indicated by lower or absent amounts of longer DNA components
diploid	possessing two alleles at each locus
drop-in	appearance of DNA component in a profile due to background contamination
drop-out	disappearance of DNA component from a profile due to random sampling of low level quantity
electrophoresis	movement of chemical through a matrix under the force of electrical field

extraction	(in DNA casework) the removal of DNA from cells
Frye	legal standard for admissibility of expert evidence in some US states
genotype	genetic composition of an individual comprising both alleles at each/all loci
haploid	possessing only one allele at each locus
haplotype	genetic composition of an individual comprising one allele at each/all loci, linked together as a inherited group
hemizygous	only one allele component present at a locus
heterozygous	two alleles at one locus are different types
homozygous	two alleles at one locus are the same type
HWE	Hardy Weinberg Equilibrium, stable frequency of alleles
ISO17025	accreditation for the general requirements for the competence to carry out tests and/or calibrations, including sampling
ladder	(allelic) quality control sample containing alleles of known size and run separately to other samples
locus/loci (pl.)	specific location/entity of DNA (marker or gene) on a chromosome, area of DNA tested in profile
low copy number (LCN)	very low amount (of DNA) in sample; specifically also the increased amplification cycle number used for PCR method
low template	very low amount (of DNA) in sample
micro	one millionth, 10^{-6}
milli	one thousandth, 10^{-3}
mitochondrion	intracellular structure containing mitochondrial DNA
mixture	more than one contributor (DNA profiling)
multiplex	chemistry analysing many loci
mutation	alteration in genetic component
nano	one thousand millionth, 10^{-9}
nucleus	intracellular structure containing nuclear DNA (used in standard DNA profiling)
odds	number of favourable outcomes/number of unfavourable outcomes

partial profile	one in which all of the components do not appear
Phadebas	presumptive test for saliva, detects amylase activity
phenotype	expressed/observed biological characteristic controlled by combination of alleles in genotype
pico	one million millionth, 10^{-12}
polygenic	controlled by several genes
polymerase	chemical that creates the amplification of DNA by PCR
polymorphic	many forms
population	in statistics, any set of items under study
presumptive	suggestive, not definitive
primer	chemical that binds to specific site (locus) of sample DNA to enable amplification in PCR
probability	number of favourable outcomes/number of possible unfavourable outcomes
pull-up	artifact seen in another part of DNA profile due to presence of a DNA component in one part of the profile
quantitation	measurement of the amount of a sample
rfu	relative fluorescence unit, measurement of peak height in an electropherogram
saliva	body fluid produced by salivary glands in mouth, containing salivary amylase
semen	body fluid produced by male ejaculation, including seminal fluid and sperm cells
seminal fluid	nutrient body fluid secreted by prostate gland of males for transmission of sperm cells in ejaculate
sensitivity	(a) a measure of how small an amount of material a technique can detect (b) the effect on the signal or measurement of a change in an input ability to detect and measure a sample
specificity	ability to discriminate an individual component of a sample
sperm	male sexual cell present in semen, produced by testes, carrying haplotype of individual
stochastic	effect due to random variation caused by sampling of low level sample
stochastic threshold	approximate level at which random sampling effects can be expected

stutter   artifact seen in DNA profile as smaller peak adjacent to main peak of real DNA component

validation   evidence of compliance/efficacy for a process being fit for purpose, with demonstration of capabilities and limits

x-axis   the horizontal axis of a graph

y-axis   the vertical axis of a graph

Abbreviations and Acronyms

A	adenine
AAFS	American Academy of Forensic Sciences
ABC	American Board of Criminalistics
ABI	Applied Biosystems
ACPO	Association of Chief Police Officers
ADO	allele dropout
AIMs	ancestry informative markers
AP	acid phosphatase
APA	American Psychological Association
ASCLD/LAB	American Society of Crime Laboratory Directors/Laboratory Accreditation Board
BKV	BK virus
bps	base pairs
C	cytosine
CCD	charged coupled device
CE	capillary electrophoresis
CF	cystic fibrosis
CODIS	Combined Offender DNA Index System
CPI	Combined Paternity Index
CPI	combined probability of inclusion
CZE	capillary zone electrophoresis
DAB	DNA Advisory Board
ds	double-stranded
DTT	dithiothreitol
EBV	Epstein–Barr virus
EDNAP	European DNA Profiling Group
emPCR	emulsion PCR
ENFSI	European Network of Forensic Science Institutes
EPG	electropherogram
ESS	European Standard Set
EVC	externally visible characteristics
FBI	Federal Bureau of Investigation
FSS	forensic science service
G	guanine
Hb	heterozygote balance ratio
HBV	hepatitis B virus
HHV-1	human herpes virus type 1
HIV-1	human immunodeficiency virus type 1
HLA	human leukocyte antigen
HPHR	heterozygous peak height ratio

HPLC	high-performance liquid chromatography
HPV	human papillomavirus
HV	hypervariable
HWE	Hardy Weinberg Equilibrium
IAI	International Association for Identification
IBD	identical-by-descent
IISNP	individual identification SNP
indel	insertion/deletion
ISFG	International Society for Forensic Genetics
ISO	International Standards Organization
JCV	polyomavirus JC
LCN	low copy number
LDO	locus dropout
LMD	laser microdissection
LoCIM	locus classification and inference of the major
LR	likelihood ratio
LT	low-template
LTDNA	low template deoxyribonucleic acid
MALDI/TOF	matrix-assisted laser desorption/ionization time-of-flight
MCMC	Monte Carlo Markov Chain
MDA	multiple displacement amplification
MGF	maternal grandfather
MGM	maternal grandmother
MHC	major histocompatibility complex
MLE	most likely estimate
MLP	multilocus probing
MP	match probability
mRNA	messenger RNA
mtDNA	mitochondrial deoxyribonucleic acid
MW	molecular weight
NAS	National Academy of Science (USA)
NCIDD	National Criminal identification DNA Database
NDIS	National DNA Index System
NDNAD	National DNA Database
NFI	Netherlands Forensic Institute
NGS	next-generation sequencing
NOAA	National Oceanic and Atmospheric Administration
NRC	National Research Council
nuDNA	nuclear deoxyribonucleic acid
OCME	Office of the Chief Medical Examiner
PCR	polymerase chain reaction
PE	probability of exclusion
PGF	paternal grandfather
PGM	paternal grandmother
PHR	peak height ratio
PHT	peak-height threshold
PML	progressive multifocal leukoencephalopathy
PoD	probability of detection
POI	person of interest
PSA	prostate-specific antigen

QA/QC	quality assurance and quality control
QAS	quality assurance standard
rCRS	revised Cambridge Reference Sequence
RFID	radio frequency identification
RFLP	restriction fragment length polymorphism
RFU	relative fluorescence unit
RHC	red hair color
RMNE	random man not excluded
RMP	random match probability
SBE	single-base extension
SDIS	State DNA Identification System
SDS	sodium dodecyl sulfate
SFGR	spotted fever group Rickettsia
SGM	second generation multiplex
SLP	single locus probes
SNP	single nucleotide polymorphism
SOP	standard operating protocol
SSM	slipped strand mispairing
STR	short tandem repeat
SWG	scientific working group
SWGDAM	scientific working group for DNA analysis methods
T	thymine
UV	ultraviolet
VNTR	variable number of tandem repeat
WGA	whole genome amplification
WTC	World Trade Center
YHRD	Y chromosome haplotype reference database

PART A
Background

Chapter 1
Introduction to Forensic Genetics

Scott Bader

The Forensic Institute, Glasgow, UK

The Ideal Forensic Material – Individualization

Forensic genetics has been touted as the gold standard of forensic analysis. This is because DNA fulfils many of the criteria that make the perfect forensic technology to establish a person's presence at a scene of crime.

Most forensic disciplines concerned with offences against the person, and some other crimes, try to establish a link between items found at the scene and items found on or associated with a suspect. In other words, to establish whether the recovered items could have originated from the same source. This process can be summarized as

1. Establishing a match
2. Calculating the significance of the match

The perfect conclusion of this exercise is to unequivocally establish that the material from the crime scene could only have come from exactly the same source as that found on or associated with the suspect and no other source. The goal of most forensic matching is to reduce the potential population from which an item could have come, to one individual within the population. This extreme is the definition of identification. The process that we are more interested in, because of its more common application, is that of *individualization*. This is the process of individualization. Individualization is a population problem as it is necessary to be able to demonstrate how many people in a population may have the match characteristics discovered by the investigator. Therefore, modern scientific individualization techniques recognize that most, if not

all, evidence is probabilistic, which is to say that we attempt to establish a *probability* or likelihood that two items had a common origin. The ideal forensic material must enable matching and probability calculations.

There are other qualities that a forensically useful material should have. *Ideally*, the material should be

1. Unique
2. Not change over time (i.e., during normal use)
3. Likely to be left at a scene in sufficient quantity to establish a match
4. Not change after being left at the scene and during subsequent examination

In this book, we shall see that DNA meets many, but not all, of these criteria and how the limitations are handled.

So what makes DNA a good material forensically?

DNA – The Molecule

DNA is sometimes called the *blueprint of life* and has characteristics that are appropriate to its role. Many, if not all, of these characteristics are important in Forensic Genetics, which is simply genetics in a legal context. These characteristics include its simplicity and yet complexity, both of which are incorporated within the polymeric chemical structure of the backbone molecule and the varied sequence of sidechain bases (the so-called letters of its information content), arranged in a double helix (*see DNA: An Overview*). The molecule is made from a relatively small number of building blocks yet contains a vast amount and range of information that can define the nature of the biological cell, and ultimately the multicellular organism,

A Guide to Forensic DNA Profiling
Edited by Allan Jamieson and Scott Bader
© 2016 John Wiley & Sons, Ltd. ISBN: 9781118751527

within which the DNA is located. The double helix structure is relatively stable in time yet is adaptable enough to "open up" to allow a living cell to use the contained information to go about its life functions (*transcription*) or to make copies of itself (*replication*). DNA is stable so as to enable transfer of the genetic information from generation to generation after replication (with cell division and mating where relevant), yet it can also change to varying extents. Some of the changes are important to only an individual organism and may be deleterious (e.g., mutation giving rise to a cancer), or are the basis for individual variation (e.g., mutation giving rise to a new variant, and the haploid segregation of chromosomes in gametes with the return of diploid pairing at fertilization to produce a new individual). Some changes affect a subpopulation (e.g., lineages) and even eventually an entire population (e.g., natural selection of mutations and new diploid combinations leading to evolutionary change).

The chapter on *DNA* describes some fundamental concepts about DNA and genetics. In summary, the genetic material of humans comprises about 3 billion nucleotides or building blocks, and is present in two copies per cell, so about 6 billion in total. This DNA is found within the nucleus of all cells other than red blood cells, in total it is called the *genome* and contains the genes that encode the proteins created by the cell to define the cell's type and characteristics and ultimately the entire organism of the human individual. It also contains other DNA sequences that are regulatory (i.e., affect the temporal or quantitative expression of the genes), structural (i.e., affect intracellular packaging and stability of DNA), or are as yet of unknown function or may even be foreign to a normal human cell (e.g., a viral infection). All of these elements are contained within 23 separate lengths of DNA, the chromosomes.

The concept that DNA contains the information for biological life using a genetic code encoded within the sequence of bases along the double helix molecule means that if we as forensic scientists can "read" that code we can question and determine the source of a given sample of DNA. The general DNA structure and constituents are the same so that with the right analytical toolkits, we are able to answer that question. So, we could test not only whether the DNA is from a human, horse, cannabis plant, or soil microbe, but in theory identify the individual human. Scientists are able to take advantage of the "adaptable stability" of

DNA and mimic the process of replication so as to make multiple copies of a DNA sample, using the polymerase chain reaction (PCR, see method). The amplified DNA is then processed and the data interpreted accordingly.

DNA in Populations

The first main concept to elaborate upon is that of Mendelian genetics (*see* Mendel mentioned in *DNA*). For a simple biological example, I will use the ABO blood group system. Here, there is a single gene involved that defines a person's blood group. The gene controls the production of a chemical on the surface of blood cells. The gene exists within the human population in one of three forms or variants: *A*, *B*, and *O*, and when referring to the gene, it is written italicized. The existence of variable forms within the population is called a *polymorphism*, and these genetic variants are known scientifically as *alleles*. They control the production of a protein that exists, respectively, as either protein variant A, variant B, or is not produced (i.e., absent) and thus called O (for null).

In any individual, the genes that encode everything that eventually produces a human being are present in two copies (not including the X and Y chromosomes), one inherited from mother and one inherited from father. It is the combination of the two copies of all the genes that will determine the final characteristics of the individual. So, while there might be just the one gene for the blood cell protein described above, there will be two copies of the gene in each person. All of the possible genetic combinations seen in different individuals are therefore *AA, BB, OO, AB, AO, BO*, and where the variants are the same, the person is called *homozygous*, where they are different, the person is called *heterozygous*. Going back to the description of the proteins that would be produced from the genetic variants, they are as follows in the table:

Gene variants	Protein variants	Blood group
AA	A only	A
BB	B only	B
OO	Nothing	O
AB	A and B	AB
AO	A only	A
BO	B only	B

The combination of gene variants possible in any human are called the *genotypes* (first column) and the final observed biological characteristics (in this instance the blood group) are called the *phenotypes*. By way of illustrating the difference – the genotypes AO and AA both have the phenotype A because only A is actually observed in blood group testing; the O is "silent." When both variants in an individual are the same, the genotype is called *homozygous*, and when different *heterozygous*.

In this example, the gene variants *A* and *B* are what is termed *codominant*, in that they are both observable in the phenotype. The *O* gene variant is termed *recessive*, in that when it is present with something else, the something else takes precedence and is the only characteristic observable. Here, the "recessiveness" is simply because *O* produces nothing, whereas *A* and *B* produce A and B proteins. Note that while we can determine the blood group phenotype of a person from his or her genotype, going in the other direction is not so simple. So, a person of blood group B, for example, may be either *BB* or *BO* genotype. Knowing the frequency of the different variants present in the population allows us to predict the percentage chance that a blood group B person has either *BB* or *BO* genotype.

As we now analyze at the DNA level, we do not need to study actual biological traits (although these are under development also, *see* **Phenotype**) like the ABO blood group, and can analyze highly polymorphic nongene sequences (*see* **DNA**; **DNA: An Overview**). This has the advantage of comprising a much larger proportion of the genome from which to select for analysis, and showing much greater variability. This greater variability leads to greater individualization such that we can identify a sample as coming from a very small handful of people if not an individual, as opposed to the large sections of the population using previous technology. So, modern DNA profiling kits use multiplex PCR methods to analyze several STR areas (called *loci*) at the same time. In the United Kingdom, in recent years until 2014, there was a standard kit called *AmpFlSTR SGM Plus* used to analyze 10 loci as well as the sex-determining region, but this has now been superseded by use of one of several kits (collectively called *DNA17*) covering the European standard 17 loci. The United States uses a set of 13 loci for criminal justice purposes, the Combined DNA Index System (CODIS), marketed and tested in two main commercial kits (*AmpFlSTR Identifiler* and *PowerPlex 16*). For paternity or kinship testing purposes (*see* **Missing Persons and Paternity: DNA**), data from these loci are supplemented by other kits (STR or single nucleotide polymorphisms (SNPs)) covering even more than the core sets used in criminal justice systems.

The Scientific Expert

This is a time of increasing stringency in the requirements of experts to establish the reliability of the techniques that they use as well as their authority in the use of those. Many systems have been and are being developed that aim to assist the court in assessing such claims. However, most of these have been by a group of experts in the same field forming themselves into some sort of group and deciding for themselves whether it is expertise, and who they will register or endorse. External validation should be a feature of any such system.

To claim a scientific basis for an expertise, the expert should be able to demonstrate for the technique(s) that they use, as a minimum (*see* **Laboratory Accreditation**; **Validation**):

1. Reliability studies of analytical technique (validation). The scientific approach to this problem is normally to put a sample through the system to see how often the sample produces the same result. This is the *reproducibility* of the technique; its ability to provide consistent results when applied to the same samples.

2. Establishment of false positive and false negative rates.
   Even if the technique is perfect, in many systems, there is not a clear difference in the measurement when it is used to separate two or more groups. A false positive occurs when something that does not have the characteristic being sought is classified as actually having them, whereas a false negative is when something should be placed in a particular class but isn't. Generally, systems are designed to minimize the number of false positives and false negatives. However, in many systems, the two are inextricably linked and as one attempts to minimize one error, the other increases.

3. Defined match criteria.
   This requires a specification for the degree of similarity that two items must have before we declare a

match. The specificity or discriminating power of a technique is, "The ability of an analytical procedure to distinguish between two items of different origin."

4. Probability of any match being a "true" match. Given that all matches are probable matches, this leads to the further requirement to know the probability that the match is to that item or material and no other.

Forensic DNA

DNA is present in many types of biological substance (*see Biological Stains; Sources of DNA*) that can be analyzed by nuclear DNA profiling methods (*see DNA: An Overview*). These substances include body fluids such as blood or semen that can be seen by the naked eye if in sufficient quantity, as well as invisible amounts of the same fluids or of other substances such as skin cells in sweat or fingermarks (*see Sources of DNA*).

The chemical stability of DNA is useful for forensic genetics because it means that the DNA of a biological sample may be analyzed long after it was deposited at a crimescene. This has been very useful, for example, in the re-examination of evidence in cold cases long after storage and with the advent of new analytical methods. If preserved under the right conditions and using the appropriate methods, DNA has even been studied from ancient samples such as Egyptian pharaohs and woolly mammoths. DNA is not stable forever, and again depending on circumstances after deposition at a crimescene and following collection and handling by forensic scientists, it can degrade and affect the ability to get useable results (*see Degraded Samples*).

Wherever possible, the nature of a biological deposit is identified or at least suggested so as to assist the evaluation of the significance of a DNA profile once it has been produced. When a body fluid suspected to be blood, semen, or saliva is present in sufficient amount so as to be visible to the naked eye, the location of the substance to be tested is clear and sampling can proceed. After the stain is located, it is usually subjected to a chemical test to try to determine what sort of stain it may be. These tests usually only suggest, rather than indicate, the presence of a biological type, requiring at least one other test to be done to confirm the result. For example, microscopic examination, of a suspected semen sample by acid phosphatase analysis,

that finds sperm cells thus confirms a sample to be or to contain semen. Often these confirmatory tests are not done, to save on time and expense, and the evidential weight of a sample is left as "probably an X stain using the relevant presumptive test, with a DNA profile matching Mr Y.". When there is little or nothing visible of a biological stain, a search for the possible location of substances must be made.

The recovered biological substance is then chemically processed so as to release whatever DNA is present (*see Extraction*). The procedure of extraction must be able to extract the DNA with minimal loss of sample due to the usually small sample collected, and can be done manually or automated. The extracted and purified DNA is then neither in sufficient quantity nor in a form so as to be studied directly, hence the succeeding stages of quantitation and amplification (*see Quantitation; Amplification*). The quantification step determines how much DNA is present in the sample so that an appropriate amount can be used in the amplification step – sufficient to be analyzed and not so much to overload the system. The amplification step involves a method called *PCR*, and makes multiple copies of the relevant areas of DNA being profiled while "marking" them chemically with markers or labels to enable detection by machine.

The amplified and labeled DNA fragments are at this point in a liquid mixture that must be separated to enable detection and measurement. It is therefore forced by an electrical voltage through a tube containing a molecular sieve or gel, a process called *electrophoresis*. This process separates the pieces of DNA according to size (length) such that smaller pieces pass more quickly through the gel than large ones. As the pieces pass a specific point in the tube, they are illuminated by light of a defined wavelength. This so-called incident or excitatory light causes the chemical labels added to the sample DNA during amplification to release light of a different wavelength, fluorescence. Different areas of DNA profiled have one of a small number of chemical labels so that depending on which fluorescent light is released at what time during electrophoresis, it is possible to know what area of DNA is being detected. The amount of fluorescence detected is used a measure of the amount of DNA passing through and thus representative of the amount of DNA in the original forensic sample. The information is captured as electronic data and analyzed using software to produce a profile (*see Introduction* to Forensic DNA Profiling – The Electropherogram (epg)).

Setting aside some of the difficulties in assessing whether a DNA component is truly present or not, a DNA profile can be matched to another DNA profile with 100% accuracy (interpretation), and with a precision dependent on the number of loci used in the match. The "match criteria" are defined; the numbers must match *exactly*.

Another parameter that may be useful to know when assessing an identification system is the sensitivity. In this context, this means how little of the material from the individual that needs to be available to enable an identification. The technology enables the profiling of the DNA from a single cell, but in forensic genetics, the presence of mixtures and degraded samples can render that ability a vice rather than a virtue (*see Interpretation of Mixtures; Graphical*, *DNA Mixture Interpretation* and *Degraded Samples*).

Many matches today are enabled by the creation of DNA databases that store the DNA profiles of people selected by a process depending on the jurisdictional rules (*see Databases*). However, there are a number of scientific and social issues that arise from the use of these databases (*see DNA Databases – The Significance of Unique Hits and the Database Controversy*; *DNA Databases and Evidentiary Issues*). Other emerging technologies have also caused debate (*see Phenotype*; *Familial Searching*).

Having established the degree to which a match exists between the crime material and the suspect, the forensic scientist must now evaluate the significance of the match (*see Identification and Individualization*; *Communicating Probabilistic Forensic Evidence in Court*). The starting point for all such calculations includes the frequency of the particular components within the population. Those frequencies for the DNA components used in forensic DNA profiling have been measured.

The use to which those frequencies are put varies with the type of profile obtained and the choice of method for calculating the significance of the evidence. This is the increasingly arcane topic of statistics, which has become so complex that some have introduced probabilistic genotyping software because the calculations are claimed to be too complex to be undertaken manually (*see Issues in Forensic DNA*).

An important concept underlying the use of frequencies in forensic work is called the *Hardy–Weinberg*

equilibrium (*HWE*). The HWE is a state in which the allelic frequencies do not change. Its forensic significance is that in the process of calculating the expected frequencies of genotypes in the population, this equilibrium, or steady state, is assumed as a starting basis.

Given that any person will normally have two alleles at each locus (although both may be the same), the allelic frequencies can be used to calculate genotype frequencies (paired combinations of alleles) by multiplication.

In a simple example, if there are only two alleles (*A* or *B*) possible at a locus, then there are only three types of individuals: *AA*, *BB*, and *AB*. If the frequency of allele *A* is *p*, and the frequency of allele *B* is *q*, it is possible to calculate the frequency of each type of person in the population *assuming the Hardy–Weinberg rules*.

These rules are

1. No selection
2. No mutation
3. No migration
4. Random mating
5. An infinitely large population

If these rules are not met, the population is not in equilibrium and the allele frequencies will be changing. There is some debate on how to accommodate this, and other possibilities, into calculating the statistics of the random match probability (RMP) for a profile (*see DNA Mixture Interpretation*). Most commonly a correction factor is incorporated into the calculation for genotype frequencies to allow for population substructures.

One of the HWE rules is "random mating." The alleles exist in pairs within men and women, but the pairs separate in the formation of sperm and egg so, in effect, the next population is a sample of drawing two alleles together, one from the male and one from the female. If *p* and *q* are the frequencies of alleles *A* and *B*, respectively (and *A* and *B* are the only two alleles at that locus), then it is quite simple algebra to calculate the result of one round of "random mating" in a population where the population of parents have the frequencies *p* and *q* for *A* and *B*:

$$(p + q) \times (p + q) = (p + q)^2 = p^2 + 2pq + q^2$$

This gives the frequency of *AA* children as p^2, *AB* children as $2pq$, and *BB* children as q^2.

A table can show the same thing perhaps more easily:

		Fathers	
		p	q
Mothers	p	$p \times p = p^2$	$p \times q = pq$
	q	$p \times q = pq$	$p \times q = q^2$

Thus, an allelic frequency database can be used to calculate an RMP to an individual: the probability that one could pick a person who would have the same genotype (profile) at random from a population of unrelated individuals.

Most professional codes of practice for forensic scientists demand that the scientist is an impartial participant in the legal process. Unfortunately, while science may be impartial in a very restricted sense, it would appear from a considerable body of research that scientists are not. There is an increasing awareness within the forensic community that biases are not only possible but also probable. We merely introduce the topic here (see *Observer Effects*).

Similarly, although routine DNA profiling of human DNA dominates the perception of forensic DNA, there are other techniques using different sources of DNA (see *Mitochondrial DNA: Profiling*; *Wildlife Crime*; *Microbial Forensics*) and different technologies (see *Single Nucleotide Polymorphism*) in addition to the more extreme application of the routine methods (see *Issues in Forensic DNA*).

The legal process may be terminated before a case gets to court, but the forensic scientist is frequently required to provide evidence for use in court. The penultimate chapters are devoted to the use of DNA profiling in court.

Finally, we consider the current debates arising from DNA profiling and consider where the future may lie for this technology that has revolutionized crime investigation and arguably the entire field of forensic science.

Related Articles in EFS Online

Short Tandem Repeats: Interpretation

Chapter 2
DNA: An Overview

Eleanor Alison May Graham

Northumbria University, Newcastle upon Tyne, UK

History of DNA Profiling

DNA profiling, as we know it today, was developed, thanks to two independent breakthroughs in molecular biology that occurred at the same time on different sides of the Atlantic. In the United States, the polymerase chain reaction (PCR) was developed by Kary Mullis of Cetus Corporation [1–3]. Almost simultaneously, the individual-specific banding patterns observed after restriction fragment-length polymorphism (RFLP) analysis of repeated DNA sequences were discovered by Professor Sir Alec Jeffreys at the University of Leicester [4–6]. In its earliest incarnation, this technique termed as *DNA fingerprinting* by its creators was performed by restriction of 0.5–10 µg of extracted DNA using the restriction enzyme *Hin*FI, followed by Southern blotting hybridization with probes termed *33.5*, *33.6*, and *33.15*, designed to bind to multiple "minisatellites" present in the restricted DNA [6]. This multilocus probing (MLP) technique would result in the binding of probes to multiple independent DNA fragments at the same time, giving rise to the traditional "bar code" pattern that is often visualized, discussing DNA profiling, even today. Differences in the number of times the probe sequence is repeated in each DNA fragment form the basis of the individual patterns observed on the autoradiogram image.

The Mendelian inheritance of these markers was established by the pedigree analysis of 54 related persons [4], and the individual nature of the banding pattern was further established by the examination of 20 unrelated persons [6]. The probability of two unrelated individuals carrying the same fingerprint was calculated from these data and was estimated as 3×10^{-11} for probe 33.15 alone, provided 15 bands could be resolved in the 4–20-kb size range on the autoradiogram. The potential application of this technique to maternity/paternity disputes and to forensic investigation was recognized immediately by Jefferys *et al.*, and was demonstrated by DNA fingerprinting of forensic-type samples, such as bloodstains and semen, in the same year [5]. Difficulties in interpretation of MLP images quickly resulted in single locus probes (SLP) with variable number of tandem repeat (VNTR) loci becoming the markers of choice for DNA profiling.

The first report concerning the use of DNA profiling in a criminal investigation was published in 1987 [7]. This investigation used two unpublished SLPs to link semen stain samples collected from two rape and murder cases that had occurred 3 years apart in 1983 and 1986 in Leicestershire, United Kingdom. The probability of this match occurring by chance was calculated as 5.8×10^{-8}. This result not only linked the two crimes but also exonerated an innocent man implicated in the murders and led to the first mass screening project undertaken for DNA profiling in the world [8].

The potential of DNA analysis for forensic science had now been demonstrated; the technology now required statistical validation by analysis of population frequencies and application to casework samples before it could progress. Early evaluation studies on MLP 33.15 provided optimistic support for the use of DNA for the personal identification and the identification of male rapists from a mixed male/female sample [9]. It does, however, also begin to uncover the limitations of this method. A mean success rate of only 62% for the DNA fingerprinting of donated vaginal swabs was observed and no typing was possible for blood or semen stains that had been stored for 4 years at room temperature, and difficulty in directly

A Guide to Forensic DNA Profiling
Edited by Allan Jamieson and Scott Bader
© 2016 John Wiley & Sons, Ltd. ISBN: 9781118751527
Also published in EFS (online edition)
DOI: 10.1002/9780470061589.fsa532.pub2

comparing related samples run on different gels was also cited as a potential problem [9]. Similar studies and European collaborations were undertaken on SLPs such as YNH24 and MS43a [10, 11]. Difficulties were again observed when interpreting gel images, with only 77.9% of 70 samples distributed between nine laboratories producing matching results when a 2.8% "window" for size differences between gel runs and laboratories was used [10]. It was recognized that subtle differences between laboratory protocols were responsible for some of the observed discrepancies, leading to a requirement for the standardization of laboratory methodology [10] and DNA profile interpretation [12, 13].

Such standardizations could improve the reproducibility of DNA typing results for MLP and SLP marker systems, but in order to be applicable to forensic investigation, DNA systems must be robust and must be applicable to samples of a less than pristine nature or that which consists of only a few cells. PCR was first applied to forensic DNA profiling for the investigation of the HLA-DQ-α1 gene, a polymorphic gene that encodes a human leukocyte antigen cell surface protein located in the major histocompatibility complex (MHC) class II region on chromosome 6 [14].

Two big breakthroughs occurred between the late 1980s and early 1990s that would form the basis of DNA profiling techniques that are recognized today. An alternative class of DNA marker, the microsatellite or short tandem repeat (STR) marker, was described by Weber *et al.* [15] and an alternative method for DNA visualization, PCR amplification, and fluorescent labeling of VNTR markers was also introduced [16, 17].

STR Analysis

STR markers are similar to the VNTR markers that were originally identified and utilized in DNA fingerprinting and SLP profiling. The difference between the classes of DNA marker lies in the length of the tandemly repeated DNA sequence. VNTRs contain 10–33-bp hypervariable repeat motifs [4] that must be observed over a size range of 4–20 kb [9] and SLP markers that are observed over a size range of 1–14 kb [10]. An STR marker repeat is composed of 1–6-bp repeat motifs [18], making the region of DNA that must be scrutinized very short (<1 kb). This length reduction is immediately beneficial to

one of the problems encountered in SLP profiling: difficulty in analyzing degraded DNA [5]. The use of the multiplex PCR to amplify target sequences before visualization significantly reduces the amount of DNA required for analysis from microgram to nanogram amounts [18, 19]. The detection and visualization method of polyacrylamide gel electrophoresis and fluorescent detection using an automated DNA sequencer (model 370, Applied Biosystems, Foster City, CA, USA), in combination with an internal size standard (GS2500, Applied Biosystems) and GENESCAN 672 software (Applied Biosystems), also allowed for precise band sizing, answering problems of intralaboratory and interlaboratory allele designation discrepancies that had been observed in SLP analysis [12, 20, 21].

One of the earliest multiplexed STR systems developed for forensic DNA analysis was a quadruplex reaction that amplified the STR markers HUMVWA31/A, HUMTHO1, HUMF131A1, and HUMFES/FPS [22]. These particular STR markers were selected from the hundreds of STRs identified throughout the human genome [23] based on a number of important parameters. Each STR must have a high level of allelic variability to maximize the discriminating power of each marker. Markers should have short PCR product length (<500 bp) to aid the analysis of degraded DNA. The chromosomal location of any potential marker should be checked to avoid closely linked loci, and tetranucleotide repeat motifs are preferred due to low artifact production during PCR amplification [24]. The overall match probability using this system was calculated as 1.3×10^{-4} for white Caucasian populations [18]. Validation studies carried out on this quadruplex system determined that 1 ng template DNA was optimal for the amplification and analysis, that stutter bands up to 11% were observed at some loci, especially HUMVWA21/A, and that DNA mixtures in a ratio of 1 : 2 or 2 : 1 could be distinguished using this system [22]. Further validation studies were carried out on extremely compromised casework samples collected from the victims of the Waco siege, which resulted in the identification of several individuals, which was not possible by any other means [25, 26].

The quadruplex system described above was next developed into a septaplex as the application of DNA profiling to forensic casework increased. The new septaplex system coamplified the tetranucleotide STR loci HUMVWFA31/A (vWA), HUMTHO1 (THO1),

D8S1179, HUMFIBRA (FGA), D21S11, and D18S51 [27]. The nomenclature used for naming these STR markers had been standardized now to allow for easy comparison between different working groups [28]. This system also included primers for the amplification of a region of the amelogenin gene, which could be used to deduce the sex of the DNA sample being analyzed [29]. Optimization and validation studies on this septaplex system reduced the amount of template required for the generation of full DNA profile to just 500 pg, with partial profiles being generated from as little as 50 pg, the equivalent of just 10 diploid cells [27]. This septaplex became known as the *second-generation multiplex (SGM)* system [30] and was used to populate the first national criminal intelligence DNA database, which became operational in the United Kingdom in April 1995 [27]. The SGM system was human specific and highly discriminating, with a probability of chance association calculated as 1×10^{-8} [31]. It could also be applied to degraded DNA samples and was capable of detecting and resolving mixed DNA profiles at ratios between $1:10$ and $10:1$ [30]. One final evolution would take place, the inclusion of a further four STR markers (D3S1358, D19S433, D16S539, and D2S1338) to produce the STR profiling kit that is currently used in the United Kingdom for forensic DNA profiling, population of the national DNA database (NDNAD), and for paternity testing.

The AmpFlSTR® SGM Plus™ System

The AmpFlSTR® SGM Plus™ system, commercially produced by Applied Biosystems (ABI), a division of Perkin Elmer, Foster City, California, USA, was introduced in June 1999, and was validated for use in forensic casework in 2000 [32]. It was designed to replace the SGM system for forensic casework in the United Kingdom to decrease the probability of a chance match occurring from 1×10^{-8} to one in trillions for unrelated individuals [32]. This greatly increased the statistical power of DNA evidence to be taken for scrutiny in the courtroom, while being back compatible with DNA profiles already stored in the NDNAD. To maintain back-compatibility, partial DNA profiles must contain data at a minimum of four of the original SGM loci to be considered for uploading to the NDNAD. The statistical power of this new system was deemed so great that instead of calculating the exact match probability for a full

DNA profile, it was recommended that an arbitrary conservative estimate of one in a billion be reported for the match probability between unrelated individuals, one in a million for parent/child relations, and 1 in 10 000 for siblings [33]. The characteristics of each STR marker are detailed in Table 1.

The AmpFlSTR® SGM Plus™ PCR amplification kit can be analyzed by two DNA separation methods: capillary electrophoresis or polyacrylamide gel electrophoresis. In this article, the analysis was performed by polyacrylamide gel electrophoresis using an ABI Prism™ 377XL DNA Sequencer (ABI). The ABI Prism™ 377XL DNA Sequencer was introduced by Applied Biosystems in 1995 and stopped its use in 2001 [44]. Automated fragment sizing of fluorescently labeled DNA fragments was achieved by the use of a scanning argon ion laser, which tracks back and forth across a "read-region" at the lower end of a vertical polyacrylamide gel. As each labeled DNA fragment passes the laser, the fluorescent dye is excited, resulting in emission of light. This light is then collected and separated by wavelength onto a charged coupled device (CCD) camera. The camera used on the 377 model is capable of detecting four different wavelengths simultaneously, allowing for the detection of three similarly sized PCR products in a single gel run, with inclusion of a separately colored size standard in each lane. The 377XL model was validated for forensic STR analysis in 1996, using the original SGM septaplex system [45]. The set of validation experiments carried out determined that complete resolution of 1 bp differences between fragments could be achieved up to 350 bp, sizing precision was increased twofold, and sensitivity was increased by one-third compared to the predeceasing 373A DNA sequencer [45].

Gel electrophoresis has now largely, if not completely, been superseded by the use of capillary electrophoresis in commercial forensic laboratories and many research institutes around the world. The market leader for provision of capillary electrophoresis equipment, Applied Biosystems, now part of Life Technologies, has produced several instruments that have been adopted for forensic use [46]. The current instrument of choice for many laboratories is the 16-capillary 3130XL Genetic Analyser, but this may itself soon be replaced by the 3500/3500XL for 8/24-cappillary capacity. The 3500 series of instruments have been designed specifically for the forensic market and include the

Table 1 Characteristics of SGM Plus STR loci[a]

Marker	Chromosome location	No. of alleles in allelic ladder	Size range (bp)	Repeat motif	Dye label	References
D3S1358	3p	8	114–142	TCA $(TCTG)_{1-3}$ $(TCTA)_n$	5-FAM	[34]
vWA[b]	12p12-pter	14	157–209	TCA$(TCTG)_{3-4}$$(TCTA)_n$	5-FAM	[35]
D16S539	16q24-qter	9	234–274	$(AGAT)_n$	5-FAM	GenBank G07925
D2S1338	2q35–37.1	14	289–341	$(TGCC)_n$$(TTCC)_n$	5-FAM	[36]
Amelogenin[b]	X p22.1–22.3 Y p11.2	NA	107 113	NA	JOE	[29]
D8S1179[b]	8	12	128–172	$(TCTR)_n$	JOE	[37]
D21S11[b]	21q11.2-q21	24	187–172	$(TCTA)_n$$(TCTG)_n$ [$(TCTA)_3$ TA$(TCTA)_3$ TCA $(TCTA)_2$ TCCA TA] $(TCTA)_n$	JOE	[38]
D18S51[b]	18q21.3	23	262–345	$(AGAA)_n$	JOE	[39]
D19S433	19q12–13.1	15	106–140	(AAGG)(AAAG)(AAGG) (TAGG)$(AAGG)_n$	NED	[40]
THO1[b]	11p15.5	10	165–204	$(AATG)_n$	NED	[41]
FGA[b]	4q28	28	215–353	$(TTTC)_3$TTTT TTCT $(CTTT)_n$ CTCC $(TTCC)_2$	NED	[42]

[a]Adapted from AmpF/STR SGM Plus PCR Amplification kit manual and [43]
[b]Loci included in the original SGM kit

addition of radio frequency identification (RFID) tags for more efficient consumable monitoring, among other features. Although not currently operational in commercial forensic laboratories, lab-on-a-chip technologies are being rapidly developed to allow for miniaturization of capillary electrophoresis devices [47], which, in the near future, may allow for rapid "at scene" DNA profiling to become a reality.

European Standard Set (ESS) of STRs. Although STRs are used as the DNA marker of choice for forensic DNA analysis and population of NDNADs throughout the world, they are not all populated with equivalent data due to the adoption of different STR marker sets in different countries. To increase the discriminatory power of each STR system and decrease the probability of adventitious matches on DNA database searches, several new kits have been produced that allow for the analysis of up to 16 STR markers in a single reaction [48, 49]. Although the new multiplex kits have not been introduced to routine casework in the United Kingdom at the time of writing, it is anticipated that they will be adopted in the near future. An additional motivation for the transition to be made comes from the desire to exchange DNA data with member states of the European Union

for the resolution of cross-border crime. The Council of the European Union resolution on the exchange of DNA analysis results, also known as the *Prüm Treaty*, identifies a core set of 12 STR markers that should be used when DNA data exchanges between EU member states (*see* Official journal). Details of the STR loci included in the new STR multiplex kits are provided in Table 2.

Alternative DNA Markers

Autosomal STR markers have become the most utilized ones in both forensic and paternity DNA profiling. However, there are numerous alternative markers that can be interrogated when required. Another class of autosomal marker, the single nucleotide polymorphism (SNP), has been investigated for application to forensic casework and identification projects. SNPs, as the name suggests, are alterations of a single base pair and occur on average every few hundred base pairs throughout the human genome [50, 51]. The major advantage of SNP markers over STRs is the small size of the DNA target, making them very useful for degraded DNA analysis and disaster victim identification projects [52]. Reduced size STR amplicons have, however,

Table 2   STR loci included in newly developed commercial STR profiling kits

ESS 12	Loci	SGM Plus®	NGM™	NGM Select™	Powerplex® ESI/X 16	Powerplex® ESI/X 17
•	D3S1358	•	•	•	•	•
•	D8S1179	•	•	•	•	•
–	D16S539	•	•	•	•	•
•	D18S51	•	•	•	•	•
•	D21S11	•	•	•	•	•
•	FGA	•	•	•	•	•
•	THO1	•	•	•	•	•
•	vWA	•	•	•	•	•
–	D2S1338	•	•	•	•	•
–	D19S433	•	•	•	•	•
•	D1S1656	–	•	•	•	•
•	D2S441	–	•	•	•	•
•	D10S1248	–	•	•	•	•
•	D12S391	–	•	•	•	•
•	D22S1045	–	•	•	•	•
–	SE33	–	–	•	–	•
–	Amelogenin	•	•	•	•	•

been developed to analyze degraded DNA while remaining compatible with current DNA databases to allow easy searching in identification projects [53].

There are a number of disadvantages associated with the use of SNP markers instead of STRs. The comparatively low discrimination power of each locus requires that approximately 50 SNPs must be investigated to give match probabilities equal to 10 STR loci [54]. Mixture analysis is also complicated, for SNP analyses are usually bi-allelic, but have also been observed to be tri- and even tetra-allelic. The use of a predominantly bi-allelic marker makes the distinction between mixtures and homozygotes difficult, especially for minor contributors, which may also display allelic dropout [54]. Owing to these problems and the financial implications of repopulating NDNADs with SNP profiles, it is unlikely that SNP markers play a major role at the forefront of forensic DNA analysis in the foreseeable future. There are still some applications in related fields in which SNP markers are proven to be useful: determination of phenotypic characteristics, such as eye color [55, 56] and hair color, by variation in the melanocortin 1 receptor (*MC1R*) gene [57–59]. SNP markers can also be used to analyze the uniparentally inherited mitochondrial DNA (mtDNA) (*see* **Mitochondrial DNA: Profiling**) and Y chromosomes (*see* **Y-Chromosome Short Tandem Repeats**), which are discussed in [60, 61].

DNA Extraction

In order for DNA from any given biological sample to be analyzed by a PCR-based method, it must first be purified from all organic and inorganic substances with which it is associated (*see* **Extraction**). This process can become complicated during forensic investigation, as DNA is often present on or in materials that are not usually encountered in the molecular biology laboratory. The extraction stage of DNA analysis is also the most susceptible stage to the occurrence of laboratory-induced contamination of sample material. For this reason, DNA extraction protocols, no matter which one is employed, must always be carried out in a dedicated laboratory, physically separated from downstream processes, especially PCR. Literature searching for DNA extraction of forensically interesting materials reveals tens of various techniques and variations on each of these. A brief listing of DNA extraction methods for commonly encountered forensic evidentiary samples is given in Table 3. Of the many techniques that have been proposed, the most commonly utilized ones are based on three techniques: organic cell lysis with phenol/chloroform purification, Chelex®100, and silica-based extractions.

The organic phenol/chloroform method is the original DNA extraction technique to be applied to forensic (and archaeological) specimens [5, 80, 81, 107]. Although many subtle variations in buffer

Table 3 List of materials commonly collected for DNA analysis during forensic investigations with reference to extraction methods

Substrate	Type of extraction	References
Blood	Silica	[62, 63]
	Chelex®	[64, 64]
Bone	Silica	[65–70]
	Lysis/precipitation	[71]
	Phenol/chloroform	[66, 67, 72, 73]
Teeth	Chelex®	[74, 75]
	Phenol/chloroform	[76–79]
Hair	Phenol/chloroform	[80, 81]
	Chelex®	[64, 82]
	Alkaline digestion	[83]
	Silica	[82, 84]
Saliva	Chelex®	[64, 85–87]
Buccal cells	Phenol/chloroform	[88, 89]
	Silica	[90]
Maggots	Phenol/chloroform	[91–93]
Feces	Silica	[94–97]
	Phenol/chloroform	[96, 97]
Urine	Silica	[69, 98, 99]
Semen	Chelex®	[100]
Trace/cells	Silica	[101, 102]
	Organic	[101, 103–105]
	Chelex®	[106]

pH, chemical concentration, incubation time, and temperature have been introduced over the years, the basis of the technique remains the same. The detergent sodium dodecyl sulfate (SDS) is used to break down cell walls and lipids present in the sample, and proteinase K, a strong protease enzyme, is used to digest the proteins that protect the DNA molecule in its natural state. An additional component dithiothreitol (DTT) can also be used to digest more robust materials such as keratinized hair and sperm cells and forms the basis of the differential extraction technique used for vaginal swabs with semen present. The differential extraction of the two cell types is possible as the sperm nuclei are impervious to SDS/proteinase K digestion because the nuclear membrane is reinforced with cross-linked thiol-rich proteins. This allows for the digestion and removal of the female component from the mixture, leaving intact sperm nuclei to be digested by the addition of an SDS/proteinase K/DTT mixture [5]. Once digested, phenol/chloroform is used to separate proteins into organic phenol layer from the nucleic acids in the aqueous chloroform layer. The nucleic acids must then be concentrated

and purified from the hazardous chloroform solvent before further analysis. This is classically achieved by ethanol precipitation but can also be carried out using a commercially available centrifugal filter device, such as the Centricon®100 system [108].

Chelex®100 was introduced as a medium for the simple extraction of DNA from forensic materials in 1991 [64]. This technique was designed specifically for use with forensic specimens and was intended to replace the organic phenol/chloroform technique. The Chelex® method has three major advantages over the organic phenol/chloroform methods: it is much faster, taking only 1 h compared to up to 24 h for the organic, it does not require multiple tube transfers, reducing the risk of laboratory-induced contamination, and it does not require the use of hazardous chemicals. Chelex® resin is composed of styrene divinylbenzene copolymers containing paired iminodiacetate ions, which act as chelating groups, binding polyvalent ions such as Mg^{2+} [64]. In this method, Chelex® resin is added directly to the sample from which DNA is to be extracted. Cell lysis and DNA liberation are achieved by a combination of alkalinity (pH 10–11) and heating at 100 °C. Initial testing performed on forensic-type samples such as blood, blood stains, semen stains, and hair demonstrated that the performance of Chelex® extraction was equal to that of phenol/chloroform methods and, in the case of blood, was less likely to allow the carryover of PCR inhibitors such as heme. Similar to organic methods, an additional DTT digestion step is required for DNA extraction from sperm [64].

Silica particles were first used for DNA extraction from human serum and urine samples. This method, similar to Chelex®, was designed to be more rapid and involves fewer tube transfer stages, to reduce the risk of sample contamination or DNA loss, than organic methods. The method uses a chaotropic agent guanidinium thiocyanate (GuSCN) to lyse cells and inactivate nucleases, while simultaneously facilitating the binding of the freed nucleic acids to silica particles [69]. Once bound, the silica–DNA complex can be pelleted, allowing cellular debris and other non-DNA components to be removed and discarded. After washing, the purified DNA can then be eluted from the silica in sterile water or TE buffer. This method is extremely sensitive due to the strong binding affinity of silica particles for nucleic acids in the presence of chaotropic agents and is subsequently adapted for use with ancient bone samples [70, 109]. The method does require some caution as GuSCN produces HCN gas on contact with acids and should therefore be kept in an alkaline solution at all times, and disposed of in 10 M NaOH.

The silica–DNA binding affinity has been utilized in the development of commercial kits such as the QIAamp® DNA kits produced by Qiagen (Qiagen, West Sussex, United Kingdom) (described in QiaAmp) and the DNAIQ™ system produced by the Promega Corporation. Both systems have been tested and validated for use with forensic casework samples [62, 63] and both systems are compatible with automated robotic workstations [110–112]. The versatility and reproducibility of such commercial DNA extraction kits, especially QIAamp® products, have made them the choice of the forensic research community over recent years, as illustrated by their usage in the majority of research articles published over recent years.

To increase sample throughput and reduce operator interaction with forensic samples, robotic workstations are now used for the majority of routine samples in commercial DNA laboratories. The first system to be adopted for mainstream commercial use was the Biorobot EZ1 from Qiagen. This system uses a silica-based DNA extraction methodology that is in principle similar to the QIAamp DNA kits, with the silica being bound to magnetic particles instead of forming a solid membrane. Due to the success of this pioneering instrument, the market leader for provision of forensic DNA profiling instruments and consumables, Applied Biosystems, has worked with Tecan (Tecan Group Ltd., Mannedorf, Switzerland) to develop and validate the AutoMate Express™ Forensic DNA Extraction System [113] for use with the PrepFiler Forensic DNA Extraction kit [114], which is another magnetic bead-based DNA extraction system now available for forensic use.

DNA Quantification

Commercially produced DNA profiling kits, such as the AmpF*l*STR® SGM Plus™ PCR amplification kit described above, are optimized to produce DNA profiles from a narrow range of template DNA concentration. AmpF*l*STR® kits produced by Applied Biosystems are optimized to amplify 1–2.5-ng template DNA. The addition of insufficient template DNA can result in stochastic amplification. Stochastic amplification manifests as unbalanced amplification of heterozygote loci and can, if severe, result in allelic dropout, making heterozygotes to appear as homozygotes at the affected loci [115]. The addition of template DNA in excess can lead to the production of large stutter peaks that complicate the interpretation of DNA profile. The term *stutter* refers to the production of natural biological artifacts during the PCR. The currently accepted model for stutter generation is by a "polymerase slippage" model that results in the addition or, more often, deletion of a single repeat unit from the actual template size. The detection and classification of stutter play an important role in profile interpretation, especially if a mixture is anticipated or observed. If the stutter characteristics are unknown for a DNA profiling system, it is possible that such artifacts may falsely be reported as "actual alleles". It has been observed that stutter does not usually exceed 10% of the associated allele peak height, but with variation between both STR loci and alleles in the locus, stutter has been observed to approach 15% [116] in some cases. Percentage stutter is calculated using the peak height in relative fluorescent units (RFU) of the observed peaks. Figure 1 shows a typical stutter pattern at the STR locus FGA.

The most commonly observed nonbiological artifacts caused by the addition of template DNA in excess are termed as *pull-up* or "bleed through" peaks. Pull-up peaks are produced when the GeneScan/GeneMapper software program is unable to distinguish between the emission spectra of the fluorescent colors in the STR system. This phenomenon is visualized by the appearance of false bands in the overamplified fragment's size range in differently colored markers.

By quantifying all DNA samples before performing DNA profiling PCR, the production of such artifacts can be reduced or completely avoided. As with DNA extraction, there are numerous methods available to perform this function. The traditional method of DNA quantitation involves measuring the absorbance of the sample at 260 nm on a spectrophotometer. This method is simple to perform and shows little sample-to-sample variation [117], making it a desirable technique. This technique does, however, suffer because of its simplicity. The technique is not species specific, indicating that any bacterial or fungal DNA that is copurified with the DNA of interest cannot be distinguished from the human target DNA. Additionally, single-stranded DNA and nucleotides cannot be distinguished from double-stranded DNA by this

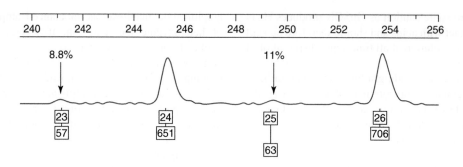

Figure 1   Example of typical stutter pattern of alleles 24 and 26 at STR locus FGA

method, which can also lead to falsely high quantitation readings [118]. A different approach to DNA quantitation is taken by the slot-blot technique. This method is based on the specific hybridization of a 40-bp probe that binds to the human alpha satellite locus D17Z1 [119]. Using this technique, DNA is quantified by visual comparison of sample band intensities, with the band intensities of standards produced from known amounts of DNA. This comparison can be performed either manually – but this allows for the subjectivity of individual interpretation, which can lead to differences between operators in quantitation – or electronically by computationally converting the band intensities into numerical values [120]. This technique shows a high degree of species specificity (human and primate) and can detect as little as 150 pg DNA in a standard assay [119]. Similar to the development of commercial DNA profiling kits, the development of commercial DNA quantitation kits has also progressed. Applied Biosystems produced the Quantiblot® human DNA quantification kit similarly to the original technique of Walsh. Walsh *et al.* use a probe that binds to the D17Z1 locus and has a lower detection limit of 150 pg [119, 121, 122].

An alternative method of DNA quantitation involves the use of a fluorescent dye PicoGreen double-stranded (ds) DNA quantitation reagent. This method was developed to allow high-throughput quantitation of multiple samples concurrently while increasing the sensitivity DNA quantitation methods. PicoGreen is a Hoechst dye that can pass through the lipid membrane of live or fixed cells to form noncovalent bonds with AT-rich areas in the minor groove of dsDNA [123]. The method utilizes the increased fluorescent intensity that is observed when PicoGreen binds to dsDNA. The fluorescent intensity of the PicoGreen dye is measured

with a spectrofluorometer capable of producing the excitation wavelength of ~480 nm and recording at the emission wavelength of ~520 nm. The DNA is then quantified by comparison of the sample fluorescence with the fluorescence of a set of standards that are included in every sample run [124]. The biggest disadvantage to this method over the hybridization methods discussed previously is that this method is not specific for human DNA. Any animal, bacterial, or fungal DNA copurified with the human DNA of interest will contribute to the final reading and could give a falsely high DNA quantification. This method is, however, much more sensitive than the previously described methods, with a reported lower detection limit of 25 pg ml^{-1} [118].

The latest development in DNA quantitation is based on the technique of real-time PCR. The methodology was first proposed 15 years ago by Higuchi and coworkers [125] who, by including ethidium bromide in the PCR reaction, were able to continuously monitor the production of dsDNA in "real time". By capturing the change in fluorescent intensity on video camera, the potential of this new development for specific DNA quantitation was realized [126]. There are several different approaches to real-time quantitation of DNA; they are all, however, based on the principle of fluorescent dye binding double-stranded DNA as it accumulates during the PCR process. As the technique is based on the PCR, DNA quantitation can be undertaken by targeting any specific region of template DNA, with many systems targeting the multicopy *Alu* sequence, which appears 500 000–1 000 000 times throughout the human genome [127–129]. This not only ensures that the technique is species specific but also has allowed numerous variations, many designed to perform additional functions, such as independent quantitation of nuclear and mtDNA in a single reaction [130–133] and assessment of DNA quality [134, 135].

Real-time PCR is the current gold standard for quantification of DNA samples prior to downstream processing and is an essential part of the laboratory process when dealing with low-template DNA (LTDNA) samples. The importance of DNA quantification was highlighted in the Review of the Science of Low Template DNA Analysis [136] in which it is considered as a "matter of best practice". As for all other aspects of the DNA laboratory process, Applied Biosystems has several kits available for real-time PCR quantification of DNA extracts. The most current system available at the time of writing is the Quantifiler® Duo DNA Quantitation kit, which allows for simultaneous analysis of human specific, via amplification of the ribonuclease P RNA component H1 and male-specific targeting a region of the sex-determining region on the Y chromosome, markers. The reported limit of reproducible detection is in the region of only 11.5 pg μl^{-1} using this system [137]. A competing kit produced by the Promega Corporation, the Plexor HY system, used the human-specific RNU2 locus and the male-specific TSPY gene as alternative DNA targets. The Plexor HY system has a reported reproducible detection limit in the region of 3.8 pg total DNA [138]. Both systems also include an internal positive control, which can be used to monitor amplification efficiency of reactions over time and indicate the presence of PCR inhibitors in DNA extracts before DNA profiling is attempted.

DNA Profile Interpretation

The methodologies, hardware, and software necessary for the generation of STR profiles are well established but constantly evolving. Regardless of the exact means of production, the interpretation of DNA profiles must remain constant. Using the earliest DNA profiling systems, based on RFLP analysis and Southern blot hybridization, it was proved to be difficult to standardize interpretations between different individuals and different laboratories. Significant differences in band sizing were regularly observed during collaborative exercises carried out by DNA testing laboratories throughout Europe [10, 11]. Although measures were taken to standardize as many variables as possible including buffer system, gel running time and temperature, and DNA visualization method, there was still an uncertainty in interpretation uniformity between laboratories [10]. The breakthrough required for standardization of DNA profile interpretation of DNA profiles came with the switch to PCR amplification [1, 2] and the introduction of fluorescent labeling allowing digitization of DNA profiling results [16, 17]. These advancements paved the way for the development of universal guidelines and validation of commercially produced kits and instruments to allow for the accurate and reliable reproducibility of DNA profiling interpretation across independent laboratories worldwide. Validation experiments, designed to demonstrate the robustness of the system, must be carried out for all commercially produced forensic DNA profiling kits before they can be used for casework. Validation data for the AmpF*l*STR® SGM Plus™ Amplification kit, used throughout this article, were published in 2000 [32].

The first step toward standardization was the adoption of a common nomenclature for STR loci, including both the name of the marker and the numerical designation of each allele observed in the human populations tested. The basis for the currently used naming systems was brought about by the European DNA Profiling Group (EDNAP), which was formed in 1989 by members of the leading police organizations and universities involved in forensic stain analysis and paternity investigation at that time [139]. The next step in achieving complete interlaboratory concordance was the addition of the allelic ladder [140]. Allelic ladders are produced by creating a mixture of DNA samples containing all observed allelic variations in the human population and then amplifying this mixture with the primers used for each locus in a given STR kit. Once created, the allelic ladder is visualized in parallel with every set of samples so that a direct comparison can be made between the amplified fragment size and the fragment size of previously observed alleles for each allele at each marker. This ensures that slight variations in running conditions, such as those observed with Southern hybridization techniques, are not misclassified based on interrun fragment sizing differences [141]. The inclusion of allelic ladders also allows for the recognition of rare and novel, full and microvariant alleles that are not present in the allelic ladders for each STR kit [142]. The final leap toward accurate DNA profile interpretation was made with the switch from "home brews" to commercially produced STR amplification kits and the use of identical or equivalent instruments in each laboratory throughout the forensic DNA typing community.

As a result of the standardization measures described above, the interpretation of single-contributor DNA profiles when sufficient template is entered into the reaction is a straightforward process. In the forensic setting, a large percentage of samples submitted for DNA analysis contain biological material from more than one source and result in mixed STR profiles. In order to produce a robust set of interpretation guidelines for mixed profiles, it is vitally important to have a thorough understanding of the amplification characteristics of biological and stochastic phenomenon in the electropherogram from which the interpretation is made. The most commonly observed artifacts in a DNA profile are termed as *stutter bands*. They are generated during the PCR by slippage of Taq polymerase, resulting in the generation of a fragment, one repeat unit shorter, or more infrequently longer, than the true allele. When the peak height of the amplified true allele is >4000 RFU in the electropherogram, stuttering is unavoidable when amplifying STR loci using Taq polymerase [143]. Each STR locus and even each allele in an STR locus has different stuttering characteristics, but stutter products are rarely observed to exceed a peak height in excess of 15% of the height of the associated allele. Any peak found in a stutter position with a height >15% of the related allele should therefore be considered as a potential true allele in a mixed DNA profile [143].

Another characteristic of the electropherogram that can mystify DNA profile interpretation is the balance of allelic amplification at heterozygotic markers. In a perfectly amplified DNA profile, the peak areas of each heterozygote allele should be equal. Differences in the amplification efficiency of each allele can, however, result in alleles being unequally amplified [143]. For a single source DNA profile produced from sufficient template (>1 ng), each shorter allele at a heterozygous locus will usually have a peak area >60% of the associated larger allele [143]. Heterozygosity balance (Hb) is calculated as relative peak area differences of heterozygote alleles (φ) for each locus. There are two similar methods used to determine Hb for forensic DNA profile interpretation, both of which use the peak area in RFU. The first is calculated as φ = smallest peak area/largest peak area, where a result of $0.67 > \varphi$ £ 1 indicates that the Hb is in the observed limits [143]. This calculation does not, however, provide any information as to which of the heterozygous alleles

has been preferentially amplified during the PCR. This information is provided when Hb is assessed by the calculation, φ = peak area shortest allele/peak area longest allele. In this case, a result of $0.67 > \varphi <1.67$ indicates a balanced amplification, with φ values < 1 indicating that the shortest allele of the pair has been preferentially amplified and φ values > 1 indicating the opposite [144].

The presence of additional bands in the electropherogram can also result from overamplification of template DNA causing saturation in fluorescent signal that cannot be resolved by the matrix files of the visualization software. These bands are termed as *pull-up* peaks due to their appearance in the raw data files, whereby a smaller peak is observed directly under the overamplified peak. When the dyes are separated to produce the electropherogram image, the smaller pull-up peak appears as an extra band, with excess blue signal producing green pull-ups and excess green signal producing yellow pull-ups. Pull-up peaks are easily recognized by the experienced DNA analyst due to their atypical morphology compared to true allele peaks and should not interfere with DNA profile interpretation [143]. If a pull-up peak is superimposed over a suspected true fragment, the sample can be diluted and reanalyzed to avoid fluorescent signal saturation.

Low Template DNA Profiling

The two biggest drives for developments in forensic DNA profiling are to improve sample throughput and technique sensitivity. Increases in sample throughput are achieved by automation of routine processes such as DNA extraction, sample loading, and DNA profiling interpretation coupled with effective laboratory management and sample tracking. While the sensitivity of DNA profiling reactions can also benefit from technological advances, the major advancements are achieved by optimization of reaction chemistries, investigation of alternate DNA markers, and use of additional stage processes.

One area of DNA profiling analysis that has received attention is the inclusion of a pre-PCR stage, designed to increase the total amount of template DNA available for STR analysis. A number of techniques, similar in their objective but differing in their means, can be described under the umbrella term of whole genome amplification (WGA). As the term indicates, these techniques are designed to replicate all DNA present in a given reaction, with the intention of generating an unlimited source of template material for multiple downstream analyses. Techniques of this kind were first described in 1989, with the publication of a universal DNA amplification method, which used restriction enzyme digestion and ligation into plasmids to achieve its goal [145]. The next generation of WGA techniques appeared in the literature during the 1990s and, like many other areas of molecular biology, it moved away from the cloning techniques to PCR amplification. The first PCR/WGA technique was termed as *primer extension preamplification polymerase chain reaction (PEP/PCR)* [146]. This technique utilizes fully degenerate 15-mer oligonucleotide primers and a range of annealing temperatures in a PCR to produce multiple copies of any template DNA present in the reaction. In his introductory article, Zhang *et al.* [146] reported a minimum amplification of 30 copies for 78% of the human genome at a 95% confidence level from a single spermatozoon. The limitations of PEP/PCR were also explored, with heterozygosity imbalance and locus dropout cited as the main concerns when the technique is applied to single-cell analysis. These observations were confirmed in the articles reporting the application of PEP/PCR to preimplantation diagnosis of single cells, whereby effects of stochastic sampling and amplification were observed for single-cell analysis [147–149]. Locus and allele dropout was also observed when PEP/PCR was applied to formalin-fixed tissues followed by microsatellite analysis [149].

Another method designed to perform the function of WGA has been termed as *multiple displacement amplification (MDA)*. This method was first introduced in 2001 and differs from the previously described techniques by the use of an alternative enzyme $\varphi29$ DNA polymerase [150]. The method of replication is based on a rolling strand-displacement model that proceeds by constantly displacing the newly generated strand of DNA to form a hyper-branched DNA replication structure, limited only by the reagents available [151]. The promise shown by this method has led to the development of several commercial WGA kits, for example, GenomiPhi WGA Amplification kit (GE Healthcare), and various publications advocating its use for human genome analysis [152–156]. All of these studies, however, have entered >10 ng DNA into the MDA reaction. Studies

conducted using <10 ng template DNA have observed unequal amplification of genomic DNA when assessed by the use of forensic DNA profiling kits, similar or identical to those used in [157–159]. Of the numerous WGA method variations that have been published to date, none have yet demonstrated the unbiased amplification of microsatellite markers when very low template material is available for entry into the WGA reaction [160–162].

An alternate approach is the use of a nested PCR strategy, which involves the use of two primer sets, one designed to prime from positions within the original amplicons. Using this approach, the initial PCR performs the function of enriching the template DNA specifically in the regions of ultimate interest. The second internal amplification reaction can then be initiated from a greatly increased initial template amount. This approach was successfully applied to the forensic DNA analysis of charred human remains [163]. This approach, however, presents a heightened risk of laboratory-introduced sample contamination by requiring the manipulation of amplified human DNA, breaking a fundamental anticontamination principle of single-direction workflow during forensic DNA analysis. A far simpler approach to increasing PCR sensitivity has, however, proven to be extremely successful and become fully integrated into forensic DNA profiling laboratories worldwide.

The term *low copy number (LCN)* DNA profiling was coined in a publication by Peter Gill of the Forensic Science Service (FSS) in 2000 and describes the analysis of <100 pg template DNA [116]. LCN has come to be associated with the use of increased PCR cycles, but there are other techniques that claim to amplify small amounts of DNA. These can be collectively termed as *LTDNA* analysis. Commercially available STR amplification kits, such as the AmpFℓSTR® SGM Plus™ kit, are optimized to produce complete and accurate DNA profiles when 1–2.5 µl template DNA is amplified for 28 cycles. Following this standard protocol, amplification of 100 pg DNA will typically result in severe allelic and locus dropout, or even complete failure. The sensitivity of this technique can be radically improved by simply increasing the number of PCR cycles, in the case of the AmpFℓSTR® SGM Plus™ kit to 34 cycles [116]. The increase in sensitivity opens up the potential of forensic DNA profiling to analyze many more sample types than had ever previously been imagined, most notably from fingerprints [164, 165], cigarette butts [103], and from the skin surface of manual strangulation victims [166–168] (*see Sources of DNA* for a further description of sources of DNA evidence).

The improved sensitivity gained by the use of an extra six PCR cycles does, however, lead to additional issues in DNA profile interpretation. When undertaking any forensic DNA analysis procedure, the importance of anticontamination protocols cannot be underestimated. This is especially true when attempting to produce LTDNA profiles, for which the template DNA may also be of a degraded nature (*see Degraded Samples*). The sensitivity of the AmpF*l*STR® SGM Plus™ PCR amplification kit when employing 34 cycles is such that laboratory-derived contamination cannot actually be completely avoided [116]. The potential to acquire DNA profile information from minute template amounts can also lead to the production of partial DNA profiles, where both allele and locus dropout are observed. To combat these problems, along with an increased size of stutter bands and unbalanced amplification of heterozygous alleles, an entirely new set of DNA profile interpretation rules is required for LTDNA analysis.

The majority of the complications observed for LTDNA profiles are due to stochastic variation. For example, a stutter band generated in an early PCR cycle, unassociated contaminating alleles, or one of two heterozygous alleles can be preferentially amplified and therefore over-represented in the final DNA profile [169]. The random nature of stochastic variation means that the same stutter products or contaminating alleles will not be amplified identically in replicate analyses [116, 170], leading to the first rule of LTDNA analysis: an allele can only be reported if it is present in at least two repeated analyses [169]. Once this rule has been applied, all remaining bands in the DNA profile can now be scrutinized. For standard 28-cycle DNA profiling reactions, stutter peaks are not observed to exceed 15% of the associated allele peak height; in LCN analysis, stutter products are much larger in the range of 20% when associated with peaks >10 000 RFU in area and 40% for associated peaks <10 000 RFU [171]. As this cannot be avoided, it must always be considered that the stutter peak could be masking an allele of a minor contributor in a mixed profile, and as such cannot be discarded simply as a stochastic artifact. Similarly for heterozygosity balance, where Hb φ values are observed to be >0.67 (when using φ = smallest peak

area/largest peak area), under standard conditions, the minimum values observed during LCN analyses for most loci in the AmpF*l*STR® SGM Plus™ PCR kit were observed at a Hb φ value of 0.2 [171]. It was also observed that, after repeated analysis, allelic dropout at known heterozygote loci occurred at a rate of approximately 10% per locus, but was not observed when the peak area of alleles was >10 000 RFU [171].

By the varying nature of LTDNA work, the majority of samples analyzed comprise DNA mixtures of dual or multiple contributors. Mixture analysis of standard or LTDNA profiles can be an extremely complex undertaking, especially when more than two or three individuals have contributed unequally to a collected sample. In a working forensic casework environment, to avoid bias, mixture analysis is carried out without any knowledge of reference DNA profiles of potential contributors. As the work carried out for inclusion in this thesis was purely research based, the interpretation permutations and mathematical rules required for unsighted mixture analysis are not further discussed in this introduction, especially as the interpretation of complex mixtures is today more likely to be performed by computational expert systems [172] to increase the speed at which the analysis can be completed and remove any subjectivity that may be introduced by individual DNA analysts.

The advantages of using an LTDNA protocol for DNA profile generation are clear when the analysis of minute trace evidence is required. These advantages do not, however, extend to the analysis of minor contributors to mixed DNA profiles. It has been noted that the use of LTDNA profiling does not convey any advantage over standard analysis when the minor:major DNA contributor ratio is below 1 : 10 [144]. This knowledge, combined with the additional complications of sporadic contamination, increased stutter and heterozygote imbalance, ensuring that LTDNA analysis is undertaken only when absolutely necessary.

Following criticism of LCN DNA profiling during the Omagh bombing trial, R. v Hoey, the Association of Chief Police Officers (ACPO) suspended the use of the method in England and Wales on 21 December 2007. The method was reinstated on 14 January 2008 following a Review of the Science of Low Template DNA Analysis [136], which found the technique to be fit for purpose. The use of LCN DNA profiling in forensic casework continues to be debated among forensic geneticists around the world [173–177].

References

[1] Saiki, R.K., Scharf, S., Faloona, F., Mullis, K.B., Horn, G.T., Erlich, H.A. & Arnheim, N. (1985). Enzymatic amplification of beta-globin genomic sequences and restriction site analysis for diagnosis of sickle cell anemia, *Science* **230**, 1350–1354.

[2] Mullis, K., Faloona, F., Scharf, S., Saiki, R., Horn, G. & Erlich, H. (1986). Specific enzymatic amplification of DNA in vitro: the polymerase chain reaction, *Cold Spring Harbor Symposia on Quantitative Biology* **51**(Pt 1), 263–273.

[3] Mullis, K.B. (1990). The unusual origin of the polymerase chain reaction, *Scientific American* **262**, 56–61, 64, 65

[4] Jeffreys, A.J., Wilson, V. & Thein, S.L. (1985). Hypervariable 'minisatellite' regions in human DNA, *Nature* **314**, 67–73.

[5] Gill, P., Jeffreys, A.J. & Werrett, D.J. (1985). Forensic application of DNA 'fingerprints', *Nature* **318**, 577–579.

[6] Jeffreys, A.J., Wilson, V. & Thein, S.L. (1985). Individual-specific 'fingerprints' of human DNA, *Nature* **316**, 76–79.

[7] Gill, P. & Werrett, D.J. (1987). Exclusion of a man charged with murder by DNA fingerprinting, *Forensic Science International* **35**, 145–148.

[8] Zagorski, N. (2006). Profile of Alec J. Jeffreys, *Proceedings of the National Academy of Sciences of the United States of America* **103**, 8918–8920.

[9] Gill, P., Lygo, J.E., Fowler, S.J. & Werrett, D.J. (1987). An evaluation of DNA fingerprinting for forensic purposes, *Electrophoresis* **8**, 38–44.

[10] Gill, P., Woodroffe, S., Bar, W., Brinkmann, B., Carracedo, A., Eriksen, B., Jones, S., Kloosterman, A.D., Ludes, B. & Mevag, B. (1992). A report of an international collaborative experiment to demonstrate the uniformity obtainable using DNA profiling techniques, *Forensic Science International* **53**, 29–43.

[11] Schneider, P.M., Fimmers, R., Woodroffe, S., Werrett, D.J., Bar, W., Brinkmann, B., Eriksen, B., Jones, S., Kloosterman, A.D., Mevag, B., Pascalij, V.L., Rittnera, C., Schmitterk, H., Thomson, J.A. & Gill, P. (1991). Report of a European collaborative exercise comparing DNA typing results using a single locus VNTR probe, *Forensic Science International* **49**, 1–15.

[12] Evett, I.W., Werrett, D.J., Gill, P. & Buckleton, J.S. (1989). DNA fingerprinting on trial, *Nature* **340**, 435.

[13] Lander, E.S. (1989). DNA fingerprinting on trial, *Nature* **339**, 501–505.

[14] Helmuth, R., Fildes, N., Blake, E., Luce, M.C., Chimera, J., Madej, R., Gorodezky, C., Stoneking, M., Schmill, N., Klitz, W., *et al.* (1990). HLA-DQ alpha allele and genotype frequencies in various human populations, determined by using enzymatic amplification and oligonucleotide probes, *American Journal of Human Genetics* **47**, 515–523.

[15] Weber, J.L. & May, P.E. (1989). Abundant class of human DNA polymorphisms which can be typed using the polymerase chain reaction, *American Journal of Human Genetics* **44**, 388–396.

[16] Ziegle, J.S., Su, Y., Corcoran, K.P., Nie, L., Mayrand, P.E., Hoff, L.B., McBride, L.J., Kronick, M.N. & Diehl, S.R. (1992). Application of automated DNA sizing technology for genotyping microsatellite loci, *Genomics* **14**, 1026–1031.

[17] Sullivan, K.M., Pope, S., Gill, P. & Robertson, J.M. (1992). Automated DNA profiling by fluorescent labeling of PCR products, *PCR Methods and Applications* **2**, 34–40.

[18] Kimpton, C.P., Gill, P., Walton, A., Urquhart, A., Millican, E.S. & Adams, M. (1993). Automated DNA profiling employing multiplex amplification of short tandem repeat loci, *PCR Methods and Applications* **3**, 13–22.

[19] Sullivan, K.M., Hopgood, R., Lang, B. & Gill, P. (1991). Automated amplification and sequencing of human mitochondrial DNA, *Electrophoresis* **12**, 17–21.

[20] Evett, I.W. & Gill, P. (1991). A discussion of the robustness of methods for assessing the evidential value of DNA single locus profiles in crime investigations, *Electrophoresis* **12**, 226–230.

[21] Evett, I.W. & Pinchin, R. (1991). DNA single locus profiles: tests for the robustness of statistical procedures within the context of forensic science, *International Journal of Legal Medicine* **104**, 267–272.

[22] Lygo, J.E., Johnson, P.E., Holdaway, D.J., Woodroffe, S., Whitaker, J.P., Clayton, T.M., Kimpton, C.P. & Gill, P. (1994). The validation of short tandem repeat (STR) loci for use in forensic casework, *International Journal of Legal Medicine* **107**, 77–89.

[23] Beckmann, J.S. & Weber, J.L. (1992). Survey of human and rat microsatellites, *Genomics* **12**, 627–631.

[24] Edwards, A., Civitello, A., Hammond, H.A. & Caskey, C.T. (1991). DNA typing and genetic mapping with trimeric and tetrameric tandem repeats, *American Journal of Human Genetics* **49**, 746–756.

[25] Clayton, T.M., Whitaker, J.P., Fisher, D.L., Lee, D.A., Holland, M.M., Weedn, V.W., Maguire, C.N., DiZinno, J.A., Kimpton, C.P. & Gill, P. (1995). Further validation of a quadruplex STR DNA typing system: a collaborative effort to identify victims of a mass disaster, *Forensic Science International* **76**, 17–25.

[26] Clayton, T.M., Whitaker, J.P. & Maguire, C.N. (1995). Identification of bodies from the scene of a mass disaster using DNA amplification of short tandem repeat (STR) loci, *Forensic Science International* **76**, 7–15.

[27] Kimpton, C.P., Oldroyd, N.J., Watson, S.K., Frazier, R.R., Johnson, P.E., Millican, E.S., Urquhart, A., Sparkes, B.L. & Gill, P. (1996). Validation of highly discriminating multiplex short tandem repeat amplification systems for individual identification, *Electrophoresis* **17**, 1283–1293.

[28] Gill, P., Brinkmann, B., d'Aloja, E., Andersen, J., Bar, W., Carracedo, A., Dupuy, B., Eriksen, B., Jangblad, M.,

Johnsson, V., Kloosterman, A.D., Lincoln, P., Morling, N., Rand, S., Sabatier, M., Scheithauer, R., Schneider, P. & Vide, M.C. (1997). Considerations from the European DNA profiling group (EDNAP) concerning STR nomenclature, *Forensic Science International* **87**, 185–192.

[29] Sullivan, K.M., Mannucci, A., Kimpton, C.P. & Gill, P. (1993). A rapid and quantitative DNA sex test: fluorescence-based PCR analysis of X-Y homologous gene amelogenin, *Biotechniques* **15**, 636–638, 640, 641

[30] Sparkes, R., Kimpton, C., Watson, S., Oldroyd, N., Clayton, T., Barnett, L., Arnold, J., Thompson, C., Hale, R., Chapman, J., Urquhart, A. & Gill, P. (1996). The validation of a 7-locus multiplex STR test for use in forensic casework. (I). Mixtures, ageing, degradation and species studies, *International Journal of Legal Medicine* **109**, 186–194.

[31] Evett, I.W., Gill, P.D., Lambert, J.A., Oldroyd, N., Frazier, R., Watson, S., Panchal, S., Connolly, A. & Kimpton, C. (1997). Statistical analysis of data for three British ethnic groups from a new STR multiplex, *International Journal of Legal Medicine* **110**, 5–9.

[32] Cotton, E.A., Allsop, R.F., Guest, J.L., Frazier, R.R., Koumi, P., Callow, I.P., Seager, A. & Sparkes, R.L. (2000). Validation of the AMPFlSTR SGM plus system for use in forensic casework, *Forensic Science International* **112**, 151–161.

[33] Foreman, L.A. & Evett, I.W. (2001). Statistical analyses to support forensic interpretation for a new ten-locus STR profiling system, *International Journal of Legal Medicine* **114**, 147–155.

[34] Li, H., Schmidt, L., Wei, M.H., Hustad, T., Lerman, M.I., Zbar, B. & Tory, K. (1993). Three tetranucleotide polymorphisms for loci: D3S1353; D3S1358; D3S1359, *Human Molecular Genetics* **2**, 1327.

[35] Kimpton, C., Walton, A. & Gill, P. (1992). A further tetranucleotide repeat polymorphism in the vWF gene, *Human Molecular Genetics* **1**, 287.

[36] Watson, A., Mazumder, A., Stewart, M. & Balasubramanian, S. (1998). Technology for microarray analysis of gene expression, *Current Opinion in Biotechnology* **9**, 609–614.

[37] Oldroyd, N.J., Urquhart, A.J., Kimpton, C.P., *et al.* (1995). A highly discriminating septaplex short tandem repeat polymerase chain reaction system suitable for human individual identification, *Electrophoresis* **16**, 334–337.

[38] Sharma, V. & Litt, M. (1992). Tetranucleotide repeat polymorphism at the D21S11 locus, *Human Molecular Genetics* **1**, 67.

[39] Urquhart, A., Oldroyd, N.J., Kimpton, C.P. & Gill, P. (1995). Highly discriminating heptaplex short tandem repeat PCR system for forensic identification, *Biotechniques* **18**, 116–118, 120, 121.

[40] Lareu, M.V., Barral, S., Salas, A., Rodriguez, M., Pestoni, C. & Carracedo, A. (1998). *Further exploration of new STRs of interest for forensic genetic analysis*, Elsevier, Oslo, in Progress in Forensic Genetics 7:

Proceedings of the 17th International ISFH Congress, pp. 192–200.

[41] Edwards, A., Hammond, H.A., Jin, L., Caskey, C.T. & Chakraborty, R. (1992). Genetic variation at five trimeric and tetrameric tandem repeat loci in four human population groups, *Genomics* **12**, 241–253.

[42] Mills, K.A., Even, D. & Murray, J.C. (1992). Tetranucleotide repeat polymorphism at the human alpha fibrinogen locus (FGA), *Human Molecular Genetics* **1**, 779.

[43] Ruitberg, C.M., Reeder, D.J. & Butler, J.M. (2001). STRBase: a short tandem repeat DNA database for the human identity testing community, *Nucleic Acids Research* **29**, 320–322.

[44] Harris, P.C. (2004). Gene hunters find cause of childhood polycystic kidney disease, *Inside iScience* **1**, 10.

[45] Frazier, R.R., Millican, E.S., Watson, S.K., *et al.* (1996). Validation of the Applied Biosystems Prism 377 automated sequencer for the forensic short tandem repeat analysis, *Electrophoresis* **17**, 1550–1552.

[46] Butler, J.M., Buel, E., Crivellente, F. & McCord, B.R. (2004). Forensic DNA typing by capillary electrophoresis using the ABI Prism 310 and 3100 genetic analyzers for STR analysis, *Electrophoresis* **25**(10–11), 1397–1412.

[47] Graham, E.A.M. (2005). DNA reviews: lab-on-a-chip technology, *Forensic Science Medicine and Pathology* **1**(2), 221–223.

[48] Barbaro, A., Cormaci, P. & Agostino, A. (2011). Validation of AmpFLSTR NGM SElectTM PCR amplification kit on forensic samples, *Forensic Science International: Genetics Supplement Series* **3**(1), e67–e68.

[49] Tucker, V.C., Hopwood, A.J., Sprecher, C.J., McLaren, R.S., Rabbach, D.R., Ensenberger, M.G., Thompson, J.M. & Storts, D.R. (2012). Developmental validation of the PowerPlex (R) ESX 16 and PowerPlex (R) ESX 17 Systems, *Forensic Science International-Genetics* **6**(1), 124–131.

[50] Risch, N. & Merikangas, K. (1996). The future of genetic studies of complex human diseases, *Science* **273**, 1516–1517.

[51] Collins, F.S., Guyer, M.S. & Charkravarti, A. (1997). Variations on a theme: cataloging human DNA sequence variation, *Science* **278**, 1580–1581.

[52] Dixon, L.A., Murray, C.M., Archer, E.J., Dobbins, A.E., Koumi, P. & Gill, P. (2005). Validation of a 21-locus autosomal SNP multiplex for forensic identification purposes, *Forensic Science International* **154**, 62–77.

[53] Graham, E.A.M. (2005). DNA reviews: mini STR's, *Forensic Science, Medicine, and Pathology* **1**, 65–68.

[54] Gill, P. (2001). An assessment of the utility of single nucleotide polymorphisms (SNPs) for forensic purposes, *International Journal of Legal Medicine* **114**, 204–210.

[55] Strum, R.A. & Frudakis, T.N. (2004). Eye colour: portals into pigmentation genes and ancestry, *Trends in Genetics* **20**, 327–332.

[56] Sturm, R.A. & Frudakis, T.N. (2004). Eye colour: portals into pignmentation genes and ancestry, *Trends in Genetics* **20**, 327–332.

[57] Grimes, E.A., Noake, P.J., Dixon, L. & Urquhart, A. (2001). Sequence polymorphism in the human melanocortin 1 receptor gene as an indicator of the red hair phenotype, *Forensic Science International* **122**, 124–129.

[58] Rana, B.K. (1999). High polymorphism at the human melanocortin 1 receptor locus, *Genetics* **151**, 1547–1557.

[59] Sturm, R.A. (2002). Skin colour and skin cancer – MC1R, the genetic link, *Melanoma Research* **12**, 405–416.

[60] Graham, E.A.M. (2006). DNA reviews: sex determination, *Forensic Science, Medicine, and Pathology* **2**, 283–286.

[61] Graham, E.A.M. (2006). DNA reviews: forensic DNA on the internet, *Forensic Science, Medicine, and Pathology* **2**, 63–66.

[62] Greenspoon, S.A., Scarpetta, M.A., Drayton, M.L. & Turek, S.A. (1998). QIAamp spin columns as a method of DNA isolation for forensic casework, *Journal of Forensic Sciences* **43**, 1024–1030.

[63] Scherczinger, C.A., Bourke, M.T., Ladd, C. & Lee, H.C. (1997). DNA extraction from liquid blood using QIAamp, *Journal of Forensic Sciences* **42**, 893–896.

[64] Walsh, P.S., Metzger, D.A. & Higuchi, R. (1991). Chelex 100 as a medium for simple extraction of DNA for PCR-based typing from forensic material, *Biotechniques* **10**, 506–513.

[65] Yang, D.Y., Eng, B., Waye, J.S., Dudar, J.C. & Saunders, S.R. (1998). Technical note: improved DNA extraction from ancient bones using silica-based spin columns, *American Journal of Physical Anthropology* **105**, 539–543.

[66] Ye, J., Ji, A., Parra, E.J., Zheng, X., Jiang, C., Zhao, X., Hu, L. & Tu, Z. (2004). A simple and efficient method for extracting DNA from old and burned bone, *Journal of Forensic Sciences* **49**, 754–759.

[67] Alonso, A., Andelinovic, S., Martin, P., Sutlovic, D., Erceg, I., Huffine, E., de Simon, L.F., Albarran, C., Definis-Gojanovic, M., Fernandez-Rodriguez, A., Garcia, P., Drmic, I., Rezic, B., Kuret, S., Sancho, M. & Primorac, D. (2001). DNA typing from skeletal remains: evaluation of multiplex and megaplex STR systems on DNA isolated from bone and teeth samples, *Croatian Medical Journal* **42**, 260–266.

[68] Evison, M.P., Smillie, D.M. & Chamberlain, A.T. (1997). Extraction of single-copy nuclear DNA from forensic specimens with a variety of postmortem histories, *Journal of Forensic Sciences* **42**, 1032–1038.

[69] Boom, R., Sol, C.J., Salimans, M.M., Jansen, C.L., Wertheim-van Dillen, P.M. & van der Noordaa, J. (1990). Rapid and simple method for purification of nucleic acids, *Journal of Clinical Microbiology* **28**, 495–503.

[70] Hoss, M. & Paabo, S. (1993). DNA extraction from Pleistocene bones by a silica-based purification method, *Nucleic Acids Research* **21**, 3913–3914.

[71] Kalmar, T., Bachrati, C.Z., Marcsik, A. & Rasko, I. (2000). A simple and efficient method for PCR amplifiable DNA extraction from ancient bones, *Nucleic Acids Research* **28**, E67.

[72] Hochmeister, M.N., Budowle, B., Borer, U.V., Eggmann, U., Comey, C.T. & Dirnhofer, R. (1991). Typing of deoxyribonucleic acid (DNA) extracted from compact bone from human remains, *Journal of Forensic Sciences* **36**, 1649–1661.

[73] Rennick, S.L., Fenton, T.W. & Foran, D.R. (2005). The effects of skeletal preparation techniques on DNA from human and non-human bone, *Journal of Forensic Sciences* **50**, 1016–1019.

[74] Tsuchimochi, T., Iwasa, M., Maeno, Y., Koyama, H., Inoue, H., Isobe, I., Matoba, R., Yokoi, M. & Nagao, M. (2002). Chelating resin-based extraction of DNA from dental pulp and sex determination from incinerated teeth with Y-chromosomal alphoid repeat and short tandem repeats, *The American Journal of Forensic Medicine and Pathology* **23**, 268–271.

[75] Trivedi, R., Chattopadhyay, P. & Kashyap, V.K. (2002). A new improved method for extraction of DNA from teeth for the analysis of hypervariable loci, *The American Journal of Forensic Medicine and Pathology* **23**, 191–196.

[76] Sivagami, A.V., Rao, A.R. & Varshney, U. (2000). A simple and cost-effective method for preparing DNA from the hard tooth tissue, and its use in polymerase chain reaction amplification of amelogenin gene segment for sex determination in an Indian population, *Forensic Science International* **110**, 107–115.

[77] De Leo, D., Turrina, S. & Marigo, M. (2000). Effects of individual dental factors on genomic DNA analysis, *The American Journal of Forensic Medicine and Pathology* **21**, 411–415.

[78] Malaver, P.C. & Yunis, J.J. (2003). Different dental tissues as source of DNA for human identification in forensic cases, *Croatian Medical Journal* **44**, 306–309.

[79] Pfeiffer, H., Huhne, J., Seitz, B. & Brinkmann, B. (1999). Influence of soil storage and exposure period on DNA recovery from teeth, *International Journal of Legal Medicine* **112**, 142–144.

[80] Higuchi, R., von Beroldingen, C.H., Sensabaugh, G.F. & Erlich, H.A. (1988). DNA typing from single hairs, *Nature* **332**, 543–546.

[81] Schreiber, A., Amtmann, E., Storch, V. & Sauer, G. (1988). The extraction of high-molecular-mass DNA from hair shafts, *FEBS Letters* **230**, 209–211.

[82] Vigilant, L. (1999). An evaluation of techniques for the extraction and amplification of DNA from naturally shed hairs, *Biological Chemistry* **380**, 1329–1331.

[83] Graffy, E.A. & Foran, D.R. (2005). A simplified method for mitochondrial DNA extraction from head hair shafts, *Journal of Forensic Sciences* **50**, 1119–1122.

[84]   Pfeiffer, I., Volkel, I., Taubert, H. & Brenig, B. (2004). Forensic DNA-typing of dog hair: DNA-extraction and PCR amplification, *Forensic Science International* **141**, 149–151.

[85]   Sweet, D. & Hildebrand, D. (1999). Saliva from cheese bite yields DNA profile of burglar: a case report, *International Journal of Legal Medicine* **112**, 201–203.

[86]   Sweet, D., Lorente, M., Lorente, J.A., Valenzuela, A. & Villanueva, E. (1997). An improved method to recover saliva from human skin: the double swab technique, *Journal of Forensic Sciences* **42**, 320–322.

[87]   Sweet, D., Lorente, M., Valenzuela, A., Lorente, J.A. & Alvarez, J.C. (1996). Increasing DNA extraction yield from saliva stains with a modified Chelex method, *Forensic Science International* **83**, 167–177.

[88]   Kato, Y., Katsumata, R., Yoshimoto, T., Tanaka, M., Huang, X.L., Tamaki, K., Kumazawa, T., Sato, K. & Katsumata, Y. (1999). Large-scale preparation of high-molecular weight DNA from buccal mucosa, *Legal Medicine (Tokyo)* **1**, 6–10.

[89]   London, S.J., Xia, J., Lehman, T.A., Yang, J.H., Granada, E., Chunhong, L., Dubeau, L., Li, T., David-Beabes, G.L. & Li, Y. (2001). Collection of buccal cell DNA in seventh-grade children using water and a toothbrush, *Cancer Epidemiology, Biomarkers and Prevention* **10**, 1227–1230.

[90]   Hanselle, T., Otte, M., Schnibbe, T., Smythe, E. & Krieg-Schneider, F. (2003). Isolation of genomic DNA from buccal swabs for forensic analysis, using fully automated silica-membrane purification technology, *Legal Medicine (Tokyo)* **5**(Suppl 1), S145–S149.

[91]   Zehner, R., Amendt, J. & Krettek, R. (2004). STR typing of human DNA from fly larvae fed on decomposing bodies, *Journal of Forensic Sciences* **49**, 337–340.

[92]   Linville, J.G., Hayes, J. & Wells, J.D. (2004). Mitochondrial DNA and STR analyses of maggot crop contents: effect of specimen preservation technique, *Journal of Forensic Sciences* **49**, 341–344.

[93]   Linville, J.G. & Wells, J.D. (2002). Surface sterilization of a maggot using bleach does not interfere with mitochondrial DNA analysis of crop contents, *Journal of Forensic Sciences* **47**, 1055–1059.

[94]   Johnson, D.J., Martin, L.R. & Roberts, K.A. (2005). STR-typing of human DNA from human fecal matter using the QIAGEN QIAamp stool mini kit, *Journal of Forensic Sciences* **50**, 802–808.

[95]   Vandenberg, N. & van Oorschot, R.A. (2002). Extraction of human nuclear DNA from feces samples using the QIAamp DNA stool mini kit, *Journal of Forensic Sciences* **47**, 993–995.

[96]   Roy, R. (2003). Analysis of human fecal material for autosomal and Y chromosome STRs, *Journal of Forensic Sciences* **48**, 1035–1040.

[97]   McOrist, A.L., Jackson, M. & Bird, A.R. (2002). A comparison of five methods for extraction of bacterial DNA from human faecal samples, *Journal of Microbiological Methods* **50**, 131–139.

[98]   Nakazono, T., Kashimura, S., Hayashiba, Y., Hara, K. & Miyoshi, A. (2005). Successful DNA typing of urine stains using a DNA purification kit following diafiltration, *Journal of Forensic Sciences* **50**, 860–864.

[99]   Yasuda, T., Iida, R., Takeshita, H., Ueki, M., Nakajima, T., Kaneko, Y., Mogi, K., Tsukahara, T. & Kishi, K. (2003). A simple method of DNA extraction and STR typing from urine samples using a commercially available DNA/RNA extraction kit, *Journal of Forensic Sciences* **48**, 108–110.

[100] Drobnic, K. (2003). Analysis of DNA evidence recovered from epithelial cells in penile swabs, *Croatian Medical Journal* **44**, 350–354.

[101] Bright, J.A. & Petricevic, S.F. (2004). Recovery of trace DNA and its application to DNA profiling of shoe insoles, *Forensic Science International* **145**, 7–12.

[102] Szibor, R., Michael, M., Plate, I. & Krause, D. (2000). Efficiency of forensic mtDNA analysis. Case examples demonstrating the identification of traces, *Forensic Science International* **113**, 71–78.

[103] Watanabe, Y., Takayama, T., Hirata, K., Yamada, S., Nagai, A., Nakamura, I., Bunai, Y. & Ohya, I. (2003). DNA typing from cigarette butts, *Legal Medicine (Tokyo)* **5**(Suppl 1), S177–S179.

[104] Esslinger, K.J., Siegel, J.A., Spillane, H. & Stallworth, S. (2004). Using STR analysis to detect human DNA from exploded pipe bomb devices, *Journal of Forensic Sciences* **49**, 481–484.

[105] Petricevic, S.F., Bright, J.A. & Cockerton, S.L. (2006). DNA profiling of trace DNA recovered from bedding, *Forensic Science International.* **159**, 21–26.

[106] Abaz, J., Walsh, S.J., Curran, J.M., Moss, D.S., Cullen, J., Bright, J.A., Crowe, G.A., Cockerton, S.L. & Power, T.E. (2002). Comparison of the variables affecting the recovery of DNA from common drinking containers, *Forensic Science International* **126**, 233–240.

[107] Hagelberg, E., Sykes, B. & Hedges, R. (1989). Ancient bone DNA amplified, *Nature* **342**, 485.

[108] Hagelberg, E. & Clegg, J.B. (1991). Isolation and characterization of DNA from archaeological bone, *Proceedings of the Royal Society of London, Series B: Biological Sciences* **244**, 45–50.

[109] Cattaneo, C., Craig, O.E., James, N.T. & Sokol, R.J. (1997). Comparison of three DNA extraction methods on bone and blood stains up to 43 years old and amplification of three different gene sequences, *Journal of Forensic Sciences* **42**, 1126–1135.

[110] Greenspoon, S.A., Ban, J.D., Sykes, K., Ballard, E.J., Edler, S.S., Baisden, M. & Covington, B.L. (2004). Application of the BioMek 2000 laboratory automation workstation and the DNA IQ System to the extraction of forensic casework samples, *Journal of Forensic Sciences* **49**, 29–39.

[111] Greenspoon, S.A., Sykes, K.L., Ban, J.D., Pollard, A., Baisden, M., Farr, M., Graham, N., Collins, B.L., Green, M.M. & Christenson, C.C. (2006). Automated PCR setup for forensic casework samples using the

Normalization Wizard and PCR Setup robotic methods, *Forensic Science International* **164**, 240–248.

[112] Montpetit, S.A., Fitch, I.T. & O'Donnell, P.T. (2005). A simple automated instrument for DNA extraction in forensic casework, *Journal of Forensic Sciences* **50**, 555–563.

[113] Brevnov, M.G., Mundt, J., Treat-Clemons, L., Kalusche, G., Meredith, J., Porter, G., Furtado, M.R. & Shewale, J.G. (2009a). Automated extraction of DNA from forensic sample types using the PrepFiler automated forensic DNA extraction kit, *Journal of the Association for Laboratory Automation* **14**, 294–302.

[114] Brevnov, M.G., Pawar, H.S., Mundt, J., Calandro, L.M., Furtado, M.R. & Shewale, J.G. (2009b). Developmental validation of the PrepFiler (TM) forensic DNA extraction kit for extraction of genomic DNA from biological samples, *Journal of Forensic Sciences* **54**(3), 599–607.

[115] Gill, P., Sparkes, R., Fereday, L. & Werrett, D.J. (2000). Report of the European Network of Forensic Science Institutes (ENSFI): formulation and testing of principles to evaluate STR multiplexes, *Forensic Science International* **108**, 1–29.

[116] Gill, P., Whitaker, J., Flaxman, C., Brown, N. & Buckleton, J. (2000). An investigation of the rigor of interpretation rules for STRs derived from less than 100 pg of DNA, *Forensic Science International* **112**, 17–40.

[117] Haque, K., Pfeiffer, R., Beerman, M., Struewing, J., Chanock, S. & Bergen, A. (2003). Performance of high-throughput DNA quantification methods, *BMC Biotechnology* **3**, 20.

[118] Singer, V.L., Jones, L.J., Yue, S.T. & Haugland, R.P. (1997). Characterization of PicoGreen reagent and development of a fluorescence-based solution assay for double-stranded DNA quantitation, *Analytical Biochemistry* **249**, 228–238.

[119] Walsh, P.S., Varlaro, J. & Reynolds, R. (1992). A rapid chemiluminescent method for quantitation of human DNA, *Nucleic Acids Research* **20**, 5061–5065.

[120] Budowle, B., Hudlow, W.R., Lee, S.B. & Klevan, L. (2001). Using a CCD camera imaging system as a recording device to quantify human DNA by slot blot hybridization, *Biotechniques* **30**, 680–685.

[121] Allen, R.W. & Fuller, V.M. (2006). Quantitation of human genomic DNA through amplification of the amelogenin locus, *Journal of Forensic Sciences* **51**, 76–81.

[122] Hayn, S., Wallace, M.M., Prinz, M. & Shaler, R.C. (2004). Evaluation of an automated liquid hybridization method for DNA quantitation, *Journal of Forensic Sciences* **49**, 87–91.

[123] Carrondo, M.A., Coll, M., Aymami, J., Wang, A.H., van der Marel, G.A., van Boom, J.H. & Rich, A. (1989). Binding of a Hoechst dye to d(CGCGATATCGCG) and its influence on the conformation of the DNA fragment, *Biochemistry* **28**, 7849–7859.

[124] Ahn, S., Costa, J. & Emanuel, J. (1996). PicoGreen quantitation of DNA: effective evaluation of samples pre- or post-PCR 10.1093/nar/24.13.2623, *Nucleic Acids Research* **24**, 2623–2625.

[125] Higuchi, R., Dollinger, G., Walsh, P.S. & Griffith, R. (1992). Simultaneous amplification and detection of specific DNA sequences, *Bio/technology (Nature Publishing Company)* **10**, 413–417.

[126] Higuchi, R., Fockler, C., Dollinger, G. & Watson, R. (1993). Kinetic PCR analysis: real-time monitoring of DNA amplification reactions, *Biotechnology (N Y)* **11**, 1026–1030.

[127] Nicklas, J.A. & Buel, E. (2003). Development of an Alu-based, real-time PCR method for quantitation of human DNA in forensic samples, *Journal of Forensic Sciences* **48**, 936–944.

[128] Urban, C., Gruber, F., Kundi, M., Falkner, F.G., Dorner, F. & Hammerle, T. (2000). A systematic and quantitative analysis of PCR template contamination, *Journal of Forensic Sciences* **45**, 1307–1311.

[129] Walker, J.A., Kilroy, G.E., Xing, J., Shewale, J., Sinha, S.K. & Batzer, M.A. (2003). Human DNA quantitation using Alu element-based polymerase chain reaction, *Analytical Biochemistry* **315**, 122–128.

[130] Alonso, A., Martin, P., Albarran, C., Garcia, P., Garcia, O., de Simon, L.F., Garcia-Hirschfeld, J., Sancho, M., de La Rua, C. & Fernandez-Piqueras, J. (2004). Real-time PCR designs to estimate nuclear and mitochondrial DNA copy number in forensic and ancient DNA studies, *Forensic Science International* **139**, 141–149.

[131] Andelinovic, S., Sutlovic, D., Erceg Ivkosic, I., Skaro, V., Ivkosic, A., Paic, F., Rezic, B., Definis-Gojanovic, M. & Primorac, D. (2005). Twelve-year experience in identification of skeletal remains from mass graves, *Croatian Medical Journal* **46**, 530–539.

[132] Andreasson, H., Nilsson, M., Budowle, B., Lundberg, H. & Allen, M. (2006). Nuclear and mitochondrial DNA quantification of various forensic materials, *Forensic Science International* **164**, 56–64.

[133] Andreasson, H., Gyllensten, U. & Allen, M. (2002). Real-time DNA quantification of nuclear and mitochondrial DNA in forensic analysis, *Biotechniques* **33**(402–404), 407–411.

[134] Timken, M.D., Swango, K.L., Orrego, C. & Buoncristiani, M.R. (2005). A duplex real-time qPCR assay for the quantification of human nuclear and mitochondrial DNA in forensic samples: implications for quantifying DNA in degraded samples, *Journal of Forensic Sciences* **50**, 1044–1060.

[135] Swango, K.L., Hudlow, W.R., Timken, M.D. & Buoncristiani, M.R. (2006). Developmental validation of a multiplex qPCR assay for assessing the quantity and quality of nuclear DNA in forensic samples, *Forensic Science International* **170**, 35–45.

[136] Caddy, B., Taylor, G. R. & Linacre, A. (2008) A Review of the Science of Low Template DNA Analysis, http://www.homeoffice.gov.uk/publications/police/790604/Review_of_Low_Template_DNA_1.pdf.

[137] Barbisin, M., Fang, R., O'Shea, C.E., Calandro, L.M., Furtado, M.R. & Shewale, J.G. (2009). Developmental validation of the quantifiler® Duo DNA quantification kit for simultaneous quantification of total human and

human male DNA and detection of PCR inhibitors in biological samples, *Journal of Forensic Sciences* **54**(2), 305–319.

[138] Krenke, B.E., Nassif, N., Sprecher, C.J., Knox, C., Schwandt, M. & Storts, D.R. (2008). Developmental validation of a real-time PCR assay for the simultaneous quantification of total human and male DNA, *Forensic Science International-Genetics* **3**(1), 14–21.

[139] Schneider, P.M. (1997). Basic issues in forensic DNA typing, *Forensic Science International* **88**, 17–22.

[140] Sajantila, A., Puomilahti, S., Johnsson, V. & Ehnholm, C. (1992). Amplification of reproducible allele markers for amplified fragment length polymorphism analysis, *Biotechniques* **12**, 16, 18, 20–22.

[141] Smith, R.N. (1995). Accurate size comparison of short tandem repeat alleles amplified by PCR, *Biotechniques* **18**, 122–128.

[142] Gill, P., Kimpton, C.P., Urquhart, A., Oldroyd, N., Millican, E.S., Watson, S.K. & Downes, T.J. (1995). Automated short tandem repeat (STR) analysis in forensic casework – a strategy for the future, *Electrophoresis* **16**, 1543–1552.

[143] Gill, P., Sparkes, R. & Kimpton, C. (1997). Development of guidelines to designate alleles using an STR multiplex system, *Forensic Science International* **89**, 185–197.

[144] Kloosterman, A.D. & Kersbergen, P. (2003). Efficacy and limits of genotyping low copy number (LCN) DNA samples by multiplex PCR of STR loci, *Journal de la Société de Biologie* **197**, 351–359.

[145] Ludecke, H.J., Senger, G., Claussen, U. & Horsthemke, B. (1989). Cloning defined regions of the human genome by microdissection of banded chromosomes and enzymatic amplification, *Nature* **338**, 348–350.

[146] Zhang, L., Cui, X., Schmitt, K., Hubert, R., Navidi, W. & Arnheim, N. (1992). Whole genome amplification from a single cell: implications for genetic analysis, *Proceedings of the National Academy of Sciences of the United States of America* **89**, 5847–5851.

[147] Kristjansson, K., Chong, S.S., Van den Veyver, I.B., Subramanian, S., Snabes, M.C. & Hughes, M.R. (1994). Preimplantation single cell analyses of dystrophin gene deletions using whole genome amplification, *Nature Genetics* **6**, 19–23.

[148] Snabes, M.C., Chong, S.S., Subramanian, S.B., Kristjansson, K., DiSepio, D. & Hughes, M.R. (1994). Preimplantation single-cell analysis of multiple genetic loci by whole-genome amplification, *Proceedings of the National Academy of Sciences of the United States of America* **91**, 6181–6185.

[149] Faulkner, S.W. & Leigh, D.A. (1998). Universal amplification of DNA isolated from small regions of paraffin-embedded, formalin-fixed tissue, *Biotechniques* **24**, 47–50.

[150] Dean, F.B., Nelson, J.R., Giesler, T.L. & Lasken, R.S. (2001). Rapid amplification of plasmid and phage DNA using Phi 29 DNA polymerase and multiply-primed rolling circle amplification, *Genome Research* **11**, 1095–1099.

[151] Dean, F.B., Hosono, S., Fang, L., Wu, X., Faruqi, A.F., Bray-Ward, P., Sun, Z., Zong, Q., Du, Y., Du, J., Driscoll, M., Song, W., Kingsmore, S.F., Egholm, M. & Lasken, R.S. (2002). Comprehensive human genome amplification using multiple displacement amplification, *Proceedings of the National Academy of Sciences of the United States of America* **99**, 5261–5266.

[152] Hosono, S., Faruqi, A.F., Dean, F.B., Du, Y., Sun, Z., Wu, X., Du, J., Kingsmore, S.F., Egholm, M. & Lasken, R.S. (2003). Unbiased whole-genome amplification directly from clinical samples, *Genome Research* **13**, 954–964.

[153] Lovmar, L., Fredriksson, M., Liljedahl, U., Sigurdsson, S. & Syvanen, A.C. (2003). Quantitative evaluation by minisequencing and microarrays reveals accurate multiplexed SNP genotyping of whole genome amplified DNA, *Nucleic Acids Research* **31**, e129.

[154] Murthy, K.K., Mahboubi, V.S., Santiago, A., Barragan, M.T., Knoll, R., Schultheiss, H.P., O'Connor, D.T., Schork, N.J. & Rana, B.K. (2005). Assessment of multiple displacement amplification for polymorphism discovery and haplotype determination at a highly polymorphic locus, MC1R, *Human Mutation* **26**, 145–152.

[155] Paez, J.G., Lin, M., Beroukhim, R., Lee, J.C., Zhao, X., Richter, D.J., Gabriel, S., Herman, P., Sasaki, H., Altshuler, D., Li, C., Meyerson, M. & Sellers, W.R. (2004). Genome coverage and sequence fidelity of phi29 polymerase-based multiple strand displacement whole genome amplification, *Nucleic Acids Research* **32**, e71.

[156] Sun, G., Kaushal, R., Pal, P., Wolujewicz, M., Smelser, D., Cheng, H., Lu, M., Chakraborty, R., Jin, L. & Deka, R. (2005). Whole-genome amplification: relative efficiencies of the current methods, *Legal Medicine (Tokyo)* **7**, 279–286.

[157] Barber, A.L. & Foran, D.R. (2006). The utility of whole genome amplification for typing compromised forensic samples, *Journal of Forensic Sciences* **51**, 1344–1349.

[158] Hughes, S., Arneson, N., Done, S. & Squire, J. (2005). The use of whole genome amplification in the study of human disease, *Progress in Biophysics and Molecular Biology* **88**, 173–189.

[159] Hughes, S., Yoshimoto, M., Beheshti, B., Houlston, R.S., Squire, J.A. & Evans, A. (2006). The use of whole genome amplification to study chromosomal changes in prostate cancer: insights into genome-wide signature of preneoplasia associated with cancer progression, *BMC Genomics* **7**, 65.

[160] Hanson, E.K. & Ballantyne, J. (2005). Whole genome amplification strategy for forensic genetic analysis using single or few cell equivalents of genomic DNA, *Analytical Biochemistry* **346**, 246–257.

[161] Lee, C.I., Leong, S.H., Png, A.E., Choo, K.W., Syn, C., Lim, D.T., Law, H.Y. & Kon, O.L. (2006). An isothermal primer extension method for whole genome amplification of fresh and degraded DNA: applications in comparative genomic hybridization, genotyping and mutation screening, *Nature Protocols* **1**, 2185–2194.

[162] Lee, C.I., Leong, S.H., Png, A.E., *et al.* (2006). An isothermal method for whole genome amplification of fresh and degraded DNA for comparative genomic hybridization, genotyping and mutation detection, *DNA Research* **13**, 77–88.

[163] Strom, C.M. & Rechitsky, S. (1998). Use of nested PCR to identify charred human remains and minute amounts of blood, *Journal of Forensic Sciences* **43**, 696–700.

[164] van Oorschot, R.A. & Jones, M.K. (1997). DNA fingerprints from fingerprints, *Nature* **387**, 767.

[165] Alessandrini, F., Cecati, M., Pesaresi, M., Turchi, C., Carle, F. & Tagliabracci, A. (2003). Fingerprints as evidence for a genetic profile: morphological study on fingerprints and analysis of exogenous and individual factors affecting DNA typing, *Journal of Forensic Sciences* **48**, 586–592.

[166] Rutty, G.N. (2002). An investigation into the transference and survivability of human DNA following simulated manual strangulation with consideration of the problem of third party contamination, *International Journal of Legal Medicine* **116**, 170–173.

[167] Wiegand, P. & Kleiber, M. (1997). DNA typing of epithelial cells after strangulation, *International Journal of Legal Medicine* **110**, 181–183.

[168] Bohnert, M., Faller-Marquardt, M., Lutz, S., Amberg, R., Weisser, H.J. & Pollak, S. (2001). Transfer of biological traces in cases of hanging and ligature strangulation, *Forensic Science International* **116**, 107–115.

[169] Gill, P. (2001). Application of low copy number DNA profiling, *Croatian Medical Journal* **42**, 229–232.

[170] Taberlet, P., Griffin, S., Goossens, B., Questiau, S., Manceau, V., Escaravage, N., Waits, L.P. & Bouvet, J. (1996). Reliable genotyping of samples with very low DNA quantities using PCR, *Nucleic Acids Research* **24**, 3189–3194.

[171] Whitaker, J.P., Cotton, E.A. & Gill, P. (2001). A comparison of the characteristics of profiles produced with the AMPFISTR SGM Plus multiplex system for both standard and low copy number (LCN) STR DNA analysis, *Forensic Science International* **123**, 215–223.

[172] Graham, E.A.M. (2005). DNA Reviews: Automated DNA profile analysis, *Forensic Science, Medicine, and Pathology* **1**, 285–288.

[173] Buckleton, J. & Gill, P. (2011). Further comment on "Low copy number typing has yet to achieve 'general acceptance'", by Budowle, B., *et al.*, 2009. Forensic Science International Genetics: Supplement Series 2, 551–552, *Forensic Science International-Genetics* **5**(1), 7–11.

[174] Budowle, B., Eisenberg, A.J. & Van Daal, A. (2009). Low copy number typing has yet to achieve 'general acceptance', *Forensic Science International: Genetics Supplement Series* **2**, 551–552.

[175] Budowle, B., Eisenberg, A.J. & van Daal, A. (2011). Response to comment on "Low copy number typing has yet to achieve "general acceptance" (Budowle *et al.*, 2009. Forensic Science International: Genetics Supplement Series 2, 551–552) by Theresa Caragine, Mechthild Prinz, *Forensic Science International-Genetics* **5**(1), 5–7.

[176] Budowle, B. & van Daal, A. (2011). Reply to comments by Buckleton and Gill on "Low copy number typing has yet to achieve 'general acceptance'" by Budowle, B., *et al.*, 2009. Forensic Science International: Genetics Supplement Series 2, 551–552, *Forensic Science International-Genetics* **5**(1), 12–14.

[177] Caragine, T. & Prinz, M. (2011). Comment on "Low copy number typing has yet to achieve 'general acceptance'" by Budowle, B., *et al.*, 2009. Forensic Science International: Genetics Supplement Series 2, 551–552, *Forensic Science International-Genetics* **5**(1), 3–4.

Related Articles in EFS Online

Autoradiograph

DQα

Low Copy Number DNA

Peak Height: DNA

Short Tandem Repeats

Variable Number Tandem Repeats

Wildlife

Whole Genome Amplification

Chapter 3
DNA

Simon J. Walsh

Australian Federal Police, Canberra, ACT, Australia

Introduction

Forensic DNA profiling combines scientific disciplines of anatomy, cell and molecular biology, genetics, mathematics, and statistics. This article aims to explain some of the fundamental science underpinning the use of DNA in a forensic context. In particular, it examines the natural attributes of DNA that contribute to its suitability for use in the forensic field and a summary of the practical tools routinely applied to extract the vital information encoded within human DNA.

Fundamental Human Anatomy

The human body is a universe of working parts and functional interactions. We observe the physical manifestations of these interactions all the time, as we walk, talk, breathe, think, or eat. These gross or macroscopic functions of the human body, however, are driven by extremely complex interactions, occurring at the cellular and subcellular level.

Our bodies are made up of trillions of cells. Each cell has a prescribed function relative to its position in the body that is essential to healthy human life. The cells themselves are extremely complex and advanced pieces of biological machinery. A cell is comprised of a cytosol, which is bound by a permeable membrane, and contains a host of miniature organs (organelles) including the nucleus. The nucleus contains DNA – the material that prescribes the cell's principal functional characteristics.

It may be useful to think of the cell as being like a factory. Membranes enclose the structure and separate different organelles, which can be thought of as departments with specialized functions. The nucleus is the central administration, containing in its DNA a library of information that determines cellular structure and processes. From it instructions are issued for proper regulation of the business of the cell. The mitochondria are the power generators. The cytosol can be thought of as the general work area, where protein machinery (enzymes) carries out the formation of new molecules from imported raw materials. There are special molecular channels in the membranes between compartments and between the cell and its external surroundings. These monitor the flow of molecules in the appropriate directions, similar to personal assistants and receptionists. Like factories, cells tend to specialize in function. For example, many of the cells in higher organisms are largely devoted to the production and export of one or a few molecular products.

Despite the diverse functions of the different types of cells that constitute the human body, each nucleated cell contains an identical copy of a common DNA molecule from which genetic information is read in a linear fashion. Since the amount of information needed to specify the structure and function of a multicellular organism such as a human is immense, the DNA molecule is extremely long. In fact, if the DNA from a single human cell were stretched end to end it would extend approximately 2 m.

Human cells live by a well-defined life cycle, itself, separated into several distinct phases. Similarly, the process of eukaryotic cell division can be divided into principle phases. Cell division can occur by mitosis that produces two diploid cells, or meiosis, which produces four haploid cells. Mitosis results in the production of two daughter cells that are identical to

A Guide to Forensic DNA Profiling
Edited by Allan Jamieson and Scott Bader
© 2016 John Wiley & Sons, Ltd. ISBN: 9781118751527
Also published in EFS (online edition)
DOI: 10.1002/9780470061589.fsa109

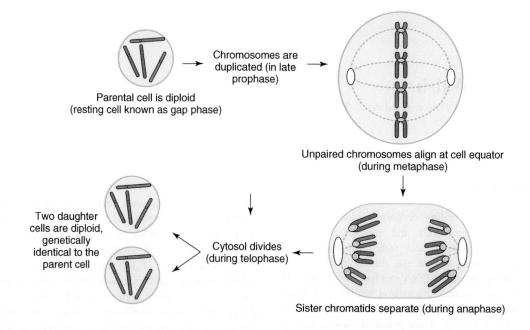

Chromosomes are
duplicated (in late
prophase)

Parental cell is diploid
(resting cell known as gap phase)

Unpaired chromosomes align at cell equator
(during metaphase)

Two daughter
cells are diploid,
genetically
identical to the
parent cell

Cytosol divides
(during telophase)

Sister chromatids separate (during anaphase)

Figure 1   Diagrammatic representation of mitosis, the process of cell replication for adult or somatic cells

each other and to the parent cell and is the process of somatic cell replication (Figure 1). Our genetic information is carried to the next generation by the haploid cells known as *gametes* (spermatozoa in the male and the oocyte in the female). These cells are produced by meiosis during gametogenesis (or specifically, spermatogenesis or oogenesis; Figure 2). In either mitosis or meiosis, the DNA (on the chromosomes) must be duplicated and distributed to each daughter cell. An error in DNA replication is called a *mutation*. If mutation occurs during replication of an adult cell only progeny cells within that person/organism are affected. This is known as *somatic mutation*. If mutation occurs in the gametes (or germinal cells) there is a possibility that it will be passed onto the offspring of the person/organism. This is referred to as a *germline mutation*.

This summary of basic cellular biology illustrates the first point as to the applicability of DNA analysis for forensic purposes. A replica DNA molecule exists in all nucleated cells in the human body. This means that cells existing in any individual's tissues, fluids, or organs carry a copy of the same DNA molecule. This means there are trillions of possible sources of DNA that can be targetted for forensic purposes. It

also means that DNA can be cross-compared among various tissue types from the same donor.

The heritable characteristic of DNA is another advantage to its use in the forensic sciences. Familial, and particularly parental, relationships can provide information to the origin of a given DNA profile due to the known presence of inherited characteristics. This application of DNA profiling technology is often used in the identification of human remains or in the investigation of crimes involving disputed paternity.

Fundamental Genetics

A striking attribute of a living cell is its ability to transmit hereditary properties from one cell generation to the next. This power of self-replication is often attributed as the defining difference between the living and the nonliving. Since the beginning of human history, people have wondered how traits are inherited from one generation to the next. Although children tend to resemble one parent more closely than the other, most offspring tend to be a blend of the characteristics of both parents. The idea of a gene, a unit of hereditary information, arose in the mid-nineteenth

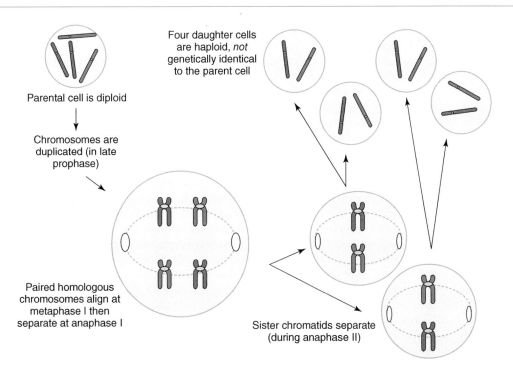

Parental cell is diploid

Chromosomes are duplicated (in late prophase)

Four daughter cells are haploid, *not* genetically identical to the parent cell

Paired homologous chromosomes align at metaphase I then separate at anaphase I

Sister chromatids separate (during anaphase II)

Figure 2   Diagrammatic representation of meiosis, the process of cell replication for germline cells or gametes

century from the famous work of an Augustinian monk named Gregor Mendel. Predominantly working in agricultural science, Mendel found that by beginning with "parents" of known genetic background one had a baseline against which the pattern of inheritance could be measured.

The total genetic information carried by a cell, all the DNA in the nucleus, is referred to as the *genome*. Strictly speaking, this DNA is referred to as *nuclear DNA*. A small amount of the cells' total DNA content exists outside the nucleus, in the mitochondria. Mitochondrial DNA (mtDNA) is also widely applied in a forensic context.

The genome of higher species is packaged into bundles known as *chromosomes*. Most nucleated human cells are diploid, meaning that the overall content of 46 chromosomes actually comprises one pair of each of the 23 chromosomes (two copies of each chromosome). Exceptions include the sex cells or gametes (spermatozoa or ova), which are haploid (a single copy of each chromosome). The human chromosomes are numbered from 1 to 22 according to their size (chromosome 1 being the largest, 2 the

second largest, and so on). These 22 chromosomes are referred to as *autosomes*, as they do not play a role in sex-determination. The 23rd pair is the X and Y chromosomes that play a direct role in sex determination. This chromosomal pair is often referred to as *nonautosomes*.

During conception, parental haploid gametes fuse and form a progenitor diploid cell that is the origin for embryonic development. Owing to this diploidy, individuals who are DNA profiled show either one or two alleles at each DNA site (or locus). If an individual shows one allele, this implies that there are two copies of the same allele present on each of the chromosomes of that particular pair. This event is referred to as *homozygosity*, and we refer to the particular individuals' profile at that DNA site (or locus) as being homozygotic. In such cases, the individual has inherited the same allele from each parent. If an individual shows two alleles at a locus, it implies that there are two different alleles present on each of the chromosomes of that particular pair. This event is referred to as *heterozygosity*, and we refer to the particular individuals' profile at that locus as being heterozygotic.

The DNA molecule encodes for the functional activities of the cells in higher organisms with the packages of genetic information on the DNA referred to as *genes*. The DNA regions containing genes are called *coding regions* (or *exons*). Genes have a dedicated role in protein synthesis, with these products being in turn linked to one or a number of biological or biochemical functions. For the most part, these essential biological functions are the same from individual to individual. As such, exonic regions are highly conserved across individuals of the same species – that is they are almost identical genetically. Another reason for DNA sequence conformity in coding regions, or genes themselves, is that alterations to DNA sequences in these areas usually have some deleterious effect on the physical well being of the individual. The health effects reduce the likelihood of survival, mate selection, and reproduction and therefore are directly linked to the propagation of this individual's particular genotype. In population genetic terms, this link between genotype and ability to survive is referred to as *genetic fitness*. By this mechanism, a genotype that affects the fitness of an individual will become less prevalent, or even extinct, within a population. This is the notion of selection.

The entire DNA molecule is not made up of genes; in fact, only a little over 5% of the genome codes for the production of proteins. The remainder of the DNA is made up of noncoding regions, or introns. Despite their prevalence, the prescribed function of noncoding regions is poorly understood. Noncoding regions were initially presumed to be functionless and as a result were commonly, but inappropriately, referred to as *junk DNA*. Recent evidence proposes some functionality for certain noncoding DNA regions [1–3]. Interestingly, large areas of noncoding DNA, many of which are not implicated in regulation, are strongly conserved between species. This may be strong evidence that they too are functional. Although some ambiguity remains as to their exact role, it is foolhardy to assume that noncoding regions are redundant.

However, as noncoding regions appear to have less responsibility when it comes to the messenger characteristics of the DNA, they have not been exposed to the same evolutionary selection pressures as the coding regions. In essence, mutations can occur in the noncoding regions without affecting the genetic fitness of the individual. Over time, this has led to a high degree of polymorphism in the noncoding regions of the human DNA molecule as mutation has been allowed to continue relatively unchecked. Hypervariable loci, such as those used for forensic identification purposes, are common in the intronic regions.

There are three major varieties of polymorphisms that exist on the genome: minisatellites, microsatellites, and single nucleotide polymorphisms (SNPs). Minisatellites (or variable number of tandem repeats (VNTRs)) are large fragments of DNA which are comprised of sequentially aligned homologous units. The individual units are typically between 20 and 100 base pairs (bps) in length and are repeated consecutively up to 100 times. The overall molecular weight (MW) of the locus is therefore determined by the number of times that the units are repeated. This is the polymorphic feature of these loci. Minisatellite loci are highly polymorphic and for that reason are powerful identification markers.

Microsatellites (or short tandem repeats: STRs), as the name suggests, are smaller versions of minisatellites. The same structural conformation exists in principle but, in comparison to minisatellites, the size of the individual units (2–8 bp) and the number of times they repeat (2–20) are reduced. Microsatellites were originally named as such as they were thought to solely be repeats of (cytosine-adenine) CA dinucleotide stretches. Microsatellites have been detected in every studied organism occurring at a higher rate than would be predicted purely on the basis of base composition. Microsatellites can be termed *simple* (an uninterrupted array of homologous repeat motifs), *compound* (repeat motif changes – two or more adjacent simple repeats), or *complex* (array is interrupted or contains several repeats of variable unit length). The overall MW of a microsatellite locus is still determined by the number of times that the units are repeated; however, the number of repeats is typically smaller for STR loci. Both VNTR and STR loci are length-based polymorphisms. This means that polymorphisms can be detected by standard electrophoretic techniques.

SNPs are loci where there is a variance in the individual base that exists at a particular position on the genome. SNPs are classified, and distinguished from single base changes, if the frequency of occurrence of the minor (less frequent) allele exceeds 1%. SNPs are the most common form of polymorphism on the genome, occurring approximately every 1000 bp (in unrelated individuals). SNPs can be bi-, tri-, or tetra-alleleic, meaning that the base that exists at a particular SNP position can vary between two, three, or four possible types. In practical terms, however,

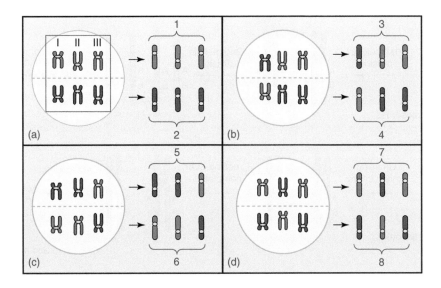

Figure 3 An example of the effect of assortment in generating haploid diversity. If there are three pairs of blue chromosomes (I, II, and III) which are duplicated during prophase to give three pink duplicate chromosome pairs. There are four different ways in which these three pairs of pairs can align at the equator of the cell during metaphase (a–d). After the two rounds of meiotic division this produces eight different possible haploid sets (1–8). The number of theoretical possibilities in a diploid organism is equal to 2^n, where n is the number of chromosomes in the haploid gamete

biallelic SNP loci are the only form of the polymorphism that are routinely detected and analyzed.

Aside from the polymorphic loci themselves, DNA has an additional level of variability that is introduced through processes such as assortment and recombination. These occur as part of the meiotic division that cells undergo during gametogenesis. Both assortment and recombination have the effect of shuffling genetic material and essentially randomizing the distribution of the diploid genotype into the haploid gametes. In assortment, the order in which chromosomal pairs align at the equator of the cell during metaphase is random. This means that the total number of gametic chromosomal combinations that can be formed from n chromosome pairs is 2^n (Figure 3). In humans ($n = 23$), meaning that over eight million combinations are possible among the haploid gametes of any individual.

Recombination, also known as *crossing-over*, involves the physical exchange of genetic material. In recombination, the arms of sister chromatids of a homologous chromosome pair can overlap during prophase I. This contact allows for the physical exchange of chromosomal segments and the genetic

material that they carry (Figure 4). Without recombination the arrangement of alleles on a particular chromosome would remain coupled together. Recombination allows new (and possibly advantageous) combinations to be produced and adds another element of variability to the inheritance of DNA.

Aside from the shuffling effect of assortment and recombination, DNA may be subject to further mutational events during meiotic or mitotic replication. At the outset of cell division the DNA must replicate itself faithfully. Any errors during this replication process will introduce a difference between the parent and progeny cells. Such a mutation occurring during meiosis can lead to a Mendellian inconsistency between the biological parent and their offspring, as the parents' gametes have mutated to a haplotype that is inconsistent with the parental genotype. These mutations are more commonly observed on the paternal side, i.e., occurring during spermatogenesis, and are an important consideration in parentage or kinship investigations.

Microsatellite loci have a high mutation rate, in comparison with other polymorphic loci such as SNPs. This trend is observed for both autosomal and nonautosomal loci. In fact, microsatellite loci are thought to be

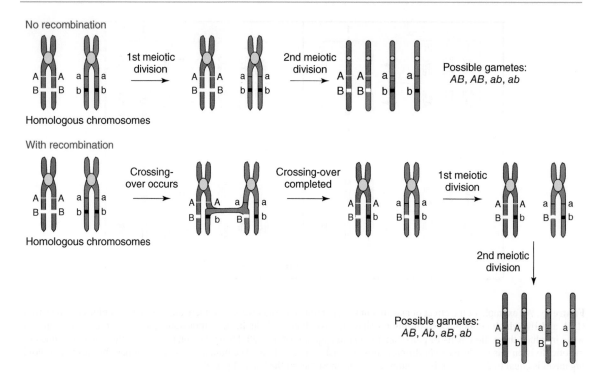

Figure 4   Representation of recombination showing its effect in shuffling the distribution of genetic material in the resultant gametes

located in mutational "hot spots" [4], that is, regions of the genome that are more susceptible to mutation due to their structure or location. A range of mutational models exist that describe the pattern of mutation of a particular locus. The model favored for microsatellite mutation is the model of slipped strand mispairing (SSM) during DNA replication.

Through the basics genetics, we understand that our genetic composition is comprised of equal proportions of DNA from each of our parents. We also understand that there are coding and noncoding segments of the molecule and types of loci that demonstrate considerable variability. We also acknowledge the role that mutation plays in shuffling and altering DNA characteristics, creating additional diversity within populations. The practical suitability of these characteristics is clear; however, it is the physical composition of the DNA molecule itself and its own inherent variation that provides scientists such a suitable template for analysis in a forensic context.

Fundamental Molecular Biology

The realization that DNA is the principle genetic molecule immediately focused attention on its structure. Likewise, the revelation that the structure of DNA was relatively simple [5] helped scientists to understand that genes had relatively similar three-dimensional structure and that differences between two genes resided in the order and number of the structural building blocks along the molecules and not in the molecules overall shape.

Structurally, DNA comprises two complementary chains of nucleotides twisted about each other in the form of a right-handed double helix. A nucleotide unit consists of a five-carbon sugar ($2'$-deoxyribose), a phosphate residue, and a nitrogenous base (either a purine or pyrimidine; Figure 5). The linking of the nucleotide units is formed via the phosphate residue through a phosphodiester bond between adjacent sugar groups. This series of bonds forms the sugar–phosphate backbone of the DNA strand and allows for the formation of extremely long

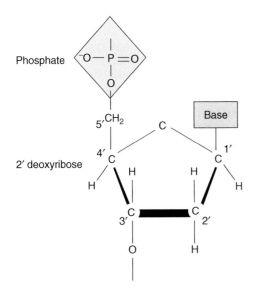

Figure 5 A nucleotide unit (or monomer). The nitrogenous base is either a purine or a pyrmidine. Nucleotide units are linked through a phosphodiester bond via successive phosphate residues and the free oxygen on the 3′ carbon

polynucleotide chains, containing upward of 3 billion nucleotide units.

The backbone of the DNA is therefore a repetitious structure, which, due to its uniformity, is incapable of encoding information. The importance of the DNA structure is derived from the bases that are attached to each of the sugars of the polynucleotide chain. There are two types of bases which attach to the sugar group of the nucleotide, the purines (adenine (A) and guanine (G)) and the pyrimidines (cytosine (C) and thymine (T)). In contrast to the regular structure of the sugar phosphate backbone, the order of the purine and pyrimidine bases along the chain is highly irregular. The order of the bases along the polynucleotide chain is referred to as the *sequence of the DNA molecule* or *DNA sequence.*

Another vital discovery of the Watson and Crick model is that the two chains of the DNA molecule are made up of complementary pairs of bases, linked together by hydrogen bonds. The pairing of the bases follows simple and strict rules. Adenine is always paired with thymine and guanine is always paired with cytosine. No other pairings are possible due to the physical structure of the bases. The strictness of the pairing rules results in a complementary relationship

between the DNA sequences on the two intertwined strands of the double helix. For example, a sequence of 5′-AAGCTG-3′ on one chain, the opposite chain must have the sequence 3′-TTCGAC-5′.

The revelation that the twisted strands of the double helix were always complementary meant that if the strands could be separated, and new DNA synthesized along each, the strict base-pairing relationship would see two identical double-stranded DNA molecules produced. In 1985, Saiki *et al.* [6] published an paper in which they described for the first time a method to simulate the DNA replication process in a laboratory environment. The technique was called the polymerase chain reaction (PCR). The PCR is essentially a sample preparation step. It allows for the continuous replication of subanalytical quantities of DNA to amplify it to a level such that routine analytical methods can be used for genotyping.

The discovery of the PCR has proven to be the catalyst for the modern biotechnology revolution. By 1988, the PCR had already ranked itself alongside cloning and DNA sequencing as an indispensable tool of molecular biology. The PCR has rapidly advanced the field of molecular biology. If the DNA sequence of a target region is known, the PCR allows for the replication and amplification of that region to the exception of the DNA, which is not required for analysis [7]. The *in vitro* replication of DNA, via the PCR, models the natural process of DNA replication. Each PCR cycle is one cycle of replication that theoretically doubles the amount of template DNA present in the sample. Each PCR cycle consists of three steps that are mediated by the temperature at which the reaction is proceeding and the relevant chemical and biological additives. The PCR is thermally controlled, readily automated, and is complete in 1–3 h.

The sequence of bases on the entire DNA molecule has now been determined [8]. It is accepted that with the exception of identical twins, no two humans contain identical DNA sequences. Therefore, an individual's DNA sequence is unique. Although extremely significant in principle, this fact does not have high practical relevance purposes as scientists are not yet able to designate the complete sequence efficiently and cost effectively. It is of more significance that differences exist on the DNA molecule and that this characteristic is another attribute of DNA that aids in its application in the forensic context.

Summary

In forensic DNA profiling, investigators collect biological evidence from crimes primarily with the purpose of assisting in the identification of the donor. The fundamental objective therefore is to differentiate individuals through analysis at the DNA level. In general, therefore, it is areas of difference on the DNA that are of more importance than those that are highly conserved. Both sequence variation and length variation have been utilized in forensic DNA profiling for many years. More recently, sophisticated techniques examining length variation at microsatellite loci are favored as the routine target of analysis.

To be useful in forensic context, the scientific procedure employed must be robust (able to produce a result from compromised samples), sensitive (able to produce a result from small amounts of original material), highly discriminating (able to provide a result which conveys a satisfactory degree of confidence), and accurate (involve minimal subjectivity or risk of error). The forensic community has many analytical tools already that satisfactorily address these requirements, but despite considerable progress the scientific community is still only beginning to understand the vast amounts of information resident on the DNA molecule and to develop technologies to allow its exploitation. Undoubtedly there is much more development to come, but already the implementation of DNA science into the forensic arena has had a tremendous and positive impact. This is primarily due to the inherent sophistication and informativeness of the DNA molecule itself.

References

[1] Johnston, M. & Stormo, G.D. (2003). Heirlooms in the attic, *Science* **302**, 997–999.

[2] Mattick, J.S. (1994). Introns: evolution and function, *Current Opinions in Genetics and Development* **4**, 823–831.

[3] Mattick, J.S. (2001). Non-coding RNA's: the architects of eukaryotic complexity, *European Molecular Biology Organisation Reports* **2**, 986–991.

[4] Chambers, G.K. & MacAvoy, E.S. (2000). Microsatellites: consensus and controversy, *Comparative Biochemistry and Physiology Part B* **126**, 455–476.

[5] Watson, J.D. & Crick, F.H.C. (1953). Molecular structure of nucleic acids: a structure for deoxyribonucleic acids, *Nature* **171**, 738–740.

[6] Saiki, R.K., Scharf, S., Faloona, F., Mullis, K.B., Horn, G.T., Erlich, H.A. & Arnheim, N. (1985). Enzymatic amplification of beta-globin genomic sequences and restriction analysis for diagnosis of sickle cell anemia, *Science* **230**, 1350–1354.

[7] Saiki, R., Gelfand, D.H., Stoffel, S., Scharf, S.J., Higuchi, R., Horn, G.T., Mullis, K.B. & Erlich, H.A. (1988). Primer-directed enzymatic amplification of DNA with thermostable DNA polymerase, *Science* **239**, 487–491.

[8] Lander, E.S., *et al.* (2001). Initial sequencing and analysis of the human genome, *Nature* **409**, 860–921.

Related Articles

Biological Stains

Sources of DNA

Chapter 4
Introduction to Forensic DNA Profiling – The Electropherogram (epg)

Allan Jamieson
The Forensic Institute, Glasgow, UK

The DNA analyst, in order to decide which alleles are present in a sample, uses a graph called the *electropherogram* (or *electrophoretogram*), usually referred to simply as the *epg*. The epg represents the separated DNA molecules that are produced after the amplification process of the original sample. It is not necessary here to detail all of the issues affecting the production of the epg as it most rarely materially affects the profile result. However, it is important to understand the general manner in which an epg is produced and how steps can be taken to verify a profiling result.

Although there are several manufacturers of kits and software, this article will use mainly GeneMapper, produced by Applied Biosystems, as illustration.

Notation and Descriptions of Profiles

A DNA profile is a series of numbers that represents the alleles found in a sample. The sample could be a body fluid obtained directly from an individual or a crimestain. The loci have been given labels or names that identify them. These are usually listed across the top of the profile and include loci such as D3, D21, FGA, and vWA. There is no special significance to the labels for forensic purposes.

The alleles also have labels. It is these labels that permit us to see the differences between individual profiles. The labels represent the length of the piece of DNA; it is a kind of shorthand. The labels are all numbers. Some of the numbers are followed by a decimal point; for example, 32.1. The number after the decimal point is part of the label and so allele 32.1 is different from allele 32.

There are many STRs in the human genome. Because there are different alleles at each STR locus, this provides the possibility to differentiate between individuals. However, there are a limited number of alleles available to choose from at each locus. So to be more forensically useful, a number of loci are examined to establish the alleles at those loci. If there were only two alleles available at a locus, let us say 28 and 29, then there would be only three possible types that a person could be;

A.   28   29
B.   28   28
C.   29   29

Notice that 29 28 is not listed. That is because all that we have is a mixture of 28s and 29s, when we examine the DNA molecules. So, all that we identify are the alleles, not whether they came from mom or dad. What we DO know is that the 28 29 person inherited a *different* allele from mom than they did from dad. When this is the case, the scientific term for that locus is heterozygous and the person is a heterozygote at that locus. When both the alleles are the same, the person is homozygous at that locus.

Separation

Theoretically, a single molecule subjected to 28 cycles of amplification will result in 2^{28} ($268\,435\,456 = \frac{1}{4}$ billion) molecules of "new" DNA, 34 cycles will produce 2^{34} ($17\,179\,869\,184 = 17$ billion). Note that one extra cycle will double that to 34 billion copies. However, in practice the process is not 100% efficient.

A Guide to Forensic DNA Profiling
Edited by Allan Jamieson and Scott Bader
© 2016 John Wiley & Sons, Ltd. ISBN: 9781118751527
Also published in EFS (online edition)
DOI: 10.1002/9780470061589.fsa1139

In the simple model provided so far, all DNA would be replicated with no start and end points on the DNA strand. To identify the specific areas of interest (the "target"), it is necessary to identify specific sequences of DNA on either side of the target STR that will enable only that DNA to be amplified. Primers are short lengths of DNA that will bind specifically to the areas on either side of the target locus. Two primers are required for each locus.

The product of the amplification process is a soup of DNA molecules of different lengths, which are the alleles at each locus. One way to visualize the components of any mixture is simply to separate the components. This is achieved in routine DNA profiling by a technique called *capillary zone electrophoresis* (CZE).

During the process of amplification, the DNA molecules are "tagged" with dyes of different colors. These enable the detection of the DNA by detection of the colored light (in reality, the dyes are illuminated by a laser and the light emitted by the dyes is then detected).

In the separation process, the charged molecules (DNA) are drawn through a very narrow tube to which a voltage has been applied from one end to the other. The tube, for historical reasons, is called a *column*. Larger molecules travel slower than smaller molecules and therefore reach the end of the column later. As the molecules leave the column they are detected by a system that then sends a signal of the detection, generally an electronic data file, to a computer. The signal from the detector is sent to a computer that will convert the signal to a graph. The computer software can then produce a visual representation of the molecules leaving the column. This type of graph is called an *epg*. The analyst then assesses the epg to establish which alleles are present from the sample.

In this way, small amounts of DNA are amplified, separated, and detected. This is the basis of the DNA-profiling technique used widely in forensic science. The most common means of performing profiling is to use a manufactured kit.

The Kit

Manufactured kits provide the key chemicals to enable the amplification and analysis of DNA extracted from a range of samples such as blood, hair, and stains. Although many kits will analyze some of the same loci, they also differ in the number and specific loci analyzed. Because each kit is actually performing amplification of a number of loci, they are called *multiplexes*.

The components of the multiplex are the individual chemicals (esp. primers), which were developed for each single locus (a "singleplex"). The process recommended for the use of the kit is the best overall compromise for the different performances of each singleplex within the multiplex. It is therefore to be expected that changes in the process may affect each locus differently.

The conversion of the signal from the detector in the analyzer to a finished epg is a complex process with a number of inputs required from the operator. These inputs have a material effect on the finished result and are the reason why many reviewing analysts require to see the raw data from the analyzer rather than the paper copy of the epg.

The task of the software is to present the data in a way that enables the analyst to decide what alleles are present in the sample. The alleles differ in size, and there must be a sufficient amount of allelic DNA to rise above the noise in the signal from the analyzer. Because the signal is produced from the light being transmitted by the DNA leaving the column, the height of the line is proportional to the amount of DNA at that point in time. The other task is to provide the length of the DNA fragment as that informs which allele it is.

Remembering that the alleles differed in their lengths (the number of carriages), it is no surprise that the analytical technique used to identify them is basically a process of separating and identifying the different lengths of DNA. That process produces a graph, the epg, from which a considerable amount of information can be gleaned.

An epg, from what was the standard kit used in the United Kingdom for many years (SGM+, manufactured by Applied Biosystems), is shown in Figure 1. Other kits may have different loci, different numbers of loci, and different numbers of colored channels, but produce similar epgs.

It is probably easier to examine a single piece of a profile in isolation to get to know the various parts.

In Figure 2 (expanded), the loci are identified by the gray boxes above the three "channels" shown on the epg (locus label). Every graph has two axes, the vertical (*y*-axis) and the horizontal (*x*-axis). In the epg, the horizontal axis generally shows the size of the DNA molecule, which appears; smaller molecules will

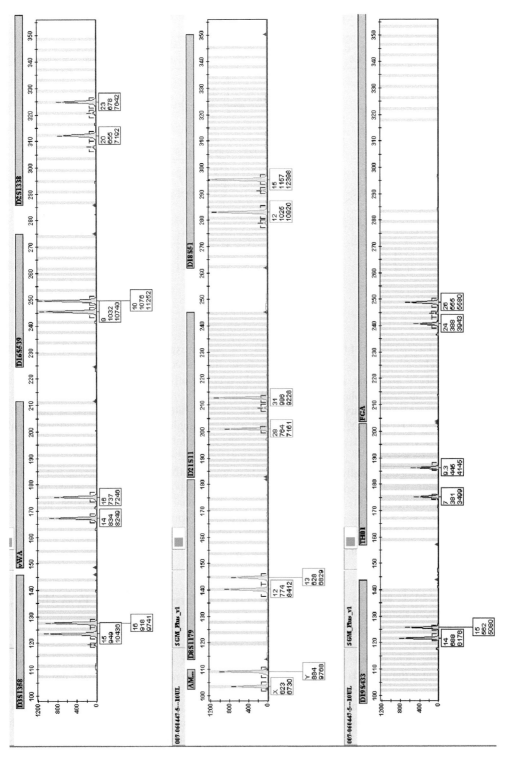

Figure 1 SGM+ epg

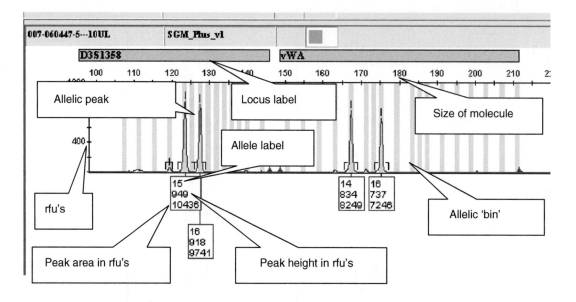

Figure 2   Portion of epg, labeled

show as peaks toward the left-hand side of the epg and larger molecules to the right.

Although the locus labels are quite long (e.g., D3S1358, D16S359) they are usually shortened for convenience in conversations or summary results to the first few characters (e.g., D3, D16, D2, and D21) except for labels such as vWA and THO1, which are complete.

The epg is produced by a computer usually with software provided by the manufacturer. The software can produce a variety of views of the data; this illustration is just one of those views. For example, the analyst can choose the scale to be used for the y-axis (vertical axis – rfu's) or the type of information that appear in the boxes attached to each allelic peak.

In this small portion of the epg, we can see that the profile is 15, 16 at D3 and 14, 16 at vWA.

If the raw or unrefined light signal from the detector is plotted on a graph, then it looks similar to Figure 3 (but without the red rectangle).

The colors represent the light output at different wavelengths. This is because the kit adds dye colors to specific loci enabling easy separation by the software of the emitted signals. Moving from left to right across represents the time passing as the different-sized pieces of DNA flow past the detector; the earliest on the left and the latest on the right.

As you would expect, the smallest DNA molecules pass through the column first and so appear to the left of the graph relative to the heavier molecules toward the right.

The area of interest to the analyst is marked by the green rectangle that contains the relevant peaks. The area to the left contains signals from the unused chemicals and debris from the reaction.

The raw data from a DNA profiling run will also include other important information about the performance of the analysis that is not visible in the epg. For example, Figure 4 shows four parameters that are important in the consistent running of an analytical process.

Relative Fluorescence Units, Peak Height, and Peak Area

The vertical axis is an approximate measure of the amount of DNA that is present. It is measured in relative fluorescence units (rfu). The raw data is a series of readings taken at regular times as the eluent (the liquid with the DNA molecules within) flow from the analyzer column. The software must join these data points together and then provide information to the operator about their size and position.

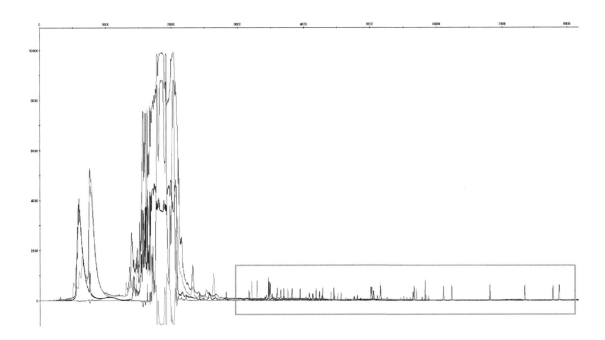

Figure 3 Raw data

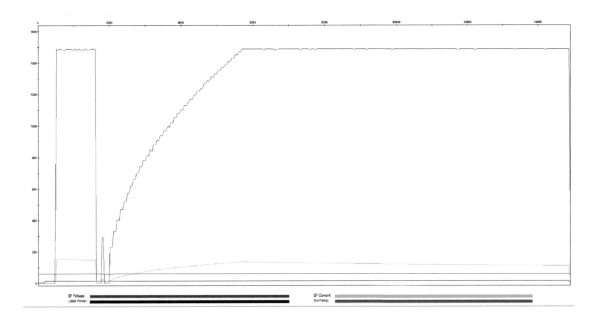

Figure 4 Operating parameters for gel run

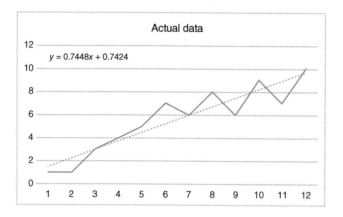

Figure 5   Example of linear regression

The epg does not show these data points, but rather a continuous line. The line is created using the data points to calculate an equation and it is the line calculated by that equation which is used to create the epg. This process may not be familiar to some and so it is illustrated here using simple examples created using an Excel spreadsheet and the trendline facility.

The simplest form of this approach is probably what is known as *linear regression*. Figure 5 illustrates linear regression. This is the sort of data that is frequently encountered in scientific analysis.

The solid line joins the actual data points. The dotted line is the line calculated to come closest to the actual data points. The equation of that line is shown in the figure. The calculation assumes that there is a linear relationship between whatever parameter is on the

x-axis and the value on the y-axis (e.g., amount of light vs amount of DNA).

Using different assumptions or procedures for calculating the line makes a difference to how it looks. Figure 6 illustrates the same data, but using different assumptions about the nature of the data.

These considerations are important when considering the entire basis of DNA interpretation – peak detection.

Within the software, there is the facility for the operator to select parameters that affect the shape and height of the peaks, and so selecting different analysis parameters may change the result of the analysis, especially at low peak heights or where peaks are very close together.

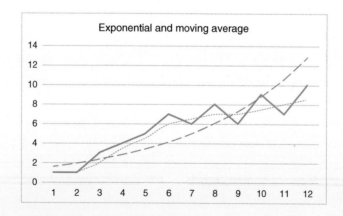

Figure 6   Illustration of exponential and moving average representations

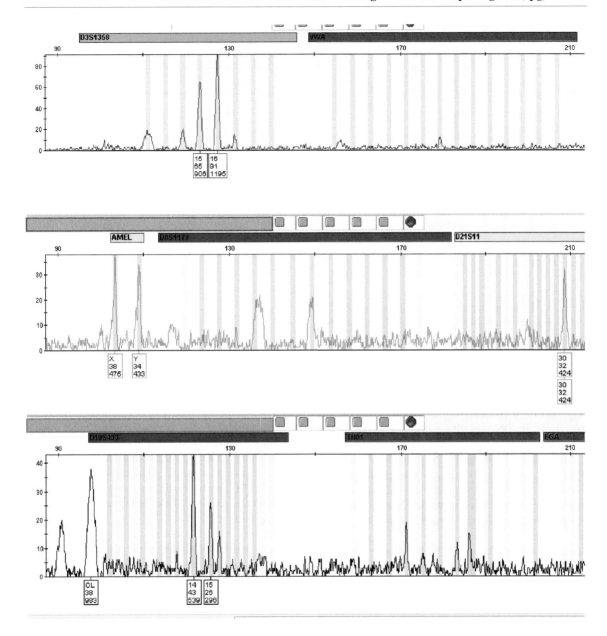

Figure 7   Baseline noise

In determining the equation that best fits the data points, one important consideration is the baseline or where zero should be. The analyzer produces a signal during the entire process, and each color may have a baseline at a different and varying height. Examples of different baseline noises within a profile are illustrated in Figure 7.

The peak height, important in interpreting the profile, is measured from the baseline, but that baseline can be calculated in different ways. The method chosen can, therefore, affect the interpretation, when fixed parameters are used for interpretation such as peak-height thresholds (PHTs) or heterozygote balance (i.e., the ratio between the peak heights of two

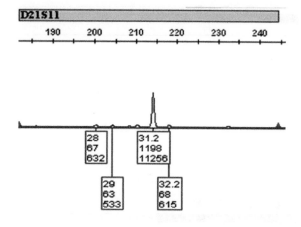

Figure 8   D21 locus at "standard" zoom

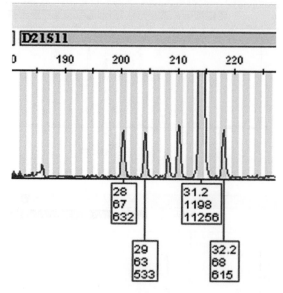

Figure 9   Zoom of D21 locus

alleles at the same locus). Within the software, the parameters for placing the baseline can be chosen by the operator introducing another operator-controlled parameter that is invisible in paper versions of an epg. The decision as to whether a peak (the signal) is above the background noise is well known in analytical chemistry and other sciences. Methods have been suggested for performing signal-to-noise calculations objectively in DNA profiling [1], but so far none appear to have been widely adopted.

The difficulty with setting an "absolute limit" or "PHT" approach can be seen in this example from casework, which coincidentally also illustrates the importance of the choice of vertical scale (changing which is called *zooming*). Figure 8 shows the "standard" zoom, where the range of the vertical axis is chosen to fit the tallest peak in the channel into the graph without exceeding the limit of the graph (there is a taller peak in the channel, which is why the 31.2 allele is only half the height of the axis. The laboratory in this case had a PHT of 75 rfu and therefore did not assess the 28 and 29 alleles as being present.

The software enables the operator to magnify or zoom particular areas of the profile. Figure 9 shows a zoomed view of the same locus as Figure 8. It can be seen that the 28, 29, and 32.2 alleles, which were discounted by the analyst in the case because of the 75 rfu PHT, are well above the background noise.

Generally speaking, laboratory guidelines in the United Kingdom use a guide of about 50 rfu to be counted as a true peak (each laboratory should determine parameters as to when to treat a peak as a true

allelic peak – most of the US labs have a fixed limit, but it is common in the United Kingdom not to have a set threshold at all). The sample in Figure 1 is a good-quality profile with the peaks being well over that figure, whereas there are clearly dubious peaks present in the sample in Figure 7. The choice of approach (eyeball, PHT, probabilistic) to assess whether a peak represents a genuine allele from the sample is an ongoing issue [2].

Peak area is rarely used nowadays in the interpretation of profiles. However, as the calculation of peak height involves the calculation of the peak height and the baseline, most of the comments applicable to peak height are applicable to peak area.

The additional complication is the issue of exactly where to consider the start and end of the peak. To assist with this, the software can mark the points that it uses to calculate the peak area. These are illustrated in Figure 10.

Sizing

The rfu deal with the *y*- or vertical-axis, the amount of DNA present. The *x*- or horizontal-axis measures the length of the DNA pieces. The shorter molecules appear to the left of the larger molecules as can be seen

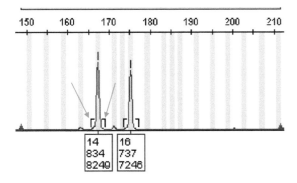

Figure 10   Peak limit markers

by the fact that at each separate locus the smaller allele number is always to the left (e.g., in Figure 2, the 14 and 15 at D3 and vWA are to the left of their respective 16 alleles).

There are a number of ways that the peak's position is on the line (strictly speaking, it is each data point that is placed – the peak follows after the calculation of the line). The data essentially comprises a series of elements, which are the time, color, and intensity of the light reading from the analyzer.

The software allows the operator to separate the signal of each color for easier visualization as illustrated in Figure 1. The initial positioning and separation of colors merely creates a time-series of dotted lines that must be translated into information about alleles.

The analyzer does not run exactly the same way every day all day. Some means must therefore be found to ensure the accuracy of the analysis each time the analyzer is used. Each manufacturer provides with the kit the means to accurately establish for each batch the length of the DNA being analyzed; an allelic ladder and internal standards.

The allelic ladder is a liquid containing DNA of many known alleles. It is analyzed in the same way and at the same time as the samples in a batch. The term *ladder* is again historical from when the analysis was performed on flat plates, and the DNA visualized a series of stripes similar to a barcode. The "ladder" appeared as a series of lines similar to the steps of a ladder. Figure 11 shows an allelic ladder.

One of the main purposes of the allelic ladder is to provide a measure for the position of each size of allele DNA molecule in a batch of samples. It is

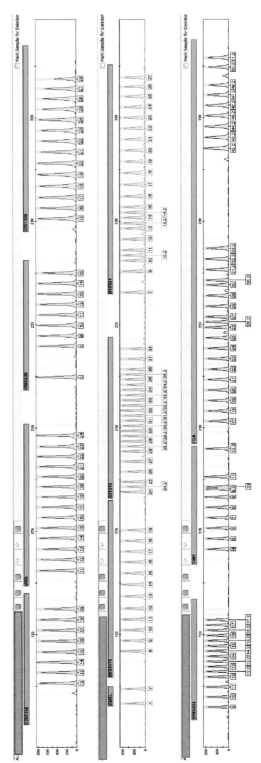

Figure 11   Allelic ladder

a very bad practice to use the results of an allelic ladder for a different batch of samples. The software knows the position of each component of the ladder and can therefore create a measure against which it can position the unknown alleles from samples. Usually, the software requires the allelic ladder sample to be identified so that it knows which sample to use as an allele size reference.

Of course it is always possible that the ladder or one of the samples is running slightly differently from the other samples in the batch, for example owing to temperature changes during the runs. Internal standards are pieces of DNA of known length, which are included in the chemicals supplied with the kit. These have a different colored dye attached to them so that they do not appear on the channels normally viewed to interpret the profile. However, they can be shown in the same way as the other channels. The software, having established the size "ruler" using the allelic ladder, can now check that each sample has been analyzed in the same way as the ladder and therefore being "sized" properly by checking that the internal standard DNA molecules are appearing in the correct positions. The channel featuring an internal standard is shown in Figure 12.

Having established the amount of DNA of a particular size, the next task is to decide whether the peak is an allele. Again, the manufacturer provides another tool to assist. The gray vertical lines in Figure 1 show the areas where the known alleles are expected to appear if they are present in the sample. They are called *bins*.

In summary, to appear in the profile as a true allele a peak has to be within one of the bins (there are exceptions such as rare mutations) and also be high enough to be clear of any spurious signal (called *noise*) that may be present in the analysis. Finally, it should not be a spurious peak.

Spurious Peaks in Profiles

Unfortunately, the profiling technique can produce peaks in the epg that do not represent alleles in the sample. These spurious peaks are problematic because it may not be possible to reliably ascertain the reason for the spurious peak; it could be an allele or it could be an artifact introduced by the process.

Stutter.   The most common additional peak artifact is called *stutter*. Stutter peaks are small peaks to the left

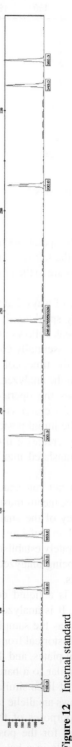

Figure 12   Internal standard

of a larger peak, but one unit less (e.g., 15 would be in the stutter position for 16). Stutter peaks are shown in Figure 13.

Each stutter peak is within a bin and in an allelic position. Stutters like these are sometimes called $n - 1$ *peaks* because they are just one repeat unit less than their "parent" peak. The software does not mark them as peaks if they are within the stutter threshold entered by the operator.

Stutter peaks tend to be much smaller in height than the parent peak and so the smaller the peak in the stutter position, the more likely it is to be stutter. The level above which the peak is considered to be certainly not stutter is called the *stutter threshold*. The stutter threshold is the ratio of height of the small peak to the parent peak, usually expressed as a percentage. The creation of these thresholds is one reason why the establishment of the baseline position is important; changes to the baseline affect heights, which affects height ratios and therefore whether a peak is excluded from a profile, because it is considered a stutter.

Each laboratory should perform experiments to determine the range of heights relative to the main peak to calculate what the appropriate stutter thresholds are within the laboratory (see, e.g., most kit user manuals and reference [3]). Ideally, this should encompass the different combinations of machines, equipment, and staff, but many labs perform only a limited set of such experiments. The stutter threshold also varies by locus so it must be calculated separately for each.

The appropriate stutter thresholds are entered as parameters in the software. They are generally less than 15%. The software uses the stutter threshold to decide whether to mark the peak. However, in some profiles involving mixed DNA, the unmarked positions may be important. The stutter threshold is not an absolute and the possibility that a stutter is a genuine allele, or that an allele above the stutter threshold is a stutter, should be considered by the analyst.

The problem for the analyst is how to differentiate a stutter peak from a genuine allele because a peak in a stutter position can be

- stutter
- stutter and an allele
- allele

Generally, analysts will look at all of the loci in a profile to assess whether the profile has been subject to

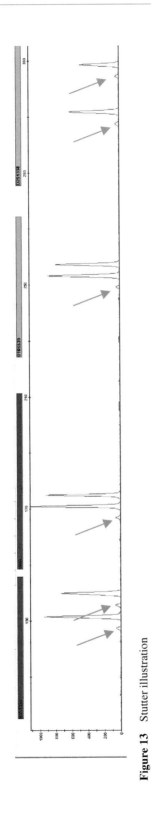

Figure 13   Stutter illustration

significant numbers of possible stutter events to assist their interpretation. This is an unsatisfactory position, as regards providing any sensible and scientifically sound decision base as to whether a peak is stutter or an allele from the sample, but it would require enormous amounts of experimentation to calculate the probability that any particular peak height ratio is stutter rather than a peak and most analysts adopt a pragmatic approach. Different expert systems treat possible stutters in different ways. Some rely on the analyst to make the decision, whereas others will use the peak height and either similar rules to those used by analysts and others using a probabilistic approach to each peak.

Less common, but still observed in casework, is a phenomenon called *forward stutter* or $n + 1$ *stutter*. This is the occurrence of a small peak one "unit" ahead of the main peak. This forward stutter also has a peak ratio threshold which is, at usually not more than 5%, generally lower than the $n - 1$ stutter threshold. It is generally considered that the mechanisms that produce $n - 1$ and $n + 1$ stutter are different and therefore they occur independently.

It is possible that $n - 2$, -3 or -4, and other $n+$ stutters occur, but they are rare.

Pull-up. Pull-up is observed as a peak, which may or may not be in an allelic position and is caused by the intrusion of the light signal from one channel to another. The general appearance is a small peak in one channel in exactly the same sizing position as a very large peak in another. Some pull-up peaks can be recognized by the software, but others may require careful manual assessment. They are not generally troublesome in most cases, but may complicate some low-level mixture assessments.

Off-ladder Peaks. An off-ladder peak is generally identified by the software as it is a peak that has a height above the PHT, but is not within a bin. An off-ladder peak (labeled OL) can be seen in Figure 7. Generally, off-ladder peaks present no problems, but the appearance of several off-ladder peaks in the same profile may suggest a sizing problem with the analysis.

The appearance of a single off-ladder peak that looks otherwise a good peak may merit investigation as a rare allele. This would entail running the sample again to see if the peak is reproducible.

Split Peaks. Split peaks are mainly a feature of increasing the number of amplification cycles or adding too much DNA to the analysis – both generally termed *over-amplification*. Improvements in technology, and perhaps a better awareness of the problems in overamplification, mean that split peaks are rarely seen in most labs nowadays and in any case even when they are present they do not usually materially affect the allele call.

Controls

A key scientific practice is the control sample. This is an experimental process used to establish that the effect that you observe is caused by the material under test and not some other component of the system. The purpose is illustrated well in clinical trials, where some people are given a tablet that looks like the drug under test, but does not contain the drug. This is because some people get better simply because they think that they have received the drug (the placebo effect). The scientist looks for a difference between the control group and the test group to establish whether it is the drug that is causing the improvement.

In forensic science, the fact to be established is that the DNA profile originated from the material recovered from a crime scene or a suspect; not the investigator, the laboratory, packaging, or analytical instruments. A "negative control" is set up by simply processing a "blank" sample that has no DNA. All being well, this control will not show any DNA. The presence of DNA in the negative control illustrates that there has been a source of contamination in the analytical method. It does not, of itself, show where that occurred, merely that it has. The tradition over many years has been, for very sound reasons, that anything found in the "negative control" invalidates the analysis.

All controls must be run at the same time (or in the same batch) as the samples for which they are to be regarded as controls. It is not acceptable to run a batch of samples, discover that one of the controls has not worked, and so create a new control to be run with the next batch of samples. To do so completely invalidates the purpose of the control.

Although the text for each is short, they are each given headings to underline the importance of appropriate and proper controls in every analysis.

Positive Control

The positive control is a sample containing a known single source profile. It is amplified using exactly the same reagents (materials) and equipment that are used for the batch of samples for which it is the control.

Extraction Control (Blank)

Extraction is the process of removing and purifying the DNA from cells. It is the first step in the amplification process and uses chemicals to disrupt the cell. Frequently, the extraction step is accomplished using kits containing all of the required materials. The purpose of the extraction blank is to demonstrate that the extraction has not added any DNA to the sample. An extraction control (usually called the *extraction blank*) is created by performing all of the steps for extraction, amplification, and electrophoresis, but without adding the sample.

The result should be a flat line on the baseline of the epg. The extraction control is a negative control.

Amplification (Reagent) Blank

In a similar way to the extraction blank, sometimes called an *amplification blank*, a control is created specifically for the PCR (amplification) process by adding all of the reagents required and going through the entire PCR process, but without any of the test sample in the tube.

The result should be a flat line on the baseline of the epg. The reagent control is a negative control.

Controls in Low-Template DNA

It has been suggested that these principles cannot be applied to the negative control in LCN DNA analysis because even in a tightly controlled analytical procedure, a significant number of negative controls (usually unknown, but has been reported in at least one paper as up to 70%) give a positive result, i.e.,

they indicate the presence of DNA. This approach has become a common practice in those laboratories performing low-template DNA analysis.

The difficulty that arises is that if it cannot be established that the DNA has been introduced during the analysis, how can any of the DNA found in the crime stains be shown NOT to have come from the procedure rather than the scene.

It is suggested by proponents that the appearance of such spurious alleles is not significant because it only occurs occasionally; tiny fragments of DNA from any material or piece of apparatus used in the analysis could have had the DNA on it, but it would be easily identifiable in a series of runs. This undesirable appearance of spurious alleles is termed *allelic drop-in*. Drop-in can of course produce spurious alleles in crimestain samples, which would be difficult to identify as drop-in rather than drop-out. One method that has been used to "identify" them is to simply subtract the profile of a suspect from the stain profile, and if there are only one or two alleles left, to claim that they must be due to drop-in, thus leaving the suspect still a suspect. Probabilistic genotyping systems claim to take account of drop-in in various ways.

References

[1] Gilder, J.R., Doom, T.E., Inman, K. & Krane, D.E. (2007). Run-specific limits of detection and quantitation for STR-based DNA testing, *Journal of Forensic Science* **52**, 97–101.

[2] Budowle, B., Onorato, A.J., Callaghan, T.F., Manna, A.D., Gross, A.D., Guerrieri, R.A., Luttman, J.C. & McClure, D.L. (2009). Mixture interpretation: defining the relevant features for guidelines for the assessment of mixed DNA profiles in forensic casework, *Journal of Forensic Science* **54**, 1–12.

[3] Gill, P., Brown, R.M., Fairley, M., Lee, L., Smyth, M., Simpson, N., Irwin, B., Dunlop, J., Greenhalgh, M., Way, K., Westacott, E.J., Ferguson, S.J., Ford, L.V., Clayton, T., Guiness, J. & Technical UK DNA working group (2008). National recommendations of the Technical UK DNA working group on mixture interpretation for the NDNAD and for court going purposes, *Forensic Science International: Genetics* **2**, 76–82.

Chapter 5
Biological Stains

Peter R. Gunn

University of Technology Sydney, Broadway, New South Wales, Australia

Introduction

Many techniques have been developed to determine the type of biological material present at a crime scene or on items pertaining to a criminal investigation. While DNA profiling is commonly perceived as the gold standard in associating a stain to an individual, it can be just as important to establish the biological source of the material to assist in the recreation of the events surrounding the commission of a crime. Expertise is required to locate possible biological material, select the most probative items for further examinations, and select those that are likely to yield DNA profiles, although there is much to learn about the last. Preliminary testing at scenes may further help in the screening, triaging, and prioritizing of items to be submitted for full biological examinations in a laboratory. Frequently, this means identifying semen or saliva in sexual assault cases and blood in assaults and homicides, but may also include other biological materials that are sometimes found at crime scenes.

Locating Potential Biological Material

It is the standard practice of the forensic biologist to first conduct a visual examination of the items or scenes of interest. Various light sources and techniques including ambient and white light, oblique lighting, ultraviolet (UV) light, alternate light sources such as multiwavelength Polilight™ examination, and

Update based on original article by Dale L. Laux, Wiley Encyclopedia of Forensic Science, © 2009, John Wiley & Sons Ltd.

A Guide to Forensic DNA Profiling
Edited by Allan Jamieson and Scott Bader
© 2016 John Wiley & Sons, Ltd. ISBN: 9781118751527
Also published in EFS (online edition)
DOI: 10.1002/9780470061589.fsa063.pub2

lasers as well as microscopy are commonly used to help locate potential biological material. Chemical and biochemical detection methods may also be used.

Broadly speaking, chemical or biochemical detection methods can be categorized as either "presumptive" or "confirmatory" tests. As a general rule, a presumptive test is very sensitive but not specific, while a confirmatory test is less sensitive but more specific for the stain it is designed to detect. Because of this, a positive result from a presumptive test cannot be used to demonstrate that a particular stain is composed of a certain body fluid, only that it might be. A presumptive test narrows the range of materials that a stain could be comprised of; it is not proof that a stain is a specific material. Conversely, a negative result from a confirmatory test cannot be taken as definitive that a stain is not of a certain type.

Presumptive and confirmatory tests will be described below under the relevant biological stains.

Blood

When blood forms a dried stain, it has a distinctive reddish-brown color, which is suggestive to the experienced analyst. Though blood does not fluoresce, alternate light sources may be used to help locate latent stains. This technique is especially useful with dilute blood staining or stains on dark and/or red backgrounds, and can usually be achieved with a bright white light source [1].

After locating potential bloodstains, presumptive color tests are utilized; most of these involve a change of color that exploits the properties of the heme molecule [2]. Heme is part of the oxygen-carrying component of red blood cells, and consists of pyrole rings surrounding an atom of iron. Heme forms part of the molecule hemoglobin, but on its own can also catalyze the oxidation of many chemicals. There is a wide range of chemicals which are used as substrates

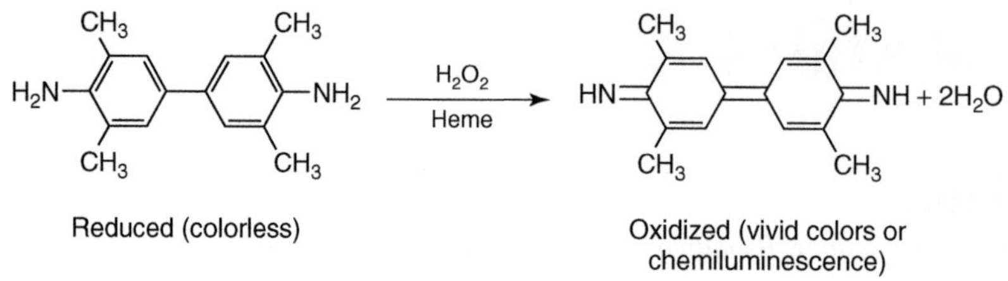

Reduced (colorless)　　　　　　　　　Oxidized (vivid colors or chemiluminescence)

Figure 1 The catalytic conversion mechanism of presumptive color reagents for the presumptive detection of blood, using tetramethylbenzidine as an typical substrate

for the detection of blood, as they undergo easily observable color changes in the presence of heme and hydrogen peroxide. The most commonly encountered of these include phenolphthalein, leucomalachite green, o-tolidine, and tetramethylbenzidine [3]. All these chemicals are colorless when in a reduced ionic state; when oxidized, these reagents change color, turning pink, green, or blue green. This color conversion occurs rapidly in the presence of an oxidant, such as hydrogen peroxide, and a catalyst, such as heme (Figure 1).

The presumptive color test is an easy test to conduct. A dry, sterile, cotton-tipped swab is rubbed against the suspected stain. A single drop of the testing reagent is added to the swab, followed by a single drop of hydrogen peroxide. An immediate color change indicates that the stain may be blood. The reagents are added in this order for a reason. A color change only after the addition of the testing reagent indicates the presence of strong oxidants and the results can be inconclusive.

A swab moistened with distilled water can be used to collect a small amount of the stain for testing; however, this may rehydrate the stain, increasing the chances of bacterial degradation.

An alternative approach is to use commercially available test strips such as Hemastix® (manufactured by Bayer), which are intended for the clinical detection of blood in (for example) urine. These work in the same manner as the tests described above, but have the advantage that all the reagents are incorporated into a dry "detection pad," which makes for convenience of use. (Note: there are similar products available from other manufacturers.)

A positive presumptive color test indicates that the stain may be blood. The tests are sensitive, reacting with bloodstains that cannot even be seen with the naked eye. However, they react with other materials such as rust, copper, and vegetable peroxidases. Oxidation of the test reagents will occur over time, so the tests must be read within seconds.

Another substrate for the presumptive detection of blood is luminol (3-aminophthalhydrazide), which produces an intense blue chemiluminescence from the oxidation process, and requires a darkened room for proper observation and photography. The chemiluminescence lasts for a matter of several seconds to few minutes. The method lends itself to scene investigation where the presence of blood is suspected, as it can be sprayed on to all surfaces [4], but the test is cumbersome in that it requires a darkened room and considerable expertise in photography to conduct efficiently. Fluorescein is sometimes used as an alternative that does not require a darkened room for detection [5].

At this point in the investigation, some laboratories will conduct DNA testing (see DNA) on the bloodstains. The primers used in DNA profiling only react with human and upper primate DNA, and so obtaining a DNA profile indicates that the presumed bloodstain is most likely of human origin. However, if the investigator wishes to confirm that the stain truly is blood (and is human), then several commercially available immunochromatographic kits have now generally replaced more time-consuming crystal tests or immunoassays. These kits not only confirm the presence of blood but also can determine whether the stains are of human origin.

The principle behind the various kits is similar, and is also found in a variety of clinical and commercial products such as home pregnancy testing kits.

The technology uses immunochromatographic membranes that incorporate monoclonal antibodies specific to human blood proteins such as hemoglobin

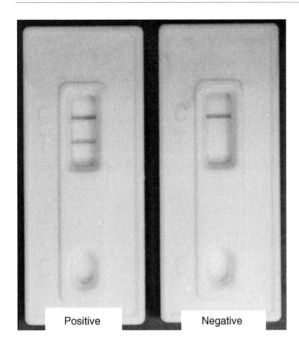

Positive   Negative

Figure 2 Immunochromatographic membrane testing of blood using monoclonal antibodies specific to human hemoglobin

[6] or glycophorin A [7]. Approximately $100\,\mu L$ of stain extract is added to a well in the cassette. The sample is absorbed onto a pad, which contains mobile monoclonal antibodies. This antigen–antibody complex migrates down the membrane where it comes into contact with an immobilized monoclonal antibody. If the extract contains human blood, a visible line will appear, indicating that the sample is human blood (Figure 2). A caveat exists here. Certain membranes are known to react with upper primate and ferret blood. Hence, this matter must be taken into consideration when conducting these tests and preparing reports.

Finally, after thorough analysis of the stain has been completed, a portion of the stain may be cut out and prepared (*see Extraction*) for DNA analysis.

Semen

Other than blood, the body fluids most commonly encountered in crimes of violence are semen and vaginal secretions. These fluids may be in wet form (vaginal aspirates, condom contents) or in dry form, as stains on clothing or on swabs used to remove material deposited on or in a person.

Semen is the fluid that is discharged from the penis during ejaculation. Semen consists of two components: a fluid portion called *seminal fluid*, a complex fluid that contains many proteins and chemicals, and *sperm cells* (usually just called *sperm*, short for spermatozoa). Sperm cells have a head and a tail, like a tadpole. Some time after discharge, the tail becomes detached from the head.

The sequence of examinations of suspected semen stains is similar to that of the examination of bloodstains described above; however, contrary to bloodstains, semen stains fluoresce when exposed to UV light. The source of this fluorescence is thought to be due to nonproteinaceous compounds found in semen, such as flavin. Whatever the source, dried semen stains frequently fluoresce intensely under UV light, thus aiding in their detection [1]. Unfortunately, the optical brighteners used in many washing powders also fluoresce when illuminated, and so can confound the examination of clothing or bed linen for semen. Hence, the observation of fluorescence must be considered a presumptive identification only.

After suspected semen stains are located, they are tested with a color test that detects the presence of acid phosphatase (AP) which is an enzyme found in large amounts in semen. AP can be found in much smaller levels in other biological fluids including vaginal secretions and saliva, as well as in a variety of nonhuman sources, so the presence of AP is also considered only a presumptive positive result [8].

AP catalyses the hydrolysis of organic phosphates such as phosphorylated choline. The reagents (materials) used in the AP test vary little from laboratory to laboratory. Slight variations in the reagents used and formulation are simply a reflection of individual preferences in terms of solubility, safety, and sensitivity.

The almost universal standard procedure is to react the soluble salt α-naphthol phosphate with the material of interest. If present, AP will liberate free α-naphthol, which is in turn coupled with a diazonium compound such as Brentamine Fast Blue or Fast Black Salt to form an insoluble colored product (Figure 3).

Where no stains are clearly visible but the presence of semen is suspected, the area where the stains are thought to be present can be covered by a large piece of wetted filter paper, removed and sprayed with reagents. The position of positive reactions on the filter paper can then be inferred on the original item.

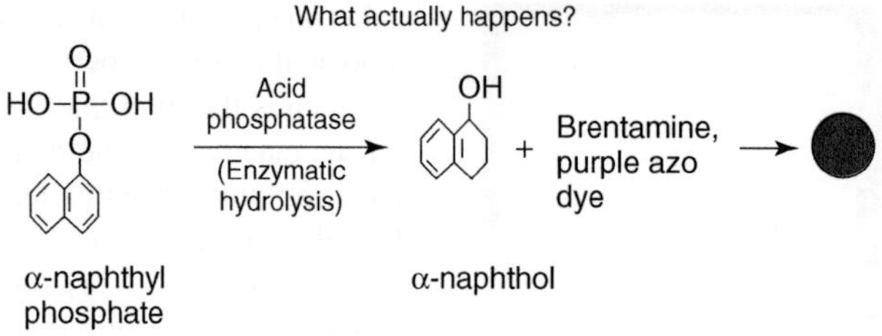

What actually happens?

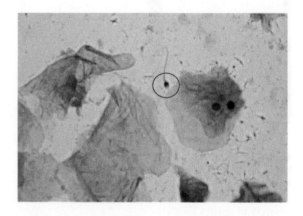

Figure 3   The enzymatic breakdown of α-naphthol phosphate by acid phosphatase is the basis for the presumptive color test for seminal fluid

The test is very sensitive and reacts with as little as two units of AP, known to exist in vaginal secretions. The stronger and faster the test result, the more likely the stain is from semen.

Alternatively, small stains can be tested with a commercial strip containing the reactants in solid form, such as Phosphatesmo KM (Macherey-Nagel GmbH & Co., Dueren Germany). The reaction is catalyzed (i.e., enabled) simply by the presence of AP and water, and the presumptive presence of semen is indicated by a change in color of the test strip.

The definitive test for the presence of human semen is a microscopic examination and the observation of spermatozoa. The morphology of the spermatozoon is unique from other cells in the body, and, with training, an investigator can readily differentiate between human sperm and other sperm types. Sperm can be visualized using a variety of microscopic examinations, including the use of contrast stains such as hematoxylin and eosin or the more popular nuclear fast red and picroindigocarmine, commonly referred to as *Christmas Tree stain* [9]. Nuclear fast red dyes the posterior portion of sperm heads a deep red and the anterior portion (acrosome) a lighter red. Picroindigocarmine dyes the spermatozoa tails as well as the cytoplasm of epithelial cells green. Frequently, the sperm tails are not visible in extracts of stains, so, depending on the protocols of individual laboratories, the number of detectable sperm heads is assessed. It is known that the longer the time interval between assault and collection of samples, the less likely sperms with tails will be found (Figure 4). With time, the number of spermatozoa decreases and they often become misshapen (Figure 5), as degradation commences soon after ejaculation, due to the hostile environment of the vagina or other environment in which the ejaculate is located.

Figure 4   A single sperm cell with its tail among vaginal cells stained with the Christmas Tree reagents

Sperm morphology

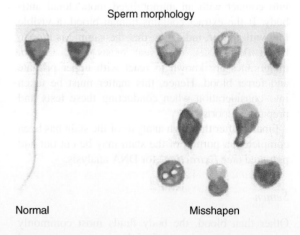

Normal   Misshapen

Figure 5   Morphological changes of sperm cells as they degrade

An alternative method of confirming the presence of semen is an immunochromatographic test specific for a component of semen, such as either prostate-specific antigen (PSA) [10] or semenogelin [11]. These tests are especially useful when semen is azoospermic (i.e., lacking in sperm), as PSA and semenogelin are found in the liquid fraction of semen. Occasionally, semen that has very low levels of sperm (oligospermia) or lacks sperm cells altogether (azoospermia) will be encountered. Oligospermia can be a temporary or a permanent condition and has multiple causes, both medical and lifestyle based (e.g., smoking, excessive alcohol consumption, bicycle riding). Azoospermia can be a result of vasectomy, or any one of a number of congenital or medical conditions. In these cases, the immunochromatographic tests will still identify the presence of semen.

The immunochromatographic tests have the advantage of being far more specific for semen than the color tests described above, but cross-reactions with other body fluids do occur, so they cannot be considered truly confirmatory. PSA and semenogelin are highly specific to seminal fluid, but recent studies have shown that small amounts of PSA can be found in female urine and breast milk [12, 13]. Likewise, semenogelin has been found, albeit at very low levels, in a wide variety of tissues [14].

It is known that DNA profiling can be accomplished on azoospermic semen samples. There are other sources of nucleated cells in semen besides spermatozoa, including epithelial cells lining the vas deferens, Sertoli cells, and white blood cells [15].

Saliva

Saliva stains are frequently found in sexual assault cases. Once again, the sequence of examinations may commence with identification of potential saliva stains with a strong light source. Saliva stains will fluoresce under UV light, albeit not as brightly as semen stains. The use of varying wavelengths and colored goggles can help distinguish saliva stains from their background [16].

Presumptive biochemical tests for saliva usually rely on the identification of the enzyme α-amylase, which is found in high concentrations in human saliva, where it aids in the digestion of starches and carbohydrates. Amylases can be found in other biological substances such as semen, feces, and in bacteria, so amylase tests are considered presumptive for the presence of saliva.

However, the levels of amylase in saliva are far higher than the levels found in other body fluids [17].

After locating possible saliva stains, the stains can either be mapped or cut out and directly analyzed. Mapping has the benefit of observing the location and distribution of saliva stains and allows for photographic documentation and assistance in the reconstruction of events at the scene. Mapping can be simply accomplished by overlaying stains with moistened starch papers, pressing them against the stains, and developing them with an iodine solution [18]. Iodine reacts with starch to produce a dark purple color. Areas that do not turn purple and remain white indicate the presence of the enzyme α-amylase (Figure 6).

A popular variant of this test is the commercial Phadebas® test, currently manufactured by Magle

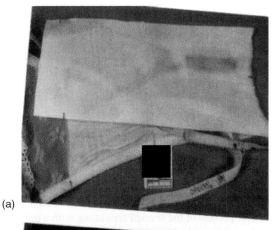

(a)

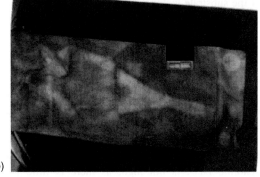

(b)

Figure 6 Mapping of underwear for acid phosphatase (a) and amylase (b). Purple (dark)-stained areas (a) demonstrate acid phosphatase distribution. (b) White (light) areas demonstrate the distribution of amylase

Life Sciences, Lund, Sweden, and available in several forms. This test detects the amylase-catalyzed release of blue dye from a starch–dye complex, thus localizing the presumptive presence of saliva [18].

At this time, no agreed confirmation test for the presence of saliva exists. Immunochromatographic membranes are available that utilize monoclonal antibodies to α-amylase; however, these have been found to react with human pancreatic amylase (albeit at a far lower level). For this reason, some human breast milk, neat liquid urine, feces, and rat saliva can also produce positive reactions [19, 20].

Urine

Occasionally, it may be necessary to determine the presence of urine at crime scenes. Assault cases have occurred in which the victims had been urinated upon, and urination frequently occurs at a variety of other crime scenes.

Light sources can be used to screen items for potential urine stains. Urine may be detected at 450 nm (orange filter), as well as at 415 nm (yellow filter) and at 505 nm (red filter). However, as with other body fluids, this technique is not specific and not all urine stains will fluoresce [16].

No confirmatory test exists for the presence of urine. All of the tests rely on the determination of various components of urine such as uric acid, urea, and creatinine. Creatinine is a component of urine and exists at a relatively high concentration ($311 - 1790 \, \text{mg} \, \text{L}^{-1}$) [21]. The classic test for creatinine is called the *Jaffe test* [22]. A portion of the stained area along with a portion of the substrate lacking the stain (a "control" area) is cut from the garment or bedding. A drop of sodium hydroxide (NaOH) is added to the stain followed by a drop of concentrated picric acid. The formation of an intense orange color is a positive indication of creatinine (Figure 7). A clear demarcation between the control area and the orange color makes the determination easier. The test can be run on sterile cotton-tipped swabbings of the stained areas as well.

DNA results from urine stains have been obtained; however, the likelihood of obtaining results using genomic DNA is not high, as there is little DNA in urine, other than in shed epithelial cells or small numbers of white blood cells.

Recently, an immunochromatographic test strip (RFID-Urine™) test has been released by Independent Forensics (IL, USA), which is claimed to be specific

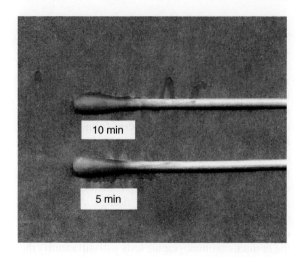

Figure 7   Creatinine color change at 5 and 10 min

for the kidney-specific protein Tamm–Horsfall glycoprotein. Early research on the specificity of this kit for urine is promising [23].

Feces

The identification of fecal matter is often important in cases of anal assault. The unique smell of feces is due to chemicals such as skatole and indole, which are by-products of bilirubin catabolism (part of the breakdown mechanism of hemoglobin). Fecal stains generally have a brown appearance and can be located visually. They can be confused with aged bloodstains and may contain traces of blood, so a positive reaction with a blood-testing reagent may occur.

Methods of analysis of fecal stains have centered on chemical and microscopic analyses. Microscopic analysis of an extract from the stain may reveal the presence of undigested plant and animal materials, which would support the conclusion of feces. A simple chemical test can be performed on an extract of the stain dissolved in distilled water. Added to this extract are a few drops of ethanol followed by a few drops of concentrated zinc chloride in ethanol. Under UV light, an intense apple green color results, indicating the presence of urobilinogen [24], a breakdown product of bilirubin and a component of feces (Figure 8). Substances other than urobilinogen, which also fluoresce, include bilirubin and porphyrin, which emit a

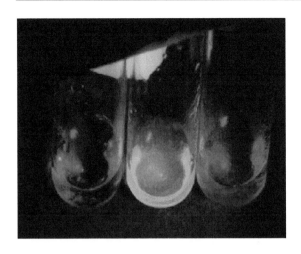

Figure 8   Urobilinogen test for the presumptive detection of fecal material. Tubes (from left) blank, positive fecal sample, and control

red fluorescence; riboflavin, acriflavin, and fluorescein, which give a yellow-green fluorescence; and eosin, mercurochrome, and erythrosin, which fluoresce a mauve color.

Alternatively, the presence in the extract of bile acid degradation products can be demonstrated by thin-layer chromatography and subsequent observation of the fluorescent products with UV light.

However, none of these methods is particularly sensitive. Hence, a negative result does not mean an absence of fecal material, particularly with an old stain.

Other Body Fluids and Secretions

It may prove necessary on very rare occasions to identify milk, pus, nasal secretions, sweat, or tears. The reader is referred to a publication of the National Institute of Justice for further details of these rarely required tests [25].

Trace Biological Material

The massive increase in the sensitivity of DNA identification techniques means that DNA profiles can be obtained from even microscopic traces of DNA invisible to the naked eye. These have been referred to as *touch* or *contact* samples, although recent research on transfer DNA indicates that these are misnomers, as touch may not be necessary for someone's DNA to be found on an item [26]. Some controversial techniques have been claimed to reliably profile just a few cells, but the location and identification of such traces impose extra difficulties and responsibilities on the forensic biologist or crime scene examiner to locate, characterize, and interpret the meaning of this material (*see* **Transfer**).

Skin cells have been targeted as a source of DNA since the mid- to late 1990s, not only on handled or worn objects [27] but also from skin-to-skin contact [28].

References

[1]   Stoilovic, M. (1991). Detection of semen and blood stains using polilight as a light source, *Forensic Science International* **51**(2), 289–296.

[2]   Spalding, R.P. (2005). Presumptive testing and species determination of blood and bloodstains, in *Principles of Bloodstain Pattern Analysis: Theory and Practice*, S.H. James, P.E. Kish & T.P. Sutton, eds, CRC Press, Boca Raton, FL.

[3]   An, J.H. & Yang, W.I. (2012). Body fluid identification in forensics, *Biochemistry and Molecular Biology Reports* **45**(10), 545–553.

[4]   Thorpe, G.H., Kricka, L.J., Moseley, S.B. & Whitehead, T.P. (1985). Phenols as enhancers of the chemiluminescent horseradish peroxidase-luminol-hydrogen peroxide reaction: application in luminescence-monitored enzyme immunoassays, *Clinical Chemistry* **31**(8), 1335–1341.

[5]   Young, T. (2006). A photographic comparison of luminol, fluorescein, and Bluestar, *Journal of Forensic Identification* **56**(6), 906.

[6]   Johnston, S., Newman, J. & Frappier, R. (2003). Validation study of the Abacus diagnostics ABAcard® Hematrace® membrane test for the forensic identification of human blood, *Canadian Society of Forensic Science Journal* **36**(3), 173–183.

[7]   Schweers, B.A., Old, J., Boonlayangoor, P. & Reich, K.A. (2008). Developmental validation of a novel lateral flow strip test for rapid identification of human blood (Rapid Stain Identification™-Blood), *Forensic Science International. Genetics* **2**(3), 243–247.

[8]   Kind, S. (1964). The acid phosphatase test, *Methods of Forensic Science* **3**, 267–288.

[9]   Leubitz, S. & Savage, R. (1984). Sensitivity of picroindigocarmine/nuclear fast red (PIC/NF) stain for detection of spermatozoa: a serial dilution study of human ejaculate, *American Journal of Clinical Pathology* **81**(1), 90–93.

[10] Hochmeister, M.N., Budowle, B., Rudin, O., Gehrig, C., Borer, U., Thali, M. & Dirnhofer, R. (1999). Evaluation of prostate-specific antigen (PSA) membrane test assays for the forensic identification of seminal fluid, *Journal of Forensic Sciences* **44**, 1057–1060.

[11] Sato, I., Kojima, K., Yamasaki, T., Yoshida, K., Yoshiike, M., Takano, S., et al. (2004). Rapid detection of semenogelin by one-step immunochromatographic assay for semen identification, *Journal of Immunological Methods* **287**(1), 137–145.

[12] Yu, H. & Diamandis, E.P. (1995). Prostate-specific antigen in milk of lactating women, *Clinical Chemistry* **41**(1), 54–58.

[13] Pollen, J.J. & Dreilinger, A. (1984). Immunohistochemical identification of prostatic acid phosphatase and prostate specific antigen in female periurethral glands, *Urology* **23**(3), 303–304.

[14] Jonsson, M., Lundwall, Å. & Malm, J. (2006). The semenogelins: proteins with functions beyond reproduction?, *Cellular and Molecular Life Sciences CMLS* **63**(24), 2886–2888.

[15] Shewale, J.G., Sikka, S.C., Schneida, E. & Sinha, S.K. (2003). DNA profiling of azoospermic semen samples from vasectomized males by using Y-PLEX™ 6 amplification kit, *Journal of Forensic Sciences* **48**(1), 127–129.

[16] Vandenberg, N. & Oorschot, R.A. (2006). The use of Polilight® in the detection of seminal fluid, saliva, and bloodstains and comparison with conventional chemical-based screening tests, *Journal of Forensic Sciences* **51**(2), 361–370.

[17] Auvdel, M.J. (1986). Amylase levels in semen and saliva stains, *Journal of Forensic Sciences* **31**(2), 426–431.

[18] Myers, J.R. & Adkins, W.K. (2008). Comparison of modern techniques for saliva screening, *Journal of Forensic Sciences* **53**(4), 862–867.

[19] Old, J.B., Schweers, B.A., Boonlayangoor, P.W. & Reich, K.A. (2009). Developmental validation of RSID™-saliva: a lateral flow immunochromatographic strip test for the forensic detection of saliva, *Journal of Forensic Sciences* **54**(4), 866–873.

[20] Pang, B. & Cheung, B.K. (2008). Applicability of two commercially available kits for forensic identification of saliva stains, *Journal of Forensic Sciences* **53**(5), 1117–1122.

[21] Spierto, F., Hannon, W., Gunter, E. & Smith, S. (1997). Stability of urine creatinine, *Clinica Chimica Acta* **264**(2), 227–232.

[22] Villena, V.P. (2010). Beating the system: a study of a creatinine assay and its efficacy in authenticating human urine specimens, *Journal of Analytical Toxicology* **34**(1), 39–44.

[23] Akutsu, T., Watanabe, K. & Sakurada, K. (2012). Specificity, sensitivity, and operability of RSID™-urine for forensic identification of urine: comparison with ELISA for Tamm-Horsfall protein, *Journal of Forensic Sciences* **57**(6), 1570–1573.

[24] Lloyd, J. & Weston, N. (1982). A spectrometric study of the fluorescence detection of fecal urobilinoids, *Journal of Forensic Sciences* **27**(2), 352–365.

[25] Gaensslen, R.E. (1983). *Sourcebook in Forensic Serology, Immunology, and Biochemistry*, Washington, USA, National institute of Justice.

[26] Meakin, G. & Jamieson, A. (2013). DNA transfer: review and implications for casework, *Forensic Science International. Genetics* **7**(4), 434–443.

[27] Van Oorschot, R.A. & Jones, M.K. (1997). DNA fingerprints from fingerprints, *Nature* **387**, 767.

[28] Wiegand, P. & Kleiber, M. (1997). DNA typing of epithelial cells after strangulation, *International Journal of Legal Medicine* **110**(4), 181–183.

Related Articles in EFS Online

Acid Phosphatase

Enzymes

Chapter 6
Sources of DNA

Sally-Ann Harbison

Institute of Environmental Science and Research Ltd., Auckland, New Zealand

Introduction

In 1987, the first report appeared in the literature describing the use of DNA profiling to assist in the investigation of a crime [1]. In this now-famous case, DNA profiling using minisatellite technology [2, 3] was used for the first time to demonstrate that semen found on the bodies of two young women was likely to be from the same man and that the young man suspected by police was excluded as the source. Further investigations, including the "blooding" of several English villages, led police to identify Colin Pitchfork, who subsequently pleaded guilty to both crimes [4].

Since then, DNA profiling has evolved through a number of stages, each one resulting in increased sensitivity or discrimination. Now, large scale DNA databases to date, where large-scale DNA databases are in use in many countries, short tandem repeat (STR) multiplexes incorporating many loci and targeting autosomal and Y chromosomes are in common use and DNA profiling is recognized as a key part of crime solution and modern policing [5].

So where does the DNA come from that produces such startling results? The answer is, almost everywhere. Today, it is well recognized that DNA profiles can be obtained from samples that are too small to be seen and sometimes difficult or impossible to attribute to a particular cell type.

The samples include the well-recognized bloodstains, semen and saliva stains, and hairs as well as less common samples such as nasal and vaginal secretions, teeth and bone, skin, including dandruff, feces, chemically treated fingerprints, plant material, and insects (for examples, see [6, 7]).

In this article, by reference to case reports and articles published over the last 20 years and by drawing on this author's personal experiences and those of others as practicing forensic scientists, attempts have been made to convey the huge variety of sources of DNA evidence that can be encountered, recognizing the infinite variety of samples, substrates, and case circumstances that exist.

Blood

Blood, splashed and smeared, is probably the most popular image conveyed of a crime scene. Blood can also be present on garments worn by individuals and on weapons such as knives and baseball bats used to inflict injury. Of course, blood can also be present as a result of innocent transfer and may have nothing to do with the alleged crime committed. The examination of the patterns of bloodstaining together with the analysis of DNA determining the likely source of blood can provide powerful forensic evidence and is often used to reconstruct events.

Of course, bloodstaining may not be visible. Various reports in the literature have investigated the effects of the luminol test on the ability to obtain DNA profiles [8, 9]. Luminol is used to visualize possible bloodstaining that has arisen from very dilute blood, typically associated with attempts to clean up a crime scene or as a result of a trail of blood left by, for example, the shoes of a participant in a crime. Application of the luminol reagent in combination with appropriate techniques to extract and amplify the trace amounts of DNA has not been found to be detrimental to the success of the DNA analysis procedure.

A Guide to Forensic DNA Profiling
Edited by Allan Jamieson and Scott Bader
© 2016 John Wiley & Sons, Ltd. ISBN: 9781118751527
Also published in EFS (online edition)
DOI: 10.1002/9780470061589.fsa539

The Vaginal Tract

Menstrual blood contains components that distinguish it from circulatory blood although these are currently difficult to quantify. A typical menstrual bleed contains, in addition to circulatory blood components, broken-down tissue from the endometrium and plasmin, a compound that prevents blood clotting. Blood associated with assault of a sexual nature may therefore contain blood derived from a menstrual bleed and/or circulatory blood caused by injury to the vagina and surrounding tissue. Menstrual blood is mixed with varying proportions of vaginal secretions.

Vaginal secretions are always located on genital swabs collected from the vagina and also on other objects used to penetrate the vaginal tract. These secretions contain miscellaneous proteins originating from the upper genital tract such as the oviduct, endometrium, and cervical mucus [10]. While difficult to identify specifically, the cellular material present provides a rich source of nuclear DNA. Thus, collection of such secretions by swabbing is often a successful source of DNA.

Semen

DNA analysis of semen formed the basis of the first reported use of DNA analysis in forensic science [1] and the use of DNA in the solution of crimes of sexual assault has had a profound effect on the effectiveness of forensic evidence in the resolution of crime. Seminal fluid or semen is a mixture of cells, spermatozoa, and a variety of organic and inorganic substances, and is a commonly encountered sample type in forensic casework.

Internal genital swabs are routinely collected from rape victims in most parts of the world. These swabs may be stained with semen, saliva, and blood as well as vaginal secretions. The DNA recovered from such swabs collected properly and stored dry or frozen is usually in good condition and the success rate from this type of sample is very high. Semen stains on clothing/bedding are also common.

Semen comprises seminal fluid with or without the presence of spermatozoa. Samples containing spermatozoa are rich in DNA and DNA analysis of such samples, where sperm are visible, is nearly always successful using polymerase chain reaction (PCR) techniques. A differential lysis treatment is commonly

used on samples of this type (*see* **Extraction**) in order to separate the female epithelial material from the spermatozoa, thus simplifying the interpretation of the resultant DNA profiles.

The advent of Y-STR profiling techniques (*see* **Y-Chromosome Short Tandem Repeats**) has led to an increase in the successful analysis of semen in the absence of spermatozoa [11]. In such circumstances, DNA is recovered and selectively profiled from the small amounts of epithelial material present in the seminal fluid even in the presence of large amounts of female DNA. Of course, Y-STR profiling is also useful when spermatozoa are present in small amounts.

Semen can be present in the mouth following oral intercourse, and is sometimes found mixed with saliva in stains on clothing. Once again, differential lysis separates the spermatozoa from the epithelial cells present enabling amplification of both spermatozoa and epithelial fractions separately and analysis of the DNA profiles.

DNA can also be recovered from cellular material on condoms although the success rates for this type of sample can be lower because of the presence of inhibitory substances in the spermicides and lubricants or because of the moist environment on the condom surfaces.

Case Study 1:

"Condom–the Critical Link in a Rape" [12] In 1993, a report appeared in the literature of the successful analysis using variable number tandem repeat (VNTR) analysis of material collected from a condom. The circumstances of the case were typical. A young girl was sexually assaulted by a man using a condom. The condom, discarded by the assailant was recovered and found to be stained with blood on one side and semen on the other. DNA analysis showed that the blood could have come from the young girl supporting the medical evidence and evidence of the girl. The DNA profile obtained from the semen was consistent with having come from the suspect.

A crucial step in the DNA profiling of evidence from cases of sexual assault is the identification of semen. This can be accomplished by the microscopic identification of spermatozoa if present, which is done by histological staining of the spermatozoa. The sensitive PCR systems used in laboratories today enable the DNA profiling of the spermatozoa on such slides and this can be enhanced using techniques such as laser microdissection [13] to facilitate the recovery of the sample. Histological slide collections made during the routine examination of sexual assault cases, over many years, provide an excellent repository of biological evidence for the investigation of old "historic" cases and many laboratories around the world are now utilizing such evidence in combination with their DNA databases to solve previously unsolved cases.

An alternative source of semen for analysis are the test papers produced during the presumptive test for semen, commonly known as the acid phosphatase (*AP*) *test* [14]. If stored in an appropriate condition, these papers can provide sufficient biological material to enable the development of DNA profiles.

It is our experience [15] that DNA profiles can still be obtained from semen stains on garments after laundering using a range of normal washing conditions. Thus, so long as the approximate location of the semen stain can be approximated (such as the crotch of a pair of underpants), then it is possible to obtain a DNA profile presumably from spermatozoa adhering to the fibers of the material.

Trace DNA

A report published in Nature in 1997 [16] demonstrated that DNA could be recovered from items held or touched for a time as brief as few seconds. This work stemmed from the observation that DNA could be successfully recovered from the blade of a tomahawk that had been submerged for 12 h and was seemingly unstained and clean. This demonstrated that DNA profiling was possible from samples such as keys, pens, and handles, and it was suggested that the success of obtaining a DNA profile may be related to the individual's propensity to "shed" DNA and not necessarily the length of time that the person was in contact with the item. The propensity of an individual to "shed" DNA has been examined [17, 18] and factors influencing the shedding of DNA by individuals investigated. It has been found that there is significant variation in the amount of DNA a person sheds at any one time and thus whether a person is a good or bad "shedder" at any particular time is currently unpredictable.

The work described above and the experiences of others [19] led to the realization that DNA recovered

from car steering wheels, computer keyboards, and other surfaces not necessarily stained with recognizable body fluids, could be an important source of DNA evidence.

One drawback with samples collected from these sources is the prevalence of mixed profiles from multiple contributors that may not be resolved into individual sources. Another is the observation that the last person to handle the item may not be the person from whom the DNA profile originated. Hence, there may be a temporal aspect to the deposition of DNA that must be considered when interpreting the DNA profiling results.

Case Study 2:

"DNA Profiling from Heroin Street Packages" [20] The authors of this study suspected that it may be possible to identify the individuals responsible for sealing the edges of the plastic packets used to contain small doses of heroin for sale. The proposition was that epithelial cells from these individuals might become trapped in the burnt edges of the packets and that this might provide useful evidence for investigators. Experimental work and analysis of case material showed that the method of sealing was crucial to the successful generation of a DNA profile and that individuals who handled the packages before and after sealing might also leave traces of DNA that could be amplified. Thus, although DNA profiles can be obtained from the sealed edges, and therefore from the sealer, they can also be obtained from other individuals who may have handled the packages.

Pipe bombs are easy to make and commonly used in America and elsewhere. When exploded, they generate a large amount of heat. During experimental trials, DNA was could be recovered and analyzed from such pipes after the explosion had taken place [21]. Critical factors of success were the ability to locate sufficient pieces of pipe and the degree of shedding of the person assembling and handling the pipe. This report serves to illustrate that what might be expected to be an extreme environmental insult may, in fact, not be as detrimental to the chance of success as expected.

Of course, legitimate transfer of DNA and/or cellular material from people to such items must be considered and never has Locard's principle "every contact leaves a trace" been truer. Its just that now, every contact leaves a trace of DNA that, if it can be collected either by visual observation, good guess work, or sometimes luck, can be compared to a reference DNA profile from an individual.

Low Copy Number and Single Cells

The successful amplification of DNA from a single cell using the second generation multiplex (SGM) multiplex and elevated cycle number [22], heralding the beginnings of low copy number (LCN) techniques [23]. In this first report, complete DNA profiles were obtained from 50% of the single source samples analyzed using elevated PCR numbers.

Subsequent to this report, there are many examples of DNA profiles being obtained from very small numbers of cells, including the use of laser microdissection to capture small numbers of sperm cells from histochemically stained microscope slides [13].

Case Study 3:

"A Tale of Two Robberies" [24] Two robberies were committed in different towns in Northern Italy. In one case, traces of saliva were detected on a pillowcase used to transport the stolen goods. In the second case, a pair of sunglasses was left behind in a bank during a robbery and cellular material was recovered from the nose and ear pieces of the frames. DNA profiles were obtained using LCN techniques and the profiles entered onto the local database. Immediately, the two DNA profiles linked together and additionally, the DNA profile of an individual on the database corresponded to the crime sample profiles.

Saliva

Saliva is a secretion of the mouth that is important in digestion and comprises cells and secretions from the salivary and parotid glands. Saliva has a high proportion of water and a low level of dissolved substances and cellular material, which can make it difficult to locate visually. Saliva is commonly encountered as a source of DNA evidence.

Perhaps the first example that springs to mind is the ubiquitous cigarette butt. Cigarette butts are often left

by suspects as they contemplate committing a crime, waiting for an opportunity, or possibly as a means to steady nerves. It is not uncommon to find DNA from multiple contributors on cigarettes, a result of sharing, and indeed on occasion three or four people may have shared the same cigarette [25].

Case Study 4:

"A New Zealand Family Affair" A car was stolen and found several days later, several hundred kilometers from home. Inside were a number of cigarette butts that should not have been there. From these butts, six different DNA profiles were obtained, five of which corresponded to five members of a "family" on a DNA database. The sixth was consistent with being from a family member not present on the database.

Perhaps a word of caution. It is not unheard of for police officers to submit numerous cigarette butts from public areas, for example, outside banks or commercial premises, in the hope of uncovering possible offenders. Such untargeted sampling approaches can lead to innocent persons being investigated and laboratories being overwhelmed with unnecessary work. As in all things, a healthy dose of common sense is helpful.

Case Study 5:

"A Body in the Water" [26] Saliva swabbed from human skin has been used to generate DNA profiles, enabling association between a bite mark and a suspect even when the body had been submerged in water for several hours. In this particular case, the deceased had suffered extensive head injuries and sexual assault as well as a bite on her right breast. Cellular material was collected by swabbing and a DNA profile obtained. The profile obtained was a mixed DNA profile containing DNA types that could be attributed to the victim as well as the suspect. The DNA evidence was produced at trial and proved crucial to the resolution of the trial.

Saliva is also prevalent among samples left at scenes of more minor crimes, for example, burglary, where it is not uncommon for offenders to help themselves from the cupboards and refrigerators of their victims. In such cases, saliva can be located on bottles and cans [27] on bitten pieces of chocolate, biscuits, and fruit, and on cutlery and the rims of glasses and cups [6].

Saliva can also be recovered from the back of licked stamps and envelopes [28]. In this case, care must be taken as a stamp can yield not only evidence of who might have licked the gum, but also evidence of DNA from skin cells transferred by touching the outer, exposed surface of the stamp. The scientist should be careful to distinguish between these two possibilities. Saliva trapped between stamp and envelope is however protected from contamination and reliable results should be obtained free from extraneous DNA. LCN techniques have aided in the effectiveness of this type of evidence as the amount of cellular material transferred to a stamp or envelope is likely to be low.

Fingernails

There are two main sources of DNA associated with fingernails. The first is the nails themselves [29]. The keratin structure of the fingernail does not contain DNA itself; therefore, the analysis of fingernails themselves is limited to recovering DNA from epithelial cells adhering to the nail. This analysis may be carried out in an attempt to determine the person from whom a nail piece came or as an alternative reference sample.

Alternatively, biological material scrapped from underneath the nail can be sampled and its source identified. The material trapped under the nails could be a variety of different body fluids or tissues such as semen, blood, saliva, skin, and vaginal secretions and could have been deposited in any number of ways. For example, a victim may scratch an offender during a violent struggle, or an offender may have digitally penetrated the victim during a sexual assault.

There are a number of reports of the successful analysis of such debris under the nails [30] including from under the nails of bodies submerged in water for periods of time [31]. Indeed, it has been shown that even repeated handwashing is not always sufficient to remove the evidence [30]. In order to interpret the results of such an analysis, it is important to know the background levels of DNA expected to be found underneath the fingernails in normal situations, one such study reports that the incidence of foreign DNA under fingernails appears to be low [32].

> **Case Study 6:**
>
> "The Persistence of DNA under Fingernails Following Submersion in Water" [31] Case one. A victim of homicide was found after submersion in bath water for 2–3 h. Mixed DNA profiles corresponding to the deceased and one other were obtained from the clipped nails. The male component of this mixture was found to correspond to the suspect, identified by a database search. Case two. A woman was seen falling into the harbor with her baby and her body was recovered 3 h later. DNA profiling was attempted on the fingernails clipped at the postmortem and the major male component was found to correspond to those of a colleague with whom an altercation had previously taken place. This information corroborated the accounts of several witnesses and no charges were laid.

Fingerprints

It is commonly understood that it is difficult but not impossible to obtain DNA profiles from fingerprints after enhancement [33]. In one comprehensive study, fingermarks were made on a variety of surfaces in blood and saliva. The fingermarks were treated to a wide range of chemical enhancement methods. In most cases, STR profiles were obtained using standard DNA profiling methods, showing that the many enhancement methods used were not significantly detrimental to the DNA profiling process. This mirrors our own experience where the difficulty arises when the fingermark is made by the greasy secretions of the skin only, in which case, elevated PCR cycle numbers may be needed because of the small amount of available biological material.

Hair

The average human head contains between 100 000 and 150 000 hair follicles [34] with hair roots present in three stages of development known as anogen, catagen, and telogen. On an average, 50–100 hairs are shed everyday, naturally or as a result of force and most of these are in the telogen phase. In the anogen phase, the hair roots are actively growing and are rich in DNA. In the catagen, or breakdown phase, nuclear DNA is still relatively abundant. Telogen hairs, however, have little or no nuclear DNA associated with them [35] and it is telogen hairs that are most often encountered in forensic casework. Unless there is additional cellular material adhering to the root structure of a telogen hair, analysis is usually unsuccessful [36], using autosomal DNA typing methods. Alternative DNA profiling methods such mitochondrial DNA typing methods [37] or LCN techniques [38] have proved to be useful for the analysis of both telogen hair roots and hair shafts, which are also known to contain very little nuclear DNA. Indeed, LCN techniques have been reported to be successful in the production of nuclear DNA profiles from hairs recovered from Siberian mummies 500 years old [38].

Teeth and Bone

The use of teeth and bone as a source of DNA for forensic work is of primary importance in the identification of human remains. Among the most challenging requirements in forensic science, in recent years, has been the requirement to identify the victims of mass disasters, commonly known as Disaster Victim Identification.

Where possible human remains are identified using dental records and fingerprints, this is not always possible. Early attempts of extracting DNA from bones from decaying and/or compromised bone samples were often unsuccessful due to the degraded nature of the DNA that was recovered and the VNTR DNA typing methodology employed. However, nuclear DNA can be recovered from these cells in sufficient amounts for DNA analysis by PCR [39].

With the advent of PCR techniques, it was possible to amplify degraded DNA and samples of bone and teeth that had been exposed to severe trauma became more useful sample types. The bodies for which identification using DNA is typically required may be from recently deceased individuals as a result of explosive or fire trauma such as following the Waco incident [40] or Spitsbergen aircraft crashes [41], or the bodies and body parts might be "old" such as those recovered from grave sites where notable historic figures such as the Romanov family [42] and Jesse James [43] were thought to be buried. Less newsworthy, but nonetheless important, are missing person cases where body identification is required [44, 45].

Success has been shown to depend less on the age of the bone and more on the conditions under which it has been kept and amplification of fragments of mitochondrial DNA from ancient bone thousands of years old has been reported [46].

Recent use of short amplicons (*see* **Mini-STRs**) and single nucleotide polymorphism (SNP) technology have increased the utility of these samples and provided increased chances of successful profiles.

An advantage of using bones and teeth for forensic purposes is that stringent washing/cleaning techniques can be employed to minimize the possibility of contamination with extraneous DNA and this is of particular importance when considering the analysis of historic or ancient specimens.

Teeth, in particular, provide a rich source of nuclear DNA within the coronal pulp and radicular canals of the tooth [47], although these sources decrease with age and disease as additional dentin is deposited on the internal surfaces.

The external structures of teeth (dentin and enamel) provide an excellent physical barrier and great protection to the mtDNA and nuclear DNA found within teeth, thus conferring teeth with a great advantage and making them a reliable source of DNA for forensic purposes in situations where other samples such as bone may prove unsuccessful.

Formalin-Fixed Paraffin-Embedded Tissue Samples

Formaldehyde-fixed and paraffin-embedded tissues provide a valuable resource for forensic analysis [48, 49]. Such tissues, stored by hospital departments, can provide direct reference material for late comparison with human remains. In addition, forensic examination can be employed to determine whether or not tissue samples showing signs of disease have been wrongly attributed to patients following allegations of mislabeling or similar.

Fecal Material

Fecal material in the form of stools or stained tissue paper is found in a small but not insignificant number of associated with burglary scenes, in particular. Fecal material contains, among other things, solid indigestible remains of consumed food, large amounts of microbial material, and other compounds known to inhibit the PCR reaction. Early attempts to recover DNA from fecal samples relied upon the use of mtDNA analysis; however, the introduction of DNA extraction methods capable of substantially removing PCR inhibitors [50, 51] has enabled nuclear DNA-based PCR methods to be utilized improving the evidentiary usefulness of this sample type.

Unusual Sources

Lice, Flies, Mosquitoes, and Maggots

Insects, particularly flies, are frequently associated with crime scenes, and the colonization of bodies by insects after death is used to determine the post-mortem interval [52]. It has been shown that it is possible to recover sufficient human DNA from the crop contents of maggots recovered from corpses to obtain DNA profiles, using not only mtDNA techniques but also conventional autosomal STR typing methods [53]. Results were obtained from maggots recovered from corpses showing putrefaction and from maggots of several different fly families. Thus results were obtained from blow flies, flesh flies, and house flies.

Case Study 7:

"Body on the Beach" [55] The body of a woman was found on a beach. Inquiries led investigators to a suspect, and, upon examination of his home, a mosquito and a small bloodstain corresponding to a blood meal were found on an inside wall. The STR DNA profile obtained corresponded to that of the victim indicating that she had been in the vicinity of the address. When taken into account with other scientific evidence, a strong case was made and the suspect was convicted.

In a similar investigation, mtDNA profiling results were could be obtained from individual human crab lice that corresponded to their human source. In other words, successful mtDNA analysis has been reported of the blood meals of the human louse, thus providing an alternative avenue of investigation when such lice are found on clothing [54].

The Contact Lens

The vacuum cleaner bag has long been regarded as a source of possible fiber evidence, but due to the sensitivity of current DNA profiling techniques, trace amounts of biological material vacuumed away either deliberately or by chance can now be recovered from this most unexpected source.

Case Study 8:

"The Contact Lens" [56] Following a report of a sexual assault committed three days earlier, investigators searched the contents of a dust bag from a vacuum cleaner and retrieved numerous fragments of a contact lens, allegedly knocked from the complainant's eye. A DNA profile, from a single source, and corresponding to that of the complainant was obtained, confirming her presence at the address and the loss of a contact lens as described by her. Faced with this evidence, a guilty plea was entered and a new avenue for potential DNA evidence was uncovered.

Plant Material as Forensic Evidence

In recent years, the suitability of plant material as forensic evidence has begun to be recognized. A number of publications have appeared in the literature describing its application.

Cannabis

A number of alternative methods have been described for the analysis of *Cannabis sativa* L. [57] including DNA sequencing of specific regions of the chloroplast DNA [58] genome suggested as a method to confirm the presence of cannabis. Other studies [59] have utilized STR typing to investigate genetic variability of cannabis plant material. While their findings were unable to fully distinguish between drug and fiber accessions, the STR markers were highly polymorphic and showed significant differentiation between individual plants that had not been clonally produced.

Grasses

Recently, PCR-based methods to distinguish between grass species have been reported. By investigating the mitochondrial sequences of 20 phylogenetically representative grass species, researchers were able to identify sufficient informative sequences (indels) in the grass mitochondrial genome to enable correct identification of 25 unknown grass samples. Thus, grass collected from items associated with crime scenes promises potential as an investigative tool [60].

Magic Mushrooms

Possession of hallucinogenic fungi is a criminal offense in many countries; however, not all closely related fungi contain the hallucinogenic ingredients and, therefore, unambiguous determination of a particular species can be of value in a criminal investigation. PCR-based DNA methods have been described [61] that in combination with phylogenetic approaches, specimens can be separated into hallucinogenic or nonhallucinogenic species.

Trees

A number of genetic approaches can be used to analyze leaf and other plant tissue from trees and this can be used to provide associative evidence in criminal casework.

Case Study 9:

"Disassociation with a Burial Site" [62] A pregnant woman's body was found buried within a few meters of a group of three sand live oak trees, *Quercus geminata*. Dried leaf material was found in the boot of a suspect's car. STR markers were developed that enabled a comparison between the dried leaf material from the car and the trees at the burial site. In this case, the DNA evidence showed that although the leaves in the suspect vehicle appeared to have come from three different trees, the results were not consistent with them having come from the three trees at the burial site.

Other groups have used different approaches to analysis. The amplified fragment length polymorphism technique has been used to investigate the potential of association of plant material from the red maple, *Acer rubrum* [63]. The results showed that within a closed set of trees, identification was possible but that interpretative difficulties arose when considering a larger group or geographical area.

Summary

Since the first reports of the use of DNA profiling to solve a forensic case, DNA profiling has evolved through a number of stages, each one resulting in increased sensitivity or discrimination, to date, where large-scale DNA databases are in use in many countries, STR multiplexes incorporating many loci, and targeting autosomal and Y chromosomes are in common use, and DNA profiling is recognized as a key part of crime solution and modern policing. The seemingly limitless nature of the sources of DNA for forensic analysis continues to impress and as forensic scientists cast their net wider into the plant and animal kingdoms, the possibilities for the future seem endless.

References

[1] Gill, P. & Werrett, D.J. (1987). The exclusion of a man charged with murder by DNA fingerprinting, *Forensic Science International* **35**, 145–148.

[2] Jeffreys, A.J., Wilson, V. & Thein, S.L. (1985). Individual-specific "fingerprints" of human DNA, *Nature* **316**, 76–79.

[3] Gill, P., Jeffreys, A.J. & Werrett, D.J. (1985). Forensic application of DNA fingerprints, *Nature* **318**, 577–579.

[4] Wambaugh, J. (1989). *The Blooding. The true story of the Narborough Village Murders*, A Perigord Press Book, New York.

[5] Butler, J.M. (2005). *Forensic DNA Typing: Biology, Technology and Genetics of STR Markers*, 2nd Edition, Elsevier Academic Press, USA.

[6] Kuperus, W.R., Hummel, K.H., Roney, J.M., Szakacs, N.A., Macmillan, C.E. & Wickenheiser, R.A., Hepworth, D., Hrycak, T.L., Fenske, B.A. & De Gouffe, M.J. (2003). Crime scene links through DNA evidence: the practical experience from saskatchewan casework, *Canadian Society of Forensic Science Journal* **36**, 19–28.

[7] Kratzer, A., Brun, C., Haas, C., Voegeli, P. & Bar, W. (2004). Evaluation of stain cases of the swiss DNA database, *International Congress Series* **1261**, 479–481.

[8] Gross, A.M., Harris, K.A. & Kaldun, G.L. (1999). The effect of luminol on presumptive tests and DNA analysis using the polymerase chain reaction, *Journal of Forensic Sciences* **44**, 837–840.

[9] Quinones, I., Sheppard, D., Harbison, S.A. & Elliot, D. (2006). Comparative analysis of luminol formulations, *Canadian Society for Forensic Science Journal* **40**, 53–63.

[10] Itoh, Y. & Manaka, M. (1988). Analysis of human vaginal secretions by SDS-polyacrylamide gel electrophoresis, *Forensic Science International* **37**, 237–242.

[11] Sibille, I., Duverneuil, C., de la Grandmaison, G.L., Guerrouache, K., Teissiere, F., Durigon, M. & de Mazancourt, P. (2002). Y STR DNA amplification as biological evidence in sexually assaulted female victims

with no cytological detection of Spermatozoa, *Forensic Science International* **125**, 212–216.

[12]   Brauner, P. & Gallili, N. (1993). A Condom- the critical link in a rape, *Journal of Forensic Sciences* **38**, 1233–1236.

[13]   Elliot, K., Hill, D.S., Lambert, C., Burroughes, T.R. & Gill, P. (2003). Use of laser micro-dissection greatly improves the recovery of DNA from sperm on microscope slides, *Forensic Science International* **137**, 28–36.

[14]   Pizzamiglio, M., Mameli, A., Maugeri, G. & Garofano, L. (2004). Identifying the culprit from LCN DNA obtained from saliva and sweat traces linked to two different robberies and the use of a database, *International Congress Series* **1261**, 443–445.

[15]   Reshef, A., Barash, M., Gallili, N., Michael, A. & Brauner, P. (2005). The use of acid phosphatase test papers for DNA profiling, *Science and Justice* **45**, 97–102.

[16]   Crowe, G., Moss, D. & Elliot, D. (2000). The effect of laundering on the detection of acid phosphatase and spermatozoa on cotton t shirts, *The Canadian Society of Forensic Science Journal* **33**, 1–5.

[17]   Van Oorschot, R.A.H. & Jones, M.K. (1997). DNA fingerprints from fingerprints, *Nature* **387**, 767.

[18]   Lowe, A., Murray, C., Whitaker, J., Tully, G. & Gill, P. (2002). The propensity of individuals to deposit DNA and secondary transfer of low levels of DNA from individuals to inert surfaces, *Forensic Science International* **129**, 25–34.

[19]   Phipps, M. & Petricevic, S.F. (2007). The tendency of individuals to transfer DNA to handled items, *Forensic Science International* **168**, 162–168.

[20]   Wickenheiser, R.A. (2002). Trace DNA: a review, discussion of theory and application of the transfer of trace quantities of DNA through skin contact, *Journal of Forensic Sciences* **47**, 442–450.

[21]   Zamir, A., Cohen, Y. & Azoury, M. (2007). DNA profiling from heroin street dose packages, *Journal of Forensic Sciences* **52**, 389–392.

[22]   Esslinger, K.J., Siegel, J.A., Spillane, H. & Stallworth, S. (2004). Using STR analysis to detect human DNA from exploded pipe bomb devices, *Journal of Forensic Sciences* **49**, 1–4.

[23]   Findlay, I., Taylor, A., Quirke, P., Farzier, R. & Urquhart, A. (1997). DNA fingerprinting from single cells, *Nature* **389**, 555–556.

[24]   Whitaker, J.P., Cotton, E.A. & Gill, P. (2001). A comparison of the characteristics of profiles produced with the AMPFLSTR® SGM Plus™ multiplex system for both standard and low copy number (LCN) STR DNA analysis, *Forensic Science International* **123**, 215–223.

[25]   Hochmeister, M.N., Budowle, B., Jung, J., Borer, U.V., Comey, C.T. & Dirnhofer, R. (1991). PCR based typing of DNA extracted from cigarette butts, *International Journal of Legal Medicine* **104**, 229–233.

[26]   Sweet, D. & Shutler, G.G. (1999). Analysis of salivary DNA evidence from a bite mark on a body submerged in water, *Journal of Forensic Sciences* **44**, 1069–1072.

[27]   Abaz, J., Walsh, S.J., Curran, J.M., Moss, D.S., Cullen, J., Bright, J., Crowe, G.A., Cockerton, S.L. & Power, T.E.B. (2002). Comparison of the variables affecting the recovery of DNA from common drinking containers, *Forensic Science International* **126**, 233–240.

[28]   Fridez, F. & Coquoz, R. (1996). PCR DNA typing of stamps: evaluation of the DNA extraction, *Forensic Science International* **78**, 103–110.

[29]   Kaneshige, T., Takagi, K., Nakamura, S., Hirasawa, T., Sada, M. & Uchida, K. (1992). Genetic analysis using fingernail DNA, *Nucleic Acids Research* **20**, 5489–5490.

[30]   Lederer, T., Betz, P. & Seidl, S. (2001). DNA analysis of fingernail debris using different multiplex systems: a case report, *International Journal of Legal Medicine* **114**, 263–266.

[31]   Harbison, S.A., Vintiner, S.K. & Petricevic, S.F. (2003). The persistence of DNA under fingernails following submersion in water, *International Congress Series* **1239**, 809–813.

[32]   Cook, O. & Dixon, L. (2007). The prevalence of mixed DNA profiles in fingernail samples taken from individuals in the general population, *Forensic Science International Genetics* **1**, 62–68.

[33]   Grubweiser, P., Thaler, A., Kochl, S., Teissl, R., Rabl, W. & Parson, W. (2003). Systematic study on STR profiling on blood and saliva traces after visualisation of fingerprint marks, *Journal of Forensic Sciences* **48**, 733–741.

[34]   Olsen, E.S. (ed.) (1994). *Disorders of Hair Growth, Diagnosis and Treatment*. McGraw-Hill, Inc, New York.

[35]   Linch, C.A., Smith, S.L. & Prahlow, J.A. (1998). Evaluation of the human hair root for DNA tying subsequent to microscopic comparison, *Journal of Forensic Sciences* **43**, 305–314.

[36]   Higuchi, R.G., von Beroldingen, C.H., Sensabaugh, G.F. & Ehrlich, H.A. (1988). DNA typing from single hairs, *Nature* **332**, 543–546.

[37]   Wilson, M.R., DiZinno, J.A., Polensky, D., Replogie, J. & Budowle, B. (1995). Validation of mitochondrial DNA sequencing for forensic casework analysis, *International Journal of Legal Medicine* **108**, 68–74.

[38]   Amory, S., Keyser, C., Crubezy, E. & Ludes, B. (2007). STR typing of ancient DNA extracted from hair shafts from siberian mummies, *Forensic Science International* **166**, 218–229.

[39]   Hochmeister, M.N., Budowle, B., Borer, U., Eggmann, U., Comey, C. & Dirnhofer, M.D. (1991). Typing of deoxyribonucleic acid (DNA) extracted from compact bone from human remains, *Journal of Forensic Sciences* **36**, 1649–1661.

[40]   Clayton, T.M., Whitaker, J.P., Fisher, D.L., Lee, D.A., Holland, M.M., Weedn, V.W., Maguire, C.N., DiZinno, C.P., Kimpton, C.P. & Gill, P. (1995). Further validation of a quadruplex STR DNA typing system: a collaborative effort to identify victims of a mass disaster, *Forensic Science International* **76**, 17–25.

[41]   Olaisen, B., Stenersen, M. & Nevag, B. (1997). Identification by DNA analysis of the victims of the August

1996 Spitsbergen civil aircraft disaster, *Nature Genetics* **15**, 402–405.

[42] Gill, P., Ivanov, P.L., Kimpton, C., Peircy, R., Benson, N., Tully, G., Evett, I., Hagelberg, E. & Sullivan, K. (1994). Identification of the remains of the Romanov family by DNA analysis, *Nature Genetics* **6**, 130–135.

[43] Stone, A.C., Starrs, J.E. & Stoneking, M. (2001). Mitochondrial DNA analysis of the presumptive remains of Jesse James, *Journal of Forensic Sciences* **46**, 173–176.

[44] Hagelberg, E., Gray, I.C. & Jeffreys, A.J. (1991). Identification of the skeletal remains of a murder victim by DNA analysis, *Nature* **352**, 427–429.

[45] Crainic, K., Paraire, F., Leterreux, M., Durigon, M. & de Mazancourt, P. (2002). Skeletal remains presumed submerged in water for three years identified using PCR STR analysis, *Journal of Forensic Sciences* **47**, 1025–1027.

[46] Hagelberg, E., Sykes, B. & Hedges, R. (1989). Ancient bone DNA amplified, *Nature* **342**, 485.

[47] Smith, B.C., Fisher, D.L., Weedn, V.W., Warnosk, G.R. & Holland, M.M. (1993). A systematic approach to the sampling of dental DNA, *Journal of Forensic Sciences* **38**, 1194–1209.

[48] Shibata, D.K., Arnheim, N. & Martin, W.J. (1988). Detection of human papilloma virus in paraffin-embedded issue using the polymerase chain reaction, *Journal of Experimental Medicine* **167**, 225–230.

[49] Gill, P., Kimpton, C.P. & Sullivan, K. (1992). A rapid polymerase chain reaction method for identifying fixed specimens, *Electrophoresis* **13**, 173–175.

[50] Johnson, D.J., Martin, L.R. & Roberts, K.A. (2005). STR-typing of human DNA from human fecal matter using the qiagen qiaamp® stool mini kit, *Journal of Forensic Sciences* **50**, 802–808.

[51] Roy, R. (2003). Analysis of human fecal material for autosomal and y chromosome STRs, *Journal of Forensic Sciences* **48**, 1035–1040.

[52] Catts, E.P. & Goff, M.L. (1992). Forensic entomology in criminal investigations, *Annual Review of Entomology* **37**, 253–272.

[53] Zehner, R., Amendt, J. & Krettek, R. (2004). STR typing of human DNA from fly larvae fed on decomposing bodies, *Journal of Forensic Sciences* **49**, 337–340.

[54] Lord, W.D., DiZinno, J.A., Wilson, M.R., Budowle, B., Taplin, D. & Meinking, T.L. (1998). Isolation, amplification and sequencing of human mitochondrial DNA obtained form human crab louse, Pthirus Pubis (l.), blood meals, *Journal of Forensic Sciences* **43**, 1097–1100.

[55] Spitaleri, S., Romano, C., Di Luise, E., Ginestra, E. & Saravo, L. (2006). Genotyping of human DNA recovered from mosquitos found on a crime scene, *International Congress Series* **1288**, 574–576.

[56] Wickenheiser, R.A. & Jobin, R.M. (1999). Comparison of DNA recovered from a contact lens using PCR DNA typing, *The Canadian Society of Forensic Science Journal* **2/3**, 67–73.

[57] Gigliano, G.S. & Cannabis Sativa, L. (2001). Botanical problems and molecular approaches in forensic investigations, *Forensic Science Review* **13**, 1–17.

[58] Linacre, A. & Thorpe, J. (1998). Detection and identification of cannabis DNA, *Forensic Science International* **91**, 71–76.

[59] Gilmore, S., Peakall, R. & Robertson, J. (2003). Short tandem repeat (STR) DNA markers are hypervariable and informative in Cannabis sativa: implications for forensic investigations, *Forensic Science International* **131**, 65–74.

[60] Ward, J., Peakall, R., Gilmore, S.R. & Robertson, J. (2005). A molecular identification system for grasses: a novel technology for forensic botany, *Forensic Science International* **192**, 121–131.

[61] Nugent, K.G. & Saville, B.J. (2004). Forensic analysis of hallucinogenic fungi: a DNA based approach, *Forensic Science International* **140**, 147–157.

[62] Craft, K.J., Owens, J.D. & Ashley, M.V. (2007). Application of plant DNA markers in forensic botany: genetic comparison of *Quercus* evidence leaves to crime scene trees using micro-satellites, *Forensic Science International* **165**, 64–70.

[63] Bless, C., Palmeter, H. & Wallace, M.M. (2006). Identification of *Acer rubrum* using amplified fragment length polymorphism, *Journal of Forensic Sciences* **51**, 31–38.

Related Articles in EFS Online

Bloodstain Pattern Interpretation

Botany

Disaster Victim Identification: Process in United Kingdom

Entomology

Hair: Microscopic Analysis

Luminol

Low Copy Number DNA

Microsatellites

Short Tandem Repeats

Variable Number Tandem Repeats

Wood

Chapter 7
Identification and Individualization

Christophe Champod

University of Lausanne, Institut de Police Scientifique, Lausanne, Switzerland

Identity, Identification, and Individualization

Prof Paul Kirk [1] introduced these terms as they relate to forensic science in a very elegant manner:

> *Identity* is defined by all philosophical authorities as uniqueness. A thing can be identical to only with itself, never with any other object, since all objects in the universe are unique. […] Bowing to general scientific usage, we must however accept the term identification in a broader context, referring only to placing the object in a restricted class. […] The real aim of all forensic science is to establish individuality, or to approach it as closely as the present state of science allows. *Criminalistics is the science of individualisation.*

An individualization can be viewed as a special case of identification, where the restricted class is populated by one object only.

Definitions of individualization in the forensic literature (e.g., fingerprint, footwear marks, or toolmarks) systematically refer to the capability of pointing to the right source *to the exclusion of all others* (objects or persons). Hence, by default, the size of the population of relevant sources considered at the outset of the examination is systematically set to its maximum, regardless of the specific circumstances of the case. We call this the *Earth population* paradigm. In that paradigm, the individualization conclusion cannot be reached in a deductive manner, but is *de facto* probabilistic in nature [2–4]. This is well spelled out by Tuthill and George [5]:

> The individualisation of an impression is established by finding agreement of corresponding individual characteristics of such number and significance as to preclude the possibility (or probability) of their having occurred by mere coincidence, and establishing that there are no differences that cannot be accounted for.

At the end of the examination process, the quantity of features observed in agreement between two objects (without discrepancies) is such that the examiner is prepared to rule out the possibility of a coincidental match, whatever the initial population of sources involved. That has been described by Stoney as a "leap of faith" [6].

If we ask ourselves the order of magnitude of the probability of adventitious matches in the mind of an examiner at the moment of its decision, we can derive it simply using the odds form of the Bayes theorem, another formal analysis can also be found elsewhere [7]:

$$\frac{\Pr(H_p|E,I)}{\Pr(H_d|E,I)} = \mathrm{LR} \times \frac{\Pr(H_p|I)}{\Pr(H_d|I)} \qquad (1)$$

where E stands for the evidence, e.g., a correspondence between a mark and a print, H_p stands for the proposition that the mark has been left by the same source as the print, H_d stands for the proposition that the mark has been left by another source (here $H_d = H_p$), and I stands for the background information; here, the adoption of the Earth population paradigm dominates all other information.

If the prior probability of H_p is set as the inverse of the size of the Earth population of sources (e.g., 1 in 7 billion), then the likelihood ratio (LR) required to achieve a posterior probability for H_p that is close to 1 (e.g., 0.9999) can be derived from the

A Guide to Forensic DNA Profiling
Edited by Allan Jamieson and Scott Bader
© 2016 John Wiley & Sons, Ltd. ISBN: 9781118751527
Also published in EFS (online edition)
DOI: 10.1002/9780470061589.fsa140

following:

$$\frac{0.9999}{1 - 0.9999} = \text{LR} \times \frac{1/(7 \times 10^9)}{1 - 1/(7 \times 10^9)} \qquad (2)$$

This can be re-arranged to give:

$$\text{LR} = \frac{0.9999}{1 - 0.9999} \times \frac{1 - 1/(7 \times 10^9)}{1/(7 \times 10^9)} \qquad (3)$$

For a posterior probability of 0.9999, the LR should at least be above 7×10^{13} or a match probability (MP) (if we assume for the sake of argument that LR = 1/MP) below 1.43×10^{-14}.

Leaving aside the consideration that the assignment of a given posterior probability is outside the duty of the scientist, we face, in the Earth population paradigm, the prospect of having to articulate probabilities out of reach of the current systematic research. Taking fingerprints as an example, the recent published statistical research [8] would allow us to quote MPs on the order of one in a billion confidently. Articulating any smaller number (down to the probability of zero) is nothing more than an unsupported leap of faith. In the above context, we agree with Saks and Koehler [9] that: "The concept of 'individualisation', which lies at the core of numerous forensic science subfields, exists only in a metaphysical or rhetorical sense."

DNA Evidence and Individualization

Current DNA short tandem repeat (STR) profiling techniques are typically based on 10–15 loci, so that the MPs for individuals unrelated to the defendant are extremely small, often less than one in a billion. This is enough for some commentators to suggest that the profile can be considered as unique "with reasonable scientific certainty" [10]. Apart from the technical issues for computing such posterior probabilities [11,12], there are four arguments that call for a more humble approach here: (i) the threshold (e.g., above 99% as proposed by the FBI in [10] amounts to quantifying the concept of reasonable doubt and is outside the realm of the scientist; (ii) invoking a very large population (such as 260 million for the FBI policy) or the population of the Earth is hardly meaningful in a forensic context; (iii) the levels of relatedness within this population with regards to the defendant

are generally not available; and, (iv) more importantly, Foreman and Evett [13] argue that an order of magnitude of 1 in a billion is a fair and reasonable approach, given the current state of knowledge of dependence effects. Hence, we should discourage anyone from believing that a matching DNA profile amounts to definitive attribution of sources – committing the *uniqueness* fallacy according to Balding [14] – but to encourage the interpretation of DNA evidence within the specific context of the case. The fact that absolute certainty is not achievable does not prevent the findings from being useful in court.

Uniqueness

Considerable confusion exists among laymen, indeed amongst forensic scientists about the use of a word such as unique also. The phrase "all portions of friction ridge skin are unique" is no more than a statement of the obvious – every entity is unique and identical to itself only.

What matters is how two objects left in forensic contexts (as an inked print and as a latent mark for example) can be distinguished from each other; either in the case where they have come from the same source or in the case where they have come from different sources. This distinguishability or variability of prints/marks not only depends crucially on the examination method but also on the intrinsic qualities of the prints/marks to display selective features (extensiveness, clarity, etc.). One striking feature in most forensic identification fields is the constant confusion between the between-*persons/objects variability* (which may be infinite) with the *variability* that is expressed in *marks* left by these persons or objects. The loss of information from a complete three-dimensional organ or object to a two-dimensional mark detected on a surface needs to be investigated specifically. The crux of the matter is not really the uniqueness of the sources involved, but the ability of an examiner to distinguish reliably marks and prints left by these sources.

Hence, invoking statements such as "Nature never repeats itself" [15] while referring to the uniqueness of the organs under examination and by consequences to the strength of the conclusion that can be derived from their examination is not legitimate. Cole named this tendency the *fingerprint examiner's fallacy* [16].

Reporting Identification Evidence in Court

The above analysis suggests that scientists should refrain from reporting categorical opinions of individualization, but should report the strength of the findings and leave the integration of that element into the overall context of the case to the jury.

For fingerprint evidence, a systematic analysis of the standards for conclusions (either in terms of criteria for sufficiency or in terms of a range of authorized conclusions by the profession) shows how the evaluation phase has been dominated by policy and pragmatic decisions instead of the application of a scientific approach [17]. The practice of reporting only individualizations and exclusions, leaving all other corroborative evidence under the heading of "inconclusive", cannot be justified on scientific grounds.

Other identification fields have suggested the use of scales of conclusion that are focused on posterior probabilities by either following the Earth population paradigm [18–22] or by applying the Bayes theorem incorporating a highly debatable 0.5 prior probability [23,24]. All these proposals fall short of providing a logical framework for the reporting task. For a discussion on the scales of conclusions, the reader can refer to the following papers [25–27].

All identification evidence types (DNA included) should be governed by the same principles when it comes to their interpretation.

There is an urgent need to find a common, coherent, and harmonized framework to report such evidence in court. The one proposed here is not new and is already embraced in other forensic fields. Broadly speaking, in all forensic areas seeking to help address issues of identity of sources, there are three inter-related factors that determine the nature of the inference that may be made: the quantity and quality of relevant detail, within-source variation, and between-source variation. These three factors impact on the LR defined as follows:

$$LR = \frac{\Pr(E|H_p, I)}{\Pr(E|H_d, I)} \quad (4)$$

The weight of forensic findings is essentially a relative and conditional measure that helps move a case in one direction or the other, depending on the magnitude of the LR. The numerator of the LR considers the within-source variability of the features defined by E and the denominator of the LR deals with their between-sources variability.

Reporting identification evidence in court could be viewed as simply assigning and reporting an LR without the need to claim individualization and set any operational threshold to reach it. All items of evidence for which the LR differs from one then becomes relevant [28].

It is a matter of principle that the scientist may not express an opinion with regard to the hypotheses themselves – that is a matter for the jury. That principle no doubt influenced the English Court of Appeal in the judgment in *R.v. Doheny. G. Adams* [29] which states "The scientist should not be asked his opinion on the likelihood that it was the Defendant who left the crime stain […]."

Conclusions that use terms such as very likely or almost certain in relation to a proposition are only logically possible when the nonscientific evidence is taken into account. Then, the statement follows from the combined effect of the scientific observation and an assessment of the prior probability that encapsulates all the evidence available to the court. The inferential process used here goes far beyond forensic science. Moreover, most of the time, the forensic scientist is not aware of the other pieces of evidence available in a case, and clearly does not have the information at hand to make inferences such as these. Forensic scientists should not make any assessment of the prior information because that ought to remain a matter for the court. To avoid such situations, we need to adopt a reporting convention that allows the scientific statement to remain consistent within a given framework irrespective of other evidence at hand. The LR provides the means for achieving this objective.

References

[1] Kirk, P.L. (1963). The ontogeny of criminalistics, *The Journal of Criminal Law, Criminology, and Police Science* **54**, 235–238.

[2] Meuwly, D. (2007). Forensic individualisation from biometric data, *Science & Justice* **46**(4), 205–213.

[3] Kwan, Q.Y. (1977). Inference of Identity of Source [D. Crim. Dissertation], University of California, Berkeley.

[4] Champod, C. & Evett, I.W. (2001). A probabilistic approach to fingerprint evidence, *Journal of Forensic Identification* **51**(2), 101–122.

[5] Tuthill, H. & George, G. (2002). *Individualization – Principles and Procedures in Criminalistics*, 2nd Edition, Lightning Powder Company, Jacksonville.

[6] Stoney, D.A. (1991). What made us ever think we could individualize using statistics, *Journal of the Forensic Science Society* **31**(2), 197–199.

[7]   Champod, C. (2000). Identification/individualization: overview and meaning of ID, in *Encyclopedia of Forensic Sciences*, J. Siegel, P. Saukko & G. Knupfer, eds, Academic Press, London, pp. 1077–1083.

[8]   Neumann, C., Champod, C., Puch-Solis, R., Egli, N., Anthonioz, A. & Bromage-Griffiths, A. (2007). Computation of likelihood ratios in fingerprint identification for configurations of any number of minutiae, *Journal of Forensic Sciences* **52**(1), 54–64.

[9]   Saks, M.J. & Koehler, J.J. (2008). The individualization fallacy in forensic science evidence, *Vanderbilt Law Review* **61**, 199–219.

[10] Budowle, B., Chakraborty, R., Carmody, G. & Monson, K.L. (2000). Source attribution of a forensic DNA profile, *Forensic Science Communications* **2**(3), http://www.fbi.gov/hq/lab/fsc/backissu/july2000/source.htm.

[11] Weir, B. (2001). DNA match and profile probabilities: comment on Budowle *et al.* (2000) and Fung and Hu (2000), *Forensic Science Communications* **3**(1), http://www.fbi.gov/programs/lab/fsc/current/weir.htm.

[12] Balding, D.J. (1999). When can a DNA profile be regarded as unique, *Science and Justice* **39**(4), 257–260.

[13] Foreman, L.A. & Evett, I.W. (2001). Statistical analysis to support forensic interpretation of a new ten-locus STR profiling system, *International Journal of Legal Medicine* **114**, 147–155.

[14] Balding, D.J. (2005). *Weight of Evidence for Forensic DNA Profiles*, John Wiley & Sons, Chichester.

[15] McRoberts, A.L. (1996). Nature never repeats itself, *The Print* **12**(5), 1–3. http://www.iinet.com/market/scafo/library/120501.html.

[16] Cole, S.A. (2004). Grandfathering evidence: fingerprint admissibility rulings from *Jennings* to *Llera Plaza* and back again, *The American Criminal Law Review* **41**(3), 1189–1276.

[17] Champod, C. (2000). Fingerprints (dactyloscopy): standard of proof, in *Encyclopedia of Forensic Sciences*, J. Siegel, P. Saukko & G. Knupfer, eds, Academic Press, London, pp. 884–890.

[18] AFTE Criteria for Identification Committee (1992). Theory of identification, range of striae comparison reports and modified glossary of definitions, *AFTE Journal* **24**(2), 336–340.

[19] SWGTREAD (2006). Standard terminology for expressing conclusions of forensic footwear and tire impression examinations, *Journal of Forensic Identification* **56**(5), 806–808.

[20] Broeders, A.P.A. (1999). Some observations on the use of probability scales in forensic identification, *Forensic Linguistics* **6**(2), 228–241.

[21] Totty, R.N. (1991). Recent developments in handwriting examination, *Forensic Science Progress* **5**, 91–128.

[22] ASTM (2004). *Standard Terminology for Expressing Conclusions of Forensic Document Examiners*, Standard E 1658-04, West Conshohocken.

[23] ENFSI Expert Working Group Marks Conclusion Scale Committee (2006). Conclusion scale for shoeprint and toolmarks examination, *Journal of Forensic Identification* **56**(2), 255–280.

[24] Deinet, W. & Katterwe, H. (2007). Comments on the application of theoretical probability models including Bayes theorem in forensic science relating to firearm and tool marks, *AFTE Journal* **39**(1), 4–7.

[25] Champod, C. & Evett, I.W. (2000). Commentary on: Broeders, A.P.A. (1999) some observations on the use of probability scales in forensic identification, *Forensic Linguistics* **6**(2), 228–241; *Forensic Linguistics* **7**(2), 238–243.

[26] Champod, C., Evett, I.W., Jackson, G. & Birkett, J. (2000). Comments on the scale of conclusions proposed by the ad hoc committee of the ENFSI marks working group, *The Information Bulletin for Shoeprint/Toolmark Examiners* **6**(3), 11–18.

[27] Biedermann, A., Taroni, F. & Garbolino, P. (2007). Equal prior probabilities: can one do any better? *Forensic Science International* **172**(2–3), 85–93.

[28] Lempert, R.O. (1977). Modeling relevance, *Michigan Law Review* **75**, 1021–1057.

[29] *R. v Alan James Doheny, R. v Gary Adams Court of Appeal - Criminal Division* [1996]. E.W.C.A. Crim 728, (31st July, 1996).

Related Articles in EFS Online

Evidence Interpretation: A Logical Approach

Short Tandem Repeats: Interpretation

Chapter 8
Transfer

Georgina E. Meakin

University College London, London, UK

Introduction

The DNA that is routinely targeted in forensic DNA profiling is contained within the nucleus (pl. nuclei) of the cells that make up our bodies (*see DNA*). Most cells have a nucleus (with the notable exception of red blood cells) and it is DNA from these cells that can be recovered from a crime scene. Sometimes, so few cells can be left on a surface of interest that it is not possible to identify the biological source of those cells, be it skin, other tissue, or body fluids, such as blood or semen (*see Sources of DNA*).

When the biological source of the DNA recovered is unknown, the DNA is commonly referred to as *trace DNA* or *touch DNA*. The use of the term *touch DNA* has led to the common misconception that trace DNA recovered from a surface of interest got there via that surface being touched. However, outside of controlled experiments, i.e., at a crime scene, this is usually not known. The term *trace DNA* allows for the fact that DNA can be transferred by other means, directly or indirectly.

Transfer of Trace DNA

Direct DNA Transfer

We can directly transfer our DNA on to a surface through contact, such as touching a surface with our bare hands, activities near the surface, such as speaking or coughing, or by leaving traces of body fluids, such as

blood, that are so dilute that they cannot be identified by routine body fluid testing (*see Biological Stains*). These instances of transfer are referred to as direct, or primary, DNA transfer. Knowing whether the DNA is from skin cells or a body fluid might help us to establish how that DNA was left on that surface.

Each gene within our DNA contains a code that provides the instructions to make a specific protein. Although cells from different tissues or body fluids have the same genes, they require different proteins at different times. This means that the genes switched on to make particular proteins at particular times can differ between cells from different biological sources. When genes are switched on, molecules of messenger RNA (mRNA) are made; these molecules translate the genetic code in the DNA to the specific protein that is made. Analyzing the types of mRNA in cells of the unknown trace material recovered could indicate the type of tissue or body fluid that those cells are from. Such mRNA profiling is being developed to identify cells from specific body fluids or tissues [1] and from skin [2]. Other techniques being developed to identify trace body fluids or tissues include analyzing micro RNA, DNA methylation, and microbial markers [3]. While these developments are promising, further research and validation studies are still required to enable these techniques to be reliably employed in forensic casework.

When we touch something, we can leave anywhere between 0 and 170 ng (170×10^{-9} or 0.00000017 g) of DNA on that surface [4]. This means we are regularly leaving our DNA on surfaces that we come into contact with, particularly those that we handle on a regular basis, such as pens, keys, and phones [5] (*see Sources of DNA*). This DNA could come from skin cells that are left behind during touching. The average person sheds approximately 400 000 skin cells per day [6], demonstrating the ease with which DNA could

Update based on original article by Allan Jamieson, Wiley Encyclopedia of Forensic Science, © 2009, John Wiley & Sons, Ltd.

A Guide to Forensic DNA Profiling
Edited by Allan Jamieson and Scott Bader
© 2016 John Wiley & Sons, Ltd. ISBN: 9781118751527
Also published in EFS (online edition)
DOI: 10.1002/9780470061589.fsa526.pub2

potentially be left on surfaces, along with the potential for onward transfer of that DNA (as discussed later). However, it is debated in the scientific literature as to whether these shed skin cells actually contain DNA. Cells in the top layer of our skin are essentially "dead", which results in the loss of their nuclei and hence their DNA. Studies show that DNA deposited by touch is actually likely to come from a combination of: some skin cells that retain nuclei [7], fragmented DNA present on the surface of the skin [8], and cell-free DNA present in sweat [9]. In addition, we often rub our face and eyes, and scratch other areas of our skin. Acts such as these might allow cells with nuclei to be transferred from those areas to our hands, effectively 'loading' our hands with DNA-bearing material, ready to be left on a surface that we subsequently touch [6]. Work is therefore required to further characterize the biological material recovered from touched surfaces, with the view of using mRNA profiling to identify evidence of contact [2].

Touching a surface is not the only way in which trace DNA can be directly transferred. We can also deposit detectable levels of DNA by speaking or coughing in the vicinity of the surface. However, there is little research published on how and to what extent activities such as these can transfer DNA. Published experiments tend to be limited to the context of crime scene or laboratory contamination [10, 11]. We know that DNA can be present in saliva and nasal mucous, therefore these body fluids may be the biological source of DNA deposited via these activities. Once again, knowing the biological source of the trace DNA could help to see whether an activity, such as speaking, caused the DNA to be left on the surface of interest.

Indirect DNA Transfer: The Onward Transfer of Directly Transferred DNA

When we leave DNA on a surface, be it via touch or some other activity, that DNA can be transferred onward to another surface. This is an example of indirect DNA transfer. Such transfer can be via one intermediary surface (secondary transfer), two intermediary surfaces (tertiary transfer), or potentially via more surfaces. Whether the surface on which we leave DNA is a person or an object, that DNA is potentially available for onward transfer.

The observation of indirect DNA transfer was first published in 1997. An experiment showed that DNA could be transferred from one person to another via a plastic tube that they had both held at different times [5]. In the years that followed, debate ensued in the scientific literature as to whether indirect DNA transfer really occurred, and if so, how relevant was it to forensic casework [6]. Since then, however, many empirical studies have been published to demonstrate that secondary DNA transfer can occur in casework-relevant scenarios, be it from person to person to object or person to object to object (several such studies are reviewed in Refs [4] and [12]). Furthermore, recent studies show that tertiary and possibly further onward transfer of DNA can occur, depending on factors described in the following text. One such study records a social setting, in which three people sat on chairs around a table, drinking and chatting, while pouring juice from a communal jug into their individual glasses [13]. DNA from the different people was indirectly transferred among themselves, the jug, glasses, table, and chairs in a bi-directional manner [13]. Indirectly transferred DNA from unknown people was also introduced into the setting, presumably from the hands of the participants [13]. A different study examining the recovery of trace DNA from ammunition casings and cartridges used in gun crime found many instances of DNA from more than one person, that is, not just DNA from the person who fired or loaded the weapon [14]. This led the authors to suggest that secondary and tertiary DNA transfer may occur at higher rates than previously thought. It is now clear that indirect DNA transfer can occur in casework-relevant situations, and it is imperative that this is considered when assessing how trace DNA got on a particular surface in a forensic case.

Factors Affecting the Detection of Transferred DNA

Experiments investigating trace DNA show extremely varied results, in terms of both DNA yield and DNA profile quality, from apparently similar trace DNA samples. The detection of trace DNA is therefore a complex issue that is dependent on many factors [4]. Such factors can be loosely grouped into three categories: deposition (the amount of DNA left on a surface of interest), persistence (how long that DNA remains on the surface), and recovery (the amount of DNA that can be taken from the surface and is subsequently available for DNA profiling).

Deposition and Persistence of Trace DNA

Some of the factors affecting the transfer and persistence of trace DNA, such as the duration of any contact, are the same as those for other types of trace evidence, such as fibers and paint. Other factors affecting how much DNA we leave on a surface via direct transfer include: our ability to shed DNA, the condition of our skin, the nature of any contact between us and the surface, and the type of surface [4]. It is also possible that our age might affect the amount of DNA we leave behind [15]. Indirect transfer of DNA is also affected by these factors, since the availability of DNA that could be transferred from one surface to the next depends on the amount and quality of DNA left on the initial surface [4]. Indirect DNA transfer is additionally affected by the type of surfaces involved in the transfer events, the nature of contact between surfaces resulting in indirect transfer, and the time between and the number of transfer events [16, 17].

How long our DNA can persist on a surface is irrespective of whether our DNA was directly or indirectly deposited. Factors that do affect trace DNA persistence include the type of surface on which the DNA is deposited and various environmental conditions [4]. For regularly used items, subsequent handling by a different person limits the persistence of DNA from the regular user [18].

Analytical Recovery of Trace DNA

From a crime scene or laboratory perspective, how we choose to recover and process trace DNA affects the amount of DNA recovered and the availability of DNA for profiling. The type of sampling method employed and how well the DNA is extracted from that sample affect its recovery [4], along with the efficiency and sensitivity of the DNA profiling technique used [12] (*see DNA: An Overview*). The latter is particularly important as, within the past year or so, extremely sensitive technologies for standard DNA profiling have been rolled out in casework laboratories. These technologies are optimized and validated for use with 0.5 ng of DNA and below, instead of with 1 ng, as was the case for the older standard profiling technologies.

We can sample a surface for DNA by using various types of swabs (consisting of buds of cotton or nylon on the end of wooden or plastic shafts) or mini-tapes (small pieces of adhesive tape) to collect the DNA or cells, or through application of lysis solution (which breaks cells up to release the DNA) directly to the surface. The choice of sampling method is usually based on the biological source of the DNA and the surface that is being sampled. For example, we commonly use mini-tapes to recover trace DNA from fabrics [19] and ridged surfaces [20], as higher yields can be achieved than by swabbing.

Making the DNA from the obtained sample available for profiling usually requires an extraction process. We use a number of different extraction processes in casework; our choice of process is dependent on its efficiency and the nature of the biological material being extracted (*see Extraction*; *DNA: An Overview*). We can also directly profile the DNA from the surface of interest, which omits the DNA extraction step and thereby increases the amount of DNA available for profiling. For example, this method can generate good quality DNA profiles from fabrics [21] and fingernails [22].

Evaluation of DNA Transfer in Forensic Casework

Distinguishing Between Different Modes of DNA Transfer

The many ways in which we can leave our DNA, and the factors affecting its transfer and persistence, need to be considered when assessing how trace DNA came to be on a surface of interest in forensic casework. In the initial instance, we should consider whether we might expect there to be any background levels of DNA present on that surface. For example, in cases of physical or sexual assault, we might investigate whether there is any DNA that could have come from the assailant present on the victim's skin or beneath their fingernails. If DNA is recovered that is not from the victim (*foreign DNA*), then we need to assess whether that DNA got there during the assault or through some other innocent means. Background studies show that foreign DNA can be recovered from a person's skin and fingernails, even when no such assault has occurred, particularly from people who cohabit with others [4]. However, physical contact, particularly of a sexual nature, may increase the level of foreign DNA detected.

In forensic casework, when we evaluate the finding of trace DNA, or any other potential evidence for that matter, it is imperative that a logical and transparent approach is taken. Central to this is ensuring that forensic experts do not solely rely on their experience, but instead turn to empirical data to help support their opinion on how the DNA got there. Some scientists believe that the available empirical data can only help a forensic expert provide an opinion on the possibilities, rather than probabilities, of DNA transfer [4], while other scientists believe that inferences regarding DNA transfer can be made in many casework situations [13]. It is agreed by both "sides" that further research is required to improve the reliability and usefulness of interpretations regarding DNA transfer, and the range of situations in which such empirical data may assist.

Issues Relating to DNA from Handled or Worn Items

As hinted above with the range of amounts of DNA that you might leave when you touch something, it is possible to touch something and not leave any DNA behind. It is also possible that you might touch someone (e.g., shake their hand) and then touch an item and not leave your DNA, but leave theirs instead. However, for touched or handled items, it is more common to recover DNA from more than one person, i.e., mixed DNA profiles. In many occurrences observed, the main profile of the mixtures obtained comes from the last person to touch the item, although instances are observed in which the last person to touch the surface is not the main contributor [13]. Therefore, it is difficult to use the nature of the mixed DNA profiles to determine the last person to handle the item of interest.

However, such research studies are usually conducted using pre-cleaned items, for example, plastic tubes or glasses that have been specifically treated to remove any DNA present. We know that we leave DNA on items that we regularly use, so in a casework situation, it is likely that the item examined would have had a certain level of DNA present on it, before its use in the crime. In fact, objects or items of clothing that are likely to have been regularly handled or worn are routinely examined for trace DNA in casework. The DNA samples obtained are believed to contain DNA from the regular user or wearer, known as *regular user DNA* or *wearer DNA*, respectively. When mixed DNA profiles are obtained, the same issues arise as described above, that is, how do we know which of the DNA profiles in the mixture comes from the regular wearer/user, the most recent

wearer/user (i.e., at the time of the crime), or indeed from indirectly transferred DNA?

Recent research is beginning to address some of these questions. It has been reported that when regularly used pens [18] or worn T-shirts [23] are used/worn by someone else, the main contributor to mixed DNA profiles initially recovered is the regular, and not the most recent, user/wearer. However, with increasing time of use, the contribution of regular user DNA to the mixtures decreases and the main contributor becomes that of the most recent user [18]. Furthermore, these studies also show that indirectly transferred DNA is detected in DNA mixtures obtained from regularly used items [18, 23, 24]. Once again, it is difficult to use the nature of mixed DNA profiles to establish how the different DNA profiles got on to the item in question.

Potential Contamination Issues

Given the apparent ease with which DNA can be transferred, potential for contamination with extraneous DNA must be considered both at the crime scene and in the laboratory. Contaminating DNA can enter the DNA detection process at any stage, including the sampling, processing, and profiling of the DNA. Examination equipment, such as fingerprinting brushes, forceps and scissors, and protective clothing, such as gloves, can act as vectors to transfer DNA from one surface to another, thereby potentially resulting in contamination [4]. There are many procedures that should be followed to try to prevent such contamination, such as ensuring appropriate cleaning protocols are in place, changing gloves on a regular basis, and performing regular monitoring of any potential background DNA levels within the laboratory. Such procedures are particularly crucial currently, as the new, more sensitive, DNA profiling technologies now being used by casework laboratories can detect DNA when the older technologies could not [25]. There is therefore a heightened need to employ more stringent decontamination procedures, with some laboratories implementing improved cleaning practices [26].

Conclusion

Touch DNA, better referred to as *trace DNA*, can be transferred to a surface in a multitude of ways, both directly and indirectly. It is currently not possible to reliably identify the biological source of trace DNA, making it particularly difficult for forensic experts to assess how trace DNA might have been transferred to the surface of interest. The detection of such transferred trace DNA, although dependent on many factors, is likely to increase in forensic casework, now that DNA profiling is routinely being conducted by extremely sensitive techniques. As such, forensic experts must consider issues of DNA transfer, and any potential risks of contamination, when evaluating findings of trace DNA in casework. To do so, the basis of their opinions must be logical and transparent, and ideally informed by empirical research. Such research continues to underline the complexity of DNA transfer, emphasizing the need for more research and increased caution against unsupported inferences from DNA evidence in casework.

References

[1] van den Berge, M., Carracedo, A., Gomes, I., Graham, E.A.M., Haas, C., Hjort, B., Hoff-Olsen, P., Maroñas, O., Mevåg, B., Morling, N., Niederstätter, H., Parson, W., Schneider, P.M., Court, D.S., Vidaki, A. & Sijen, T. (2014). A collaborative European exercise on mRNA-based body fluid/skin typing and interpretation of DNA and RNA results, *Forensic Science International: Genetics* **10**, 40–48.

[2] Haas, C., Hanson, E., Banemann, R., Bento, A.M., Berti, A., Carracedo, Á., Courts, C., Cock, G.D., Drobnic, K., Fleming, R., Franchi, C., Gomes, I., Hadzic, G., Harbison, S.A., Hjort, B., Hollard, C., Hoff-Olsen, P., Keyser, C., Kondili, A., Maroñas, O., McCallum, N., Miniati, P., Morling, N., Niederstätter, H., Noël, F., Parson, W., Porto, M.J., Roeder, A.D., Sauer, E., Schneider, P.M., Shanthan, G., Sijen, T., Syndercombe Court, D., Turanská, M., Van Den Berge, M., Vennemann, M., Vidaki, A., Zatkalıková, L. & Ballantyne, J. (2015). RNA/DNA co-analysis from human skin and contact traces – results of a sixth collaborative EDNAP exercise, *Forensic Science International: Genetics* **16**, 139–147.

[3] Sijen, T. (2015). Molecular approaches for forensic cell type identification: On mRNA, miRNA, DNA methylation and microbial markers, *Forensic Science International: Genetics*, in press.

[4] Meakin, G. & Jamieson, A. (2013). DNA transfer: Review and implications for casework, *Forensic Science International: Genetics* **7**, 434–443.

[5] Van Oorschot, R.A.H. & Jones, M.K. (1997). DNA fingerprints from fingerprints [6], *Nature* **387**, 767.

[6] Wickenheiser, R.A. (2002). Trace DNA: A review, discussion of theory, and application of the transfer of trace quantities of DNA through skin contact, *Journal of Forensic Sciences* **47**, 442–450.

[7] Balogh, M.K., Burger, J., Bender, K., Schneider, P.M. & Alt, K.W. (2003). Fingerprints from fingerprints, *International Congress Series* **1239**, 953–957.

[8] Kita, T., Yamaguchi, H., Yokoyama, M., Tanaka, T. & Tanaka, N. (2008). Morphological study of fragmented DNA on touched objects, *Forensic Science International: Genetics* **3**, 32–36.

[9] Quinones, I. & Daniel, B. (2012). Cell free DNA as a component of forensic evidence recovered from touched surfaces, *Forensic Science International: Genetics* **6**, 26–30.

[10] Finnebraaten, M., Granér, T. & Hoff-Olsen, P. (2008). May a speaking individual contaminate the routine DNA laboratory?, *Forensic Science International: Genetics Supplement Series* **1**, 421–422.

[11] Rutty, G.N., Hopwood, A. & Tucker, V. (2003). The effectiveness of protective clothing in the reduction of potential DNA contamination of the scene of crime, *International Journal of Legal Medicine* **117**, 170–174.

[12] van Oorschot, R.A.H., Ballantyne, K.N. & Mitchell, R.J. (2010). Forensic trace DNA: A review, *Investigative Genetics* **1**, 17 p.

[13] Goray, M. & van Oorschot, R.A.H. (2015). The complexities of DNA transfer during a social setting, *Legal Medicine* **17**, 82–91.

[14] Montpetit, S. & O'Donnell, P. (2015). An optimized procedure for obtaining DNA from fired and unfired ammunition, *Forensic Science International: Genetics* **17**, 70–74.

[15] Poetsch, M., Bajanowski, T. & Kamphausen, T. (2013). Influence of an individual's age on the amount and interpretability of DNA left on touched items, *International Journal of Legal Medicine* **127**, 1093–1096.

[16] Goray, M., Eken, E., Mitchell, R.J. & van Oorschot, R.A.H. (2010). Secondary DNA transfer of biological substances under varying test conditions, *Forensic Science International: Genetics* **4**, 62–67.

[17] Verdon, T.J., Mitchell, R.J. & Van Oorschot, R.A.H. (2013). The influence of substrate on DNA transfer and extraction efficiency, *Forensic Science International: Genetics* **7**, 167–175.

[18] Van Oorschot, R.A.H., Glavich, G. & Mitchell, R.J. (2014). Persistence of DNA deposited by the original user on objects after subsequent use by a second person, *Forensic Science International: Genetics* **8**, 219–225.

[19] Verdon, T.J., Mitchell, R.J. & Van Oorschot, R.A.H. (2014). Evaluation of tapelifting as a collection method for touch DNA, *Forensic Science International: Genetics* **8**, 179–186.

[20] Williams, G., Pandre, M., Ahmed, W., Beasley, E., Omelia, E., World, D. & Yu, H. (2013). Evaluation of low trace DNA recovery techniques from ridged surfaces, *Journal of Forensic Research* **4**, 199.

[21] Linacre, A., Pekarek, V., Swaran, Y.C. & Tobe, S.S. (2010). Generation of DNA profiles from fabrics without DNA extraction, *Forensic Science International: Genetics* **4**, 137–141.

[22] Ottens, R., Taylor, D. & Linacre, A. (2015). DNA profiles from fingernails using direct PCR, *Forensic Science, Medicine, and Pathology* **11**, 99–103.

[23] Meakin, G.E., Boccaletti, S. & Morgan, R.M. (2014). DNA as Trace Evidence: Developing the Empirical Foundations for Interpretation, *Poster at 22nd International Symposium on the Forensic Sciences of the Australian and New Zealand Forensic Science Society*.

[24] Meakin, G.E., Butcher, E.V., van Oorschot, R.A.H. & Morgan, R.M. (2015). The Deposition and Persistence of Indirectly-Transferred DNA on Regularly-Used Knives, *Oral Presentation at 26th Congress of the International Society for Forensic Genetics*.

[25] Szkuta, B., Harvey, M.L., Ballantyne, K.N. & Van Oorschot, R.A.H. (2015). DNA transfer by examination tools – A risk for forensic casework?, *Forensic Science International: Genetics* **16**, 246–254.

[26] Ballantyne, K.N., Salemi, R., Guarino, F., Pearson, J.R., Garlepp, D., Fowler, S. & van Oorschot, R.A.H. (2015). DNA contamination minimisation – finding an effective cleaning method, *Australian Journal of Forensic Sciences* 1–12.

Related Articles in EFS Online

Biological Swabs

Evidence Interpretation: A Logical Approach

Low Template DNA Analysis and Interpretation

Trace Evidence: Transfer, Persistence, and Value

Chapter 9
Laboratory Accreditation

Allan Jamieson

The Forensic Institute, Glasgow, UK

Introduction and Background

For the purposes of this work, accreditation will refer to organizational assessment, certification will be taken to refer to an individual's assessment.

Accreditation

Accreditation is primarily a means by which methods and procedures are set to paper, and a system put in place to ensure that those methods are followed. There are a large number of accreditation systems available in the forensic arena. This is probably inevitable, given the range of skills deployed in disciplines as disparate as handwriting and DNA profiling. The comments here, therefore, cannot include all of the accreditation systems and schemes present worldwide. They are necessarily general and intended to introduce the meaning and in particular the limitations of what can be inferred from accreditation.

Probably, the most widespread standards for accreditation worldwide emanate from the International Standards Organization (ISO). For ISO, accreditation is primarily set by "customer requirements", not by scientific accuracy or reliability.

In 2009, the stated purpose of the ISO standards was to:

- make the development, manufacturing, and supply of products and services more efficient, safer, and cleaner

Update based on original article by Kenneth E. Melson, Ralph Keaton and John K. Neuner, Wiley Encyclopedia of Forensic Science, © 2009, John Wiley & Sons, Ltd.

A Guide to Forensic DNA Profiling
Edited by Allan Jamieson and Scott Bader
© 2016 John Wiley & Sons, Ltd. ISBN: 9781118751527
Also published in EFS (online edition)
DOI: 10.1002/9780470061589.fsa440.pub2

- facilitate trade between countries and make it fairer
- provide governments with a technical base for health, safety and environmental legislation, and conformity assessment
- share technological advances and good management practice
- disseminate innovation
- safeguard consumers, and users in general, of products and services
- make life simpler by providing solutions to common problems.

In 2015, those have disappeared from the ISO website. The "benefits" of ISO standards are now listed as

- Cost savings – International Standards help optimize operations and therefore improve the bottom line
- Enhanced customer satisfaction – International Standards help improve quality, enhance customer satisfaction, and increase sales
- Access to new markets – International Standards help prevent trade barriers and open up global markets
- Increased market share – International Standards help increase productivity and competitive advantage
- Environmental benefits – International Standards help reduce negative impacts on the environment[a] [my underline].

From a scientific perspective, these appear to deliver little or nothing in terms of accuracy or precision of results. Nevertheless, forensic science has been caught up in the general drive toward accreditation in almost every commercial activity.

The UK Forensic Science Regulator notes,[b]

There is no requirement for an organisation, or individual, to be accredited to any national, or international, standard before results they generate are admissible as evidence.

However, a few lines further on;

The European Union has adopted Council Framework Decision 2009/905/JHA on the accreditation of forensic service providers carrying out laboratory activities. This requires that laboratories providing DNA analysis services to the CJS be accredited to ISO 17025 [4] by December 2013.

Accreditation Schemes

In the United States, the most widespread accreditation standard for forensic laboratories is the ASCLD/LAB scheme (American Society of Criminal Laboratory Directors Laboratory Accreditation Board – "the first organization in the world dedicated to accrediting crime labs – and we're still the only accrediting body that focuses 100% on laboratories performing testing for criminal justice the largest forensic science accrediting body in the world"[c]). ASCLD-LAB is a not-for-profit organization that offers

an enhanced ISO program of Crime Laboratory Accreditation for both forensic testing disciplines and breath alcohol calibration, based on ISO/IEC 17025 and enhanced by ASCLD/LAB-*International* Supplemental Requirements. Our accreditation of testing labs is recognized by both the Inter American Accreditation Cooperation (IAAC) and the International Laboratory Accreditation Cooperation (ILAC).[d]

These standards are based on

- ISO/IEC 17025:2005 Internationally developed and approved
- ASCLD/LAB developed supplemental requirements specific to forensic science testing laboratories
- ASCLD/LAB policies for laboratories
- Board interpretations for specific program applications.[e]

The ASCLD-LAB standard is based on ISO17025. This is also the base standard intended to be used by the Forensic Science Regulator in the United Kingdom, and has been in use in Australia for some time.

Australia was, in the early 1990s, linked to ACLD-LAB, but ultimately adopted a solely ISO17025 accreditation system.

ISO17025

ISO17025 is the standard for, "General requirements for the competence of testing and calibration laboratories". It has five principal sections, only one of which addresses technical issues:

1. Scope
2. Normative references
3. Terms and definitions
4. Management requirements
5. Technical requirements.

To understand the system it is necessary to examine in some detail the standard as set out in the ISO documentation.

The laboratory shall use test and/or calibration methods, including methods for sampling, which meet the needs of the customer and which are appropriate for the tests and/or calibrations it undertakes. Methods published in international, regional or national standards shall preferably be used.

The choice of analytical method is of course crucial for any scientific test. Two things are notable as regard the standard; the standard is set by the customer, and there is only a suggestion that published methods are used. The customer in the forensic environment would appear to be in most instances law-enforcement agencies and, ultimately, the Courts. It is widely recognized that these have not been especially discriminating or knowledgeable about science.

If a method has not been described in the published literature, then it most likely has been developed in-house. The standard states,

When it is necessary to use methods not covered by standard methods, these shall be subject to agreement with the customer and shall include a clear specification of the customer's requirements and the purpose of the test and/or calibration. The method developed shall have been validated appropriately before use.

Again, the customer.

In addition, a word that seems to pervade modern documentation when it would appear that a real definition is elusive or simply too difficult; "appropriately". It is not defined within the standard how appropriateness is to be judged and by whom.

As to the role of the customer in defining requirements;

> The amount of direct input from the CJS [criminal justice system] end-user should be determined by the provider[f]

Accreditation should not be confused with validation. Validation is the scientific definition of the parameters of an analytical method, and accreditation is a system of documentation describing what should be done. Validation is a component of accreditation and accreditation has therefore been used to support claims of validation *because of* the accreditation of the organization.

The ISO17025 standard defines validation as,

> the confirmation by examination and the provision of objective evidence that the particular requirements for a specific intended use are fulfilled.

It goes on,

> The validation shall be as extensive as is necessary to meet the needs of the given application or field of application.

The decision as to the extent of any validation is therefore placed with the laboratory. There are no objective criteria set for the validation parameters. This is not a criticism of the ISO standard, which must of necessity be general. It is a caution that the mere possession of accreditation does not mean that any particular scientific standard has necessarily been met because that standard would appear to be "in the eye of the beholder".

Accreditation in the Forensic Context

If it is intended that accreditation will be adduced as evidence of the correctness of the results and opinion delivered to Courts, then it will be a necessary consequence that the defense will seek to scrutinize not only the production of those results, but the accreditation process. To date, the accreditation process has not been scrutinized thoroughly in Court, despite the frequent claims of accredited organizations that their opinion is to be relied upon because of accreditation. Indeed, there are documented instances of errors, some serious, by accredited laboratories.[g,h] This is inevitable and only reinforces two things; first, that accreditation is no guarantee of the reliability of a specific result and second, that practitioners should not, therefore, claim that it does. If accreditation will be used to underpin the reliability of results, then the process used will need to be more open to inspection than it would appear to be at the moment.

Of importance in the forensic environment is the ISO17025 section on opinions;

> When opinions and interpretations are included, the laboratory shall document the basis upon which the opinions and interpretations have been made. Opinions and interpretations shall be clearly marked as such in a test report.

It should be noted that this, as in most of the standard, is a description of what should be done, not a description of the parameters that would form part of a validation exercise such as accuracy, precision, reliability, reproducibility, and limitations.

Section 5.10 of the ISO17025 standard states,

> Each test report or calibration certificate shall include at least the following information, <u>unless the laboratory has valid reasons for not doing so</u>

So there would appear to be considerable latitude and subjectivity in the application of the requirements to meet the ISO17025 standard.

The main output of a forensic laboratory is the opinion formed on the basis of the analytical results. ISO17025 does not accredit such opinion. The UK Forensic Science Regulator, in a footnote, states;

> Where this [opinion] it [sic] to be included in a provider's schedule of accreditation, they will need to ensure that they are in compliance with the UKAS publication LAB 13.[f]

LAB 13 is explicit;

> UKAS will <u>assess the processes</u> put in place by the laboratory for the purposes of making statements of opinions or interpretations in order to evaluate the laboratory's competence to do

so,   but will not accredit or otherwise endorse the statements themselves.[i]

This would appear to merely codify the rationale that the expert uses to derive an opinion. While that is a worthwhile and an important aim, it is nevertheless difficult to see how this is not simply part of professional practice and would be subject to examination in court as a matter of routine; accreditation will neither strengthen nor weaken the expert's opinion.

The problems of attempting to accredit without fundamental scientific standards (as opposed to processes) is recognized in at least one aspect of DNA profiling;

> David Balding in his paper – "evaluation of mixed-source, low template DNA profiles in forensic science" outlines the problems related to the interpretation of such profiles. In the introduction he refers to a review by the UK regulator of LTDNA evidence as follows, "The report found the underlying science to be "sound" and LTDNA profiling to be "fit for purpose" although admitting that there was lack of agreement "on how LTDNA profiles" are to be interpreted." Balding suggests that these comments are somewhat contradictory. How can a technique be fit for purpose without valid methods to assess evidential strength? I suggest that this is a classic example of the use of technology where standards or norms hadn't been established [1].

Care should be exercised to avoid confusing an accredited opinion with an accurate opinion. While accreditation has some meaning, nothing can be deduced about an organization's or individual's competence from a lack of such accreditation. In particular, it is clear from case experience that most of the differences in opinion between scientists in Court arise from different evaluations of the data (i.e., what does it mean in the context of the case) rather than whether the physical analysis has been properly performed. Accreditation does not remove that area of dispute.

Defense Expert Accreditation

It is apparently implicit in most discussions on accreditation that the defense expert will operate under the same conditions as the prosecution expert. This is probably a consequence of the fact that, historically,

most defense experts have simply sought to repeat the work performed by the prosecution laboratory. This has undoubtedly been reinforced by the lawyers' "fight fire with fire" approach. However, there is an emerging trend recognizing a new, and possibly more effective, role for the defense expert; the review of the work of the prosecution.

There is a view [2] that the main purpose of a competent scientific defense expert is, rather than to simply repeat the Prosecution tests, to review the processes, procedures, and conclusions of the prosecution experts. This includes verification that what has been claimed to have been done *has* been done, and whether it has been done according to validated procedures and standards.

Unless the validation and standards are clearly scientifically defined, and the information is disclosed to the expert, the purpose of this process is entirely compromised.

The final output of the review of the Prosecution scientific case may be in the form of briefing papers and reports to instructing lawyers or Counsel. In some cases the briefings or reports may concur with the methods, interpretations, and evaluations employed by the prosecution experts, in other cases there are differences between the prosecution and defense conclusions. As has been illustrated, this is not an area currently covered by accreditation. In fact such review is explicitly banned from being accredited;

> Expression of opinions and interpretations relating to results is considered to be an inherent part of testing/calibration and UKAS will not accredit expression of opinions and interpretations in reports as a separate activity.[i]

The question remains as to if, how, and whether, and for what, defense experts (who are frequently academic scientists with relevant scientific skills) will be accredited.

Conclusion

Accreditation is a limited mechanism for examining and certifying some aspects of forensic science. This does not affect the necessity for proper scrutiny in individual cases and cannot be a substitute for proper verification and discovery. The current ISO17025 requirements are deficient in several important respects as a suitable system for forensic science, but are capable of being improved. Validation is and should remain a scientific function because accreditation does not and cannot verify all aspects of the underlying science, the competence of the scientists, the reliability, validity or accuracy of the methods or how they are applied, and how scientific results are evaluated and presented in court.

To suggest that accreditation is able to do so, is a superficially appealing solution to minimize the costs and uncertainties associated with science and expert evidence. It is also, however, a dangerous and unwarranted elevation of accreditation to a status beyond its capabilities. Until rigorous scientific standards are developed, the merit of any form of assessment is questionable [1]. Organizational accreditation should not be used as the criterion to justify any forensic practice or area of expertise in a criminal trial or civil proceeding. It cannot be used as a cover for the identified deficiencies in the scientific underpinning of many forensic practices.

Accreditation in its present form, and even in ideal conditions, can never provide a guarantee of sound science. Science requires rigorous and on-going international validation. This cannot be encompassed within accreditation schemes, which in order to be rigorous would necessarily be cumbersome, time consuming, and expensive (although some have argued that is already the case [1]).

Even if accreditation provided a comprehensive and thoroughly reliable indication of how scientific evidence should be interpreted and evaluated, the fact remains that two scientists may have legitimately opposing views as to the significance of the evidence in a legal context. While existing accreditation schemes may address the interpretation of results (i.e., how laboratories get actual results, for example, the amount of alcohol or drug in a sample or the alleles in a DNA profile), it does not adequately deal with the evaluation phase (i.e., the assessment of the evidential value of those results within the context of a specific case). The forensic evaluation of analytical results, rather than the results, is by far the most common challenge to scientific evidence. The perspective of a prosecution scientist is necessarily informed by the material provided to them by law enforcement and the prosecution service. The defense perspective, in contrast, is informed by the fact that they are not obliged to present a particular view, but rather to test the view of the prosecution. For this reason, accreditation cannot be used as an alternative to the proper scrutiny of scientific evidence by the prosecution and defense.

Realistically, it is difficult to see how evaluation could ever be accredited, given that different experts can rationally hold different views on the evaluation of the same evidence. (It goes almost without saying that it would be no solution to set up an accreditation regime in forensic science for the evaluation phase by allowing the "customer" to decide whether the evaluation is "fit for purpose". In forensic science, a focus on "customer requirements", the main parameter in ISO17025, is problematic because while both prosecution and defense experts are legally intended to be experts "for the court", as a matter of practicality they are "instructed" by the prosecution or the defense. Accreditation of forensic providers by the ISO is therefore fundamentally awkward because of the underlying philosophical tensions between the need for utility and value-for-money for the prosecution or defense, and the courts' need for scientific reliability, validity, and accuracy. While the demands of the parties and the court are not necessarily mutually exclusive, the admissibility and credibility of expert witnesses should not be rubber-stamped by inadequate accreditation.

There is no evidence that accredited organizations provide a more reliable and accurate service than nonaccredited organizations. None of the high-profile failures in forensic science of the past would necessarily have been prevented by accreditation. Indeed, arguably most of the most recent errors have occurred within accredited systems. The evidence for any tangible improvement, and in particular any improvements in cost efficiency or cost effectiveness, is absent or scanty. Commentators have recognized that ISO and other existing accreditation schemes are no panacea:

> Accreditation is just one aspect of an organization's quality assurance program, which also should include proficiency testing where relevant, continuing education, and other programs to help the organization provide better overall services. In the case of laboratories, accreditation does not mean that accredited laboratories do not make mistakes, nor does it mean that a laboratory utilizes best practices in every case, but rather, it means that the laboratory adheres to an established set of standards of quality and relies on acceptable practices within these requirements. An accredited laboratory has in place a management system that defines the various processes by which it operates on a daily basis,

monitors that activity, and responds to deviations from the acceptable practices using a routine and thoughtful method. This cannot be a self-assessing program.[j] [my underline]

However accreditation, as operated at the moment, does not satisfy all the needs of forensic science and it would be wrong to consider that miscarriages will be avoided when all parties in the scientific process are accredited [1].

End Notes

[a.] http://www.iso.org/iso/home/standards/benefitsof standards.htm

[b.] Information – Legal Obligations FSR-I-400 Issue 3.

[c.] http://www.ascld-lab.org/about-ascldlab/

[d.] http://www.ascld-lab.org

[e.] http://www.ascld-lab.org/international-testing-program

[f.] Forensic Science Regulator. Codes of Practice and Conduct *for forensic science providers and practitioners in the Criminal Justice System* Version 2.0 August 2014 available at https://www.gov.uk/government/publications/forensic-science-providers-codes-of-practice-and-conduct-2014

[g.] http://www.sfgate.com/bayarea/article/Technician-boss-in-S-F-police-lab-scandal-6169230.php

[h.] https://www.washingtonpost.com/local/crime/national-accreditation-board-suspends-all-dna-testing-at-district-lab/2015/04/26/2da43d9a-ec24-11e4-a55f-38924fca94f9_story.html

[i.] UKAS Guidance on the Application of ISO/IEC 17025 Dealing with Expressions of Opinions and Interpretations [UKAS Publication ref: LAB 13].

[j.] "Strengthening Forensic Science in the United States: A Path Forward." Committee on Identifying the Needs of the Forensic Sciences Community; Committee on Applied and Theoretical Statistics, National Research Council, National Academy of Sciences of the US. Published February 2009.

References

[1] Willis, S. (2014). Accreditation – Straight belt or life jacket? Presentation to Forensic Science Society Conference November 2013, *Science and Justice* **54**, 505–507.

[2] Jamieson, A. (2011). The case for full disclosure of laboratory case files, *Journal of the Law Society of Scotland* http://www.journalonline.co.uk/Magazine/56-3/1009322.aspx

Chapter 10
Validation

Campbell A. Ruddock

Oklahoma City Police Department, Forensic DNA unit, Oklahoma City, OK, USA

Introduction

Forensic science like all scientific disciplines is dependent upon a solid framework of reproducible and reliable data from which observations, credible interpretations, and conclusions can be supported.

DNA testing remains at the forefront of the forensic disciplines as a standard bearer of reliable testing procedures both in the scientific community and the legal system. This level of integrity as a testing standard is founded on the many stringent quality assurance policies and practices that DNA testing has adopted over time. The discipline is subject to many quality assurance components including guidelines and recommendations established by scientific working groups (SWG's), annual audit process, proficiency testing, in depth peer review of casework, testing controls, validations, and established interpretation criteria based on observed empirical data.

In its brief existence, DNA testing has flourished and established itself as a crucial and commonly utilized method of individualization in criminal investigations. As is the nature of science, there is a constant state of evolution and progressive development as technologies advance, novel methods are pioneered and limits of detection are pushed to ever increasing sensitivities.

As a result, today's crime laboratory is expected to keep pace with these changes while maintaining a strict commitment to quality. Critical to the establishment of new technology or approaches to DNA testing is the validation process to demonstrate the integrity of a method before utilization in case work.

Validation is achieved through documented testing and can be viewed as a critical aspect of any laboratory's quality assurance program. With regards to forensic short tandem repeat STR analysis, delineation of boundaries and thresholds from validation data contribute to sound interpretation [1]. Validation is necessary to create confidence in testing results, operating procedure, and assurance in quality, all of which play an important part in reassuring the reliability and impartiality required of DNA testing.

To be admissible in the courtroom, scientific testing must prove itself reliable. DNA testing evolved alongside the Daubert standard [2] dictates that scientific testing methods must be reliable and that testing standards and error rates have been applied appropriately. Validation is a critical step to meeting this admissibility ruling (and the alternative in some states – Frye).

Validation Defined

A validation study is a body of data generated to test and demonstrate the reliability, reproducibility, robustness, and limitations of a given method [3].

With this in mind it is useful to establish early on that validations pertain directly to the testing of methods and procedure. Validation in this sense serves as a process to test and ultimately demonstrate a method's success in measuring what it is intended to measure.

So What Actually Requires Validation in a DNA Testing Facility?

Any new process coming into the DNA laboratory affecting the results (chemistry, instrumentation, interpretation, or testing) is subject to requiring validation. Each laboratory identifies the critical components of the testing process and will ensure each component is adequately tested in and for the entire process, and its performance validated for casework.

A Guide to Forensic DNA Profiling
Edited by Allan Jamieson and Scott Bader
© 2016 John Wiley & Sons, Ltd. ISBN: 9781118751527
Also published in EFS (online edition)
DOI: 10.1002/9780470061589.fsa1125

This involves planning of a validation strategy, having a testing goal, designing experiments to test an assays performance, consideration of the end use as well as an in depth examination of the data generated during the validation testing to establish thresholds and operating protocols – the documented technical steps and components of the method, or simply how the laboratory should conduct this particular test.

The validation process for a new application provides the laboratory with a thorough understanding of the subject matter, theory, performance parameters, limitations, and predictability of a method. This understanding of the validation data provides a comprehensive understanding of the application and ensures confidence in the results as well as an understanding of when and how the method may go awry, and potentially the corrective actions when this occurs.

From a legal perspective, validations are the body of work that demonstrates confidence in a method's results. A validation study of a new method typically tests several important quality aspects of the subject in question [3]:

(a) Robustness – ability to obtain results successfully a high percentage of the time
(b) Reliability – ability to produce accurate results and perform consistently under stated conditions
(c) Reproducibility – ability to produce the same result from different testing times, instruments, or operators
(d) Range – upper and lower limits of a methods operational capability

Each of these is crucial to understanding the fundamental operation and performance of a method.

Types of Validations

Validations within the DNA discipline require two distinct types of validation (i) developmental validations and (ii) internal validations.

Both categories of validation studies are important quality tests; each type can be considered as a separate layer in establishing validity with both types serving their own function to the forensic laboratory.

At its core, a validation is a quality process and integral to establishing any new assay. The general strategy of where the validation process sits from creation to casework implementation is summarized in Figure 1.

Examining each type of validation study allows their function in the overall process to become clear.

1. *Developmental validations* – These types of validation studies can be considered the genesis point for any novel DNA technique, approach, chemistry or instrument establishing its function, and reliability scientifically.
   Developmental validations are traditionally, although not exclusively, conducted by manufacturers or developers who have designed and made a new application. When considering forensic DNA applications examples of developmental validations would be the validation of an entirely new STR chemistry kit considering species specificity studies, polymorphisms, mapping, characterization of genetic markers, detection methods, inheritance, reaction conditions, or development of optimized primers. Developmental validations will often include working crime laboratories to assist with interlaboratory concordance studies to support consistency of results. [4]
   This manner of validation study can be considered the initial body of work conducted to test the framework of operability and performance reliably within an established range. It is critical that all these testing parameters have been established during a developmental validation before recommendation for casework assessment.
   The outcome of the developmental validation is the basis for which the manufacturer can publish recommendations for the use, limitations, and considerations of the end user purchasing the product and establish support for recognition as a new method. Although this pertains to new methods, this does not require that an established method be put through a developmental validation if it is being transferred to a forensic application. For example, the use of an assay originally developed for nonhuman applications (such as PCR) being considered for human forensic DNA testing could utilize the original validation data as part of its developmental validation.
   All this must be based on an often exhaustive body of data examining rigorous testing at extreme ends of the capabilities of the chemistry. The new method must be function tested much in the same way any machinery goes through detailed testing before manufacturing.

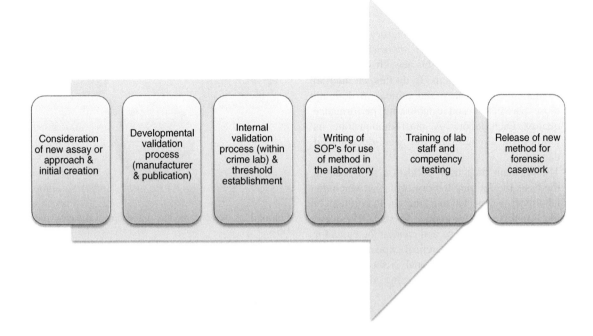

Figure 1   Process map of validation considerations

Data from developmental validations is published in scientific literature or presented at meetings to receive acceptance within the scientific and forensic DNA communities to be available in support of its establishment as a new assay or approach. Support of method reliability and literature is important when considering court admissibility rules also (such as the U.S Frye & Daubert admissibility standards).

Most forensic laboratories use manufactured kits as the basis of their DNA profiling. The laboratory depends on the manufacturer to conduct the developmental validation on new kits for several practical reasons: limited research time or capabilities, staff, and funding restrictions or the manufacturer developing an assay as a proprietary product. As the name suggests, this manner of validation generally relates to new product development. Although it is acceptable for end user laboratories to rely on manufacturer developmental validations, the laboratory must still have access to the published developmental validation. The laboratory these need only conduct an in house internal validation to ensure the kit works

in its hands before putting it to casework use. The developmental validation can be considered as the foundation work on guidelines and establishment of any new method.

2. *Internal validations* – The purpose of an internal validation is to test the limitations of a new method within a specific workflow, verify that a kit or product functions appropriately for routine casework applications, and confirm that results can be reproduced by trained analysts in that specific laboratory.

Although the principles, chemistries, and instruments used in forensic DNA testing laboratories are well established, each laboratory can have a degree of freedom and interchangeable testing options with what assays and instruments are utilized in a testing method. Also to be considered is that each instrument or assay although designed for a specific task will display variations in sensitivity and "personality" between instruments, environments, users etc., so ultimately each laboratory set up is different from any other and the new kit must undergo validation in each laboratory – even different laboratories in the same building or different equipment in the same laboratory.

This necessitates that each laboratory authors its own *standard operating protocols* (SOP's) and guidelines detailing how this new kit will operate within its specific system. To do this, an internal validation is necessary and critical to defining those parameters and establishing performance quality. Each laboratory must demonstrate its journey by an accurate and well documented dataset.

The resultant data from validation will become the basis for defining the protocols for which the laboratory is expected to adhere to, and ultimately the limitations of testimony. These SOP's document the technical steps and contain the bases for interpretations. The theoretical expectation from an SOP is that any trained analyst should be able to reproduce results under the same conditions by following the protocol.

Governing Bodies and Guidelines

Before undertaking any validation project, it is crucial to understand the governing standards and guidelines as they relate to quality assurance and validations of forensic DNA methods.

Validation standards allow for a degree of uniformity in the recognized approach to what is critical with regards to data and documentation from a validation study, and assist in ensuring quality within the discipline.

In the United States forensic DNA testing laboratories adhere to a set of quality standards established in the quality assurance standard's (QAS) document. These standards were developed by the DNA Advisory Board (DAB) under the review of guidelines recommended by SWGDAM (scientific working group for DNA analysis methods) to establish appropriate quality measures and documentation within forensic laboratories. All laboratories should be audited annually in accordance to this document, and additional external evaluation every second year to further assesses compliance to the established standards. In Europe, the European Network of Forensic Science Institutes (ENFSI) also has a DNA working group establishing similar guidelines (Figure 2).

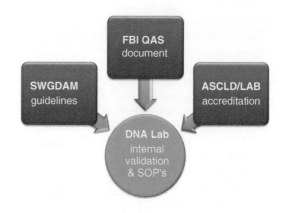

Figure 2   Governing bodies influencing validations in the USA

QAS Document

The QAS document dictates that the laboratory must have thoroughly validated any new technologies before their release for casework [5]. Part of this, although not a direct part of the validation itself, also includes that all personnel undergo and pass a competency test and get trained in each newly validated technique to demonstrate an understanding in this new process.

The QAS document standards cover many general elements of quality assurance documentation and are not solely aimed toward validations. However, Section 8 of the QAS document [5] specifically relates to the validation standards and outlines the minimal expectations of what each validation must successfully document.

The laboratory must show that sufficient data exists to support any limitations and use of a new technique and adequately document its validation.

The SWGDAM Validation Guidelines

The SWGDAM validation guidelines are a set of recommendations and approaches to DNA testing put forth by a working group of academics, technical leaders, and DNA analysts involved in the field. The guidelines served as the framework for the creation of the QAS document published by the FBI. As an active peer body in the discipline of forensic DNA testing, SWGDAM will review the QAS document and recommend updates or changes to this document; however the QAS document holds ultimate authority over the guideline recommendations. The latest revision of the validation guidelines were published in December 2012 [6].The guidelines were intended to assist testing laboratories and set forth a uniform and accepted framework as a baseline for laboratories embarking on new validations to create and document reliable methods in compliance to the QAS document [6].

At a minimum, the guidelines recommended that each validation study should display data under the following study areas to assist in establishing reliable protocols:

- Studies with known and non-probative case work samples
- Repeatability studies
- Reproducibility studies
- Sensitivity studies
- Mixture studies
- Contamination studies
- Stochastic studies (for STR chemistry)

This framework allows compilation of data necessary to display that the assay being tested has been examined for reliability, robustness, and reproducibility.

Accreditation

Following the QAS standards as they apply to validation is critical to maintaining accreditation status and allowing the laboratory to participate in the NDIS (National DNA Index System) data basing system. Many laboratories are accredited under the ASCLD/LAB ISO/IEC 17025 program (American Society of Crime Laboratory Directors/Laboratory Accreditation Board – International Standards Organization/International Electrotechnical Commission 17025). Accreditation promotes confidence in quality and ensures laboratory conformance to established testing standards. Although ASCLD/LAB has its own section of guidelines pertaining to general validation and testing standardization, it again conforms to the QAS document for DNA validations. ASCLD/LAB also serves to govern that the laboratory is complying with its own established protocols and that new methods have been appropriately documented and followed.

Internal Validations Process

Embarking on an internal validation project is often viewed as a substantial undertaking for a laboratory owing to the stringent quality standards and auditing process. The challenge most laboratories are faced with is time frame vs. data analysis.

Important to the success of any validation project is establishing the project goals and time frame. The guiding strategy of validation is to establish scientific confidence in the new method as swiftly as possible to bring it online for casework purposes.

Much of this depends on the particular method or kit being examined, and the aspects tested define the conclusions that can be determined.

The basic DNA workflow can be organized as several critical stages each encompassing its own set of methods and in turn its own specific requirements for validation:

- DNA extraction
- DNA quantification
- Normalization and PCR amplification
- Capillary electrophoresis
- Data analysis and interpretation

Although these are each independent components of the DNA analysis process, validation is not the same as the troubleshooting process where instrumentation operation often requires isolation from the process to identify and resolve specific issues.

New methods can be validated simultaneously if more efficient for the laboratory such as validation of a new STR kit and genetic analyzer within the same project.

Conducting a full internal validation plan, the laboratory would follow studies recommended in the SWGDAM guidelines and consider manufacturers recommendations [7].

On the basis of this framework, the laboratory can now develop a strategy to examine the operational limits of each aspect tested. The studies should also show that the results obtained are similar to those obtained with any currently employed methods. For example, introducing an automated extraction method should produce results consistent with or better than current manual method. Laboratories are free to conduct more in-depth testing of each method; however these categories reflect the minimum standards required for established internal validations by SWGDAM. The goal of the validation should be to confirm and document the new method functions successfully.

Examining the study categories allow us to see the role each test series plays in validation and performance testing.

Repeatability study – provides data on whether a set of samples can produce similar results consistently in apparently identical conditions (e.g., using the same machines, lab, and staff). This directly relates to displaying precision and accuracy.

Reproducibility study – whether this set of results be demonstrated reliably again under the same conditions but different times or by different analysts.

Sensitivity study – allows for the determination of a dynamic range over which reliable results can be obtained (e.g., the upper and lower limits of detection of a positive result, limits of where a reliable quantity can be measured).

Concordance study – whether the method produces similar results when compared with an existing method.

Mixture study – particular to forensic DNA applications, it is critical to assess the behavior of mixtures. Forensic samples often contain DNA from two or more people. The laboratory must determine at what point can genotypes be either resolved as individual contributors or an uninterpretable mixture of contributors. Part of this study involves determining balance between genotypes and interlocus performance. This ultimately allows for the establishment of mixture interpretation guidelines, such as deconvoluting profiles (i.e., separating the contributing profiles in, for example, major/minor mixtures), establishing stutter percentages, major and minor component ratios or simply identifying a mixture. The laboratory can utilize this study set to define threshold of how mixtures behave and at what point contributors cannot be successfully resolved by the laboratory.

Contamination study – with increasing sensitivity of DNA detection methods it becomes necessary to assess if an assay introduces any possibility of contamination, or can detect any contaminant [8, 9]. The laboratory is responsible for demonstrating the ability of the assay to perform contamination free.

Stochastic study – the PCR process is subject to stochastic events (random sampling errors) that will interfere with the ability to successfully interpret many samples especially with very low amounts of DNA. Stochastic studies will assess at what point data in the assay may be liable to stochastic or random events such as allelic drop in or drop out, peak height imbalances, elevated stutter, allele masking, and false homozygotes. These require caution in interpretation and the so-called calling thresholds (e.g., when a peak can be inferred to be from a homozygote) to be set. By examining data from the validation a laboratory can safely determine the minimum peak heights necessary to ensure stochastic events are not interfering with the genotypes presented and allelic calls are correct.

Sample Selection

An internal validation is composed of two sample type subsets. The laboratory is required to test the new method on both "known" reference and "non-probative casework" type samples. Probative samples categorize any sample type that may be encountered as biological evidence in casework or ultimately develop investigative leads. For example cigarette butts, blood stains, or trace DNA from firearm triggers. The outcome from analysis of such samples are often unknown, and thus reflect true case simulation. Non-probative samples are usually, but not always, represented by reference type samples such as known buccal or blood samples from individuals, collected only for comparison purposes and not anticipated to introduce any interpretation complexities such as mixtures or allelic drop out and have more predictable results (Figure 3).

Reference samples such as commercial standard references, blood or buccal swabs of a known genotype can be expected to result in high quality, higher yield DNA and are therefore ideal candidates for testing the performance of the assay and reproducibility. Utilization of samples with an expected outcome allows variables to be tested one at a time during the validation process.

Different dilutions of a known high-quality DNA sample allow for testing sensitivity ranges – the limits of detection of an assay and determine parameters such as at what point the system becomes overloaded, or fails to detect material present in very low amounts. Examination of this data allows the laboratory to define thresholds based on a set of observed data within their process. Often the developmental validation data

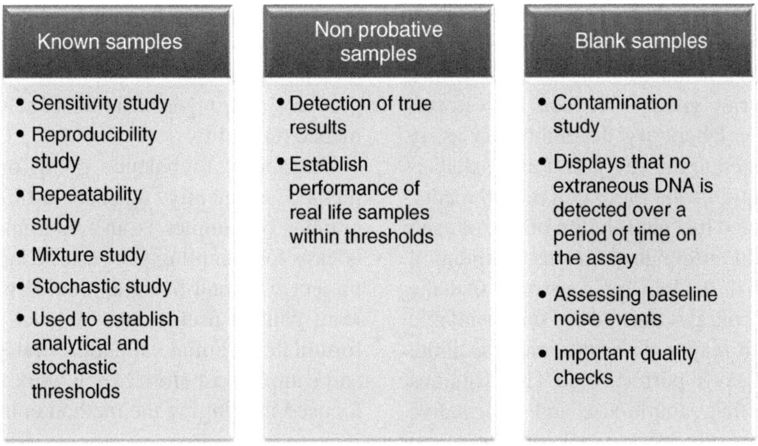

Figure 3   Testing sample categories

serves as a good template for initial sensitivity ranges to be tested. For example, validation of a new STR kit would usually cover a range of 31.2 to 1000 pg (1 ng) of template DNA and this range would be selected based on developmental recommendations of expected performance [4, 7].

Known samples can be prepared to set parameters and confirm data falls within the stated recommendations of the initial developmental validation study.

Non-probative casework samples are designed to mimic the real world forensic type samples that the laboratory commonly encounters during case work. This may include sample sets such as cigarette butts, chewing gum, trace DNA, or compromised samples from clothing or any substrate type the laboratory views as commonly encountered.

Although these samples are of an unpredictable and variable quality, giving results that can vary drastically, the advantage to utilizing these samples is to validate that no false results are obtained and simulate how real world or complex samples may behave with regards to the method being tested. It is necessary that the laboratory examines all commonly encountered sample types to generate an idea of sample behavior. This is especially true with trace or low level DNA samples that present additional complexities and interpretational considerations [8].

Through simulation of how typical samples respond to the new assay, the scientist can engage in a more comprehensive appreciation of the limitations of the assay, and how compromised data will look. All of these observations will become critical in determining thresholds, trouble shooting, and identifying bad data. As much of forensic DNA analysis encompasses complex, degraded, inhibited, low template, or other challenging samples, the ability to identify "bad" data is a critical interpretation skill that is a discussion chapter in itself.

Although it is impossible to predict every casework scenario, part of the value in testing non-probative samples allows a degree of confidence in identifying the differences between actual true compromised, low copy template or degraded DNA samples, and instrument errors and artifacts.

The range and design of the non-probative type samples utilized in an internal validation are at the testing laboratories' discretion. However the compiled data should strive to be representative of samples the laboratory would commonly expect to see during routine casework.

Sample Size

Although the QAS document and SWGDAM guidelines outline a framework for studies that must be conducted in a comprehensive validation, the sample size used for testing often varies among laboratories [10]. The question often arises how many samples constitute a comprehensive or acceptable validation study? Studies have shown that standardization of sample size between laboratories for validation projects is non-uniform and somewhat problematic [11]. The depth and amount of samples utilized in a validation study varies greatly between laboratories and even within the laboratory depending on assay tested, time committed to the study, and user satisfaction that the data supports the minimum requirements. It is generally accepted that a minimum of five of each sample group should suffice to populate a validation study set; however it is often misconstrued that the more samples used enlarges the body of data available to the laboratory and may assist with a more accurate snapshot of the assay's performance [11]. Studies have demonstrated that sample size and informative data will plateau quickly after 5–10 replicates and extensive sampling is often unnecessary to a validation [12]. In general, the more variable the data obtained, the more samples are necessary to identify the population parameters (i.e., if the data in five samples is highly variable then more needs to be done to establish the extent of the variability such as average and range whereas if five samples produce almost identical results it can be inferred that more testing would contribute relatively less information about the range and average result).

The benefit is frequently represented more by the range of sample types investigated during the validation as opposed the quantity of each sample type.

The standard validation of a new STR kit including all the outlined studies required by the QAS document may consist of ~90–100 samples in total, and the SWGDAM guidelines recommends a minimum of 50 samples per validation project [6]. The laboratory should have some objective parameter to decide the appropriate number of samples of each type that require to be assessed in the validation.

Likewise selection of dilution ranges for sensitivity studies are dependent upon laboratory observations or narrowed by manufacturer recommendations.

Some validation studies will require less samples and data points to generate confidence in the reliability when compared to other studies, such as the validation of a new STR kit that involves establishing more thresholds and therefore examination of more parameters. Surveys of laboratories show that while the range of sample numbers chosen varies, most laboratories aim to run less than 10 sensitivity samples, and 5 different two-person mixture samples and 5–10 non-probative samples during validation [10]. Examining two- and three-person mixture samples with

minimal allelic sharing allows for better examination of stochastic artifacts and allelic dropout phenomena.

Running samples in duplicate or triplicate sets [7] provides a stronger basis for conclusions and performance reliability.

The ability to balance going online with a new method efficiently against testing an appropriate number of samples is an important consideration. It is easy for sampling to consume large portions of the project time and become bloated without any significant gain in useful data. As such it is important to formulate an initial validation strategy, goal, deadline, and sample set before bench work analysis to remain focused in bringing the method online successfully.

Setting Thresholds

A critical component to any internal validation study is the ability to ultimately define thresholds for data interpretation; this is especially important during STR data analysis. Establishing these thresholds ensure consistency within the laboratory for interpretation, allelic calls, and an ability to decide what data is viable for interpretation. This again plays a role in quality, ensuring interpretations are uniform and calls are not made on weak unsupported data. The goal of setting thresholds is to determine the point at which there is too little, or cautionary zones for interpretation.

Keeping with our example of the validation of a new STR kit, the laboratory must decide upon first an analytical or signal to noise threshold, and then select a stochastic threshold for interpretation [13]. These are established directly from validation study data.

Analytical threshold – can be described as the limit of detection or defining signal to noise ratios. What is the minimum signal at which a data point can be identified as being detected as a potential allele as opposed to an artifact?

From here, a dynamic range can be determined by establishing the point at which data exhibits oversaturation, and the range wherein ideal data can be consistently observed.

Finally in assisting with interpretation, the laboratory needs to establish a stochastic threshold. The purpose of which is to determine a point below which a potential partner allele may be lost from a heterozygous pair. This leaves a gray area between upper and lower thresholds of what can be detected, what can be comfortably called as heterozygous, detection of allelic drop in events [8, 9], and serves as a cautionary flag alerting the interpreting analyst that anything below this threshold may be suffering from stochastic events and potentially affecting the interpretation.

Performance Checks and Material Modifications

Additional quality components related to validation include performance checks and material modifications. Although these are usually simpler in nature than full internal validation, they are also integral quality assurance processes.

A laboratory must decide when a full validation, performance check, or material modification is the appropriate quality step.

A *performance check* is designed to demonstrate the consistent operability of an instrument, and differs from the validation of a method. For example, a genetic analyzer is identified as a critical piece of equipment in the laboratory and will undergo a full internal validation first. However if a second identical instrument is installed, a performance check would be a suitable approach to rapid implantation as the thresholds were established on an identical model during internal validation.

Thus the requirement for the second instrument is simply to demonstrate concordance with the validated procedure.

A performance check also functions as an additional quality measure if an instrument undergoes a repair or calibration before releasing it for active casework again to ensure it is operating as expected.

A *material modification* would be pertinent in a situation where an existing assay is modified in some manner, for example, reducing input DNA volumes for quantification or increasing injection times on a genetic analyzer. The general validated method in place still exists but a single aspect may be altered. The laboratory would be required to document testing to show the modification is reliable, but would not be required to test each parameter as outlined in the complete validation process. If there is a possibility that the modification will alter the process then it requires assessment of data.

Strategies for these quality checks are often left to each laboratory to assess the degree of testing but all records should be well documented.

These approaches are important as is often necessary to "revalidate" a process as the use of the method evolves with the needs of the laboratory. In this regard, it is true that the working crime laboratory is never truly complete with the validation process as the methods change over time and the validation must also evolve to support those changes.

Challenges of Validation Process

Validation of any new method within the DNA analysis process is a critical step that must be planned, implemented, and documented diligently and thoroughly. Familiarity with the validation data is the opportunity to become confident with the scientific boundaries of the method.

A particular challenge, and the one that validation is intended to meet, is ensuring that the interpretation of a profile is supported by sufficient data. Validation work is frequently subject to the external audit process and scrutiny from other experts. As such it is in the best interests of the laboratory to conduct organized, detailed, and well-documented validations and build a core body of reliable data to support the interpretation guidelines of the laboratory.

The length of time devoted to internal validation projects are often viewed as the most challenging aspect to the crime laboratory. They can quickly become expansive (and expensive) projects and can be perceived as hindering a laboratory's ability to quickly utilize a new method.

The laboratory must balance the desire to implement the new method with ensuring reliable results and interpretation. Strategy, appropriate sampling, and focus on the parameters being tested can prevent validations from becoming disoriented.

Even if it not possible to have all case work analysts involved directly in the validation work, there should be an emphasis on ensuring that time is taken to review and discuss each validation outcome and report. This is to the advantage of each individual when considering interpretation ability, testimony, and communicating an understanding of the principles behind the protocols.

Outsourcing validation projects can relieve the laboratory of the burden of time-consuming validation work, and also can often offer additional external expertise when dealing with a new process. Outsourcing also allows the laboratory staff to focus on casework which some managers may consider as higher priority.

Although this is beneficial it is important that the laboratory does not overlook the data presented. In this aspect it is vital the laboratories remain involved in their own validation processes to keep abreast of the process and assay and take time to study any validation project that is outsourced.

Laboratories also have additional validation resources available to help ensure their own internal validations are appropriate. The website STRbase [g] maintains a reference library of STR kit validation studies, and the SWGDAM (or ENSFI) guidelines themselves are a vital resource for planning a validation correctly which was the intentional goal of the publication.

The core science behind DNA testing is seldom challenged in most courts today. However the legal community should understand the importance of validation studies in corroborating a laboratory's ability to produce sound scientific results. As the validation studies are the basis for operating procedures and discoverable, they should be reference points for establishing confidence in all testing methods and demonstrating that the laboratory can adequately support its conclusions.

Testimony and Training

While training is not technically part of the actual validation itself it remains a critical component of the quality process. Once a method has been validated, it is imperative that all analysts become competent in its use. An important part of this training should be a fundamental understanding of how the method works and the data generated to support it. As analysts ultimately testify to the methods used, it is in the interest of every expert to have confidence in the thresholds of interpretation and its limitations to succeed in giving the most effective, balanced, and informed testimony.

As such, review of validation data, or summary of internal validation data should be included as part of the training each analyst receives in the new method.

References

[1] Holt, C.L., Buoncristiani, M., Wallin, J.M., Nguyen, T., Lazaruks, K.D. & Walsh, P.S. (2002). TWGDAM Validation of AmpFiSTR PCR Amplification Kits for Forensic DNA Casework, *J Forensic Sci.* **47**(1), 66–96.

[2] M. W. Perlin (2006). Scientific Validation of Mixture Interpretation Methods. Proceedings, 17th International Symposium on Human Identification, December 5, 2006.

[3] Butler, J.M. (2001). Forensic DNA Typing: Biology and Technology Behind STR Markers, in *Laboratory Validation*, 2nd Edition, Elsevier Academic Press, Chapter 16, San Diego, pp. 389–412.

[4] Oostdik, K., Lenz, K., Nye, J., Schelling, K., Yet, D., Bruski, S., Strong, J., Buchanan, C., Sutton, J., Linner, J., Frazier, N., Hays, Y., Matthies, L., Sage, A., Hahn, J., Wells, R., Williams, N., Price, M., Koehler, J., Staples, M., Swango, K.L., Hill, C., Oyerly, K., Duke, W., Katzilierakis, L., Ensenberger, M.G., Bourdeau, J.M., Sprecher, C.J., Krenke, B. & Storts, D.R. (September 2014). Developmental validation of the PowerPlex® Fusion System for analysis of casework and reference samples: A 24-locus multiplex for new database standards, *FSI: genetics* **12**, 69–76.

[5] Standards for forensic DNA testing laboratories, FBI homepage (accessed Jul. 2014): http://www.fbi.gov/about-us/lab/biometric-analysis/codis/stds_testlabs

[6] Revised validation guidelines for DNA analysis methods, SWGDAM homepage (accessed Jul. 2014): http://swgdam.org/SWGDAM_Validation_Guidelines_APPROVED_Dec_2012.pdf

[7] Internal validation Guide of Autosomal STR Systems for Forensic Laboratories (2013) Reference manual, Promega Corporation, Madison, Wisconsin.

[8] Gill, P. (2001). Application of Low Copy Number DNA Profiling, *Croat. Med. J.* **42**, 229–232.

[9] Validation of Testing & interpretation Protocols for Low template DNA Samples Using AmpFiSTR Identifiler. Caragine T, Mikulasovich R., Tamariz J., Bajda E., Sebestyen J., Baum H. and Prinz M. *Croat Med J.* 2009 Jun; **50**(3): 250–267.

[10] Can the Validation Process in Forensic DNA Typing be standardized? Butler J. M., Tomsey C. S. and Kline M. C. 15th international Symposium on Human Identification (October 6, 2004)

[11] Butler, John. (2006). Debunking some urban legends surrounding validation within the forensic DNA community. (Profiles in DNA, Sept. 2006 p3-6) http://projects.nfstc.org/workshops/resources/literature/debunking%20validation%20butler.pdf

[12] ENFSI DNA working group homepage (accessed Jul. 2014) Recommended minimum criteria for the validation of various aspects of the DNA profiling process (2010): http://www.enfsi.eu/sites/default/files/documents/minimum_validation_guidelines_in_dna_profiling_-_v2010_0.pdf

[13] Validation. Butler, John & McCord, Bruce, STRbase website (accessed Jul. 2014) Validation, Albany DNA academy workshop (Butler & McCord June 13–14 2005) http://www.cstl.nist.gov/strbase/pub_pres/Albany_Validation.pdf

Further Reading

ASCLD/LAB International standard document ISO/IEC 17025 (second edition)

NIJ validation information for public DNA laboratories: http://www.nij.gov/topics/forensics/lab-operations/Pages/validation.aspx

STRbase website (accessed Jul 2014) STRbase validation project: http://www.cstl.nist.gov/strbase/validation.htm

Related Articles

DNA

Degraded Samples

Discovery of Expert Findings

Introduction to Forensic Genetics

Laboratory Accreditation

Related Articles in EFS Online

Low Template DNA Analysis and Interpretation

PART B
Analysis & Interpretation

Chapter 11
Extraction

Campbell A. Ruddock

Oklahoma City Police Department, Forensic DNA unit, Oklahoma City, OK, USA

Introduction

One of the most crucial stages in the development of a DNA profile is the ability of the scientist to recover cellular material from a substrate and to extract DNA from it in a manner that is suitable for further processing steps such as polymerase chain reaction (PCR). Forensic samples are, however, not always easy to deal with. Samples can be deposited in the most inconvenient of places (*see* **Sources of DNA**), exposed to the harshest of environments, and mixed with many potential inhibitors of DNA profiling. Many of these factors are outside the control of the scientist.

An Ideal Method

A method suitable for the extraction of forensic samples requires the following:

- DNA is efficiently recovered from the biological sample.
- The extracted DNA is protected from further fragmentation or nuclease action.
- The extracted DNA is free of inhibitory substances that may have a detrimental effect on further processing.
- The method minimizes the risks of cross contamination from other samples or sources.

In recent years, new techniques have been developed and implemented, methods are also required that enable the following:

- The coextraction of DNA and RNA and
- The extraction of DNA from plant material of various kinds.

Typical steps in the process are as follows:

- Visual examination and presumptive tests to identify the biological source of the sample
- Recovery of biological material
- Lysis (i.e., bursting) of the cells and release of the DNA into solution
- Removal of inhibitory compounds
- Determination of the amount of DNA recovered
- If necessary, concentration of the DNA extract.

Any method developed for forensic use must be validated according to the accreditation or other quality system in place in the laboratory. Each of the methods described in this article can include numerous, small, laboratory-specific variations, such as incubation times and temperatures; however, the basic steps are common to all procedures.

Most laboratories will maintain several different extraction methods as it is important to select the most appropriate extraction strategy that is best tailored to the biological sample type to increase the quality of DNA recovered. For example, recovery of DNA from bone requires a much more involved and aggressive demineralization chemistry to improve recovery success. Buccal (i.e., mouth) swabs for databases may be better suited for more efficient automated protocols.

However, most extraction methods follow the basic approach of separating cells from other material, and lysis of cell membranes to free DNA followed by purification of the DNA itself.

Update based on original article by Sally-Ann Harbison, Wiley Encyclopedia of Forensic Science, © 2009, John Wiley & Sons, Ltd.

A Guide to Forensic DNA Profiling
Edited by Allan Jamieson and Scott Bader
© 2016 John Wiley & Sons, Ltd. ISBN: 9781118751527
Also published in EFS (online edition)
DOI: 10.1002/9780470061589.fsa554.pub2

Proteinase K/Organic Extraction

The earliest method described for the recovery of DNA from forensic samples involved the use of the enzyme proteinase K, followed by an organic extraction with a solution of phenol and chloroform [1]. Despite the fact that this is a time-consuming method, has multiple transfer steps, and uses hazardous chemicals, it remains a favorite in many forensic laboratories owing to the high-quality nucleic acid yield and purification capabilities.

Cellular material is recovered from the substrate (e.g., garment, weapon) by scraping, soaking, swabbing, or other means (*see Sources of DNA*). A simple Tris/HCl buffer containing proteinase K and a detergent such as sodium dodecyl sulfate (SDS) is added to the cell pellet. The proteinase is an enzyme that breaks open the cell and nuclear membranes, releasing the cell contents including the DNA into solution. The phenol/chloroform step coupled with an ethanol precipitation or alternate concentration step such as MicroCon concentration devices successfully separates nucleic acid from heavier protein molecules, removes proteinaceous waste and inhibitors and results in a purified DNA extract amenable for further analysis. It is particularly useful when small amounts of DNA are expected, such as swabs taken from car steering wheels or touched items.

The DNA that is recovered is double-stranded DNA, relatively free of impurities, and can be used for many applications (*see DNA: An Overview*; *DNA*).

Differential Extraction

Forensic laboratories typically employ a differential extraction method for the separation of spermatozoa from other cells such as vaginal epithelia [1]. Strong disulfide bonds prevent lysis (bursting or breaking up) of the spermatozoa nuclei in the presence of proteinase K and SDS, (a detergent), allowing the more fragile epithelial and other cells to lyse and release their DNA. Separation of the spermatozoa from the lysed cells is achieved by centrifugation and removal of the supernatant (the liquid portion sitting above the separated solids) containing the lysed cellular components. The spermatozoa can then be lysed by the addition of a reducing agent such as dithiothreitol (DTT) in the presence of the extraction buffer, proteinase K, and SDS. DTT serves to break and prevent the reformation of the disulphide bonds present in the proteins and DNA of the sperm cells, and can also be incorporated into standard extraction chemistry to ensure no residual male DNA remains undetected.

Exploitation of the different cellular membrane resilience between epithelial and sperm cells is the fundamental principle behind differential extractions.

Each fraction, the "sperm" and "epithelial" fractions, can then be processed one by one typically by organic extraction, phenol/chloroform extraction, ethanol precipitation, or other methods (see the following).

Although a pure separation between fractions is not always possible, it remains the standard process for separating male and female components in sexual assault mixtures.

Alternative approaches to the separation of sperm cells from epithelial cells include the use of laser microdissection [2] and cell sorting using a glass microdevice method [3]. These approaches have potential for integration into more automated extraction protocols and direct amplification approaches. Using a laser to target and remove sperm cell directly also allows for a cleaner separation than is often possible with traditional differential extraction and a semi-quantitative approach as the number of sperm heads collected can be counted during collection.

Chelex®

With the advent of PCR, Chelex® extraction became widely used [4]. This method generates single-stranded DNA suitable for PCR and became the method of choice in many laboratories because of its simplicity, low cost, and lack of harmful reagents.

Chelex® 100 is a resin composed of styrene divinylbenzene copolymers containing paired iminodiacetate ions that act as chelating groups. These chelating groups have a high affinity for polyvalent (multiple charges) metal ions such as Mg^{2+} ions.

Thus, degradation of DNA in the sample is minimized by chelation of the metal ions inactivating the nuclease enzymes that digest DNA. Chelex® beads in suspension are added to cells recovered from a substrate, and after incubation, the DNA is released from the cells by boiling. The alkalinity of the solution and the high temperature cause the cell membranes to burst, releasing the DNA.

Chelex® is inhibitory to the PCR reaction and it has been observed [5] that long-term storage of samples containing Chelex® beads results in a deterioration of the DNA profile quality.

While Chelex® is suitable for a wide range of sample types, additional clean up and concentration steps are often required for dirty or samples containing very small amounts of DNA. Nevertheless, Chelex® extraction remains a popular choice in forensic laboratories.

Solid-Phase Extraction Technologies

In recent years, alternative technologies suitable for manual or automated applications have become more widely used. These methods can also be employed after the separation of spermatozoa and epithelial cells. One of the earliest such methods to be used was DNA IQ™ [6–9].

DNA IQ™

The DNA IQ™ system utilizes a two-step method. First, the cellular material is recovered from the substrate by incubation of the sample to 95 °C with a lysis buffer. Then DNA IQ™, a silica-coated, paramagnetic resin is added to the sample. The resin binds to DNA with high affinity in the presence of chaotropic elements such as guanidinium, which lyse the cells, denature proteins, and inhibit DNAses.

A magnet is then applied, which causes the resin, with DNA attached, to congregate on the tube wall nearest to the magnet. DNA is then recovered from the resin using an elution buffer. DNA can be recovered from most forensic sample types, using proteinase K to assist in the extraction of DNA from hair, bone, and spermatozoa [9] and is reported to be particularly suitable for very small samples. The amount of DNA captured by the resin is roughly proportional to the amount of resin used and can be varied according to the sample type. This has advantages when extracting DNA from DNA database samples where the amount of starting material is large, as a consistent amount of DNA can be extracted and further expensive quantitation steps may not be required [8]. The DNA IQ™ system has been successfully implemented onto robotic platforms [10] and has been used by many laboratories to extract DNA from casework samples, for example, from volume crime cases [7] and envelope flaps [11].

MagAttract™

The MagAttract™ system (Qiagen Inc.) also utilizes paramagnetic silica beads to capture DNA after release from cells using chaotropic agents. A similar lyse, bind, wash, and elute protocol is followed [12, 13]. Again, the final elution volume can be altered depending on the concentration of DNA likely to be recovered. This technology has been optimized for use on several robotic platforms, enabling laboratories to customize specific protocols.

Charge Switch™ Technology

Charge Switch™ (DNA Research Innovations Ltd., UK) also uses magnetic bead technology. In this case, however, the magnetic beads are coated with a unique chemical compound that acts as an ionic switch that is dependent on pH. The overall process is the same as that employed by other magnetic technologies. First, the cells are recovered from the substrate and lysed. Then at pH below 6.5, the DNA from lysed cells binds to the particles that are subsequently captured using a magnet. The pH is raised to 7 to allow a washing step to take place before the pH is raised again to 8. At this pH, the charge is neutralized and the DNA is eluted. Again, modifications to the elution volume can be made to alter the concentration of the recovered DNA and the technology has been shown to be applicable to a wide variety of forensic samples [14].

QIAamp Technology

In 1998, Greenspoon et al. [5] described the use of QIAamp® spin columns (Qiagen Inc.) as an alternative extraction method for the extraction of DNA from database samples resulting in DNA that survived long-term storage at −20 °C. In this process, cells are lysed and then placed into a spin column containing a silica-gel-based membrane to which the DNA binds. Following washing steps, aided by centrifugation or vacuum suction depending on the protocol being followed, the DNA is eluted into solution ready for quantitation and/or amplification. A recent addition to the QIAamp® spin columns is the use of an additional column, known as a *QIAshredder® homogenizing column*, after cell lysis and before the binding of the sample to the silica membrane [15]. The use of such columns enhanced the effectiveness of the QIAamp® spin column process, increasing the performance of

this extraction system relative to either a Chelex®
extraction or an organic extraction.

Solutions for Specific Sample Types

FTA Card

Whatman FTA® cards are extensively used for the
collection of reference samples for forensic analysis.
The FTA® technology lyses cells on contact, releasing,
and immobilizing the DNA. An added advantage is
that infectious pathogens and other microorganisms
are deactivated, enabling long-term room temperature
storage of samples [16].

Once the sample is immobilized onto the card,
a small punch is taken typically 2 mm across. A
simple series of washing steps follows, which removes
any inhibitory substances that might be present. The
washed punch is then placed directly into the amplification. This method is easily automated [17].

Feces

The extraction of DNA from fecal remains presents
particular challenges. It has been shown that swabbing of the outer surface of the stool [18] or collection of tissue paper smeared with feces [19] offers
the best chance of success. In the extraction process,
it is important to remove as much inhibitory material
as possible, particularly the polyphenolic compounds
[20]. A number of specific solutions have been developed for the successful extraction of DNA from feces;
these include the QIAamp® DNA stool Mini Kit
(Qiagen Inc.) and the Ultraclean™ Fecal DNAIsola-
tion Kit (MO BIO Laboratories Inc.).

Extraction from Bone

There are many methods described in the literature
for the extraction of DNA from samples of bone (see
[21–23]). The most significant difference between the
methods described is whether or not a demineralization step is used. There are common themes to most
of the methods. First, most bones can be successfully cleaned of surface dirt and potential contaminating substances including extraneous DNA using
one or more of the following methods; abrasion with
sandpaper and so on The cleaned pieces of bone are
then crushed into small fragments, often with the

aid of a freezer mill and liquid nitrogen until a fine
powder is obtained. The powder can be demineral-
ized using several changes of 0.5M ethylene diamine
tetraacetic acid (EDTA), pH 7.5 at 4 °C with agita-
tion over 1–2 days [21, 22] or as part of the lysis
procedure [23]. For most of the methods described,
subsequent organic extraction and concentration with a
column-based method such as a Centricon™ 30 micro-
concentrator is suggested.

Teeth

Like bones, teeth are relatively easy to clean before
extraction. Some complexity is introduced when it is
necessary to preserve the external hard surfaces of the
tooth, which is important if physical and biochemical
tests are also to be carried out. Methods of extraction
that do not crush or damage the physical structure of
the tooth are required, although this may reduce the
maximum recovery of DNA [24].

Hair

As with teeth and bones, hair can be cleaned before
extraction. One suggestion is the use of sonication in
2% SDS, followed by rinsing in water before extraction as an effective method [25]. One method used to
optimize the recovery of DNA from root and shafts of
telogen is to grind the hair after washing using glass
grinders, followed by Chelex® extraction. Alternatively, organic extraction methods [26] or solid-phase
extraction methods such as DNA IQ™ can be used.

Formaldehyde-fixed and Paraffin-embedded Tissues

Formaldehyde-fixed and paraffin-embedded tissues
provide a valuable resource for forensic analysis.
Removal of the paraffin can be accomplished by
washing the tissue in xylene [27] or by microwave
treatment of the paraffin blocks to "melt" the paraffin
[28]. A variety of extraction methods can then be used,
including organic extraction and Chelex® procedures.

Coextraction of DNA and RNA

Recently, there has been interest shown in the development of RNA-based methods for the identification of
body fluids in forensic samples [29].

To maximize the usefulness of such techniques, it is important that both DNA and RNA can be obtained simultaneously from the same sample and methods that accomplish this have been published [30, 31]. In brief, these methods include steps to protect the fragile RNA from RNAses and methods to selectively precipitate DNA in the presence of RNA. As the development of the RNA-based methods is in its infancy and has not been widely adopted by forensic laboratories to date, it is likely that refinements to these methods will be made.

Extraction of Plant Material

The use of plant material as a source of forensic DNA evidence has also been recognized. Many methods for the extraction of DNA from plant material are based on the use of hexadecyltrimethlyammonium bromide (CTAB) [32], although these have been more recently replaced by custom-designed commercial kits such as DNeasy Plant Kits from Qiagen Inc. [33].

As the sensitivity and robustness of STR amplification chemistry has improved dramatically in recent years, and smaller target regions identified, many of the inhibitors which are often copurified with DNA extracts (e.g., heme from blood), and sample degradation have become less problematic. Additional extraction strategies such as sample concentration and dilution of inhibited samples allow for amplification to overcome these challenges in many instances.

Contamination

No account of the extraction of DNA from forensic samples would be complete without some mention of contamination. Lessons learned from the study of ancient specimens [34] describe the risks of contamination and precautions that can be taken to minimize the risks. As DNA is recovered from ever smaller amounts of cellular material, this is of utmost importance. Recent adoption of low copy number DNA (*see* **Transfer**) techniques in laboratories typically includes the monitoring of the laboratory environment for extraneous DNA, which has highlighted the importance of protective clothing, frequent changes of gloves, and the decontamination of equipment and surfaces.

Control samples known as reagent blanks are included with each set of extractions to assist with contamination monitoring and serve as an additional quality assurance check during the extraction process. The purpose of the blank is to detect any contaminant DNA that may have been introduced via reagents or operator.

Automated Extraction

It has been possible to incorporate robotic platforms into the extraction process to assist with reducing the more laborious steps of extraction. Automation allows DNA samples to be processed in batches and extracted with improved efficiency, consistency and reliability, decreased frequency of contamination incidents, and a recovery comparable to manual technique [35]. Automated extraction platforms such as the Maxwell 16, AutoMate Express™, Qiagen EZ1, and QIAcube allow multiple samples to be extracted and purified simultaneously within shorter time frames and reducing analyst sample handling time. Although each robot uses different chemistries and optimized lysis buffers as described previously, each allows for automation of the extraction process. While this process still includes a manual initial incubation step to free cellular material from the substrate, the robotic platform handles the purification steps that are repetitive and ideal for automation.

Another advantage to automation of the extraction process is reducing the number of steps in which an analyst has to handle the sample, thus also reducing potential for user contamination events or sample switches as the process works within a contained system. Single tube devices such as the PrepFiler Lysep™ columns further simplify the transfer steps and thus reduce contamination possibilities between cell lysis and robotic extraction [36].

With a view to the future, incorporation of automated extraction tools assists in streamlining laboratory process and improving capacity, consistency, and efficiency.

References

[1] Gill, P., Jeffreys, A.J. & Werrett, D.J. (1985). Forensic application of DNA fingerprints, *Nature* **318**, 577–579.

[2] Elliot, K., Hill, D.S., Lambert, C., Burroughes, T.R. & Gill, P. (2003). Use of laser micro-dissection greatly improves the recovery of DNA from sperm on microscope slides, *Forensic Science International* **137**, 28–36.

[3] Horsman, K., Barker, S.L.R., Ferrance, J.P., Forrest, K.A., Koen, K.A. & Landers, J.P. (2005). Separation of sperm

and epithelial cells on micro-fabricated devices: potential application to forensic analysis of sexual assault evidence, *Analytical Chemistry* **77**, 742–749.

[4]   Walsh, P.S., Metzger, D.A. & Higuchi, R. (1991). Chelex® 100 as a medium for the simple extraction of DNA for PCR-based typing of forensic material, *Biotechniques* **10**, 506–513.

[5]   Greenspoon, S.A., Scarpetta, M.A., Drayton, M.L. & Turek, S.A. (1998). QIAamp spin columns as a method of DNA isolation for forensic casework, *Journal of Forensic Sciences* **43**, 1024–1030.

[6]   Greenspoon, S.A., Ban, J.D., Sykes, K., Ballard, E.J., Edler, S.S., Baisden, M. & Covington, B.L. (2004). Application of the Biomek® 2000 laboratory automation workstation and the DNA IQ™ system for use in the DNA extraction of high volume forensic casework, *Journal of the Canadian Society for Forensic Science* **49**, 29–39.

[7]   Komonski, D.J., Marignani, A., Richard, M.L., Frappier, J.R.H. & Newman, J.C. (2004). Validation of the DNA IQ IQ™ system for use in the DNA extraction of high volume forensic casework, *Journal of the Canadian Society for Forensic Science* **37**, 103–109.

[8]   Promega Corporation (2002). *DNA IQ™ System – Database Protocol*, Promega Corporation, Madison, WI.

[9]   Promega Corporation (2002). *DNA IQ™ System – Small Sample Casework Protocol*, Promega Corporation, Madison, WI.

[10]   McLaren, B. (2006). Automation in a forensic laboratory: an update, *Profiles in DNA* **9**, 19–20.

[11]   Ng, L.-K., Ng, A., Cholette, F. & Davis, C. (2007). Optimization of recovery of human DNA from envelope flaps using DNA IQ™ system for STR genotyping, *Forensic Science International Genetics* **1**, 283–286.

[12]   Kishore, R., Hardy, W.R., Anderson, V.J., Sanchez, N.A. & Buoncristiani, M.R. (2006). Optimisation of DNA extraction from low yield and degraded samples using the Bio Robot® EZ1 and Bio Robot® M48, *Journal of Forensic Sciences* **51**, 1055–1061.

[13]   Montpetit, S.A., Fitch, I.T. & O'Donnell, P.T. (2005). A simple automated instrument for DNA extraction in forensic casework, *Journal of Forensic Sciences* **50**, 1–9.

[14]   Taylor, M., Bridge, C. & Baker, M. (2005). Improved sensitivity for forensic DNA purification using Charge Switch® Technology, *DNA Research Innovations Ltd. Quest* **2**, 51–54.

[15]   Castella, V., Dimo-Simonin, N., Brandt-Casadevall, C. & Mangin, P. (2006). Forensic evaluation of the QIAshredder/QIAamp DNA extraction procedure, *Forensic Science International* **156**, 70–73.

[16]   Burgoyne, L., Kijas, J., Hallsworth, P. & Turner, J. (1994). *Proceedings from the Fifth International Symposium on Human Identification*, Promega Corporation, Madison, WI, p. 163.

[17]   Belgrader, P., Del Rio, S.A., Turner, K.A., Marino, M.A., Weaver, K.R. & Williams, P.E. (1995). Automated DNA purification and amplification from blood-stained cards using a robotic workstation, *Biotechniques* **19**, 426–432.

[18]   Johnson, D.J., Martin, L.R. & Roberts, K.A. (2005). STR-typing of human DNA from human fecal matter using the Qiagen QIAamp® Stool mini kit, *Journal of Forensic Sciences* **50**, 802–808.

[19]   Roy, R. (2003). Analysis of human fecal material for autosomal and Y chromosome STRs, *Journal of Forensic Sciences* **48**, 1035–1040.

[20]   Monteiro, M., Bonnemaison, D., Vekris, A., Petry, K.G. & Bonnet, J. (1997). Complex polysaccharides as PCR inhibitors in feces, *Journal of Clinical Microbiology* **35**, 995–998.

[21]   Hochmeister, M.N., Budowle, B., Borer, U.V., Comey, C.T. & Dirnhofer, R. (1991). Typing of deoxyribonucleic acid (DNA) extracted from compact bone from human remains, *Journal of Forensic Sciences* **36**, 1649–1661.

[22]   Hagelberg, E., Sykes, B. & Hedges, R. (1989). Ancient bone DNA amplified, *Nature* **342**, 485.

[23]   Loreille, O.M., Diegoli, T.M., Irwin, J.A., Coble, M.D. & Parson, T.J. (2007). High efficiency DNA extraction from bone by total demineralisation, *Forensic Science International Genetics* **1**, 191–195.

[24]   Smith, B.C., Fisher, D.L., Weedn, V.W., Warnosk, G.R. & Holland, M.M. (1993). A systematic approach to the sampling of dental DNA, *Journal of Forensic Sciences* **38**, 1194–1209.

[25]   Linch, C.A., Smith, S.L. & Prahlow, J.A. (1998). Evaluation of the human hair root for DNA typing subsequent to microscopic comparison, *Journal of Forensic Sciences* **43**, 305–314.

[26]   Hellmann, A., Rohleder, U., Schmitter, H. & Wittig, M. (2001). STR typing of human telogen hairs – a new approach, *International Journal of Legal Medicine* **114**, 269–273.

[27]   Banerjee, S.K., Makdisi, W.F., Weston, A.P., Mitchell, S.M. & Campbell, D.R. (1995). Microwave-based DNA extraction from paraffin-embedded tissue for PCR amplification, *Biotechniques* **18**, 768–773.

[28]   Gill, P., Kimpton, C.P. & Sullivan, K. (1992). A rapid polymerase chain reaction method for identifying fixed specimens, *Electrophoresis* **13**, 173–175.

[29]   Juusola, J. & Ballantyne, J. (2003). Messenger RNA profiling: a prototype method to supplant conventional methods for body fluid identification, *Forensic Science International* **135**, 85–96.

[30]   Alvarez, M., Juusola, J. & Ballantyne, J. (2004). An mRNA and DNA co-isolation method for forensic casework samples, *Analytical Biochemistry* **335**, 289–298.

[31]   Chromczynski, P. (1993). A reagent for the single step simultaneous extraction of RNA, DNA and proteins from cell and tissue samples, *Biotechniques* **15**, 532–534.

[32]   Doyle, J.J. & Doyle, J.L. (1987). A rapid DNA isolation procedure for small quantities of fresh leaf tissue, *Phytochemistry Bulletin* **19**, 11–15.

[33] Bless, C., Palmeter, H. & Wallace, M.M. (2006). Identification of *Acer rubrum* using amplified fragment length polymorphism, *Journal of Forensic Sciences* **51**, 31–38.

[34] Lindahl, T. (1997). Facts and artifacts of ancient DNA, *Cell* **90**, 1–3.

[35] Phillips, K., McCallum, N. & Welch, L. (2012). A comparison of methods for forensic DNA extraction: Chelex-100® and the QIAGEN DNA Investigator Kit (manual and automated), *Forensic Science International: Genetics* **6**(2), 282–285.

[36] Stangengaard, M., Borsting, C., Ferrero-Milani, L., Frank-Hansen, R., Poulsen, L., Hansen, A.J. & Morling, N. (2013). Evaluation of four automated protocols for extraction of DNA from FTA cards, *Journal of Laboratory Automation* **18**(5), 404–410.

Related Articles in EFS Online

Low Template DNA Analysis and Interpretation

[26] Shangguan, M., Keating, C., Ferrari-Milan, J., Frank Hansen, R., Bogdan, L., Hansen, A., & Murillo, N. (2013). Evaluation of four automated protocols for extraction of DNA from FTA cards. Journal of Laboratory Automation 18(5), 404–410.

[25] Bille, C., Fitzgerald, J., Walbroehl, M. (2000). Identification of Alter Zhirysu single amplified fragment length polymorphism. Journal of Forensic Sciences 51, 40–45.

[24] Lindahl, T. (1993). Instability and decay of the primary structure of DNA.
Nature 362, 1–8.

[23] Phillips, K., McCallum, N. A., Welch, L. (2012). A comparison of methods for forensic DNA extraction: Chelex 100° and the QIAGEN DNA Investigator kit (manual and automated). Forensic Science International: Genetics 6(2), 182–185.

Related Articles in EFS Online

Low Template DNA Analysis and Interpretation

Chapter 12
Quantitation

Robert I. O'Brien[*]

National Forensic Science Technology Center (NFSTC), Largo, FL, USA

Introduction

The DNA quantification process, also referred to as DNA quantitation, is conducted to determine how much DNA is contained within a given biological sample. Biological samples are submitted to the forensic laboratory with the intention of developing a DNA profile to either place a suspect or victim at a scene, connect them to a specific piece of evidence, or demonstrate that the party had no connection to a crime.

To develop a high-quality DNA profile, it is important that the analyst first determines the quantity of DNA present in a sample. If too much DNA is present, this can cause what is known as *off-scale data* in the final detection process of DNA analysis. Off-scale data tends to be littered with artifacts and extra peaks that make interpretation of the resulting profiles difficult, if not impossible. As a result, most laboratories will not allow DNA analysts to use off-scale data. By contrast, if too little DNA is available, then data retrieved at the detection process will be incomplete, often resulting in what is known as *drop-out* where information is missing and the result is an incomplete profile. Quantifying the DNA that is collected after extracting cells residing within the evidence addresses both of these issues.

Once the amount of DNA is established, the DNA analyst can make any adjustments required before the amplification process. Samples with excess concentrations of DNA can be diluted; samples where

the concentration of DNA is too low can either be concentrated or a new sample can be taken from the evidence so that it contains more of the biological material of interest. Even if this is not possible, quantification of the DNA available at this point provides an expectation to the DNA analyst of what can be expected in the final results. This data can even be used to guide investigators to submit additional pieces of evidence if the evidence submitted does not yield enough data to provide usable profiles.

For these reasons, DNA quantification is a crucial step in the analysis process. Its importance has been stressed by the Federal Bureau of Investigation (FBI) in the Quality Assurance Standards against which forensic laboratories are audited. Standard 9.4 of the latest version of the audit document directs auditors to examine whether the laboratory quantifies the amount of human DNA in forensic samples before nuclear amplification [1]. Laboratories audited against this standard must not only demonstrate the quantified DNA but also show that the quantification process is specific for human DNA.

However, simply performing DNA quantification is not sufficient. The methods employed must provide a specific degree of accuracy. If the processes are not accurate then it is no better than proceeding without quantifying DNA. The need for increasingly accurate techniques has influenced the methods used for DNA quantification over the years.

As new methods in processing DNA have become more sensitive, allowing DNA profiles to be developed from smaller and smaller samples, there is now a need to determine how much DNA is contained in these very low-level samples. For some laboratories, being able to detect how much DNA is present in these samples is imperative because it will dictate the type of amplification process to be used, or, if the sample does not contain sufficient DNA, whether the analysis process should even continue.

*Written by Robert O'Brien in his capacity as an employee of National Forensic Science Technology Center, Inc.

A Guide to Forensic DNA Profiling
Edited by Allan Jamieson and Scott Bader
© 2016 John Wiley & Sons, Ltd. ISBN: 9781118751527
Also published in EFS (online edition)
DOI: 10.1002/9780470061589.fsa1104

Background

One of the earliest and most widely used processes to quantify DNA was "Slot Blot quantification [2]." This test is specific for human and other primate DNAs using a 40-basepair probe that is complementary to a primate-specific alpha satellite DNA sequence D17Z1 on chromosome 17 [3, 4]. Radioactive probes were initially used, but modifications to colorimetric and chemiluminescent detection methods were later employed to make the technique safer and more widely acceptable.

During the Slot Blot process, genomic DNA was captured on a nylon membrane followed by the addition of a human-specific probe. The more DNA the membrane contained, the more probes attached, and in turn the intensity of the color or chemiluminescence of the bands of DNA on the membrane increased. The intensity of the bands was then compared to the intensities of bands of DNA of known concentrations. The process was labor intensive because several steps in the process required manipulation by an individual.

The method was also very subjective as the quantity of DNA was determined by visually comparing intensities of color or luminescence. If the intensity of the band of DNA from the evidence did not exactly match up with the known concentrations on the membrane, then the quantity was an estimate at best. If the bands from the DNA tested were darker than the darkest DNA band of known concentration or lighter than the lightest DNA band of known concentration then the analyst was forced to make dilutions or concentrations based solely on a best estimate. It was not apparent until the end of this process whether the guesswork was accurate or not. Apart from the lack of accuracy, subjectivity also played a part as analysts reading the results would read different intensities at different levels, often leading to confusion in the interpretation of these results.

In addition, Slot Blot quantitation could falsely lead the analyst to believe that he or she could develop a full DNA profile because inhibitors in these samples could go undetected during quantitation, leaving the analyst with no DNA profile at the conclusion of the process.

The Slot Blot process was soon replaced by a new method that made the process more accurate, objective, and one where inhibitors would be detected. This method was real-time polymerase chain reaction (PCR) [5]. Real-time PCR addressed these problems by increasing sensitivity of the quantitation process, thereby removing subjectivity in data interpretation. The quantity of sample no longer depended on visual estimations, and because it was PCR-based, any inhibitors that would affect amplification would affect this quantitation process [6]. A side benefit was that man hours were greatly reduced. The process itself took approximately the same time as Slot Blot quantitation; however, once the samples were loaded and the process was initiated, the analyst could perform other tasks.

Principles of Real-Time PCR

There are two types of PCR used in forensic DNA analysis. The more common form of PCR used during amplification is endpoint PCR. In endpoint PCR, as the name suggests, the user is only interested in the final result of the PCR process. Specific pieces of DNA are targeted using primers and probes supplied and those pieces go through a fixed number of cycles of copying. The user is only interested in how much DNA is present at the end of the PCR process. Once the PCR process is complete, the amplified DNA is subsequently put through a detection process.

With real-time PCR, however, it is not the final product that is of interest, but rather the continuous monitoring of the PCR process. After every cycle of PCR, the resulting quantity of DNA is monitored either by the presence or absence of fluorescence depending on what quantitation kit is used. Monitoring is required because what is being examined is not the final amount of DNA achieved, but at what cycle in the PCR process a specific quantity of DNA is achieved. This is called the *cycle threshold* or C_T value [7].

The threshold in the real-time PCR process is equivalent to a specific quantity of DNA. After every cycle in the PCR process, the instrument and software check to observe if the amount of DNA present after that cycle has reached the set threshold. Once the DNA is copied enough times to reach the threshold, then the software is able to deduce, based on the number of cycles it took to reach that quantity, the quantity of starting DNA. So there is a direct correlation between the cycle threshold and the quantity of starting DNA.

This correlation is achieved by the construction of a standard curve. The standard curve is constructed by taking known concentrations of DNA starting from a high amount and putting it through a serial dilution and running it through the real-time process along with the samples of unknown DNA concentration. The cycle thresholds are plotted against the logarithm of the concentration of DNA to produce a standard curve (see Figure 1). Using this standard curve, concentrations of DNA of unknown samples can be deduced based on where they fall along the standard curve.

This method of DNA quantitation is much more accurate than the Slot Blot method described earlier. At the end of the process, the software deduces the concentration of DNA so there is no subjectivity introduced into the interpretation process. However, even with these advantages over the older methods there are still problems with the accuracy of the real-time PCR process.

Accuracy Within the Standard Curve

The standard curve as previously mentioned is constructed based on known concentrations of DNA that are put through a serial dilution. The standard curve has between 7 and 8 points of known concentration depending on which manufacturer's quantitation kit is being used. The belief is that any point that lies within that curve constructed from those various points will be highly accurate.

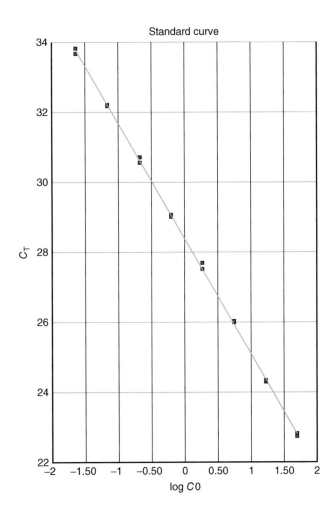

Figure 1   Cycle thresholds plotted against the logarithm of the concentration of DNA produce a standard curve

After the quantitation process is complete, three factors are reviewed to determine if the curve produced was of acceptable quality to be used to calculate the quantity of the samples being measured:

1. R^2 value – this is a measure of the fit of the data points to the regressed line [8].
2. Slope value – this is an indication of the PCR efficiency [8].
3. Y-intercept – this is the Y value when the log of the concentration equals 0. Therefore, the Y-intercept corresponds to the C_T value of a sample with a concentration of $1\,\mathrm{ng\,\mu l^{-1}}$ [8].

The R^2 value is important because it will indicate how well the data points generated from the serial dilution correspond with each other. If the serial points do not follow in a straight line then at some point during the serial dilutions pipetting errors may have occurred. Typically the kits require an R^2 value of ≥ 0.990 [7–9].

The importance of the slope is to show the efficiency of the PCR process. A slope of -3.3 [7–9] indicates 100% efficiency, meaning that there is a doubling during the PCR process. There are three phases of amplification during the PCR process [7]: the geometric phase, the linear phase, and the plateau. In the geometric phase, there is a high and constant efficiency and it is during this phase that there is a doubling of the amount of DNA at every cycle [7]. A slope of -3.3 or within that range shows that the PCR process achieved that efficiency during the quantitation process.

The question to be asked is "How do any of the factors being looked at correspond to the accuracy of the quantitation process?" To determine this, plots of these three factors vs. the concentration of data were examined (see Figures 2–4) [10].

Despite all the benefits of real-time PCR, the final determination of quantity is still based on a standard curve that is manmade. The problem is not with the creation of the serial dilution because this would be seen with the R^2 value, but rather with the starting

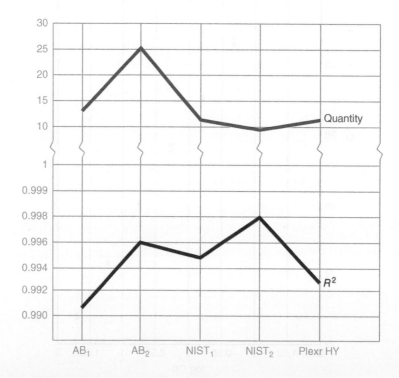

Figure 2 Quantity vs. the R^2 value. As the R^2 value changes there is no corresponding change in the measurement of the quantity of DNA in the corresponding run. Therefore, R^2 is not a good measure of accuracy [10]

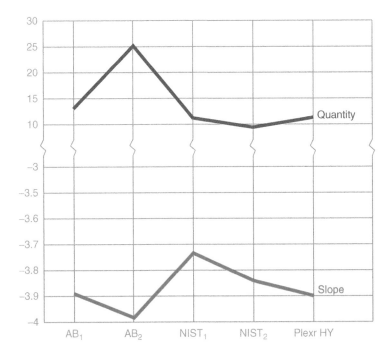

Figure 3   Quantity vs. slope. From this plot variations in the values of the slope do not correlate to changes in the corresponding quantity of DNA [10]

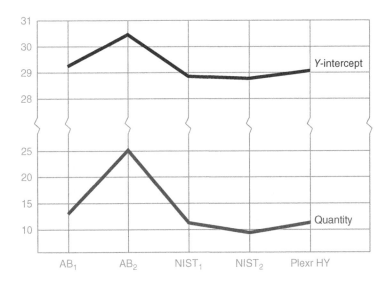

Figure 4   *Y*-intercept vs. quantity. Unlike the other two factors, there is a direct correlation between the quantity of DNA and the curves corresponding to the *Y*-intercept [10]

initial concentration of the DNA standard provided by the manufacturer, as well as the stability of this standard over time. If the starting concentration is not exactly what it is purported to be then all the serial dilutions made from it will also be inaccurate. This inaccuracy will be reflected in the Y-intercept because the software's C_T value for a concentration of $1 \, \text{ng} \, \mu\text{l}^{-1}$ for DNA would be incorrect. All quantities of DNA measured off of this curve will also be inaccurate.

To rectify this problem, it must first be determined what C_T value corresponds to a true concentration of $1 \, \text{ng} \, \mu\text{l}^{-1}$. If there is reason to suspect that the standard provided by the manufacturer of the kit is inaccurate, then separate standards of known concentrations may be purchased. In the United States, these can be purchased through NIST (National Institute of Standards and Technology). Once the C_T value for $1 \, \text{ng} \, \mu\text{l}^{-1}$ is determined, then the Y-intercept from future runs can be measured against the known C_T value. A correction factor can then be applied if necessary. During the validation process of the kit it must also be determined how long the DNA standards remain stable in solution. Over time, DNA will break down in solution and this can lead to inaccurate results. During the validation of any quantitation chemistry, the C_T value of the Y-intercept must be examined over time and observed at what point it changes. When the C_T value of the Y-intercept begins to fluctuate, this indicates that the concentration of the diluted DNA standard is beginning to change, and with this change comes a loss of accuracy.

Some manufacturers adopt a range that the C_T value of the Y-intercept can fall within. However, it must be noted that an increase in 1 point in the C_T value of the Y-intercept example from a 28 to a 29 correlates to a twofold increase in the estimated quantitation value [10]. The laboratory must determine if the range provided by the manufacturer is acceptable for their analysis.

Quantitation of Low-Level DNA Analysis

Even though there are challenges to ensuring the quantitation of samples within the dynamic range of the standard curve, these can be overcome with additional work on the part of the user. If the C_T value of the sample measured is outside the range of the standard curve, the curve is extrapolated to provide an estimate of the quantity. However, the further the extrapolation, the less accurate the result.

For concentrations above the highest concentration of the standard curve, the recommendation of most manufacturers is to dilute the sample and quantify it again. On the basis of the value provided, a $1:10$ dilution and/or a $1:100$ dilution will bring the sample down into the dynamic range of the standard curve providing a more accurate estimate of the quantity. Because these samples have such a high concentration of DNA, there is no risk of consuming all of the samples by repeating the quantitation process.

This is not the case when the concentration of DNA is below the dynamic range of the standard curve. At such low concentrations of DNA, there is often not enough sample left over to repeat the quantitation process if necessary. The need for accurate quantitation of low-level samples has increased as the other methods of DNA analysis have become more sensitive. Special techniques for the amplification process (e.g., low copy number (LCN) analysis) [11] are employed based on the quantity of input DNA. If the quantity of input DNA is not accurate then the laboratory may proceed with DNA analysis using techniques that would not be ideal for yielding a DNA profile at the end of the process.

The manufacturers of the three major DNA quantification kits used in forensic DNA analysis have attempted to make their kits more accurate for use with low-level samples. Two primary approaches are used to determine an accurate quantitation of low-level samples: (i) to target an amplicon of the same basepair size as the pieces that are targeted in the next step of the process; and (ii) to increase the dynamic range of the standard curve at lower concentrations, so extrapolation of the curve is not required.

Amplicon size is important because if the piece targeted during quantitation is much smaller than the sizes targeted during endpoint PCR in the next phase of DNA analysis then the quantity may not accurately depict whether the amount of DNA in the sample is sufficient to be taken further. For example, a small amplicon size is targeted and the resulting quantity is in an acceptable range where it would be expected for a DNA profile to be developed. However, at the end of the process all that is retrieved is a partial profile. This could occur because the sample was degraded. The amplicon size targeted could be as small as a piece of degraded DNA so there was amplification of the piece of DNA during quantitation producing a quantity. However, in the next step of the process, the pieces targeted were bigger and because they were not present in the sample, no amplification occurred. The major kits on the market currently use techniques targeting amplicons in the range of 99–214 base pairs [7, 12–16].

The other technique to improve accuracy of lower-level samples was to increase the dynamic range of the curve. When extrapolation occurs then there is a loss of accuracy; when dealing with low-level samples, slight changes in accuracy can have a big impact on the final result. By lowering the lowest concentration on the dynamic curve there is no need to extrapolate the standard curve. This is because any sample with less DNA than the lowest concentration will not provide a DNA profile. The three current quantitation kits in use have their lowest concentration in the single-digit picogram range [8, 9, 12–14]. The lowest range in their standard curve is less DNA than is found in one diploid human cell [17].

The importance of quantitation systems has often been overlooked in the grand scheme of DNA analysis. Quantitation results are not usually reported in DNA reports or questioned in court. Yet without an accurate method of quantitation there could be no results, or worse yet, low-level DNA could be consumed without any results. Improvements in the quantitation systems have come a long way to ensure that as long as usable DNA is present a profile can be developed from it. However, forensic scientists must undergo proper training and use their knowledge and experience to ensure that human error does not undo the advances in technology and any errors introduced by the technology are detected and corrected.

References

[1] Federal Bureau of Investigation (2011). Quality assurance standards for forensic DNA testing laboratories effective 9-1-2011. http://www.fbi.gov/about-us/lab/biometric-analysis/codis/qas-standards-for-forensic-dna-testing-laboratories-effective-9-1-2011 (accessed 21 Jan 2014).

[2] Butler, J.M. (2001). DNA quantification, in *Forensic DNA Typing*, Academic Press, p. 33.

[3] Waye, J.S., Presley, L.A., Budowle, B., Shutler, G.G. & Fourney, R.M. (1989). A simple and sensitive method for quantifying human genomic DNA in forensic specimen extracts, *BioTechniques* **7**, 852–855.

[4] Walsh, P.S., Varlaro, J. & Reynolds, R. (1992). A rapid chemiluminescent method for quantitation of human DNA, *Nucleic Acids Research* **20**, 5061–5065.

[5] Horsman, K.M., Hickey, J.A., Cotton, R.W., Landers, J.P. & Maddox, L.O. (2006). Development of a human-specific real-time PCR assay for the simultaneous quantitation of total genomic and male DNA, *Journal of Forensic Sciences* **51**, 758–765.

[6] Kontanis, E.J. & Reed, F.A. (2006). Evaluation of real-time PCR amplification efficiencies to detect PCR inhibitors, *Journal of Forensic Sciences* **51**, 795–804.

[7] Applied Biosystems (2008). Phases of amplification, in *Quantifiler® Duo DNA Quantification Kit User's Manual*, pp. 1–13.

[8] Promega (2013). Generating a standard curve and determining concentrations of unknowns, in *Plexor® HY System for the Applied Biosystems 7500 and 7500 FAST Real-Time PCR Systems Technical Manual*, p. 39.

[9] Qiagen (2011). *Investigator Quantiplex Handbook for Quantification of Human DNA in Forensic Samples*, p. 34, pp. 56–59.

[10] O'Brien, R. & Figarelli, D. (2010) Evaluation of Three Parameters for Assessing DNA Quantitation. National Forensic Science Technology Center, technology evaluation report.

[11] Budowle, B., Eisenberg, A.J. & van Daal, A. (2009). Validity of low copy number typing and applications to forensic science, *Croatian Medical Journal* **50**, 207–217.

[12] Qiagen (2012). Principle and procedure, in *Investigator Quantiplex HYres Kit Validation Report*, p. 2.

[13] Krenke, B.E., Nassif, N., Sprecher, C.J., Knox, C., Schwandt, M. & Storts, D.R. (2008). Developmental validation of a real-time PCR assay for the simultaneous quantification of total human and male DNA, *Forensic Science International. Genetics* **3**, 14–21.

[14] Holt, A., Mulero, J., Shewale, J., Muehling, J., Benfield, J., Olson, S., Fenesan, K. & Green, R. (2013). *Development of an Innovative DNA Quantification and Assessment System*, Life Technologies, Human Identification Group, South San Francisco, CA.

[15] Ballantyne, J. & Hanson, E., Green, R., Holt, A., Mulero, J. (2013). Enhancing the sexual assault workflow: testing of next generation DNA assessment and Y-STR systems, in *Forensic Science International: Genetics Supplement Series*, http://dx.doi.org/10.1016/j.fsigss.2013.10.117 (accessed 21 Jan 2014).

[16] De Leeuw, W., Olson, S., Green, R., Holt, A. & Schade, L. (Aug/Sep 2013). Development of an innovative DNA quantification and assessment system: streamlining workflow using intelligent tools, *Forensic Magazine*, http://www.forensicmag.com/articles/2013/08/development-innovative-dna-quantification-and-assessment-system-streamlining-workflow-using-intelligent-tools

[17] McCord, B. (2011). Presentation: DNA quantitation by real-time PCR: advanced issues. International Forensic Research Institute, Florida International University. http://dna.fiu.edu/Advanced%20DNA%20Typing%20lectures/An%20introduction%20to%20principles%20of%20QPCR-D.pdf (accessed 22 Jan 2014).

Chapter 13
Amplification

Campbell A. Ruddock

Oklahoma City Police Department, Forensic DNA unit, Oklahoma City, OK, USA

The polymerase chain reaction (PCR) method is a biochemical process by which a small amount of one or more specific sections of DNA can be increased to a larger amount that is then usable for another purpose. This purpose can simply be detection and interpretation as for DNA profiling or manipulation as for biotechnological or biomedical purposes. It was originally developed in the 1980s by K. Mullis and colleagues for research purposes and has since been used as the main basis for modern forensic DNA profiling. The term covers a method in principle, the details of which can vary considerably between different applications and requirements.

The generic PCR method can be summarized as a three-step process: Denaturation, Annealing, and extension. It starts with a solution of purified DNA (or biological material containing DNA) to which a mixture of chemicals is added. The mixture is then heated to a temperature that separates the two entwined strands of the DNA (a process called denaturation). DNA is normally double stranded and when denatured becomes single stranded. The temperature is then dropped for the second step to a level that allows small pieces of DNA (called primers) that "recognize" and bind to specific areas of the single-stranded sample DNA (annealing). Primers recognize and bind to sections of DNA upstream and downstream of the region of interest, thereby flanking that site. The temperature is then raised slightly for the third step during which an enzyme or chemical, called a polymerase, starts from the primers

and makes new copies of the DNA region of interest using building blocks of chemicals in the mixture (extension), ending with a piece of DNA of interest (*see **DNA: An Overview***), now double stranded again. The three steps of denaturation, annealing, and extension/synthesis are repeated many times in a cyclical manner, theoretically doubling the amount of the DNA region of interest each cycle. This increase in amount of DNA is called "amplification". The ability of PCR amplification to exponentially copy very small target regions of human DNA is advantageous in forensic analysis as many samples are of a degraded or compromised nature. This led to PCR replacing RFLP (restriction fragment length polymorphism) and genetic fingerprinting, and allowed for a more robust assay with increased sensitivity. As PCR required less input DNA (0.5–1 ng) much smaller biological samples could now be considered for DNA profiling. Standard kits used for forensic DNA profiling (e.g., Identifiler (*see **DNA: An Overview***), Profiler, Powerplex, SGMplus (*see **DNA: An Overview***)) typically involve 28 cycles that would create about 250 million copies from one sample piece of DNA under ideal conditions.

Newer generation expanded loci short tandem repeat (STR) chemistries such as Globalfiler and Powerplex Fusion 6C are capable of amplifying even more target loci, some of which are smaller fragments, further enhancing the ability to work with compromised samples while increasing the discriminatory power. PCR has been applied and modified in various ways for standard forensic DNA profiling. The DNA regions of interest (loci) for profiling are a selection of STRs (*see **DNA: An Overview***) that show a high level of variability or polymorphism (*see **DNA**; **DNA: An Overview***) in the human population and for which the allelic frequencies (*see **Introduction to Forensic Genetics***) are known. Primers for these STR loci (*see **Introduction to Forensic Genetics***) have been

Update based on original article by Scott Bader, Wiley Encyclopedia of Forensic Science, © 2009, John Wiley & Sons, Ltd.

A Guide to Forensic DNA Profiling
Edited by Allan Jamieson and Scott Bader
© 2016 John Wiley & Sons, Ltd. ISBN: 9781118751527
Also published in EFS (online edition)
DOI: 10.1002/9780470061589.fsa1029.pub2

combined into multiplexes as commercially available kits. These kits contain at least the loci (*see DNA*) used for the reported DNA profile of any particular jurisdiction, if not more. For example, the SGMplus kit contains primers for the 10 loci reported in the United Kingdom, and PowerPlex16 (*see Introduction to Forensic Genetics*) contains primers for the 13 loci used by CODIS Database (*see Databases*) in the United States plus three others. The kits also include primers that will detect the Amelogenin sex locus that will identify X and Y alleles. Expanded loci kits contain mini STR loci and additional Y chromosome male markers. Another advantage of the expanded loci capabilities are increased statistical discriminatory powers and standardization of target loci worldwide, as these kits contain target loci used in North American, European, and Asian databases [1]. The kits have been validated for forensic use as shown in publications in the scientific literature, and recommended protocols are given by the manufacturer of each kit. These define the amount of starting sample (or template) DNA, the number of cycles of PCR to be used, and guidelines for interpretation of results.

Primer pairs are designed to match specific DNA sequences in the regions flanking each STR site of interest. These primers allow amplification of the DNA at the locus independent of the STR length present in the DNA sample.

So one set of primers (per locus) can profile the DNA sample of any person, irrespective of the alleles of that individual (*see DNA*). To enable the PCR products to be detected by a machine, the primers are modified to include a color tag or marker. The tag is a chemical that will fluoresce with light of a known wavelength when it is illuminated by a laser of a known wavelength. The emission of the fluorescence is measured by a photodetector within the DNA profiling machine, the detected light indicating the presence of PCR product, the amount of PCR product (intensity of fluorescence), and the size of PCR product (when data about the time of analysis or electrophoresis (*see Introduction to Forensic Genetics*) is incorporated). Tagging different primer pairs with chemicals that fluoresce with different colors allows mixtures of primers to be used to test for multiple loci (*see Introduction to Forensic Genetics*) at the same time. The electronic data output from the profiling machine is then fed into a computer using appropriate software that, using a set of chosen parameters, will produce a graphical representation or electrophoretogram (or electropherogram,

epg) (*see DNA: An Overview*) showing the detected DNA components within a sample, i.e., the profile.

PCR amplification of a DNA sample may not always work at some or all loci, giving a partial epg or profile, or no result at all. Reasons for these events include, for example, mutation, stochastic artifacts, inhibition, and degradation. If a mutation (*see DNA: An Overview*) has occurred within the STR of a person's DNA, the PCR product will still work but it will simply show an allele size different from the one expected, as the primers for the locus are designed to amplify whatever lies between. A mutation of this kind will be of particular significance, for example, in paternity cases. If, however, the mutation occurred within the binding site sequence for the primer, there will be a reduced ability of the primer to recognize and bind to its target sequence, thus reducing the efficiency of the amplification and so the amount of PCR product for that locus, the actual amount depending on the severity of the mutation [2].

Although a sensitive technique, limited amount of template DNA used in PCR can result in amplification artifacts or stochastic events [3]. When too few template copies are available to begin with, the process can introduce stochastic artifacts such as peak imbalances, allelic drop in and drop out, increased stutter, and preferential locus amplification. All these PCR artifacts can impede interpretation of data and complicate low template analysis.

Inhibition of PCR amplification can be because of the presence of chemicals within the DNA sample that have not been adequately separated from the DNA during chemical extraction, either because of inadequate laboratory processing or the nature of chemicals within the samples themselves. These chemicals then interfere with the ability of the DNA polymerase enzyme within the PCR kit to make new DNA, either by interfering with the enzyme or by binding to the DNA, so that the yield of PCR product for profiling purposes can be reduced or below detectable levels. Known inhibitors that can be commonly encountered in casework include organic components of soil, heme (a component of red blood cells), humic acids, and indigo dye (denim fabric) [4].

Degradation (*see Degraded Samples*) of DNA occurs when DNA has been exposed to chemicals or conditions that cause breakdown of the DNA molecules into smaller fragments, analogous to someone using a pair of scissors to cut up a ball of string. This can be physical environmental factors such as extreme heat (e.g., fires) or irradiation (e.g., direct sunlight) or biological environmental factors such as microbial digestion or self-derived biochemical digestion of decomposing body parts or fluids.

The extent to which any given DNA-containing sample will degrade is a complex process and will depend on its exposure to these various factors and the length of time involved. This is true whether the sample is still at a scene of crime or being kept in storage by criminal justice agents. Once DNA has been extracted into a pure DNA solution (in preparation for analysis), it will in theory be at a greatly reduced risk of degradation, but again, this will depend on the quality of the laboratory procedure and handling. In order to minimize degradation of purified DNA samples, they will be stored frozen; the longer the period of expected storage the lower the temperature. Some DNA, however, can be kept for very long periods and still generate usable PCR products when tested, for example, DNA studied from certain archaeological specimens or dried semen stains on microscope slides. The effect of degradation can be severe enough that nothing is PCR amplified, or it may only partly reduce the quality of the PCR product. The latter situation will give rise to a phenomenon seen on the epg as a slope or decreasing height of peaks from left to right sides of the chart. This can be simply explained as a result of larger pieces of DNA being fewer than smaller pieces in a sample to be amplified. The larger the piece of DNA the greater the chance that it will suffer degradation, leading to a breakage of the DNA molecule between the two primers used to amplify a given locus. Partially degraded DNA samples can still generate useable data but often produce only partial profiles [5].

Utilization of mini STRs (such as the minifiler kit) which target even smaller target sequences than conventional STR's during PCR have been successful in overcoming degradation [6], thus presenting an alternative strategy when conventional STR analysis fails.

Mini STR's are smaller target regions where the PCR primers have been moved closer to the repeat region to reduce the overall target size, thus increasing the potential for successful amplification even when the template DNA is degraded. However, this can also result in concordance issues owing to insertion/deletions between mini STR data and conventional STR data when the same target regions are tested [6].

PCR is a sensitive method that, when optimized according to requirements and methods of detection, will give interpretable results within validated or specified limits. Owing to the flexible nature of the method, there are slight differences as applied in forensic science contexts, for example, as part of the kits commercially available from different companies. In other words, no single detailed method is prescribed or used for all analyses. This is not a problem as long as the particular method has been tested, validated, and reported to the scientific community to show that that method works and that when it is subsequently used the analyst is working within the recommended guidelines.

Although PCR is the key component for amplification of the STRs utilized in forensic DNA profiling, it has been adapted for other uses. The most often encountered of which is as a quantative assay known as real time, or qPCR (*see Quantitation*). qPCR incorporates quenching and florescent probes attached to the primers during the cycling process and can measure changes in florescent intensity as the target sequences are amplified. As the quantity of replicated DNA increases, fluorescent signal is released and detected. This allows the number of replicated copies to be calculated. By multiplexing different primers and florescent probes, qPCR chemistries can quantify both autosomal and male specific Y DNA simultaneously [7], and gain insight into any anticipated male to female DNA mixture ratios prior to full STR profiling analysis.

Additional approaches to improving the amplification process include adding more cycles to increase sensitivity, increasing polymerase, sample concentration, and reduced reaction volumes.

Recent advances in direct amplification, a technique that involves releasing DNA from an substrate and directly amplifying it without involved extraction/purification and quantification steps has aided in decreasing sample processing and analysis times. Direct amplification utilizes optimized primers and reaction mixture capable of overcoming specific inhibitors and is well suited for high template samples such as blood and saliva [8–10]. As a result, this application has been useful for high throughput solutions such as databasing improving overall efficiency of the process.

Nested PCR is another modified amplification approach that utilizes a dual set of optimized primers to reduce nonspecific binding artifacts and allow amplification of single cells. This has proved to be an especially useful application when considering problematic samples such as charred human remains identification [11] and fetal DNA detection .Scientific knowledge and analytical methods are constantly evolving, but the use of PCR to amplify ever smaller quantities of casework DNA samples is currently a topic of debate (*see **Degraded Samples***).

PCR is being used routinely in forensic science to assist individualization of a sample of biological material left at a crime scene. The type of biological material may be indicated by one or more other tests that can presumptively or specifically type the sample. There is ongoing research and development of PCR-based methods that are intended to identify the type of biological material, specifically the body fluid that is in a forensic sample. One advantage of such PCR methods would be the ability to make body fluid identification possible from a very small amount of material and perhaps perform profiling in the same process. In the same way that the human identification kits use a multiplex of primers to test for several loci in one PCR amplification, a single analytical kit could be used to identify several different types of biological sources and whether the stain was from a single or mixed source [12].

The quest for faster, real time results has also led to a growing interest in rapid DNA chemistry. This technology utilized microfluidic, chip technology [13] to allow for single cartridge all in one technology that can type 15 loci profiles (28 cycles) rapidly and with minimal user interaction. Their potential use at booking sites for arrestees and rapid database searching would be advantageous to law enforcement and immigration agencies to assist in detaining persons of interest. Such application takes PCR from the laboratory directly into the field.

Although PCR is a staple in STR analysis the future will look to improving the process speed, assay sensitivity, and robustness of PCR for field applications.

References

[1] Hares, D.R. (2012). Expanding the CODIS Core Loci in the United States, *Forensic Science International: Genetics* **6**, e52–e54.

[2] Clayton, T.M., Hill, S.M., Denton, L.A., Watson, S.K. & Urquhart, A.J. (2004). Primer binding site mutations affecting the typing of STR loci contained within the AMPFlSTR SGM Plus kit, *Forensic Science International* **139**, 255–259.

[3] Budowle, B. & van Daal, A. (2009). Extracting evidence from forensic DNA analyses: future molecular biology directions, *BioTechniques* **46**, 339–350 (April 2009 Special Issue).

[4] Radstrom, P., Knutsson, R., Wolffs, P., Lovenklev, M. & Lofstrom, C. (2004). Pre-PCR processing: strategies to generate PCR-compatible samples, *Molecular Biotechnology* **26**, 133–146.

[5] Hughes-Stamm, S.R., Ashton, K.J. & van Daal, A. (2011). Assessment of DNA degradation and the genotyping success of highly degraded samples, *International Journal of Legal Medicine* **125**, 341–348.

[6] Andrade, L., Bento, A.M., Serra, A., Carvalho, M., Gamero, J.J., Oliveira, C., Batista, L., Lopes, V., Balsa, F., Corte-Real, F. & Anjos, M.J. (2008). AmpFlSTR® MiniFiler™ PCR amplification kit: The new miniSTR multiplex kit, *Forensic Science International: Genetics Supplement Series* **1**(1), 89–91.

[7] Nicklas, J.A. & Buel, E. (2006). Simultaneous Determination of Total Human and Male DNA using a Duplex Real-Time PCR Assay, *Journal of Forensic Sciences* **51**(5), 10005–100015.

[8] Wang, D.Y., Chien-Wei, C., Oldroyd, N.J. & Hennessy, L.K. (2009). Direct amplification of STRs from blood or buccal cell samples, *Forensic Science International: Genetics Supplement Series* **2**(1), 113–114.

[9] Brito, P., Lopes, V., Bogas, V., Balsa, F., Andrade, L., Serra, A., Sao Bento, M., Bento, A.M., Cunha, P., Carvalho, M., Corte-Real, F. & Anjos, M.J. (2011). Amplification of non-FTA samples with AmpFlSTR® Identifiler® Direct PCR Amplification Kit, *Forensic Science International: Genetics Supplement Series* **3**(1), e371–e372.

[10] Wieczorek, D. & Krenke, B.(2009). *Direct Amplification from Buccal and Blood Samples Preserved on Cards Using the PowerPlex® 16 HS System*. Promega Corporation Web site. http://www.promega.com/resources/profiles-in-dna/2009/direct-amplification-from-buccal-and-blood-samples-preserved-on-cards-using-powerplex-16-hs/ Updated 2009. (accessed April 29, 2015).

[11] Strom, C.M. & Rechitsky, S. (1998). Use of Nested PCR to Identify Charred Human Remains and Minute Amounts of Blood, *Journal of Forensic Sciences* **43**(3), 696–700.

[12] Fleming, R.I. & Harbison, S.A. (2010). The development of a mRNA multiplex RT-PCR assay for the definitive identification, *Genetics* **4**, 244–256.

[13] Peter, M., Fleming, R.I. & Harbinson, S.A. (2010). Rapid amplification of commercial STR typing kits Vallone, *Forensic Science International: Genetics Supplement Series* **2**(1), 111–112.

Chapter 14
Interpretation of Mixtures; Graphical

Allan Jamieson

The Forensic Institute, Glasgow, UK

As forensic DNA profiling encounters more types of crime stains in terms of complex mixtures and sources, it becomes almost impossible to present all of the circumstances that an analyst may have to interpret.

As the User Manual for many kits states,

> A sample containing DNA from two sources can be comprised (at a single locus) of any of the seven genotype combinations listed below.

- heterozygote + heterozygote, no overlapping alleles (four peaks)
- heterozygote + heterozygote, one overlapping allele (three peaks)
- heterozygote + heterozygote, two overlapping alleles (two peaks)
- heterozygote + homozygote, no overlapping alleles (three peaks)
- heterozygote + homozygote, overlapping allele (two peaks)
- homozygote + homozygote, no overlapping alleles (two peaks)
- homozygote + homozygote, overlapping allele (one peak)

Increasing the number of sources increases the complexity of the interpretation and reasonable inferences that can be drawn from a profile. The aim of this article is to illustrate the type of profiles that can be found and some of the problems in interpreting them. None of the examples are comprehensive or definitive because of the range of profiles found in casework and the continuing uncertainty as to assessing the actual number of contributors and how dubious peaks should be interpreted.

Identifying and Interpreting Mixtures

A profile is usually represented by a series of numbers describing the alleles present at each locus. The number of alleles at a locus can also identify the minimum number of contributors of the DNA at that locus, and therefore possibly the entire profile. The more alleles that can be identified in a single source profile (i.e., one coming from one person), the less becomes the probability that it would be found by chance in the general population. Mixtures of DNA can create difficulties in identifying the actual contributors.

By way of illustration: if I have profile 28 29 and you have profile 30 31 at a locus, our mixed cells would have a profile 28 29 30 31. However, the same profile could be produced by two people with profiles 28 30 and 29 31, or 28 31 and 29 30. If this mixture was found at a crime scene, we now have six "suspect" heterozygote profiles (we call them "potential contributors", including homozygotes would increase that number). In fact, a mixed profile usually generates many thousands of "suspects" and sometimes many millions.

There are two circumstances when it can be easier to interpret a mixture. The first is, when there is a known potential contributor, and the second is, when one contributor has provided a lot more DNA to the profile than all of the other contributors put together. This last can become important when there are several contributors.

In some forensic circumstances, one of the likely contributors may be known. For example, when an intimate swab is obtained from a rape victim, it can be assumed that her alleles will be within the profile; the mixture may be 11 12 13 and the person from whom the swab was taken be 11 13. The "foreign" 12 allele could not have come from the complainer.

A Guide to Forensic DNA Profiling
Edited by Allan Jamieson and Scott Bader
© 2016 John Wiley & Sons, Ltd. ISBN: 9781118751527
Also published in EFS (online edition)
DOI: 10.1002/9780470061589.fsa1146

Table 1   Hypothetical scenario from intimate swab

	AMEL	D3	vWA	D16	D2	D8	D21	D18	D19	THO1	FGA
Swab	X Y	15	15	11	17	11	24.2	12	13	6 9.3	19
		17	16	12	19	13	28	18	14.2		21
		18	18		20		30		16		
			19		24		32				
Complainer	X X	18	15	11	19	11	24.2	12	13	6 9.3	19
		18	18	12	20	13	32	12	13		21

Table 2   Calculation of "foreign" alleles from swab

	AMEL	D3	vWA	D16	D2	D8	D21	D18	D19	THO1	FGA
Swab	X Y	15	15	11	17	11	24.2	12	13	6 9.3	19
		17	16	12	19	13	28	18	14.2		21
		18	18		20		30		16		
			19		24		32				
Complainer	X X	18	15	11	19	11	24.2	12	13	6 9.3	19
		18	18	12	20	13	32	12	13		21
"Foreign" alleles	Y	15	16	–	17	–	28	18	14.2	–	–
		17	19		24		30		16		

We take an example from a hypothetical crime-stain profile (using SGM+ profile in Table 1).

Some loci, even though they are mixtures of two persons' DNA (known in this case because we have invented it!), show only two alleles (e.g., D16, D8, D18, THO1, and FGA), so the number of alleles alone is not a reliable indicator of the actual number of contributors (without other information)

It is because of this last fact that when the known source is subtracted to identify the "foreign" alleles, it has been a common practice to remove all of their alleles from the crime-stain profile whether they are present in the suspect or not. Using the same profiles as in Table 1, Table 2 is shown.

The resultant profile is a partial profile because of the possibly shared alleles at several loci. The Y at Amel demonstrates that there is a male contributor.

The foreign alleles can now be compared with the suspect (Table 3).

It can be seen that at every locus for which a profile is available, the genotype of the suspect matches the genotype identified from the crime stain. Obviously, the greater the number of matches between the foreign alleles and the suspect, the greater the evidential value will be. This is reflected in the ability to use more numbers in the product rule to calculate the random match probability (RMP). Lack of the appearance of alleles at any locus is not *in itself* a reason to reject a profile match, but a statistic is required to assess the significance of the match, and consideration must be given to other reasons for the apparent match and nonmatching alleles.

In some instances, there may be evidence from the remaining alleles or from other evidence (e.g.,

Table 3   Comparison of foreign alleles with suspect

	AMEL	D3	vWA	D16	D2	D8	D21	D18	D19	THO1	FGA
Suspect	X Y	15	16	11	17	11	28	12	14.2	6 9.3	21
		17	19	11	24	13	30	18	16		21
"Foreign" alleles	Y	15	16	–	17	–	28	18	14.2	–	–
		17	19		24		30		16		

Y-STR profiling) that there is potentially more than one contributor to the remaining profile; in other words, the sample contains DNA from at least three people, the source plus at least two others. In these circumstances there is no way to reliably separate the additional contributors.

Remembering that the number of alleles only indicates the minimum number of contributors, it is always possible that the calculated partial profile is actually not from a single source (person), but from more than one who share alleles with each other. Another possibility is that the amount of DNA from one or more people was just too low for the complete profiles to be detected by the kit. This is called *drop-out*.

Peak Heights and Mixtures; Background

The expert must assess many aspects of the profile to come to a conclusion that will almost always involve making some assumptions. The usual form used in statements is that the scientist will estimate the minimum number of potential contributors to a profile. The eventual conclusion is usually a probable one, not a certainty.

Figure 1 illustrates a situation where the 15 allele has a much higher peak than the 16 allele. It has been shown by experiment that one allele may be as low as about 60% of the height of its "partner" allele and yet still be from the same person. If the profile shows only two alleles at a locus and one is, say, more than twice the height of the other, then it is most likely that each comes from a different person.

This provides another method to assist in deciding how many contributors there are to a profile. This measure (the difference in the peak heights) is called *peak height balance* or *heterozygote balance*. The annotation normally used to describe this is heterozygote balance ratio (Hb). In Figure 1 the most obvious explanation for this result may be that the 15 allele comes from a different person than the 16 allele. One possible interpretation is a mixture of DNA from a person who is 15 15 and one who is 16 16?

There are other possibilities. If there are indeed two contributors, then it is possible that both of them contributed to the 15 peak. So the 15 peak could be made up of DNA from a 15 15 person and a 15 16 person; two possible explanations for the same profile.

When one contributor shares an allele with another, or is thought to do so, so that only a single peak is seen despite the fact that there are at least two contributors

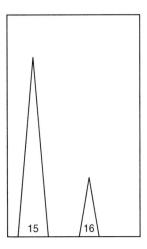

Figure 1 Profile with unequal peak heights: 15 15 and a 16 16, or a 15 16 and a 15 15?

to the peak, the phenomenon is called *masking*. This creates yet another difficulty in assessing the presence or absence of alleles from a specific individual.

Interpretation of a profile requires the analyst to consider the entire profile, but in coming to almost any opinion it will have been necessary to make some assumptions about, for example, the number of contributors.

Figure 2 illustrates a single locus with three alleles in the profile; the 16 and 17 peaks are less than 50% of the height of the 15 peak.

Because there are three alleles, there must be *at least* two contributors as each person can only contribute a maximum of two alleles. Perhaps, an obvious solution to this profile is a combination of a 15 15 (homozygous) individual with a 16 17 (heterozygous) individual. However, there are other possibilities, including a 15 16 and a 15 17 individual. This is what makes the reliable identification of the contributors to many mixtures impossible.

These considerations apply mostly to "good quality" DNA available in sufficient amounts to be easily detected by the kit. In the examples above it is assumed that all of the DNA types in the sample have been detected. Not all DNA found at a crime scene is of good quality, or quantity. This can affect the interpretation of the resultant profiles.

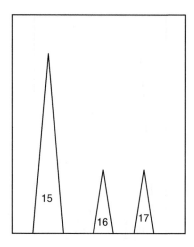

Figure 2   A three-allele locus

Mixed Samples; Analysis of Mixtures

With the increasing sensitivity of the profiling techniques, mixed samples are probably the most common type of sample seen by a forensic laboratory. The statistical interpretation of these mixed samples is an ongoing debate. It should be noted that the information regarding the number of contributors obtained solely from the electropherogram (epg) can only establish the *minimum* number of contributors. Without further information even the inference of a single contributor is just that; an inference.

In the epg, the decision as to whether a sample is mixed can be made by any or all of

- more than two alleles at a locus
- imbalanced alleles at a locus.

More than Two Alleles at a Locus

This is probably one of the easiest methods to determine the presence of more than one contributor as it is based on the fact that a person can contribute at most two alleles per locus to a profile. Figure 3 shows a two-person (minimum) mixture at THO1.

The allelic peaks in Figure 3 are 7, 8, 9, and 9.3. There is a smaller peak in position 6, which in this instance the software has allocated as a stutter peak; it is not considered further for the moment.

The normal task of the forensic analyst is to determine the source of the profile; i.e., what are the profiles

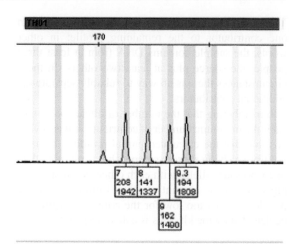

Figure 3   Two-person mixture at a single locus (the unlabeled peak is considered stutter)

Table 4   Possible contributors to two-person profile

Contributor 1	Contributor 2
7 8	9 9.3
7 9	8 9.3
7 9.3	8 9

of the contributors. Assuming that this is indeed a two-person mixture, the possible genotypes that can be derived from this profile are shown in Table 4.

This is the simplest inference from such a profile, but of course it may be that the profile has other contributors who are "masked" by the contribution of others and/or there are homozygote contributors. Either of these increases the number of possible contributor profiles.

Peak Height Imbalance

When two different alleles at the same locus come from the same person they are expected to be approximately of the same height because they should both have the same amount of DNA. In Figure 4, the peak heights of the 11 and 12 alleles are 226 and 95, respectively. There are only two alleles and therefore, using only allele counting, this sample could be considered to have come from one person The expected ratio of the peak heights, given the expected equal contributions of DNA from each allele, is 50/50 or 1. This is calculated

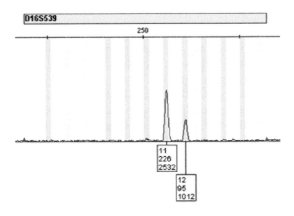

Figure 4   Peak height imbalance

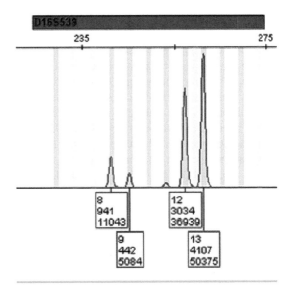

Figure 5   Major/minor locus

by dividing the height of the higher peak of the pair by the height of the lower peak and multiplying to give a percentage value. This ratio is called the *peak height ratio* (PHR) or Hb. Because of the variance in results and the only approximate relationship between peak height and amount of DNA, each laboratory must conduct experiments as part of the validation process to establish the expected range of imbalance expected from a heterozygote PHR. For most labs this will be above about 60%, but for mathematical convenience 50% is often the chosen working threshold.

In Figure 4, for example, the PHR is $((95/226) \times 100)$, which is 42% and below the accepted threshold for the DNA to have come from one person. Considering this aspect alone, this profile can therefore be considered to come from at least two people.

In terms of possible contributors, this can affect the inferences as to the possible genotypes of the contributors. If only the alleles are considered, and the necessity to have two contributors, then one must consider the obvious 11 11 with a lesser amount from a 12 12, but also the possibility of an amount of about 100 rfu (relative fluorescence units) at each locus from a 11 12 contributor and about 50 rfu from a 11 11 contributor.

(In a real case, and depending on the results at other loci and the fact that peak height variation between runs increases markedly below about 100 rfu, it is likely that this result would not be considered definitive and the run repeated or the other loci taken into consideration. This merely underlines the variable and the subjective aspects of profile interpretation.)

Major/Minor Mixtures

One form of peak imbalance is caused when the amount of DNA from one contributor is much larger than the amount contributed by the other(s). At a single locus, this could look much like Figure 5.

This locus is interesting for a number of reasons connected with the use of peak height balance.

Considering only the two highest peaks: they have a PHR of about 74% and therefore could be considered to have come from the same heterozygote contributor with a 12 13 genotype. If we consider this to be a two-person mixture, then neither of the lower alleles (8 and 9) could have come from the same person who contributed either of the 12 or 13 alleles (if a 8 12, 8 13, 9 12, or 9 13 genotype is proposed) because of PHR considerations (all of those combinations produce a PHR of much less than 50%). So, *if we assume a two-person mixture*, then the major contributor is 12 13 and the minor contributor is 8 9.

Complex Mixtures

You may have noticed in Figure 5 that there is a further complication in this particular profile; the 8 and 9 are unbalanced also, with a PHR of 47%. Applying the normal accepted cut-off for the PHR of at least 60%

implies that there are two minor contributors and this is a three-person mixture and not a two-person mixture.

Now a new assessment is necessary.

If we wish to consider that one of the contributors is 8 13, we infer their contribution to be about 950 rfu on the basis of the 8 allele that we can see, then the contribution of the 13 allele from the other contributor(s) can be estimated to be about 3150 (4100 − 950). We can use approximations because we know that the peak heights are not accurate regarding the amount of DNA anyway. At a height of about 3150, the 13 allele is now very close in height to the 13 allele at 3107 and so that is a proposition that fits the observed results quite well. It does not affect the conclusion that the major contributor is 12 13, but it does leave the 9 allele unaccounted for and so requires the inference of a third contributor, which also happens to agree with the 8 9 imbalance.

The 9 may be a small contribution from a 9 9 homozygote. It could also be part of a poorly balanced 8 9 heterozygote. Using the same logic as we applied to the 8 allele, it could also be part of a 9 12 or 9 13 heterozygote profile. If the 9 contributes about 450 rfu to the 13 peak, then the 12 13 PHR is now about 83% and presents no problem in terms of the major profile being 12 13.

If the 9 allele contributes about 450 rfu to the 12 peak, the 12 13 PHR becomes about 63%. Over the line … just!

We may wish to consider the different proposition that one of the contributors is 8 12. Using the same logic as for the 8 13, the other(s) contribution to the 12 allele is about 2100. This produces a 12 13 PHR of 51%, which is now below the 60% cut-off and so changes the interpretation of the major profile; i.e., there is no major profile.

So, if we assume a two-person mixture, then this must be 12 13 major contributor with an 8 9 minor; nothing else works given that assumption. The evidence against the two-person mixture hypothesis at this locus is the PHR between the 8 allele peak and 9 allele peak, but we know that this is not a hard and fast rule and so there is doubt. One interpretation of the mixture if we now assume that it is a three-person mixture is that there is no major contributor; the opposite conclusion to our first inference. If the suspect is a 12 13 at this locus, then the significance of the evidence against him is significantly different depending on how we treat the 8 9 PHR and the number of other possible contributors.

It should be noted that a four-person mixture is also possible from this locus by invoking a homozygous contribution at any allele along with a heterozygote contribution to the same allele (e.g., 13 13, 8 12, 9 13, and 12 13).

Most analysts will consider the entire profile when assessing the most likely interpretation. Some authors believe that this interpretation should be done before the analyst has any knowledge of the suspect profile(s), [1] while others believe that this is difficult to achieve practically and there is no evidence of bias affecting the interpretation [2]. Statistics such as the RMP, random man not excluded (RMNE), and combined probability of inclusion (CPI) do not require any suspect profile to be specified, but can be inferred from a profile. The likelihood ratio (LR) requires the definition of a profile as a proposition and therefore normally requires knowledge of the suspect's profile.

The assessment of the profile from Figure 5 to the D2 locus can now be extended. The analyst in the case stated that the alleles of the defendant were, "prominent in the majority of loci" with the inference that even in the absence of a statistic, it was their view that this was stronger evidence against the defendant because there was a larger amount of the defendant's DNA present.

Figure 6 shows the D21 locus (from the same sample used for Figure 5) at which the 16 and 19 alleles are the two highest peaks. There are only four alleles detected. On the basis of allele counting, this is therefore a two-person mixture.

The 16 and 19 alleles have a PHB of 69% $((898/1300) \times 100)$, which is within the normal parameter for them having come from the same individual. The 23/26 PHB is 49% and therefore, using the 60% threshold, they could not have come from the same person. The conclusion is that this is better considered as a three-person mixture. Dealing with the single issue as to whether the prominent peaks should be considered to come from a single person (and assuming that the defendant is 16 19), it can be seen that one possible contributor genotype is 16 23. If that is so, and there are at least two other contributors, then the 16 peak could comprise DNA from the 16 23 contributor and at least one other contributor. If we use the height of the 23 peak (about 480 rfu) as before to provide an estimate of the contribution of the 16 23 contributor to the 16 peak, then the remaining height of the 16 peak is about 418 rfu (898 − 480). The 16 19 PHB now becomes 32% and the defendant's profile

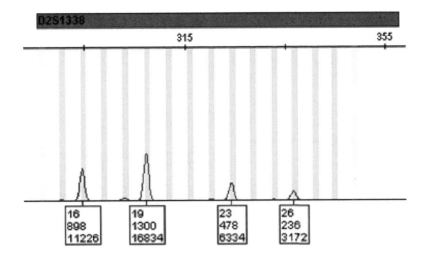

Figure 6   D2 locus

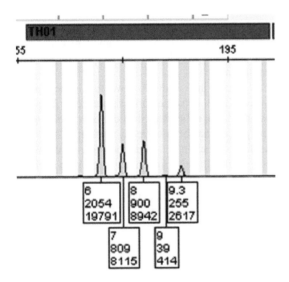

Figure 7   THO1 locus

is excluded unless there is another contributor to the 19 peak.

Despite the PHR considerations (using a 60% threshold) pointing to a three-person mixture, there was only a single locus in this entire profile that had more than four alleles. The THO1 locus is illustrated in Figure 7.

Considering the 9 allele with a peak height of 39: with the parameters that the software is using for this

profile, the 39 allele is assessed as an allele. If the PHT was adjusted to 50 rfu, it would be below the threshold and not counted. The difference is significant when considering the possible genotypes using only the presence of alleles because for every combination possible from the 6, 7, 8, and 9.3 alleles must be added another including the 9 allele. Even if we exclude homozygous contributors, the number of genotypes (or "suspect profiles" who could be contributors) possible from 4 alleles is 6, but the number possible from 5 is 10 (for the mathematically minded this is the calculation of the number of combinations possible when choosing r items from n of them; $(n!/(n-r)!$ where r is 2 and n is the number of observed alleles. The number of possible homozygotes is n).

So, the attribution of peak height and the setting of peak height thresholds are important in the interpretation of forensic DNA profiles because they can cause a particular genotype to be included or excluded from consideration.

Some probabilistic methods take no account of peak height in assessing the weight of evidence. The consequence of that can be counter-intuitive conclusions. Figure 8 shows the vWA locus in one of four runs of a particular casework sample. All runs showed the 17 allele well above the height of any other allele. In two 28-cycle runs, no other alleles were called at vWA, and in the other 31-cycle run the 17 allele was at 1273 rfu, the 15 was absent, the 16 below the stutter threshold and 18 at 306 rfu and the 19 again at 114 rfu.

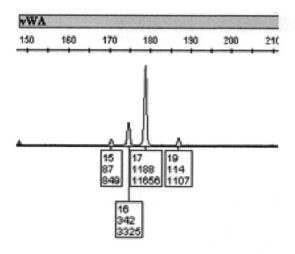

Figure 8   vWA locus where defendant is 17 17

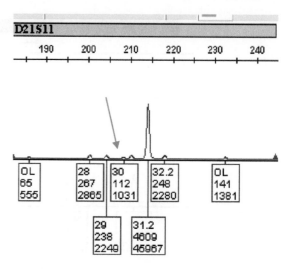

Figure 9   Allelic peaks at the same level as stutter

The most obvious interpretation of this locus was that it contained the DNA from a 17 17 homozygote – the genotype of the defendant.

The software (LikeLTD) was of the type that does not take account of peak height. The LR at this locus was 0.12, favoring the defense proposition that the DNA came from two unknown persons rather than the defendant (who was 17 17 at that locus) and an unknown person.

In casework, there are a number of other considerations that can assist to provide more confidence in the estimated number of contributors. For example, the presence of a known contributor.

Stutter

While stutter can generally be easily recognized in single source samples, they can cause serious difficulties in mixture interpretation. In Figure 9 there are a series of peaks (28 29 30 and 32.2) with heights between 100 and 300 rfu. There is another peak, in the 31.2 position and marked with an arrow, which has been treated as stutter by the software because of its PHR compared to the 31.2 peak. Given that the minor contributors to this profile are producing peak heights at about the level of the stutter peak, it is possible that the stutter is in fact an allele. In this instance there would, therefore, be five alleles in the minor profile leading to an inference of at least three contributors to the minor profile rather than two. This significantly changes the statistics of the minor profile(s).

The inclusion or exclusion of the 30.2 "stutter" will, or should, make a difference to any statistical interpretation of this profile and others exhibiting similar phenomena.

This locus also exhibits two off-ladder peaks (marked "OL"). In a casework sample these off-ladder peaks may cause the analyst to consider whether the sizing process has been correctly performed.

As the peak height in a stutter position increases it is to be expected that the probability that it is an allele, or an allele plus stutter, increases. It is currently unclear how "expert profile interpretation" by other software systems can provide any more reliability to the decision as to which is true or even more likely given that the research has shown that it is not possible to provide any estimate of the uncertainty in such decisions. Simply being "objective" is not enough if the objective rules are unsupported by experimental data.

Consider the 16 peak at the D3 locus in Figure 6. It has an allocated height of 91 rfu and protrudes well above the noise of the baseline. The baseline or zero will therefore normally have little effect on any calculation involving the peak area. Now consider the 30 peak at D21. There is baseline noise about 10 rfu in height just to the left of the 30 peak, which has an allocated height of 32. The peak may therefore have a significant contribution of noise to the peak height depending on how the position of the baseline is calculated. As the peak height reduces, this effect will become more pronounced, and more caution should be applied to peak heights (and areas) as the peak height approaches the baseline.

Low-Template Mixtures

The user manuals for Applied Biosystems kits include

> When the total number of allele copies added to the PCR is extremely low, unbalanced amplification of the two alleles of a heterozygous individual may occur due to stochastic fluctuation in the ratio of the two different alleles. The PCR cycle number and amplification conditions have been specified to produce low peak heights for a sample containing 20-pg human genomic DNA. Low peak heights should be interpreted with caution.
>
> Individual laboratories may find it useful to determine an appropriate minimum peak height threshold based on their own results and instruments using low amounts of input DNA.

Notwithstanding that caution, there has been a constant drive to improve the sensitivity of DNA profiling to detect smaller amounts of DNA. Three general approaches, insofar as the current loci are concerned, have been to increase the number of amplification cycles, improve the "quality" of the samples by a clean-up procedure, and to increase the amount of DNA added to the separation process. Some laboratories have attempted combining all the three. Originally termed *low copy number* (LCN), referring to the increased cycle number method, the general technique is now more widely termed *low-template DNA* (LT or LTDNA). Laboratories sometimes describe the process as high-sensitivity testing or some other label to differentiate it from the procedure for the kit used and as recommended by the manufacturer of the kit.

The main features of the increased-cycle method were set out in two papers published in 2000 and 2001 [3, 4] (referring to LCN with the SGM+ kit). Others have used different kits and cycle numbers [5].

Gill *et al.* [3] stated,

> At 28 cycles neither SGM nor SGM plus produced alleles at DNA concentrations below 100 pg. At 34 cycles, full profiles could be obtained down to approximately 25–50 pg – the equivalent of four to ten cell nuclei.

However, a number of difficulties were apparent from the use of the technique. The technique is claimed to be so sensitive that it will identify single alleles that are in fact a contaminant not associated with the sample under test. These single alleles are called *drop-in*. Because these drop-in alleles should be rare events, the technique requires two runs to reduce or eliminate the possibility that such contamination will not be counted as "true" alleles. The LT process, therefore, requires at least two runs. A "consensus profile" is created by including any allele that is observed at least twice, regardless of the number of runs. Two runs are most common in practice. The creation of a consensus profile is the alternative to a probabilistic approach, which usually involves software implementing one of the proposed statistical models for the interpretation of such mixtures. Here, we look only at the epg to illustrate some of the problems of LT analysis. These have been summarized [6];

> all methods used to analyze low copy number DNA suffer from several disadvantages that are primarily derived from stochastic variation.
>
> … there are several consequences that cannot be avoided:
>
> (i) allele drop-out may occur because one allele of a heterozygote locus can be preferentially amplified;
>
> (ii) stutters may be preferentially analyzed – these are sometimes known as *false alleles*;
>
> (iii) the method is prone to sporadic contamination, amplifying alleles that are unassociated with the crime stain or sample.
>
> (iv) This means that different DNA profiles may be observed after replicate PCR analyses.

Although there have been a number of proposed methods for the statistical interpretation of LT samples, there is an ongoing debate as to which, if any, is a reliable method at the present time.

Figure below shows the results of two runs from an illustrative casework sample and comments about the changes between the runs. Probabilistic genotyping software was used in the case to calculate an LR.

There is a relationship between the amount of input DNA and peak height using the manufacturer's recommended and validated method. In LT analysis this relationship breaks down with consequent problems in interpretation, In fact, it is the main issue in challenging such analyses in court.

It can be seen that, even where alleles are reproduced, there is considerable variation in the peak heights and PHR's between runs. Some authors have proposed methods to deal with this variation, but there is insufficient experimental data to support such proposals in casework.

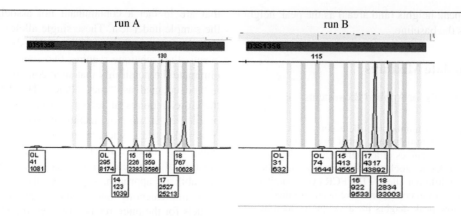

run B vs run A: 14 absent, all PHB's changed

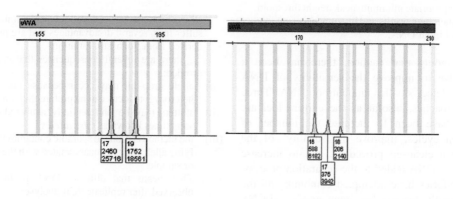

17 no longer highest peak, 16 is highest in one run but absent in the other, 18 present in one run absent in the other, all PHBs changed

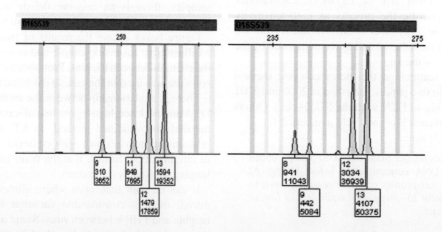

11 third highest in one run but absent in the other, 8 absent in one run but higher than 9 in the other, all PHBs changed (although 12 13 PHB probably within acceptable limits of variation)

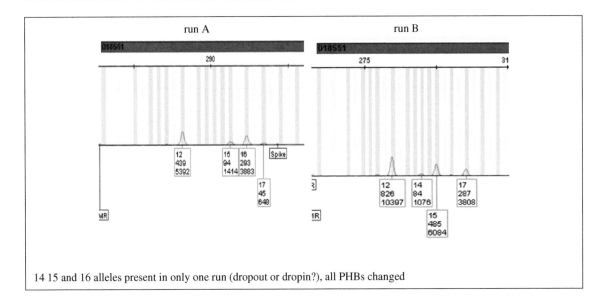

14 15 and 16 alleles present in only one run (dropout or dropin?), all PHBs changed

The technique also suffers from a phenomenon called *drop-out* whereby alleles that should be present in the sample are not observed.

Dealing with just two problems that arise from profiles of this type;

1. drop-in versus dropout,
2. peak height balance.

Drop-in versus Drop-out

Very low amounts mean that some alleles are not detected in every run, and possibly not at all. When an allele should appear but does not, the phenomenon is called *drop-out*. That problem of course is only apparent if an interpreter knows what DNA is supposed to be present in the sample, or if more than one run is performed and the allele is absent in one or more of the runs, or in the extreme if an entire locus has no alleles present in the profile.

Drop-out is the extreme form of peak height variability. In standard DNA profiling with the recommended amount of DNA (0.5–1.5 ng; 500–1500 pg), the peak heights are expected to be consistent between runs. When very low amounts of DNA are used, the peak heights can vary considerably between runs. This causes problems, *inter alia*, in estimating the number of contributors to the profile.

An additional complication of analyzing very low amounts of DNA is that spurious alleles, supposedly from the environment, are detected. These are termed *drop-in* and are again identified primarily by the fact that they do not belong to a known or expected DNA profile. They were detected in the original validation studies from pre-2000 performed by the FSS Ltd.

One difficulty that is immediately apparent is that if an allele occurs only once, then it could be either drop-out or drop-in. Examples from the figure above include the 19 allele at vWA. Another difficulty for systems that claim to "take account of" the uncertainty is how one evaluates just how much uncertainty can be associated with any finding. For example, are the single occurrences of the 16, 18, and 19 alleles at vWA more or less likely to represent genuine alleles than the 11 at D16, which actually appears twice, but is treated as stutter in the second run? If so, by how much? On what basis?

Partial Profiles

There are a number of kits available for forensic DNA profiling. Kits may analyze more or fewer loci. This is important when considering whether a profile is a full profile or a partial profile. As each kit measures a different number of loci, a full profile in one kit may

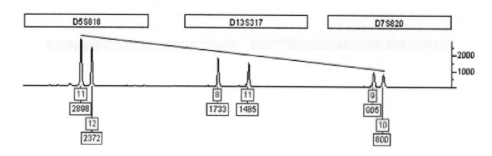

Figure 10   Illustration of one channel of a profile from "degraded" DNA [7]

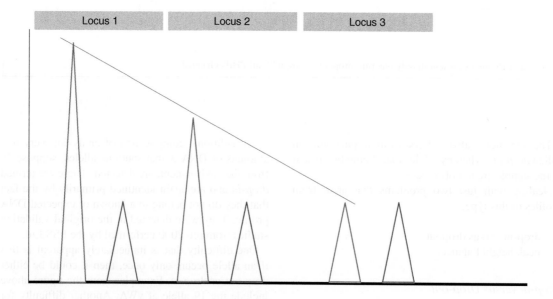

Figure 11   Illustration of mixture with one contributor degraded

be only a partial profile when compared to the results from another kit. For example, the SGM kit measures only six loci, but the SGM+ kit measures the same six, plus another four. So a full profile from the SGM kit will be, at most, about 60% of a full SGM+ profile of the same individual. A full SGM+ profile will be a partial Identifiler profile (Identifiler has 16 including the Amelogenin locus).

The concept of a partial profile is therefore applied only to the results from a specific kit and simply means that a result has not been obtained at every locus, or that an allele that should have been detected was not detected. The evidential value of a partial profile is less than the evidential value of a full profile, but a valid statistic can nevertheless be calculated in accord with the generally accepted approaches to full profiles.

Degraded Samples

DNA is a chemical. It is carried in the cells that make up the body. If those cells that were shed from our body were not somehow destroyed, then we would quickly be knee-deep in discarded body cells. Although cells, tissues, and DNA can be preserved for thousands of years, it is more likely that they will not last that long. Light, humidity, heat, bacteria, and some chemicals will all hasten the disruption of cells and the degradation of DNA. Degradation, in DNA terms, means that the long chains of DNA are chopped into smaller lengths.

The DNA profiling kit only recognizes the complete version of each allele. Remember that the alleles vary in their length. The longer alleles are therefore more likely to be chopped than the smaller ones. Remember that the loci with the longer pieces of DNA are at the right-hand side of the graph (e.g., D2, D18, and FGA). A degraded sample will show smaller peaks as one progresses from left to right looking along the graph (Figure 10).

In some instances alleles may not appear at all because so much of the DNA of that allele has degraded that there are insufficient molecules to be detected by the kit. The effect on the epg is that no peak, or sometimes a very small peak, appears on the epg and the allele cannot be regarded as "true".

The difficulties that degraded samples can create are illustrated in Figure 11.

Figure 11 is a schematic illustration of a mixture of a degraded major contributor (blue) and a nondegraded minor contributor (red). In such a case, the major contributor *may* be identified at some loci but not all, and the high molecular weight loci (i.e., at the right-hand side of the epg) may show no major contributor, and a mixture of two people appear as a single heterozygous contributor. In some cases, the alleles from the degraded contributor(s) may have completely

dropped out (i.e., disappeared) from the larger loci.

References

[1] Krane, D.E., Ford, S., Gilder, J.R., Inman, K., Jamieson, A., Koppl, R., Kornfield, I.L., Risinger, D.M., Rudin, N., Taylor, M.S. & Thompson, W.C. (2008). Sequential unmasking: a means of minimizing observer effects in forensic DNA interpretation. Letter to the editor, *Journal of Forensic Science* **53**, 1006–1007.

[2] Thornton, J.I. (2010). Letter to the editor – a rejection of "working blind" as a cure for contextual bias, *Journal of Forensic Science* **55**, 1663.

[3] Gill, P., Whitaker, J., Flaxman, C., Brown, N. & Buckleton, J. (2000). An investigation of the rigor of interpretation rules for STRs derived from less than 100 pg of DNA, *Forensic Science International* **112**, 17–40.

[4] Whitaker, J.P., Cotton, E.A. & Gill, P. (2001). A comparison of characteristics of profiles produced with the SGM Plus multiplex system for both standard and Low Copy Number (LCN) STR DNA analysis, *Forensic Science International* **123**, 215–223.

[5] Caragine, T., Mikulasovich, R., Tamariz, J., Bajda, E., Sebestyen, J., Baum, H. & Prinz, M. (2009). Validation of testing and interpretation protocols for low template DNA samples using AmpFlSTR® Identifiler®, *Croatian Medical Journal* **50**, 250–267.

[6] Gill, P. (2002). Role of short tandem repeat DNA in forensic casework in the UK – past, present, and future perspectives, *Bio Techniques* **32**, 366–385.

[7] Gilder, J. (2008). Computational methods for the objective review of forensic DNA testing results. PhD Thesis.

Chapter 15
DNA Mixture Interpretation

Dan E. Krane

Wright State University, Dayton, OH, USA

Introduction

Short tandem repeat (STR) sequences have become the genetic markers of choice for the purpose of human identification in forensic investigations [1–3]. In the case of a high-quality, single-source sample and barring the possibility of error, STR analysis can provide compelling statistical evidence that an observed correspondence between an evidentiary sample and a particular individual is very unlikely to be the result of coincidence [4].

However, many evidentiary samples are composed of mixtures of two or more individuals' DNA and their interpretation can be significantly more challenging [5]. Consider a locus where three alleles (such as the D3S1358 locus in Figure 1 with a 13, 17, and 18 allele) are observed. Even if it is known that exactly two persons contributed genetic material to this sample, six different pair-wise combinations of genotypes are qualitatively consistent with the observation of these three alleles: (i) 13, 13 and 17, 18; (ii) 13, 17 and 18, 18; (iii) 13, 17, and 17, 18; (iv) 13, 17 and 13, 18; (v) 13, 18 and 17, 17; and (vi) 13, 18 and 17, 18. Interpretation becomes even more difficult when no assumptions are made regarding the number of contributors to a mixed sample (e.g., the three alleles observed at the D3S1358 locus in Figure 1 could represent a mixture of three individuals with genotypes: 13, 13; 13, 17; and 17, 18). Unfortunately, the potential for alleles to be shared between individuals limits the ability of simple counting techniques to correctly infer the number of contributors to mixed samples [5]. The difficulties are compounded even more dramatically if there is a possibility that the information available

for analysis is incomplete (e.g., a 15 allele might have also been present in the sample that gave rise to the D3S1358 locus shown in Figure 1 but failed to be detected, it may have "dropped out").

Despite intense interest on the part of the forensic science community, there is still no generally accepted means of attaching a statistical weight to a mixed sample with an unknown number of contributors where allelic drop-out may have occurred. Because a number of statistical approaches can be relied upon to attach weights to single-source samples, many testing laboratories endeavor to deconvolute or separate mixed DNA samples into their component parts. Currently available deconvolution approaches are hampered by the uncertainties that are associated with low-level samples (e.g., distinguishing between signal and noise and determining the impact of stochastic effects).

Emerging probabilistic approaches may eventually provide an alternative to the deconvolution of mixed samples using standard operating procedures and simple mathematical formulae. These probabilistic approaches generate likelihood ratios that have the potential to capture uncertainties related to ranges of possible rates of drop-in and drop-out and can be divided into two categories: semi-continuous (relying exclusively on the alleles that are deemed to be present; peak height information is not utilized by the approach) and fully continuous (molecular biological parameters are incorporated such as peak height ratio, hypothetical mixture ratios, and the expectation of stutter artifacts).

The computational complexity associated with fully continuous probabilistic approaches in particular is introducing an important, unprecedented set of challenges to the criminal justice system that requires careful consideration. To date, computer software (be it a word processing program or a software package

A Guide to Forensic DNA Profiling
Edited by Allan Jamieson and Scott Bader
© 2016 John Wiley & Sons, Ltd. ISBN: 9781118751527

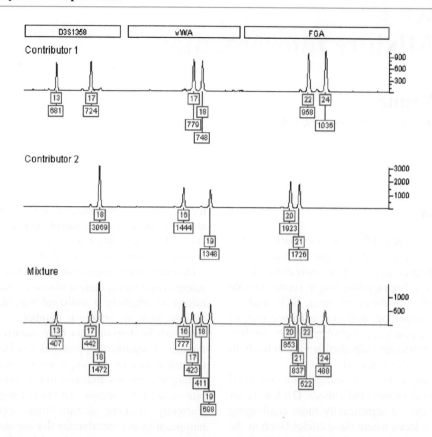

Figure 1   Partial electropherograms of two single-source samples and their corresponding 1:2 mixture. Allelic designations for each peak appear immediately below it with corresponding peak height information (in relative fluorescence units, RFUs) immediately below that. Locus names are in the boxes above.

that converts the raw electronic data of a DNA profiling analysis into an easily interpreted graphical format) has been used simply to assist humans during the course of activities that they could have performed less efficiently without that assistance. We may be on the cusp of a new era where computer programs take on the role of exercising judgment and arriving at conclusions that cannot be confirmed or replicated by human experts due to the sheer number and complexity of the analyses that are performed.

Conventional Mixture Deconvolution

The rarity of single-source samples among unrelated individuals is commonly estimated as a random match probability (RMP) using the following equations:

$$\text{homozygotes} : A_iA_i : P_{ii} = p_i^2 + p_i(1 - p_i)\theta_{ii} \quad (1a)$$

$$\text{heterozygotes} : A_iA_j : P_{ij} = 2p_ip_j(1 - p_i)\theta_{ij} \quad (1b)$$

where p_i and p_j are the frequencies of alleles in a relevant population of alternative suspects and θ is an allowance for population substructure [4]. The possibility of numerous alternative hypotheses dramatically reduces the probative value of mixed evidentiary samples. The chance of a randomly selected, unrelated individual not being excluded as a possible contributor to a mixed evidentiary sample (the combined probability of inclusion or CPI) [6,7] is arrived at with the equation:

$$\text{CPI} = A_iA_j \ \dots \ A_n : P_{ij\dots n} = (p_i + p_j + \ \dots \ + p_n)^2 \quad (2)$$

where p_i through p_n are the frequencies of alleles in a relevant population of alternative suspects [6,7]. Typical RMP values for single-source samples that have been genotyped at the 13 standard CODIS STR loci are in the range of 1 in 10^{12} to 10^{50} [8] while CPI values for 13 locus mixed STR genotypes where no more than four alleles are observed across all tested loci (and thus are consistent with being a two person mixture) are typically in the range of 1 in 10^6 to 10^{10}. For example, in the case of the D3S1358 locus shown in Figure 1, the RMP value for "contributor 1" using a Caucasian database [9] is 1 in 192 and 1 in 38 for "contributor 2" as single-source samples, while the CPI value for their mixture is 1 in 7.

The striking difference in the weight of the DNA evidence associated with single-source and mixed evidentiary samples has motivated the development of approaches that attempt to elucidate the genotypes of the individual contributors from mixed evidentiary samples [10–17]. These existing approaches have generally attempted to formalize and objectify a series of *ad hoc* rules employed by DNA analysts tasked with assessing which peaks at each tested locus are associated with each other and, thereby, with individual contributors. The most obvious approach to resolution involves grouping pairs of alleles according to their respective peak heights. For example, in the mixture at the D3S1358 locus in Figure 1, the heights of the 13 and 17 allele peaks are similar to each other, whereas the 18 allele is approximately three times greater in size. This approach is ultimately based on the assumption that a pair of peaks from a heterozygote should contribute relatively equal amounts of DNA. This assumption is supported in part by numerous validation studies [18–21] that suggest that when an individual is heterozygous at a locus the peak heights of the alleles tend to be within a certain percentage of each other (peak height balance). An extension of this approach attempts to eliminate further genotype combinations from the mixture by assessing the DNA contribution ratio for all contributors to a sample (the mixture proportion/ratio), and then minimizing the variance from this ratio among all contributors across *all* tested loci [15,22]. Erroneous assignment of peaks to contributors can occur as the result of potentially incorrect assumptions (e.g., peak heights are strictly additive, similar amounts of genomic template will yield similar peak heights, artifacts can be reliably identified, and mixture ratios are constant across all loci) and/or complications arising from similar amounts of DNA being contributed by two or more individuals (in which case the correct assignment

may not be any more likely than other potential assignments).

The reality of mixed STR DNA profiles is that some loci cannot be resolved into two single genotypes by these methods because the observed electropherogram data provides equivalent or very similar support for two or more of the competing alternative hypotheses of genotype combinations that could account for all the detected alleles. An approach that rests primarily upon the two principal assumptions of mixture resolution methods (1: that the number of contributors is known or at least explicitly hypothesized, and 2: that alleles from the same individual will be present at approximately the same intensity within a stated margin of error) can be used to provably determine which alternative hypotheses of genotype combinations are mathematically feasible (in light of peak height balance and summation expectations) and which should be eliminated from consideration due to their failure to satisfy one or more objective rules. When only a single combination of genotypes is supported by the underlying data, RMP calculations can be used to describe the rarity of those individual genotypes. In instances where some but not all alternative hypotheses of contributor genotypes can be eliminated from consideration, a CPI-with-constrained-hypotheses value for a mixed DNA profile can be calculated.

The ability for mixtures to be resolved diminishes when the ratio is either very similar (close to 1:1) or far apart (greater than 1:5). One reason for the latter is the preferential amplification of major contributors. Another reason is that for small amounts of template DNA, a minor contributor can be masked by or mistaken for commonly encountered stutter artifacts. It may be necessary to consider certain mixtures with the stutter filters turned off in order to identify all possible mixture contributors. Contributor peaks in stutter position may also be observed to be higher than if they were observed in nonstutter positions. Care should be taken when examining such contributor profiles as the contribution from stutter may put the minor contributor peaks out of balance.

The mixture resolution method outlined here is implemented in a freely downloadable software package called *GenoStat®* [23]. Once a user has entered the RFU values for a given DNA sample, GenoStat® performs the mixture resolution method as well as calculates the RMP for each contributor's fully resolved loci, the unconstrained CPI, and the CPI for constrained loci using only the contributor hypotheses that the resolution method has deemed plausible. While GenoStat® makes the process of mixture deconvolution easier, it works only for samples where it is explicitly assumed that there are two and only two contributors with no other phenomena such as drop-out. The computations that it performs are ones that a human expert could relatively easily confirm by hand if necessary but that would not be the case for mixtures of three or more individuals.

Probabilistic Approaches

Numerous approaches that promise to attach statistical weights to mixed samples where drop-out may have occurred have been put forward in the past few years. These approaches take into account (and sometimes use data from evidence samples to infer) drop-out and drop-in rates to generate likelihood ratios between prosecution and defense hypotheses. These emerging probabilistic approaches may eventually provide an alternative to the deconvolution of mixed samples using standard operating procedures and simple mathematical formulae. Probabilistic approaches to date can generally be divided into two broad categories: semi-continuous (relying exclusively on the alleles that are deemed to be present and peak height information is not utilized by these approaches) and fully continuous (molecular biological parameters are incorporated such as peak height ratio, hypothetical mixture ratios, and the expectation of stutter artifacts).

In conventional STR DNA profiling, where recommended amounts of template DNA for all contributors insure that all alleles in an evidence sample have been detected, it is expected that the probability assigned to the prosecution's theory of the case is 1 (meaning that the test results would appear as they do if the prosecution's theory of the case is, in fact, correct). The defendant's theory of the case (typically that contributions from some other, randomly chosen, unrelated individuals have together given rise to what is seen in the evidence sample) usually has a much lower probability. In these cases, the ratio of the likelihoods (with the probability of the prosecution's theory in the numerator and the probability of the defense's theory in the denominator) is essentially the reciprocal of the probability of the defense's theory of the case. If allele drop-out/in is a possibility (e.g., in a partial profile), then there is uncertainty in whether or not an allele

is present in the sample – and therefore what genotype combinations are possible. Simply ignoring loci where it is necessary to invoke drop-out to include an individual as a possible contributor to a mixed sample is a solution that brings with it a significant risk of producing apparently strong evidence against an innocent suspect [24].

In cases where it is necessary to invoke drop-out (or drop-in) for the evidence sample to be consistent with the prosecution's theory of the case, the evidence is much less consistent with what would be expected if the prosecution's theory was correct. Drop-out constitutes a failure of the carefully designed STR DNA test kits to generate a complete, correct result and should be expected to be a relatively rare event if the kits themselves are to be generally considered to be reliable. In some instances, the prosecution's theory of the case could be very poorly supported by the actual test results yet be relatively more likely than a defense hypothesis for the same case.

One helpful analogy might be to consider "who stole my biscuit?" We can accept that it is exceedingly unlikely that Father Christmas (being a person widely admired for his good character) stole my biscuit. However, it is much less likely that a unicorn (which are widely known to not actually exist) stole my biscuit. The ratio of those two hypotheses might suggest that the prosecution's theory is a much better explanation of the loss of my biscuit – unless and until we consider that alternative defense theories (e.g., that my brother stole my biscuit; who came up with the idea of a unicorn being involved in the first place?) are more consistent with the test results. When it is necessary to invoke drop-out (and/or drop-in) for test results to be consistent with a prosecution's theory of a case, it is critically important that both the numerator and the denominator be fully disclosed – yet, some probabilistic approaches currently provide only the ratio of the two likelihoods.

Semi-Continuous Probabilistic Genotyping Approaches

Generally speaking, semi-continuous probabilistic genotyping approaches require a human expert to determine what peaks are present or absent (or "questionable") in a test result. Determining and applying a rate at which drop-out (and drop-in) has occurred then becomes the primary challenge for a semi-continuous probabilistic genotyping approach. First-generation software approaches to deconvolution like GenoStat® avoid the issue by explicitly requiring that all information associated with a sample has been detected. But numerous software packages have since emerged such as LoCoMotion [25], likeLTD (likelihoods for low-template DNA profiles) [26], FST [27], Lab Retriever [28], LiRa/LiRT [23], and GenoProof Mixture (Qualitype) that require a specific drop-out/in rate in order to generate their likelihood ratios. For any of these approaches (including those that are fully continuous), a drop-out probability of 0 for the suspect of interest would translate directly to an outright rejection of any prosecution hypothesis for which it is necessary to posit the test failed to obtain complete information from an evidence sample. By the same token, a drop-out probability of 1 delivers unhelpful likelihood ratios in that no one could be excluded as a possible contributor to a sample and all conceivable defense hypotheses become well-supported.

Three general (not necessarily mutually exclusive) strategies at estimating drop-out/in rates have emerged in currently available software: (1) inference from template quantitation, (2) "completeness" of the test results themselves, and (3) use of a range of values with preference given to those that deliver a likelihood ratio most favorable to a defendant. All three strategies have proven to be controversial. Quantitation methods do not perform well in ranges where drop-out/in rates are highest [29] and deliver only estimates of total human DNA associated with a sample (not that of individual contributors). Inference of drop-out/in rates based on comparisons between evidence and reference profiles can be argued to be self-fulfilling and suspect-centric. Alternatively, reliance on allele count and/or observation of locus drop-out will typically underestimate the number of contributors (especially minor contributors) to a mixture. And, approaches that use a range of values must use artificial/arbitrary limits to those ranges because drop-out/in probabilities close to 0 and 1 dramatically reduce the probative value of an evidence sample – which is often the objective of one of the two parties involved in criminal proceedings. Layered on top of the debate regarding these different strategies is an on-going debate regarding the importance of using locus-specific drop-out/in rates rather than a single probability used across an entire test result. That question is significantly complicated by consideration of the possibility that the contribution of one or more contributors to a mixed sample may be degraded and/or inhibited.

Some semi-continuous probabilistic genotyping approaches such as likeLTD are available as open source software. While more complicated than the calculations for a mathematically provable approach to deconvolution like that in GenoStat, it should be possible for all approaches that use estimates of drop-out/in rates to be performed by hand if necessary at least for two-person mixtures.

Fully Continuous Probabilistic Genotyping Approaches

Fully continuous probabilistic genotyping approaches endeavor to use more of the data associated with DNA profile test results than just the presence and absence of alleles. Some approaches claim to extract and use hundreds of features to evaluate electrophero-grams though less than two dozen (which also have been the subject of debate among analysts for years) have been alluded to in the peer-reviewed literature to date. Most current fully continuous probabilistic geno-typing approaches rely upon computationally intensive Markov Chain Monte Carlo (MCMC) analyses of the data associated with evidence samples. Analyses of samples can easily take hours or even days to complete.

The forensic DNA profiling community has been engaged in vigorous debate for many years about the most appropriate way to recognize and take into account a number of features that might be utilized by fully continuous probabilistic genotyping approaches. Among these contentious issues is the most appropriate way to distinguish between signal and noise with proposed solutions ranging from: run-specific, statistically based limits of detection and quantitation [30] to static limits of detection and quantitation [31] to stochastic and analytical thresholds rooted in template quantities and sampling error considerations to arbitrary minimum peak height thresholds. A significant challenge to fully continuous probabilistic geno-typing is the lack of consensus within the scientific community about which of a number of possible solutions is correct. In those instances where the forensic science community cannot be persuaded that a particular approach is correct, it will not be possible for a probabilistic genotyping algorithm that uses that approach to reasonably assert that that probabilistic genotyping approach itself is generally accepted. And, if a probabilistic genotyping approach professes to have finally solved the difficult issue of distinguishing between signal and noise in DNA test results it would be irresponsible for that solution to not be shared in the peer-reviewed literature so that it could be applied by those using conventional approaches to interpret test results.

Debates similar to those regarding signal and noise continue to a greater or a lesser extent for many of the features of a test result that a human analyst or a continuous probabilistic genotyping approach might consider. A partial list includes the implications and recognition of both $n-1$ and $n+1$ (for consistency with other articles) stutter artifacts; peak height balance/imbalance thresholds; peak height addition; peak height measurement variability; recognition of commonly encountered artifacts such as "pull-up/bleed through", "spikes", and "blobs"; laboratory error rates; and intra- and interlocus drop-out/in rates. It is reasonable to expect that many of these features will be highly correlated and that they should be given very different relative weights in different circumstances [32]. Probabilistic genotyping approaches will need to disclose not only which features are considered but specifically how they are utilized in order for them to achieve general acceptance.

These on-going debates have little if any impact on the interpretation of some samples (e.g., unmixed, complete profiles from human remains from mass disasters or genocides). Probabilistic genotyping approaches could significantly increase laboratory throughput by being used to characterize such samples, thereby freeing human analysts to focus their attention on more difficult test results (e.g., complicated mixtures with degradation/inhibition). However, when human experts agree that a test result is "not suitable for interpretation" or "inconclusive", it is unsafe to invoke probabilistic genotyping approaches until all these issues have been resolved.

Proponents of some fully continuous probabilistic genotyping approaches such as STRMix [33–35] and TrueAllele [36–38] have suggested that validation studies that show that their approaches consistently arrive at correct conclusions are sufficient to ensure the reliability of their approaches. That position is at odds, however, with the long-standing expectation both in forensic science and other disciplines such as computer science that validation studies are primarily intended to determine the boundaries beyond which

an approach cannot be expected to generate reliable results. Validation results cannot be extrapolated to say that a method can generate a reliable interpretation for all manner of samples. No validation study could be performed to demonstrate that a probabilistic genotyping approach is "fit for all purposes". Instead, they need to deliver explicit limits such as "while output for up to three-person mixtures and where degradation/inhibition has not occurred are correct for more than 99% of samples, this approach is presently not suitable for use with: mixtures of four or more individuals, where degradation/inhibition may have occurred, or where close relatives may have been contributors to a mixed sample."

Among the boundaries that need to be explored separately and in concert are the number of contributors to a sample (the larger the number of contributors, the more computationally challenging an evaluation), the degree of degradation/inhibition of the DNA from each of the contributors to a sample, the degree of relatedness of possible contributors to a sample (a match probability for a pair of siblings to a sample will be much less impressive than for a pair of unrelated individuals), and the quantity of useful information in a test result (some samples simply will not have appreciably more information associated with them than negative controls and reagent blanks). Validation studies with dozens or even hundreds of samples cannot suffice given that evidence samples come in a very wide variety (of number of contributors, degrees of degradation, and mixture ratios) and are unlikely to be well represented in any validation work.

It is important to note that there is no correct answer to the likelihood ratios generated by probabilistic genotyping approaches for any given sample. It should not be surprising that two different approaches generate different likelihood ratios because they may be addressing different questions and they may be expressing different levels of confidence given the features they are evaluating. Proponents of probabilistic genotyping software packages should scrupulously avoid succumbing to market pressures to have their programs simply "get bigger numbers". [39]

Black Boxes and Due Process: Transparency in Expert Software Systems

Software has generally been used to assist the analysis of forensic evidence via two main routes: data visualization (such as spectrograms or electropherograms) and statistical calculations (such as PopStats and GenoStat®). Both of these routes have served primarily to expedite the work performed by human experts during their evaluations of complex data sets.

Methods for conventional analysis of evidence such as breath alcohol or DNA (and even ballot counting) are widely known, take a specific set of known input values, and produce results that can be independently confirmed by other experts using generally accepted approaches. Processes performed by humans are inherently subject to review by other humans. Human experts are rightly required to testify as to the validity of their conclusions by revealing their underlying measurements, calculations, and approaches.

Advances in our understanding of complex chemical and biological processes, statistics, and computational methods have brought us to the cusp of a new era – the development of expert software systems intended to evaluate evidence that cannot be interpreted by conventional human analysis. Where forensic scientists might summarize test results as "uninterpretable" or "inconclusive", expert software systems have begun to provide very definitive conclusions. This evolution of the use of software (from improving workflow to actually interpreting evidence) has critically important implications for the criminal justice system.

When computer software rather than human experts make decisions regarding the evaluation of evidence, an effective review of these software systems is required in order to fully evaluate the performance of the system. Expert systems must, necessarily, incorporate assumptions about the operating characteristics of the tests being evaluated. The accuracy of the conclusions reached by these systems depends on the accuracy of those underlying assumptions – *and* their implementation. If independent experts cannot identify those assumptions (ideally, by examining the underlying source code), then it is very difficult to assess the reliability of the expert systems. An early proof of this point came from an in-depth, independent review of the source code used by the Alcotest 7110 MKIII-C breath alcohol analyzer software (not even an expert system). The use of this software as an unscrutinized "black box" allowed simple programming mistakes to go undetected for years.

Unlike human analysts who can sometimes struggle to explain how their approaches are objective and based on experimentally validated rules, expert systems have the distinct advantage of being based

on source code that unambiguously details the exact means by which they arrive at conclusions. If an adversary objects to some portion of an expert system's approach to solving a problem, it should be possible to scrutinize the validation study, algorithm, or source code and to precisely identify the basis of the disagreement. While it may be difficult to critically review the source code of some expert systems, failure to have the opportunity to review the entire basis of an expert computer system's conclusions raises serious and legitimate concerns about due process. Lack of access in these contexts operates, in essence, as a failure to fully have the opportunity to understand or confront significant, perhaps even the most significant, evidence in a case. Expert software systems must be held to the same standards of transparency that we have come to expect of human experts.

If the source code of a black box system were disclosed, the box would be open to independent scrutiny. The main justification for maintaining black box software is the protection of intellectual property. Courts will need to decide whether the desire for secrecy (in order to protect a perceived commercial advantage) outweighs the right of defendants to fully examine the evidence against them.

References

[1] Edwards, A., Hammond, H.A., Lin, J., Caskey, C.T. & Chakraborty, R. (1992). Genetic variation at five trimeric and tetrameric tandem repeat loci in four human population groups, *Genomics* **12**, 241–53.

[2] Frégeau, C.J. & Fourney, R.M. (1993). DNA typing with fluorescently tagged short tandem repeats: a sensitive and accurate approach to human identification, *BioTechniques* **15**, 100–19.

[3] Kimpton, C.P., Gill, P., Walton, A., Millican, E.S. & Adams, M. (1993). Automated DNA profiling employing multiplex amplification of short tandem repeat loci, *PCR Meth. App.* **3**, 13–22.

[4] National Resource Council (NRC) (1996). *The evaluation of forensic DNA evidence*, National Academy Press, Washington DC.

[5] Paoletti, D.R., Doom, T.E., Krane, C.M., Raymer, M.L. & Krane, D.E. (2005). Empirical analysis of the STR profiles resulting from conceptual mixtures, *Journal of Forest Science* **50**(6), 1361–1366.

[6] Devlin, B. (1992). Forensic inference from genetic markers, *Statistical Methods in Medical Research* **2**, 241–262.

[7] Ladd, C., Lee, H., Beiber, F., Probability of exclusion estimates in forensic analysis of complex DNA mixtures. In Proceedings of the American Academy of Forensic Sciences 52nd annual meeting. 2000.

[8] Butler, J.M. (2005). *Forensic DNA typing*, 2nd Edition, Academic Press, San Diego.

[9] Budowle, B., Moretti, T.R., Baumstark, A.L., Defenbaugh, D.A. & Keys, K.M. (1999). Population data on the thirteen CODIS core short tandem repeat loci in African Americans, U.S. Caucasians, Hispanics, Bahamians, Jamaicans, and Trinidadians, *Journal of Forest Science* **44**(6), 1277–1286.

[10] Curran, J.M., Triggs, C.M., Buckleton, J. & Weir, B.S. (1999). Interpreting DNA mixtures in structured populations, *Journal of Forest Science* **44**(5), 987–995.

[11] Evett, I.W., Gill, P.D. & Lambert, J.A. (1998). Taking account of peak areas when interpreting mixed DNA profiles, *Journal of Forest Science* **42**(1), 62–69.

[12] Evett, I.W., Foreman, L.A., Lambert, J.A. & Emes, A.E. (1998). Using a tree diagram to interpret a mixed DNA profile, *Journal of Forest Science* **43**(3), 472–476.

[13] Gill, P., Sparkes, R., Pinchin, R., Clayton, T.M., Whitacker, J.P. & Buckleton, J. (1998). Interpreting simple STR mixtures using allele peak area, *Forensic Science International* **91**, 41–53.

[14] Clayton, T.M., Whitaker, J.P., Sparkes, R. & Gill, P. (1998). Analysis and interpretation of mixed forensic stains using DNA STR profiling, *Forensic Science International* **91**, 55–70.

[15] Perlin, M.W. & Szabady, B. (2001). Linear mixture analysis: a mathematical approach to resolving mixed DNA samples, *Journal of Forest Science* **46**(6), 1372–1378.

[16] Wang, T., Xue, N., Rader, M., Birdwell, J.D., Least Square Deconvolution (LSD) of STR/DNA mixtures. Association of Forensic DNA Analysts and Administrators Winter Meeting. January 17-18, 2001. Austin, TX.

[17] Weir, B.S., Triggs, C.M., Starling, L., Stowell, L.I., Walsh, K.A.J. & Buckleton, J. (1997). Interpreting DNA mixtures, *Journal of Forest Science* **42**(2), 213–222.

[18] Frank, W.E., Llewellyn, B.E., Fish, P.A., Riech, A.K., Marcacci, T.L., Gandor, D.W., Parker, D., Carter, R.R. & Thibault, S.M. (2001). Validation of the AmpFLSTR™ Profiler Plus PCR amplification kit for use in forensic casework, *Journal of Forest Science* **46**(3), 642–646.

[19] Holt, C.L., Buoncristiani, M., Wallin, J.M., Nguyen, T., Lazaruk, K.D. & Walsh, P.S. (2002). TWGDAM validation of AmpFLSTR™ PCR amplification kits for forensic DNA casework, *Journal of Forest Science* **47**(1), 66–96.

[20] Leclair, B., Frégeau, C.J., Bowen, K.L. & Fourney, R.M. (2004). Systematic analysis of stutter percentages and allele peak height and peak area ratios at heterozygous STR loci for forensic casework and database samples, *Journal of Forest Science* **49**(5), 1–13.

[21] Perkin-Elmer, Applied Biosystems AmpFlSTR Profiler Plus PCR amplification kit user's manual. Foster City:1997.

[22] Perlin, M.W., US Patent No. 5876933. Washington, DC: U.S. Patent and Trademark Office. 1999.

[23] Puch-Solis, R., Rodgers, L., Mazumder, A., Pope, S. & Evett, I. (2013). Evaluating forensic DNA profiles using peak heights, allowing for multiple donors, allelic dropout and stutters, *Forensic Science International: Genetics* **7**, 555–63.

[24] Curran, J.M. & Buckleton, J. (2010). Inclusion probabilities and dropout, *Journal of Forest Science* **55**(5),

[25] Gill, P., Kirkham, A. & Curran, J. (2007). LoComationN: A software tool for the analysis of low copy number DNA profiles, *Forensic Science International* **166**, 128–38.

[26] Balding, D. (2013). Evaluation of mixed-source, low-template DNA profiles in forensic science, *PNAS* **110**(30), 12241–12246.

[27] Mitchell, A.A., Tamariz, J., O'Connell, K., Ducasse, N. & Budimlija, Z. (2012). Validation of a DNA mixture statistics tool incorporating allelic drop-out and drop-in, *Forensic Science International: Genetics* **6**, 749–761.

[28] Lohmueller, K. & Rudin, N. (2012). Calculating the weight of evidence in low-template forensic DNA casework, *Journal of Forest Science* **12017**, 1–7.

[29] Grgcak, C.M., Urban, Z.M. & Cotton, R.W. (2010). Investigation of reproducibility and error associated with qPCR methods using Quantifiler® Duo DNA Quantification kit, *Journal of Forest Science* **55**(5), 1331–1339.

[30] Gilder, J., Doom, T., Inman, K. & Krane, D. (2007). Run-specific limits of detection and quantitation for STR-based DNA testing, *Journal of Forest Science* **52**(1), 97–101.

[31] http://www.dfs.virginia.gov/wp-content/uploads/2014/08/210-D1100-FB-PM-VIII-Capillary-Electrophoresis.pdf

[32] Gill, P., Brenner, C.H., Buckleton, J.S., Carracedo, A., Krawczak, M., Mayr, W.R., Morling, N., Prinz, M., Scheider, P.M. & Weir, B.S. (2006). DNA Commission of the International Society of Forensic Genetics: Recommendations on the interpretation of mixtures, *Forensic Science International* **160**, 90–101.

[33] Bright, J.A., Taylor, D., Curran, J. & Buckleton, J. (2013). Degradation of forensic DNA profiles, *Australian Journal of Forensic Sciences* **45**(4), 445–449.

[34] Bright, J.A., Curran, D. & Buckleton, J. (2013). Developing allelic and stutter peak height models for a continuous method of DNA interpretation, *Forensic Science International: Genetics* **7**, 296–304.

[35] Taylor, D., Bright, J.A. & Buckleton, J. (2013). The interpretation of single source and mixed DNA profiles, *Forensic Science International: Genetics* **7**, 516–528.

[36] Perlin, M.W., Sinelnikov, A. An information gap in DNA evidence interpretation. *PLoS One* **4**:e8327

[37] Perlin, M.W., Legler, N.M., Spencer, C.E., Smith, J.L. & Allan, W.P. (2011). Validating TrueAlleleQR mixture interpretation, *Journal of Forensic Science* **56**, 1430–47.

[38] Perlin, M.W. & Belrose, J.L. (2013). B.W Duceman. New York State TrueAllele casework validation study, *Journal of Forensic Science* **58**, 1458–1466.

[39] Coble, M., Mixture Interpretation Using Probabilistic Genotyping. Science, Cell Phones & Social Media – Finding & Using Evidence of Innocence in Post-Conviction Cases. Orlando, National Association of Criminal Defense Lawyers, April 30, 2015.

Chapter 16
Degraded Samples

Jason R. Gilder

Forensic Bioinformatics, Fairborn, OH, USA

Introduction

DNA is a relatively stable macromolecule and under certain circumstances has been known to persist for tens of thousands of years (*see* **DNA**; **Mitochondrial DNA: Profiling**) [1–3]. Samples of human DNA that are decades [4–6] and even centuries [2] old have been amenable to genotyping for forensic purposes as well. However, the environmental conditions to which most evidentiary samples are exposed are usually much less conducive to the preservation of the information content of DNA molecules. Exposure to UV irradiation from sunlight, as well as to warm, moist environments, has been found to result in degradation of DNA within a matter of hours [7]. Evidence samples that begin with only trace amounts of DNA are particularly at risk of only being partially detected due to degradation and/or inhibition of polymerase chain reaction (PCR) amplification.

Characteristics of Degraded DNA Samples

It has been widely observed that alleles corresponding to larger fragments of DNA typically exhibit weaker signals/intensity than smaller alleles after exposure to some environments, ostensibly because they provide a larger target for damage to be accumulated [1].

In the absence of degradation and stochastic effects because of small sample sizes, the amount of genomic template associated with any given locus in an evidence sample should be equivalent (stoichiometric). Given that the amount of product generated during PCR amplification is generally proportional to the amount of starting template in multiplex reactions [8], total peak height, or area between alleles and loci should be roughly equivalent. As a result, progressively falling peak heights from small to large (left to right) DNA fragments on electropherograms are commonly considered by forensic DNA testing laboratories to be an indication of degradation (Figure 1). However, the absence of laboratory quantitative thresholds associated with these trends has made declarations of degradation subjective and commonly supported simply by an examiner's past training and experience. Difficulties in distinguishing between the effects of physical damage to DNA molecules, the presence of chemicals that inhibit the PCR process [9, 10], and the fact that smaller DNA fragments are more efficiently amplified than larger ones during the PCR process [8] have complicated efforts to develop objective standards of identifying degradation.

Objectively Identifying Potential Degradation/Inhibition

The downward slope characterizing degraded or inhibited single-source samples can be measured. First, a best-fit linear regression through the heights of the peaks is drawn [11]. The data collection point is the position on the x-axis and the height of the peak is the position on the y-axis (homozygotes are divided in half). A slope is then calculated for the angle of the regression line and compared to a population of non-degraded samples (a collection of positive controls whose slopes have been separately calculated). If a given sample falls outside of the population of nondegraded samples at a given level of significance (e.g., $\alpha = 0.05$), then it can be flagged as being potentially degraded or inhibited. Such samples should be evaluated to determine the potential for allelic dropout,

A Guide to Forensic DNA Profiling
Edited by Allan Jamieson and Scott Bader
© 2016 John Wiley & Sons, Ltd. ISBN: 9781118751527
Also published in EFS (online edition)
DOI: 10.1002/9780470061589.fsa522.pub2

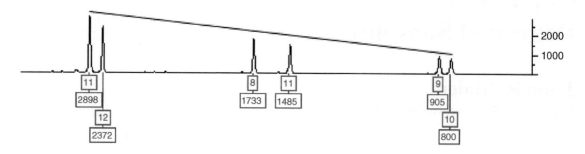

Figure 1   An electropherogram exhibiting signs of degradation or inhibition. Degradation and inhibition are marked by observing progressively falling peak heights as the size of the DNA product increases (left to right)

reduced assumptions for mixture components, and other issues.

Mini-STRs

A new set of mini-short tandem repeat (STR) primers have been developed to address the issue of degradation [12]. The distance between the primer sequence and the STR repeats has been shortened so that the amplified DNA product is significantly smaller. Smaller amplicons are less likely to be affected by the effects of degradation and inhibition. Life Technologies (formerly Applied Biosystems) produces the MiniFiler™ test kit, which examines eight of the STR loci (D13S317, D7S820, D2S1338, D21S11, D16S539, D18S51, CSF1PO, and FGA) and the sex-determining locus Amelogenin [13]. All of the MiniFiler™ amplicon sizes are less than 300 bp. More recently, Life Technologies released their Global-Filer™ test kit, which evaluates 21 STR loci, a Y-STR (DYS391), the sex-determining locus Amelogenin, and a Y chromosomal indel marker used to help eliminate the possibility of detecting the presence of a Y chromosome [14]. GlobalFiler® includes 10 Mini-STR loci (D3S1358, TH01, D13S317, D19S433, vWA, D5S818, D10S1248, D22S1045, D2S441, and D1S1656) and an optimized buffer to reduce inhibition.

Mini-STRs can successfully detect alleles in some degraded samples, but the tests present their own challenges [13]. In some instances, the Mini-STR primer sets have revealed primer binding site mutations, in which the PCR primer cannot effectively bind to the sample. A primer binding site mutation can result in either a reduced number of allele copies (creating a peak height imbalance) or the failure to copy the

allele altogether (null alleles). In addition, it is possible to produce slightly different testing results between a traditional STR testing kit and one that employs Mini-STR loci. In some instances, there is a 4 bp deletion in the region between the standard STR primer sequence and the beginning of the Mini-STR primer sequence. In those cases, the reported allele from a traditional STR kit would be one less than what would be reported by a Mini-STR kit. For example, an Identifiler® test at the locus D13S317 might produce a profile of (8, 10), whereas the MiniFiler™ test kit might produce a profile of (9, 10) or (8, 11). A study comparing the results of 532 US population samples between the Identifiler® and MiniFiler™ test kits found 15 discrepancies in the 6384 genotypes compared [13].

Y-STR Testing

Y-STR testing identifies the male contribution to a sample by targeting the Y chromosome (*see Y-Chromosome Short Tandem Repeats*). Y-STR testing also has the feature of producing small amplicons for a subset of the tested loci. For example, 6 of the 17 loci examined by the Applied Biosystems Yfiler® test kit produces product sizes less than 200 bp (DYS456, DYS389I, DYS458, DYS393, DYS391, and YGATAH4) [15]. Therefore, Y-STR testing may be a reasonable alternative when working with degraded samples (at the cost of less probative results).

Low Copy Number Testing

Samples containing low amounts of DNA often exhibit signs of degradation. However, it is not recommended that Mini-STRs or Y-STRs be used to alleviate the issues observed in the analysis of low copy number (LCN) DNA samples. Both the Yfiler and MiniFiler™ test kits recommend a minimum starting template of 0.5 ng. The GlobalFiler™ kit recommends an optimal starting template of 1 ng. Using less than the recommended amount of input DNA can still produce results at or below the stochastic threshold. The issues present with standard LCN DNA test results may still be observed, including allelic dropout, allelic drop-in, exaggerated stutter, and exaggerated peak height imbalance.

Addressing Inhibition

In some instances, it may be possible to distinguish between the effects of degradation and inhibition in that further purification of template DNA followed by reamplification can remedy problems associated with the presence of inhibitors. It is also possible that new extraction and amplification strategies will minimize the trends observed in peak heights for degraded/inhibited samples analyzed with currently popular methods [16]. Reformulation of the buffer in modern STR testing kits has helped reduce the frequency of inhibition [14].

Electropherograms can also appear degraded if the amplification mix is created improperly. Adding too little Taq polymerase can result in a profile that appears to be degraded. Adding too much EDTA in TE buffer can sequester the magnesium ions, turning off the Taq, and again creating a profile that appears to be degraded or inhibited. Further, adding too much template DNA will cause the PCR reagents to compete for template strands. The shorter fragments will be preferentially amplified, again resulting in a profile that appears to be degraded or inhibited [8]. All of these issues can be identified by comparing the samples with the controls and references run in the same amplification. If the other samples appear to be normal, then it is likely the amplification setup is correct. In addition, reamplification can rectify the appearance of degradation or inhibition.

The Coroner's Inquest into the Death of Jaidyn Leskie

The Victoria Police Forensic Services Centre in Australia used the Profiler Plus® test kit to generate STR DNA profiles from two evidentiary samples associated with the deceased [17]. The DNA profiles that were detected were subsequently found to be consistent with the DNA profile of a rape victim associated with a distinctly separate investigation for which DNA testing was performed by the same laboratory less than 1 week earlier. Evidence at the inquest suggested that the rape victim could not have been involved in the death of Jaidyn Leskie. The testing laboratory suggested that the correspondence between DNA profiles of at least seven (and as many as 12, after additional testing and review) STR loci associated with the evidence samples in the two cases may be a result of an "adventitious" (coincidental) match rather than due to contamination between the two analyses.

The small quantities of template available for PCR amplification from the investigation samples associated with the deceased, coupled with apparent degradation/inhibition resulted in several peaks associated with the largest amplification products falling below 200 relative fluorescent units (RFUs). One issue raised during the course of the Coroner's inquest was whether the most likely source of contamination from the rape investigation (an unmixed sample of the complainant on a condom) also qualified as being degraded/inhibited.

Comparison of the trends in peak height versus data collection point for the condom sample (Figure 2) were found to be significantly different than those of the sampling of 164 ostensibly nondegraded/inhibited positive control samples or the positive control associated with the rape investigation. The condom falls below the threshold for variance in the sampling of positive controls at the $\alpha = 0.01$ level. Thus, there is less than a 1% chance that a sample consistent with the sampling of positive controls (and thus presumably undegraded) would, by chance, exhibit the significant difference noted in the condom.

The Coroner ruled that the DNA testing result in the Leskie investigation was caused by contamination:

> The match to the bib occurred as a result of contamination in the laboratory and was not an adventitious match. The samples from the two cases were examined by the same scientist within a close time frame [17].

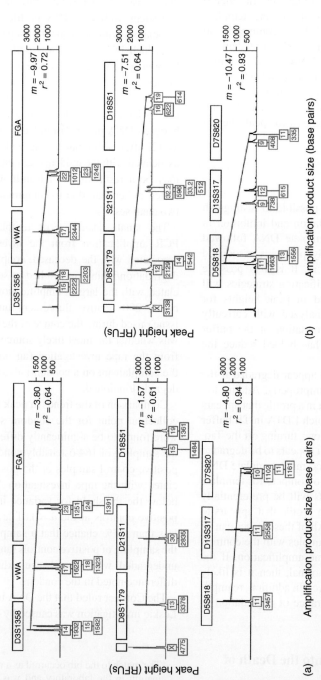

Figure 2 Electropherograms associated with a high-quality genomic DNA template (a) and with the condom sample from the rape investigation (b) that qualifies as being inconsistent with the sampling of positive controls

Conclusions

Degradation and inhibition are common issues encountered during the course of forensic DNA casework review. Peak height is no longer a reliable measure of the relative quantities of DNA and the risk of allelic dropout is greatly increased. Objective measures can be used to identify when a sample may be subject to degradation or inhibition based on linear regression slopes using the electropherogram. Inhibitors can be removed with an added purification step during the amplification process. Newer technologies like Mini-STRs and some Y-STR profiling kits have the ability to resolve some DNA profiles that have been compromised by degradation. No matter how a degraded profile is resolved, the analyst must consider a variety of alternative interpretations (and have those additional alternatives reflected in a lessening of the statistical weight associated with an evidence sample).

References

[1] Handt, O., Hoss, M., Krings, M. & Paabo, S. (1994). Ancient DNA: methodological challenges, *Experientia* **50**(6), 524–529.

[2] von Wurmb-Schwark, N., Harbeck, M., Wiesbrock, U., Schroeder, I., Ritz-Timme, S. & Oehmichen, M. (2003). Extraction and amplification of nuclear and mitochondrial DNA from ancient and artificially aged bones, *Legal Medicine (Tokyo)* **5**(1), S169–S172.

[3] Poinar Jr, G.O. (1994). The range of life in amber: significance and implications in DNA studies, *Experientia* **50**(6), 536–542.

[4] Kevles, D.J. (2003). Ownership and identity, *The Scientist* **17**(1), 22.

[5] Gill, P., Ivanov, P.L., Kimpton, C., Piercy, R., Benson, N., Tully, G., Evett, I., Hagelberg, E. & Sullivan, K. (1994). Identification of the remains of the Romanov family by DNA analysis, *Nature Genetics* **6**, 130–135.

[6] Ivanov, P.L., Wadhams, M.J., Roby, R.K., Holland, M.M., Weedn, V.W. & Parsons, T.J. (1996). Mitochondrial DNA sequence heteroplasmy in the Grand Duke of Russia Georgij Romanov establishes the authenticity of the remains of Tsar Nicholas II, *Nature Genetics* **12**(4), 417–420.

[7] Adams, D.E., Presley, L.A., Baumstark, A.L., Hensley, K.W., Hill, A.L., Anoe, K.S., Campbell, P.A., McLaughlin, C.M., Budowle, B., Giusti, A.M., Smerick, J.B. & Baechtel, F.S. (1991). Deoxyribonucleic acid (DNA) analysis by restriction fragment length polymorphisms of blood and other body fluid stains subjected to contamination and environmental insults, *Journal of Forensic Science* **36**(5), 1284–1298.

[8] Walsh, P.S., Erlich, H.A. & Higuchi, R. (1992). Preferential PCR amplification of alleles: mechanisms and solutions, *PCR Methods and Applications* **1**, 241–250.

[9] DeFranchis, R., Cross, N.C.P., Foulkes, N.S. & Cox, T.M. (1988). A potent inhibitor of Taq polymerase copurifies with human genomic DNA, *Nucleic Acids Research* **16**(21), 10355.

[10] Akane, A., Matsubara, K., Nakamura, H., Takahashi, S. & Kimura, K. (1994). Identification of the heme compound copurified with deoxyribonucleic acid (DNA) from bloodstains, a major inhibitor of polymerase chain reaction (PCR) amplification, *Journal of Forensic Science* **39**(2), 362–372.

[11] Draper, N.R. & Smith, H. (1998). *Applied Regression Analysis*, Wiley Series in Probability and Statistics.

[12] Coble, M.D. & Butler, J.M. (2005). Characterization of new MiniSTR loci to aid analysis of degraded DNA, *Journal of Forensic Science* **50**(1), 43–53.

[13] Hill, C.R., Kline, M.C., Mulero, J.J., Lagace, R.E., Chang, C.W., Hennessy, L.K. & Butler, J.M. (2007). Concordance study between the AmpFlSTR MiniFiler PCR amplification kit and conventional STR typing kits, *Journal of Forensic Science* **52**(4), 870–3.

[14] Martin, P., de Simon, L.F., Luque, G., Farfan, M.J. & Alonso, A. (2014). Improving DNA data exchange: validation studies on a single 6 dye STR kit with 24 loci, *Forensic Science International: Genetics* **13C**, 68–78.

[15] Mulero, J.J., Chang, C.W., Calandro, L.M., Green, R.L., Li, Y., Johnson, C.L. & Hennessy, L.K. (2006). Development and validation of the AmpFlSTR® Yfiler™ PCR amplification kit: a male specific single amplification 17 Y-STR multiplex system, *Journal of Forensic Science* **51**(1), 64–75.

[16] Schmerer, W.M., Hummel, S. & Herrmann, B. (1999). Optimized DNA extraction to improve reproducibility of short tandem repeat genotyping with highly degraded DNA as target, *Electrophoresis* **20**(8), 1712–1716.

[17] G. Johnstone, Inquest into the death of Jaidyn Raymond Leskie. Coroner's Case Number: 007/98. July 31, 2006.

Related Articles in EFS Online

Archaeology

Chapter 17
Ceiling Principle: DNA

Simon J. Walsh

Australian Federal Police, Canberra, ACT, Australia

Introduction

The National Research Council (NRC) committee was assembled in 1990 to assess the general applicability and suitability of using DNA technology in forensic science. The NRC Report [1] provided recommendations in six areas related to the DNA typing process: technical issues, statistical interpretation, laboratory standards, databanks and privacy, legal issues, and societal and ethical issues.

Assessing the probability of observing a particular multilocus genotype is a pursuit that is only attempted in forensic science. At the time of the NRC deliberations, this was already a controversial issue and a fundamental reason for the committee's existence. However, the NRC recommendations in the area of statistical interpretation actually provoked further controversy, rather than allaying it. Arguably the most controversial recommendations were those known as the *ceiling principle* and *interim ceiling principle*.

Much of the early debate surrounding DNA evidence interpretation involved the need to account for population substructure in statistical estimates. Owing to population-level differences in allele frequencies, statistical estimates can vary depending upon the source of population data. In a criminal case it is not usually known what database is the most appropriate to apply as this depends on, firstly, being able to assess the community of persons that had opportunity to commit the crime, and secondly, to have access to a representative database of this community.

At its simplest, it was the belief in population heterogeneity and its potentially discriminating effect on statistical evidence that led to the justification for the ceiling principle. It was believed that the ceiling principle would yield conservative estimates, even for a substructured population, provided the allele frequencies used in the calculation exceed the allele frequencies in any of the population subgroups. To apply the ceiling principle, the upper bound for the frequency of each allele is required, irrespective of the population of origin. The largest frequency in any of these populations, or a fixed figure of 5%, whichever is larger, should be taken as the ceiling frequency. The ceiling frequencies are then multiplied using the product rule to obtain the genotype frequency. This product of maximal frequency values serves as an upper bound for the product of all other unknown frequencies. To determine the frequencies themselves, the NRC recommended that random samples of 100 persons be drawn from each of 15–20 populations that each represents a relatively homogeneous genetic group.

Both the population genetic and statistical basis of the ceiling principle recommendation and the study proposed by the NRC were subsequently criticized in the literature (see for example [2–6]). It also caused conjecture in court by undermining the use of population-specific estimates [7, 8] or provoking significant controversy that it failed the general acceptance test and was ruled inadmissible [9]. In the second report produced by the NRC [10], the ceiling method was described as unnecessarily conservative and was abandoned in favor of recommended methods to obtain population-specific frequency estimates that account for population subdivision.

A Guide to Forensic DNA Profiling
Edited by Allan Jamieson and Scott Bader
© 2016 John Wiley & Sons, Ltd. ISBN: 9781118751527
Also published in EFS (online edition)
DOI: 10.1002/9780470061589.fsa593

References

[1] National Research Council (1992). *National Research Council Report: DNA Technology in Forensic Science*, National Academy Press, Washington, DC.

[2] Weir, B.S. (1992). Population genetics in the forensic DNA debate, *Proceedings of the National Academy of Science, USA* **89**, 11654–11659.

[3] Weir, B.S. (1993). Forensic population genetics and the NRC, *American Journal of Human Genetics* **52**, 437–439.

[4] Devlin, B., Risch, N. & Roeder, K. (1994). Comments on the statistical aspects of the NRC's report on DNA typing, *Journal of Forensic Sciences* **39**(1), 28–40.

[5] Cohen, J.E. (1992). The ceiling principle is not always conservative in assigning genotype frequencies for forensic DNA testing, *American Journal of Human Genetics* **51**(5), 1165–1168.

[6] Slimowitz, J.R. & Cohen, J.E. (1993). Violations of the ceiling principle: exact conditions and statistical evidence, *American Journal of Human Genetics* **53**, 314–323.

[7] State v. Sivri, 646 A.2d 169 (Conn. 1994).

[8] State v. Carter, 246 Neb. 953, 524 N.W.2d 763 (1994).

[9] People v. Wallace, 14 Cal. App. 4th 651, 17 Cal. Rptr. 2d 721 (1993).

[10] National Research Council (1996). *National Research Council Report: The Evaluation of Forensic DNA Evidence*, National Academy Press, Washington, DC.

Related Articles in EFS Online

Interpreting Expert Opinions: History of

Chapter 18
Y-Chromosome Short Tandem Repeats

Jack Ballantyne and Erin K. Hanson

University of Central Florida and National Center for Forensic Science, Orlando, FL, USA

Introduction

The physical map of the Y chromosome consists of three distinct regions: the euchromatin, the heterochromatin and pseudoautosomal regions (PARs). The PARs are located at the telomeric ends of the chromosome and constitute ~5% of the Y chromosome sequence. PARs are the only regions of the chromosome to undergo recombination with the X chromosome during male meiotic events. The remaining 95% of the Y chromosome does not undergo recombination referred to as the nonrecombining region of the Y chromosomes (*NRY*) and comprises euchromatin sequences (that contain all of the chromosome's known genes) and the functionally inert heterochromatin. Thus, the entire NRY is inherited in a patrilinear manner, with a haplotype of physically and genetically linked genetic markers passed essentially unchanged, barring any rare mutations, from father to son [1].

The unique biology of the genetic markers present on the NRY region has resulted in their widespread use in determining patrilineal relationships within and between populations to aid in understanding of human migration and evolution [2, 3]. Y-chromosome microsatellites or short tandem repeats (STRs) are one class of these genetic markers that have been incorporated into a variety of multiplex PCR assays for potential forensic casework applications [4–12]. Their intended use is not to replace autosomal STR loci but to employ them in casework situations in which the traditional autosomal loci would not be expected to yield sufficient probative information. For example, Y-chromosome short tandem repeats

(Y-STRs) are particularly useful for cases involving admixed male and female DNA for which a separation of the male- and female-derived cells is unsuccessful or not feasible [13–15].

Commonly Used Y-STR Markers

A major international multicenter study of 13 candidate Y-STR markers resulted in recommendations for the use of nine core loci for standard forensic haplotyping [3]. These loci are referred to as the minimal haplotype loci (*MHL*), and include DYS19, DYS385 (a) and (b), DYS389 (I and II), DYS390, DYS391, DYS392, and DYS393 (*see Mini-STRs* for a description of the naming conventions for different loci and alleles). Despite the initial utility of this set of markers in forensic casework, there was a need for additional Y-STR loci to be used in conjunction with these markers to improve the discriminatory capacity of Y-STR testing. In 2003, the use of two additional loci, DYS438 and DYS439, was recommended by the Scientific Working Group on DNA Analysis Methods (SWGDAM) [16]. The MHL loci plus the two additional loci are referred to as the "SWGDAM core loci."

Various combinations of the common Y-STR loci have been incorporated into commercially available multiplex systems (Table 1) [6, 7, 10–12]. The Promega PowerPlex® Y kit, which contains the SWDGAM core loci plus DYS437, and the Applied Biosystems AmpF*l*STR® Yfiler™ kit, which also contains the SWGDAM core loci plus several additional markers (DYS437, DYS448, DYS456, DYS458, C4 (DYS635), and H4) are two of the most commonly used multiplex kits in the US [6, 7]. Figure 1 gives an example of a 17-locus Y-STR profile from an individual obtained using the Yfiler™ kit. Three additional Y-STR systems were developed by Reliagene

A Guide to Forensic DNA Profiling
Edited by Allan Jamieson and Scott Bader
© 2016 John Wiley & Sons, Ltd. ISBN: 9781118751527
Also published in EFS (online edition)
DOI: 10.1002/9780470061589.fsa120

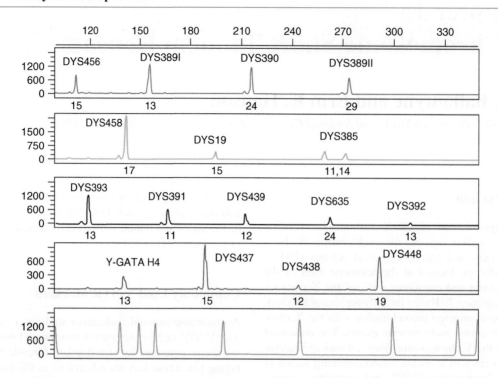

Figure 1   Y-STR profile using the Applied Biosystems AmpF*l*STR® Yfiler™ Amplification Kit. 17 Y-STR loci are coamplified in a single reaction, separated by capillary electrophoresis, and displayed as an electropherogram. The *x* axis represents fragment size (base pairs) and the *y* axis represents signal intensity (relative fluorescence intensity (RFU)). Each locus is labeled with a fluorescent dye: top channel – 6-FAM (blue); second channel – VIC (green); third channel – NED (black); fourth channel – PET (red); bottom channel – LIZ (orange) – internal size standard

Table 1   Commercial Y-STR Multiplex Amplification Kits

Commercial kit	Manufacturer	Incorporated loci
Commonly used commercial kits		
PowerPlex® Y	Promega Corporation, Madison, WI, USA	DYS19, DYS385a/b, DYS389I, DYS389II, DYS390, DYS391, DYS392, DYS393, DYS437, DYS438, DYS439
AmpF*l*STR® Yfiler™	Applied Biosystems, Foster City, CA, USA	DYS19, DYS385a/b, DYS389I, DYS389II, DYS390, DYS391, DYS392, DYS393, DYS437, DYS438, DYS439, DYS456, DYS458, DYS448, DYS635(C4), H4
Previously available commercial kits		
Y-Plex™ 5	Reliagene Technologies Inc., New Orleans, LA, USA	DYS19, DYS385a/b, DYS389II, DYS390, DYS391, DYS393
Y-Plex™ 6	Reliagene	DYS389I, DYS389II, DYS392, DYS393, DYS438, DYS439
Y-Plex™12	Reliagene	DYS19, DYS385a/b, DYS389I, DYS389II; DYS390, DYS391, DYS392, DYS393, DYS437, DYS438, DYS439

Technologies (Y-Plex™ 5, Y-Plex™ 6, and Y-Plex™ 12) but are no longer commercially available [10–12]. All of these kits have been fully validated for forensic use as required by US national DNA standards and in accordance with SWGDAM validation guidelines [6, 7, 10–12]. They have been optimized to exhibit a high degree of sensitivity and specificity for male DNA, even in the presence of a vast excess of female DNA.

Interpretation of a Y-STR Match

Since the loci in the NRY region of the Y chromosome are inherited as a physical block of physically linked haplotypes, independent assortment does not occur and the loci are in linkage disequilibrium with each other. As a result the product rule cannot be used to determine multilocus Y-STR frequencies. A counting method is commonly employed in order to estimate the frequency of occurrence of a particular Y-STR haplotype. With the counting method, the frequency of the haplotype is the number of times the haplotype is observed divided by the number of samples in the database. Alternative methods for Y-STR haplotype frequency estimates have been suggested including one based upon a mismatch distribution approach that allows the evaluation of the proportion of pairs of Y-STR haplotypes that are prone to become identical by state (IBS), in one generation, by recurrent mutation [17].

To correct for possible sample effects when using databases of limited size, the use of confidence intervals around the haplotype frequency estimate has been recommended. Reporting a haplotype frequency without associated confidence intervals may still be acceptable as a factual statement regarding observations in a particular database. If a confidence interval is applied and the haplotype has been observed in the database, the upper 95% confidence limit would be calculated using the following formula

$$p + 1.96\sqrt{\frac{(p)\,(1-p)}{n}} \tag{1}$$

where p is x/n (n is the database size, x is the number of times observed in the database). If the haplotype has not been previously observed in the database, the formula used to calculate the upper 95% confidence limit would be the following

$$1 - (0.05)^{1/n} \tag{2}$$

where n is the size of the database. A simplified alternative formulation can also be used in this instance; $3/n$ (n = size of the database). This value is close to the earlier formula and for 95% of the time the real

frequency is less than that estimate. Owing to population differentiation between subpopulations within the broader ethnic groups an appropriate θ (or F_{ST}) correction, akin to the situation with autosomal STRs, may be applicable [18, 19].

Empirical studies have confirmed the nonlinkage of Y-STR haplotypes and autosomal STR profiles [18]. Therefore, in cases with both autosomal and Y-STR analysis performed, it is possible to multiply the autosomal STR profile frequency with the upper confidence limit bounded Y-STR haplotype frequency to produce an overall frequency estimate for the combined profiles.

Casework Applications

Y-STRs can be particularly useful when trying to determine the genetic profile of the male donor in a male/female DNA admixture when the female DNA component is present in vast excess (e.g., $\geq$100-fold) and when traditional autosomal STR analysis fails or is not well suited for the particular analysis [13–15]. Samples containing a mixture of body fluids other than semen, such as in saliva/saliva mixtures, saliva/vaginal secretion mixtures in cases of oral sodomy, or fingernail scrapings with cells from the perpetrator may not be suitable for autosomal STR analysis. In these types of samples, unlike sperm containing samples, a differential lysis approach to separate the male and female cells is not possible. The minor male component in nondifferentially extracted samples would often not be detectable with the PCR-based autosomal STR systems routinely used. This is due to the kinetics of the PCR process itself, which does not permit minor components to be detected at low levels (i.e., $\leq$1/20) because of titration of critical reagents by the major DNA component [20]. Autosomal STR analysis may also fail with some semen containing samples in which few sperms are present, or are present in an extremely fragile state, such as in extended interval (i.e., >48 h) postcoital samples. Differential extraction of these particular samples may not result in male profile being obtained due to a combination of premature lysis of the sperm's cellular constituents into the nonsperm fraction and to sperm loss during the physical manipulations required of the DNA isolation process. Therefore the use of Y-STR systems can eliminate the need for differential extractions (separating the male and female fractions), thus reducing the potential loss of the small amount of male DNA that may be present in such samples.

Y-STRs are hemizygous in nature, with only one allele being found at each single-copy locus. Therefore, Y-STRs can be useful in determining the number of male contributors in an admixed DNA sample [8, 21–23]. Mixture analysis using autosomal analysis becomes quite complex when the number of donors exceeds two. However, the presence of multiple alleles at each Y-STR locus in a sample can give a more precise indication of the number of male contributors.

Y-chromosome polymorphisms may also be useful in criminal paternity cases, missing persons cases, and in the identification of victims involved in mass disasters where a reference sample from the (male) victim may not be available [24–30]. Y-chromosome markers are inherited as a physical block unchanged from one generation to the next (barring any random mutation events). Therefore, a Y-STR profile obtained by typing a male relative in the same lineage should be the same as that of the victim. Additionally, Y-STR analysis may provide additional discrimination in situations where a complete autosomal profile is not obtained, such as in mixtures or partially degraded samples [20, 31–35].

Y-STR analysis may aid in familial searches, which refers to the use of low stringency autosomal STR matching of a crime scene profile with an offender DNA database to identify possible biological relatives of the donor of the crime scene sample [36, 37]. With the large number of samples present in offender databases, several individuals from different candidate families can arise as potential relatives to the donor of the crime scene profile. Subsequent Y-STR analysis of the crime scene profile and the offenders in the database identified as potential relatives should eliminate most of the adventitious candidates. This not only facilitates the efficiency of the investigative process but also precludes unnecessary invasion of the privacy of noninvolved families. However, coincidental matches between unrelated individuals still occur with the limited number of Y-STR loci typically used in forensic casework. Therefore, it may be necessary to use additional highly discriminating "noncore" Y-STR loci in order to resolve coincidental matches and provide a more accurate indication of true relatedness.

References

[1]   Tilford, C.A., Kuroda-Kawaguchi, T., Skaletsky, H., Rozen, S., Brown, L.G., Rosenberg, M. McPherson, J.D., Wylie, K., Sekhon, M., Kucaba, T.A., Waterston, R.H. & Page, D.C. (2001). A physical map of the human Y chromosome, *Nature* **409**(6822), 943–945.

[2]   De, K.P., Kayser, M., Caglia, A., Corach, D., Fretwell, N., Gehrig, C., Graziosi, G, Heidorn, F., Herrmann, S., Herzog, B., Hidding, M., Honda, K., Jobling, M., Krawczak, M., Leim, K., Meuser, S., Meyer, E., Oesterreich, W., Pandya, A., Parson, W., Penacino, G., Perez-Lezaun, A., Piccinini, A., Prinz, M. & Roewer, L. (1997). Chromosome Y microsatellites: population genetic and evolutionary aspects, *International Journal of Legal Medicine* **110**(3), 134–149.

[3]   Kayser, M., Caglia, A., Corach, D., Fretwell, N., Gehrig, C., Graziosi, G., Heidorn, F., Herrmann, S., Herzog, B., Hidding, M., Honda, K., Jobling, M., Krawczak, M., Leim, K., Meuser, S., Meyer, E., Oesterreich, W., Pandya, A., Parson, W., Penacino, G., Perez-Lezaun, A., Piccinini, A., Prinz, M., Schmitt, C. & Roewer, L. (1997). Evaluation of Y-chromosomal STRs: a multicenter study, *International Journal of Legal Medicine* **110**(3), 125–129.

[4]   Corach, D., Filgueira, R.L., Marino, M., Penacino, G. & Sala, A. (2001). Routine Y-STR typing in forensic casework, *Forensic Science International* **118**(2–3), 131–135.

[5]   Kayser, M., Brauer, S., Willuweit, S., Schadlich, H., Batzer, M.A., Zawacki, J., Prinz, M., Roewer, L. & Stoneking, M. (2002). Online Y-chromosomal short tandem repeat haplotype reference database (YHRD) for U.S. populations, *Forensic Science International* **47**(3), 513–519.

[6]   Krenke, B.E., Viculis, L., Richard, M.L., Prinz, M., Milne, S.C., Ladd, C., Gross, A.M., Gornall, T., Frappier, J.R., Eisenberg, A.J., Barna, C., Aranda, X.G., Adamowicz, M.S. & Budowle, B. (2005). Validation of a male-specific, 12-locus fluorescent short tandem repeat (STR) multiplex, *Forensic Science International* **148**(1), 1–14.

[7]   Mulero, J.J., Chang, C.W., Calandro, L.M., Green, R.L., Li, Y., Johnson, C.L. & Hennessy, L.K. (2006). Development and validation of the AmpFlSTR Yfiler PCR amplification kit: a male specific, single amplification 17 Y-STR multiplex system, *Forensic Science International* **51**(1), 64–75.

[8]   Prinz, M. & Sansone, M. (2001). Y chromosome-specific short tandem repeats in forensic casework, *Croatian Medical Journal* **42**(3), 288–291.

[9]   Roewer, L., Krawczak, M., Willuweit, S., Nagy, M., Alves, C., Amorim, A., Anslinger, K., Augustin, C., Betz, A., Bosch, E., Caglia, A., Carracedo, A., Corach, D., Dekairelle, A.F., Dobosz, T., Dupuy, B.M., Furedi, S., Gehrig, C., Gusmao, L., Henke, J., Henke, L., Hidding, M., Hohoff, C., Hoste, B., Jobling, M.A., Kargel, H.J., De, K.P., Lessig, R., Liebeherr, E., Lorente, M., Martinez-Jarreta, B., Nievas, P., Nowak, M., Parson, W,

Pascali, V.L., Penacino, G., Ploski, R., Rolf, B., Sala, A., Schmidt, U., Schmitt, C., Schneider, P.M., Szibor, R., Teifel-Greding, J. & Kayser, M. (2001). Online reference database of European Y-chromosomal short tandem repeat (STR) haplotypes, *Forensic Science International* **118**(2–3), 106–113.

[10] Shewale, J.G., Nasir, H., Schneida, E., Gross, A.M., Budowle, B. & Sinha, S.K. (2004). Y-chromosome STR system, Y-PLEX 12, for forensic casework: development and validation, *Forensic Science International* **49**(6), 1278–1290.

[11] Sinha, S.K., Nasir, H., Gross, A.M., Budowle, B. & Shewale, J.G. (2003). Development and validation of the Y-PLEX 5, a Y-chromosome STR genotyping system, for forensic casework, *Forensic Science International* **48**(5), 985–1000.

[12] Sinha, S.K., Budowle, B., Arcot, S.S., Richey, S.L., Chakrabor, R., Jones, M.D., Wojtkiewicz, P.W., Schoenbauer, D.A., Gross, A.M., Sinha, S.K., Shewale, J.G. (2003). Development and validation of a multiplexed Y-chromosome STR genotyping system, Y-PLEX 6, for forensic casework, *Forensic Science International* **48**(1), 93–103.

[13] Betz, A., Bassler, G., Dietl, G., Steil, X., Weyermann, G. & Pflug, W. (2001). DYS STR analysis with epithelial cells in a rape case, *Forensic Science International* **118**(2–3), 126–130.

[14] Dekairelle, A.F. & Hoste, B. (2001). Application of a Y-STR-pentaplex PCR (DYS19, DYS389I and II, DYS390 and DYS393) to sexual assault cases, *Forensic Science International* **118**(2–3), 122–125.

[15] Martin, P., Albarran, C., Garcia, O., Garcia, P., Sancho, M. & Alonso, A. (2000). Application of Y-STR analysis to rape cases that cannot be solved by autosomal STR analysis, *Progress in Forensic Genetics* **8**, 526–528.

[16] SWGDAM Y-STR Subcommittee (2007). Report on the current activities of the scientific working group on DNA analysis methods Y-STR subcommittee, *Forensic Science Communications* **6**(3), 1–2.

[17] Pereira, L., Prata, M.J. & Amorim, A. (2002). Mismatch distribution analysis of Y-STR haplotypes as a tool for the evaluation of identity-by-state proportions and significance of matches – the European picture, *Forensic Science International* **130**(2–3), 147–155.

[18] Budowle, B., Adamowicz, M., Aranda, X.G., Barna, C., Chakraborty, R., Cheswick, D., Dafoe, B., Eisenberg, A., Frappier, R., Gross, A.M., Ladd, C., Lee, H.S., Milne, S.C., Meyers, C., Prinz, M., Richard, M.L., Saldanha, G., Tierney, A.A., Viculis, L. & Krenke, B.E. (2005). Twelve short tandem repeat loci Y chromosome haplotypes: genetic analysis on populations residing in North America, *Forensic Science International* **150**(1), 1–15.

[19] National Research Council (1996). *The Evaluation of Forensic DNA Evidence*, National Academy Press, Washington, DC.

[20] Prinz, M., Boll, K., Baum, H. & Shaler, B. (1997). Multiplexing of Y chromosome specific STRs and performance for mixed samples, *Forensic Science International* **85**(3), 209–218.

[21] Daniels, D.L., Hall, A.M. & Ballantyne, J. (2004). SWGDAM developmental validation of a 19-locus Y-STR system for forensic casework, *Forensic Science International* **49**(4), 668–683.

[22] Hanson, E.K. & Ballantyne, J. (2004). A highly discriminating 21 locus Y-STR "megaplex" system designed to augment the minimal haplotype loci for forensic casework, *Journal of Forensic Sciences* **49**(1), 40–51.

[23] Hanson, E.K., Berdos, P.N. & Ballantyne, J. (2006). Testing and evaluation of 43 "noncore" Y chromosome markers for forensic casework applications, *Journal of Forensic Sciences* **51**(6), 1298–1314.

[24] Alshamali, F., Qader Alkhayat, A., Budowle, B. & Watson, N. (2004). Y chromosome in forensic casework and paternity testing, *Progress in Forensic Genetics* **10**, 353–356.

[25] Andelinovic, S., Sutlovic, D., Erceg, I., Skaro, V., Ivkosic, A., Paic, F., Rezic, B., Finis-Gojanovic, M. & Primorac, D. (2005). Twelve-year experience in identification of skeletal remains from mass graves, *Croatian Medical Journal* **46**(4), 530–539.

[26] Anjos, M.J., Carvalho, M., Andrade, L., Lopes, V., Serra, A., Batista, L., Oliveira, C., Tavares, C., Balsa, F., Corte-Real, F., Vieira, D.N. & Vide, M.C. (2004). Individual genetic identification of biological samples: a case of an aircraft accident, *Forensic Science International* **146**, S115–S117.

[27] Jobling, M.A., Pandya, A. & Tyler-Smith, C. (1997). The Y chromosome in forensic analysis and paternity testing, *International Journal of Legal Medicine* **110**(3), 118–124.

[28] Kayser, M., Kruger, C., Nagy, M., Geserick, G., de Knijff, P. & Roewer, L. (1998). Y-chromosomal DNA-analysis in paternity testing: experiences and recommendations, *Progress in Forensic Genetics* **7**, 494–496.

[29] Li, J. (2004). Chromosome STR genetic markers in paternity identification, *Zhong Nan Da Xue Xue Bao Yi Xue Ban* **29**(4), 432–434.

[30] Rolf, B., Keil, W., Brinkmann, B., Roewer, L. & Fimmers, R. (2001). Paternity testing using Y-STR haplotypes: assigning a probability for paternity in cases of mutations, *International Journal of Legal Medicine* **115**(1), 12–15.

[31] Berger, B., Niederstätter, H., Köchl, S., Steinlechner, M. & Parson, W. (2003). Male/female DNA mixtures: a challenge for Y-STR analysis, *Progress in Forensic Genetics* **9**, 295–299.

[32] Cerri, N., Ricci, U., Sani, I., Verzeletti, A. & De, F.F. (2003). Mixed stains from sexual assault cases: autosomal or Y-chromosome short tandem repeats? *Croatian Medical Journal* **44**(3), 289–292.

[33] Parson, W., Niederstatter, H., Brandstatter, A. & Berger, B. (2003). Improved specificity of Y-STR typing in DNA mixture samples, *International Journal of Legal Medicine* **117**(2), 109–114.

[34] Tsuji, A., Ishiko, A., Ikeda, N. & Yamaguchi, H. (2001). Personal identification using Y-chromosomal short

tandem repeats from bodily fluids mixed with semen, *American Journal of Forensic Medicine and Pathology* **22**(3), 288–291.

[35]   Yoshida, Y., Fujita, Y. & Kubo, S. (2004). Forensic casework of personal identification using a mixture of body fluids from more than one person by Y-STRs analysis, *Journal of Medical Investigation* **51**(3–4), 238–242.

[36]   Bieber, F.R., Brenner, C.H. & Lazer, D. (2006). Human genetics. Finding criminals through DNA of their relatives, *Science* **312**(5778), 1315–1316.

[37]   Greely, H.T., Riordan, D.P., Garrison, N.A. & Mountain, J.L. (2006). Family ties: the use of DNA offender databases to catch offenders' kin, *Journal of Law Medicine and Ethics* **34**(2), 248–262.

Chapter 19
Expert Systems in DNA Interpretation

Hinda Haned[1] and Peter Gill[2,3]

[1]*Netherlands Forensic Institute, The Hague, The Netherlands*
[2]*Norwegian Institute of Public Health, Oslo, Norway*
[3]*University of Oslo, Oslo, Norway*

Introduction

Expert systems have been developed as specialized software that can assist forensic scientists to interpret complex DNA profiles. They typically automate calculations of statistics that are relevant to different applications of forensic DNA profiling: kinship testing, disaster victim identification, and the analysis of crime-samples. For the latter, which represents the bulk of forensic DNA casework, the introduction has been slow, mainly because of the lack of accessible software [1]. However, a number of systems have recently become available and have been successfully introduced in casework in forensic laboratories. In this review, we describe the currently available expert systems and discuss their theoretical principles, advantages, and limitations, along with the aspects of performance and validation.

Challenges in DNA Interpretation

The increased sensitivity of DNA profiling has made complex DNA profiles commonplace in forensic casework. We define complex DNA profiles as low-template deoxyribonucleic acid (LTDNA) samples that are prone to stochastic effects such as allelic drop-out (missing alleles) and allelic drop-in (spurious alleles). For such samples, frequency-based statistics such as the probability of exclusion (PE) or the random match probability (RMP) cannot be used to evaluate the strength of the DNA evidence, because they do not take into account the stochastic phenomena that create uncertainty about the composition of the sample. Alternatively, likelihood ratio (LR)-based models offer a flexible framework for the evaluation of such samples, because they allow for uncertainties in the sample to be accounted for.

The Likelihood Ratio Framework

LRs are the preferred way to evaluate the strength of the DNA evidence [2, 3]. LRs are the ratios of the likelihoods of two hypotheses, also referred to as *propositions*. These hypotheses are conditioned statements that describe the alternative prosecution and defense hypotheses. In the forensic literature, they are traditionally labeled as the hypothesis of the prosecution (H_p) and the hypothesis of the defense (H_d). Typically, the person of interest (POI) is included in the prosecution hypothesis and is replaced by an unknown individual under the defense hypothesis. The hypotheses state the number of contributors, some of which will be known, while others are deemed unknown. The POI is often the suspect, but if there is a question of transfer of DNA from a victim to the suspect, then the POI is the victim. LRs are calculated by taking the ratio of two conditional probabilities: that of the DNA evidence (denoted E), given that the proposition of the prosecution is true, compared to the probability of the evidence, given that the proposition of the defense is true (equation 1).

$$\text{LR} = \frac{\Pr(E|H_p)}{\Pr(E|H_d)} \qquad (1)$$

In the following, it is assumed that we are interested in the suspect's DNA profile. For a crime-sample with

A Guide to Forensic DNA Profiling
Edited by Allan Jamieson and Scott Bader
© 2016 John Wiley & Sons, Ltd. ISBN: 9781118751527
Also published in EFS (online edition)
DOI: 10.1002/9780470061589.fsa1126

more than one contributor, the hypotheses may be H_p: the DNA in the crime-stain is from the suspect and the victim and H_d: the DNA in the crime-sample is from one unknown person, unrelated to the suspect, and the victim. When the LR is above one, it favors the prosecution hypothesis; when it is below one, it favors the defense hypothesis. It is worth stressing that the LRs only compare the relative likelihoods of two (or more) hypotheses but that does not preclude both of the hypotheses as false.

The use of LRs to evaluate the strength of evidence is widely discussed in the literature.

The Need for Expert Systems

When comparing a crime-sample profile to one or more reference profiles (from a suspect or a victim), there may be stochastic effects in the crime-sample profile: phenomena such as allelic drop-out and drop-in create discrepancies at several loci, making it impossible to evaluate the strength of the DNA evidence. The practice of discarding problematic loci has proven to be biased and is not recommended in casework [4]. LR-based models are flexible and allow these issues to be evaluated probabilistically. However, LR-based systems rely on algorithms that cannot be derived manually; therefore, there is a

need for expert software systems that automate the calculations. From an algorithmic standpoint, the main issue when analyzing DNA profiles, whether low- or high-template, is to derive all possible genotypes that might explain the crime-sample profile. By definition, the "true" genotypic combination is unknown in case-work; therefore, the role of the software is to derive all possibilities and to assign them statistical weights, based on a set of rules defined by the underlying probabilistic model. In the following, we only describe the currently available expert systems.

Currently Available Expert Systems

Currently available systems facilitate the analysis of single-source (single donor) and mixed DNA profiles. While all expert systems are anchored in a LR approach, the underlying mathematical models are different. A straightforward way to distinguish between the different systems is to think in terms of the weights that are assigned to the different genotype combinations that may explain the crime-sample under a given hypothesis. On the basis of how these weights are assigned, the different systems are usually classified into two main groups: continuous and semi-continuous systems [1]. Table 1 summarizes the different features of the available software.

Table 1 Summary of the currently available interpretation systems

Expert system	LTDNA	LR	Deconvolution	License	References
Continuous systems					
DNAmixtures	✓	✓	✓	Open-source	[5]
STRmix	✓	✓	✓	Commercial	[6]
TrueAllele	✓	✓	✓	Commercial	[7]
Semi-continuous systems					
Lab Retriever	✓	✓	✗	Open-source	[8]
LikeLTD	✓	✓	✗	Open-source	[9]
LRmix	✓	✓	✗	Open-source	[10]
Deconvolution systems					
GeneMapper *ID-X*	✗	✗	✓	Commercial	[11]
LoCIM	✓	✗	✓	Non-commercial	[12]
Mastermix	✗	✗	✓	Non-commercial	[13]

"LTDNA" indicates whether the software can handle samples with low template components, "LR" indicates whether the software can evaluate the evidence through likelihood ratios, and the "Deconvolution" column highlights whether the software offers mixture deconvolution possibilities. Note that DNAmixtures is an open-source R package; however, it relies on the Hugin commercial software

Semi-continuous Systems

The key parameters for these models are the drop-out and drop-in probabilities that, respectively, measure the chance that an allele may be absent or a spurious (contaminant) allele may be present. In addition, population databases are used to determine the frequency of alleles found in the crime-stain and reference samples. The drop-out, drop-in, and allelic probabilities are combined to generate the statistical weight of evidence for the hypothesized genotypic combinations. Although semi-continuous models do not make use of the peak height information explicitly, the peak height information may be used to inform the models' parameters [3, 14].

The main semi-continuous models in current use are LRmix [10], Lab Retriever [8], and LikeLTD [9]. All are used in casework applications and the software are freely distributed, under open-source licenses. The programs rely on similar theories, but they differ in the way that their parameters are informed. In LRmix and Lab Retriever, the user has to enter both drop-out and drop-in parameters; however, both programs offer possibilities to estimate the drop-out probability. In LRmix, sensitivity analyses of the LR to the drop-out parameter can be plotted and a 95% confidence interval for the dropout probabilities is plotted. Lab Retriever provides an Excel sheet to estimate drop-out probabilities using a logistic regression model based on the peak heights from the crime-sample profile [14]. LikeLTD differs, as it infers the model parameters directly using maximum likelihood estimation.

Continuous Systems

Continuous models fully evaluate allelic peak heights in order to determine the weights that are assigned to the different genotype combinations. Because they are more complex, continuous models typically have more parameters than the semi-continuous models. The currently available continuous systems are DNAmixtures [5], STRmix [6], and TrueAllele [7]. DNAmixtures is distributed under an open-source license; however, it relies on the commercial Hugin software; STRmix and TrueAllele are distributed under commercial licenses. DNAmixtures uses Bayesian networks to generate LRs. In common with the semi-continuous LikeLTD program, the model parameters are estimated using likelihood maximization algorithms. However, the system explicitly accounts for peak heights in the likelihoods.

TrueAllele and STRmix use a fully Bayesian approach to generate the LR statistics, this means that prior distributions of the model parameters lead in turn to posterior distributions, where all the unknown parameters are integrated. Certain parameters and assumptions of the models rely directly on empirical data generated during validation studies (STRmix), while others strictly rely on the data available from the crime-sample profile (DNAmixtures, TrueAllele). These parameters include the DNA quantity, locus-specific degradation parameters, and variances of the peak heights. Both STRmix and TrueAllele rely on approximation algorithms. Both systems use Markov Chain Monte Carlo (MCMC) to perform the required integrations over all the unknown parameters. MCMC algorithms are based on random sampling procedures; therefore, running these systems twice on the same case generates different results. The variability in results is typically described in validation studies; however, there are insufficient data available on the subject [15, 16].

Mixture Deconvolution Systems

Mixture deconvolution systems are useful when there is no reference sample available from a POI, i.e., a known victim or a suspect. Typically, genotypes that are extracted by deconvolution can be searched against a DNA database in order to identify potential candidates of interest to the case. These are sometimes called *speculative searches*, as the genotypes are not known with certainty.

Continuous systems described in the previous section (Table 1) can also be used for mixture deconvolution. The statistical weights computed by these systems can be used to infer the most probable genotypes explaining the crime-sample. Other available software use empirical data, either from the crime-sample itself or from controlled experiments, to derive a set of empirical rules to deconvolute the mixtures. The LoCIM (locus classification and inference of the major) tool is an automated Excel sheet that enables the inference of the major component's alleles in mixtures, it relies on a set of empirical rules and is freely available upon request from the developers [12]. The Mastermix [13] tool and Genemapper *ID-X* mixture analysis tool [11] derive the genotypes that best fit the analyzed mixture, based on an estimate of the mixture proportion (from the sample itself). Both programs follow the theory described in reference [17], and they are both limited to two-person mixtures with no allelic dropout, which limits their applicability in casework.

Systems for the Inference of the Number of Contributors

The number of contributors always has to be specified in the hypotheses evaluated in the LR framework; however, this number can never be known with certainty in forensic casework. A number of statistical methods have been developed to help estimate the number of donors to a forensic DNA sample. They either rely on empirical data to derive rules about the number of donors [18, 19] or use the maximum likelihood principle to determine which number of donors is best supported by the data [20, 21]. In this section, we focus on the methods that are currently implemented in a computer program, for use in casework.

The freely available NOC*It* software [19] computes the posterior probability of the number of contributors, given a particular crime-sample profile. The software relies on calibration data from single-donor samples to inform the components of the model that are needed to compute the posterior distribution. This program takes into account the population allele frequencies and the alleles peak heights and it also models allelic dropout and stutter. The open-source Forensim package for the R statistical software [22, 23] offers facilities to estimate the number of contributors using a maximum likelihood estimator [20]: for a given sample, the program returns the number of donors that gives the highest probability of observing the crime profile. The estimator relies on the population allele frequencies but does not take account of peak heights; therefore, it can only be used on high-template samples.

An alternative approach to estimate the number of contributors utilizes an exploratory approach to evaluate different propositions. The effect on the LR can be explored by varying the number of contributors in the model. Different sets of propositions can be evaluated and this assists forensic scientists to explore the most relevant propositions for the case. An illustration of this approach is provided in references [24, 25].

Further Evaluation of the Evidence

The principles behind LR-based interpretation are possibly more difficult to explain compared to summary statistics such as random man non excluded (RMNE) tests. Noncontributor tests, also referred to as *performance tests* [24, 26], can help with the understanding of the meaning of LRs.

Noncontributor tests evaluate LRs obtained when H_p is false (or H_d is true), i.e., when the POI is replaced by a simulated random person. Such tests are carried out n times, n is the number of simulated random profiles. The resulting distribution of the LRs indicates how much an estimated LR for a given case differs from an LR that would be obtained for a random man (unrelated to the case). Non-contributor tests based on simulation are limited by the number of profiles that can be simulated, and they can be computationally intensive for complex hypotheses. An alternative was suggested by Dørum *et al.* [27], who computed the exact probability that a non-contributor would yield an LR at least as high as the "observed LR," which is the LR obtained when the POI is evaluated under H_p. This probability is obtained conditioned on H_d is true and is also based on the evaluation of non-contributor genotypes; however, it relies on exact probabilities rather than simulations.

These tests can help further evaluate the evidence and they are useful to compare different sets of propositions or different models [24, 28, 29]. Exact probability tests are implemented in the euroMix R package [30], while noncontributor tests are available from the LRmix module of the Forensim R package [10].

Comparative Studies

Continuous models account for peak heights and in principle make the "best use" of available data [1]. However, incorporating peak heights comes at the cost of added complexity: distributional assumptions have to be made about the peak heights and this usually involves numerous parameters that must be estimated either from the crime-sample profile itself or from experimental data. For the latter, calibration is an important issue as the modeling assumptions may not always hold, particularly for LTDNA profiles that have high levels of variability [31–33]. The fewer parameters and assumptions of the semi-continuous models make them easier to implement in casework, as they are more robust to variability compared to continuous models. However, the LR ranges produced by these systems are typically lower than those produced by continuous systems.

Table 2 Summary of the published studies comparing the performance of different expert systems

Compared software	Study description	References
Lab Retriever, STRmix	25 experimental two-person mixtures, created in duplicates, with five different mixture ratios created from two donors	[15]
LikeLTD, LRmix	Two casework-examples: one two-person and one three-person mixture	[34]
LikeLTD, LiRa, LRmix	Single-source, two- to four-person mixtures examples from the literature, analyzed with different replicate numbers and variable amounts of dropouts and drop-in	[35]
Lab Retriever, LRmix, STRmix	Two virtual two-person mixtures with different ratios	[36]

Note that LiRa is currently not available for purchase or download, the software relies on a semi-continuous model, see [35] for details

It is expected that different LRs are obtained if different software are used to evaluate the same crime-sample; however, models would be expected to converge [24]. Owing to the novelty and restricted accessibility of certain software, there is little information in the literature about their relative performances. However, the limited studies available to date, described in Table 2, show that similar results are obtained from different expert systems.

Validation

The validation of an expert system usually involves a proof of the validity of the implemented model. However, model validation is not straightforward because the true weight of the DNA evidence cannot be determined: there is no "gold standard test" and no true LR that can serve as a ground truth, as the generated LRs always depend on the model's assumptions [9]. However, the basic properties of an LR-based system have been widely discussed in the forensic literature [37], and there are several ways whereby the validity of an LR-based expert system can be verified. For example, an upper bound of the LR is provided by the inverse of the match probability of the queried donor under the prosecution hypothesis (usually the suspect) [38]. A study carried out by Steele *et al.* [39] using the LikeLTD software nicely illustrates how such properties can be verified using experimental DNA samples.

Another approach consists of comparing the expert system output to a gold standard LR, which can be calculated when most parameters of the model can be estimated from known samples. Haned *et al.* [40] illustrated the use of a gold standard LR to evaluate the

performance of the LRmix program when used to evaluate complex mixtures of three to five donors. Gill and Haned [24] further suggest the use of a standard basic model against which more complex models can be compared. The authors defined the requirements for such model, which enables the evaluation of complex profiles, without using all the available information. Typically, this model can help evaluate the performance of a continuous system.

Remaining Challenges

Expert systems such as those described in this review will become increasingly commonplace in the forensic community as they increase laboratory throughput of complex cases. While some laboratories will implement expert systems, others may continue to report complex profiles as inconclusive. The ability to move to advanced interpretation models described in this review depends on resources at disposal, including training costs and/or software fees. Many of the available systems are open-source and free of charge, which makes them easy to implement in casework. These software may represent a first step for forensic laboratories, before they introduce more complex models. They also offer an ideal framework for international collaborative efforts [41].

It is expected that no one single expert system will be adopted by the entirety of the forensic DNA community: different laboratories have different needs and resources, and diversity in methodology is expected. This reflects the view that there is no one true LR and the statistics produced depend on the models' parameters and assumptions [9]. Diversity in systems is commonplace in other branches of science, for example, in population genetics, numerous software coexist, they do not compete but rather complement each other [42]. In the context of forensic science investigations, different software can be used to cross-check the results for a given case, and this is something to encourage. Comparative studies on large datasets, representative of the challenges encountered in casework, will further help the understanding of the advantages and limitations of the different systems. Such comparisons are essential, as they will assist forensic laboratories in choosing a particular system, to complement their internal procedures, validation criteria, and workflow.

References

[1] Steele, C.D. & Balding, D.J. (2014). Statistical evaluation of forensic DNA profile evidence, *Annual Review of Statistics and its Application* **1**, 361–384.

[2] Gill, P., Brenner, C.H., Buckleton, J.S., Carracedo, A., Krawczak, M., Mayer, W.R., Morling, N., Prinz, M., Schneider, P.M. & Weir, B.S. (2006). DNA commission of the International Society of Forensic Genetics: recommendations on the interpretation of mixtures, *Forensic Science International* **160**(2-3), 90–101.

[3] Gill, P., Gusmo, L., Haned, H., Mayr, W.R., Morling, N., Parson, W., Prieto, L., Prinz, M., Schneider, H., Schneider, P.M. & Weir, B.S. (2012). DNA commission of the international society of forensic genetics: recommendations on the evaluation of STR typing results that may include drop-out and/or drop-in using probabilistic methods, *Forensic Science International: Genetics* **6**, 679–688.

[4] Curran, J.M. & Buckleton, J. (2010). Inclusion probabilities and dropout, *Journal of Forensic Sciences* **55**(5), 1171–1173.

[5] Graversen, T. & Lauritzen, S. (2014). Computational aspects of DNA mixture analysis, *Statistics and Computing*, 1–15.

[6] Taylor, D., Bright, J.A. & Buckleton, J. (2013). The interpretation of single source and mixed DNA profiles, *Forensic Science International: Genetics* **7**, 516–528.

[7] Perlin, M.W., Legler, M.M., Spencer, C.E., Smith, J.L., Allan, W.P., Belrose, J.L. & Duceman, B.W. (2011). Validating TrueAllele® DNA mixture interpretation, *Journal of Forensic Sciences* **56**(6), 1430–1447.

[8] Cheng, K., Inman-Semerau, L., Rudin, N., Inman, K. & Lohmueller, K.E. (2014). Scientific Collaboration, Innovation & Education Group, Available from: www.scieg.org/lab_retriever.html (accessed Jan 2015).

[9] Balding, D.J. (2013). Evaluation of mixed-source, low-template DNA profiles in forensic science, *Proceedings of the National Academy of Sciences of the United States of America* **110**(30), 12241–12246.

[10] Haned, H. & Gill, P. (2011). Analysis of complex DNA mixtures using the Forensim package, *Forensic Science International: Genetics Supplement Series* **3**, e79–e80.

[11] GeneMapper® ID- X. Applied Biosystems, Foster City, CA, USA.

[12] Benschop, C.C.G. & Sijen, T. (2014). LoCIM-tool: an expert's assistant for inferring the major contributor's alleles in mixed consensus DNA profiles, *Forensic Science International: Genetics* **11**, 154–165.

[13] Gill, P. (2014). The Mastermix Mixture Deconvolution Tool, Available from: https://sites.google.com/site/forensicdnastatistics/

[14] Lohmueller, K.E., Rudin, N. & Inman, K. (2014). Analysis of allelic drop-out using the Identifiler® and PowerPlex® 16 forensic STR typing systems, *Forensic Science International: Genetics* **12**, 1–11.

[15] Bille, T.W., Weitz, S.M., Coble, M.D., Buckleton, J. & Bright, J.-A. (2014). Comparison of the performance of different models for the interpretation of low level mixed DNA profiles, *Electrophoresis* **35**, 3125–3133.

[16] Perlin, M.W., Belrose, J.L. & Duceman, B.W. (2013). New York State TrueAllele® casework validation study, *Journal of Forensic Sciences* **58**(6), 1458–1465.

[17] Gill, P., Sparkes, R., Pinchin, R., Clayton, T., Whitaker, J. & Buckleton, J. (1998). Interpreting simple STR mixtures using allele peak areas, *Forensic Science International* **91**, 41–53.

[18] Perez, J., Mitchell, A.A., Ducasse, N., Tamariz, J. & Caragine, T. (2011). Estimating the number of contributors to two-, three-, and four-person mixtures containing DNA in high template and low template amounts, *Croatian Medical Journal* **52**(3), 314–326.

[19] Swaminathan, H., Grgicak, C.M., Medard, M. & Lun, D.S. (2015). NOCIt: a computational method to infer the number of contributors to DNA samples analyzed by STR genotyping, *Forensic Science International: Genetics*, **16**, 172–180.

[20] Haned, H., Pontier, D., Lobry, J.R., Pène, L. & Dufour, A.B. (2010). Estimating the number of contributors to forensic DNA mixtures: does maximum likelihood perform better than maximum allele count? *Journal of Forensic Sciences* **56**(1), 23–28.

[21] Biedermann, A., Bozza, S., Konis, K. & Taroni, F. (2012). Inference about the number of contributors to a DNA mixture: comparative analyses of a Bayesian network approach and the maximum allele count method, *Forensic Science International: Genetics* **6**(6), 689–696.

[22] Haned, H. (2011). Forensim: an open source initiative for the evaluation of statistical methods in forensic genetics, *Forensic Science International: Genetics* **5**(4), 265–268.

[23] R Core Team. (2014). R: A Language and Environment for Statistical Computing. R Foundation for Statistical Computing, Vienna, Austria, Available from: http://www.R-project.org (accessed Jan 2015).

[24] Gill, P. & Haned, H. (2013). A new methodological framework to interpret complex DNA profiles using likelihood ratios, *Forensic Science International: Genetics* **7**(2), 251–263.

[25] Buckleton, J., Bright, J.A., Taylor, D., Evett, I., Hicks, T., Jackson, G. & Curran, J.M. (2014). Helping formulate propositions in forensic DNA analysis, *Science & Justice* **54**(4), 258–261.

[26] Gill, P., Curran, J.M., Neumann, C., Kirkham, A., Clayton, T., Whitaker, J. & Lambert, J. (2008). Interpretation of complex DNA profiles using empirical models and a method to measure their robustness, *Forensic Science International: Genetics* **2**, 91–103.

[27] Dørum, G., Bleka, O., Gill, P., Haned, H., Snipen, L., Sæbø, S. & Egeland, T. (2014). Exact computation of the distribution of likelihood ratios with forensic applications, *Forensic Science International: Genetics* **9**, 93–101.

[28] Taylor, D. (2014). Using continuous DNA interpretation methods to revisit likelihood ratio behaviour, *Forensic Science International: Genetics* **11**, 144–153.

[29] Mitchell, A.A., Tamariz, J., O'Connell, K., Ducasse, N., Budimlija, Z., Prinz, M. & Caragine, T. (2012). Validation of a DNA mixture statistics tool incorporating allelic drop-out and drop-in, *Forensic Science International: Genetics* **6**(6), 749–761.

[30] Dørum, G. (2014). euroMix package: forensic calculations for DNA mixtures accounting for possibly inbred pedigrees (simulations with conditioning, LR). Exact p-values, Available from: http://euromix.r-forge.r-project.org/ (accessed Jan 2015).

[31] Bright, J.A., Turkington, J. & Buckleton, J. (2009). Examination of the variability in mixed DNA profile parameters for the Identifiler® multiplex, *Forensic Science International: Genetics* **4**(2), 111–114.

[32] Westen, A., Grol, L.J.W., Harteveld, J., Matai, A.S., de Knijff, P. & Sijen, T. (2012). Assessment of the stochastic threshold, back-and forward stutter filters and low template techniques for NGM, *Forensic Science International: Genetics* **6**(6), 708–715.

[33] Whitaker, J.P., Cotton, E.A. & Gill, P. (2001). A comparison of the characteristics of profiles produced with the AMPFlSTR® SGM Plus™ multiplex system for both standard and low copy number (LCN) STR DNA analysis, *Forensic Science International* **123**(2-3), 215–223.

[34] Haned, H., Slooten, K. & Gill, P. (2012). Exploratory data analysis for the interpretation of low template DNA mixtures, *Forensic Science International: Genetics* **6**, 762–774.

[35] Puch-Solis, R. & Clayton, T. (2014). Evidential evaluation of DNA profiles using a discrete statistical model

implemented in the DNA LiRa software, *Forensic Science International: Genetics* **11**, 220–228.

[36] Bright, J.A., Evett, I.W., Taylor, D., Curran, J.M. & Buckleton, J. (2014). A series of recommended tests when validating probabilistic DNA profile interpretation software, *Forensic Science International: Genetics* **14**, 125–131.

[37] Morrison, G.S. (2011). Measuring the validity and reliability of forensic likelihood-ratio systems, *Science & Justice* **51**(3), 91–98.

[38] Cowell, R.G., Graversen, T., Lauritzen, S.L. & Mortera, J. (2015). Analysis of forensic DNA mixtures with artefacts, *Applied Statistics* **64**(1), 1–32.

[39] Steele, C.D., Greenhalgh, M. & Balding, D.J. (2014). Verifying likelihoods for low template DNA profiles using multiple replicates, *Forensic Science International: Genetics* **13**, 82–89.

[40] Haned, H., Benschop, C., Gill, P. & Sijen, T. (2015). Complex DNA mixture analysis in a forensic context: evaluating the probative value using a likelihood ratio model, *Forensic Science International: Genetics*, **16**, 17–25.

[41] Prieto, L., Haned, H., Mosquera, A., Crespillo, M., Alema, M., Aler, M., Alvarez, F, Baeza-Richer, C, Dominguez, A, Doutremepuich, C, Farfán, M.J, Fenger-Grøn, M, García-Ganivet, J.M, González-Moya, E, Hombreiro, L, Lareu, M.V, Martínez-Jarreta, B, Merigioli, S, Milans Del Bosch, P, Morling, N, Muñoz-Nieto, M, Ortega-González, E, Pedrosa, S, Pérez, R, Solís, C, Yurrebaso, I. & Gill, P. (2014). Euroforgen-NoE collaborative exercise on LRmix to demonstrate standardization of the interpretation of complex DNA profiles, *Forensic Science International Genetics* **9**, 47–54.

[42] Excoffier, L. & Heckel, G. (2006). Computer programs for population genetics data analysis: a survival guide, *Nature* **7**, 745–758.

Related Articles in EFS Online

Evidence Interpretation: A Logical Approach

Interpretation: Low Template DNA

Mixture Interpretation: DNA

Chapter 20
Paternity Testing

Burkhard Rolf[1] and Peter Wiegand[2]

[1]*Eurofins Medigenomix Forensik GmbH, Ebersberg, Germany*
[2]*University Hospital of Ulm, Ulm, Germany*

History of Markers Used for Paternity Testing

Paternity testing with genetic markers goes back to the discovery of the ABO blood group by Karl Landsteiner [1]. For many years, ABO, the rhesus system and many of the later discovered polymorphic antigens of the erythrocyte membrane, serum proteins, and erythrocyte enzymes were the markers of choice for paternity testing. Although accurate and precise, some of the early tests did not have sufficient statistical power in case of non-exclusion. The highly polymorphic human leukocyte antigen (HLA) system was later used to complement the blood group findings in such cases.

With the discovery of DNA polymorphisms, the blood group and histocompatibility era in paternity testing ended soon. The restriction fragment length polymorphisms (RFLP) described by Jeffreys [2] were the first generation of solely DNA-based markers that could be used for paternity testing. These markers were visualized after gel electrophoresis using specific probes that bind to the targeted DNA region of interest. Depending on the type of probe, one can distinguish between multilocus probes and single locus probes. The single locus probes were the marker of choice until polymerase chain reaction (PCR) revolutionized the forensic DNA typing. Currently, microsatellite markers or short tandem repeat (STR) polymorphisms, amplified by PCR, are used in almost all laboratories for paternity testing (as well as for crime scene stain investigations).

Legal Aspects of Paternity Testing

Results of a paternity test can have high impact on social, familial, and also monetary relationships between an alleged father and a child. Therefore, many countries have laws that regulate paternity testing. Such laws set a framework for legal testing. Legal paternity tests comprise all tests ordered by public authorities like family courts or that are used in such judicial proceedings. The so-called peace of mind or private tests are also regulated in most countries. Usually the laws require that all parties involved in testing have consented to testing.

Practical Process

During the sampling process for legal testing, the identity of all participants is documented by the sampler. To prove the identity of the sample donor, typically photographs are taken by the sampler (or photos provided by the participants are used) and an appropriate ID is checked and photocopied. Saliva samples collected with buccal swabs or FTA paper are the starting material in the laboratory. Most laboratories provide the sampler with forms for the documentation of the sampling process. The laboratory process starts with the extraction of the DNA from the sample. During this step, other cellular materials like proteins are removed.

The purified DNA is used as template for the PCR. Short areas of the genome, the STR polymorphisms are then amplified. These polymorphic loci vary in length between different individuals. A multiplex-PCR is used to amplify several STR loci in one reaction. This means that several primer pairs for the different loci are combined in one assay. Figure 1 shows the result

A Guide to Forensic DNA Profiling
Edited by Allan Jamieson and Scott Bader
© 2016 John Wiley & Sons, Ltd. ISBN: 9781118751527
Also published in EFS (online edition)
DOI: 10.1002/9780470061589.fsa1123

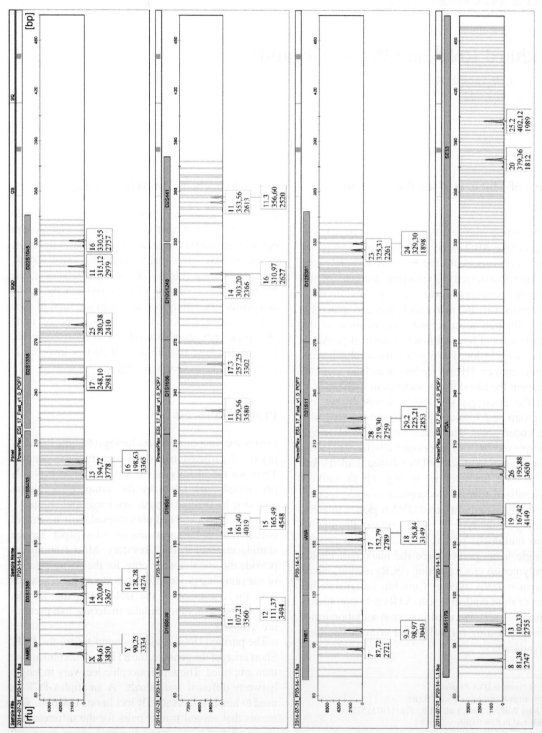

Figure 1   Male DNA profile - multiplex PCR including 16 variable STR marker and Amelogenin (gender typing marker "XY")

for a sample in the multiplex "PowerPlex® ESI17" from Promega. Promega is a supplier of laboratory reagents from Madison, WI, USA. Other companies like Qiagen from Hilden in Germany or Life Technologies/Applied Biosystems from Foster City, CA, USA offer similar products. Such commercially available marker systems (so-called kits) are premixed multiplex PCR reagents including the primers. Almost all paternity testing laboratories rely on kits from at least one of these suppliers.

Finally, the length measurement of the amplified DNA is carried out by electrophoresis to determine the genotype. The individual loci are labelled with different fluorescent dyes. Therefore loci differ in length and color/dye that allows the parallel detection of many loci at the same time. The electrophoresis is carried out in capillaries. Full automation of this step is made possible by modern electrophoresis systems like the 8-capillary "3500" or the 24-capillary "3500xL Genetic Analyzer" from Life Technologies.

Data Analysis

In a test with a mother, a child, and an alleged father, the evaluation of the laboratory results starts with a comparison of mother and child. In this step, it is determined which of the two alleles of the child is maternal and which has to be the paternal allele. Figure 2 shows four STR-loci for mother, child, and two alleged father. STR loci are repeat polymorphisms which mean that a certain DNA sequence is arranged in tandem repeats. The number of repeats is variable. The individual length variants are called alleles, and the name of the allele is derived from the repeat number. An allele "9" is therefore a 9-fold repetition of the core DNA motive, an allele "10" a 10-fold.

In Figure 2, the allele the child has not inherited from the mother can be seen in the profile of alleged father 1. Alleged father 2 has a negative test result. He does not show the compatible paternal allele in 3 of 4 of the displayed loci. Therefore, this man is excluded as father.

In a negative case, i.e., the tested man does not show the correct paternal allele in several loci, paternity can practically be excluded and no probability calculation is done in most laboratories. The minimal number of exclusive loci can vary from laboratory to laboratory and from country to country. In Germany, for example, at least four exclusive loci are required; in

some other countries, three exclusions might be sufficient. However, such differences have more formal reasons and are not really relevant for the quality of the testing in the majority of cases.

Table 1 shows an example from a paternity testing report. Two men were named as alleged fathers and had been tested.

A comparison of the results for the marker D3S1358 in the first row of the table, for mother and child reveals that allele 14 of the child must have been inherited from the alleged father. Alleged father A is showing this allele, alleged father B is not. In the next line showing the results for the marker D1S1656, it becomes obvious that the child must have inherited allele 16 from his father. Again, alleged father A is showing this allele, whereas the alleged father B is not.

After evaluation of all 20 markers, the alleged father A is showing the paternal allele in every case, whereas alleged father B can be excluded in 13 of the 20 tested loci. If the case is positive and the tested man has all paternal alleles, a probability can be calculated (see section titled "Statistical Evaluation").

Testing with or without a Sample of the Mother

Paternity tests can be carried out with and without a sample of the mother. In case the mother participates in the test, the paternal allele of the child can be determined. In a motherless case, both alleles of the child are potentially paternal. This has an impact on both the chance to detect a non-father and on the power of the probability calculation. However, with the availability of multiplex kits that allow the simultaneous detection of several loci, this drawback of motherless tests can be easily compensated by testing a higher number of markers that ensures reliable results without a maternal sample. Nevertheless, including the mother in the test can increase the amount of information on the identity of the tested child. Because the samples from mother and child have to show genetic relation, the documentation of the identity of the mother also identifies the child.

Mutation Events

In rare cases, the alleged father and the child (or the mother and the child) might exhibit an isolated

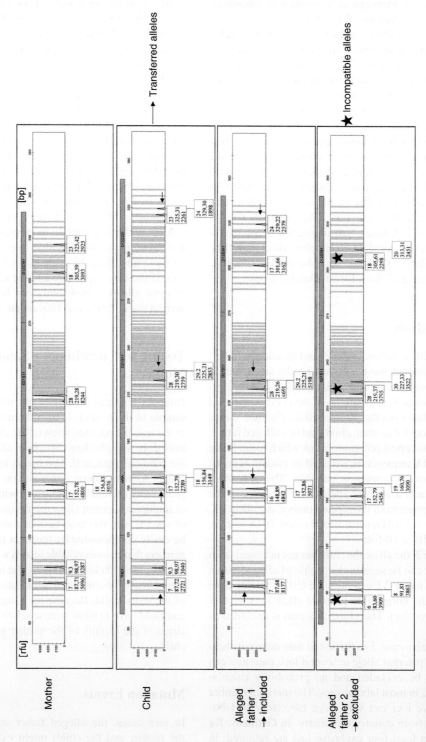

Figure 2 Examples of DNA profiles from a mother, a child and two alleged fathers.

Table 1 Results of a paternity test involving a mother, a child, and two alleged fathers

DNA-system	DNA-criteria Alleged father A	DNA-criteria Alleged father B	DNA-criteria Child	DNA-criteria Mother
AMEL	X/Y	X/Y	X/Y	X/X
D3S1358	14/16	15/16	14/17	16/17
D1S1656	16/17.3	11/17	15/16	12/15
D6S1043	11/12	12/17	11/11	11/13
D13S317	11/12	9/11	12/12	11/12
Penta E	7/12	7/9	12/13	12/13
D16S539	13/14	9/12	11/14	9/11
D18S51	13/18	13/18	13/14	14/15
D2S1338	16/19	20/24	16/23	17/23
CSF1PO	10/12	12/13	12/12	11/12
Penta D	10/13	10/12	11/13	11/13
TH01	6/9.3	7/9.3	9.3/9.3	9/9.3
vWA	16/19	17/19	16/16	16/18
D21S11	29/30.2	28/30	29/31.2	29/31.2
D7S820	8/11	8/9	9/11	9/11
D5S818	12/13	11/11	11/12	9/11
TPOX	8/8	8/8	8/8	8/11
D8S1179	13/15	13/15	13/14	13/14
D12S391	19/21	18/19	15/19	15/22
D19S433	15/16	14/16	15/17.2	13/17.2
FGA	19/24	20/20	19/21	21/21

exclusion at only one locus. A reason for such an observation can be a mutation event in the germ line. However, one has also to consider the possibility that the alleged father is not the father and that the other loci do not show exclusion only by chance. These alternatives have to be compared in a biostatistical calculation. Locus specific mutation rates are known, and the mutation is considered as negative evidence for the paternity probability [3, 4]. As mutation rates are small, ($<1 \times 10^{-3}$), mutations are only seen in ca. 1 of 100 cases.

Molecular basis of the mutation events is most likely the so-called replication slippage. It is supposed that both strands of the DNA separate and re-anneal subsequently during replication under the formation of a loop. This loop consists of one or more repeat units. The reparation of this loop results in the gain or loss of repeats [5]. In most cases, mutations have a "one-step" character, which means that the number of repeats is changed by +1 or −1 [6].

It is also important to exclude first-grade relatives of the alleged father from being the true father of the child in cases with single exclusions/mutations. Owing to the genetic similarity in families, a first-grade relative

of the true father will show less exclusions to the child than a unrelated man.

Gonosomal Marker and Paternity Testing

Besides autosomal chromosomes, sex chromosomes carry STR markers as well. Both the Y-chromosomal markers as well as the X-chromosomal markers [7] are useful for paternity and kinship testing.

As there is no recombination of the Y chromosome, the information of several markers can be combined and analyzed as haplotype. Due to the paternal segregation, it is possible to follow male lineages over many generations [8].

In kinship testing, it is therefore possible to compare the Y chromosome of a child with those of distant relative from the paternal line. In case the alleged father has died, an uncle, the grandfather, or the granduncle can be tested instead. In contrast to the genetic information of the autosomal markers, which is "diluted" from generation to generation, a test with distant relatives can be successfully solved with Y markers.

The other sex chromosome, the X, is interesting for paternity tests with daughters. Females inherit

Table 2   Results of a half-sibling test using X-chromosomal markers

DNA-system	DNA-criteria Alleged sibling A	DNA-criteria Alleged sibling B
AMEL	X/X	X/X
DXS10103	17/19	19/19
DXS8378	10/13	10/11
DXS7132	14/15	13/15
DXS10134	32/37	35/38
DXS10074	9/17	8/8
DXS10101	29.2/31	27.2/28.2
DXS10135	22/23	20.1/31
HPRTB	12/13	11/13
DXS10148	20/26.1	24.1/28.1
DXS7423	15/15	14/15
DXS10146	25/41.2	26/29
DXS10079	20/22	19/19

Table 3   Genotypes of the child, the mother, and the alleged father and the resulting paternity index formulas

Child	Mother	Alleged father	PI
A_i/A_i	A_i/A_i	A_i/A_i	$1/p_i$
		A_i/A_j	$1/2p_i$
	A_i/A_j	A_i/A_i	$1/p_i$
		A_i/A	$1/2p_i$
$A_i/A_j\ (i{\neq}j)$	A_i/A_i	A_j/A_j	$1/p_j$
		A_j/A_k	$1/2p_j$
	A_i/A_j	A_i/A_j	$1/(p_i+p_j)$
		A_i/A_j	$1/(p_i+p_j)$
		A_j/A_k	$1/(2p_i+2p_j)$
	A_i/A_k	A_j/A_j	$1/p_j$
		A_j/A_l	$1/2p_j$

Modified from [9] and reproduced with permission from Ref. [10] © Springer Science and Business Media 2007. $K{\neq}i{\neq}j{\neq}l$

the X chromosome of the father. Kinship cases with the grandmother instead of the alleged father are an example for the use of the X chromosome markers. In this constellation, the X-chromosomal markers are as powerful as the autosomal markers.

If two daughters with different mothers want to know if they have the same father, a test of the X-chromosomal markers can also reveal exclusions, as the daughters must share at least one X-chromosomal marker allele for each locus in case of relation. Table 2 is showing an example of such a half-sibling test.

A test of 12 loci resulted in 7 exclusions and thus proved the two females are unrelated. Such a clear result would not have been possible with a test of the "regular" autosomal markers. During the biostatistical evaluation of the X-chromosmal makers, a linkage has to be considered as well. Owing to the close proximity of the markers, some are segregated as linkage groups.

Statistical Evaluation

In case of non-exclusion of the alleged father, a statistical evaluation of the laboratory results is carried out. For this, a likelihood ratio is calculated. In a normal case involving mother, child, and alleged father, or a child and an alleged father, the probability of two alternative hypotheses is determined. The hypotheses are

X : the alleged father is the father of the child

and

Y : the alleged father and the child are unrelated

The second hypothesis is often formulated as "someone else, unrelated with the alleged father, is father of the child", which is equal to the wording given earlier. The probabilities of both hypotheses are set into relation. For the first hypothesis, the frequency of the genotype constellation in a theoretical group of real families is calculated. For the second hypothesis, the frequency of the genotype constellation in a theoretical group of "false" families (in which the alleged father is not the father) is calculated. After simplifying the resulting equations, the decisive factor is the population frequency of the allele which the child inherited from the father. A rare characteristic leads to a high paternity probability, a frequent one is less indicative for the paternity.

Table 3 shows the formulas relevant for the calculation of X/Y in cases with father, mother, and child. Typically, computer software that derives the respective formulas from the genotype constellation and that has access to the allele frequency data tables is used for the calculations. Table 4 shows the same formulas for motherless cases.

The likelihood ratio X/Y is also called Paternity Index (PI), a value above 1 means that the paternity of the tested man is more likely than the non-paternity. The likelihood ratios of the individual markers are combined by multiplication. The combined likelihood ratio is also called Combined Paternity Index (CPI). Experts in many countries convert the paternity index into a percentage value with the so-called

Table 4   Genotypes of the child and the alleged father and the resulting paternity index formulas

Child	Alleged father	PI
A_i/A_i	A_i/A_i	$1/p_i$
	A_i/A_j	$1/2p_i$
A_i/A_j $(i{\neq}j)$	A_j/A_j	$1/p_j$
	A_i/A_k	$1/4p_i$
	A_i/A_j	$(p_i{+}p_j)/4p_ip_j$

$K \neq i \neq j$

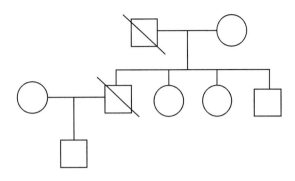

Figure 3   Schematic presentation of a family tree in a deficiency case. [Reproduced with permission from Ref. [10]. © Springer Science and Business Media, 2007.]

Essen-Möller Formula [11]:

$$W = 1/(1 + Y/X) \qquad (1)$$

A figure above 50% means that the paternity of the tested man is more likely. This calculation contains the assumption of the so-called *a priori* probability of 50%. This means that the chance of the tested man to be the father before the laboratory test was 50%. Most laboratories use a reporting threshold in a way that above a certain, predefined probability, the paternity is considered as "proven".

It is important to keep in mind that the second hypothesis (see earlier) considers unrelatedness between the tested man and the child. In cases where a close relative of the alleged father could be the true father as well, the above-described statistics is not applicable. A modified statistical approach is necessary, as well as an expanded testing scheme using more markers. However, also cases in which for example the brother of the tested man can be the alleged father are nevertheless solvable.

Kinship Cases

If the alleged father is not available for testing, different strategies can followed to solve such a case. In case he has passed away, one might find a pathological tissue specimen stored in a hospital from the deceased. Such samples have an independent record on the identity and are well suited for genetic testing in most cases [12].

If there are no pathological specimens, relatives of the alleged father might be tested and the paternity case becomes a kinship case. First grade relatives like parents, siblings, or children of the alleged father are suitable for such an approach. Figure 3 shows a

pedigree where instead of the alleged father three of his siblings are tested. Depending on the pedigree, no exclusion constellations may be observed. In such cases, the non-paternity has to be proven by a probability calculation. Furthermore, one has to keep in mind that a negative test result might also be caused by so far unknown non-paternity somewhere else in the pedigree. Sometimes, an exhumation is the last alternative in such cases without relatives or tissue samples.

Paternity Tests in Case of Immigration

Besides paternity tests for family reasons, many countries request a paternity test from visa applicants. If legal alien residents request the subsequent immigration of family members or if relatives of legal alien residents apply for a visa, they are requested in many countries to prove the relation with a genetic test. From a laboratory's perspective, organizing a sampling abroad can be a challenging, as the sampler may have no or little previous experience with the requirements necessary for taking samples. However, the legal requirements have to be met by the sampler. Therefore a detailed instruction sent with the forms is certainly helpful.

Quality Management in Paternity Testing Laboratories

To ensure the quality of the laboratory process, paternity testing laboratories are subject to quality management rules. One aspect of the quality management system is accreditation. National laboratory accreditation bodies monitor participating laboratories according to international norms like ISO/IEC 17025 [13]. It is an international standard for the technical competency of a laboratory and covers every aspect of the process from sample preparation to analytical testing and the reports. One step of the quality management system and the requirement of the norm ISO/IEC 17025 is the participation in proficiency testing programs. Regular audits by the National laboratory accreditation bodies ensure that the quality management system is applied by the laboratory.

References

[1] Landsteiner, K. (1901). Über Agglutinationserscheinungen normalen menschlichen Blutes, *Wien klin Wschr* **14**, 1132–1134.

[2] Jeffreys, A.J., Wilson, V. & Thein, S.L. (1985). Individual-specific 'fingerprints' of human DNA, *Nature* **316**, 76–79.

[3] Henke, J., Fimmers, R., Baur, M.P. & Henke, L. (1993). DNA-minisatellite mutations, recent investigations concerning distribution and impact on parentage testing, *International Journal of Legal Medicine* **105**, 217–222.

[4] Rolf, B., Keil, W., Brinkmann, B., Roewer, L. & Fimmers, R. (2001). Paternity testing using Y-STR haplotypes: Assigning a probability for paternity in cases of mutations, *International Journal of Legal Medicine* **115**, 12–15.

[5] Levinson, G. & Gutman, G.A. (1987). Slipped-strand mispairing: a major mechanism for DNA sequence evolution, *Molecular and Biological Evolution* **4**, 203–221.

[6] Brinkmann, B., Klintschar, M., Neuhuber, F., Hühne, J. & Rolf, B. (1998). Mutation rate in human microsatellites: influence of the structure and length of the tandem repeat, *The American Journal of Human Genetics* **62**, 1408–1415.

[7] Szibor, R., Krawczak, M., Hering, S., Edelmann, J., Kuhlisch, E. & Krause, D. (2003). Use of X-linked markers for forensic purposes, *International Journal of Legal Medicine* **117**, 67–74.

[8] Foster, E.A., Jobling, M.A., Taylor, P.G., Donnelly, P., de Knijff, P., Mieremet, R., Zerjal, T. & Tyler-Smith, C. (1998). Jefferson fathered slave's last child, *Nature* **396**, 27–28.

[9] Krüger, J., Fuhrmann, W., Lichte, K.H. & Steffens, C. (1968). Zur Verwendung des Polymorphismus der sauren Erythrocytenphosphatase, *Deutsche Zeitschrift für die Gesamte Gerichtliche Medizin* **64**, 127–146.

[10] Rolf, B. & Wiegand, P. (2007). Abstammungsbegutachtung, Rechtsmedizin 17, pp 109–119.

[11] Essen-Möller, E. (1938). Die Beweiskraft der Ähnlichkeit im Vaterschaftsnachweis; theoretische Grundlagen, *Mitt Anthr Ges (Wien)* **68**, 9–53.

[12] Gjertson, D.W., Brenner, C.H., Baur, M.P., Carracedo, A., Guidet, F., Luque, J.A., Lessig, R., Mayr, W.R., Pascali, V.L., Prinz, M., Schneider, P.M. & Morling, N. (2007). ISFG: Recommendations on biostatistics in paternity testing, *Forensic Science International: Genetics* **1**, 223–231.

[13] Wiegand, P., Madea, B. & Musshoff, F. (2014). International Guidelines and Accreditation in Forensic Medizin, in *Handbook of Forensic Medicine*, B. Madea, ed., John Wiley & Sons, Ltd, Chichester.

Related Articles

DNA

Familial Searching

Introduction to Forensic DNA Profiling – The Electropherogram (epg)

Introduction to Forensic Genetics

Missing Persons and Paternity: DNA

Chapter 21
Observer Effects

William C. Thompson

University of California, Irvine, CA, USA

Introduction

The term observer effect generally describes circumstances in which the results of an observation are affected by the observer. In physics, the term has been used to describe circumstances in which the act of observation changes the phenomenon being observed, as where measurement of electrical current in a circuit changes the current flow. By contrast, in the social sciences and in forensic science, the term is used to describe circumstances in which the observer's preconceptions or motives influence conclusions drawn from data [1]. The preconceptions and motives are thought to influence the perception and interpretation of the evidence rather than changing the evidence itself. Observer effects are sometimes also called examiner bias [2, 3] although it important to note that the "bias" entailed in the phenomenon may occur without the observer intending or even being aware of it [4, 5].

Observer effects are closely related to context effects and the two terms are sometimes used synonymously [4]. The term context effect originated in psychology and has been used to describe circumstances in which the perception of a stimulus is affected by the surrounding context, as where a gray object looks lighter against a dark background than against a light background (see, e.g., http://web.mit.edu/persci/people/adelson/checkershadow_illusion.html). In forensic science, the term context effect has been used more broadly to describe situations in which the results of a forensic analysis are affected by the circumstances in which it is performed, and particularly by the information available to the

analyst, as when an analyst becomes more likely to identify a latent print as that of a suspect when told that another analyst has already made the identification or when told that other evidence indicates the suspect made the print. The "other evidence" might be said to provide a "context" that changes the analyst's interpretation of the data contained in the prints. Alternatively, the "other information" might be said to have changed the analyst's expectations about the data and hence to have induced an observer effect.

The same phenomenon is sometimes described as confirmation bias. In psychology and cognitive science, the term confirmation bias refers to a human tendency to evaluate evidence in a manner that supports or confirms one's preconceptions, such as a tendency to search out and give more weight to evidence that supports a favored hypothesis than to evidence that contradicts it [5]. In forensic science, the term confirmation bias has been used in a manner that is roughly interchangeable with the terms observer effect and context effect [6, 7].

Underlying Psychological Phenomenon

Underlying all of these terms is a basic phenomenon of human psychology – the tendency of observers to interpret data in a manner consistent with their expectations and desires. The existence of this phenomenon is well established – it has been called *one of the most venerable ideas of traditional epistemology* as well as *one of the better demonstrated findings of twentieth century psychology* [8]. An early discussion of the phenomenon can be found in the writings of Francis Bacon, who commented in 1620 that

> The human understanding when it has once adopted an opinion draws all things else to support and agree with it. And though there be a greater number and

A Guide to Forensic DNA Profiling
Edited by Allan Jamieson and Scott Bader
© 2016 John Wiley & Sons, Ltd. ISBN: 9781118751527
Also published in EFS (online edition)
DOI: 10.1002/9780470061589.fsa144

weight of instances to be found on the other side, yet these it either neglects and despises, or else by some distinction sets aside and rejects, in order that by this great and pernicious predetermination the authority of its former conclusions may remain inviolate [9].

Even earlier, Julius Caesar [10] famously noted men's tendency to "believe quite readily that which they wish to be true". In the twentieth century, psychologists confirmed the existence and strength of these phenomena with innumerable experiments in which people's interpretation of a variety of stimuli, data, and forms of evidence were shown to be influenced by preconceptions and desires. The effects are greatest when the underlying data are somewhat ambiguous and when observers are influenced by strongly held expectations and motives. Extensive reviews of this literature are found in [1, 4, 5, 8, 11, 12].

The most relevant studies relate to the interpretation of scientific data. Like everyone else, scientists have a tendency to interpret data in a manner that supports theories that they favor. The tendency of academic scientists to cling to pet theories, well past the point at which such adherence could be justified by the evidence, has been widely noted [13–15]. In his iconic book *Galileo's Revenge: Junk Science in the Courtroom* [16], Peter Huber traced several false scientific theories to misinterpretation of data arising from uncontrolled observer effects. A scientist who is committed to a pet theory inevitably (and unconsciously) interprets data in a manner consistent with that theory. By Huber's account, uncontrolled observer effects are one of the hallmarks of junk science.

Minimizing Observer Effects

Allowing preconceptions to influence the interpretation of data is said to be the "cardinal sin for the formal, pure scientist" [8]. Accordingly, when scientists must rely on subjective judgment to interpret the results of an experiment, they routinely take careful steps to mask or shield the person interpreting data from extraneous information that might improperly influence the interpretation. For example, scientists in most fields use "blind" or "double-blind" procedures when relying on subjective judgment to interpret data. Blind procedures are also widely used for peer-review of scientific articles, for grading of written examinations, and for other functions for which it is important to minimize observer effects.

The field of forensic science has been criticized for failing to take adequate steps to minimize observer effects [1, 4]. Through communications with police, lawyers, and other experts, forensic scientists often are exposed to information that may influence their expectations and perhaps even their hopes and desires about what a particular examination might reveal [1]. Moreover, when performing examinations forensic scientists often rely in part on subjective judgment to evaluate potentially ambiguous data [17]. Even seemingly objective procedures like DNA testing sometimes require analysts to use subjective judgment to resolve crucial ambiguities and hence could potentially be influenced by observer effects [3, 18–21]. Yet forensic scientists rarely take steps to shield themselves from extraneous information – i.e., information unnecessary for making a scientific assessment – when making comparisons or interpreting test results [1] (*see* **Degraded Samples**).

The difference between forensic science and other scientific fields may stem in part from uncertainty about what types of information are necessary and relevant to a forensic science assessment. In some forensic disciplines consideration of nonscientific evidence is not only accepted but required by professional norms. For example, fire investigators are trained to consider whether a suspect had a motive for setting a fire when deciding whether to classify a fire as arson [22]. There have been reports of forensic scientists relying on nonscientific evidence in other disciplines as well, such as a DNA analyst who defended a "match" that implicated the defendant in a rape case by saying: "I know I am right. They found the victim's purse in [the defendant's] apartment" [21]. In 1997 the US Justice Department's Office of Inspector General reported that FBI explosives experts had relied on extraneous evidence when making key scientific determinations in a number of important cases [23]. In the first World Trade Center bombing in 1993, for example, FBI examiners had relied on the fact that the suspects had access to urea nitrate to reach the conclusion that urea nitrate had been used to make the bomb. The Inspector General condemned this reasoning as circular and biased. The FBI laboratory management agreed and pledged to take steps to ensure that the problem never happened again. Academic commentators have been unanimous in condemning the use of such nonscientific evidence as a basis for scientific conclusions [1, 6, 7, 17, 18]. They argue that the role of the forensic scientist is to offer conclusions derived from a scientific discipline, not to offer conclusions based in part on analysis of other evidence in the case.

Forensic scientists have become more aware of the importance of addressing observer effects as a result of a high-profile error by the FBI's fingerprint identification unit in the Madrid train bombing case [6, 7, 24]. Three highly trained FBI latent print examiners, and a well regarded independent examiner, all identified a latent print associated with the Madrid bombing as having come from Brandon Mayfield, a resident of Portland, Oregon. The error came to light when Spanish authorities determined the latent print actually matched an Algerian suspected terrorist. The FBI acknowledged the error and apologized to Mr Mayfield. In a subsequent analysis, the agency attributed the error in part to confirmation bias. After an initial erroneous identification, each subsequent examiner was fully aware that the latent print had previously been matched to Mayfield. This knowledge may have led them to place too much weight on similarities between the two prints while ignoring or discounting discrepancies.

Empirical Studies of Observer Effects in Forensic Science

Empirical studies have confirmed that observer effects can influence the interpretation of latent prints, leading to errors [25–28]. For example, in one clever study, psychologists asked five highly experienced latent print examiners to compare pairs of prints [26]. The examiners were not told that they had previously individualized these pairs (i.e., found them to match) during casework. Each examiner was instead told (incorrectly) that the prints were those that the FBI had erroneously matched in the Madrid train bombing case. Although they were instructed to "ignore all the contextual information and focus solely on the actual prints", three of the five examiners changed their previous judgment of "match" to "no match" and a fourth changed from "match" to "cannot tell". Only one of the five examiners consistently maintained that the prints were a "match". In other words, after exposure to "extraneous information" suggesting that the prints should *not* match, four of five examiners reached a different conclusion than they had reached previously when comparing the same prints.

Studies in other forensic science domains have also found evidence of observer effects on examiners'

judgments [29]. Research on the precise mechanisms by which observer effects influence interpretation are just beginning to emerge [30]. Additional research in this important area is clearly needed.

Case Managers and Sequential Unmasking

There are a number of procedures for minimizing observer effects [1, 4, 31]. One method is to separate various laboratory functions and assign them to different people. A case manager who is fully informed of the facts of the case decides what to test and how to test it; a laboratory analyst who is "blind" to extraneous information analyzes and interprets the test results. To the extent possible, the analyst remains "blind" to extraneous information, such as information about the legal consequences of the judgment and nonscientific evidence in the case, when deciding whether samples "match". Once the analyst interprets and records the test results, the case manager (who is aware of the broader facts of the case) is then responsible for placing the test results in context and assessing the compatibility of forensic observations with various theories of what occurred.

Another approach is simply to perform the analysis and evaluation of various samples in a sequence so that analysis and interpretation of early samples cannot be influenced by knowledge of the later samples. Evidentiary samples, which are generally more difficult evaluate, are analyzed first, before the analyst knows the features of the reference samples. For example, fingerprint examiners can decide whether a latent print is interpretable and which features of the latent print constitute reliable data before knowing whether those features are consistent or inconsistent with a reference print. Similarly, DNA analysts can decide which "alleles" in an evidentiary sample profile are real and which are spurious before knowing whether those alleles match up with a suspect's. Information required to draw an ultimate conclusion is "unmasked" when needed but the analyst performs as much work as possible while "blind" to unnecessary facts [31].

References

[1] Risinger, D.M., Saks, M.J., Thompson, W.C. & Rosenthal, R. (2002). The Daubert/Kumho implications of observer effects in forensic science: hidden problems of expectation and suggestion, *California Law Review* **90**(1), 1–56.

[2] Beckham, J.C., Annis, L.V. & Gustafson, D.J. (1989). Decision making and examiner bias in forensic expert recommendations for not guilty by reason of insanity, *Law and Human Behavior* **13**(1), 79–87.

[3] Thompson, W.C. (1998). Examiner bias in forensic RFLP analysis, *Scientific Testimony: An Online Journal*, http://www.scientific.org/case-in-point/articles/thompson/thompson.html.

[4] Saks, M.J., Risinger, D.M., Rosenthal, R. & Thompson, W.C. (2003). Context effects in forensic science, *Science and Justice* **43**(2), 77–90.

[5] Plous, S. (1993). *The Psychology of Judgment and Decision Making*, McGraw-Hill, New York.

[6] Stacey, R.B. (2004). Report on the erroneous fingerprint individualization in the Madrid train bombing case, *Journal of Forensic Identification* **54**(6), 706–718.

[7] Office of the Inspector General U.S. Department of Justice (2006). *A Review of the FBI's Handling of the Brandon Mayfield Case*, Office of the Inspector General U.S. Department of Justice, Washington, DC, pp. 1–330.

[8] Nisbett, R. & Ross, L. (1980). *Human Inference*, Prentice Hall, Englewood Cliffs, p. 67.

[9] Bacon, F. (1620). Novum Organum, Book I, 109, point 46, reprinted, in *Great Books of the Western World*, R.M. Hutchins ed. Vol. 30, Britannica Publishing, New York.

[10] Caesar, G.J. (1873). *Commentaries on the Gallic War 155* (51 BCE), John Wiley & Sons.

[11] Schneider, D.J., Hastorf, A.H. & Ellsworth, P.C. (1979). *Person Perception*, 2nd Edition, Addison-Wesley Publishing, Reading.

[12] Gilovich, T. (1991). *How We Know What Isn't So: The Fallibility of Human Reason in Everyday Life*, The Free Press, New York.

[13] Barber, B. (1952). *Science and the Social Order*, Collier, New York.

[14] Kuhn, T.S. (1962). *The Structure of Scientific Revolutions*, University of Chicago Press, Chicago.

[15] Mahoney, M.J. (1976). *Scientist as Subject: The Psychological Imperative*, Ballinger, Cambridge.

[16] Huber, P.W. (1991). *Galileo's Revenge: Junk Science in the Courtroom*, Basic Books, New York.

[17] Thompson, W.C. & Cole, S.A. (2007). Psychological aspects of forensic identification evidence, in *Expert Psychological Testimony for the Courts*, M. Costanzo, D. Krauss & K. Pezdek, eds, Lawrence Erlbaum and Associates, New York.

[18] Thompson, W.C. (1995). Subjective interpretation, laboratory error and the value of forensic DNA evidence: three case studies, *Genetica* **96**, 153–168.

[19] Thompson, W.C. (1997). A sociological perspective on the science of forensic DNA testing, *UC Davis Law Review* **30**(4), 1113–1136.

[20] Thompson, W.C. (1997). Accepting lower standards: the National Research Council's second report on forensic DNA evidence, *Jurimetrics Journal* **37**(4), 405–424.

[21] Thompson, W.C., Ford, S., Doom, T., Raymer, M. & Krane, D. (2003). Evaluating forensic DNA evidence: essential elements of a competent defense review: part 1, *The Champion* **27**(3), 16–25.

[22] Lentini, J. (2006). *Scientific Protocols for Fire Investigation*, CRC Press, Boca Raton.

[23] Office of the Inspector General, U.S. Department of Justice (1997). *The FBI Laboratory: An Investigation into Laboratory Practices and Alleged Misconduct in Explosives-Related and Other Cases*, Office of the Inspector General, U.S. Department of Justice, Washington, DC.

[24] Thompson, W.C. & Cole, S.A. (2005). Lessons from the Brandon Mayfield case, *The Champion* **29**, 32–34.

[25] Dror, I.E., Peron, A., Hind, S.L. & Charlton, D. (2005). When emotions get the better of us: the effect of contextual top-down processing on matching fingerprints, *Applied Cognitive Psychology* **19**(6), 799–809.

[26] Dror, I.E., Charlton, D. & Peron, A. (2006). Contextual information renders experts vulnerable to making erroneous identifications, *Forensic Science International* **156**, 74–78.

[27] Dror, I.E. & Charlton, D. (2006). Why experts make errors, *Journal of Forensic Identification* **56**(4), 600–616.

[28] Dror, I.E. & Rosenthal, R. (2008). Meta-analytically quantifying the reliability and biasability of forensic experts, *Journal of Forensic Sciences* **53**(4), 900–903.

[29] Miller, L.S. (1987). Procedural bias in forensic examination of hair, *Law and Human Behavior* **11**(2), 157–163.

[30] Schiffer, B. & Champod, C. (2007). The potential (negative) influence of observational biases at the analysis stage of fingermark individualization, *Forensic Science International* **167**, 116–120.

[31] Krane, D.E., Ford, S., Gilder, J.R., Inman, K., Jamieson, A., Koppl, R., Kornfield, I.L., Risinger, D.M., Rudin, N., Taylor, M.S. & Thompson, W.C. (2008). Sequential unmasking: a means of minimizing observer effects in forensic DNA interpretation (letter), *Journal of Forensic Sciences* **53**(4), 1006–1007.

Related Articles

Identification and Individualization

Related Articles in EFS Online

PART C
Applications

Chapter 22
Databases

Simon J. Walsh

Australian Federal Police, Canberra, ACT, Australia

Introduction

Typically, forensic DNA databases consist of two separate collections of profiles: a database of the profiles of individuals who have either volunteered or been compelled to submit samples and a database of profiles obtained from samples from crime scenes or from exhibits associated with an alleged offense (Figure 1). The administrator of a database typically has capacity to compare profiles from

1. individuals to individuals;
2. crime samples to individuals; and
3. crime samples to other crime samples.

The overall database comprises (at least) two separate indices. One contains the DNA profiles from individuals, whereas the other stores DNA profiles from crimes. These separate databases can be matched internally (as depicted by arrows (a) and (c) in Figure 1). These matches seek to locate duplicate entries on the "offender database" or crimes with a common DNA profile, respectively. The databases are also matched against each other (as depicted by arrow (b) in Figure 1). This is often regarded as the most informative match process, as it links individuals on the "offender database" with profiles associated with crimes.

In a relatively short period, the growth of DNA databases internationally has been rapid with tens of millions of short tandem repeat (STR) profiles now held from convicted offenders, suspects, and unsolved crimes. Links provided through DNA database searches have contributed valuable intelligence to literally millions of criminal investigations. Often links are provided for crimes that are notoriously difficult to resolve, such as property crime (such as burglary and vehicle theft) and historic unsolved crimes (commonly referred to as *cold cases*). The global scale of DNA database use, its relative infancy, the complexity of addressing requisite socio-legal concerns, and the expanding capability of forensic DNA profiling combine to create a challenging law enforcement tool that demands careful assessment and management. This section introduces the emergence of forensic DNA databases in more detail and isolates aspects of their development for more detailed consideration.

A Brief Summary of National DNA Database Programs

Over the past two decades, the establishment of a forensic DNA database has been an important development for police and forensic agencies. There has been wide acceptance of the concept, and large-scale DNA database operations now exist in most developed countries.

As the initial National DNA Database, the United Kingdom has benefited from a broad legislative regime and consistent funding and has grown remarkably since 1995. The UK National DNA Database (NDNAD) now contains about 5 million person profiles (as at December 2014) and about 480 000 crime profiles. In 2013–2014 alone, 17 152 crimes were solved (detected) following an NDNAD match, giving a detection rate of 58% from the 29 351 crimes where scene profiles were loaded to the NDNAD. National DNA databases also exist in 27 European Union countries, including Austria, Belgium, Croatia, Cyprus, Czech Republic, Denmark, Estonia, Finland, France, Germany, Hungary, the

A Guide to Forensic DNA Profiling
Edited by Allan Jamieson and Scott Bader
© 2016 John Wiley & Sons, Ltd. ISBN: 9781118751527
Also published in EFS (online edition)
DOI: 10.1002/9780470061589.fsa108.pub2

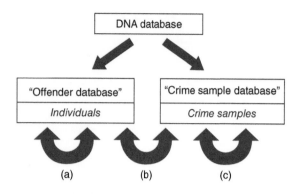

Figure 1   Summary of functionality of a standard DNA database system

Netherlands, Norway, Portugal, Slovenia, Spain, Sweden, Switzerland, and Ukraine (data provided by European Network of Forensic Science Institutes (ENFSI), see http://www.enfsi.eu/).

In 1989, the Federal Bureau of Investigation (FBI) launched the Combined Offender DNA Index System (CODIS) as a pilot program. This was fortified in 1994 with the creation of the *DNA Identification Act*. The technology was standardized to a panel of 13 STR loci (known colloquially as the *CODIS loci*). All 50 states have enacted legislation to establish a State Index, and once uploaded at the State level, the data are combined at the National level through CODIS. In May 2015, there were over 11 780 000 individual profiles and 632 000 crime profiles on CODIS. There have been more than 270 000 investigations aided through CODIS. The information management system that operates CODIS is made freely available by the FBI and has been adopted in at least 28 countries.

The Canadian Government committed to DNA databasing by introducing the *DNA Identification Act in 1998*, and implementing the national database in June 2000. The National DNA Database of Canada has shown consistent growth over its eight-year history. Currently (July 2015), the National DNA Database holds over 313 000 person profiles and 108 000 crime profiles and has contributed links to over 36 000 crimes.

Australia is a federation of six states and two territories. Each has implemented a DNA database, with the first (Victoria) beginning in 1997. Because of difficulties, harmonizing laws data was only combined onto a National system in 2007. The National Criminal Identification DNA Database (NCIDD) is managed by the Federal agency CrimTrac. In 2012–2013, 135 992 DNA samples from crime scenes were matched to individuals, and 51 600 crime scenes to other crime scenes, linking together police investigations. The New Zealand National DNA database began in 1995 as the second national database in the world. It now has about 160 000 person samples and 34 000 crime profiles. The New Zealand DNA database has a high "hit" rate with nearly 70% of all unsolved cases loaded on the case sample database successfully linked to individuals, and 30% linked to another crime.

An appealing aspect of forensic DNA technology has always been the potential for the standardized STR outputs to be shared widely by police and/or forensic agencies. While this widespread international exchange is yet to be reached, the recent heightened awareness around the threat of transnational crime and terrorism has precipitated significant early steps toward the formation of international DNA database capabilities. In Europe, the Council of the European Union released the first resolution covering the exchange of DNA analysis results in 1997. The resolution called on Member States to consider establishing their own national DNA databases and to agree common standards for DNA profiling to *facilitate the exchange of data*. This approach was acknowledged as an important tool for investigating and combating cross-border crime. Work on agreeing common standards for DNA profiling was being advanced under the umbrella of the ENFSI. The Prüm Treaty, signed by Belgium, Germany, France, Luxembourg, the Netherlands, Austria, and Spain in March 2006, provides for enhanced cross-border cooperation of the police and judicial authorities. The signatories agreed to give one another access to their DNA and fingerprint files using a *hit/no hit* system. This approach creates a necessary distinction between databasing and speculative searching of DNA profiles between states and the preferred process of exchanging specific profiles during serious international investigations. More countries have embraced the EU-Prüm-Decision (2008/615/JHA) and now regularly exchange profiles: Austria, Germany, Spain, Luxembourg, Slovenia, Finland, France, Bulgaria, Slovakia, Latvia, Lithuania, Romania, Hungary, Poland, Cyprus, and the Netherlands.

An example of bona fide international databasing is the Interpol DNA Database, set up by the Interpol General Secretariat in 2003. The database (or Gateway) provides a resource through which Interpol's member countries can exchange and compare DNA profile data. Access to the Interpol database (by what are termed *beneficiaries* or *users*) is allowable only following a written undertaking. Existing users can also object to any new beneficiary being granted access. The submitting countries retain ownership of the profiles and have direct control of submission, access, and deletion, in accordance with (their own) national legislation. Once a match occurs and the submitting country has been notified, then that country can communicate or request additional material to or from another country, subject to restrictions imposed by that country. This framework is aimed at meeting understandable concerns about privacy of, and control of, profiles once they leave national borders.

To date, wholesale contributions to the Interpol Database have been limited to a few countries. Presumably, this is due to the realization that for most crime types there is limited intelligence value in exporting large quantities of DNA profiles for international searching. By the end of 2013, Interpol's DNA database (known as *DNA Gateway*) held just over 140 000 profiles from 69 countries. Searches of the database in 2013 alone had produced 86 hits. Given that in all cases the act of searching involved only adding a profile already collected and analyzed, each of these instances of success must be seen as adding quite significant value toward achieving an otherwise improbable identification.

The many millions of profiles from the many countries around the world, and the links with over a million crimes represent the product of considerable investment from national governments and the police and forensic agencies responsible for law enforcement in these territories. While this progress is impressive, DNA database operations are still relatively recent additions to the criminal justice system and the principal focus to date has been on their establishment and growth. It is important that we also examine the operational and socio-legal impact the databases have had on the criminal justice system and how we can learn from experiences to date and ensure that continued positive outcomes will flow from their future use.

Operational Impact of Forensic DNA Databases

As the technology that forms the basis for DNA intelligence databases is specialized, the operational components have remained the responsibility of forensic biology laboratories. In general, the database and its products are the property of law enforcement agencies with the analytical and matching processes administered on their behalf by forensic institutions. All aspects of the process, whether handled by police or scientists, are subject to governing legislation. Often, this legislation contains clauses that facilitate external review of operations by delegated parliamentary authorities. From a forensic scientist's perspective, the legal basis for the administration of DNA databases represents an additional level of governance over their work. DNA laws typically contain sections that prescribe the appropriate conditions under which a DNA sample can be collected, analyzed, and stored, and the criminal sanctions that are enforceable for individuals in breach of these requirements. Although not possible to itemize all the various offense categories here, they generally include intentionally or recklessly supplying forensic material for analysis, improperly accessing or disseminating information stored on the DNA database, and matching profiles on the database unlawfully. Penalties can include fines and/or prison sentences.

In a practical context, the impact of the operational management of forensic DNA databases has had a much more profound effect on forensic organizations than the need to adjust processes to adhere to the governing legislation. The snapshot of global database models provided above illustrates that a unifying trend in major jurisdictions has been a steady increase in the scale of database operations. While this has occurred in concert with increasingly broad legislative regimes, it is more likely to have been a critical impetus for iterative legislative expansion.

The workload generated through DNA database operations has compelled forensic laboratories to find efficiency gains in the analytical process. The workload generated through DNA database operations has been a major burden on forensic DNA providers. Many have simply not coped with the volume of submissions and have experienced considerable backlogs and case processing delays. In the United States, in 2003, there were over 540 000 unsolved homicide, rape, and property crime cases in the hands of police or forensic agencies awaiting DNA testing [1]. Considerable resources have been directed toward this issue by the US Government (USDoJ, 2003) [2], the National Institute of Justice, and the American Society of Crime Laboratory

Directors (ASCLD) [3], but the issue remains an intractable one and one that commonly effects major forensic organizations. A more recent 2011 report from the National Institute of Justice (ref Mark Nelson, *Making Sense of DNA Backlogs – Myths vs. Reality*, U.S. Department of Justice, Office of Justice Programs, National Institute of Justice, NCJ 323197, Washington, DC, February 2011, p. 3, http://www.ncjrs.gov/pdffiles1/nij/232197.pdf) estimated the backlog in state and local laboratories, and found that the backlog in forensic casework continues to grow due to a disparity in demand and laboratory capacity.

This circumstance has compelled forensic laboratories to find efficiency gains in the analytical process and has resulted in a vastly different model of case management. Historically, police and forensic scientists have had a focus on clearing one crime at a time. Cases were submitted to the forensic laboratory after considerable investigation had occurred and, in most cases, a suspect had been identified. The role of the scientist was to process these cases and determine whether there was evidence that could assist either the prosecution or the defense of that specific crime. Occasionally, there were cases where the forensic analysis contributed vital investigative information that assisted the location and arrest of a suspect. The broad utilization of DNA technology and, in particular, the advent of DNA databasing has seen this paradigm change. Essentially, the analysis of evidence items occurs earlier in the investigative process with the hope that the scientist can produce intelligence information (such as a database link) in crimes for which no suspect has been identified through other means. The increased volume of submissions has also seen a trend away from individual case management and toward batch processing. It has also led to a greater prevalence of automated laboratory techniques that seek to achieve high-throughput analysis without extensive human involvement at all.

The combination of high analytical demand and the considerable funding associated with forensic DNA analysis has created an opportunity for commercial genetic testing providers to enter the forensic market. This is a common feature of the US landscapes. "Forensic" samples (exhibits relating to the alleged offense) typically remain the responsibility of the crime lab, but private companies are contracted to analyze offender samples on behalf of the State. With the demise of the Forensic Science Service (FSS) in

the United Kingdom, almost all of the DNA profiling for casework and databasing is now done by private companies. Even where most of the forensic scientific investigation is done by police scientists, the DNA profiling is still performed by private companies as an analytical laboratory service.

Another trend associated with the emergence of DNA database operations has been the broadening range of crimes submitted to forensic biology laboratories for analysis, contributing to the backlog of DNA profiling work in the United States. In the 1980s, DNA profiling was primarily used to solve serious crimes. It now contributes to the investigation of a broad spectrum of crimes, including property offenses such as burglary. The variation in jurisdictional, legislative, and operational frameworks can impact the case submission profile; for example, certain countries in Europe initially focused on the investigation of serious violent and sexual offenses [4]. In general, there has been a clear pattern of decrease in the proportion of cases from serious crime categories and an increase in the proportion of cases submitted from volume crime categories [5].

The changing nature of case submissions, represented above, has also been accompanied by an associated change in the type of exhibit located, and hence the type of sample(s) presented for DNA analysis. For example, serious, violent crimes would be expected to result in injuries and bleeding from those associated and therefore a higher likelihood of receiving blood as the principal evidence type. Likewise, crimes of a sexual nature predominantly involve a male offender and hence will typically be associated with semen evidence. Property crimes and drug crimes are less simple to classify in this way and are not thought to be strongly associated with a characteristic evidence (or sample) type. A general trend, however, is that these types of incidents often result in the submission of more discrete evidence types, such as cigarette butts, drinking containers, food remnants, tools or swabs from surfaces, or objects that the offenders are believed to have touched or handled (commonly referred to as *trace DNA*) [6].

Investigative and Intelligence Use of Forensic DNA Databases

As mentioned earlier, the establishment of forensic DNA databases has been a contributor to a change in thinking within forensic science. Historically, each case was processed as a unit or perhaps as a small series. The analyst adopted a *cradle-to-grave* approach and usually sought to refute or corroborate the version(s) of events suggested during either the investigation or the trial. Typically, a suspect had been identified through other means and the forensic analysis was comparative rather than suggestive.

This model has changed significantly. Forensic DNA databases have catalyzed profound changes in the volume and profile of forensic case submissions, meaning that with the exception of certain serious crimes, the focus has shifted to a batch-processing model within which the DNA database is an embedded component and where all cases and individual samples are viewed as potentially linked. At an organizational level, the critical objective is efficiency: maximizing the processing capacity in the minimal time and with the minimal associated expense. These objectives have typically been set and driven by police users as they align best with their investigative priorities.

The ability to link cases and identify a crime series has been an effective strategy in law enforcement for some time [7]. Incorporating DNA outcomes into the existing array of investigative data provides an additional mechanism to link cases committed by the same individual or organization, adding also a highly discriminating mechanism for identification. Through the ability to provide technical information capable of directing police investigations (such as by identifying a suspect or a crime-to-crime link), DNA databases are able to operate as an intelligence tool. Another important investigative feature of DNA databases is their ability to transcend jurisdictional boundaries, which may have hampered abilities of law enforcement agencies to link crimes and offenders which transcend such boundaries. This is particularly true in large countries, for example, the United States, Canada, and Australia, where states or provinces have the responsibility for law enforcement within particular physical and legislative boundaries. This more proactive use of forensic DNA outcomes also presents opportunities for more integrated and intuitive use of the technology. Achieving this relies upon a complete understanding of the nature and scope of the investigative contribution that forensic DNA profiling can make, presently and in the future.

The amalgamation of DNA profile data from numerous crimes also provides a means to examine forensic outcomes holistically for tactical or operational intelligence. The cases and crime information residing on forensic DNA databases (and indeed other forensic holdings) contain vast records of links made through scientific analyses, covering an amalgamation of crime types and localities that often remain separate in police investigative and intelligence structures. Analyzed collectively, database outcomes also offer significant value to fields such as criminology. A future step in the use of forensic DNA databases could be to extend the operational success of DNA databases to allow greater analysis of trends in criminal behavior. This could lead to proactive policing strategies that are based on a contemporary understanding of criminality.

Familial Searching

Recently, DNA databases have been utilized to assess profiles that are returned after a search with a high level of allele sharing. This is due to the increased likelihood that such a result would be returned from a person related to the donor of the comparison profile, than from an unrelated, random individual. This application of the use of forensic DNA databases is known as *familial searching* and was pioneered by the UK FSS as a legitimate investigative use of the UK NDNAD. These searches produce leads that are refined through combination with other investigative information such as geography, age of the donor, Y-chromosome testing, and so on.

Familial searching was first applied by the FSS in 2002 in the case of serial murder of three women in South Wales, which had occurred in 1973. A DNA profile taken from crime scene evidence was used for comparison and provided investigators with a familial match to Paul Kappen. Police investigation then led them to his father, Joseph Kappen, who was identified as the rapist and murderer of the three women.

While there have been celebrated examples of success from cases of familial searching, a degree of challenge and adverse commentary has begun to surface. For example, concerns have been raised that minority groups will be unfairly targeted when from a sweep of partial matches, as these groups are overrepresented in convicted offender databanks. Other opponents to this technique claim that law enforcement will waste time and resources following up on a variety of leads, many of which may be false and have no bearing on the case. However, when investigating a crime, a variety of leads must be considered and pursued; some will have merit and others will not. Through this technique, forensic science has the potential to generate leads for investigative consideration, some of which return results of great significance.

Cold Case Review and Postconviction Testing

Forensic DNA testing and state and national databases have been used retrospectively to re-examine evidence from historic, unsolved offenses originating as far back as the 1970s. In some circumstances, this analysis has not only identified a suspect for the crime in question but has proven the innocence of an already incarcerated person. In America, the New York Innocence Project (http://www.innocenceproject.org/) based at the Cardozo School of Law, New York, record that 330 persons have been exonerated (as on July 2015) following DNA testing of exhibits related to their original convictions. The Innocence Project was directly involved in 176 of these cases. Collectively, these men (and four women) have served over 2500 years in prison for crimes that they never committed, with the average jail term being in excess of 14 years. In 20 cases, the death penalty had been imposed before an individual's innocence was proved. About 70% of those exonerated were members of minority groups. Additionally, in over 40% (140 of 330) of cases involving postconviction DNA exoneration, the true perpetrator was also correctly identified through the use of DNA testing.

In 2012, only the state of Oklahoma in the United States did not have some form of law allowing postconviction access to DNA testing. The legislative models vary in the extent of provisions they afford to inmates seeking DNA retesting. In some states, all incarcerated felons are granted access to postconviction DNA testing with the associated costs borne by state authorities. In others, there are restrictions on the eligibility of certain inmates: for example, those who pleaded guilty or whose lawyers failed to request DNA testing at trial. In some models, there are time limits on when an application can be made, and the petitioning inmate must meet the cost of reanalysis. As with all laws, there is a need to strike a balance, in this case between the rights of incarcerated felons to have their convictions reviewed, and the potential for misuse of state

resources and the protracted continuation of criminal matters.

The revelations of programs such as the Innocence Project provide an example of the potential for DNA testing to uncover the truth – whether it does so on the "side" of the victim or their wrongly convicted attacker. However, it is important that we also remember that DNA is simply another example of forensic evidence. While it allows a high level of certainty regarding its conclusions, it is not infallible and does not have the same effect when used in a stand-alone capacity, in the absence of support from investigative outcomes or other forensic evidence. Also, obtaining meaningful DNA evidence relies on the accurate localization of biological material at the crime scene and the demonstration of appropriate chain of custody and procedural handling of the subsequent analysis. Operating in this way is commonplace in contemporary investigations; however, it is less assured in historic investigations, and in some cases, the lower level of rigor applied through outdated practices can jeopardize the usefulness or admissibility of forensic evidence recovered later using contemporary techniques.

For postconviction testing to be of future use, it is incumbent that all relevant evidence be collected and stored appropriately so as to allow for subsequent reanalysis. Again, it is necessary to strike a balance between collecting and storing everything indefinitely and destroying vital items of evidence too hurriedly. This is another area to be considered in postconviction legislative models and in best-practice policies and procedures for police and forensic agencies.

The realization of the ability of a "new" technology such as DNA analysis to provide greater clarity and certainty in historic investigations tells us something else about our field of science. That is, we should continue to strive to adapt and develop our technical capability. The impressive outcomes of postconviction use of DNA testing provide a stark reminder of how the technologies of tomorrow may well provide the ability to reflect with more clarity and certainty on cases occurring today.

Socio-Legal Issues Associated with Forensic DNA Databases

It is important to remember that although DNA profiling is arguably the most powerful and rapidly developing forensic investigative tool, its use is not without controversy. This is due largely to its enormous potential to implicate individuals in a crime and the risk of its deliberate or accidental misuse. The present and future uses of forensic DNA profiling are a worrying prospect for some members of the international criminal justice community and for members of the public as well.

Almost ubiquitously, the establishment of DNA databases on a state or national level has required substantial changes in legislation. There is considerable variation in the legislative models applied in different jurisdictions. Initially, offenders convicted of serious violent or sexual crimes were seen as the most suitable candidates for DNA database inclusion. Over time, the gamut of offenses for which a compulsory DNA sample can be obtained has increased to include property crimes and, in some places, summary offenses. In addition, the need for an individual to be convicted is no longer mandatory in many jurisdictions, and individuals can be sampled upon suspicion or arrest. In all cases, the legislation seeks to strike a balance between the desire for the state to develop and utilize a significant forensic resource for the purpose of more effective crime resolution and reduction, and the rights of individuals exposed to the criminal justice system.

Legislative amendments of the type that lead to the establishment of forensic DNA database nature are destined to be controversial. In some cases, observers feel that these new laws have been enacted too hastily, have lacked suitable public and legal scrutiny, and have been justified under misleading, populist "law and order" politicking. Others worry that extending police powers to allow the collection of DNA samples represents an encroachment into the previously sacred territory of criminal law and a diminution of basic individual rights, in particular, the right to silence and the right against self-incrimination. Other observers are concerned by the storage of human genetic information and its potential for future misuse.

Forensic scientists utilizing forensic DNA databases have an increased need for awareness of relevant socio-legal issues. In a practical context, DNA-based legislation represents an additional level of governance for forensic professionals and one of the first pieces of law that places direct requirements on the manner in which they undertake their professional work. In addition, it prescribes sanctions for individuals or institutions who contravene the administrative processes detailed in these laws. The debate that has continued on many of the issues associated with the use of forensic DNA profiling in the criminal justice system has expanded to encompass applications of the scientific process that are primarily the responsibility of the forensic community. Forensic professionals (and particularly the administrators of forensic institutions) must acquaint themselves with these issues and enter the existing debate. Failure to do so could mean that the direction for the application of our scientific tools will become the responsibility of people from outside the forensic community itself.

Summary

Despite the rather spectacular results that have emerged from the use of forensic DNA databases, the technology remains a relatively recent development and one that will continue to develop over time. It is important to remember that as databases grow and age, they will become more challenging to manage, as much of the information stored on them will become increasingly redundant. It is important that forensic practitioners and administrators continue to research and refine DNA database applications to ensure they continue to have an effective, positive impact.

Acknowledgment

The data in this article was updated by Scott Bader in July 2015.

References

[1] Lovrich, N.P., Gaffney, M.J., Pratt, T.C., Johnson, C.L., Asplen, C.H., Hurst, L.H. & Shellberg, T.M. (2003). *National Forensic DNA Study Report*, 12 December 2003.

[2] Office of the Inspector General (2004). *Report on the No Suspect Casework DNA Backlog Reduction Program*, Audit Report No. 05–02, November 2004.

[3] 180 Day Study Report: Status and Needs of United States Crime Laboratories, Report of the American Society of Crime Laboratory Directors, 28 May 2004.

[4] Schneider, P.M. & Martin, P.D. (2001). Criminal DNA databases: the European situation, *Forensic Science International* **119**, 232–238.

[5] Walsh, S.J. (2007). Current and future trends in forensic molecular biology, in *Molecular Forensics*, R. Rapley & D. Whitehouse, eds, John Wiley & Sons, London, pp. 1–20.

[6] Raymond, J.J., Walsh, S.J., van Oorschot, R.A., Gunn, P.R. & Roux, C. (2004). Trace DNA: an underutilised resource or Pandora's Box?, *Journal of Forensic Identification* 56(4), 668–686.

[7] Gotleib, S. (1998). *Crime Analysis – From First Report to Final Arrest*, Alpha Publishing, Montclair, CA.

Related Articles

DNA

DNA Databases and Evidentiary Issues

DNA: An Overview

Chapter 23
Missing Persons and Paternity: DNA

Bruce S. Weir

University of Washington, Seattle, WA, USA

Introduction

Matching DNA profiles have proved to be of great value in forensic science when they link a person to evidence associated with a crime. The chance of a coincidental match between the profiles of two different people is so small that matches are rightly regarded as strong evidence. This has led to the increasing use of searches for a particular profile in databases of profiles previously obtained by law enforcement agencies. These forensic applications make little appeal to an essential nature of DNA profiles – genetic markers are heritable, meaning that a parent passes on one copy of his or her marker genes to a child. This leads to the similarity of profiles between related individuals and the application of DNA profiling to parentage disputes and missing person searches. The strength of the evidence from matching or partially matching profiles depends in large degree on the degree of relatedness of the people whose DNA is examined and calculations can be complex. There is simplification, however, in the situation where the people are not inbred and where their population can be regarded as being in a state of evolutionary equilibrium. These simplifications are described in this article.

The calculations described here are all within the framework of likelihood ratios of the probabilities of an observed set of DNA profiles under alternative hypotheses about the relatedness of the people whose DNA has been examined.

A Guide to Forensic DNA Profiling
Edited by Allan Jamieson and Scott Bader
© 2016 John Wiley & Sons, Ltd. ISBN: 9781118751527
Also published in EFS (online edition)
DOI: 10.1002/9780470061589.fsa129

Measures of Inbreeding and Relatedness

The use of DNA profiles in parentage and missing persons situations rests on the comparisons of profiles from people who may be related. The greater the degree of relatedness, the more likely it is that profiles will be similar but it is necessary to be able to quantify such statements. Are father and son more related than are two brothers? How can profiles from two men be used to favor the explanation that they are brothers over the claim they are unrelated? Such questions require a means for attaching numbers to the degree of relatedness, and these numbers refer to the chance that alleles, the components of DNA profiles, are identical by descent (ibd).

People are related when they have ancestors in common and this means that relatives may share genes – the genes that descended from those ancestors. Two copies, or alleles, of the same genetic marker that have descended from the same ancestral allele are said to be identical by descent (ibd). Two individuals that have ibd alleles are said to be related, and individuals that receive ibd alleles from their parents are said to be inbred. In the classical theory of population genetics, there is an implied reference population: ibd alleles are copies of the same allele in the reference population and their histories further back in time are not considered. The probability that an allele taken at random from one individual is ibd to an allele taken at random from another individual is the coancestry coefficient θ of those two individuals. The inbreeding coefficient F of a child has the same value as the coancestry θ of its parents.

There is a simple "path-counting" method for determining coancestry coefficients. For individuals X and Y, the number of individuals in the path linking them through their common ancestor(s) A is written as α. This number includes the individuals themselves.

If F_A is the inbreeding coefficient of the ancestor, generally zero, the coancestry coefficient is given by $\theta_X = \sum_A (0.5)^\alpha (1 + F_A)$. For people related on only the maternal or paternal side of their family, there is likely to be only one ancestor A and the simplest example is that of parent Y and child X. Their common ancestor is Y and their coancestry is $(0.5)^2 = 0.25$. If Z is one of the parents of Y, then the grandparent (Z)–grandchild (X) coancestry is $(0.5)^3 = 0.125$, and so on. The two paths linking full-sibs X and Y through their parents G and H are XGY and XHY so $\theta_{XY} = (0.5)^3 + (0.5)^3 = 0.25$.

The equality of the coancestries for parent–child and full-sib pairs suggest that a more detailed quantification of relatedness is needed, and the first step is to use the number of pairs of alleles two relatives have that are ibd. There can be zero, one, or two such pairs depending on whether the individuals are unrelated, unilineal relatives (e.g., parent–child) or bilinear relatives (e.g., full-sibs). This description requires that an individual's two alleles are not themselves ibd. Calculating the probabilities k_0, k_1, k_2 that two individuals have 0, 1, 2 ibd pairs is fairly straightforward. If X has alleles a, b and Y has alleles c, d then it is necessary to ask how many of the four pairs ac, ad, bc, bd are ibd. If c is the allele that is copied by parent Y to transmit to child X, then it must be that either a or b is ibd to c. There are no other ibd relationships and $k_0 = 0$, $k_1 = 1$, $k_2 = 0$. If a, c are the alleles that full-sibs have received from parent G and b, d are the alleles they receive from parent H, then each of these pairs has equal chances of being copies of the same or different parental alleles and so being ibd or not. This leads to $k_0 = 0.25$, $k_1 = 0.50$, $k_2 = 0.25$. The coancestry coefficient θ is a summary of the three k coefficients: $\theta = k_1/4 + k_2/2$. Values of these measures are shown in Table 1 for some common relatives. Note that they all refer to the unobservable property of identity by descent. It is the expected values for those degrees of relatedness that are shown in the table.

The k-coefficients are sufficient for describing the relatedness for noninbred individuals. There is a more elaborate set of 15 coefficients for the situation with inbreeding when any two or three of four of the alleles carried by two people may be ibd. These coefficients were discussed in a review by Weir *et al.* [1]. For a random-mating population and genetic markers that have reached a state of equilibrium between the opposing evolutionary force of genetic drift that reduces genetic variation and

Table 1 Identity by descent measures for noninbred relatives

Relationship	k_2	k_1	k_0	θ
Identical twins	1	0	0	$\frac{1}{2}$
Full sibs	$\frac{1}{4}$	$\frac{1}{2}$	$\frac{1}{4}$	$\frac{1}{4}$
Parent/child	0	1	0	$\frac{1}{4}$
Half-sibs	0	$\frac{1}{2}$	$\frac{1}{2}$	$\frac{1}{8}$
First cousins	0	$\frac{1}{4}$	$\frac{3}{4}$	$\frac{1}{16}$
Unrelated	0	0	1	0

the force of mutation that increases variation, all 15 of these more complicated ibd measures can be expressed in terms of the quantity θ. This θ is the probability that any two alleles in a population are ibd and it refers to the effect of past evolutionary events rather than immediate family membership. The probability that any three alleles are ibd is $2\theta^2/(1 + \theta)$ and the chance that any four alleles are ibd is $6\theta^2/[(1 + \theta)(1 + 2\theta)]$. The probability that two pairs of alleles are ibd (whether or not all four are ibd) is $\theta^2(1 + 5\theta)/[(1 + \theta)(1 + 2\theta)]$. These results were all derived by Evett and Weir [2].

Frequencies of Sets of Alleles

Setting up a set of identity measures was the first step in allowing observed DNA profiles to be used to make inferences about relatedness of the people represented by those profiles. Identity measures describe the relationship and they can also be used to express how likely it is that two people with a specified degree of relatedness have particular profiles. In other words, if the relationship is known, then the profile types can be predicted. Some results from statistical theory can then be used to reverse the argument: if the profiles are known, what can be inferred about the relatedness?

Identity by descent cannot be observed, but the ibd probabilities allow the probabilities of sets of alleles to be expressed as functions of allele frequencies. Without any inbreeding or relatedness, the probability P_{ii} that an individual is homozygous for allele A_i is

Table 2 Genotype-pair probabilities for noninbred relatives (different subscripts denote different alleles)

Genotype pair	Probability
A_iA_i, A_iA_i	$k_2\, p_i^2 + k_1\, p_i^3 + k_0\, p_i^4$
A_iA_i, A_jA_j	$k_0\, p_i^2\, p_j^2$
A_iA_i, A_iA_j	$k_1\, p_i^2\, p_j + 2k_0\, p_i^3\, p_j$
A_iA_i, A_jA_k	$2k_0\, p_i^2\, p_j p_k$
A_iA_j, A_iA_j	$2k_2\, p_i p_j + k_1\, p_i p_j(p_i + p_j) + 4k_0\, p_i^2\, p_j^2$
A_iA_j, A_iA_k	$k_1\, p_i p_j p_k + 4k_0\, p_i^2\, p_j p_k$
A_iA_j, A_kA_l	$4k_0 p_i p_j p_k p_l$

given by the Hardy–Weinberg result $P_{ii} = p_i^2$ where p_i is the frequency of the allele. The genotype frequency P_{ij} for heterozygote A_iA_j is $P_{ij} = 2p_ip_j, j \neq i$.

For individuals with inbreeding level F, these Hardy–Weinberg frequencies are modified to $P_{ii} = p_i^2 + Fp_i(1 - p_i)$ and $P_{ij} = 2(1 - F)p_ip_j$. Of more importance in the present context are the probabilities that two related individuals have specified genotype frequencies. The probability that two noninbred members of the same family are both homozygous A_iA_i has to take into account that they may share zero, one, or two pairs of alleles ibd. This means that their four copies of allele A_i may represent four, three, or two independent (non-ibd) alleles. The required probability is

$$\Pr(A_i A_i, A_i A_i) = k_0\, p_i^4 + k_1\, p_i^3 + k_2\, p_i^2 \qquad (1)$$

and the complete set of probabilities is shown in Table 2.

To take into account the evolutionary relatedness quantified by the parameter θ, there is a very convenient result first described in the forensic context by Balding and Nichols [3]. The probability that an allele is of type A when n_A of the previous n alleles examined were of that type is $[n_A\theta + (1 - \theta)p_A]/[1 + (n - 1)\theta]$ and this can be called the *Dirichlet sampling formula*. For the first allele examined, the probability is just p_A. The probability an allele is A, given that an A has already been seen, is $[\theta + (1 - \theta)p_A]$ so the chance they are both A is $p_A[\theta + (1 - \theta)p_A] = p_A^2 + \theta p_A(1 - p_A)$. The "background" or "evolutionary" relatedness produces the same effect as an inbreeding coefficient of $F = \theta$.

The probability that an allele is A, given that the previous two alleles were A, is $[2\theta + (1 - \theta)p_A]/(1 + \theta)$

and this is of immediate use in paternity testing: it is the probability that a random man provides paternal allele A, given that the alleged father is homozygous for the allele (but see Table 4).

As one further example, the probability that an allele is A, given that the previous three alleles examined were also A, is $[3\theta + (1 - \theta)p_A]/(1 + 2\theta)$. In the forensic context where a crime stain, left by the perpetrator, is of type AA this leads to the probability that a suspect is also of type AA:

$$\Pr(AA|AA) = \Pr(A|AAA)\ \Pr(A|AA)$$
$$= \frac{[3\theta + (1 - \theta)p_A]\ [2\theta + (1 - \theta)p_A]}{(1 + \theta)\ (1 + 2\theta)} \qquad (2)$$

Note the use of the conditional probability symbol |.

The results just described for relatives, meaning familial relationships among people in the same family or evolutionary relatedness among people in the same population, are employed in the likelihood ratios for comparing alternative hypotheses about sets of observed DNA profiles. Whether the context is in the forensic situation involving a suspect and a crime stain, or the parentage situation of a child and an alleged father, or the missing person situation involving a stain or some remains and the relatives of the missing person, there is the evidence E of two or more DNA profiles and there are alternative hypotheses H that specify the relationship(s) among the sources of those profiles. One hypothesis, H_p, may be identity in the forensic case, father–child in the parentage case, and sibships in the missing person case. An alternative, H_d, may be unrelatedness in each case. The strength of the evidence is expressed as a likelihood ratio $LR = \Pr(E|H_p)/\Pr(E|H_d)$.

The identity measures and expressions for joint genotypic probabilities also allow another type of calculation that has recently arisen in studies of databases [4]. When all profiles in a database are compared to all other profiles, there are often quite striking degrees of similarity observed. It is helpful to be able to predict the degree of such similarity, taking into account familial and evolutionary relatedness, in order to determine whether or not the observed similarities indicate any unusual features of the database. To date, the observations have been consistent with expectations [4], and these expectations are now described.

The probability P_2 that two profiles match is [4]

$$P_2 = \sum_i \Pr(A_i A_i, A_i A_i) + \sum_i \sum_{j \neq i} \Pr(A_i A_j, A_i A_j)$$

$$= \sum_i \Pr(A_i A_i A_i A_i) + 2 \sum_i \sum_{j \neq i} \Pr(A_i A_i A_j A_j)$$

$$= \frac{1}{D} \, [6\theta^3 + \theta^2(1 - \theta) \, (2 + 9S_2) +$$

$$2\theta(1 - \theta)^2(2S_2 + S_3) + (1 - \theta)^3(2S_2^2 - S_4)] \quad (3)$$

The first line specifies the genotypes, the second shows the corresponding sets of alleles, and the third shows the value from the Dirichlet assumption. Random mating is assumed for the second line. The third line employs the notation $S_k = \sum_i p_i^k, k = 2, 3, 4$ and $D = (1 + \theta)(1 + 2\theta)$. Partial matches occur when two individuals share one allele at a locus, rather than the two required for a match. The probability that two individuals partially match is

$$P_1 = 2 \sum_i \sum_{j \neq i} \Pr(A_i A_i, A_i A_j)$$

$$+ \sum_i \sum_{j \neq i} \sum_{k \neq i,j} \Pr(A_i A_j, A_i A_k)$$

$$= 4 \sum_i \sum_{j \neq i} \Pr(A_i A_i A_i A_j)$$

$$+ 4 \sum_i \sum_{j \neq i} \sum_{k \neq i,j} \Pr(A_i A_i A_j A_k)$$

$$= \frac{1}{D} \, [8\theta^2(1 - \theta) \, (1 - S_2) + 4\theta(1 - \theta)^2(1 - S_3)$$

$$+ 4(1 - \theta)^3(S_2 - S_3 - S_2^2 + S_4)] \quad (4)$$

with the same meaning for the three rows as for P_2. Finally, for two individuals to mismatch, i.e., have no alleles in common,

$$P_0 = \sum_i \sum_{j \neq i} \Pr(A_i A_i, A_j A_j)$$

$$+ 2 \sum_i \sum_{j \neq i} \sum_{k \neq i,j} \Pr(A_i A_i, A_j A_k)$$

$$+ \sum_i \sum_{j \neq i} \sum_{k \neq i,j} \sum_{l \neq i,j,k} \Pr(A_i A_j, A_k A_l)$$

$$= \sum_i \sum_{j \neq i} \Pr(A_i A_i A_j A_j)$$

$$+2 \sum_i \sum_{j \neq i} \sum_{k \neq i,j} \Pr(A_i A_i A_j A_k)$$

$$+ \sum_i \sum_{j \neq i} \sum_{k \neq i,j} \sum_{l \neq i,j,k} \Pr(A_i A_j A_k A_l)$$

$$= \frac{1}{D} \, [\theta^2(1 - \theta) \, (1 - S_2)$$

$$+2\theta(1 - \theta)^2(1 - 2S_2 + S_3)$$

$$+(1 - \theta)^3(1 - 4S_2 + 4S_3 + 2S_2^2 - 3S_4)] \quad (5)$$

If, in addition to membership in the same population, two individuals have family relatedness described by k_0, k_1, k_2:

$$\Pr(\text{Match}) = k_2 + k_1 \, [\theta + (1 - \theta)S_2] + k_0 \, P_2$$

$$\Pr(\text{Partial Match}) = k_1 \, (1 - \theta) \, (1 - S_2) + k_0 \, P_1$$

$$\Pr(\text{Mismatch}) = k_0 \, P_0 \quad (6)$$

It is important to stress that these matching probabilities P_0, P_1, P_2 do not refer to specific profiles. They represent similarities over all profile types and so they apply to studies of databases rather than to specific parentage or missing person situations.

Parentage Testing

The usual situation in paternity disputes is that mother, child, and alleged father are genotyped. The alleged father is declared "not excluded" if he carries an allele that is inferred to be the child's paternal allele and the strength of the evidence against him is quantified as the paternity index (PI). The two simplest explanations for the genetic evidence E are

H_p: the alleged father is the father.
H_d: the alleged father is not the father.

and the PI is

$$\text{PI} = \frac{\Pr(E|H_p)}{\Pr(E|H_d)} \quad (7)$$

If there is a prior probability π_0 of paternity, the posterior probability π should be changed to Bayes' theorem:

$$\frac{\pi}{1-\pi} = \text{PI} \times \frac{\pi_0}{1-\pi_0} \qquad (8)$$

The PI can be expressed in terms of probability of genotype G_C of child, conditional on genotypes G_M, G_{AF} of mother, and alleged father:

$$\begin{aligned}
\text{PI} &= \frac{\Pr(G_C|G_M, G_{AF}, H_p)\ \Pr(G_M, G_{AF}|H_p)}{\Pr(G_C|G_M, G_{AF}, H_d)\ \Pr(G_M, G_{AF}|H_d)} \\
&= \frac{\Pr(G_C|G_M, G_{AF}, H_p)}{\Pr(G_C|G_M, G_{AF}, H_d)} \qquad (9)
\end{aligned}$$

since the adult probabilities do not depend on the hypotheses. Provided the mother and alleged father are not related, so that the child's maternal and paternal alleles A_M and A_P are independent, it is more convenient to work with the alleles than the child's genotype. Noting that A_M depends only on the mother's genotype:

$$\begin{aligned}
\text{PI} &= \frac{\Pr(A_M\, A_P|G_M, G_{AF}, H_p)}{\Pr(A_M\, A_P|G_M, G_{AF}, H_d)} \\
&= \frac{\Pr(A_M|G_M, H_p)\ \Pr(A_P|A_M, G_M, G_{AF}, H_p)}{\Pr(A_M|G_M, H_d)\ \Pr(A_P|G_M, G_{AF}, H_d)} \\
&= \frac{\Pr(A_P|A_M, G_M, G_{AF}, H_p)}{\Pr(A_P|G_M, G_{AF}, H_d)} \qquad (10)
\end{aligned}$$

because $\Pr(A_M|G_M)$ does not depend on H.

Suppose first that familial or evolutionary relatedness is not considered. Under explanation H_p, the alleged father has provided the paternal allele, of type A_i say, and the probability of the allele is 1.0 or 0.5, depending on whether he is homozygous or heterozygous for that allele. Under explanation H_d some other

man, the true father TF, has provided the paternal allele and the probability of this unknown man providing the paternal allele is just the population allele frequency p_i. The PI is $1/p_i$ or $1/(2p_i)$ for homozygous A_iA_i or heterozygous A_iA_j alleged fathers.

Alleged Father Related to True Father

There are situations, including those of incest, where the alternative hypotheses involve relatives. There may be reason to suspect that either the alleged father or his brother is the true father of a child. The two hypotheses become

H_p: the alleged father is the father.
H_d: the alleged father is related to the father.

and then it is necessary to determine the probability of the paternal allele, given that it came from a relative of the alleged father. Provided there is no inbreeding, the calculations follow from the joint probabilities for relatives given in Table 2 and are shown in Table 3. These lead to the probabilities of paternal allele A_i under H_d that it came from a relative, and the PI values are $1/[2\theta_{AT} + (1 - 2\theta_{AT})p_i]$ for homozygous alleged fathers and $1/\{2[\theta_{AT} + (1 - 2\theta_{AT})p_i]\}$ for heterozygous alleged fathers. The quantity θ_{AT} is the coancestry of alleged and (under H_d) true fathers.

It is also possible to construct a likelihood ratio for a different pair of alternative explanations for situations when the alleged father is either deceased or otherwise not available for testing but his relative can be tested. If X is the tested man, the hypotheses are

H_p: X is a relative of the father Y.
H_d: X is unrelated to the father Y.

Table 3 Paternity index calculations when H_d is that alleged father is related to the father

Alleged father	$\Pr(A_i \mid H_p)$	Relative	$\Pr(\text{Relative}|\text{Alleged father})$	$\Pr(A_i \mid H_d)$
A_iA_i	1.0	A_iA_i	$(k_0 p_i^4 + k_1 p_i^3 + k_2 p_i^2)/p_i^2$	1.0
		A_iA_j	$(2k_0 p_i^3\, p_j + k_1 p_i^2\, p_j)/p_i^2$	0.5
A_iA_j	0.5	A_iA_i	$(2k_0 p_i^3\, p_j + k_1 p_i^2\, p_j)/(2p_i p_j)$	1.0
		A_iA_j	$[4k_0 p_i^2\, p_j^2 + k_1 p_i p_j(p_i + p_j) + 2k_2 p_i p_j]/(2p_i p_j)$	0.5
		A_iA_k	$(4k_0 p_i^2\, p_j p_k + k_1 p_i p_j p_k)/(2p_i p_j)$	0.5

The paternal allele is A_i and A_j, A_k are any other distinct alleles

If the degree of relatedness in H_p is specified by θ_{XY}, then the PI, often called the *Avuncular Index*, when the paternal allele is A_i is $[1 - 2\theta_{XY} + 2\theta_{XY}/p_i]$ when the tested man is homozygous A_iA_i, $[1 - 2\theta_{XY} + \theta_{XY}/p_i]$ when the tested man is heterozygous A_iA_j, and it is $(1 - 2\theta_{XY})$ when the tested man does not carry A_i.

Evolutionary Relatedness

For populations in which there is a (low) level of relatedness of individuals because of the evolutionary history of the population, there is a need to consider the relatedness of mother, alleged father, and father. This does not affect $\Pr(A_P|G_M, G_{AF}, H_p)$ because that is determined by the genotype of the alleged father. Under H_d, however, the Dirichlet sampling formula can be used. The probability of the paternal allele depends on the four alleles already seen: those of the mother and the alleged father. The resulting PI values are shown in Table 4.

Missing Person Calculations

Many of the issues involved in missing person calculations are the same as those for paternity disputes. Instead of a paternal allele being known, a biological sample from the missing person is available. Suppose a person is missing; the genetic evidence E consists of the genotype from a sample that has come from some person X who may be the missing person Y, together with the genotypes from the spouse M and child C of the missing person. Two explanations of the evidence are

H_p: the sample is from the missing person.
H_d: the sample is not from the missing person.

A general approach for calculating the likelihood ratio is to work with probabilities of genotypes conditional on those in the previous generation(s):

Table 4 Paternity index values for a population with evolutionary relatedness

G_M	G_C	A_M	A_P	G_{AF}	PI
A_iA_i	A_iA_i	A_i	A_i	A_iA_i	$\dfrac{1+3\theta}{4\theta + (1-\theta)p_i}$
				A_iA_j	$\dfrac{1+3\theta}{2[3\theta + (1-\theta)p_i]}$
	A_iA_j	A_i	A_j	A_jA_j	$\dfrac{1+3\theta}{2\theta + (1-\theta)p_j}$
				A_iA_j	$\dfrac{1+3\theta}{2[\theta + (1-\theta)p_j]}$
				A_jA_k	$\dfrac{1+3\theta}{2[\theta + (1-\theta)p_j]}$
A_iA_k	A_iA_i	A_i	A_i	A_iA_i	$\dfrac{1+3\theta}{3\theta + (1-\theta)p_i}$
				A_iA_k	$\dfrac{1+3\theta}{2[2\theta + (1-\theta)p_i]}$
	A_iA_j	A_i	A_j	A_jA_j	$\dfrac{1+3\theta}{2\theta + (1-\theta)p_j}$
				A_iA_j	$\dfrac{1+3\theta}{2[\theta + (1-\theta)p_j]}$
				A_jA_l	$\dfrac{1+3\theta}{2[\theta + (1-\theta)p_j]}$

Different subscripts denote different alleles

$$LR = \frac{\Pr(E|H_p)}{\Pr(E|H_d)}$$

$$= \frac{\Pr(G_C, G_M, G_X|H_p)}{\Pr(G_C, G_M, X|H_d)}$$

$$= \frac{\Pr(G_C|G_M, G_X, H_p) \ \Pr(G_M, G_X|H_p)}{\Pr(G_C|G_M, G_X, H_d) \ \Pr(G_M, G_X|H_d)}$$

$$= \frac{\Pr(G_C|G_M, G_X, H_p)}{\Pr(G_C|G_M, H_d)} \tag{11}$$

since the genotype of the child does not depend on that of X when H_d is true (ignoring evolutionary relatedness within the population). This likelihood ratio is the same as in the paternity case where X is alleged to be the father of child C who has mother M. Similar extensions can be made to allow for X to be a relative of the missing person, or to allow for evolutionary relatedness among all members of a population.

It may be the case that people apart from the spouse and child of the missing person are typed. The general procedure is the same: the probabilities of the set of observed genotypes under two explanations are compared. Suppose the parents P, Q as well as the child C and spouse M of the missing person Y are typed, and that a sample is available that has come from some person X thought under H_p to be Y. Under explanation H_d, the sample from X did not come from Y, and therefore the genotype of X does not depend on the genotypes of P and Q and the genotype of C does not depend on the genotype of X.

$$LR = \frac{\Pr(E|H_p)}{\Pr(E|H_d)}$$

$$= \frac{\Pr(C, M, X, P, Q|H_p)}{\Pr(C, M, X, P, Q|H_d)}$$

$$= \frac{\Pr(C|M, X, P, Q, H_p) \ \Pr(M, X, P, Q|H_p)}{\Pr(C|M, X, P, Q, H_d) \ \Pr(M, X, P, Q|H_d)}$$

$$= \frac{\Pr(C|M, X, H_p) \ \Pr(M, X|P, Q, H_p)}{\Pr(C|M, X, P, Q, H_d) \ \Pr(C, M, X, P, Q|H_d)} \cdot \frac{\Pr(P, Q|H_p)}{\Pr(P, Q|H_d)}$$

$$= \frac{\Pr(C|M, X, H_p) \ \Pr(M|H_p) \ \Pr(X|P, Q, H_p)}{\Pr(C|M, X, P, Q, H_d) \ \Pr(M|H_d) \ \Pr(X|H_d)}$$

$$= \frac{\Pr(C|M, X, H_p) \ \Pr(X|P, Q, H_p)}{\Pr(C|M, P, Q, H_d) \ \Pr(X|H_d)} \tag{12}$$

Table 5   An example of a missing person calculation

Child	G_C	A_1A_2
Sample	G_X	A_1A_3
Spouse	G_M	A_2A_4
Mother	G_P	A_1A_5
Father	G_Q	A_3A_6
$\Pr(C \mid M, X, H_p)$	$=$	$\frac{1}{4}$
$\Pr(X \mid P, Q, H_p)$	$=$	$\frac{1}{4}$
$(C \mid M, P, Q, H_d)$	$=$	$\frac{1}{8}$
$\Pr(X \mid H_d)$	$=$	$2p_1p_3$
LR	$=$	$\frac{1}{4p_1p_3}$

An example is shown in Table 5.

Evolutionary relatedness can be accounted for by modifying the terms involving allele frequencies. In this case, the term $\Pr(X|H_d)$ needs to take into account the alleles already seen in P, Q, M, and C. For the example in Table 5, where $X = A_1A_3$, this probability is that of obtaining A_1 after having seen two copies of A_1 and A_2 and one copy of A_3, A_4, A_5, and A_6, and then of obtaining A_3 after having seen three copies of A_1, two copies of A_2, and one copy of A_3, A_4, A_5, and A_6. From the Dirichlet sampling formula, this probability is

$$\Pr(A_1 A_3|A_1 A_1 A_2 A_2 A_3 A_4 A_5 A_6)$$

$$= \frac{2\theta + (1 - \theta)p_1}{1 + 8\theta} \ \frac{\theta + (1 - \theta)p_3}{1 + 7\theta} \tag{13}$$

As a final example, consider the case where profiles are available from one parent P, four siblings S, the spouse M, and a child C of a missing person, as well as from a sample X that may be from that missing person. Sample profiles are shown in Table 6. Write the evidence as $E = (C, M, X, S, P)$ and the hypotheses H_p, H_d that X is or is not from the missing person. It is necessary to introduce the untyped parent Q and add over all possible genotypes for this parent that are consistent with P and S under H_d, and consistent with P, S, X under H_p. The probability of any specific genotype of Q does not depend on the hypotheses. The general procedure is still to write the probabilities for people conditional on those in the previous generations:

$$LR = \frac{\Pr(C,M,X,S,P|H_p)}{\Pr(C,M,X,S,P|H_d)}$$

$$= \frac{\sum_Q \Pr(C,M,X,S,P|Q,H_p)\ \Pr(Q|H_p)}{\sum_Q \Pr(C,M,X,S,P|Q,H_d)\ \Pr(Q|H_d)}$$

$$= \frac{\sum_Q \Pr(C|M,X,S,P,Q,H_p)}{\sum_Q \Pr(C,M,X,S,P|H_d)}$$

$$= \frac{\dfrac{\Pr(M,X,S,P|Q,H_p)\ \Pr(Q)}{\sum_Q \Pr(C,M,X,S,P|H_d)}}{\Pr(M,X,S,P|Q,H_d)\ \Pr(Q)}$$

$$= \frac{\dfrac{\sum_Q \Pr(C|M\ X\ H_p)\ \Pr(M|H_p)}{\Pr(X\ S\ P|Q\ H_p)\ \Pr(Q)}}{\sum_Q \Pr(C|M\ S\ P\ Q\ H_d)\ \Pr(M|H_d)}$$

$$= \frac{\dfrac{\Pr(X|H_d)\ \Pr(S\ P|Q\ H_d)\ \ \Pr(Q)}{\sum_Q \Pr(C|M\ X\ H_p)\ \Pr(X\ S|P\ Q\ H_p)}}{\Pr(P|Q\ H_p)\ \Pr(Q)}$$

$$= \frac{\dfrac{\sum_Q \Pr(C|M\ P\ Q\ H_d)\ \Pr(X|H_d)}{\Pr(S|P\ Q\ H_d)\ \Pr(P|Q\ H_d)\ \Pr(Q)}}{\Pr(C|M,X,H_p)\ \sum_Q \Pr(X,S|P,Q,H_p)}$$

$$= \frac{\Pr(Q)}{\dfrac{\Pr(X|H_d)\ \sum_Q \Pr(C|M,P,Q,H_d)}{\Pr(S|P,Q,H_d)\ \Pr(Q)}} \tag{14}$$

Details for the specific profiles are shown in Table 6.

Discussion

Interpreting DNA evidence for situations involving parentage or missing person identification rests on the profile probabilities for sets of related individuals. When relatedness is a consequence of membership in the same family, there is a set of three parameters that are the probabilities two people share zero, one, or two pairs of ibd alleles. For the relatedness resulting from the shared evolutionary history of all members of a population, there is a convenient formulation in terms of a general coancestry coefficient θ. This formulation has become widely used in single-contributor

Table 6 An example of a missing person calculation

P	mother, with genotype A_3A_4
S	sibs, with genotypes $A_2A_4, A_2A_4, A_2A_4, A_3A_4$
Q	untyped father who must have genotype A_2A_3 or A_2A_4
M	spouse, with genotype A_5A_6
C	child, with genotype A_3A_5
X	sample, with genotype A_3A_3

$$\Pr(C|M, X, H_p) = 1/4$$

$$\Pr(X, S|P, Q, H_p) = \begin{cases} \dfrac{1}{1024}, & Q = A_2A_3 \\ 0, & Q = A_2A_4 \end{cases}$$

$$\Pr(X|H_d) = p_3^2$$

$$\Pr(C|M, P, Q, H_d) = \begin{cases} \dfrac{1}{2}, & Q = A_2A_3 \\ \dfrac{1}{4}, & Q = A_2A_4 \end{cases}$$

$$\Pr(S|P, Q) = \begin{cases} \dfrac{1}{256}, & Q = A_2A_3 \\ \dfrac{1}{256}, & Q = A_2A_4 \end{cases}$$

$$\Pr(Q) = \begin{cases} 2p_2p_3, & Q = A_2A_3, \\ 2p_2p_4, & Q = A_2A_4 \end{cases}$$

$$LR = \frac{(1/4) \times (1/1024) \times 2p_2p_3}{(p_3^2)[(1/2) \times (1/256)\ 2p_2p_3 + (1/4) \times (1/256)\ 2p_2p_4]}$$

$$= \frac{1}{4p_3(2p_3 + p_4)}$$

forensic calculations and it should also be used in paternity calculations. The identification of remains in missing person situations can be quite complicated when many family members are typed, but the use of likelihood ratios to compare evidence probabilities under alternative hypotheses provides a general approach. The probabilities need to be written for individuals in one generation conditional on individuals in previous generations.

Relatedness coefficients allow the probabilities of DNA profiles for sets of individuals to be written out explicitly. Although increasing relatedness is expected to result in increasing profile similarity, the probability expressions in Tables 1 and 2 make it clear that even unrelated people may have very similar profiles, whereas related people may have quite dissimilar profiles. For example, unrelated people may both be homozygous A_1A_1 at a locus and full-sibs may have completely different genotypes A_1A_1, A_2A_2. It is more appropriate to compare evidence probabilities under alternative hypotheses than it is to have arbitrary rules that deny the possibility of relatedness, once some threshold level of allelic dissimilarity is reached.

Acknowledgment

This work was supported in part by NIH grant GM 75091.

References

[1]   Weir, B.S., Anderson, A.D. & Hepler, A.B. (2006). Genetic relatedness analysis: modern data and new challenges, *Nature Reviews Genetics* **7**, 771–780.

[2]   Evett, I.W. & Weir, B.S. (1998). *Interpreting DNA Evidence–Statistical Genetics for Forensic Scientists*, Sinuaer Associates, Sunderland.

[3]   Balding, D.J. & Nichols, R.A. (1994). DNA profile match probability calculations: how to allow for population stratification, relatedness, database selection and single bands, *Forensic Science International* **64**, 125–140.

[4]   Weir, B.S. (2007). The rarity of DNA profiles, *Annals of Applied Statistics* **1**, 358–370.

Related Articles in EFS Online

Interpretation of Mitochondrial DNA Evidence

Short Tandem Repeats: Interpretation

Chapter 24
Familial Searching

Klaas Slooten[1,2] and Ronald Meester[1]

[1]*VU University Amsterdam, Amsterdam, The Netherlands*
[2]*Netherlands Forensic Institute, The Hague, The Netherlands*

Familial Searching: Definition

Familial searching is the act of deliberately searching a DNA database with the purpose of identifying biological relatives of the unknown donor of a DNA profile. Typically, this profile is obtained from crime scene evidence, but it may also belong, for example, to an unidentified newborn and abandoned child with the purpose of identifying its parents. A familial search can be carried out if no direct match with the crime scene profile has been found in the database.

As DNA databases maintained for criminal justice purposes contain mostly autosomal DNA, a familial search will mostly involve comparisons of autosomal DNA. In that case, the search concentrates on close biological relatives: parents, children, and siblings of the unknown offender. Comparisons of Y-chromosomal data, if available, may indicate relatedness (albeit potentially distant) in the paternal lineage; and similarly, mitochondrial DNA may be used for the maternal lineage. In this article, we will focus mostly on the search for first-degree relatives using autosomal STR data, these being typically the data stored in a DNA database. In principle, autosomal DNA is sufficiently discriminatory to differentiate quite well between first-degree relatives and unrelated individuals. However, a search will necessarily have some chance of overlooking an existing relationship and it may also produce candidate relatives that later turn out to be unrelated. We will review different strategies for finding such relatives and discuss their

properties. We will also discuss how to deal with databases that contain DNA profiles obtained from different multiplexes.

Familial searching, if permitted, is usually restricted to attempt the resolution of serious crimes only. There are several jurisdictions where familial searching is regularly carried out, most notably the United Kingdom. The paper by Pope *et al.* [1] gives an overview of UK experience in the period 2003–2009. A more recent overview of the familial searching procedures and results in the United Kingdom is given in [2]. According to [2], in the United Kingdom (where about 6 million profiles are stored in the national DNA database representing almost 10% of the population), 32 out of the 188 familial searches carried out by the FSS in the period 2003–2011 resulted in the identification of a close relative of the offender. In the United Kingdom, an initial list is based on the information derived from autosomal DNA, which is subsequently rearranged taking other information into account, such as age, ethnicity, and geography. According to both [1] and [2], adding geographical information had the highest impact.

In countries where a smaller fraction of the population has been added to the DNA database, one would expect fewer successes. In the Netherlands, where the database represents a little more than 1% of the population, familial searching has been introduced in 2012. About 15 familial searches have been carried out so far, one of which led to an arrest in a vice case.[a] In addition, a population survey aimed at finding paternal relatives in a rape and homicide case, led to the identification of the offender.

For an overview of the attitude toward familial searching elsewhere around the world, we refer the

---

A Guide to Forensic DNA Profiling
Edited by Allan Jamieson and Scott Bader
© 2016 John Wiley & Sons, Ltd. ISBN: 9781118751527
Also published in EFS (online edition)
DOI: 10.1002/9780470061589.fsa1122

reader to [2]. In the United States, legislation differs between states, an overview of the state policies is given in [3]. We only mention here that in California, several investigative successes have been reported with the technique including the arrest of the so-called Grim Sleeper (cf. [4]).

Kinship Indices

In familial searching, we want to quantify the support for two individuals (crime scene profile and a database profile) to have a certain biological relationship. This is usually done by computing the likelihood ratio: we compare the probability to see these two profiles if they belong to individuals who are related in a specified way, to the probability to observe these profiles if they belong to two unrelated individuals. For example, the likelihood ratio in favor of sibship for persons with genotypes G_1 and G_2 is given by:

$$\mathrm{SI}(G_1, G_2)$$

$$= \frac{P(G_1, G_2 \mid \text{profiles are from full siblings})}{P(G_1, G_2 \mid \text{profiles are from unrelated individuals})} \tag{1}$$

where SI stands for Sibling Index. Similarly, the likelihood ratio in favor of being parent–child (as opposed to unrelated) is called PI. We will write KI (Kinship Index) to denote the choice of either PI or SI, or perhaps another form of relatedness.

The KI, and in fact all likelihood ratios for relatedness between two individuals assuming that they are not inbred, are easy to compute and depend only on the form of relatedness and the allele frequencies of the alleles that the two profiles have in common. Indeed, suppose we postulate a biological relationship between (i.e., the pedigree connecting) two persons with genotypes $g_1 = (a_1, a_2)$ and $g_2 = (b_1, b_2)$ on a certain locus. Then the Mendelian inheritance of alleles allows us to calculate

$$\kappa = (\kappa_0, \kappa_1, \kappa_2)$$

where κ_i is the probability that the two persons have i pairs of identical-by-descent (IBD) alleles on a locus. For any hypothesis H, we can compute the probability $P(g_2 = (b_1, b_2)|g_1 = (a_1, a_2), H)$ by looking at the IBD

possibilities:

$$P(g_2 = (b_1, b_2)|g_1 = (a_1, a_2), H) = \kappa_0 f_{g_2}$$
$$+ \kappa_1 P(g_2 = (b_1, b_2)|g_1 = (a_1, a_2), PC) + \kappa_2 1_{g_1, g_2}$$

Here, f_{g_2} is the population frequency of g_2. In the middle term, PC stands for parent–child: it corresponds to the situation where there is one pair of IBD alleles between the two individuals. In the last term, $1_{g_1, g_2}$ is equal to one if $g_1 = g_2$ and zero otherwise: if there are two IBD alleles, the genotypes must be identical. Thus, we see that all likelihoods of the genetic data can be reduced to calculating parent–child genotype probabilities, plus some constant terms. The kinship index is then

$$\mathrm{KI}(g_1, g_2) = \kappa_0$$
$$+ \kappa_1 \frac{P(g_2 = (b_1, b_2)|g_1 = (a_1, a_2), PC)}{f_{g_2}} + \kappa_2 \frac{1_{g_1, g_2}}{f_{g_2}}$$

If we disregard mutation, then this can be rewritten as

$$\mathrm{KI}(g_1, g_2) = \kappa_0$$
$$+ \frac{\kappa_1}{4} \left(\frac{1_{a_1, b_1} + 1_{a_2, b_1}}{p_{b_1}} + \frac{1_{a_1, b_2} + 1_{a_2, b_2}}{p_{b_2}} \right)$$
$$+ \frac{\kappa_2}{2} \frac{1_{a_1, b_1} 1_{a_2, b_2} + 1_{a_1, b_2} 1_{a_2, b_1}}{p_{b_1} p_{b_2}} \tag{2}$$

where p_x denotes the population frequency of the allele x. The KI on several loci, if they are unlinked, is just the product of the KI's per locus. Furthermore, this is still true for PI with linked markers if these are in linkage equilibrium.

The KI are readily adapted to take background relatedness into account (by taking a θ-correction). Mutation can also be incorporated, although this is only relevant for PI as for the other types of relatedness, mutations cannot be detected. As mutations are rare (cf. [5]), ignoring them altogether has only a very limited effect on the effectiveness of a familial search.

Strategies for Autosomal Familial Searches

Familial searching relies on the fact that close relatives tend to share more alleles than unrelated individuals.

Therefore, one may consider to limit the number of database profiles that are subjected to an evaluation of the possibility of relatedness by only considering profiles that have sufficiently many alleles IBS (identical by state, i.e., indistinguishable by repeat length) with the crime scene profile. For example, the UK search strategy described in [1] sets the threshold at a minimum of nine IBS alleles on a comparison of SGMPlus profiles. For profiles that pass this threshold, likelihood ratios for being parent–child and for being siblings are computed. This procedure has as advantage that fewer LR calculations are needed. However, it was already noted in [6] that LR computations are more effective than using a count of IBS alleles only. This is not surprising, as the likelihood ratio does not only take into account which alleles are shared but also how rare these alleles are. Thus, assuming one knows the allele frequencies, LR computations discriminate better between relatives and nonrelatives. Ge *et al.* [7] conducted a simulation study to estimate the probability with which a true relative would be selected for various combined KI- and IBS-thresholds. By invoking the Neyman–Pearson lemma, [8] showed a KI-threshold is superior to any other type of threshold. Furthermore, computational power nowadays is sufficient to calculate millions of KI's efficiently. Indeed, as the KI only depend on the shared alleles with the crime scene profile (cf. equation (2)), at most six possible KI per locus occur. This makes it possible to efficiently calculate the KI and the distribution of KI for the crime scene profile (cf. [9]). Therefore, we will in this article suppose that likelihood ratios are computed for every database profile. The main problem following these computations is how to select a candidate list for further investigation.

Profile-Dependent Variation

It was observed already in [10] that the ease by which relatives can be found in a database not only depends on the database size but also, for fixed database size, on the crime scene profile. This is not surprising, as if the crime scene profile has only alleles that are common in the population, then by definition these alleles will be shared by relatively many individuals, and the resulting likelihood ratio based on such shared alleles is relatively small. Conversely, rare alleles in a genotype will be shared by fewer unrelated individuals, and the LR for such shared alleles is relatively big. The extent to which the SI-distribution varies

between profiles is illustrated in Figure 1 in which the SI-distribution for a thousand randomly generated genotypes are depicted, both with actual brothers and with unrelated individuals.

We also note that although the exceedance probabilities $P(KI \geq t \,|\, \text{related})$ and $P(KI \geq t \,|\, \text{unrelated})$ may differ from profile to profile, the false positive probabilities are bounded by the inequality (cf. [11])

$$P(\text{KI} \geq t \mid \text{unrelated}) \leq \frac{1}{t} \qquad (3)$$

regardless of the type of kinship index KI or threshold $t > 0$. Thus, a search for any type of relatedness with threshold t in a database with N profiles of actually unrelated individuals will, in expectation, yield less than N/t candidate relatives, irrespective of the requested type of relatedness or the set of loci on which the calculation is based. On the other hand, the probability that an actual relative will exceed that threshold does of course depend on these parameters. It is the objective of a familial search to carry out searches for types of relatedness where both the probability to find relatives is large enough for the search to be worthwhile, while at the same time maintaining a tolerable amount of false positives.

Strategies

When the likelihood ratios between the crime scene profile and the database have been computed, it is not always practically possible to further – genetically or otherwise – follow up on all persons with a likelihood ratio in favor of relatedness. For example, when a sibling search is conducted on the SGMPlus loci, Figure 1a shows that the list of database profiles with $SI \geq 1$ may contain a few percent of the database. Therefore, a decision has to be made which persons are going to be further investigated. Several such strategies are possible. In [12], the following four strategies are compared:

Top-k. This strategy selects the database members making up the top-k of KIs. The largest KIs give the strongest indication for relatedness, so working down the list of KIs means that the most promising profiles are treated first. This method is used by the state of California (cf. [13]) with $k = 168$ chosen for practical reasons.

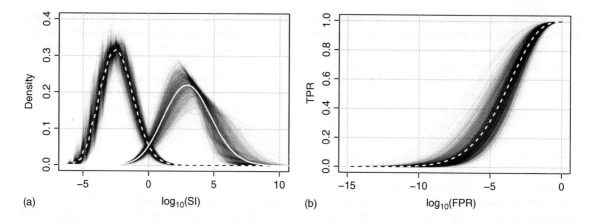

Figure 1   Distribution of SI (a) and corresponding ROC curves (b) for SGMplus profiles. (a) Density estimates of $\log_{10}(SI)$ for full siblings and unrelated profiles for 1000 profiles. Means are indicated by white curves (dashed for unrelated and solid for full siblings). (b) ROC curves corresponding to decision rules based on an SI-threshold for 1000 profiles. The mean (over profiles) is indicated by a dashed white curve

Fixed KI-threshold. This strategy selects all database members with a KI above some threshold. That is, for some fixed threshold t (e.g., 1000 or 10 000), select all database members for which KI > t. In contrast with the top-k strategy, the number of profiles that is selected is not fixed when implementing a KI-threshold.

Profile-centered. This method, introduced in [11], first determines the KI-distribution of the crime scene profile. Given a desired probability with which a relative, if present, must appear on the candidate list, the method selects all database profiles that exceed the relevant quantile of the KI-distribution of the crime scene profile.

Conditional method. This method, also introduced in [11], computes the posterior probability of relatedness for all database members, given prior probabilities for relatedness and assuming that the database contains at most one relative of the type we are looking for.

These strategies have quite different properties. The top-k method fixes the workload but one has no control over the probability of detection (PoD), by which we mean the probability that a relative, if present in the database, is detected by the method. This strategy has been studied, either in actual or in simulated DNA databases, in various places in the literature, e.g., [6, 10, 14, 15].

The fixed KI-threshold by definition only investigates sufficiently promising leads, but the workload nor the PoD are fixed, as for different profiles the probabilities for actual relatives and for unrelated individuals to exceed the same threshold may differ.

The profile-centered method by definition fixes the PoD, as one investigates everyone until the probability to find a relative, if one was present, is satisfactorily high. While this means that every case is treated such that the success probability is equal, it also implies that one loses control over the workload.

Finally, the conditional method has advantage that it takes all the obtained likelihood ratios into account and provides a full Bayesian analysis; but this means that prior probabilities are needed. In [11], a comparison of the profile-centered and the conditional method is carried out including a discussion of a frequentist interpretation of the involved probabilities.

In [12], it is shown that the strategy which is most efficient in the long run is the KI-threshold. Intuitively, this makes sense: if one only further investigates leads that are sufficiently strong based on the data in the database, then this will provide the lowest number of false positive leads for the obtained true positive rate.

Fortunately, it is also shown in [12] that for practical purposes, the top-k method performs almost as good as the fixed KI-threshold method. In Figure 2 taken from [12], we compare the observed lengths of candidate lists obtained with the four methods described above

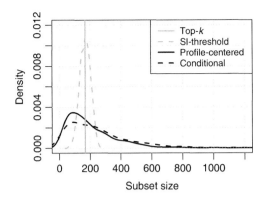

Figure 2 Empirical and candidate list length for a sibling search with the four strategies with tuning parameters chosen such that the average PoD is equal for all strategies

in a (mock) database of 10^5 SGMPlus profiles, where the parameters of the methods have been chosen to have the same PoD as that obtained with the top-168 strategy.

It is observed that the KI-threshold on average yields 167.8 false positives, which almost coincides with the number that was used for the top-k strategy. Note also that the profile-centered and conditional method can yield very large candidate lists. This is not true for the fixed KI-threshold method, where this number is bounded for all profiles by the same bound (equation 3).

The top-k strategy and the fixed KI-threshold are therefore the most suitable strategies if a familial search is set up as a separate investigative process, carried out once and for all. A further advantage of the KI-threshold method is that in principle, a newly added profile to the database may immediately be compared with familial search case profiles from active cases and submitted to further testing if a KI is observed at least as large as the threshold. This can also be realized, of course, for the profile-dependent strategy and also for the conditional method. In the latter case, one could be alerted if a person is added to the database whose probability of relatedness exceeds a certain minimum.

As the top-k and the fixed KI-threshold seem to be most suitable, we review the performance of these methods when a search for siblings is carried out, for several database sizes and sets of loci. In Figure 3 (cf. [12]), we plot the PoD, i.e., the probability that

a true sibling is encountered in the top-k, for various database sizes and both for the SGMPlus multiplex (10 autosomal loci) and for the NGM multiplex (15 autosomal loci, including those in SGMPlus). It again becomes clear that the PoD is very case-dependent, and we observe that this effect becomes stronger as the database size increases. Some profiles have sufficiently rare alleles to make chance matches unlikely enough to be able to find relatives highly ranked even in very large databases, whereas for others, chance matches are more likely and the probability to find a relative highly ranked diminishes much more quickly as the database becomes larger. We also observe, as has also been remarked in [10], that for each profile the PoD is almost linear in $\log(k)$, and the profile's population frequency is a good predictor for the precise fit. Thus, the marginal gain in PoD from increasing k diminishes rather quickly, making it not sensible to consider ever longer candidate lists. Finally, we remark that raising the number of loci from the 10 of the SGMplus multiplex to the 15 in the NGM kit makes it possible to increase the database size approximately one order of magnitude at the same PoD.

In Figure 4 (cf. [12]), we investigate the strategy of fixing an SI-threshold in the three mock databases. For 1000 case profiles, we evaluate the PoD and the length of the candidate list for three thresholds (10^2, 10^3, and 10^4). Figure 4 shows the results, where each point represents a case profile, each cloud corresponds to a threshold. The white crosses indicate averages in each cloud. The candidate list grows linearly with the database size. We also remark that the variance of the length of the candidate list is much larger for $t = 10^2$ than for the two larger thresholds, whereas the variance of the PoD has opposite behavior.

Further Statistical Issues

Heterogeneous Databases

In many countries, not all database profiles have the same amount of genetic data. For example, at the time of writing,[b] the Dutch DNA database contains about 200 000 profiles of convicted offenders and suspects. About half of these are typed on the SGMPlus loci and the remainder on the NGM loci, while a limited

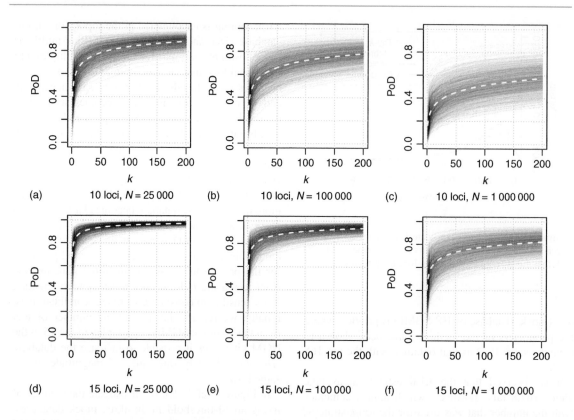

Figure 3 PoD of top-k strategies for sibling searches in mock databases of sizes $N = 25\,000$, $100\,000$, and $1\,000\,000$ for 1000 case profiles on 10 and 15 loci. Dashed white lines indicate the means over profiles

number had been typed for even more loci. Therefore, a KI-threshold t will lead to different true positive probabilities $P(KI \geq t \mid \text{related})$ and false positive probabilities $P(KI \geq t \mid \text{unrelated})$. One may wonder if the threshold should be chosen differently depending on the loci on which the calculation is based (thus regarding the database as a collection of different databases and performing a separate search in each). In [12], it was shown that, under the condition that we may assume that the number of loci for which a database profile has been typed is independent of the probability that this profile is from a relative of the crime scene profile, the most efficient strategy is to apply the same KI-threshold throughout. That is, a database profile is selected for further consideration based on the strength of the obtained evidence in favor of relatedness, regardless of the nature of that evidence. Increasing the true positive rate on a less informative part of the database, while maintaining the same overall true positive rate, leads to more extra

false positives in the less informative part than are economized on the more informative part. Thus, other choices, such as the strategy to fill in expected values for missing loci, or to work with separate lists as investigated in [13] cannot result in a lower false positive rate for the same true positive rate on the database as a whole.

Nongenetic Information

Similar considerations apply when nongenetic additional information can be taken into account, such as age, geographical information, or ethnicity. For example, an age range of the offender may be known from eye witness testimony, and consequently, a probability distribution on the age pf offender's siblings and other relatives can be determined. This can give rise to a likelihood ratio based on the age of the database member, which can be combined with the autosomal likelihood ratio. Provided the likelihood

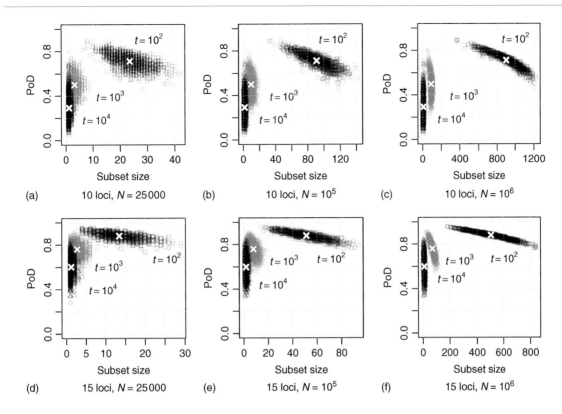

Figure 4 PoD versus length of candidate list for full sibling searches with fixed SI-thresholds (SI $> 10^2, 10^3, 10^4$) in mock databases of sizes $N = 25\,000$, 100 000, and 1 000 000 for 1000 case profiles on 10 and 15 loci. White crosses indicate the means over profiles

ratio calculation corresponding to age is accurate, selecting according to a threshold on the total LR is most efficient.

Population Heterogeneity

A forensic database generally contains DNA profiles of persons from different populations, each with their own allele frequencies. The population of the donor of the case profile is generally unknown, although it's mitochondrial and (if relevant) Y-chromosomal haplotype may be indicative about it. For the database profile, the ethnicity may also not be certain. Therefore, when a KI is computed between the case profile and a database profile, we may not know either ethnicity.

A first attempt to account for population heterogeneity in the database may be to apply a θ-correction with a large value for θ. However, this is not

very useful. First of all, computing a KI using a θ-correction implies that we consider these profiles to belong to individuals who come from the same subpopulation – which cannot possibly be true for all database members. The effect of this correction is to increase the allele frequencies of the alleles in the profile of the unknown offender. As the KI only depend on these frequencies because only the matching alleles are involved in equation 2, the effect is that a lower value of the likelihood ratio is obtained whenever there are matching alleles compared to when $\theta = 0$.

A concern remains that, if the case profile originates from a population with a relatively low diversity of alleles, the KI is not conservative even if applied with a θ-correction. Indeed, if incorrect allele frequencies are used for such a case profile, this will usually increase the number of false positives with database members from that population (cf. [16]).

Therefore, one may choose to compute the KI for multiple choices of allele frequencies, belonging to groups known to be present in the database. The SWGDAM committee has recommended to do so, and to investigate a possible lead only if $KI \geq N$ for all populations and $KI \geq N/10$ for the other populations, thereby setting database-dependent thresholds both on the maximum and minimum obtained KI. As Ge and Budowle (cf. [17]) observe, the minimum KI is most likely to be with the population from which the case profile originates. This is intuitively reasonable, as the KI depends only on the allele frequencies shared with the case profile. More common alleles are, by definition, likely to be observed the most which explains why the KI tends to be lowest when computed with allele frequencies corresponding to the population of the case profile. In [17], it is concluded that the SWGDAM recommendation is too stringent, especially for large databases (with a million or more profiles): the division by N in the KI-threshold drastically reduces the false negative and false positive rates. They recommend to use a minimum KI-threshold independent of the database size.

Familial Searching on Mixtures

So far, we have been concerned with familial searches where the profile of the unknown offender has been determined without uncertainty. Even though this is of course the ideal starting point for a familial search, there is no conceptual reason to limit the procedure to such profiles. For mixtures, one may for example consider hypothesis H_p: victim and brother of database member are the contributors, versus H_d: the victim and an unknown person are the contributors.

For two person mixtures without drop-out and drop-in, where one of the contributors is known (say, victim) and the other contributor is the target of the search, the power of a familial search has been investigated in [18]. More generally, familial searching on two and three person mixtures, with and without known contributors, and considering also the possibility of allelic dropout, has been investigated in [19]. Forensically, mixtures in which the unknown offender is the only unknown contributor to the mixture are most relevant. It has been shown that a familial search on a mixture using 15 loci in many cases, especially the forensically relevant ones, has true and false positive rates comparable to those obtained from a single source profile using 10 loci. This last type of search is routinely done, but the former is not; we conclude that from a statistical point of view, there is no reason to discard mixtures as being too little informative.

Ethical Aspects

Familial searching also brings new ethical issues: the inclusion of a person in the database automatically entails the virtual inclusion of that person's first-degree relatives. These persons, contrary to the database members themselves, are effectively added without their consent to the database without having been suspected of or convicted for a crime. Also, if further genetic tests to investigate a possible relationship are not or not effectively carried out, a family may become the object of interest in a criminal investigation purely by chance. Especially in the United States, the concern has been formulated that if an ethnic group is overrepresented in the database, then a disproportionate amount of the leads generated by familial searching–both true and false–will be with persons of that ethnic group, thus furthering their over-representation. We refer the reader to Sonia Suter [20] for a study of the ethical considerations involved.

End Notes

a. http://www.ad.nl/ad/nl/1039/Utrecht/article/detail/3777682/2014/10/28/Serie-aanrander-Utrechtse-binnenstad-aangehouden.dhtml, accessed November 17, 2014.

b. http://dnadatabank.forensischinstituut.nl/dna_databanken/dna_databank_strafzaken/samenstelling_en_werkwijze/groei-dna-12m.aspx, accessed 26 November 2014.

References

[1] Pope, S., Clayton, T., Whitaker, J., Lowe, J. & Puch-Solis, R. (2009). More for the same? *Enhancing the investigative potential of forensic DNA databases, Forensic Science International: Genetics Supplement Series* **2**, 458–459.

[2] Maguire, C., McCallum, L., Storey, C. & Whitaker, J. (2014). Familial searching: a specialist forensic DNA profiling service utilising the National DNA Database to identify unknown offenders via their relatives – the UK experience, *Forensic Science International: Genetics* **8**, 1–9.

[3] Kim, J., Mammo, D., Siegel, M. & Katsanis, S. (2011). Policy implications for familial searching, *Investigative Genetics* **2**, 22.

[4] Miller, G. (2010). Familial DNA testing scores a win in serial killer case, *Science* **329**, 262.

[5] AABB (2008). Annual Report Summary for Testing in 2008 of Blood Banks Relationship Testing Program Unit, A. A., http://www.aabb.org/sa/facilities/Documents/rtannrpt08.pdf (accessed Aug 2015).

[6] Curran, J. & Buckleton, J. (2008). Effectiveness of familial searches, *Science Justice* **84**, 164–167.

[7] Ge, J., Chakraborty, R., Eisenberg, A. & Budowle, B. (2011). Comparisons of familial DNA database searching strategies, *Journal of Forensic Science* **56**, 1448–1456.

[8] Balding, D., Krawczak, M., Buckleton, J. & Curran, J. (2013). Decision-making in familial database searching: KI alone or not alone? *Forensic Science International: Genetics* **7**(1), 52–54.

[9] Kruijver, M. (2015). Efficient computations with the likelihood ratio distribution, *Forensic Science International: Genetics* **14**, 116–124.

[10] Cowen, S. & Thomson, J. (2008). A likelihood ratio approach to familial searching of large DNA databases, *Forensic Science International: Genetics Supplement Series* **1**, 643–645.

[11] Slooten, K. & Meester, R. (2014). Probabilistic strategies for familial DNA searching, Journal of the Royal Statistical Society Series C 1–25, to appear.

[12] Kruijver, M., Meester, R. & Slooten, K. (2014). Optimal strategies for familial searching, *Forensic Science International: Genetics* **13**, 90–103.

[13] Myers, S., Timken, M.D., Piucci, M.L., Sims, G.A., Greenwald, M.A., Weigand, J.J., Konzak, K.C. & Buoncristiani, M.R. (2011). Searching for first-degree familial relationships in California's offender DNA database: validation of a likelihood ratio-based approach, *Forensic Science International: Genetics* **5**(5), 493–500.

[14] Bieber, F., Brenner, C. & Lazer, D. (2006). Finding criminals through DNA of their relatives, *Science* **312**, 1315–1316.

[15] Hicks, T., Taroni, F., Curran, J., Buckleton, J., Castella, V. & Ribaux, O. (2010). Use of DNA profiles for investigation using a simulated national DNA database: Part II. *Statistical and ethical considerations on familial searching, Forensic Science International: Genetics* **4**(5), 316–322.

[16] Rohlfs, R., Fullerton, S. & Weir, B. (2012). Familial identification: population structure and relationship distinguishability, *PLoS Genetics* **8**(2), e1002469.

[17] Ge, J. & Budowle, B. (2012). Kinship index variations among populations and thresholds for familial searching, *PLoS ONE* **5**(2), e37474.

[18] Chung, Y.-K., Hu, Y.-Q. & Fung, W. (2010). Familial database search on two-person mixture, *Computational Statistics and Data Analysis* **54**, 2046–2051.

[19] de Ronde, A. (2014). The use of complex mixtures for DNA database searches when relatives are present in the database. Master's thesis, Universiteit van Amsterdam, http://dare.uva.nl/cgi/arno/show.cgi?fid=542815 (accessed Aug 2015).

[20] Suter, S. (2010). All in the family: privacy and DNA familial searching, *Harvard Journal of Law & Technology* **23** (2), 309–399.

Chapter 25
Single Nucleotide Polymorphism

Claus Børsting, Vania Pereira, Jeppe D. Andersen, and Niels Morling

University of Copenhagen, Copenhagen, Denmark

Introduction

Genetic variations in specific base pair positions in the genome (Figure 1) are called *single nucleotide polymorphisms* (SNPs) if at least two variants (alleles) have frequencies of more than 1% in a large, random population. The haploid human genome consists of approximately 3000 million base pairs and the most recent count of SNPs is 38 million [1], which gives an average of one SNP per 80 base pairs. However, identification of new SNPs happens at a rapid rate and, as more human genomes are sequenced in full, the number of SNPs will also increase. The density of SNPs across the genome varies up to tenfold [2] because of variations in selection pressure as well as local recombination and mutation rates [3]. The vast majority of SNPs have only two alleles because the mutation rate at a particular base pair position in the genome is extremely low (on average 1 mutation per 100 million generations) and it is highly unlikely that two point mutations happen at the same position.

The human genome consists of 30 000–35 000 genes. However, the coding regions of these genes only comprise 1.1–1.5% of the genome. SNPs located outside coding regions can influence gene expression if they are located in regulatory DNA sequences. However, the majority of SNPs probably have very little or no functional consequences for the organism. A SNP located in a gene may have diverse effects on the cellular function of the protein encoded by the gene. A SNP in the coding region of a gene may change the protein sequence because the trinucleotide sequence (the codon) that codes for one amino acid in the protein will be different for different SNP alleles. For example, the codon TGC can be changed to TGT, TGG, or TGA by point mutations in the third position of the codon (Figure 1). The original C allele codes for the amino acid cysteine. The T allele also codes for the amino acid cysteine (known as a *silent mutation*), whereas the G allele codes for the amino acid tryptophan (known as a missense mutation) and the A allele codes for termination of protein synthesis (known as a nonsense mutation). Obviously, the nonsense mutation is the most severe form of mutation and will almost always result in a nonfunctional protein. A missense mutation can have all kinds of consequences on the protein, including misfolding, misplacement, decreased or increased activity, which again may affect the organism in various ways. Even a silent mutation may not be neutral for the cell, because a silent mutation may affect the efficiency of protein synthesis and, thus, alter the cellular concentration of the protein.

Forensic Genetic Markers

Ever since the first human "DNA fingerprint" was made [4] and the first DNA evidence was presented at court [5], tandem repeat sequences have been the favored targets for forensic DNA analyses. Mutations happen frequently in tandem repeat sequences (on average 1 mutation per 300 generations) and, therefore, it is highly likely to find different alleles in different individuals, which make tandem repeat sequences very suitable for identification purposes. Today, short tandem repeats (STRs) with four base pair repeat units are preferred and the forensic community has selected a subset of STRs [6, 7] that are included in commercial kits used by forensic laboratories across the globe. These kits have facilitated the development

A Guide to Forensic DNA Profiling
Edited by Allan Jamieson and Scott Bader
© 2016 John Wiley & Sons, Ltd. ISBN: 9781118751527
Also published in EFS (online edition)
DOI: 10.1002/9780470061589.fsa1113

DNA sequence	GAC	TG**C**	AAA
Protein sequence	Asp	Cys	Lys

DNA sequence	GAC	TG**T**	AAA
Protein sequence	Asp	Cys	Lys

DNA sequence	GAC	TG**G**	AAA
Protein sequence	Asp	Trp	Lys

DNA sequence	GAC	TG**A**	AAA
Protein sequence	Asp	Stop	

Figure 1 Examples of how point mutations in the last nucleotide of codons can alter the protein sequence

of standardized databases, which have proved to be highly valuable tools for national and international law enforcement.

With the exception of SNPs in the mitochondrial genome [8] (*see **Mitochondrial DNA: Profiling***), it was not until the late 1990s that SNPs were considered as potential forensic genetic markers [9, 10]. In this chapter, we will discuss the use of SNPs in forensic genetics and we will look into the future where modern sequencing techniques, known as *next-generation sequencing* (NGS), may transform the way forensic genetic investigations are conducted, not only at the technical level in the laboratories but also by providing the opportunity to extract more information from the trace samples and allow combined analyses of STRs and SNPs.

Challenges in Forensic Genetics

The Sample Material

Forensic genetic investigations are typically faced with two major challenges. First of all, the unique trace sample(s) collected from the crime scene often contain very small amounts of DNA and, thus, it is pivotal to maximize the amount of information obtained from each investigation performed on the DNA. This is usually done by simultaneously amplifying as many DNA loci as possible using the polymerase chain reaction (PCR) [11]. However, it is very challenging to develop multiplex PCR assays and, historically, this has been one of the major limitations of forensic

genetic investigations. As the number of desired PCR products increases, there is an increased risk of primer-dimer formations and unwanted amplification products. Furthermore, it becomes increasingly difficult to ensure that all fragments are amplified with equal efficiency and extensive optimization of large multiplexes is usually required. Second, DNA is quickly degraded into smaller pieces when a cell dies and the content is spilled to the surroundings. The rate of the degradation process varies depending on temperature, humidity, pH, light, presence of microorganisms, and other environmental factors. DNA in nucleosome complexes are better protected from degradation and a distinct pattern of nucleosome-sized fragments is observed as the degradation progress [12, 13]. The length of DNA in the nucleosome core is 146 base pairs (bps) and it is difficult to amplify longer fragments by conventional PCR in highly degraded DNA.

The amount and general condition of the DNA influences which type of DNA marker may be used to obtain the maximum level of information from the sample. If very little DNA is available, STRs are the best choice of marker, because one SNP locus is less informative than one STR locus. The probability P of a match between the SNP profiles from two randomly selected individuals typed for n SNP loci can be approximated by assuming that all SNPs are in Hardy–Weinberg equilibrium and that the frequency of the least common allele, ρ, is constant for all loci.

$$P = (\rho^2)^n + (2\rho(1-\rho))^n + ((1-\rho)^2)^n \quad (1)$$

This is a simple function of ρ and n. The match probability has the highest value for $\rho = 0.5$, but does not change very much when ρ is 0.3–0.5 [10]. Thus, equation (1) is a good estimate for the real match probability of a set of SNPs if the allele frequencies of the selected SNP loci are within this range, even though equation (1) was calculated under the assumption that ρ is constant for all loci. If ρ is 0.2–0.5, 50 SNPs give a combined match probability equivalent to that of 12 STRs [10]. For paternity casework, it is estimated that 4–8 SNPs are needed to obtain the same power of exclusion as one STR locus [9]. Thus, 50–60 SNPs with a minimum heterozygosity of 0.32 ($\rho = 0.2$) and preferably with a heterozygosity of 0.42 ($\rho = 0.3$) or higher have the same discriminatory power for analysis of stains (match probability) and disputed family relations (power of exclusion) as the 13 Combined

DNA Indexing System (CODIS) STR loci or the 12 European Standard Set (ESS) STR loci [6, 7].

Two SNP panels developed for human identification have been multiplexed to a level that matches the discriminatory power of the commercial STR kits. The SNP*for*ID assay amplifies 52 SNPs in one PCR [14]. This assay has been tested in interlaboratory exercises within the SNP*for*ID consortium [15] and the European DNA Profiling Group (EDNAP) [16], and it has been implemented in a few forensic genetic laboratories mainly as a supplementary tool in relationship testing [17–19]. The lengths of the PCR products range from 59 to 115 bp and 38 of the amplicons are shorter than 100 bp.

A panel of 92 individual identification SNPs (IISNPs) has been selected [20] and 44 of these SNPs have been successfully multiplexed [21]. The lengths of the PCR products range from 69 to 125 bp and 17 of the amplicons are shorter than 100 bp. The selection criteria for the two panels were slightly different, but the mean match probabilities of the assays are similar (approximately 10^{-16}–10^{-21} depending on the investigated population). Both assays employ the PCR-single-base extension (SBE)-capillary electrophoresis (CE) method described in the next section.

If the DNA is degraded, successful genotyping depends on the sizes of the PCR products. The length of the PCR product containing a SNP locus only needs to be the length of the PCR primers plus one base pair (the SNP position). In theory, a DNA sequence is unique if it is 16 bp long (4^{16} = 4295 million combinations, which is more than the number of base pairs in the human genome). Thus, a PCR product containing a SNP locus only needs to be $(2 \times 16) + 1 = 33$ bp long. In reality, the PCR primer design restrains the positioning of the PCR primer and the PCR product must be longer. Nevertheless, most SNPs can be amplified on PCR products that are less than 100 bp in length. In contrast, the commonly used STR alleles have up to 40 tandem repeat units and, consequently, PCR products containing an STR locus can be 200 bp or longer. Furthermore, STR alleles are typically identified by fragment size using electrophoresis and in order to separate and identify all the loci in one experiment, the longest PCR products in the commercial multiplexes may be as long as 400–450 bp [22, 23]. Consequently, partial STR profiles are frequently observed when the DNA is highly degraded, whereas SNP typing of the same material results in complete profiles [14, 21, 24, 25].

Mutations

Mutations in the DNA create variations that make it possible to identify individuals based on their DNA profiles. However, mutations are not welcome in relationship testing, where the purpose is to determine whether and/or how individuals are related. If the investigated man and a child in a typical paternity case do not share any alleles at a given locus (genetic inconsistency), it indicates that the man is not the father. However, mutation events in the sperm of the true father may create genetic inconsistencies between the father and child. Mutations are observed in approximately $100 \times (13 \times 0.003) = 3.9\%$ of the cases, where the 13 CODIS STR loci are investigated. This is a highly unfortunate, but unavoidable, consequence of the relatively high mutation rate of tandem repeats. Even though the father matches the child at all other investigated loci, the inconsistency will speak against paternity and statistical weight calculations for alternative scenarios may indicate that the alternative scenario is more likely. In rare cases where relatives (e.g., two brothers, or father and son) are investigated, it may be impossible to draw a conclusion, because relatives share a high number of genetic markers and few genetic inconsistencies are expected between an investigated relative, who is not the father, and a child [26–30]. For comparison, one genetic inconsistency between the father and the child will be observed in approximately $100 \times (50 \times 0.0000001) = 0.0005\%$ of the cases, if 50 SNPs are investigated.

In mass disasters such as the World Trade Center terrorist attack in 2001 or the South Asian Tsunami in 2004, the victims may be impossible to identify by visual inspection because the human remains are highly fragmented, decomposed, or burned. Recovered DNA may be highly degraded, and unless reference materials from the missing persons are available, the victims must be identified via reference samples from close relatives. The low mutation rate of SNPs and the possibility of typing highly degraded DNA make SNPs very useful in mass disaster investigations.

Mixtures

Many trace samples collected from crime scenes contain DNA from more than one contributor (mixtures). These samples are particularly difficult to analyze, because it is not simple to deduce which alleles originate from which contributor. If the sample is typed for STRs, it is possible to estimate the number of contributors in the mixture from the number of detected alleles and sometimes it is even possible to estimate the STR profiles of the minor and major contributor based on the amplification strength (allele balance) of the alleles [31–34]. None of this is possible if the sample is typed for SNP loci. If both SNP alleles are detected in the mixture, it is usually possible to deduce that the sample is a mixture based on the allele balance [17, 30]. However, it is not possible to estimate how many people have contributed to the mixture or deduce the profiles of any of them except perhaps for the major contributor. The most useful SNPs for human identification are highly polymorphic and, therefore, there is a high probability that both alleles will be detected in mixtures of two or more individuals. If one of the individuals that contributed to the mixture is homozygous at a particular locus, there is $\rho^2 + 2\rho(1 - \rho)$ percent probability (75%, if $\rho = 0.5$) that another individual in the mixture has the other allele. If both alleles are detected in a mixture, there is no discriminatory power of a SNP locus since any individual may have contributed to the mixture and no one can be excluded.

PCR Artifacts

PCR amplification of STRs generates artifacts known as stutters. They are formed when an unfinished PCR product disassociates from the target DNA strand during DNA synthesis and subsequently anneal to another position (known as slipped strand mispairing) [35]. Stutters are usually one repeat shorter than the original allele; however, stutters of other lengths are also formed. Usually, the stutter signal is much weaker (<10%) than the signal from the true allele. However, if the amount of DNA is low and the stutter is formed during the first critical cycles of the PCR, there is a risk that the signal from the stutter may be as strong as the signal from the true allele and it may be assigned to the sample (drop-in allele) [36, 37]. If the target DNA is highly degraded, unfinished PCR products may also be formed when PCR primers anneal to DNA strands where the target sequences are interrupted. These products will generate artifacts of more random sizes in subsequent PCR cycles, because the 3′-end of the unfinished PCR product may anneal to any section of the tandem repeat. Stutters are a major problem in the analysis of mixtures, because it can be difficult to conclude whether a weak signal in a typical stutter

position is in fact a stutter or an amplification product from the minor contributor to the mixture.

Stutters are not formed in the amplification of SNP loci. Even if unfinished extension products are formed by slippage or because the target DNA is highly degraded, the unfinished extension products can only anneal to one unique position and it will simply function as a primer in the next PCR cycle.

SNP Typing Methods

Several high-throughput platforms that can type thousands of SNPs from a few individuals or a few SNPs from thousands of individuals at the same time and at a low cost have been developed in the last 20 years [38, 39]. Unfortunately, these platforms use relatively large amounts of DNA (10–200 ng) per sample per experiment, which is not applicable with the amount of DNA typically recovered from trace samples at crime scenes. Therefore, the attempts to implement high-throughput SNP platforms for routine forensic genetic investigations have so far been unsuccessful. Modern sequencing techniques may change that. Below, we describe the SNP typing assay used today and the sequencing methods that may revolutionize the field of forensic genetics in the near future.

SNP Typing by PCR-SBE-CE

SNP typing assays developed for forensic genetics during the last 10–15 years usually involve an initial multiplex PCR followed by a multiplex SBE reaction and detection of the SBE products by CE. The SBE reaction is a cycle reaction similar to the PCR (Figure 2).

Analysis of the electropherograms with SBE results may be challenging [15, 16] and it is important to introduce a quality assessment of each genotype call by defining locus-specific rules based on the signal strengths. The relative signal strengths of the two possible alleles at a locus are reproducible from experiment to experiment and from sample to sample [17]. Usually, the acceptable peak height ratio of a heterozygous allele call may be defined as $m \pm 40\%$, where m is the mean of observed ratios in approximately 100 unrelated heterozygous individuals. Similarly, the signal to noise ratio of homozygous allele calls can be clearly defined. Usually, a signal to noise ratio of 5–20 : 1 is adequate [17, 30]. The rules for data analysis are

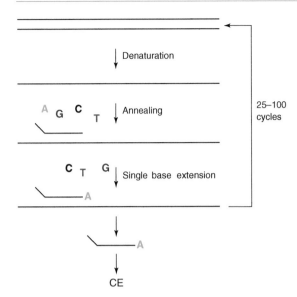

Figure 2 The cyclic SBE reaction. Double-stranded PCR products are denatured at high temperature, the SBE primers anneal to the PCR products at low temperature, and single base extension of the SBE primer is made at the optimal temperature of the Taq DNA polymerase. The SBE primer anneals to the single-stranded PCR product immediately upstream of the SNP position, and a fluorescently labeled dideoxyribonucleotide complimentary to the nucleotide in the SNP position is added to the SBE primer. The dideoxyribonucleotides are labeled with four different fluorophores. The SBE products can be analyzed by CE where the length of the SBE primer identifies the SNP locus and the color of the fluorescent label identifies the SNP allele

important for the evaluation of the sample itself. With biallelic SNPs, it is not possible to detect more than two alleles and it is not immediately evident whether the typing results originate from one or more individuals. The only method for determining whether the sample is contaminated or contains DNA from more than one individual is to look at the signal strengths (allele balance). An individual may have an unusual allele balance at a given locus because the signal from one allele is weak. This is typically caused by a mutation in one of the PCR or SBE primer binding sites [30]. However, if the peak height ratios are unusual at several loci, it is a strong indication that the sample contains DNA from more than one individual. Applying rules for data analysis makes it possible to readily identify mixtures even in 20 : 1 ratios [30].

PCR-SBE-CE assays are very sensitive and SNP profiles may be obtained from as little as 50–100 pg DNA (the amount of DNA found in 7–14 human cells) if the assay is fully optimized [25, 40]. Nevertheless, PCR-SBE-CE assays are only validated for casework in a few forensic genetic laboratories [17–19, 40]. This is mainly due to the lack of commercial kits and dedicated software solutions for analysis of SBE products, which requires that the local laboratories handle all of the quality control measures themselves. This may be a considerable task, especially if the laboratory is accredited according to an international standard, e.g., ISO 17025.

Next-Generation Sequencing (NGS)

The invention of emulsion PCR (emPCR) and bridge PCR marked the beginning of a new era in genetic sciences [41, 42]. These methods allow *in vitro* amplification of individual DNA molecules (clonal amplification) attached to a primer on either a bead (emPCR) or a solid surface (bridge PCR). Millions of different DNA molecules (clones) may be amplified in the same reaction and, after amplification, millions of copies of each original DNA molecule form a "cluster of DNA" that is immobilized on the bead or the solid surface. Subsequently, each DNA cluster of identical molecules can be efficiently sequenced by various methods and platforms [41, 42].

Addition of one nucleotide (dATP, dCTP, dGTP, or dTTP) to a growing DNA strand releases pyrophosphate and a proton (Figure 3). On the 454 pyrosequencing platforms, the pyrophosphate is used to generate light in a secondary reaction catalyzed by the enzyme luciferase. The light is detected by a camera and translated into a DNA sequence. On the Ion Torrent platform, the protons are detected directly by an ion sensor. On the Illumina platforms, the nucleotides are fluorescently labeled and detected by a camera. Furthermore, the nucleotides are blocked in the 3' position, which prevents incorporation of more than one nucleotide at the time. This is an advantage when the sequence contains stretches of the same nucleotide (homopolymer stretches). On the 454 pyrosequencing and the Ion Torrent platforms, several nucleotides will be incorporated at homopolymer stretches and more light and protons will be detected, respectively. However, if the stretch is longer than five nucleotides, it may be difficult to deduce the correct number of nucleotides in the homopolymer [43, 44].

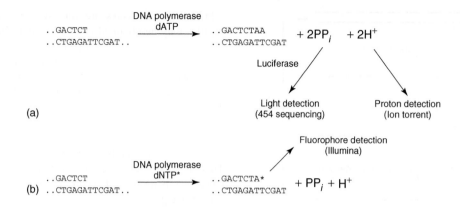

Figure 3 Next-generation sequencing. (a) Nucleotides are added sequentially to the sequencing reaction and incorporated into the DNA strand by the DNA polymerase. In the example, dATP is added to the reaction and the DNA is extended with two dATPs. This releases two pyrophosphates (PP_i) and two protons (H^+) that may be detected by the 454 sequencer and the Ion Torrent platform, respectively. (b) All nucleotides are added to the sequencing reaction. The nucleotides are labeled with four different fluorophores and blocked to prevent further extension. In the example, the DNA strand is extended with one fluorescent dATP. The fluorophore is detected by the Illumina platform and the block is subsequently removed prior to a new round of extension

Whole genomes or targeted regions of DNA may be used for the NGS workflows. Several methods for enrichment of specific regions for sequencing are available [45, 46] and they either use probes to capture the selected regions or amplify the regions by a PCR-based method. The latter will most likely be the preferred method for forensic genetic applications, because PCR ensures high sensitivity and speed, and because the number of relevant loci will be limited to a few hundred.

Electrophoresis puts restraints on the number of loci that may be detected at the same time and, today, there are forensic genetic CE-based assays for autosomal STRs, Y chromosome STRs, X chromosome STRs, insertion/deletion (indel) markers, mitochondrial DNA (mtDNA) SNPs, autosomal SNPs, Y chromosome SNPs, ancestry informative markers (AIMs), phenotypical markers, mRNA markers, etc. All of these assays may be combined into a single NGS assay if it is possible to develop a multiplex PCR that can amplify the relevant loci. One large and sensitive assay will reduce the amount of DNA used and, at the same time, increase the information obtained from a sample.

The output from the various NGS platforms ranges from 0.1 to 3000 million individual sequences (reads). Sequencing of a few hundred, relatively short (<200 bp) PCR products is a simple task even for the smallest platforms. Sequencing of, e.g., 500 loci with an average coverage of 100 reads per locus in 100 individuals requires 5 million reads and will be possible with already available benchtop machines.

One of the major challenges will be to develop a forensic tool for analysis and reporting of the sequence data. The future software must be completely reliable, because the sheer number of sequences will prevent manual analysis of the data. Results from typing of forensic samples can be difficult to interpret even with the current PCR-CE technology. With NGS, all of the PCR artifact including all types of stutters will be visible and need to be identified and sorted. This will be a difficult task, particularly from mixtures and samples with low amounts of DNA, where the errors introduced in the first cycles of the PCR will create drop-in alleles.

Currently, the forensic genetic laboratories are exploring the possibilities provided by NGS and reports on STR and SNP sequencing are beginning to emerge [43, 44, 47–52]. Furthermore, two of the major manufacturers of NGS platforms are working on forensic applications and the first forensic NGS assay, the HID-Ion AmpliSeq™ Identity Panel, was launched in January 2014. With this assay, it is possible to sequence 48 SNP*for*ID SNPs, 43 IISNPs, and 30 Y chromosome SNPs in a single reaction.

SNPs as Investigative Leads

In the last two decades, a large portion of forensic genetic research has explored DNA markers that are associated with physical traits (phenotypes) of individuals. Prediction of human phenotypes are rarely used in real casework today, but it is likely that future NGS assays will include phenotypical markers in addition to the traditional markers and that forensic DNA phenotyping will play substantial roles in future forensic genetic investigations. Conventional forensic DNA identification relies on a match between the DNA profile found at the crime scene and the DNA profile of the suspect. Often, no suspect matches the DNA profile found in the trace sample and no match is found in a criminal DNA database. In such cases, information about the ancestry or the externally visible traits of the perpetrator can be valuable information that can be used to reduce the number of suspects and allow the police investigators to focus on specific groups of individuals. Human sex determination is an example of a forensic phenotype that is accurately predicted with the use of a single genetic marker (amelogenin) [53]. The amelogenin-based sex determination is routinely carried out in casework today, because amelogenin is typed together with the commercially available STR-kits.

In the following sections, we discuss the use of DNA markers for the prediction of biogeographic ancestry and pigmentary traits, which are two of the most important phenotypes used to describe an individual.

SNPs, Population Genetics, and Ancestry Inference

Population genetics focuses on the distribution of the allele frequencies in different populations. This is done in the light of demographic processes that shape patterns of genetic diversity in populations, such as selection pressure, genetic drift, migrations, and mutations.

The criteria to define a human population vary. However, they usually refer to a group of individuals that live in geographical proximity, have common language and culture, and tend to mate more frequently with each other than with individuals from other groups [54].

The analysis of contemporary human populations can offer insights into the aspects of human history and it has been used to study both large-scale and microscale patterns of genetic variation [54].

Phylogeography refers to the study of the relationship between different genes or genome sequences and the genetic diversity detected in a temporal and geographic frame. This field of research grew rapidly in the 1970s and 1980s together with the development of molecular biology techniques and the observation that genetic lineages can be classified into groups of similar molecular haplotypes (haplogroups) that often have different and specific geographical locations (Figure 4) [55]. The fact that it focuses on the biogeographic history of a species or population is one of the aspects that separates the phylogeography from conventional population genetics.

The interest in the study of genetic diversity and ancestry has surpassed the boundaries of the scientific community and research. Nowadays, DNA testing companies are offering online information on ancestry or genetic history to the average public in a fast and easy way. The most appropriate markers to perform such studies are AIMs and uniparental markers (mtDNA and Y chromosome).

Ancestry Informative Markers (AIMs). The study of autosomal ancestry informative markers (AIMs) has become the method of choice when handling individual ancestry. The interest in this kind of marker has increased in the last decades because they can be very effective in many different areas of applied science, from population and forensic genetics to association studies and other clinical applications [56, 57].

The term *AIMs* refer to *genetic polymorphisms*, usually autosomal biallelic SNPs, which exhibit large allele frequency divergence between major ethnic groups [57].

In order to infer ancestry, the loci are studied in various human populations and the allele frequency distributions assessed. The best AIMs will be those markers that present large differences in allele frequencies between populations and can capture the genetic variation between groups.

The majority of reported AIM panels are capable of estimating the proportion of admixture of individuals and populations, and capable of predicting the ancestry of an individual to one of five continents: Europe, Africa, Asia, Australia, or America [57–59]. However, the genetic differences within continental groups are smaller than those between continents and fine-scale studies of, e.g., north and south European populations require analysis of many more markers [57, 60].

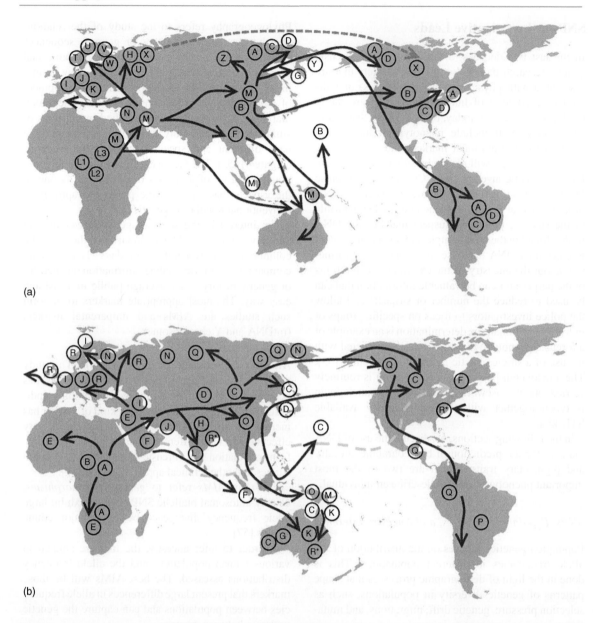

Figure 4 Phylogeographic studies allow a detailed picture of the mtDNA (a) and Y chromosome (b) haplogroups and their geographical distribution. The letters used to designate the mtDNA and Y chromosome haplogroups were defined independently of each other and, therefore, there is no geographical or genetic relationship between, e.g., the mtDNA haplogroup A and the Y chromosome haplogroup A

Besides tracing back individual genealogies, AIMs can also aid in forensic genetic casework. AIMs may be useful in the identification of missing persons and victims of mass disasters, and when there is no reliable information on a suspect or only few investigative leads. In these situations, the analysis of AIMs can provide information on the biogeographic ancestry of the individual and help to redirect the course of the investigations [57, 60, 61] as in the Madrid bombings in 2004 [62].

In medical applications, known as "admixture mapping", AIMs may identify candidate loci that could be linked to different diseases. AIMs can also have a prominent role in identification of possible false associations in association studies. Before these studies can be undertaken, there has to be a proper assessment of cases and controls, since underlying population substructure in cases/controls can produce spurious associations due to differences in allele frequencies between the two groups [63]. Ancestry assessment may also be important in therapeutics, since drug response and metabolism also vary between ethnic groups [64].

Uniparental Markers. Female and male lineage markers, mtDNA, and Y chromosome markers, respectively, have also been used in the reconstruction of the evolutionary history. Unlike autosomal markers that undergo recombination in each generation, lineage markers are transmitted directly from parent to child without recombination (Figure 5). Due to

their specific pattern of inheritance, mtDNA and Y chromosome analyses inform about the history of female or male lineages, respectively, and can be used to study population genetic differences between males and females [65]. These markers have a low effective population size (one fourth of the autosomes) and, therefore, the effects of genetic drift will be more evident and result in even more accentuated genetic differences between continental groups and a better correlation with geography [60, 66].

The mtDNA and Y chromosome profiles used in forensic genetic investigations typically consist of many different loci (SNPs and/or STRs). The many loci are inherited from one of the parents as a whole and, therefore, they are not independent loci. Instead, they form a mtDNA or Y chromosome haplotype that will be identical in all children of the same woman (and the children of her daughters and their daughters, etc.) and all male members of the family, respectively

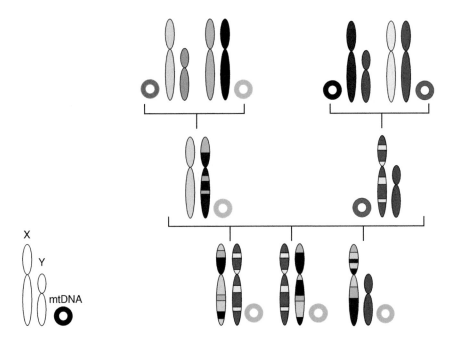

Figure 5 Transmission patterns of the sex chromosomes (X and Y) and the mtDNA (relative sizes are for illustration only and are not to scale). Unlike autosomes, lineage markers are transmitted directly without any recombination. The Y chromosome is only transmitted from fathers to sons, while the mtDNA is transmitted from mothers, to both sons and daughters. Regarding the X chromosome, there is difference in the number of chromosomes present in each sex: females have two copies while males have only one X chromosome and one Y chromosome. Therefore, men inherit the X chromosome from their mothers (an X chromosome that has suffered recombination before being transmitted), whereas women inherit one X chromosome from each parent. The paternal X chromosome is transmitted to the daughters without suffering recombination in the majority of its extension

(Figure 5). This makes uniparental markers very useful in relationship testing, especially for identification of disaster victims when samples from close relatives are available. The disadvantages of uniparental markers are that they identify the parental lineage, but not the individual, and that the power of discrimination is relatively low compared to that of autosomal markers. Furthermore, mutations will alter the haplotype and may lead to exclusion of true relatives.

It is important to emphasize that uniparental markers only reveal information on the parental lineage. If ethnical admixture has happened several generations ago, any phenotypical traits associated with a particular ethnic group may be lost. However, the uniparental marker remains the same. Thus, an individual with a mtDNA or Y chromosome haplotype that is found frequently in, e.g., African individuals may look European or *vice versa*.

Mitochondria and Mitochondrial DNA. Mitochondria are subcellular organelles that are responsible for energy production in animal cells. They contain genetic information in the form of a circular mtDNA molecule of about 16 569 bps [67]. The number of mtDNA copies varies from 100 to 10 000 per cell depending on the energy demands of the tissue. The high number of mtDNA copies improves the chance of isolating mtDNA, which makes analysis of mtDNA particularly useful if the sample is ancient or degraded (*see **Mitochondrial DNA: Profiling**) [68]. In addition, mtDNA can be collected from hair shafts, which contain only small amounts of highly degraded nuclear DNA.

The mtDNA comprises 37 genes and a 1122-bp noncoding sequence known as the mtDNA control region. Most of the variations in the mtDNA are located in the hypervariable (HV) regions of the control region [69, 70]. There are at least three HV regions with a high number of SNPs and these regions can be amplified by PCR and sequenced. Historically, the preferred targets for forensic genetic and phylogenetic investigations have been HV1 (position 16024–16400) and HV2 (position 44–340). However, with the invention of NGS methodologies, it is now possible to sequence the complete mtDNA molecule in a fast and cost-effective manner [43, 44].

In 1999, the European DNA Profiling (EDNAP) Group's mtDNA population database project (EMPOP) was initiated with the purpose of creating a common forensic standard for mtDNA sequencing and an online mtDNA database with high quality mtDNA population data. Only laboratories qualified by successful participation in EMPOP collaborative exercises have permission to submit mtDNA sequences into EMPOP [68]. With release 11 (October 2013), the EMPOP database contains 34 617 mtDNA sequences from populations all over the world.

Y Chromosome. The Y chromosome is the smallest human chromosome and contains only about 58 million bps [71] (*see **Y-Chromosome Short Tandem Repeats**). It is composed of two different types of chromatin: hetero- and euchromatin. The heterochromatic region is located in the distal part of the long arm and contains highly repetitive sequences. There are considerable size differences in the heterochromatin. In some males, it constitutes more than half of the chromosome, while in others it may not even be detectable. The remaining portion of the Y chromosome consists of euchromatin and contains sequences that are homologous to the X chromosome, repetitive sequences, and all known genes on the Y chromosome. The Y chromosome also has two pseudoautosomal regions (PAR1 and PAR2) at both ends that pair and recombine with the X chromosome. The male specific region of the Y chromosome contains the sex determining region as well as genes involved in spermatogenesis [72].

The Y chromosome has greater diversity than the mtDNA. In addition to biallelic polymorphisms like SNPs, there are also many STRs scattered throughout the chromosome that are of interest in population studies and ancestry inference. They are very useful to resolve male genealogies and for studying the structure of populations and reconstruct their evolutionary history [73, 74]. The combined analysis of Y-SNPs and Y-STRs is a common approach in population genetic studies. Fast-evolving markers with high mutation rates are very useful for the study of fine-scale processes that occurred in a recent time frame such as recent migrations or expansions. Furthermore, these markers are very informative for investigation of the relationship between individuals since they are characterized by high levels of diversity. However, when the study focuses on past events that occurred a long time ago, slowly evolving markers with low mutation rates are more informative [75, 76].

Y-STR typing is frequently used in forensic genetic case work and can be very useful for mixture interpretation [77, 78]. Especially in cases where the major contributor is female and the minor contributor is male, which is a situation that is often encountered in rape cases.

In 2000, the Y chromosome haplotype reference database (YHRD) was formed with the purpose of collecting human Y-STR haplotypes for estimation of haplotype frequencies and assessment of Y chromosome variation [79]. With release 46 (December 2013), the YHRD database contains 126 931 Y-STR haplotypes from populations all over the world.

Prediction of Pigmentary Traits

Genetic markers associated with skin, hair, and eye colors have been studied intensively [80–82] and much is known about the genetics underlying the pigmentary traits. Eye, hair, and skin colors are among the phenotypes with the largest visible variations. Eye colors can vary from blue to brown. Hair colors can be in the range from white to red, brown and black, and skin color is found in the range from pale white to dark brown. The great variation in colors and the high heritability of the pigmentary traits [83, 84] make prediction of eye, hair, and skin colors applicable for routine forensic genetic investigations.

The pigmentary traits are the only forensic phenotypes besides sex where validated assays have been developed for routine use in forensic genetic casework. The forensic SNP assays include assays for eye color prediction [85–87], hair color prediction [88], simultaneously hair and eye color prediction [82], simultaneously eye and skin color prediction [89], and simultaneously hair, eye, and skin color prediction [90]. All of these assays employ the PCR-SBE-CE method described above.

Eye Color. Eye color is currently the best investigated pigmentary trait. A study from 2009 systematically investigated the predictive values of SNPs associated with eye color in Europeans [81] and six SNPs (*HERC2* rs12913832, *OCA2* rs1800407, *SLC24A4* 12896399, *SLC45A2* rs16891892, *TYR* rs1393350, and *IRF4* rs12203592) from this study have been selected to form an assay for prediction of eye color. The assay is named the IrisPlex and an eye color prediction model has been developed [40, 86] that predicts blue and brown eye color across European populations with a very high accuracy (blue eye color: 94% and brown eye color: 94%). However, the sensitivity (true positive rate) for prediction of intermediate eye color (eye colors that are neither blue

nor brown) is low (1.1%) and the vast majority of the true intermediate eye colors are falsely predicted as blue or brown. The prediction accuracy of the IrisPlex prediction model is greatly dependent on the genotype of *HERC2* rs12913832. Indeed, it has been argued that for practical purposes, prediction of blue and brown eye colors based on the genotype of *HERC2* rs12913832 performs as good as the IrisPlex prediction model [91]. *HERC2* rs12913832 is the only IrisPlex SNP that has a known biological function. It is located in an enhancer element of the oculocutaneous albinism type II (*OCA2*) promoter [92] and regulates expression of *OCA2*.

The intermediate eye color category contains a wide range of eye colors not classified as either blue or brown, including eye colors perceived as green or hazel. Often, intermediate eye colors also contain regions of different colors, e.g., brown color areas around the pupil and blue areas at the outer iris boundary (Figure 6). These complex color patterns make the prediction difficult. Future work should focus on SNPs that are informative for the non-blue and non-brown eye colors in order to increase the prediction accuracy for the intermediate eye colors.

Hair Color. The first assay for prediction of hair color was published in 2001 [88]. It was based on SNPs in the melanocortin 1 receptor (*MC1R*) gene and the assay predicted red or non-red hair color. More recently, a systematic study analyzed the predictive power of 45 SNPs previously described to be associated with hair color in Polish Europeans [93]. A predictive model was developed based on a subset of 13 SNPs that were merged with the IrisPlex assay into a single assay capable of predicting both eye and hair color simultaneously [82]. The assay is named

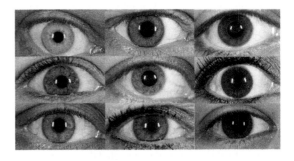

Figure 6 Examples of eye colors

the HIrisplex and includes a prediction model that has been assessed in various European populations. The HIrisPlex prediction model has a prediction accuracy of 69.5% for blond hair, 78.5% for brown hair, 80% for red hair, and 87.5% for black hair color. For prediction of eye color, the HIrisPlex uses the same prediction model as the IrisPlex.

Variations in hair color are restricted to individuals of European ancestry and hair can be dyed easily, which limits the practical use of hair color prediction in forensic genetic casework. Furthermore, some hair colors are age dependent [82, 94], e.g., blond hair is known to develop into light brown after childhood in some individuals and red hair color is known to fade with increasing age. The low prediction accuracy for blond hair in the HIrisPlex study may be related to the age-dependent effect [82]. Also, hair graying (loss of pigment) and male baldness is highly age dependent [95, 96]. Therefore, age determination should be part of future assays for hair color prediction. Obviously, prediction of chronological age would be highly relevant for forensic genetic casework, and early studies on DNA-based estimation of age are promising [97, 98]. However, more research is needed before it can be part of the forensic toolbox.

Skin Color. Prediction of skin color is the least developed research area among the pigmentary traits. The reason is the large genetic complexity of skin color, the high correlation to ancestry and the strong environmental influence of UVR [99]. Skin color and ancestry are closely correlated and it may be argued that the prediction of ancestry also will give a prediction of skin color. However, this is only the truth in non-admixed populations.

The high genetic complexity of skin color has been illustrated by a systematic study of 75 SNPs in 24 pigmentary genes [90]. The study found that three SNPs, *SLC45A2* rs16891982, *SLC24A5* rs1426654, and *ASIP* rs2424984 explained 45.8% of the variations in skin color when skin color was measured on a continuous scale. In another study, seven SNPs were typed to predict categorical skin color as nonwhite or non-brown in various populations [89]. A prediction accuracy of 72% was obtained. The prediction of eye color and hair color has shown the way ahead for prediction of skin color, but due to the genetic complexity of skin color, it is expected than many more SNPs are required to achieve sufficiently high prediction accuracy for use in forensic genetic casework.

Description of a Pigmentary Phenotype. All pigmentary traits are continuous. Therefore, the use of color categories (e.g., blue, brown, or white) over-simplifies the actual variation. Even though categories are generally accepted, there is a very large subjective element of individual assessment in studies that employ categories and this will affect the conclusions that may be drawn. The individual classification into different categories have either been self-declared using questionnaires [85, 100, 101] or assessed by trained professionals to minimize interpersonal differences [102]. Especially, the questionnaire-based approach is likely to introduce large variations because of individual differences in perception of colors. The use of trained professionals will yield a better classification of the pigmentary traits but will make it hard for other research groups to reproduce the conditions of the study unless the assessments are performed by the same professionals. Measuring the traits in question as continuous variables is a way to eliminate the use of categories. Skin color can be treated as a continuous variable by a noninvasive measurement of the melanin content [103], reflectance [104, 105] or digital photography [106]. For eye color and hair color measurements, spectroscopy or digital photography can be employed to objectively measure these traits [101, 105, 107–109]. Obviously, the more accurate and more detailed the trait can be measured, the better the chance is to find the underlying genetics.

In contrast, it is preferable for police investigators that the reporting is done in categories, because colors are well known and immediately recognized by the public. Therefore, the DNA genotype generated from the trace sample must first be translated into a pigmentation interval on a continuous scientific scale and, second, the interval must be translated into a color category. The range of possible colors may furthermore be presented to the investigators with visual examples covering the predicted interval. This will require recognized standards and large validation studies. Fortunately, the forensic genetic community has a long successful record of developing international standards for DNA typing and reporting of evidence.

The introduction of NGS technology in forensic genetics will make ancestry and pigmentary markers part of commonly used kits. This will certainly lead to a general discussion on how investigative leads should be evaluated and reported to the police, and it will increase the need for interpretation guidelines from the community.

References

[1] The 1000 genome project consortium (2012). An integrated map of genetic variation from 1,092 human genomes, *Nature* **491**, 56–65.

[2] International SNP Map Working Group (2001). A map of human genome sequence variation containing 1.42 million single nucleotide polymorphisms, *Nature* **409**, 928–933.

[3] Reich, D.E., Schaffner, S.F., Dalby, M.J., McVean, G., Mullikin, J.C., Higgins, J.M., Richter, D.J., Lander, E.S. & Altshuler, D. (2002). Human genome sequence variation and the influence of gene history, mutation and recombination, *Nature Genetics* **32**, 135–142.

[4] Jeffreys, A.J., Wilson, V. & Thein, S.L. (1985). Individual-specific 'fingerprints' of human DNA, *Nature* **316**, 76–79.

[5] Gill, P., Jeffreys, A.J. & Werrett, D.J. (1985). Forensic application of DNA 'fingerprints', *Nature* **318**, 577–579.

[6] Budowle, B., Moretti, T.R., Baumstark, A.L., Defenbaugh, D.A. & Keys, K.M. (1999). Population data on the thirteen CODIS core short tandem repeat loci in African Americans, U.S. Caucasians, Hispanics, Bahamians, Jamaicans, and Trinidadians, *Journal of Forensic Sciences* **44**, 1277–1286.

[7] Welch, L.A., Gill, P., Phillips, C., Ansell, R., Morling, N., Parson, W., Palo, J.U. & Bastisch, I. (2012). European Network of Forensic Science Institutes (ENFSI): evaluation of new commercial STR multiplexes that include the European Standard Set (ESS) of markers, *Forensic Science International: Genetics* **6**, 819–826.

[8] Parson, W. & Dür, A. (2007). EMPOP – a forensic mtDNA database, *Forensic Science International: Genetics* **1**, 88–92.

[9] Krawczak, M. (1999). Informativity assessment for biallelic single nucleotide polymorphisms, *Electrophoresis* **20**, 1676–1681.

[10] Gill, P. (2001). An assessment of the utility of single nucleotide polymorphisms (SNPs) for forensic purposes, *International Journal of Legal Medicine* **114**, 204–210.

[11] Saiki, R.K., Gelfand, D.H., Stoffel, S., Scharf, S.J., Higuchi, R., Horn, G.T., Mullis, K.B. & Erlich, H.A. (1988). Primer-directed enzymatic amplification of DNA with a thermostable DNA polymerase, *Science* **239**, 487–491.

[12] Cockerill, P.N. (2011). Structure and function of active chromatin and DNase I hypersensitive sites, *FEBS Journal* **278**, 2182–2210.

[13] Thanakiatkrai, P. & Welch, L. (2011). Evaluation of nucleosome forming potentials (NFPs) of forensically important STRs, *Forensic Science International: Genetics* **5**, 285–290.

[14] Sanchez, J.J., Phillips, C., Børsting, C., Balogh, K., Bogus, M., Fondevilla, M., Harrison, C.D., Musgrave-Brown, E., Salas, A., Syndercombe-Court, D., Schneider, P.M., Carracedo, A. & Morling, N. (2006). A multiplex assay with 52 single nucleotide polymorphisms for human identification, *Electrophoresis* **27**, 1713–1724.

[15] Musgrave-Brown, E., Ballard, D., Balogh, K., Bender, K., Berger, B., Bogus, M., Børsting, C., Brion, M., Fondevila, M., Harrison, C., Oguzturun, C., Parson, W., Phillips, C., Proff, C., Ramos-Luis, E., Sanchez, J.J., Diz, P.S., Rey, B., Stradmann-Bellinghausen, B., Thacker, C., Carracedo, A., Morling, N., Scheithauer, R., Schneider, P.M. & Court, D.S. (2007). Forensic validation of the SNP*for*ID 52-plex assay, *Forensic Science International: Genetics* **1**, 186–190.

[16] Sanchez, J.J., Børsting, C., Balogh, K., Berger, B., Bogus, M., Butler, J.M., Carracedo, A., Court, D.S., Dixon, L.A., Filipovic, B., Fondevila, M., Gill, P., Harrison, C.D., Hohoff, C., Huel, R., Ludes, B., Parson, W., Parsons, T.J., Petkovski, E., Phillips, C., Schmitter, H., Schneider, P.M., Vallone, P.M. & Morling, N. (2008). Forensic typing of autosomal SNPs with a 29 SNP-multiplex–results of a collaborative EDNAP exercise, *Forensic Science International: Genetics* **2**, 176–183.

[17] Børsting, C., Rockenbauer, E. & Morling, N. (2009). Validation of a single nucleotide polymorphism (SNP) typing assay with 49 SNPs for forensic genetic testing in a laboratory accredited according to the ISO 17025 standard, *Forensic Science International: Genetics* **4**, 34–42.

[18] Schwark, T., Meyer, P., Harder, M., Modrow, J. & von Wurmb-Schwark, N. (2012). The SNP*for*ID assay as a supplementary method in kinship and trace analysis, *Transfusion Medicine and Hemotherapy* **39**, 187–193.

[19] Phillips, C., García-Magariños, M., Salas, A., Carrecedo, A. & Larau, M.V. (2012). SNPs as supplements in simple kinship analysis or as core markers in distant pairwise relationship tests: when do SNPs add value or replace well-established and powerful STR tests, *Transfusion Medicine and Hemotherapy* **39**, 202–210.

[20] Pakstis, A.J., Speed, W.C., Fang, R., Hyland, F.C., Furtado, M.R., Kidd, J.R. & Kidd, K.K. (2010). SNPs for a universal individual identification panel, *Human Genetics* **127**, 315–324.

[21] Lou, C., Cong, B., Li, S., Fu, L., Zhang, X., Feng, T., Su, S., Ma, C., Yu, F., Ye, J. & Pei, L. (2011). A SNaPshot assay for genotyping 44 individual identification single nucleotide polymorphisms, *Electrophoresis* **32**, 368–378.

[22] Tucker, V.C., Kirkham, A.J. & Hopwood, A.J. (2012). Forensic validation of the PowerPlex® ESI 16 STR multiplex and comparison of performance with AmpFlSTR® SGM Plus®, *International Journal of Legal Medicine* **126**, 345–356.

[23] Green, R.L., Lagacé, R.E., Oldroyd, N.J., Hennessy, L.K. & Mulero, J.J. (2013). Developmental validationof the AmpFℓSTR® NGM SElect™ PCR Amplification Kit: a next-generation STR multiplex with the SE33 locus, *Forensic Science International: Genetics* **7**, 41–51.

[24] Fondevila, M., Phillips, C., Naveran, N., Fernandez, L., Cerezo, M., Salas, A., Carrecedo, A. & Lareu, M.V. (2008). Case report: identification of skeletal remains using short-amplicon marker analysis of severely degraded DNA extracted from a decomposed and charred femur, *Forensic Science International: Genetics* **2**, 212–218.

[25] Børsting, C., Mogensen, H.S. & Morling, N. (2013). Forensic genetic SNP typing of low-template DNA and highly degraded DNA from crime case samples, *Forensic Science International: Genetics* **7**, 345–352.

[26] Wurmb-Schwark, N.V., Mályusz, V., Simeoni, E., Lignitz, E. & Poetsch, M. (2006). Possible pitfalls in motherless paternity analysis with related putative fathers, *Forensic Science International* **159**, 92–97.

[27] Karlsson, A.O., Holmlund, G., Egeland, T. & Mostad, P. (2007). DNA-testing for immigration cases: the risk of erroneous conclusions, *Forensic Science International* **172**, 144–149.

[28] Nothnagel, M., Schmidtke, J. & Krawczak, M. (2010). Potentials and limits of pairwise kinship analysis using autosomal short tandem repeat loci, *International Journal of Legal Medicine* **124**, 205–215.

[29] Børsting, C. & Morling, N. (2011). Mutations and/or relatives? Six case work examples where 49 autosomal SNPs were used as supplementary markers, *Forensic Science International: Genetics* **5**, 236–241.

[30] Børsting, C., Mikkelsen, M. & Morling, N. (2012). Kinship analysis with diallelic SNPs – experiences with the SNP*for*ID multiplex in an ISO17025 accreditated laboratory, *Transfusion Medicine and Hemotherapy* **39**, 195–201.

[31] Haned, H., Pène, L., Lobry, J.R., Dufour, A.B. & Pontier, D. (2011). Estimating the number of contributors to forensic DNA mixtures: does maximum likelihood perform better than maximum allele count?, *Journal of Forensic Sciences* **56**, 23–28.

[32] Tvedebrink, T., Eriksen, P.S., Mogensen, H.S. & Morling, N. (2012). Identifying contributors of DNA mixtures by means of quantitative information of STR typing, *Journal of Computational Biology* **19**, 887–902.

[33] Kelly, H., Bright, J.A., Curran, J. & Buckleton, J. (2012). The interpretation of low level DNA mixtures, *Forensic Science International: Genetics* **6**, 191–197.

[34] Gill, P. & Haned, H. (2013). A new methodological framework to interpret complex DNA profiles using likelihood ratios, *Forensic Science International: Genetics* **7**, 251–263.

[35] Ellegren, H. (2000). Microsatellite mutations in the germline: implications for evolutionary inference, *Trends in Genetics* **16**, 551–558.

[36] Benschop, C.C.G., van der Beek, C.P., Meiland, H.C., van Gorp, A.G.M., Western, A.A. & Sijen, T. (2011). Low template STR typing: effect of replicate number and consensus method on genotyping reliability and DNA database search results, *Forensic Science International: Genetics* **5**, 316–328.

[37] Cowen, S., Debenham, P., Dixon, A., Kutranov, S., Thomson, J. & Way, K. (2011). An investigation of the robustness of the consensus method of interpreting low-template DNA profiles, *Forensic Science International: Genetics* **5**, 400–406.

[38] Kwok, P. (2001). Methods for genotyping single nucleotide polymorphisms, *Annual Review of Genomics and Human Genetics* **2**, 235–258.

[39] Sobrino, B., Brion, M. & Carracedo, A. (2005). SNPs in forensic genetics: a review on SNP typing technologies, *Forensic Science International* **154**, 181–194.

[40] Walsh, S., Lindenbergh, A., Zuniga, S.B., Sijen, T., de Kniff, P., Kayser, M. & Ballantyne, K.N. (2011). Developmental validation of the IrisPlex system: determination of blue and brown iris colour for forensic intelligence, *Forensic Science International: Genetics* **5**, 464–471.

[41] Mardis, E.R. (2008). Next-generation DNA sequencing methods, *Annual Review of Genomics and Human Genetics* **9**, 387–402.

[42] Metzker, M.L. (2010). Sequencing technologies – the next generation, *Nature Reviews* **11**, 31–46.

[43] Parson, W., Strobl, C., Huber, G., Zimmermann, B., Gomes, S.M., Souto, L., Fendt, L., Delport, R., Langit, R., Wootton, S., Lagacé, R. & Irwin, J. (2013). Evaluation of next generation mtGenome sequencing using the ion Torrent Personal Genome Machine (PGM), *Forensic Science International: Genetics* **7**, 543–549.

[44] Mikkelsen, M., Frank-Hansen, R., Hansen, A.J. & Morling, N. (2014). Massively parallel pyrosequencing of the mitochondrial genome with the 454 methodology in forensic genetics, *Forensic Science International: Genetics*. DOI: 10.1016/j.fsigen.2014.03.014

[45] Mamanova, L., Coffey, A.J., Scott, C.E., Kozarewa, I., Turner, E.H., Kumar, A., Howard, E., Shendure, J. & Turner, D.J. (2010). Target-enrichment strategies for next-generation sequencing, *Nature Methods* **7**, 111–119.

[46] Hagemann, I.S., Cottrell, C.E. & Lockwood, C.M. (2014). Design of targeted, capture-based, nex generation sequencing tests for precision cancer therapy, *Cancer Genetics* **206**, 420–431.

[47] Fordyce, S.L., Avila-Arcos, M.C., Rockenbauer, E., Børsting, C., Frank-Hansen, R., Petersen, F.T., Willerslev, E., Hansen, A.J., Morling, N. & Gilbert, M.T.

(2011). High-throughput sequencing of core STR loci for forensic genetic investigations using the Roche Genome Sequencer FLX platform, *Biotechniques* **51**, 127–133.

[48] Seo, S.B., King, J.L., Warshauer, D.H., Davis, C.P., Ge, J. & Budowle, B. (2013). Single nucleotide polymorphism typing with massively parallel sequencing for human identification, *International Journal of Legal Medicine* **127**, 1079–1086.

[49] Warshauer, D.H., Lin, D., Hari, K., Jain, R., Davis, C., LaRue, B., King, J.L. & Budowle, B. (2013). STRait razor: a length-based forensic STR allele-callling tool for use with second generation sequencing data, *Forensic Science International: Genetics* **7**, 409–417.

[50] Van Neste, C., Vandewoestyne, M., Van Criekinge, W., Deforce, D. & Van Nieuwerburgh, F. (2014). My-Forensic-Loci-queries (MyFLq) framework for analysis of forensic STR data generated by massive parallel sequencing, *Forensic Science International: Genetics* **9**, 1–8.

[51] Rockenbauer, E., Hansen, S., Mikkelsen, M., Børsting, C. & Morling, N. (2014). Characterization of mutations and sequence variants in the D21S11 locus by next generation sequencing, *Forensic Science International: Genetics* **8**, 68–72.

[52] Dalsgaard, S., Rockenbauer, E., Buchard, A., Mogensen, H.S., Frank-Hansen, R., Børsting, C. & Morling, N. (2014). Non-uniform phenotyping of D12S391 resolved by second generation sequencing, *Forensic Science International: Genetics* **8**, 195–199.

[53] Kayser, M. & Schneider, P.M. (2009). DNA-based prediction of human externally visible characteristics in forensics: motivations, scientific challenges, and ethical considerations, *Forensic Science International: Genetics* **3**, 154–161.

[54] Jobling, M.A., Hurles, M. & Tyler-Smith, C. (2003). *Human Evolutionary Genetics: Origins, Peoples & Disease*, Garland Science, New York.

[55] Gonder, M.K., Mortensen, H.M., Reed, F.A., de Sousa, A. & Tishkoff, S.A. (2007). Whole mtDNA genome sequence analysis of ancient African lineages, *Molecular Biology and Evolution* **24**, 757–768.

[56] Kidd, J.R., Friedlaender, F.R., Speed, W.C., Pakstis, A.J., De La Vega, F.M. & Kidd, K.K. (2011). Analyses of a set of 128 ancestry informative single-nucleotide polymorphisms in a global set of 119 population samples, *Investigative Genetics* **2**, 1.

[57] Pereira, R., Phillips, C., Pinto, N., Santos, C., dos Santos, S.E., Amorim, A., Carracedo, A. & Gusmão, L. (2012). Straightforward inference of ancestry and admixture proportions through ancestry-informative insertion deletion multiplexing, *PLoS One* **7**, e29684.

[58] Galanter, J.M., Fernandez-Lopez, J.C., Gignoux, C.R., Barnholtz-Sloan, J., Fernandez-Rozadilla, C., Via, M., Hidalgo-Miranda, A., Contreras, A.V., Figueroa, L.U., Raska, P., Jimenez-Sanchez, G., Zolezzi, I.S., Torres, M., Ponte, C.R., Ruiz, Y., Salas, A., Nguyen, E., Eng, C., Borjas, L., Zabala, W., Barreto, G., González, F.R., Ibarra, A., Taboada, P., Porras, L., Moreno, F., Bigham, A., Gutierrez, G., Brutsaert, T., León-Velarde, F., Moore, L.G., Vargas, E., Cruz, M., Escobedo, J., Rodriguez-Santana, J., Rodriguez-Cintrón, W., Chapela, R., Ford, J.G., Bustamante, C., Seminara, D., Shriver, M., Ziv, E., Burchard, E.G., Haile, R., Parra, E., Carracedo, A. & Consortium, L.A.C.E. (2012). Development of a panel of genome-wide ancestry informative markers to study admixture throughout the Americas, *PLoS Genetics* **8**, e1002554.

[59] Phillips, C., Parson, W., Lundsberg, B., Santos, C., Freire-Aradas, A., Torres, M., Eduardoff, M., Børsting, C., Johansen, P., Fondevila, M., Morling, N., Schneider, P., the EUROFORGEN-NoE Consortium, Carracedo, A. & Lareu, M.V. (2014). Building a forensic ancestry panel from the ground up: The EUROFORGEN Global AIM-SNP set, *Forensic Science International: Genetics*. DOI: 10.1016/j.fsigen.2014.02.012

[60] Phillips, C., Salas, A., Sánchez, J.J., Fondevila, M., Gómez-Tato, A., Alvarez-Dios, J., Calaza, M., de Cal, M.C., Ballard, D., Lareu, M.V., Carracedo, A. & SNPforID Consortium (2007). Inferring ancestral origin using a single multiplex assay of ancestry-informative marker SNPs, *Forensic Science International: Genetics* **1**, 273–280.

[61] Budowle, B. & van Daal, A. (2008). Forensically relevant SNP classes, *Biotechniques* **44**, 603–608.

[62] Phillips, C., Prieto, L., Fondevila, M., Salas, A., Gómez-Tato, A., Alvarez-Dios, J., Alonso, A., Blanco-Verea, A., Brión, M., Montesino, M., Carracedo, A. & Lareu, M.V. (2009). Ancestry analysis in the 11-M Madrid bomb attack investigation, *PLoS One* **4**, e6583.

[63] Sankararaman, S., Sridhar, S., Kimmel, G. & Halperin, E. (2008). Estimating local ancestry in admixed populations, *American Journal of Human Genetics* **82**, 290–303.

[64] Enoch, M.A., Shen, P.H., Xu, K., Hodgkinson, C. & Goldman, D. (2006). Using ancestry-informative markers to define populations and detect population stratification, *Journal of Psychopharmacology* **20**, 19–26.

[65] Schaffner, S.F. (2004). The X chromosome in population genetics, *Nature Reviews Genetics* **5**, 43–51.

[66] Zakharia, F., Basu, A., Absher, D., Assimes, T.L., Go, A.S., Hlatky, M.A., Iribarren, C., Knowles, J.W., Li, J., Narasimhan, B., Sidney, S., Southwick, A., Myers, R.M., Quertermous, T., Risch, N. & Tang, H. (2009). Characterizing the admixed African ancestry of African Americans, *Genome Biology* **10**, R141.

[67] Tully, G., Bar, W., Brinkmann, B., Carracedo, A., Gill, P., Morling, N., Parson, W. & Schneider, P. (2001). Considerations by the European DNA profiling (EDNAP) group on the working practices, nomenclature and interpretation of mitochondrial DNA profiles, *Forensic Science International* **124**, 83–91.

[68] Parson, W., Brandstatter, A., Alonso, A., Brandt, N., Brinkmann, B., Carracedo, A., Corach, D., Froment, O., Furac, I., Grzybowski, T., Hedberg, K., Keyser-Tracqui, C., Kupiec, T., Lutz-Bonengel, S., Mevag, B., Ploski, R., Schmitter, H., Schneider, P., Syndercombe-Court, D., Sorensen, E., Thew, H., Tully, G. & Scheithauer, R. (2004). The EDNAP mitochondrial DNA population database (EMPOP) collaborative exercises: organisation, results and perspectives, *Forensic Science International* **139**, 215–226.

[69] Carracedo, A., Bar, W., Lincoln, P., Mayr, W., Morling, N., Olaisen, B., Schneider, P., Budowle, B., Brinkmann, B., Gill, P., Holland, M., Tully, G. & Wilson, M. (2000). DNA Commission of the International Society for Forensic Genetics: guidelines for mitochondrial DNA typing, *Forensic Science International* **110**, 79–85.

[70] Parson, W. & Bandelt, H.J. (2007). Extended guidelines for mtDNA typing of population data in forensic science, *Forensic Science International: Genetics* **1**, 13–19.

[71] Morton, N. (1991). Parameters of the human genome, *Proceedings of the National Academy of Sciences of the United States of America* **88**, 7474–7476.

[72] Graves, J.A. (2005). Recycling the Y chromosome, *Science* **7**, 50–51.

[73] Roewer, L., Croucher, P., Willuweit, S., Lu, T., Kayser, M., Lessig, R., Knijff, P., Jobling, M.A., Tyler-Smith, C. & Krawczak, M. (2005). Signature of recent historical events in the European Ychromosomal STR haplotype distribution, *Human Genetics* **116**, 279–291.

[74] Sajantila, A., Salem, A.-H., Savolainen, P., Bauer, K., Gierig, C. & Paabo, S. (1996). Paternal and maternal DNA lineages reveal a bottleneck in the founding of the Finnish population, *Proceedings of the National Academy of Sciences of the United States of America* **93**, 12035–12039.

[75] Steiper, M.E. (2010). DNA markers of human variation, in *Human Evolutionary Biology, MP Muehlenbein*, Cambridge University Press, New York, pp. 238–264.

[76] Schlotterer, C. (2000). Evolutionary dynamics of microsatellite DNA, *Chromosoma* **109**, 365–371.

[77] Mulero, J.J., Chang, C.W., Calandro, L.M., Green, R.L., Li, Y., Johnson, C.L. & Hennessy, L.K. (2006). Development and validation of the AmpFlSTR Yfiler PCR amplification kit: a male specific, single amplification 17 Y-STR multiplex system, *Journal of Forensic Sciences* **51**, 64–75.

[78] Thompson, J.M., Ewing, M.M., Frank, W.E., Pogemiller, J.J., Nolde, C.A., Koehler, D.J., Shaffer, A.M., Rabbach, D.R., Fulmer, P.M., Sprecher, C.J. & Storts, D.R. (2013). Developmental validation of the PowerPlex® Y23 System: a single multiplex Y-STR analysis system for casework and database samples, *Forensic Science International: Genetics* **7**, 240–250.

[79] Willuweit, S. & Roewer, L. (2007). Y chromosome haplotype reference database (YHRD): update, *Forensic Science International: Genetics* **1**, 83–87.

[80] Sulem, P., Gudbjartsson, D.F., Stacey, S.N., Helgason, A., Rafnar, T., Magnusson, K.P., Manolescu, A., Karason, A., Palsson, A., Thorleifsson, G., Jakobsdottir, M., Steinberg, S., Palsson, S., Jonasson, F., Sigurgeirsson, B., Thorisdottir, K., Ragnarsson, R., Benediktsdottir, K.R., Aben, K.K., Kiemeney, L.A., Olafsson, J.H., Gulcher, J., Kong, A., Thorsteinsdottir, U. & Stefansson, K. (2007). Genetic determinants of hair, eye and skin pigmentation in Europeans, *Nature Genetics* **12**, 1443–1452.

[81] Liu, F., van Duijn, K., Vingerling, J.R., Hofman, A., Uitterlinden, A.G., Janssens, A.C. & Kayser, M. (2009). Eye color and the prediction of complex phenotypes from genotypes, *Current Biology* **5**, R192–R193.

[82] Walsh, S., Liu, F., Wollstein, A., Kovatsi, L., Ralf, A., Kosiniak-Kamysz, A., Branicki, W. & Kayser, M. (2013). The HIrisPlex system for simultaneous prediction of hair and eye colour from DNA, *Forensic Science International: Genetics* **7**, 98–115.

[83] Clark, P., Stark, A.E., Walsh, R.J., Jardine, R. & Martin, N.G. (1981). A twin study of skin reflectance, *Annals of Human Biology* **6**, 529–541.

[84] Posthuma, D., Visscher, P.M., Willemsen, G., Zhu, G., Martin, N.G., Slagboom, P.E., De Geus, E.J. & Boomsma, D.I. (2006). Replicated linkage for eye color on 15q using comparative ratings of sibling pairs, *Behavior Genetics* **1**, 12–17.

[85] Mengel-From, J., Børsting, C., Sanchez, J.J., Eiberg, H. & Morling, N. (2010). Human eye colour and HERC2, OCA2 and MATP, *Forensic Science International: Genetics* **4**, 323–328.

[86] Walsh, S., Liu, F., Ballantyne, K.N., van Oven, M., Lao, O. & Kayser, M. (2011). IrisPlex: a sensitive DNA tool for accurate prediction of blue and brown eye colour in the absence of ancestry information, *Forensic Science International: Genetics* **5**, 170–180.

[87] Ruiz, Y., Phillips, C., Gomez-Tato, A., Alvarez-Dios, J., Casares de, C.M., Cruz, R., Maronas, O., Sochtig, J., Fondevila, M., Rodriguez-Cid, M.J., Carracedo, A. & Lareu, M.V. (2013). Further development of forensic eye color predictive tests, *Forensic Science International: Genetics* **1**, 28–40.

[88] Grimes, E.A., Noake, P.J., Dixon, L. & Urquhart, A. (2001). Sequence polymorphism in the human melanocortin 1 receptor gene as an indicator of the red hair phenotype, *Forensic Science International* **122**, 124–129.

[89] Spichenok, O., Budimlija, Z.M., Mitchell, A.A., Jenny, A., Kovacevic, L., Marjanovic, D., Caragine, T., Prinz, M. & Wurmbach, E. (2011). Prediction of eye and skin color in diverse populations using seven SNPs, *Forensic Science International: Genetics* **5**, 472–478.

[90] Valenzuela, R.K., Henderson, M.S., Walsh, M.H., Garrison, N.A., Kelch, J.T., Cohen-Barak, O., Erickson, D.T., John, M.F., Bruce, W.J., Cheng, K.C.,

Ito, S., Wakamatsu, K., Frudakis, T., Thomas, M. & Brilliant, M.H. (2010). Predicting phenotype from genotype: normal pigmentation, *Journal of Forensic Sciences* **2**, 315–322.

[91] Pietroni, C., Andersen, J.D., Johansen, P., Andersen, M.M., Harder, S., Paulsen, R., Børsting, C. & Morling, N. (2014). The effect of gender on eye colour variation in European populations and an evaluation of the IrisPlex prediction model, *Forensic Science International: Genetics*. DOI: 10.1016/j.fsigen.2014.02.002

[92] Visser, M., Kayser, M. & Palstra, R.J. (2012). HERC2 rs12913832 modulates human pigmentation by attenuating chromatin-loop formation between a long-range enhancer and the OCA2 promoter, *Genome Research* **22**, 446–455.

[93] Branicki, W., Liu, F., van Duijn, K., Draus-Barini, J., Pospiech, E., Walsh, S., Kupiec, T., Wojas-Pelc, A. & Kayser, M. (2011). Model-based prediction of human hair color using DNA variants, *Human Genetics* **4**, 443–454.

[94] Rees, J.L. (2003). Genetics of hair and skin color, *Annual Review of Genetics* **37**, 67–90.

[95] Nyholt, D.R., Gillespie, N.A., Heath, A.C. & Martin, N.G. (2003). Genetic basis of male pattern baldness, *Journal of Investigative Dermatology* **6**, 1561–1564.

[96] Panhard, S., Lozano, I. & Loussouarn, G. (2012). Greying of the human hair: a worldwide survey, revisiting the '50' rule of thumb, *British Journal of Dermatology* **4**, 865–873.

[97] Zubakov, D., Liu, F., van Zelm, M.C., Vermeulen, J., Oostra, B.A., van Duijn, C.M., Driessen, G.J., van Dongen, J.J., Kayser, M. & Langerak, A.W. (2010). Estimating human age from T-cell DNA rearrangements, *Current Biology* **22**, R970–R971.

[98] Bocklandt, S., Lin, W., Sehl, M.E., Sanchez, F.J., Sinsheimer, J.S., Horvath, S. & Vilain, E. (2011). Epigenetic predictor of age, *PLoS One* **6**, e14821.

[99] Shriver, M.D., Parra, E.J., Dios, S., Bonilla, C., Norton, H., Jovel, C., Pfaff, C., Jones, C., Massac, A., Cameron, N., Baron, A., Jackson, T., Argyropoulos, G., Jin, L., Hoggart, C.J., McKeigue, P.M. & Kittles, R.A. (2003). Skin pigmentation, biogeographical ancestry and admixture mapping, *Human Genetics* **4**, 387–399.

[100] Han, J., Kraft, P., Nan, H., Guo, Q., Chen, C., Qureshi, A., Hankinson, S.E., Hu, F.B., Duffy, D.L., Zhao, Z.Z., Martin, N.G., Montgomery, G.W., Hayward, N.K., Thomas, G., Hoover, R.N., Chanock, S. & Hunter, D.J. (2008). A genome-wide association study identifies novel alleles associated with hair color and skin pigmentation, *PLoS Genetics* **5**, e1000074.

[101] Mengel-From, J., Wong, T.H., Morling, N., Rees, J.L. & Jackson, I.J. (2009). Genetic determinants of hair and eye colours in the Scottish and Danish populations, *BMC Genetics* **10**, 88.

[102] Walsh, S., Wollstein, A., Liu, F., Chakravarthy, U., Rahu, M., Seland, J.H., Soubrane, G., Tomazzoli, L., Topouzis, F., Vingerling, J.R., Vioque, J., Fletcher, A.E., Ballantyne, K.N. & Kayser, M. (2012). DNA-based eye colour prediction across Europe with the IrisPlex system, *Forensic Science International: Genetics* **6**, 330–340.

[103] Kongshoj, B., Thorleifsson, A. & Wulf, H.C. (2006). Pheomelanin and eumelanin in human skin determined by high-performance liquid chromatography and its relation to in vivo reflectance measurements, *Photodermatology, Photoimmunology and Photomedicine* **3**, 141–147.

[104] Stokowski, R.P., Pant, P.V., Dadd, T., Fereday, A., Hinds, D.A., Jarman, C., Filsell, W., Ginger, R.S., Green, M.R., van der Ouderaa, F.J. & Cox, D.R. (2007). A genomewide association study of skin pigmentation in a South Asian population, *American Journal of Human Genetics* **6**, 1119–1132.

[105] Candille, S.I., Absher, D.M., Beleza, S., Bauchet, M., McEvoy, B., Garrison, N.A., Li, J.Z., Myers, R.M., Barsh, G.S., Tang, H. & Shriver, M.D. (2012). Genome-wide association studies of quantitatively measured skin, hair, and eye pigmentation in four European populations, *PLoS One* **10**, e48294.

[106] Jacobs, L.C., Wollstein, A., Lao, O., Hofman, A., Klaver, C.C., Uitterlinden, A.G., Nijsten, T., Kayser, M. & Liu, F. (2012). Comprehensive candidate gene study highlights UGT1A and BNC2 as new genes determining continuous skin color variation in Europeans, *Human Genetics* **2**, 147–158.

[107] Shekar, S.N., Duffy, D.L., Frudakis, T., Sturm, R.A., Zhao, Z.Z., Montgomery, G.W. & Martin, N.G. (2008). Linkage and association analysis of spectrophotometrically quantified hair color in Australian adolescents: the effect of OCA2 and HERC2, *Journal of Investigative Dermatology* **12**, 2807–2814.

[108] Liu, F., Wollstein, A., Hysi, P.G., Ankra-Badu, G.A., Spector, T.D., Park, D., Zhu, G., Larsson, M., Duffy, D.L., Montgomery, G.W., Mackey, D.A., Walsh, S., Lao, O., Hofman, A., Rivadeneira, F., Vingerling, J.R., Uitterlinden, A.G., Martin, N.G., Hammond, C.J. & Kayser, M. (2010). Digital quantification of human eye color highlights genetic association of three new loci, *PLoS Genetics* **6**, e1000934.

[109] Andersen, J.D., Johansen, P., Harder, S., Christoffersen, S.R., Delgado, M.C., Henriksen, S.T., Nielsen, M.M., Sørensen, E., Ullum, H., Hansen, T., Dahl, A.L., Paulsen, R.R., Børsting, C. & Morling, N. (2013). Genetic analyses of the human eye colours using a novel objective method for eye colour classification, *Forensic Science International: Genetics* **7**, 508–515.

Related Articles

Mitochondrial DNA: Profiling

Y-Chromosome Short Tandem Repeats

Related Articles in EFS Online

Mixture Interpretation: DNA

Short Tandem Repeats

Chapter 26
Mini-STRs

Michael D. Coble and Rebecca S. Just

The Armed Forces DNA Identification Laboratory, Rockville, MD, USA

Disclaimer: The opinions and assertions contained herein are solely those of the authors and are not to be construed as official or as views of the US Department of Defense, the US Department of the Army, or the Armed Forces Institute of Pathology.

For well over a decade, short tandem repeat (STR) markers have played an important role in advancing the field of forensic DNA typing. In the United States, there are two commercial companies that produce multiplex STR kits used by forensic laboratories: Applied Biosystems (Foster City, CA) and Promega Corporation (Madison, WI). Each company has produced a "megaplex" autosomal STR kit containing 16 markers: the 13 Combined DNA Index System (CODIS) loci [1, 2]. Two markers specific to each company's kit, and the amelogenin marker for sex determination. Both 16-plex kits have amplicon sizes ranging from 100 to 450 base pairs (bp). The availability of commercial kits has helped to standardize the STR markers used by the forensic community.

The conventional STR kits perform well when an optimal quantity (approximately 1 ng) of high-quality DNA is used, exhibiting peak height balance both within loci (heterozygous alleles) and between each marker. However, biological evidence at crime scenes is often exposed to the elements and/or microbial agents that may cause DNA to degrade. Inhibitor molecules, such as heme in blood or humic acid in soil, can also copurify with DNA and prohibit the generation of a full STR profile. Degradation and inhibition may result in amplification failure especially of high-molecular weight loci, resulting in a "partial profile" in which only a subset of the core

13 CODIS loci are obtained (*see **Degraded Samples***). The loss of multiple forensic markers as a result of degradation and inhibition reduces the overall statistical significance of any observed match. If a biological sample is too highly degraded for STR analysis, the forensic scientist may have to turn to mitochondrial DNA (mtDNA), which can be expensive and time consuming to test, and may result in limited information, especially for common mtDNA haplotypes (*see **Mitochondrial DNA: Profiling***).

One strategy to recover the genetic information lost due to DNA degradation would be to reduce the size of the PCR (Polymerase Chain Reaction) amplicons for the "larger" loci. By designing PCR primers to bind closer to the core tandem repeat (Figure 1), it is possible to create a smaller PCR product, a "mini-STR", while still retaining the core repeat information. The reduced-size PCR amplicon then has a greater chance (relative to conventional STR primers) of generating a profile when genetic material is degraded.

Emergence of Mini-STRs as a Forensic Tool

During the mid-1990s, Dr John Butler (presently at the National Institute of Standards and Technology, NIST) and his colleagues at GeneTrace Systems developed a system to rapidly genotype STR profiles using matrix-assisted laser desorption/ionization time-of-flight (MALDI/TOF) mass spectrometry. The rapid detection of multiple unlabeled PCR products using MALDI/TOF represented a significant reduction in sample processing and analysis time as compared to standard STR profiling. One limitation of the MALDI/TOF technology, however, was related to the size of PCR fragment analyzed; amplicons larger than 140 bp were difficult to resolve with the method. To make the commonly used forensic STR markers

A Guide to Forensic DNA Profiling
Edited by Allan Jamieson and Scott Bader
© 2016 John Wiley & Sons, Ltd. ISBN: 9781118751527
Also published in EFS (online edition)
DOI: 10.1002/9780470061589.fsa544

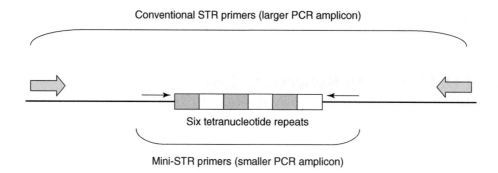

Conventional STR primers (larger PCR amplicon)

Six tetranucleotide repeats

Mini-STR primers (smaller PCR amplicon)

Figure 1   An example of a mini-STR compared to conventional STR primers. The mini-STR primers are adjacent to the six nucleotide repeats producing a smaller PCR product compared to the conventional STR primers

more amenable to MALDI/TOF detection, Butler and colleagues redesigned the primers to create smaller amplicons. Significantly, Butler and colleagues noted in their 1998 publication that these reduced-size amplicons could be utilized to increase the recovery of STR profiles from degraded samples [3, 4].

A few years later, laboratories began publishing information on reduced-size PCR amplicons for (mostly CODIS) loci [5–8]. These early studies demonstrated the forensic potential of mini-STRs, sometimes with very significant results. For example, Hellmann *et al.* [5] reduced the amplicon size of the TPOX locus by 160 bp to test telogen hairs. This group was able to recover the correct genotype over 77% of the time compared to only about 18% of the time with conventional primers – a fourfold improvement.

Additional advances in mini-STR research and application also came as a result of the terrorist attack on the World Trade Center (WTC) towers on September 11, 2001. Shortly after the attacks, the New York Office of the Chief Medical Examiner (NY-OCME) was charged with the task of identifying the nearly 3000 victims of the disaster. Knowing that many of the samples recovered from the crime scene would be highly degraded and of poor quality, the NY-OCME investigated new technologies, such as single nucleotide polymorphism (SNP) typing and reduced-size STR amplicons, to increase the success rate on the compromised samples. Through work at NIST and a private laboratory (the Bode Technology Group) all of the core CODIS markers were redesigned as mini-STRs [9]. Protocols were developed and validated at NIST [9], and samples from the disaster were tested at the Bode Technology Group

[10]. Mini-STRs proved to be valuable for the identification efforts: nearly 20% of the 850 DNA-only identifications from the WTC disaster were made using mini-STRs [11].

Following the success of mini-STRs in recovering genetic information from CODIS loci, additional research into other markers of forensic interest has included autosomal loci unlinked to the CODIS markers [12]. Additional markers not linked to the CODIS loci can be useful for resolving complex paternity cases such as incest. A set of X-chromosome mini-STRs [13] have been developed for select forensic scenarios where linked X-STR markers can provide additional discrimination relative to autosomal loci. Finally, Y-chromosome mini-STRs [14] have been developed to amplify male-specific loci (*see* **Y-Chromosome Short Tandem Repeats**).

In 2007, the first commercial mini-STR kit, AmpF*l*STR® MiniFiler™ (Applied Biosystems), became available to the forensic community. A 9-plex, MiniFiler™ includes amelogenin and eight of the largest loci from the AmpF*l*STR® Identifiler® and SGM Plus® (Applied Biosystems) STR typing kits. The MiniFiler™ amplicon sizes generally range up to 250 bp (290 bp for the extended FGA locus alleles), and represent an approximate 30–200 bp size reduction as compared to the Identifiler® and SGM Plus® amplicons for the included loci. In addition to the reduced-size amplicons, the MiniFiler™ amplification protocol, which increases (relative to other AmpF*l*STR® kits) the number of thermal cycles to 30, and proprietary amplification buffer, which already contains the DNA polymerase, are kit optimizations designed to overcome inhibition and recover loci from compromised samples. MiniFiler™ is thus intended for use as a supplement to other megaplex STR kits when an insufficient number of loci are recovered, or as a stand-alone kit when extremely limited sample quantities would prevent multiple attempts to develop a genetic profile [15].

A second commercial mini-STR kit, PowerPlex® S5 (Promega Corporation), is also now available to forensic practitioners. Like MiniFiler™, the S5 kit utilizes small amplicons (under 260 bp) and a proprietary amplification buffer optimized to overcome inhibition. In contrast to MiniFiler™, however, PowerPlex® S5 includes only four loci in addition to amelogenin. Rather than as a means to recover additional loci when large-amplicon loci fail, the S5 kit is marketed as a reliable, lower-cost exclusionary tool for criminal casework and population screening.

Challenges to Mini-STR Development

With the availability of commercially available mini-STR kits, many forensic laboratories can now take advantage of using these markers on casework samples without the need to produce "in-house" multiplexes that must pass high quality control standards for use in forensic casework. However, challenges remain to the development and use of both in-house and commercial mini-STR kits. These include repeat size limitations, limited multiplex real estate, and the potential for profile discordance as a result of primer design.

Some of the current CODIS loci are difficult to develop as true mini-STRs because of the size of the repeat region. For example, the FGA locus has a rather large allele spread – ranging from 17 to 33 repeats (and up to 51 repeats among the extended alleles). A large allele spread is advantageous for a high-diversity marker, but successful amplification of a 50 tetranucleotide repeat (200 bp) along with an additional 40–50 bp for the flanking primer sequence (240–250 bp total amplicon) in a highly degraded sample is unlikely. Ideally, mini-STR multiplexes would be composed of markers with amplicons sizes no larger than 150 bp.

However optimal from a profile recovery standpoint, the restriction of mini-STRs to amplicons sizes less than 150 bp greatly limits the number of markers that can be tested in a four or five fluorescent dye system. To overcome the limited multiplex real estate,

a few multiplexes, with each dye channel containing 1–2 mini-STR markers, could be constructed for use in tandem. However, a disadvantage to typing with multiple assays is the consumption of additional, often limited, DNA template. This could be especially problematic when typing samples under "low copy number" conditions where multiple replicates are required for data analysis and interpretation [16, 17]. Although a greater number of fluorescent dyes could be used to increase the number of loci amplified in a single reaction, this is not at present a viable option because of capillary electrophoresis (CE) detection limitations.

Alternately, nonnucleotide linker molecules that shift the electrophoretic mobility of the amplified product could be used to construct a mini-STR multiplex with more than 1–2 markers per dye channel. For example, suppose that two mini-STR loci, A and B, have the amplicon size ranges 72–112 and 96–136 bp, respectively. In constructing a multiplex, it would be necessary to position these two loci in separate dye channels since there is potential for overlap between the higher molecular weight alleles of locus A and the lower molecular weight alleles of locus B. Using non-nucleotide linkers equivalent to approximately 2.5 bp [18], the addition of 10 such linkers between the primer and the fluorescent dye for locus B would shift the apparent size of the amplicon by +25 bp. As a result, locus B would migrate at 121–161 bp and provide enough separation to be included in the same dye channel as locus A. Although non-nucleotide linker molecules can increase the electrophoretic separation between overlapping loci as described, there is a limit to the number of linkers that can be added to a primer and still result in consistently high-quality data.

Primer design presents an additional challenge to the development of mini-STRs from standard STR loci. A necessity for the creation of reduced-size STR amplicons is a clean sequence region flanking the repeat motif. Not all of the industry-standard STR markers have clean flanking regions, which can make the design of mini-STRs a challenge, and may result in nonconcordant alleles when typing the same loci with different STR multiplexes. For example, the CODIS marker D7S820 has a polyT stretch found 13 nucleotide bases downstream of the core tetranucleotide repeat. Designing a primer adjacent to the repeat and avoiding the polyT repeat would potentially miss a number of microvariants created by the addition

(X.1) or subtraction (X.3) of thymidine nucleotides in this region. In other words, if a sample tested with a conventional kit typed as a 15.1 allele, a mini-STR designed to avoid this polyT region (through placement of an amplification primer between the core repeat and the T-stretch) would result in a 15 allele.

There are several additional ways in which newly designed STR primers may result in allele discordance with standard STR typing kits. For example, suppose that at some STR locus an individual is genotyped as 4, 5 using a commercial kit. We shall focus only on the chromosome possessing the "5" allele (Figure 2, bottom allele). Interestingly, this particular allele has six core repeats. but between the core repeat and the forward primer of the commercial kit is a 4 bp deletion on the chromosome. The net effect of this deletion (equivalent to a single tetranucleotide repeat) is that

the commercial kit scores this allele as having five repeats (Figure 2A; the sample types as a 4, 5). If the newly designed mini-STR primer is designed to hybridize between the commercial kit primer and the 4 bp deletion, then both genotypes will be concordant (Figure 2B; the sample types as a 4, 5). If, however, the mini-STR primer binding site includes the 4 bp deletion region, it is possible that little or no hybridization will occur. This would be especially true if the 3' end of the mini-STR primer did not match the target sequence on the chromosome. If a "null allele" were to result due to the primer binding site mutation (Figure 2C; the sample types as 4, 4), the mini-STR genotype will be discordant with the kit genotype. Finally, if the mini-STR primer is adjacent to the core repeat and thus well within the 4 bp deletion, the genotype resulting from the mini-STR amplification will be 4,

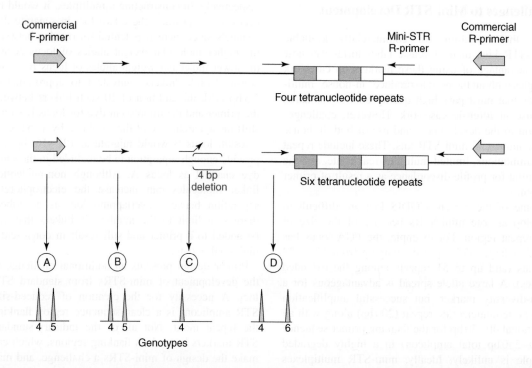

Figure 2   An example of discordance among mini-STR primers compared to a commercial kit. The top chromosome has four tetranucleotide repeats and the bottom chromosome has six tetranucleotide repeats. In the flanking region of the forward primer, there is a 4 bp deletion. Amplification using the commercial STR primers (A) results in a genotype of 4, 5 the deletion effectively "subtracts" one of the core repeats. (B) The mini-STR primer binding site is also outside of the 4 bp deletion region, and produce a 4, 5 genotype. (C) The 3' end of the mini-STR primer produces no PCR product from the bottom chromosome resulting in a "null allele" genotype of 4, 4 and be discordant with the conventional kit. (D) The mini-STR primer is adjacent to the core repeat and is well within the 4 bp deletion, the genotype will be 4, 6 and be discordant with the conventional kit

6 (Figure 2D) and again discordant with the conventional kit.

Because of the mutations that result in insertions, deletions, and SNPs in the flanking regions of forensic STRs, laboratories should always test any new mini-STR primer set against the conventional kit on a set of population samples to assure concordance between the two systems. In most cases discordance is not a major issue since typically only one allele of the total 26 CODIS alleles would be affected. That is, a moderate stringency database search would still identify a profile typed with the conventional kit when compared to the mini-STR-generated profile with a single allele difference.

Conclusions

Mini-STRs have already proven effective for the recovery of genetic information from highly compromised samples, such as those encountered in mass disasters. Beyond the increased power of discrimination offered by the recovery of more genetic loci, mini-STRs have also proven valuable for the sorting and reassociation of highly commingled remains [17] from mass graves according to the International Commission on Missing Persons [19]. The European forensic community has recently recommended that current forensic loci should be reduced in size as much as possible and that new mini-STRs be incorporated into the next generation STR multiplexes to increase the number of shared Interpol loci [20, 21]. In the future, mini-STRs may play an important role in the analysis of forensic evidence normally reserved for mtDNA analysis, such as skeletal remains [22] and shed telogen hairs [23]. The potential utility of mini-STRs is high and their frequency of use in forensic casework is likely to increase as both new and familiar autosomal, X-chromosome, and Y-chromosome loci are designed with reduced-size amplicons.

References

[1] FBI's Combined DNA Index System (CODIS) Homepage. http://www.fbi.gov/hq/lab/codis/index1.htm

[2] Budowle, B, Moretti, T.T., Niezgoda, S.J. & Brown, B.L. (1998). CODIS and PCR-based short tandem repeat loci: law enforcement tools. *Proceedings of the Second European Symposium on Human Identification*, June 1998. Innsbruck, Austria, Madison, WI. Promega Corporation.

pp. 73–88. http://www.promega.com/geneticidproc/eusymp2proc/17.pdf

[3] Butler, J.M., Li, J., Shaler, T.A., Monforte, J.A. & Becker, C.H. (1998). Reliable genotyping of short tandem repeat loci without an allelic ladder using time-of-flight mass spectrometry, *International Journal of Legal Medicine* **112**(1), 45–49.

[4] Butler, J.M. & Becker, C.H. (2001). *Improved Analysis of DNA Short Tandem Repeats with Time-of-Flight Mass Spectrometry*, Science and Technology Research Report. National Institute of Justice, http://www.ncjrs.gov/pdffiles1/nij/188292.pdf

[5] Hellmann, A., Rohleder, U., Schmitter, H. & Wittig, M. (2001). STR typing of human telogen hairs – a new approach, *International Journal of Legal Medicine* **114**(4–5), 269–273.

[6] Wiegand, P. & Kleiber, M. (2001). Less is more – length reduction of STR amplicons using redesigned primers, *International Journal of Legal Medicine* **114**(4–5), 285–287.

[7] Ohtaki, H., Yamamoto, T., Yoshimoto, T., Uchihi, R., Ooshima, C., Katsumata, Y. & Tokunaga, K. (2002). A powerful, novel, multiplex typing system for six short tandem repeat loci and the allele frequency distributions in two Japanese regional populations, *Electrophoresis* **23**(19), 3332–3340.

[8] Tsukada, K., Takayanagi, K., Asamura, H., Ota, M. & Fukushima, H. (2002). Multiplex short tandem repeat typing in degraded samples using newly designed primers for the TH01, CSF1PO, and vWA loci, *Legal Medicine (Tokyo)* **4**, 239–245.

[9] Butler, J.M., Shen, Y. & McCord, B.R. (2003). The development of reduced size STR amplicons as tools for analysis of degraded DNA, *Journal of Forensic Science* **48**(5), 1054–1064.

[10] Holland, M.M., Cave, C.A., Holland, C.A. & Bille, T.W. (2003). Development of a quality, high throughput DNA analysis procedure for skeletal samples to assist with the identification of victims from the World Trade Center attacks, *Croatian Medical Journal* **44**, 264–272.

[11] Biesecker, L.G., Bailey-Wilson, J.E., Ballantyne, J., Baum, H., Bieber, F.R., Brenner, C., Budowle, B., Butler, J.M., Carmody, G., Conneally, P.M., Duceman, B., Eisenberg, A., Forman, L., Kidd, K.K., Leclair, B., Niezgoda, S., Parsons, T.J., Pugh, E., Shaler, R., Sherry, S.T., Sozer, A. & Walsh, A. (2005). DNA Identifications after the 9/11 World Trade Center attack, *Science* **310**(5751), 1122–1123.

[12] Coble, M.D. & Butler, J.M. (2005). Characterization of new miniSTR loci to aid analysis of degraded DNA, *Journal of Forensic Sciences* **50**(1), 43–53.

[13] Asamura, H., Sakai, H., Kobayashi, K., Ota, M. & Fukushima, H. (2006). MiniX-STR multiplex system population study in Japan and application to degraded DNA analysis, *International Journal of Legal Medicine* **120**(3), 174–181.

[14] Park, M.J., Lee, H.Y., Chung, U., Kang, S.C. & Shin, K.J. (2007). Y-STR analysis of degraded DNA using

reduced-size amplicons, *International Journal of Legal Medicine* **121**(2), 152–157.

[15] Mulero, J.J., Chang, C.W., Lagacé, R.E., Wang, D.Y., Bas, J.L., McMahon, T.P. & Hennessy, L.K. (2008). Development and validation of the AmpFlSTR MiniFiler PCR Amplification Kit: a MiniSTR multiplex for the analysis of degraded and/or PCR inhibited DNA, *Journal of Forensic Science* **53**(4), 838–852.

[16] Gill, P., Whitaker, J., Flaxman, C., Brown, N. & Buckleton, J. (2000). An investigation of the rigor of interpretation rules for STRs derived from less than 100 pg of DNA, *Forensic Science International* **112**(1), 17–40.

[17] Irwin, J.A., Leney, M.D., Loreille, O., Barritt, S.M., Christensen, A.F., Holland, T.D., Smith, B.C. & Parsons, T.J. (2007). Application of low copy number STR typing to the identification of aged, degraded skeletal remains, *Journal of Forensic Science* **52**(6), 1322–1327.

[18] Butler, J.M. (2005). *Forensic DNA Typing: Biology and Technology behind STR Markers*, 2nd Edition, Academic Press, London.

[19] Parsons, T.J., Huel, R., Davoren, J., Katzmarzyk, C., Milos, A., Selmanovic, A., Smajlovic, L., Coble, M.D. & Rizvic, A. (2007). Application of novel "mini-amplicon" STR multiplexes to high volume casework on degraded skeletal remains, *Forensic Science International: Genetics* **1**, 175–179.

[20] Gill, P., Fereday, L., Morling, N. & Schneider, P.M. (2006a). The evolution of DNA databases – recommendations for new European loci, *Forensic Science International* **156**, 242–244.

[21] Gill, P., Fereday, L., Morling, N. & Schneider, P.M. (2006b). Letter to editor – new multiplexes for Europe: amendments and clarification of strategic development, *Forensic Science International* **163**, 155–157.

[22] Opel, K.L., Chung, D.T., Drabek, J., Tatarek, N.E., Jantz, L.M. & McCord, B.R. (2006). The application of miniplex primer sets in the analysis of degraded DNA from human skeletal remains, *Journal of Forensic Sciences* **51**(2), 351–356.

[23] Müller, K., Klein, R., Miltner, E. & Wiegand, P. (2007). Improved STR typing of telogen hair root and hair shaft DNA, *Electrophoresis* **28**(16), 2835–2842.

Related Articles in EFS Online

Disaster Victim Identification: Process in United Kingdom

Low Copy Number DNA

Short Tandem Repeats

Chapter 27
Phenotype

Tony Frudakis

DNAPrint Genomics, Inc., Sarasota, FL, USA

Introduction

The genomics and bioinformatics era has enabled the recent development of systems and methods for the derivation of human phenotype from the genotyping of crime stain DNA evidence. This is accomplished through an empirical process of inference, either directly through genotypes for the functionally relevant genetic positions (loci) or indirectly through an appreciation of the genetic heritage of the donor. Forensic scientists are accustomed to using DNA sequence polymorphisms as identifiers. On the basis of the frequency of the identifier, we can statistically link individuals with samples associated with criminal investigations. Microsatellites, such as the short tandem repeats (STRs) employed for the Federal Bureau of Investigation (FBI's) combined DNA index system (CODIS) have been most commonly used for this purpose because they are multiallelic. That is to say, they have many alleles (varieties per location, or locus) and so relatively few loci are necessary to produce sequence signatures. Microsatellites are not chosen from the human genome based on their human ancestry or phenotype information, since this type of information would render them more or less powerful as identification tools among different human subpopulations. Thus, they are relatively useless for inferring phenotype. If we find that a suspect or a database entry matches the STR profile, we can extract probative value from the profile, otherwise, we have traditionally employed nongenetic investigative processes designed to produce the suspects necessary to achieve this objective.[a]

For many cases, the investigative process begins with an attempt to ascribe characteristics or features to the perpetrator that can lead to identification. If a human eyewitness were available, we would query the witness about physical appearance – what the suspect was wearing, the suspects "race" and, more specifically, we would obtain estimates and ranges for the basic anthropometric phenotypes such as skin color, eye color, height, etc. In the best-case scenario, we might obtain the basic physical descriptors or features such as those that might be present on a work identification card for the suspect, and, in a suboptimal scenario, we might obtain descriptors that are inaccurate or misleading. Unfortunately, the best-case scenario with human eyewitnesses is rarely achieved; unreliable information is sometimes provided by design (perhaps the witness has a motive to deceive) or by circumstance such as might be the case if the witness observed from afar on a darkly lit street. Assuming that the integrity of the witness is intact, and the witness had a clear view of a suspect, we are still left with fundamental problems created by the subjective nature of the human experience. Human testimony is generally not objective, almost always unstandardized, and never formally quantitative. Physical descriptions provided by one witness may or may not comport with those from another – not necessarily because one is wrong, but because one witness' opinion on what it is to look "dark" or "Asian", for example, may be different from the other. These basic problems translate into a fundamental defect associated with the extraction of phenotype data from human eyewitnesses – namely, that the testimony is not falsifiable, meaning that an investigator cannot verify its accuracy through independent examination. Nonetheless, there is a reason investigators consider themselves lucky to have access to eyewitness testimony. An investigation is much like a classification

A Guide to Forensic DNA Profiling
Edited by Allan Jamieson and Scott Bader
© 2016 John Wiley & Sons, Ltd. ISBN: 9781118751527
Also published in EFS (online edition)
DOI: 10.1002/9780470061589.fsa598

problem, where one attempts to make the most specific classification possible (the ascription of identity). Given the number of variables, and the fact that the number of incorrect classifications far outnumbers those that are correct (one) the classification problem is complex and we need classification features in order to delimit the likely possibilities. Here, data from witness testimony is analogous to a classification feature, and information theory (e.g., Bayes theorem) teaches us that even suboptimally informative (as opposed to uninformative or misleading) "features" are better than no features at all [1, 2]. Clearly, it would be far better to extract physical information on the donor using empirical techniques that lend themselves to the scientific method – techniques based on the observations of unperturbed nature, producing objective, quantitative and falsifiable data that can be communicated logically to others using standardized terms. It happens that if DNA is available from a crime scene, we now have access to new methods meeting these criteria for the inference of certain aspects of physical appearance (human traits or phenotypes).

The recent completion of the first human genome draft has provided a foundation for the development of empirical processes by which a partial physical portrait of a DNA donor can be constructed. In this chapter, we discuss certain overt phenotypes that are highly heritable, which are required if we hope to draw connections between DNA sequences and trait values. For example, parents with dark skin tend to have children with similarly dark skin and blue-eyed parents tend not to have brown-eyed offspring, suggesting that if we knew which and how genetic regions controlled or were informative for skin and eye color, we could predict these phenotypes simply through genetic observation. In fact, since most anthropometric (comparative human) phenotypes are determined by inherited gene sequences, much of a crime-scene DNA donor's physical information is imbedded in their DNA – we have only to figure out how to extract it. The inheritance of some phenotypes is relatively simple, and this information can be extracted with the investment of time and money. For others of more complex inheritance, the information is not currently extractable and may never be with existing technology.

There are two basic methods for inferring phenotypes from DNA. If we desire to infer phenotype from DNA using *direct methods*, we need to understand at least the major elements of the genetic architecture of the phenotype – that is, which genes and gene variants (as well as environmental factors) underlie variable expression of the phenotype. These genes are called phenotypically active loci, and their variants *phenotypically active variants*. With the direct method, we relate genotypes to specific phenotypes through our understanding of the genetic architecture, or if we do not fully understand the genetic architecture, through an empirical process based on prior experience and the use of databases. Of course, at least some of the genetic architecture must be understood or captured by our databases for the direct method to be possible. Even for "relatively simple" phenotypes, the expression tends to be extraordinarily complex, involving multiple variants per gene, sometimes more than one gene and sometimes even environmental factors. As basic genetics research powered to identify these genes and factors must involve many hundreds, even thousands or tens of thousands of subjects (depending on the phenotype, the number of loci, and their frequency in the relevant populations), arriving at the requisite level of understanding is very expensive and time consuming. As a result, we can so far only use direct methods with a couple of the overt human phenotypes that have so far proven amenable – hair color, iris color and, possibly soon, skin color as well (at least within some human populations).

Another method of inferring phenotype from DNA is based not on any understanding of the genetic architecture of the phenotype, but based on the recognition that expression of the phenotype is correlated with certain elements of human population structure. This is called the indirect method of DNA-based phenotype inference. Indirect methods are based on an appreciation of individual genomic ancestry in terms of admixture. We choose the term admixture, rather than mixture, because the distribution of ancestry within populations and individuals tends toward amalgamation and the preservation of structure rather than dilutive blending and homogenization (by analogy, the colors yellow and red combining to produce an amalgamation of yellow and red, rather than orange). The correlation between elements of ancestry and phenotype within populations of individuals allow for an inference of the latter on an individual-by-individual basis. If skin color, for example, is systematically and quantitatively darker among individuals with increasing levels of African genetic ancestry, and if we have a good database of individuals of varying African ancestry and their skin color measurements, we can infer the skin color of a crime-scene donor from a precise genomic ancestry estimate of the donor's African admixture. The use of databases makes the process both objective and empirical in that the inference is based strictly on observation (as opposed to based on a model such as a model of the genetic architecture). As we describe, in this chapter, depending on the phenotype and its distribution among the world's various populations, we can employ the empirical method with reference databases to not only infer trait value but also to do so quantitatively and with predefined levels of confidence (based on the likelihood that the inference is correct). In what follows, we first describe the currently available methods for indirectly inferring phenotype from DNA, then those for direct inference. We then discuss some of the first cases that have employed these methods with success and close with a brief discussion on the issues associated with the penetration of these new methods into the modern forensics investigative process. Most of our discussion here is necessarily brief and significantly more details can be found in Frudakis *et al.* [3] which represents the first text to discuss this topic in depth.

Indirect Method of Phenotype Inference

The indirect method of phenotype inference relies on the empirical process, which itself is driven by observation. With this method, we rely on observations of correlations between phenotypes and ancestry, rather than direct relationships with gene sequences. This focuses our attention to certain phenotypes unevenly distributed among the world's various populations, which arose either because they conferred selective advantage among our ancestors in certain geographical regions or through sampling and genetic drift. Reproductive barriers such as oceans, geographical extremes, and assortative mating helped to solidify a global amalgamation of populations as and after our ancestors expanded out of Africa some 200 000 years ago (reviewed in [4, 5]).

The main phenotypes distributed as a function of genetic ancestry and of interest to the forensic investigator are those that are overt, such as skin color, certain facial features, hair/iris color, stature, etc. To infer them accurately, we thus need an accurate tool with which to measure an individual's ancestry, and we need to measure this ancestry (and phenotype) among large population of individuals. Polymorphism of the Y and mtDNA chromosomes are the gold standard for reconstructing human population histories and measuring the apportionment of genetic diversity among the world's populations (Figure 1), but these chromosomes are uniparental (e.g., the Y is inherited by males from their father, who inherited it from his father, and his father) and as such, they are of little use to the forensic scientist. For example, from measures of Y chromosome mixes among various worldwide populations, we might note that the distribution of higher eumelanin index values (darker skin colors,

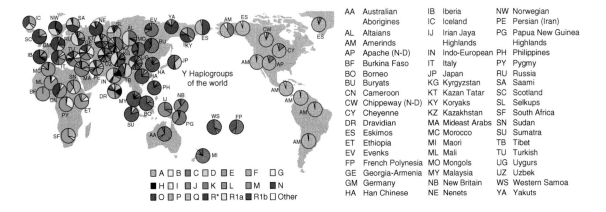

Figure 1 Global apportionment of Y haplogroup diversity. Pie charts illustrate the proportion of haplogroups as identified in the legend at the bottom. Populations are identified with a two-letter code/defined by the legend to the right [Reproduced with permission from J. D. McDonald. © 2004]

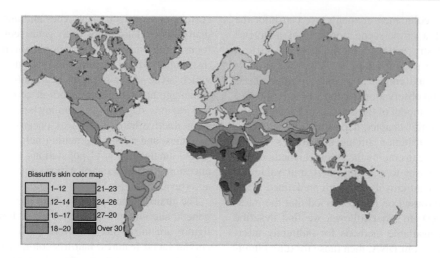

Figure 2   Geographical distribution of skin melanin levels. Higher values correspond to darker colors [Reproduced with permission from Cengage Learning © 2000]

Figure 2; [8]) is correlated with certain Y-haplogroups such as E that dominates in present-day Africa, or the L of South Asia and that lighter eumelanin index values correlated with those such as R or I shared among Europeans (compare Figures 1 and 2). Armed with this data, we might predict light European-like skin color for 28% of African Americans based on Y haplogroup sequence alone because no fewer than 28% of African Americans in the United States have a European Y chromosome as a result of recent admixture [3, 6, 7]. Indeed, the history of many other populations involves the admixture of those parental populations within which our anthropometric phenotype differences evolved and the ancestry for any one individual is best considered as a unique point along a sliding scale of admixture among these populations. In the field, we call this "sliding scale" a multidimensional continuum of admixture, based on the graphical methods we use to display the results (Figure 3). Uniparental chromosome polymorphisms are not useful for predicting phenotype because they do not tell us enough about the ancestry of any given individual, which is a complex function of all of the ancestors not just their patrilineal or matrilineal lines.

To indirectly infer a phenotype from the DNA of an individual, we must first have a method by which to quantitatively estimate individual genetic ancestry admixture, contributed by all the ancestors of an

individual (e.g., an individual might register with 80% "European" and 20% "African" admixture or some other mix). To do this, we measure ancestry informative markers (AIMs) on all 23 chromosomes of an individual. Secondly, we need to derive our understanding of the relationship between phenotype and ancestry from the same type of data – individual phenotype measurements and individual genomic ancestry admixture estimates. Note that we are therefore working on the level of the individual (within and/or between populations) rather than on the level of the population and so rather than using uniparental polymorphisms we must use AIMs distributed among all 23 chromosomes. Though binning or assigning an individual to a single population (such as "Caucasian") is conceptually easier than estimating the admixture of ancestry, it is not suitable for this purpose for the same reason we cannot use inferences of ancestry from uniparental chromosome polymorphisms. Specifically, we need to know what percentage of an individual's karyotype is derived from the ancestors of a given population, if we hope to compute the probability that the individual expresses a phenotype that is highly characteristic of that population.

AIMs are polymorphisms showing significant allele frequency differences between human populations. For example, an AIM may come in two "flavors" – a G allele and an A allele, with G rarely found in

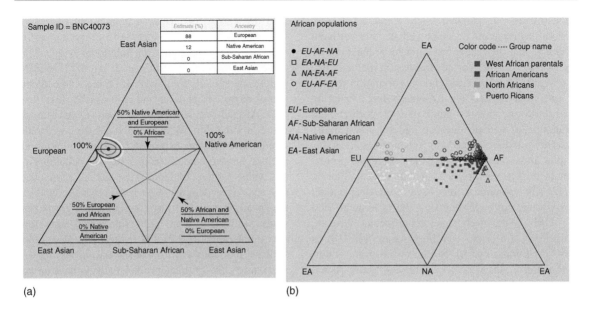

(a)　　　　　　　　　　　　　　　　　　　　(b)

Figure 3 Individual genomic ancestry estimates portrayed with a tetrahedron plot. (a) The most likely estimate (MLE) for an individual is shown with a spot (red) which corresponds to specific percentages shown in the upper right-hand box. The percentages are obtained in four-dimensional space with an algorithm, but can be displayed on a two-dimensional piece of paper using this plot diagram; projecting the MLE spot perpendicularly on the each of the three axes within any of the four subtriangles (arrows) gives the corresponding percentage. The closer the spot is to the triangle vertices (labeled European, sub-Saharan African, East Asian, or Native American), the higher the percentage admixture corresponding to that type of ancestry. (b) Plot of numerous MLEs for individuals of color-coded self-described ancestry (legend upper right) obtained using the 176 AIM panel described in the text. Though continental Africans show predominantly African admixture, this African-American sample shows considerable European admixture and the Puerto Rican sample shows even more

European or Eurasian populations but commonly found among various African populations. Most AIMs are single nucleotide polymorphisms (SNPs) such as this, with only two alleles, and SNP–AIMs constitute about 0.04% of the 2 million or so SNPs in the human genome. To construct an admixture panel, the most informative AIMs are selected from those that have been databased via the human genome (or similar other) project and the allele frequencies/frequency differentials among our founding parental populations is inferred through analysis of modern-day representative descendants. Using the AIM genotypes of any one individual, we invert the frequency of these alleles in various populations in order to calculate the likelihood that the individual's ancestry was derived proportionally from these populations. The likelihood for all possible proportions is calculated, we select the best as the most likely estimate (MLE), and select those within two – tenfold likelihood values fall within the confidence intervals for the

MLE (Figure 3a). If the admixture panel is to address the global population, worldwide population models are usually chosen on the basis of hypothesis-free clustering results (e.g., see [9]). One panel that has been well characterized incorporates a four-population model; this panel (developed in the laboratory of the author) was the first to be extensively characterized and applied for forensic cases ([3, 10]; discussed further below). Since individuals derived mainly from the Eurasian continent share one element of ancestry, we can arbitrarily name this element "European" or "Eurasian", and so on for the other three elements. Other more complex global models are possible but whatever the model, the choice of nomenclature is arbitrary, and usually based on either the modern-day origin of the parental representatives or geographical origin of the parental population (estimated from paleoarcheological, linguistics, and/or uniparental chromosome analyses). Mathematical methods allow for an accommodation of uncertainty with regard to the estimation of parental allele frequencies from modern-day representatives, as well as other pertinent variables, and the reader can refer to Frudakis *et al.* [3] for more details. For this discussion, here, suffice it to say that whatever the chosen population model, as long as it is based on hypothesis-free clustering results, an individual's admixture proportions are a function of genetic distance and thus potentially relevant for indirectly predicting phenotype. As of this chapter, three panels are available to forensic professionals through a company located in Sarasota Florida (DNAPrint genomics, Inc., see www.dnaprint.net or www.ancestrybydna.com) – the aforementioned 176-AIM continental panel (European, African, Indigenous American, and East Asian; [3, 10]), a 320-AIM Eurasian panel (Northern European, Southeastern European, Middle Eastern, and South Asian; [3]) and a 1476-AIM European panel (Figure 4; [3]).

Discerning whether particular elements of individual ancestry are correlated with certain phenotypes is accomplished through databases and regression analyses, where we plot one variable (such as a trait value) against another (such as percent admixture for a given ancestry type) and note whether or not there is a statistical dependence of the former on the latter. Regression analyses have shown correlations for skin eumelanin content and individual African ancestry levels using a 30-AIM ([12], African-American population) and the aforementioned 176-AIM panels ([10],

Puerto Rican Afro-Caribbean population; Figure 5). For example, we could conclude from the regression analyses in Figure 5 that an individual with >75% African admixture determined using the 176-AIM panel is most likely to have an *M* (eumelanin content) value above 40 and an individual with less than 50% African ancestry is most likely to have an *M* value less than 40. With larger databases, we could provide not only an expected *M* value by taking an average but we could also quantify the reliability of this value with confidence intervals. A correlation has also been demonstrated between iris color and European ancestry [13]; we can see from Figure 6 that while individuals with high "European" admixture have light (color > 2.2) and darker iris color (color < 2.2), individuals with substantial non-European admixture (20% or greater) almost always have darker iris colors. Thus, a crime-scene DNA sample determined to have been deposited by an individual with 40% East Asian and 60% European admixture, or 50% African and 50% European admixture can be inferred to have an iris color on the darker end of the range observed in the human population. With larger databases, we could even quantify the likelihood that this type of conclusion is wrong. For example, if we see that the conclusion is true for 999 of 1000 individuals, we could estimate that the conclusion is correct with 99.9% certainty and that only 1 in 1000 such conclusions would be wrong. As of this chapter, the indirect method can only be used for

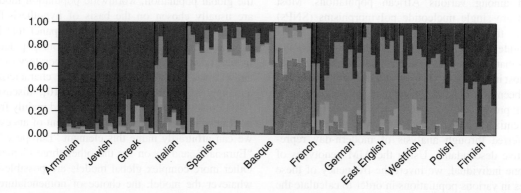

Figure 4 Individual genomic ancestry admixture estimates among Europeans with respect to a five-population European model. The 1346 European AIM panel described in the text was used to generate the data. For each individual, the proportional ancestry derived from these five parental European populations is represented with a bar, using colors coding for each ancestry type and the scaling on the left. Markers and genotype data were derived from the work published by Bauchet *et al.* [11] [Reproduced from Ref. [11]. © Elsevier, 2007]

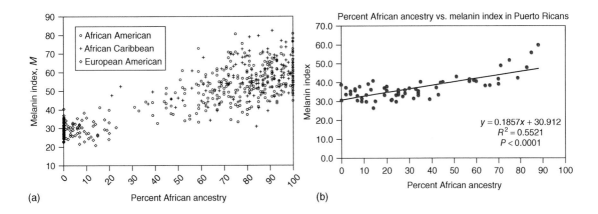

(a) Percent African ancestry

(b)

Figure 5   Regression of eumelanin value (*M*) from skin measurement on African individual genomic ancestry estimates in a population of (a) African Americans, European Americans, and Afro-Caribbean samples, obtained using a 30-AIM panel [12] and (b) Puerto Ricans, obtained using the 176-AIM panel described in the text [3, 10]. Each spot represents the point estimate of African admixture for an individual. Higher *M* values correspond to darker skin colors (higher concentration of eumelanin per unit skin area)

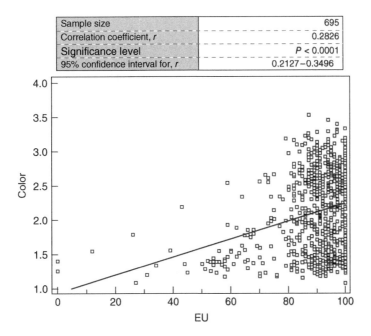

Figure 6   Regression of iris eumelanin scores from digital photographs on European individual genomic ancestry estimates in a population predominantly of self-described "Caucasians". Each spot represents a point estimate of European admixture for an individual. Higher color scores correspond to lighter colors (less eumelanin)

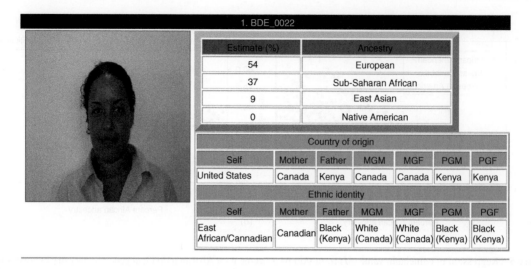

Figure 7   Example of an admixture database entry. Entries in this particular database (www.dnawitness.net) included a digital photograph taken under standardized conditions, country of origin, that of their mother, father, and their maternal grandmother (MGM) and paternal grandmother (PGM) as well as maternal grandfather (MGF) and paternal grandfather (PGF). Similarly, the self-reported "ethnic identity" is provided by each subject. The laboratory that administers this database took the photograph and determined the admixture profile with respect to a global four-population model using the 176-AIM panel discussed in the text. The database had 4700 entries as of August 2007

these two phenotypes but through the construction and use of admixture databases, we may soon learn of others. For example, if we construct an admixture database of individuals, which included the self-described "ethnicity" and a digital photograph for each entry, and then query the database with a particular admixture profile (± a reasonable range), we might get a return of several entries like that shown in Figure 7. From these returns, we could discern whether the individuals are more likely to refer to themselves as belonging to one particular population than another, and how reliable such an inference can be expected to be. Using software biometric tools, we might learn that the average distance between the eyes (for example) is significantly different from that of a random collection of individuals, or a group of individuals with a different type of admixture profile. Some investigators may be able to use collections of digital photographs corresponding to an admixture profile to mentally compile a composite sketch, though the future promises to provide software for identifying all of the phenotypes statistically characteristic of the profile (compared to randomly specified samples) as well as the ranges of trait values, we can expect algorithms to construct an *in silico* "rendering"

of the suspect similar to that provided by a human eyewitness.

A very important point that needs to be highlighted is that if our admixture methods are insensitive or inaccurate, if there are problems with the population model or parental representatives we have built our test on, or if there are glitches with the database software, there will be error. However, assuming that the size of the database is adequate, this error is expected to result in an increase rather than a decrease in entropy of the system [3]. The increase in entropy leads to a loss of information and an inability to recognize correlations in regression analyses (false negatives) rather than an ability to recognize false correlations (false positives). For example, an admixture assay based on only a few AIMs covering only one chromosome would produce a large standard error in admixture estimates and the imprecise estimates may be so scattered about their true values in a regression plot that the relationship between trait value and ancestry is concealed (e.g., in Figure 5b, imagine the spots so far scattered above and below the line at low as well as high African admixture values that the sum of squared distance to a line indicating no correlation is similar to that for one indicating a good correlation).

False positives can only obtain if false positive correlations are produced between phenotypes and elements of ancestry, which equates to the creation of false pattern, but random error that we would expect from a poorly performing assay would, by definition, obfuscate pattern and increase the entropy. It is possible to create false pattern from an assay that produces estimates with biased error, but with admixture/phenotype databases even these tend to result in a decrease rather than an increase in entropy. For example, consider an assay that has a tendency to erroneously estimate low levels of African admixture for South Asians (but not for other "European" populations such as Middle Eastern or Continental Europeans). It might seem that this error could lead to the mistaken conclusion that low levels of African admixture for individuals of primarily European ancestry is correlated with very dark skin color, even though most Continental Europeans with low levels of African admixture exhibit lighter skin colors (Figure 5). However, note that all of the Europeans would be present in the database, and using the high European/low African profile to query the database would result in a jumble of various light and dark skin color phenotypes rather than the shade that would be observed, were the error not present. Thus, we have an increase in entropy over which we would expect without the error, leading to an inability to make an accurate inference and false negative (type I) error rather than the creation of a false positive. Nonetheless, admixture panels that produce biased estimates are easily identified if they are properly validated and characterized [3]. A properly constructed and validated admixture panel should exhibit single-digit percentage accuracy (total error from statistical imprecision and bias combined). The laboratory of the author operates such a validated admixture/phenotype database ($n = 4700$ samples as of August 2007) and has used it in several homicide cases, but as we discuss later, so far only to indirectly infer skin color and iris color. Finding other phenotypes for which the indirect method will be useful in the future and the development of more advanced data mining and composite sketch software tools will require significantly greater investment.

Direct Method

Though they can be correlated with phenotypes, ancestry and markers of ancestry do not cause phenotypes – genes do. In contrast with the indirect method, the direct method relies on measurements of the actual genes underlying the phenotype of interest. Though far more satisfying in a theoretical sense, since we expect to be able to do a better job of predicting trait value (more accuracy and tighter confidence intervals), the direct method is rarely practicable because it requires an understanding of the dominant aspects of the genetic architecture of a phenotype, and acquiring this understanding is a very expensive and time-consuming endeavor. To date, research on the genetic basis for only human iris color and one aspect of hair color has been productive enough to enable direct phenotyping from DNA. The objective with the direct method is to define polymorphisms associated strongly enough with the phenotype that they are predictive for that phenotype with good sensitivity and specificity. Note that hundreds of good gene/phenotype associations have been described in the literature over the past decade or so (mostly for clinical phenotypes), but few of them are sufficiently strong or detailed enough within each gene to enable "genetic classification". Given the complexity of human phenotypes, useful polymorphisms are likely to be found for phenotypes where expression is controlled by one to a few genes at most, and will almost always be useful in the context of diplotypes (diploid pairs of haplotypes, where a haplotype is a chromosomal string of SNP alleles). Which diplotypes are associated with which trait values would be best determined through an empirical process of database construction and query, as with the indirect method, except we query with diplotypes rather than admixture profiles.

Iris Color

The best example of an effective direct system for inferring a human phenotype is human iris color. Linkage screens and association scans have shown that variable human iris color in humans is primarily determined by polymorphism in the Oculocutaneous Albinism 2 (OCA2) gene [13–15]. OCA2 was first discovered by researchers studying the human albino phenotype as a locus with mutations that affected iris melanin production but not skin melanin production (as well as other mutations that affect both). Recently, Frudakis [13] built upon earlier reports [14–17] to identify 33 OCA2 SNPs associated with digitally quantified iris color independent from their ancestry information. As it is with many phenotypes (e.g., Figure 5), ancestry was itself correlated with the phenotype (Figure 6) and correcting the associations with respect to population structure was crucial for demonstrating that they were *bona fide* (i.e., that the association was with iris color, not an element of population structure that is itself correlated with iris color; [3]). Though each of the 33 SNPs were marginally (independently) associated with iris color, none were very useful on their own as iris color classification features. However, when assembled into diplotypes, the alleles for these 33 SNPs were highly predictive for the overall eumelanin content of the iris; among 1100 diplotypes from individuals of European descent, there existed 96% concordance of iris colors among those samples with the same diplotypes [3, 13]. To predict the iris color of a given sample, this team thus built a database of phenotyped diplotypes, and then queried the database much as we do with the indirect method of phenotyping – though, in this case, with test diplotypes rather than admixture profiles. The return for this query provides an average iris color and range of iris colors as a point estimate and range of inferred color for the test diplotype. The results were satisfying; a validation sample provided a 96% accuracy rate (the inferred or predicted iris color for the unknown iris fell within the predicted range 96% of the time; Figure 8) and demonstrated that the method was capable of pinpointing the overall eumelanin content of the iris and often the particular shade, though not the pattern of iris pigmentation [13].

Particularly interesting from this work on iris color is what it teaches us to expect for other phenotypes.

The predictive power of these SNPs required a consideration within the context of diplotypes. Not only were SNPs unable to provide predictive power on their own, haplotypes were equally insufficient and even diplotypes composed using smaller numbers of SNPs than these 33 (such as hap-tag SNPs) were insufficient to achieve good prediction results [13]. This illustrates the apparent historical and mechanistic complexity of even this relatively simple (predominantly single-gene) phenotype. A by-product of this complexity is the need for a massive database in order to handle most test samples; with so many SNPs part of the equation, the number of diplotypes in the human population is very large and the chances that a test sample from a crime scene would have a match in the database at its current size ($n = 1100$, Summer, 2007) is about 10%. Nonetheless, the inferences for these 10% are highly accurate and based on this utility, the iris color diplotype database system has been developed as a forensic service by DNAPrint genomics under the trade name Retinome™ (DNAPrint genomics is the laboratory within which the author conducted much of the work described here and throughout this chapter). So far the method has been applied to several homicide cases; however, due to the currently small size of the database, many detectives desiring to use Retinome™ have been unable to do so because their crime-scene samples did not have a match in the database. For this method of predicting iris color to have more of a broad impact on the investigative process, the size of the database will have to be increased substantially.

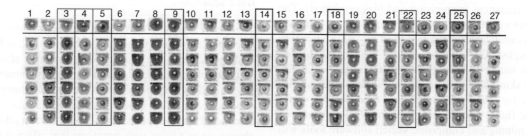

Figure 8   Examples of iris color inference enabled with the 33 marker/iris color database described in the text. Iris color is inferred using the average color exhibited by samples in the database with matching diplotypes and an interval is provided around this point estimate using the range of colors exhibited or a default range, whichever is larger. This inferred range is then used to query the database and all of the irides falling within the range are presented. This typically produces tens or hundreds of irides of similar overall color from a distance (determined by eumelanin content) though of different pattern, depending on the color and database size. Shown here are returns for 27 test subjects. Six representatives of the inferred iris color score range are provided for each of the 27 test irides below the line and the actual color of the test iris is shown above the line

In spite of its limitations, the Retinome™ system was the first system for the direct inference of a complex human phenotype. Since its introduction on the lecture circuit in 2004, other OCA2 systems involving additional single nucleotide polymorphisms (SNPs) were described [23], and eventually, a single SNP was discovered in 2008 [24–26] that was so powerfully associated with the light/dark iris color dichotomy that it was posited to represent no less than a founder mutation – an evolutionarily instrumental mutation that not only explains but also represents the historical genesis of the crude light versus dark dichotomy extant throughout the world today. The strength of the association (nearly perfect, with respect to the dichotomy), functional studies with cultured melanocytes, the universality of the association (the C allele associated with lighter colors in individuals from around the world), and the location of the SNP in an important regulatory region of the OCA2 gene all combined to suggest that this hypothesis is indeed true. Although the SNP is only useful for crude predictions (lighter vs. darker colors), the founder status of the mutation meant that prediction was suddenly possible for all samples – not merely a small fraction. Indeed, it is likely that some of the previously described SNPs were useful as components of a predictive tool through linkage with this founder mutation. However, others are likely to represent important pieces of the final solution for predicting precise colors and shades with economy and practicality. For example, one of the 33 Retinome™ SNPs (rs1800407) was demonstrated to be a penetrance modifier of the newly discovered founder mutation, and a minimalist set of OCA2 polymorphisms for the "ultimate" in forensics utility (precise color, perhaps pattern as well, for all crime-scene samples) will likely require a composite diplotype system involving the founder mutation and some number of the previously described SNPs in Frudakis et al. [3] and Duffy et al. [23]. This "ultimate" system has not yet been developed, though integration of the founder mutation with those of the Retinome™ system in a newly available forensic service called Retinome™ 2.0 (DNAPrint genomics, Inc., Sarasota, Florida) represents a step toward this goal.

Hair Color

Hair color cannot yet be comprehensively predicted from pigmentation gene genotypes. The iris color polymorphisms just described are not associated with human hair color and association and linkage scans have so far been relatively fruitless in identifying other useful associations ([3]; Zhu G. and Martin N., Queensland Institute of Medical Research, Brisbane AU, personal communication, and T. Frudakis unpublished results). This may be due to the fact that unlike the crudest aspect of iris color – the quantity of eumelanin in the iris – the genetic basis for hair color is a function of significant locus heterogeneity and complex historical origin. However, it appears that red color may be an exception. Valverde et al. [27] was the first to identify MC1R associations with pheomelanogenic red hair color (RHC), and subsequently, several other authors have extended these results to identify what are today called the RHC phenotype alleles (all SNPs, Box et al. [28, 32]; Duffy et al. [29]; Smith et al. [30]; Palmer et al. [31]; Bastiaens et al. [33, 34]; Kennedy et al. [35]; Flanagan et al. [36], and reviewed by Sturm, [37]). The associations are sufficiently strong to enable good predictive power – with odds ratios ranging from 2.3 to over 100 (reviewed in Sturm, 2002; [3]). The United Kingdom's forensic science service (FSS) has condensed the major MC1R red-hair polymorphisms into a 12-marker test that is sold to the forensics community. This test is generally only useful in cases of homozygosity; individuals who are homozygous for any of these mutations, or heterozygous for any two separate mutations (called compound heterozygotes) are accurately predicted to be redheaded (accuracy $= 96\%$, from a test with $n = 48$ subjects) and those without a mutation (homozygous wild type) are almost always not redheaded (accuracy $= 100\%$, from a test with $n = 35$ subjects; [18]). Approximately 84% of redheads are detectable by these criteria. Predictive ability is lower in the case of simple heterozygotes (only one mutation present, in the heterozygous state), which is by definition the state in which most of these RHC SNP alleles are expected to be found, in which case 88% are not redheaded while 12% are redheaded ($n = 33$). Indeed, we might expect that each of these mutations will have varying influences on the phenotype depending on the MC1R context within which it is found, and application of diplotype databases as described for iris color may be helpful in teasing more predictive power.

Other Phenotypes

Databases are not yet available for the direct inference of skin color, but this may change soon. Shriver *et al.* [12] and Bonilla *et al.* [38] used a process called admixture mapping to identify variants in the OCA2, MATP, ASIP, and TYR pigmentation genes associated with skin color in a manner that is independent from their ancestry information content. None of these appear to be strong enough to enable accurate prediction, but [19] convincingly described additional variants of the SLC24A5 gene that underlie additional variable skin pigmentation in humans (as well as other vertebrates). Diplotypes involving SNPs in these five genes may be sufficient for accurate inference of skin color within the context of the database systems we have been discussing, though such as database has not yet been constructed. Promising markers for human stature have also been identified in the RUNX2 gene [20] and RANK gene [21], but its unclear whether these two genes are sufficient for predicting this phenotype (especially since environment is likely to play such a role) and RUNX2/RANK variant databases for this phenotype have also not yet been constructed.

Ethical/Procedural Issues and Case Studies. Were the STR profile for each of the world's human inhabitants deposited into an international forensic DNA database, there would be no need to infer phenotype from crime-scene DNA since we would always be able to achieve a database match. Owing to ethical and procedural concerns, this is unlikely to come to pass in the foreseeable future. The ethical issues surrounding the inference of phenotype are extensively covered in Frudakis *et al.* [3], but for our purposes here, we can simply note that there is not a fundamental difference between learning about phenotype from human eyewitnesses versus DNA, except when DNA is available, it is more likely to provide reliable and falsifiable information. At some point, ethicists that decry the use of DNA for predicting phenotype as part of the investigative process will have to choose between the rights of DNA donors to remain anonymous and uncharacterized and the rights of future victims of these donors not to be future victims. Phenotype profiles may cause the inclusion of innocent individuals into suspect pools, which would cause inconvenience to these individuals but not increase the likelihood of a false conviction (their CODIS profile must still match that of the crime-scene sample, the probability of which is not reasonably a function of whether or not they are tested using the current state-of-the-art

CODIS assays, and is irrespective of their phenotype). It could be argued that many such individuals would or should become suspects for other reasons – such as a life of crime, proximity to the crime scene and/or relation to the victim – and that information about phenotype merely hones attention to a subset of these individuals. Indeed, many investigators consider these other reasons adequate priors (bases) on their own for defining who is and is not of interest in an investigation and honing attention to a subset of them with DNA-based phenotype information could reduce unnecessary inconvenience for many not fitting the phenotype "profile". Notwithstanding, weighted against the death of innocent victims that could be caused by not applying intelligence provided by DNA-based methods, inconvenience caused to innocent individuals subsequently proven not to match the CODIS profile of a given crime-scene sample pales toward insignificant in comparison. Indeed, we seem to have made the decision to use physical information to shape investigations already – as it pertains to human eyewitness testimony; even with all of its pitfalls, its subjectivity, and poor performance rate, eyewitness testimony currently represents one of the most important cornerstones of the investigative process. The use of DNA-based methods promise only to improve this performance using DNA as an additional and/or alternative source for information, at least for cases where DNA is available. Even so, ethicists have complained that DNA-based phenotyping methods are akin to "racial profiling", but the difference between using physical information gleaned from a crime-scene specimen and "racial profiling" is the application of falsifiable science rather than prejudice. For example, focusing on an individual based on information extracted from a crime scene is an exercise based on evidence and data and the conclusions are falsifiable by other laboratories. In contrast, focusing on an individual based on a belief that individuals of "group X" are more likely to be criminals – lacking specific data derived from a crime scene – is based more on prejudice and subjectivity than the scientific method and generally speaking, such correlations are not adequately powerful in a predictive sense to constitute meaningful priors when determining the likelihood of an individual's involvement in a crime.

The methods described in this chapter have been applied to numerous criminal investigations. The first application of the indirect method was for the

Louisiana Multiagency Homicide Task Force Investigation (Louisiana Serial Killer Case) in the spring of 2003 [3, 22]. Investigators had adequate DNA from various rape/murder scenes throughout the state, but without a CODIS match, they were forced to target their investigation based on two eyewitness accounts that subsequently proved irrelevant to the case. Over a year passed with the task force looking for a "Caucasian" male (not only with standard investigative practices but also with DNA sampling dragnets) until a 73-AIM version of the DNAPrint 176-AIM genomic ancestry panel described in this chapter (which was also sold under the trade name DNAWITNESS™ as version 2.0) was applied and indicated that the donor was an individual of primarily African ancestry (85%) with a small amount of Indigenous American admixture (15%). In this particular case, the lack of European admixture was used to infer a relatively dark skin shade with respect to the average African-American in the United States (Figure 5a). The investigation was refocused with this data and within a couple of months, the newly refocused investigation lead to an ex-con in the area fitting this profile whose CODIS STR profile was subsequently matched to the crime scene. Were it not for the application of the phenotyping methods, the investigation would have continued on its misdirected path, and others would likely have been raped and murdered [22].

Another murder case in Napa California was initially focused on Hispanic suspects based on an eyewitness account. Napa detectives applied the 176-AIM panel discussed in this chapter and obtained a continental admixture result that was found from DNAPrint genomics' DNAWITNESS 2.5 database to be consistent with individuals of Continental European as well as Middle Eastern descent – not Hispanic. They then applied the DNAPrint Eurasian panel of 320 AIMs and the RETINOME™ iris color panel described earlier in this chapter and learned from database searches that the individual was most likely of Northern European ancestry and of light-colored irides. The investigation was focused appropriately, and the perpetrator of the crime in this particular case (who was of Northern European descent with blue eyes) was eventually identified and linked to the crime scene via the CODIS profile. As with human eyewitness data, DNA-based phenotype information does not always result in quick arrests of course, and of the hundred or so investigations that have employed the methods described

herein, the majority remain open. However, even for these cases, investigators have saved money and time that would have been spent investigating individuals with phenotypes very different from the crime-scene DNA donor.

To advance the field, the SNP and AIM associations and databases currently available need to be amplified so that an inference for every sample can be obtained, and more research is needed so that additional phenotypes can be considered. In the near future, this may be an uphill battle, at least in the United States. For example, many US grant-funding agencies have not embraced much of the work described in this chapter – particularly those associated with indirect methods of phenotype inference and it seems most likely that the task of expanding this field will likely to be left to private enterprise or public laboratories outside the United States. Indeed, the work described in this chapter was funded with private capital, and though commercial demand for the products has not so far economically justified the investment, the work has at least provided some public service and could prove just as useful for other more commercially lucrative areas of research such as in drug development (where constructing a portrait of an ideal patient for a given drug could have a significant impact on the likelihood of clinical trial success). The institutional resistance in the United States toward the type of work discussed in this chapter is interesting and deserves some thought here. Some argue that the US justice system is not built for efficiency and is biased toward the interests of the accused. If true, this may explain why US budgets for solving crimes are often limited such that US investigators have difficulty funding basic CODIS processing of their crime-scene samples (which should always be done first since identity testing provides probative, not merely presumptive results). For example, backlogs of a year or more and anecdotal reports of rape kits stacked to the ceiling awaiting funding for CODIS processing are not uncommon in the United States. For agencies experiencing such backlogs, budget allocation for phenotyping is likely to remain de-prioritized and until phenotyping methods have had more time to penetrate the field through continued demonstration of utility. Until the problems underlying the CODIS backlogs have been solved, the application of DNA-based phenotyping methods is likely to continue on a case-by-case basis, with emphasis on high-profile cases that investigators are under unusual pressure to quickly solve (such as serial homicide cases).

Acknowledgments

I would like to thank all of the volunteers who provided their informed consent to be part of our forensic databases here at DNAPrint genomics, Inc.

End Notes

[a.] Though, since all loci carry some ancestry information, calculations on the statistical certainty of such a match requires the use of appropriate population databases since they are based on allele frequencies that vary subtly from population to population.

References

[1] Theodoridis, S. & Koutroumbas, K. (1999). *Pattern Recognition*, Academic Press Publishers, London.

[2] Robert, C. (2001). *The Bayesian Choice*, 2nd Edition, Springer-Verlag New York Inc., New York.

[3] Frudakis, T., Terravainen, T. & Thomas, M. (2007). Multilocus OCA2 genotypes specify human iris colors, *Human Genetics*, **122**(3–4), 311–324.

[4] Cavalli-Sforza, L. & Bodmer, W. (1999). *The Genetics of Human Populations*, Dover Publications, Mineola, NY.

[5] Jobling, M., Hurles, M. & Tyler-Smith, C. (2004). *Human Evolutionary Genetics. Origins, Peoples and Disease*, Garland Publishing, New York, NY.

[6] Lind, J., Hutcheson-Dilks, H., Williams, S., Moore, J., Essex, M., Ruiz-Pesini, E., Wallace, D., Tishkoff, S., O'Brien, S. & Smith, M. (2007). Elevated male European and female African contributions to the genomes of African American individuals, *Human Genetics* **120**(5), 713–722.

[7] Chakraborty, R. (1986). Gene admixture in human populations: models and predictions *Yearbook of Physical Anthropology* **29**, 1–43.

[8] Jurmain, R., Nelson, H., Kilgore, L. & Trevathan, W. (2000). *Introduction to Physical Anthropology*, Wadsworth/Thomson Learning, Belmont, CA.

[9] Rosenberg, N., Pritchard, J., Weber, J., Cann, H., Kidd, K., Zhivotovsky, L. & Feldman, M. (2002). Genetic structure of human populations, *Science* **298**, 2381–2385.

[10] Halder, I., Shriver, M., Thomas, M., Fernandez, J. & Frudakis, T. (2007). A panel of ancestry informative markers for estimating individual biogeographical ancestry and admixture from four continents: utility and applications, *Human Mutation* **29**(5), 648–658.

[11] Bauchet, M., McEvoy, B., Pearson, L., Quillen, E., Sarkisian, T., Hovhannesyan, K., Deka, R., Bradley, D. & Shriver, M. (2007). Measuring European population stratification using microarray genotype data, *American Journal of Human Genetics* **80**(5), 948–956.

[12] Shriver, M., Parra, E., Dios, S., Bonilla, C., Norton, H., Jovel, C., Pfaff, C., Jones, C., Massac, A., Cameron, N., Baron, A., Jackson, T., Argyropoulos, G., Jin, L., Hoggart, C., McKeigue, P. & Kittles, R. (2003). Skin pigmentation, biogeographical ancestry and admixture mapping, *Human Genetics* **112**(4), 387–399.

[13] Frudakis, T. (2007). *Molecular Photofitting: Predicting Phenotype and Ancestry from DNA*, Elsevier Academic Press Publishers, Burlington, MA.

[14] Zhu, G., Evans, D., Duffy, D., Montgomery, G., Medland, S., Gillespie, N., Ewen, K., Jewell, M., Liew, Y., Hayward, N., Sturm, R., Trent, J. & Martin, N. (2004). A genome scan for eye color in 502 twin families: most variation is due to a QTL on chromosome 15q, *Twin Research* **7**, 197–210.

[15] Frudakis, T., Thomas, M., Gaskin, Z., Venkateswarlu, K., Chandra, S., Ginjupalli, S., Gunturi, S., Natrajan, S., Ponnuswamy, V. & Ponnuswamy, K. (2003). Sequences associated with human iris pigmentation, *Genetics* **165**, 2071–2083.

[16] Rebbeck, T., Kanetsky, P., Walker, A., Holmes, R., Halpern, A., Schuchter, L., Elder, D.E. & Guerry, D. (2002). P gene as an inherited biomarker of human eye color, *Cancer Epidemiology Biomarkers and Prevention* **11**(8), 782–784.

[17] Sturm, R. & Frudakis, T. (2004). Eye colour: portals into pigmentation genes and ancestry, *Trends in Genetics* **20**(8), 327–332.

[18] Grimes, E., Noake, P., Dixon, L. & Urquhart, A. (2001). Sequence polymorphism in the human melanocortin 1 receptor gene as an indicator of the red hair phenotype, *Forensic Science International* **122**, 124–129.

[19] Lamason, R., Mohideen, M., Mest, J., Wong, A., Norton, H., Aros, M., Jurynec, M., Mao, X., Humphreville, V., Humbert, J., Sinha, S., Moore, J., Jagadeeswaran, P., Zhao, W., Ning, G., Makalowska, I., McKeigue, P., O'donnell, D., Kittles, R., Parra, E., Mangini, N., Grunwald, D., Shriver, M., Canfield, V. & Cheng, K. (2005). SLC24A5, a putative cation exchanger, affects pigmentation in zebrafish and humans, *Science* **310**(5755), 1782–1786.

[20] Ermakov, S., Malkin, I., Kobyliansky, E. & Livshits, G. (2005). Variation in femoral length is associated with polymorphisms in RUNX2 gene, *Bone* **38**(2), 199–205.

[21] Chen, Y., Xiong, D.H., Yang, T.L., Yang, F., Jiang, H., Zhang, F., Shen, H., Xiao, P., Recker, R.R. & Deng, H.W. (2007). Variations in RANK gene are associated with adult height in Caucasians, *American Journal of Human Biology* **19**(4), 559–565.

[22] Stanley, S. (2006). *An Invisible Man: The Hunt for a Serial Killer Who Got Away with a Decade of Murder*, Berkley Books, New York.

[23] Duffy, D.L., Montgomery, G.W., Chen, W., Zhao, Z.Z., Le, L., James, M.R., Hayward, N.K., Martin, N.G. & Sturm, R.A. (2007). A three-single-nucleotide polymorphism haplotype in intron 1 of OCA2 explains most human eye-color variation, *American Journal of Human Genetics* **80**(2), 241–252.

[24] Eiberg, H., Troelsen, J., Nielsen, M. & Mikkelsen, M. (2008). Blue eye color in humans may be caused by a perfectly associated founder mutation in a regulatory element located within the HERC2 gene inhibiting OCA2 expression, *Human Genetics* **123**(2), 177–187.

[25] Sturm, R.A., Duffy, D.L., Zhao, Z.Z., Leite, F.P., Stark, M.S., Hayward, N.K., Martin, N.G., & Montgomery, G.W. (2008). A single SNP in an evolutionary conserved region within intron 86 of the HERC2 gene determines human blue-brown eye color, *American Journal of Human Genetics* **82**(2), 424–431.

[26] Kayser, M., Liu, F., Janssens, A.C., Rivadeneira, F., Lao, O., van Duijn, K., Vermeulen, M., Arp, P., Jhamai, M.M., van Ijcken, W.F., den Dunnen, J.T., Heath, S., Zelenika, D., Despriet, D.D., Klaver, C.C., Vingerling, J.R., de Jong, P.T., Hofman, A., Aulchenko, Y.S., Uitterlinden, A.G., Oostra, B.A. & van Duijn, C.M. (2008). Three genome-wide association studies and a linkage analysis identify HERC2 as a human iris color gene, *American Journal of Human Genetics* **82**(2), 411–423.

[27] Valverde, P., Healy, E., Jackson, I., Rees, J., Thody, A. (1995). Variants of the melanocyte-stimulating hormone receptor gene are associated with red hair and fair skin in humans, *Nature Genetics* **11**, 328–330.

[28] Box, N., Wyeth, J., O'Gorman, I., Martin, N. & Sturm, R. (1997). Characterization of melanocyte stimulating hormone variant alleles in twins with red hair, *Humman Molecular Genetics* **6**, 1891–1897.

[29] Duffy, D., Box, N., Chen, W., Palmer, J., Montgomery, G., James, M., Hayward, N.K., Martin, N.G. & Sturm, R.A. (2004). Interactive effects of MC1R and OCA2 on melanoma risk phenotypes, *Human Molecular Genetics* **13**(4), 447–461.

[30] Smith, R., Healy, E., Siddiqui, S., Flanagan, N., Steijlen, P., Rosdahl, I., Jacques, J.P., Rogers, S., Turner, R., Jackson, I.J., Birch-Machin, M.A., & Rees, J.L. (1998). Melanocortin 1 receptor variants in an Irish population, *The Journal of Investigative Dermatology* **111**, 119–122.

[31] Palmer, J., Duffy, D., Box, N., Aitken, J., O'Gorman, L., Green, A., Hayward, N.K., Martin, N.G., & Sturm, R.A. (2000). Melanocortin-1 receptor polymorphisms and risk of melanoma: is the association explained solely by pigmentation phenotype? *American Journal of Human Genetics* **66**(1), 176–186.

[32] Box, N., Duffy, D., Irving, R., Russell, A., Chen, W., Griffyths, L. Parsons, P.G., Green, A.C., & Sturm, R.A. (2001). Melanocortin-1 receptor genotype is a risk factor for basal and squamous cell carcinoma, *The Journal of Investigative Dermatology* **116**, 224–229.

[33] Bastiaens, M., ter Huurne, J., Kielich, C., Gruis, N., Westendorp, R., Vermeer, B. & Bouwes Bavinck, J.N. (2001a). The melanocortin-1-receptor gene is the major freckle gene, *Human Molecular Genetics* **10**(16), 1701–1708.

[34] Bastiaens, M., ter Huurne, J., Kielich, C., Gruis, N., Wetendorp, R., Vermeer, B. & Bavinck, J.N.B. (2001b). Melanocortin-1 receptor gene variants determine the risk of nonmelanoma skin cancer independently of fair skin and red hair, *American Journal Human Genetics* **68**(4), 884–894.

[35] Kennedy, C., ter Huurne, J., Berkhout, M., Gruis, N., Bastiaens, M., Bergman, W., Willemze, R., & Bavinck, J.N. (2001). Melanocortin 1 receptor (MC1R) gene variants are associated with an increased risk for cutaneous melanoma which is largely independent of skin type and hair color, *The Journal of Investigative Dermatology* **117**(2), 294–300.

[36] Flanagan, N., Healy, E., Ray, A., Philips, S., Todd, C., Jackson, I. (2000). Pleiotropic effects of the melanocortin 1 receptor (MC1R) gene on human pigmentation, *Human Molecular Genetics* **9**, 2531–2537.

[37] Sturm, R. (2002). Skin colour and skin cancer – MC1R, the genetic link, *Melanoma Research* **12**(5), 405–416.

[38] Bonilla, C. Parra, E., Pfaff, C., Dios, S., Marshall, J., Hamman, R., Ferrell, R.E., Hoggart, C.L., Mckeigue, P.M., & Shriver, M.D. (2004). Admixture in the Hispanics of the San Luis Valley, Colorado and its implications for complex trait gene mapping, *Annals of Human Genetics* **68**, 139–153.

Chapter 28
Mitochondrial DNA: Profiling

Terry Melton

Mitotyping Technologies, State College, PA, USA

Introduction

Mitochondrial deoxyribonucleic acid (mtDNA) analysis is a routine adjunct to crime scene investigation. Introduced in the early 1990s to aid with the identification of military remains and implemented since then by the Armed Forces DNA Identification Laboratory in Rockville, MD, in all military conflicts [1], it was first used in criminal justice proceedings by the FBI in 1996 in *Tennessee v. Paul William Ware* [2]. In that case, a single hair located in the throat of a victim linked Ware to a homicide. mtDNA provides a valuable locus for forensic DNA typing in certain circumstances, especially for skeletal remains, shed hairs or hair fragments, and degraded samples of all types. In general, it is used when short tandem repeat (STR) testing is not possible owing to limited or degraded nuclear deoxyribonucleic acid (nuDNA) because mtDNA is naturally abundant and resistant to degradation [3]. mtDNA cannot be a unique identifier, as can nuDNA, because of its pattern of maternal inheritance nor does it provide the statistical power of a nuDNA match; as such, it is used as supplementary circumstantial evidence in criminal cases. mtDNA analysis has played a large role in the identification of missing persons when applied to skeletal remains as well as in postconviction exonerations where crime scene hairs previously attributed to a defendant via microscopy are found to be exclusions via this form of testing.

A Guide to Forensic DNA Profiling
Edited by Allan Jamieson and Scott Bader
© 2016 John Wiley & Sons, Ltd. ISBN: 9781118751527
Also published in EFS (online edition)
DOI: 10.1002/9780470061589.fsa111.pub2

mtDNA Biology

DNA is found in two locations in all human cells except red blood cells. nuDNA, inherited from both parents, makes up 26 pairs of chromosomes in the nucleus. mtDNA, inherited only from the mother, is located in the mitochondria, which are small, peanut-shaped cytoplasmic organelles that generate cellular energy. The full complement of nuDNA has about 3 billion of the four chemical bases of DNA (adenine, guanine, thymine, and cytosine, abbreviated as A, G, T, and C; also known as nucleotides) in a linear array within the chromosomes. Human mtDNA contains approximately 16 569 nucleotides in a double-stranded circular molecule. While each cell contains two copies of nuDNA, there are hundreds to thousands of mtDNA molecules within dozens to hundreds of mitochondria per cell, depending on the particular tissue. With some exceptions, all tissues in an individual have a dominant mtDNA type, or sequence, of DNA nucleotides.

The mtDNA types, sequences, or "profiles" present among humans have been generated by mutational changes occurring in this DNA over many generations. All living humans can be linked by their profiles into a single large tree and share a common maternal ancestor; individuals with similar types are most closely clustered in the tree. mtDNA reflects the biogeographical ancestry of a particular maternal lineage. For example, certain types may be readily recognizable as having originated in Asia, Africa, or Europe. mtDNA is passed intact from a mother to all her children; males inherit their mother's mtDNA but do not pass it on to their children. For this reason, all maternally related individuals share the same mtDNA profile.

The natural abundance of mtDNA is the key to its forensic utility. mtDNA recovery from small or degraded biological samples is greater than nuDNA recovery owing to the high copy number (there are many mitochondria in a cell, but one nucleus) and because the molecule's small circular structure may protect it from damage by heat, humidity, acidity, and ultraviolet (UV) light. In addition, nuDNA in naturally shed hairs and hair shafts is extremely limited even when these samples are freshly collected [4].

The mtDNA molecule codes for 13 proteins, 2 ribosomal RNAs, and 22 transfer RNAs, and also contains a 1122-nucleotide "noncoding" region, sometimes called *the control region* or *D-loop*, that is forensically informative [5]. As the DNA sequence differs so much among individuals in two "hypervariable" sections of the control region, the likelihood of choosing two people at random with the same mtDNA sequence is very low [6]. About 8–12 nucleotide differences on average are observed between two maternally unrelated individuals for the regions that are analyzed comprised of DNA sequence about 700 nucleotides long [7].

Candidates for forensic mtDNA typing analyses are (i) shed hairs with no follicle, tissue, or root bulb attached; (ii) hair shaft fragments; (iii) bones or teeth that have been subjected to long periods of high acidity, high temperature, or high humidity; (iv) stain or swab material that has been unsuccessfully typed for nuDNA markers; and (v) tissue (skin, muscle, and organ) that has been unsuccessfully typed for nuDNA markers. While mtDNA typing of blood, semen, and saliva crime scene stains from clothing and floors is possible, it is likely that mixtures will be obtained due to the extreme sensitivity of this form of typing in samples that, unlike hairs and bones, are difficult to clean before DNA extraction. On the other hand, degraded samples collected from near-sterile or UV radiation-exposed surfaces, such as the exterior of a vehicle, may easily provide single-source mtDNA profiles. Current developments in methodology, including deep sequencing, may improve the ability to deconvolute mtDNA mixtures [8], increasing the potential sample pool in future cases.

The Analytical Process

An mtDNA analysis begins when total genomic DNA is extracted from biological material such as a tooth, blood sample, or hair. Extraction methods, such as grinding of hair or bone or complete dissolution of proteinaceous material, are designed and validated in order to optimize the yield of DNA for specific sample types. In addition, the external surfaces of samples are thoroughly cleaned via sanding with a rotary drill bit (for bones) or ultrasonic water baths (for hairs). Approximately 2 cm of a single hair is used in the average case, although success has been achieved with much less; for skeletal remains, approximately 0.1–0.5 g of bone is used [9–11].

Following extraction, the polymerase chain reaction (PCR) is used to amplify the two hypervariable portions of the noncoding region using flanking primers. Primers are small bits of DNA that identify and hybridize to or adhere to the ends of the region one wishes to PCR amplify, therefore targeting a region for amplification. Primer pairs have been designed and manufactured to encompass virtually any region of mtDNA in humans, and may include "miniprimer pairs" that can recover the smallest fragments of DNA from a degraded sample, usually under 150 bp in length [12] (*see **Degraded Samples***).

Because the natural abundance of mtDNA as well as the creation of PCR product introduces many copies of mtDNA into the laboratory, care is taken to eliminate the introduction of exogenous (contaminating) DNA during both the extraction and amplification steps by methods such as the use of prepackaged sterile equipment and reagents, aerosol-resistant barrier pipette tips, gloves, masks, and lab coats, separation of pre- and post-amplification areas in the laboratory using dedicated reagents for each, UV irradiation of equipment, and autoclaving of tubes and reagent stocks. In forensic casework, questioned samples are processed at different times than known samples and in different laboratory rooms. Most importantly, several negative controls that would indicate the presence of contamination introduced during testing are run in parallel with all samples. Overall, contamination is more of a concern for the mtDNA laboratory than the nuDNA laboratory; however, each laboratory determines through internal validation studies how contamination and its control, detection, and interpretation can impact casework and still result in a defensible outcome [13].

When adequate amounts of PCR product are amplified from the two hypervariable regions, as determined from either a yield gel or other quantitation method, Sanger sequencing reactions are performed. These chemical reactions use each PCR product as a template to create a new complementary strand of DNA in which some nucleotides are labeled with dye. The strands created at this stage are then separated according to size by an automated sequencer that uses a laser to "read" the sequence. Where possible, the sequences of both hypervariable regions (called *HV1* and *HV2*) are determined on both strands of the double-stranded DNA molecule and in overlapping PCR products, with sufficient redundancy to confirm the nucleotide sequence that characterizes that particular sample. Sequencing products are electrophoresed on gel capillary instruments with single or multiple capillaries; dedicated software analyzes and stores the nucleotide information for later examiner analysis.

Forensic examiners assemble the mtDNA sequence via computer and then compare it to a standard published reference sequence called the revised Cambridge Reference Sequence (rCRS; [14, 15]), denoting all the nucleotide differences. The entire process is then repeated with a known sample, usually blood, saliva, or a buccal swab, collected from a known individual. The sequences from both samples, about 700 nucleotides each, are compared to determine whether they match. Depending on data quality or ambiguities, portions of the analysis may be repeated.

Heteroplasmy

Heteroplasmy is defined as the presence of two or more types of mtDNA within an individual [16]. There are two forms of heteroplasmy: length heteroplasmy and site (or sequence) heteroplasmy. mtDNA composition in humans, with the exception of individuals with some tissue-specific mitochondrial diseases, is characterized by a dominant high-frequency single type with ubiquitous low-frequency site heteroplasmy. The overwhelming majority of mtDNA-containing cells within an individual contain the same 16 569 bp mtDNA molecule throughout; however, it has been experimentally determined that a vast number of other types, usually differing from the dominant type by only a single nucleotide for the region examined, and generated by mutation during life or germline cell development, coexist at very low frequencies within all cells. There is also frequent occurrence of length heteroplasmy in certain control region strings of cytosine residues ("C-stretches") which creates populations of mtDNA molecules in each cell that differ slightly in length. Length heteroplasmy occurs in about 50% of all individuals. Site or sequence heteroplasmy, where at a single nucleotide address there are two different DNA bases such as T and C, has

been observed in approximately 1% of blood samples and 10–15% of hair samples during routine forensic mtDNA analysis, with other tissues such as bone believed to be intermediate with respect to frequency. The frequency estimate of site heteroplasmy is highly dependent on the detection method, with methods such as Sanger sequencing able to detect minor variants at the 5–10% level in most cases and methods such as high-performance liquid chromatography (HPLC) detecting heteroplasmy down to less than 1% of molecules analyzed. Newer deep sequencing methods can detect heteroplasmy at the single molecule level; the utility of this approach to detect heteroplasmy may prove helpful in forensic casework in the future. Regardless of detection method, forensic guidelines are derived from each laboratory's validation studies to allow for conservative interpretations of heteroplasmy such that false failures to exclude cannot occur when it is present.

Interpretation. Within the forensic community that performs mtDNA analysis, the following guidelines are generally used for forensic interpretations:

- *Exclusion* If samples differ at two or more nucleotide positions (excluding length heteroplasmy), they can be excluded as coming from the same source or maternal lineage.
- *Inconclusive* The comparison should be reported as inconclusive if samples differ: (i) at a single position only (whether or not they share a common length variant between positions 302–310); (b) only by not sharing a common length variant between positions 302–310 (all other positions are concordant).
- *Cannot exclude* If samples have the same sequence, or are concordant (sharing a common DNA base at every nucleotide position, including common length variants), they cannot be excluded as coming from the same source or maternal lineage.

In the event of a "cannot exclude" result, a forensic mtDNA database is searched for the mitochondrial sequence that has been observed for the samples. The most comprehensive and freely available mtDNA forensic database is found at www.empop.org [17]; this database contains mtDNA profiles from around the world and is subdivided by metapopulation and geography, permitting searches appropriate to the case at hand. The current convention in the event of a failure to exclude is for the analyst to report the number of times the observed sequence is present in the database in order to estimate its relative frequency in the population. A frequency statistic is calculated, and a 95% or 99% confidence interval (or upper bound) is placed around the estimated frequency to account for the inherent uncertainty in the frequency calculation as one would never be able to type all living humans. Several statistical approaches are appropriate for placing a failure to exclude in a population context, including Holland and Parsons upper bound, Clopper and Pearson upper bound, or likelihood ratio.

While the majority of mtDNA types occurs at low frequencies within forensic ethnic subdatabases, (African origin, Asian origin, European origin, or Hispanic), there is one mtDNA control region sequence that is seen in around 7% of Caucasians. Interestingly, the status of this type as "most common" has continued as forensic databases have grown over the past 20 years. However, additional single nucleotide polymorphisms (SNP) in the coding region create subtypes of this common type, and SNP methods can be applied in forensic missing person cases to increase discriminatory potential when this common control region type is present. Despite the existence of this and other more common types, many newly typed samples have novel sequences, indicating that all the mtDNA variation present in humans has not yet been identified. One exception to the high diversity that is present within ethnic databases has been observed: due to founder effects, mtDNA diversity in Native Americans is limited, and certain types in this group are observed at high frequencies [18]. Depending on the population history of other isolated groups, other population-specific types may be observed at high frequencies as well.

In addition to samples within forensic databases, over 100 000 human mtDNA control region sequences have been characterized in other research contexts (see the many references to human mtDNA populations that have been studied at http://www.mitomap.org/, as well as reference [19]). In general, the pattern observed in most populations around the world, with the exception of some populations of anthropological interest, is that most of the sequences are uncommon, and a few types are present at frequencies greater than 1%. Because of this fact, it is possible to exclude greater than 99% of a population as potential contributors of a sample in most cases, except where one is dealing with

a more common type. In contrast, a multilocus nuDNA typing profile provides vastly superior discriminatory power and statistics that permit source attribution. For this reason, mtDNA can never provide the resolution of individuality that nuDNA typing can.

As mentioned earlier, mtDNA is maternally inherited, so that any maternally related individuals would be expected to share the same mtDNA sequence. This fact is useful in cases where a long deceased or missing individual is not available to provide a reference sample but any living maternal relative might do so. Because of meiotic recombination and the diploid (biparental) inheritance of nuDNA, the reconstruction of a nuDNA profile from even first-degree relatives of a missing individual is rarely this straightforward. This feature has allowed some important historical mysteries to be solved, such as the identification of the remains of the assassinated Romanov family [20], the Vietnam Unknown Soldier [21], and American outlaw gunfighter Wild Bill Longley [22]. However, the maternal inheritance pattern of mtDNA might also be considered problematic. Because all individuals in a maternal lineage share the same mtDNA sequence, mtDNA cannot be considered a unique identifier. In fact, apparently unrelated individuals might share an unknown maternal relative at some distant point in the past. For this reason, it is important that judges, attorneys, and juries in criminal proceedings are educated about the maternal inheritance pattern of mtDNA.

Nonforensic Uses

While mtDNA is useful for forensic examinations, it has also been used extensively in two other major scientific realms. First, there are a number of serious inherited diseases caused by deleterious mutations in gene-coding regions of the mtDNA molecule [23]. In addition, molecular anthropologists have been using mtDNA for four decades to examine both the extent of genetic variation in humans and the relatedness of populations all over the world [24]. An mtDNA maternal inheritance pattern can reveal ancient population histories, which might include migration patterns, population sizes, expansion dates, and geographic homelands. mtDNA has been recovered from numerous Denisovan and Neanderthal skeletons, and the resulting population genetics studies have allowed anthropologists to better evaluate modern humans' relationship with our distant ancestors in the human evolutionary tree [25]. The general methods for performing all mtDNA analyses, including forensic methods, are identical to those used in molecular biology laboratories all over the world for studying DNA from any living organism.

Laboratory Practices

mtDNA analysis is offered by many forensic laboratories worldwide within both the public and private sectors. All practicing laboratories are guided in application of mtDNA analysis by national and international standards and guidelines for DNA testing and various accrediting bodies. In addition, all practices must be validated at an individual laboratory prior to implementation in casework.

mtDNA matching has become an extremely valuable process for missing persons programs including the FBI's National Missing Persons DNA Database program and the International Commission on Missing Persons, owing to the likely recovery of mtDNA from even the most degraded skeletal remains. Under these programs, maternal relatives submit samples for typing and inclusion in the database for eventual comparison to profiles obtained from recovered skeletal remains.

Although mtDNA is still undergoing admissibility hearings in the rare US jurisdiction, several hundred cases have been litigated in the United States since 1996. All convictions in which mtDNA has played a role have been upheld at the appellate level. In addition, numerous postconviction endeavors have been aided by mtDNA analysis of crime scene hairs which had been evaluated previously only via hair microscopy. For more information on court cases and appellate decisions, see http://www.denverda.org/DNA/Mitochondrial_DNA_Legal_Decisions.htm.

References

[1]   Holland, M.M. & Parsons, T.J. (1999). Mitochondrial DNA sequence analysis – validation and use for forensic casework, *Forensic Science Reviews* **11**, 21–50.

[2]   Davis, C.L. (1998). Mitochondrial DNA: *State of Tennessee v. Paul Ware*, *Profiles in DNA* **1**, 6–7.

[3]   Budowle, B., Adams, D.E., Comey, C.C. & Merrill, C.R. (1990). Mitochondrial DNA: a possible genetic material suitable for forensic analysis, in *Advances in Forensic Sciences*, H.C. Lee & R.E. Gaensslen, eds, Year Book Medical Publishers, Chicago, pp. 76–97.

[4]   Wilson, M.R., Polanskey, D., Butler, J., DiZinno, J.A., Replogle, J. & Budowle, B. (1995). Extraction, PCR amplification and sequencing of mitochondrial DNA from human hair shafts, *Biotechniques* **18**, 662–669.

[5]   Taanman, J.-W. (1999). The mitochondrial genome: structure, transcription, translation, and replication, *Biochimica et Biophysica Acta* **1410**, 103–123.

[6]   Vigilant, L., Stoneking, M., Harpending, H., Hawkes, K. & Wilson, A.C. (1991). African populations and the evolution of human mitochondrial DNA, *Science* **253**, 1503–1507.

[7]   Budowle, B., Wilson, M.R., DiZinno, J.A., Stauffer, C., Fasano, M.A., Holland, M.M. & Monson, K.L. (1999). Mitochondrial DNA regions HVI and HVII population data, *Forensic Science International* **103**, 23–35.

[8]   Melton, T., Holland, C. & Holland, M. (2012). Forensic mitochondrial DNA: current practice and future potential, *Forensic Science Review* **24**(2), 110–122.

[9]   Melton, T. & Nelson, K. (2005). Forensic mitochondrial DNA analysis of 691 casework hairs, *Journal of Forensic Sciences* **50**, 73–80.

[10] Nelson, K. & Melton, T. (2007). Forensic mitochondrial DNA analysis of 116 casework skeletal samples, *Journal of Forensic Sciences* **52**, 557–561.

[11] Melton, T., Dimick, G., Higgins, B., Yon, M. & Holland, C. (2012). Mitochondrial DNA analysis of 114 hairs measuring less than one centimeter from a 19-year-old homicide, *Investigative Genetics* **3**, 12.

[12] Gabriel, M.N., Huffine, E.F., Ryan, J.H., Holland, M.M. & Parsons, T.J. (2001). Improved mtDNA sequence analysis of forensic remains using a "mini-primer set" amplification strategy, *Journal of Forensic Sciences* **46**, 247–253.

[13] Carracedo, A., Bär, W., Lincoln, P., Mayr, W., Morling, N., Olaisen, B., Schneider, P., Budowle, B., Brinkmann, B., Gill, P., Holland, M., Tully, G. & Wilson, M. (2000). DNA Commission of the International Society for Forensic Genetics: guidelines for mitochondrial DNA typing, *Forensic Science International* **110**, 79–85.

[14] Andrews, R.M., Kubacka, I., Chinnery, P.F., Lightowlers, R.N., Turnbull, D.M. & Howell, N. (1999). Reanalysis and revision of the Cambridge Reference Sequence for human mitochondrial DNA, *Nature Genetics* **23**, 147.

[15] Anderson, S., Bankier, A.T., Barrell, B.G., de Bruijn, M.H.L., Coulson, A.R., Drouin, J., Eperon, I.C., Nierlich, D.P., Roe, B.A., Sanger, F., Schreier, P.H., Smith, A.J.H., Staden, R. & Young, I.G. (1981). Sequence and organization of the human mitochondrial genome, *Nature* **290**, 457–465.

[16] Melton, T. (2004). Mitochondrial DNA heteroplasmy, *Forensic Science Reviews* **16**, 1–20.

[17] Parson, W. & Dür, A. (2007). EMPOP – a forensic mtDNA database, *Forensic Science International: Genetics* **1**(2), 88–92.

[18] Budowle, B., Allard, M.W., Fisher, C.L., Isenberg, A.R., Monson, K.L., Stewart, J.E.B., Wilson, M.R. & Miller, K.W.P. (2000). HVI and HVII mitochondrial DNA data

in Apaches and Navajos, *International Journal of Legal Medicine* **116**, 212–215.

[19] Parson, W., Brandstätter, A., Alonso, A., Brandt, N., Brinkmann, B., Carracedo, A., Corach, D., Froment, O., Furac, I., Grzybowski, T., Hedberg, K., Keyser-Tracqui, C., Kupiec, T., Lutz-Bonengel, S., Mevag, B., Ploski, R., Schmitter, H., Schneider, P., Syndercombe-Comb, D., Sorensen, E., Thew, H., Tully, G. & Scheithauer, R. (2004). The EDNAP mitochondrial DNA population database (EMPOP) collaborative exercises: organisation, results, and perspectives, *Forensic Science International* **139**, 215–226.

[20] Gill, P., Ivanov, P.L., Kimpton, C., Piercy, R., Benson, N., Tully, G., Evett, I., Hagelberg, E. & Sullivan, K. (1994). Identification of the remains of the Romanov family by DNA analysis, *Nature Genetics* **6**, 130–135.

[21] Daoudi, Y., Morgan, M., Diefenbach, C., Ryan, J., Johnson, T., Conklin, G., Duncan, K., Smigielski, K., Huffine, E., Rankin, D., Mann, R., Holland, C., McElfresh, K., Canik, J., Armbrustmacher, V. & Holland, M. (1998). Identification of the Vietnam Tomb of the Unknown Soldier: the many roles of mitochondrial DNA, in *Proceedings of the Ninth International Symposium on Human Identification*, Promega Corporation, Scottsdale.

[22] Owsley, D.W., Ellwood, B.B. & Melton, T. (2006). Search for the grave of William Preston Longley, hanged Texas gunfighter, *Historical Archaeology* **40**, 50–63.

[23] Wallace, D.C., Brown, M.D. & Lott, M.T. (1999). Mitochondrial DNA variation in human evolution and disease, *Gene* **238**, 211–230.

[24] Stoneking, M. (1990). Mitochondrial DNA variation and human evolution, in *Human Genome Evolution*, M. Jackson, T. Strachan & G. Dover, eds, BIOS Scientific Publishers, Oxford, pp. 263–281.

[25] Krings, M., Stone, A., Schmitz, R.W., Krainitzki, H., Stoneking, M. & Pääbo, S. (1997). Neandertal DNA sequences and the origin of modern humans, *Cell* **90**, 1–12.

Related Articles in EFS Online

Hair: Microscopic Analysis

Interpretation of Mitochondrial DNA Evidence

Wrongful Convictions and the Role of Forensic Science

Chapter 29
Geographical Identification by Viral Genotyping

Hiroshi Ikegaya[1], Pekka J. Saukko[2], Yoshinao Katsumata[3,4], and Takehiko Takatori[3]

[1]*Kyoto Prefectural University of Medicine, Kyoto, Japan*
[2]*University of Turku, Turku, Finland*
[3]*National Institute of Police Science, Tokyo, Japan*
[4]*Nagoya Isen, Nagoya, Japan*

Introduction

Major genetic differences between human populations must have evolved when they expanded, originating from Africa, across the earth in the course of the last 100 000 years [1, 2]. The theory of isolation by distance, that is, the decrease of genetic similarity with increasing geographic distance, has been supported by data on genetic polymorphism [3, 4]. In the course of this evolution, humans have carried many parasites that have coevolved with humans, resulting in different types of relationship, that is, commensal, mutualistic, or pathogen to humans [5]. Therefore, evolution and genomic diversity of viruses have been used to gain better insight into patterns of ancient human migration [6]. Studies with human papillomavirus (HPV-16), polyomavirus JC (JCV), and also the bacterium *Helicobacter pylori* have shown a similar pattern of evolution to humans with origins in Africa and subsequent migration of ethnic groups to the other continents in prehistoric times [7–10].

This association of parasitic genomic diversity with geographic area has also attracted forensic scientists. Recently, Ikegaya *et al.* [11] reported a novel method of applying genetic diversity of the JC virus to forensic case work. After that report, several other parasites have been examined to find out whether their genotype and geographical region correlate to such an extent that would allow them to be used as aids to the process of human identification.

Relations between Parasitic Genotype and Geographic Area

JCV, a member of the *Polyomaviridae* family, was first isolated in 1971 from the brain of a patient with progressive multifocal leukoencephalopathy (PML) and was eventually found to be ubiquitous in the human population [12, 13]. After primary asymptomatic infection in childhood, JCV persists in the renal tissue of most adults, excreting its progeny virus in urine. JCV strains worldwide can be classified into more than 30 genotypes from 18 main genotypes by phylogenetic analyses [14] of viral 5100p DNA sequences [15]. Each genotype is distributed in relatively small distinct areas of different parts in the world (Table 1).

BK virus (BKV) belongs to the same family of *polyomaviridae* as JCV, and was first detected from a renal transplant patient in 1971 [16]. Primary infection with this virus usually occurs in childhood and the seroprevalence rate reaches the adult rate (65–90%) at the age of 5–10 years [17]. BKV is also known to persist in the kidneys and to excrete progeny virus in urine [18]. BKV strains worldwide can be classified into seven main genotypes

A Guide to Forensic DNA Profiling
Edited by Allan Jamieson and Scott Bader
© 2016 John Wiley & Sons, Ltd. ISBN: 9781118751527
Also published in EFS (online edition)
DOI: 10.1002/9780470061589.fsa464.pub2

Table 1   Distribution of JCV genotypes in the Old World

Genotype	Geographic region where indicated genotype is mainly detected[a]
EU-a	Europe
EU-b	Southern Europe
EU-c	Northeast Siberia, Arctic circle
B1-c	Europe, Mediterranean
Af1	Central and western Africa
Af2-a	Southern Africa
Af2-b	Northern Africa, western Asia
Af3	Central Africa
B1-a	China
B1-b	Central and western Asia
B1-d	Saudi Arabia, Greece
B2	India, Mauritius
CY-a	Korea
CY-b	Northeastern China, southern Japan
SC	Southeast Asia, southern China
MY	Northern Japan, Korea
8A	New Guinea, Oceania
2E	Oceania

[a] Areas of geographic distribution indicated according to reports by Yogo *et al.* and Takasaka *et al.*

according to phylogenetic analyses of viral DNA sequences [19, 20]. Each genotype occupies distinct areas of distribution in different parts of the world (Table 2).

So far, a correlation between the geographic area and genotypes has also been noted in other parasites, such as Epstein–Barr virus (EBV) [20], human herpes virus type 1 (HHV-1), *H. pylori* [21], hepatitis B virus (HBV) [22], and *Candida albicans* [23]. Figures 1 and 2 show the phylogenetic tree of the JC virus and HHV-1 virus, respectively. These phylogenetic trees, constructed from worldwide isolates, show close

Table 2   Distribution of BKV genotypes in the Old World

Subtype	Subgroup	Geographic region where an indicated genotype is mainly detected[a]
I	Ia	Africa
	Ib-1	Southeast Asia
	Ib-2	Europe
	Ic	Northeast Asia
IV		Continental Asia
II, III		Rarely detected

[a] Areas of geographic distribution indicated according to Zheng *et al.*

correlations to the geographic areas; however, the relation between the area and genotypes is much closer in JC virus than HHV-1 virus. The reason for this is that the evolutional history of JCV is almost synchronized to the history of humans, whereas HHV-1 is not, as a host change may have occurred; therefore, not only geographic correlations but also evolutional history of the parasite in question has to be analyzed.

Detection of Parasitic Genotypes from Forensic Samples

Polymerase chain reaction (PCR) amplification of a 610 bp region (VT intergenic region: IG region) of the viral genome was used for JCV detection from forensic autopsy cases. The detection rate was 45% when 200 mg of renal tissue was used as template and somewhat lower, 33%, from 5 ml of urine. The detection rate was higher (>50%) with elderly subjects. Multiple samples taken from the same kidney and the contralateral one from the same cadaver showed identical sequences. The JCV detection rate was not related to the cause of death and was hardly affected by postmortem decomposition [24]. Detection of JCV from formalin-fixed and paraffin-embedded tissue has also been reported [25]. In formalin-fixed, paraffin-embedded samples, not only the original sequences but also those with 1% of base substitution were detected and no genotype change was found. In formalin-soaked samples, the original sequences and those with more than 1% of substitution causing genotype change were detected; thereafter, genotype was determined only using specimens in a frozen state or that had been formalin-fixed for a short time. There is a report that JCV was detectable from 50 μl of urine. When 200 μl of urine was used for detection, 54.9% was JCV positive, and JCV DNA was highly detectable from minute urine stains prepared three months earlier using 100 μl of JCV-positive urine [26]. These findings show that this method could be used for urine stain samples left at the scene and small amounts of urine taken from autopsies. Although there are several chemical or immunological methods to identify urine stains, it can be problematic to confirm that they are of human origin. However, detection of JCV or BKV from urine stains automatically confirms that they are human, because these viruses only infect the human urinary tract.

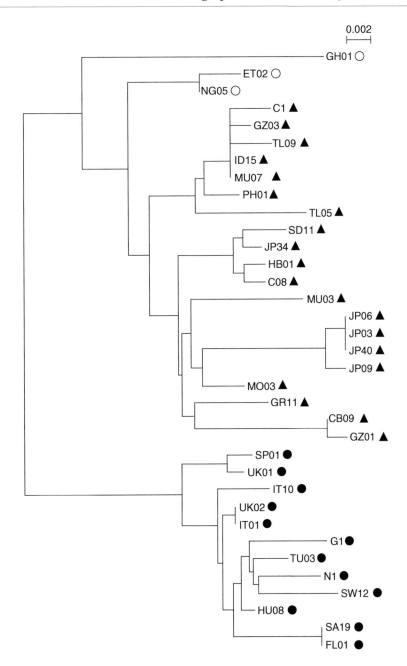

Figure 1 Phylogenetic analysis of JCV genome; 610 bp hypervariable region (IG region) of JCV genome was phylogenetically analyzed. Open circle, African isolates; closed circle, European isolates; and closed triangle, Asian isolates

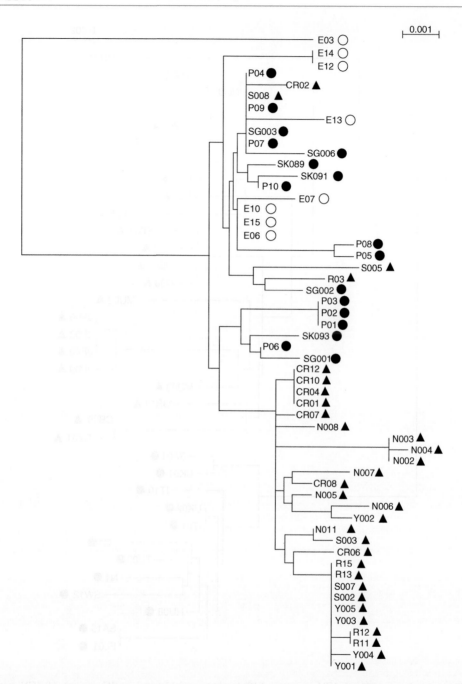

Figure 2 Phylogenetic analysis of HHV-1 genome; 666 bp hypervariable region of HHV-1 genome was phylogenetically analyzed. Open circle, African isolates; closed circle, European isolates; and closed triangle, Asian isolates

BKV DNA was also detectable in 30.5% of postmortem cases [27]. In addition, JCV DNA was detected in 47.2% of the same postmortem cases. Overall, BKV or JCV was detectable in 69.8% of postmortem cases. Additionally, the distribution of the two viruses is slightly different. Therefore, it is possible to narrow down the geographic region of human remains according to the geographic distribution of different viruses.

As EBV infects human leukocytes, it might, at least in principle, be a good tool to identify using blood samples; however, the detection rate from postmortem blood samples was only 16% and globally the number of genotype varieties found is limited [20]. Similarly to EBV, HBV is detectable from human blood samples. HBV, as is the case for JCV, is one of the viruses that shows a very close relationship between virus genotypes and geographic regions [22]. However, because of its low detection rate (about 1%), its effectiveness in actual police investigations is unknown. Therefore, a high detection rate is also necessary for actual use. Also HHV-1 DNA has been detected postmortem in forensic cases from the trigeminal nerve by PCR method with a detection rate of 61% [28], as well as *H. pylori* from gastric mucosa, with a detection rate of 56% [29]. However, there have been no reports of these genotypes being used to determine the geographic origin of humans.

Estimation of Geographic Origin

After JCV infection, the same viral strains are maintained in the kidneys and urine throughout life, irrespective of the host's relocation; therefore, the estimated geographical origin from the JCV genotype is closely related to the area where the host grew up. Among all the parasites described above, the JCV genotype has been classified in most detail. The applicability of these methods depends in particular on the distribution of the genotype, subtypes, and subgroups within the geographic area in question. Especially in Asia, many genotypes and their subtypes are found in small domains; for instance, mainly two genotypes are found in Japan, with one genotype prevailing in the north and the other in the south. We can therefore estimate from which area a cadaver originated from and the probability of a cadaver originating from the place where it was found. Japanese police started to use JCV method in 2005

and BKV method in 2007. So far, these methods have been applied to more than 10 cases and in some of them with good results. For other parasites, it is not clear whether double infection or genotypic change might occur during life; therefore, further studies are necessary.

Potential New Approaches toward Geographical Identification Using Human Parasites

In addition to the genomic diversity of human parasites, another approach that may have potential to be used in similar way in the future, but has to our knowledge not been investigated, is the impact of antibiotics. The widespread use of antimicrobial agents worldwide has led to an increasing prevalence of drug-resistant strains of bacteria that can show distinct patterns both geographically and over time. In 1992 established Alexander Project is a continuing surveillance study examining the antimicrobial susceptibility of bacterial pathogens of community-acquired respiratory tract infections with participating centers in many countries in Europe, Africa, Latin America, Middle East, Far East, and the United States [30]. As this type of bacterial resistance is under continued evolution, it would presuppose the existence of a global online database for comparison and additionally a sufficient stability of the bacterial strains to be detected in postmortem material.

References

[1] Hinkes, M.J. (2008). Migrant deaths along the California-Mexico border: an anthropological perspective, *Journal of Forensic Sciences* **53**(1), 16–20.

[2] Cattaneo, C., Ritz-Timme, S., Schutz, H.W., Collins, M., Waite, E., Boormann, H., Grandi, M. & Kaatsch, H.J. (2000). Unidentified cadavers and human remains in the EU: an unknown issue, *International Journal of Legal Medicine* **113**(3), N2–N3.

[3] Cavalli-Sforza, L.L., Menozzi, P. & Piazza, A. (1993). Demic expansions and human evolution, *Science* **259**(5095), 639–646.

[4] Ramachandran, S., Deshpande, O., Roseman, C.C., Rosenberg, N.A., Feldman, M.W. & Cavalli-Sforza, L.L. (2005). Support from the relationship of genetic and geographic in human populations for a serial founder effect originating in Africa, *Proceedings of the National Academy of Sciences of the United States of America* **102**(44), 15942–15947.

[5] Dethlefsen, L., McFall-Ngai, M. & Relman, D.A. (2007). An ecological and evolutionary perspective on human-microbe mutualism and disease, *Nature* **449**(7164), 811–818.

[6] Cavalli-Sforza, L.L. & Feldman, M.W. (2003). The application of molecular genetic approaches to the study of human evolution, *Nature Genetics* **33**(Suppl), 266–275.

[7] Ho, L., Chan, S.Y., Burk, R.D., Kiviat, N., Lancaster, W., Mavromara-Nizos, P., Labropoulou, V., Mitrani-Rosenbaum, S., Norrild, B., Pillai, R.M., Stoerker, J., Syrjaenen, K., Wheeler, C.M., Williamson, A.L. & Bernard, H.U. (1993). The genetic drift of human papillomavirus type 16 is a means of reconstructing prehistoric viral spread and the movement of ancient human populations, *Journal of Virology* **67**(11), 6413–6423.

[8] Sugimoto, C., Kitamura, T., Guo, J., Al-Ahdal, M.N., Shchelkunov, S.N., Otova, B., Ondrejka, P., Chollet, J.Y., El-Safi, S., Ettayebi, M., Grésenguet, G., Kocagöz, T., Chaiyarasamee, S., Thant, K.Z., Thein, S., Moe, K., Kobayashi, N., Taguchi, F. & Yogo, Y. (1997). Typing of urinary JC virus DNA offers a novel means of tracing human migrations, *Proceedings of the National Academy of Sciences of the United States of America* **94**(17), 9191–9196.

[9] Covacci, A., Telford, J.L., Del Giudice, G., Parsonnet, J. & Rappuoli, R. (1999). Helicobacter pylori virulence and genetic geography, *Science* **284**(5418), 1328–1333.

[10] Ikegaya, H., Zheng, H.Y., Saukko, P.J., Varesmaa-Korhonen, L., Hovi, T., Vesikari, T., Suganami, H., Takasaka, T., Sugimoto, C., Ohasi, Y., Kitamura, T. & Yogo, Y. (2005). Genetic diversity of JC virus in the saami and the finns: implications for their population history, *American Journal of Physical Anthropology* **128**(1), 185–193.

[11] Ikegaya, H., Iwase, H., Sugimoto, C. & Yogo, Y. (2002). JC virus genotyping offers a new means of tracing the origins of unidentified cadavers, *International Journal of Legal Medicine* **116**(4), 242–245.

[12] Padgett, B.L., Walker, D.L., ZuRhein, G.M., Eckroade, R.J. & Dessel, B.H. (1971). Cultivation of papova-like virus from human brain with progressive multifocal leucoencephalopathy, *Lancet* **1**(7712), 1257–1260.

[13] Kunitake, T., Kitamura, T., Guo, J., Taguchi, F., Kawabe, K. & Yogo, Y. (1995). Parent-to-child transmission is relatively common in the spread of the human polyomavirus JC virus, *Journal of Clinical Microbiology* **33**(6), 1448–1451.

[14] Yogo, Y., Sugimoto, C., Zheng, H.Y., Ikegaya, H., Takasaka, T. & Kitamura, T. (2004). JC virus genotyping offers a new paradigm in the study of human populations, *Reviews in Medical Virology* **14**(3), 179–191.

[15] Cole, C.N. & Conzen, S.D. (2001). Polyomaviridae: the viruses and their replication, in *Field's Virology*, D.M. Knipe & P.M. Howley, eds, Lippincott Williams & Wilkins, Philadelphia, Vol. 2, p. 3280.

[16] Gardner, S.D., Field, A.M., Coleman, D.V. & Hulme, B. (1971). New human papovavirus (B.K.) isolated from urine after renal transplantation, *Lancet* **1**(7712), 1253–1257.

[17] Knowles, W.A. (2001). The epidemiology of BK virus and the occurrence of antigenic and genomic subtypes, in *Human Polyomaviruses: Molecular and Clinical Perspectives*, K. Khalili & G.L. Stoner, eds, Wiley, New York, p. 704.

[18] Zhong, S., Zheng, H.Y., Suzuki, M., Chen, Q., Ikegaya, H., Aoki, N., Usuku, S., Kobayashi, N., Nukuzuma, S., Yasuda, Y., Kuniyoshi, N., Yogo, Y. & Kitamura, T. (2007). Age-related urinary excretion of BK polyomavirus by nonimmunocompromised individuals, *Journal of Clinical Microbiology* **45**(1), 193–198.

[19] Zheng, H.Y., Nishimoto, Y., Chen, Q., Hasegawa, M., Zhong, S., Ikegaya, H., Ohno, N., Sugimoto, C., Takasaka, T., Kitamura, T. & Yogo, Y. (2007). Relationships between BK virus lineages and human populations, *Microbes and Infection* **9**(2), 204–213.

[20] Ikegaya, H., Motani, H., Sakurada, K., Sato, K., Akutsu, T. & Yoshi, M. (2008). Forensic application of Epstein-Barr virus genotype: correlation between viral genotype and geographical area, *Journal of Virological Methods* **147**(1), 78–85.

[21] Kersulyte, D., Mukhopadhyay, A.K., Velapatiño, B., Su, W., Pan, Z., Garcia, C., Hernandez, V., Valdez, Y., Mistry, R.S., Gilman, R.H., Yuan, Y., Gao, H., Alarcón, T., López-Brea, M., Balakrish Nair, G., Chowdhury, A., Datta, S., Shirai, M., Nakazawa, T., Ally, R., Segal, I., Wong, B.C., Lam, S.K., Olfat, F.O., Borén, T., Engstrand, L., Torres, O., Schneider, R., Thomas, J.E., Czinn, S. & Berg, D.E. (2000). Differences in genotypes of Helicobacter pylori from different human populations, *Journal of Bacteriology* **182**(11), 3210–3218.

[22] Kao, J.H. (2011). Molecular epidemiology of hepatitis B virus, *Korean Journal of Internal Medicine* **26**(3), 255–261.

[23] Xu, J. & Mitchell, T.G. (2003). Geographical differences in human oral yeast flora, *Clinical Infectious Diseases* **36**(2), 221–224.

[24] Ikegaya, H., Iwase, H. & Yogo, Y. (2004). Detection of identical JC virus DNA sequences in both human kidneys, *Archives of Virology* **149**(6), 1215–1220.

[25] Ikegaya, H., Iwase, H., Zheng, H.Y., Nakajima, M., Sakurada, K., Takatori, T., Fukayama, M., Kitamura, T. & Yogo, Y. (2005). JC virus genotyping using formalin-fixed, paraffin-embedded renal tissues, *Journal of Virological Methods* **126**(1–2), 37–43.

[26] Sakurada, K., Ikegaya, H., Motani, H., Iwase, H., Sekiguchi, K., Akutsu, T., Yoshino, M., Takatori, T. & Sakai, I. (2005). JC virus genotyping can be used to narrow down the native place of persons from urine stains, *Japanese Journal of Forensic Science and Technology* **10**(2), 111–117.

[27] Ikegaya, H., Motani, H., Saukko, P., Sato, K., Akutsu, T. & Sakurada, K. (2007). BK virus genotype distribution offers information of tracing the geographical origins of unidentified cadaver, *Forensic Science International* **173**(1), 41–46.

[28] Motani, H., Sakurada, K., Ikegaya, H., Akutsu, T., Hayakawa, M., Sato, Y., Yajima, D., Sato, K., Kobayashi, K. & Iwase, H. (2006). Detection of herpes simplex virus type 1 DNA in bilateral human trigeminal ganglia and optic nerves by polymerase chain reaction, *Journal of Medical Virology* **78**(12), 1584–1587.

[29] Nagasawa, A., Azuma, K., Motani, H., Hayakawa, M., Yajima, D., Kobayashi, K., & Iwase, H. (2007). Detection of helicobacter pylori from postmortem gastric mucosa – application to the geographic identification of unidentified cadavers, *76th Kanto meeting of Japanese Society of Legal Medicine*, Yokohama.

[30] Jacobs, M.R., Felmingham, D., Appelbaum, P.C. & Grüneberg, R.N. (2003). The Alexander project 1998–2000: susceptibility of pathogens isolated from community-acquired respiratory tract infection to commonly used antimicrobial agents, *The Journal of Antimicrobial Chemotherapy* **52**(2), 229–246.

Further Reading

Jernberg, C., Löfmark, S., Edlund, C. & Jansson, J.K. (2007). Long-term ecological impacts of antibiotic administration on the human intestinal microbiota, *ISME Journal* **1**(1), 56–66.

Related Articles in EFS Online

Anthropology

Disaster Victim Identification: Process in United Kingdom

Chapter 30
Microbial Forensics

Bruce Budowle and Phillip C. Williamson

University of North Texas Health Science Center, Fort Worth, TX, USA

Introduction

Immediately following the terrorist attacks on September 11, 2001, an act of bioterrorism occurred in the United States. In a simple and deliberate manner, *Bacillus anthracis* spores were sent through the mail to media and political offices, and resulted in 22 infections and five deaths [1–6]. As the result of this attack, the world became aware of a vulnerability in which many in the field of counterterrorism were quite cognizant. Bioterrorism is a real threat. The use of the US mail as a dissemination vehicle heightened concerns because it demonstrated that a simple delivery mechanism could be used to expose people to a deadly pathogen (a disease-causing agent). The naïve concept that successful delivery of a bioweapon was difficult was no longer viable. The United States and specifically the Federal Bureau of Investigation (FBI), the agency with the primary responsibility to investigate this crime, were ill-prepared to undertake the forensic analyses related to the investigation of the anthrax attack; supporting forensic science analysis of microbial evidence was extremely limited at that time [7, 8]. The goal in a criminal investigation is usually the identification of the perpetrator of the crime (i.e., attribution). Science can play a role in supporting attribution as well as providing information for developing investigative leads. Evidence is any material, physical or electronic, that can associate with or exclude individuals from a crime. In an investigation of bioterrorism or biocrime, microbial evidence as well as traditional evidence is sought. Since 2001, the government, in partnership with academia and

industry, has responded to the dearth of capabilities and analytical tools for forensic analyses of microbial evidence by developing the field of Microbial Forensics [7–14]. Microbial Forensics is the scientific discipline dedicated to analyzing evidence from a bioterrorism act, biocrime, hoax, or inadvertent release of microorganism/toxin for attribution purposes [10]. Microbial evidence may include microbes, toxins, nucleic acids, protein signatures, inadvertent microbial contaminants, stabilizers, additives, dispersal devices, and so on.

A forensic investigation of any case where the weapon is a pathogen or toxin will initially attempt to determine the identity of the causative agent and source of the bioweapon in much the same manner as an epidemiologic investigation. Microbial forensics and epidemiology are integrated in the context of a crime (Figure 1). For many decades, epidemiologists have used general forensic approaches to identify the causative agents and the etiology of diseases of public health concerns. Epidemiology investigates the combination of clinical presentation of disease, identification of the pathogen, the distribution in a population, and anecdotal factors to deduce where an infection began and how it spread throughout a population [13–16]. Indeed, epidemiologists have been practicing microbial forensic scientists well before the existence of a defined field known as *Microbial Forensics*. In microbial forensics, the epidemiologic concerns are identification and characterization of specific disease-causing pathogens or their toxins, their modes of transmission, and any manipulations that may have been done intentionally to increase their effects against human, animal, or plant targets. Microbial forensics goes one step further than most epidemiologic investigations; evidence is characterized to assist in determining the specific source of the sample, in ways that are as individualizing as possible, and the methods, means, processes, and locations

A Guide to Forensic DNA Profiling
Edited by Allan Jamieson and Scott Bader
© 2016 John Wiley & Sons, Ltd. ISBN: 9781118751527
Also published in EFS (online edition)
DOI: 10.1002/9780470061589.fsa1031

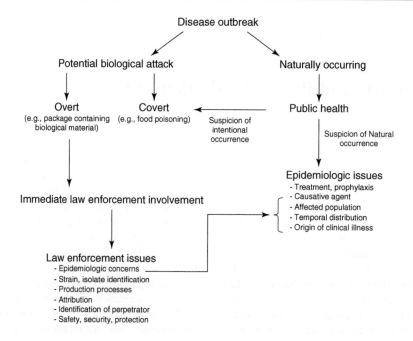

Figure 1   General schematic approach to a disease outbreak involving public health and/or law enforcement

involved in the determination of the identity of the perpetrator(s) of the attack [9, 14].

Most people tend to believe that the anthrax attack of 2001 is the first known attack using bioweapons. Nature has produced a plethora of bacteria, viruses, and fungi that pose serious health risks to humans, animals, and plants and has thus already engineered bioweapons, of which many are readily accessible. Accessibility makes the threat of an attack a viable concern. Many uses of bioweapons have been witnessed throughout human history, dating back many millennia. For example, the ancient Romans and Assyrians poisoned the water supplies of their enemies with carrion; the Spanish and the British colonists used blankets and clothing contaminated with measles and smallpox against the Native Americans; and there are many twentieth century accounts including the attempt by the Aum Shinrikyo Cult to disseminate *B. anthracis* spores on the Tokyo populace [17–21] (see [21] for an account of bioterrorism in the twentieth century). Moreover, technology has developed to such a point that there is a significant potential for access to biothreats, which may have been impossible to acquire in the recent past. For example, synthetic biology may soon make it possible to create inaccessible pathogens,

no longer thought to be available in nature, that have been historically proven to be devastating to human health [22–24].

Agriculture is a desirable target because it can disrupt food supplies and have significant impact on the economy. One only needs to consider the outbreak of foot-and-mouth disease in England to appreciate the economic impact that may result from a single outbreak (estimated to be greater than $12 billion [25–27]). Plants and animals are likely targets as well. The moral threshold for a potential perpetrator of an attack against plants and animals may be lower than that for a human target. In addition, the risk of harm to the perpetrator can be greatly reduced. An attack on a country that relies predominantly on a single food crop could be catastrophic because it could create famine, economic upheaval, and political instability. Attacks on agriculture have occurred and are well documented; they range from the cyanide-tainted Chilean grape scare of 1989 [28] to the pesticide-tainted cattle feed of the 1980s and 1990s [29] to the potential use of mycoherbicides (fungi) to control coca and poppy production [30, 31]. The challenge for law enforcement regarding agriculture is that it is a highly vulnerable target with meager security measures.

There is a long list of targets and other sectors of society that are impacted from farm to fork, including livestock, livestock producers, crops, water supplies, food processors, food handlers, processing facilities, food and agriculture transportation systems, farm workers, food in grocery stores, restaurants, and local communities. This security deficiency almost guarantees unchallenged and unhindered access by a determined bioterrorist.

Lastly, toxins, produced by some plants, fungi, and bacteria, may also be used by the bioterrorist and as weapons in traditional crimes, such as extortion. Toxins are readily accessible and easy to produce and transport. Botulinum toxin, for example, is one of the most lethal toxins known [32–35]. A single gram of the toxin is sufficient to kill more than 1 million people. Most toxin-related crimes in the United States involve ricin, a readily accessible toxin that is derived from bean of *Ricinus communis*, the castor plant [36]. The convenient access to castor beans and the fact that recipes for purifying the toxin can be found on the Internet make ricin an appealing bioweapon. In fact, ricin has also been used in well-known assassinations [21, 37, 38].

Because the number and variety of potential biological weapons are large, a number of pathogens are readily obtainable, and there are many potential targets that are not well protected, it is nearly impossible to prevent all attempts at bioterrorism. Another successful bioterrorism attack is inevitable. In order for law enforcement to respond adequately to identifying the perpetrator(s) and bringing them to justice or for justification of a government to take appropriate action, an effective microbial forensic science program is needed. An investigative response capability is essential for public safety and security and that includes the ability to analyze evidence found at crime scenes where bioweapons have been used.

Detection and Identification Capabilities

Attribution is a primary goal of microbial forensics and requires acquisition of data that can distinguish an individual isolate or sample from similar samples, to the most precise level possible. A microbial forensics toolbox requires procedures that enable detection and identification. Analytical capabilities include nucleic-acid-based analytical systems, culture, immunoassays, protein characterization, and the use

of bioassays in animals and tissue culture. Culturing (the growing of the microorganism in the laboratory) has been the gold standard in traditional microbiology laboratories for detection and identification of viable pathogens [39]. However, culture-based pathogen identification may be ineffective in some forensic situations for some types of bacteria and fungi samples [40–46]. It is often several days before results are obtained by culture for slow-growing microorganisms. For investigations relying on an immediate and rapid response, culturing time could be a drawback. Moreover, culturing often cannot provide attribution beyond a genus or species level. Another limitation is that up to 99% of microbial species cannot be cultured by current methods. Lastly, some evidence samples may not be viable, particularly old and degraded materials, and thus are not amenable to culture methods.

A major analytical endeavor for attribution is the analysis of genetic signatures that can associate or eliminate a pathogen sample with a specific source. The use of molecular biology for microbial identification, characterization, and attribution purposes in many ways is analogous to that for human DNA forensic analysis, which associates or excludes a suspect or victim as the source of a biological specimen(s) found at crime scenes [47–49]. However, in contrast, current microbial forensics is unlikely to achieve the same level of attribution as is possible for human identification in most cases and, in fact, may not ever be able to achieve individualization. The inheritance patterns of microorganisms, particularly asexual reproduction, limit individualization. Also, data are lacking on the diversity, endemicity, and complex inheritance strategies of microorganisms. These range from clonal to horizontal gene flow, and the history and manipulations of the bioweapon, all of which complicate the analysis and interpretation of bioterrorism and biocrime evidence.

Regardless of all this, molecular biology techniques continue to develop such that the specificity, sensitivity, and speed of testing are improving. Even without the ability to individualize, some critical information can be generated, which will allow, to some degree, the deduction of the nature and source of an evidentiary sample and the exclusion of potential candidate sources or isolates. Basically, genetics can eliminate some investigative leads that would likely prove fruitless. For example, multilocus variable-number tandem repeat assay (MLVA), a research tool in 2001, was used to confirm that the strain of *B. anthracis* in the letter attack was the Ames strain [4, 50]. While hardly individualizing, this strain level attribution information was sufficient to focus the law enforcement investigation on samples that were accessible to laboratories rather than the environmentally accessible isolates. Ames is not commonly found in nature [4, 51, 52].

Genetic markers that may be exploited for forensic attribution include single nucleotide polymorphisms (SNPs), repetitive sequences, insertions and deletions, mobile elements, pathogenicity islands, virulence and resistance genes, house keeping genes, and structural genes [53]. However, given the advances that have occurred in the past several years, whole-genome sequencing may become routinely feasible and cost effective, at least for viable, cultural microbes and, to some extent, for nonviable or nonculturable microorganisms. In theory, all genetic marker classes can be simultaneously assayed by whole-genome sequencing.

Whole-genome sequencing was used to genetically characterize the *B. anthracis* spores in the letters used in the attack of 2001 [54]. Initially, no variation between the evidence and a reference sample was observed. Thus, the technology did not provide any investigative value for the case. The technology, which, just a few years ago, had limited the depth of coverage, was extremely laborious, time consuming, and costly (up to $250 000 to sequence a single sample genome). Only a few genomes could be reasonably sequenced and therefore only crucially defining individualizing genetic variants could be identified within a population of samples. However, the process ushered in new approaches for the investigation of microbial forensic evidence [4, 54].

Fortunately, because of an astute microbiologist who identified some late spore-forming morphology (i.e., shape) variant colonies in the forensic evidence, some genetic variants associated with the morphotypes were identified from purified colonies to assist in excluding many potential sources [4]. Whole-genome sequencing technology at the time would not have been able to detect the variants from evidence in the letters or from the putative ancestral source of the bioweapon, known as RMR1029, the flask of *B. anthracis* maintained at USAMRIID (United States Army Medical Research Institute for Infectious Diseases) [4]. The flask contained a concoction of Ames-strain culture samples, contributed from a number of collaborating laboratories. From isolated morphology subpopulations, four variants were selected, whole-genome sequenced, and real-time polymerase chain reaction (PCR) assays were developed to detect the distinguishing genetic variants. These four genetic assays were used to scan the repository of candidate source samples ($N = 1077$) collected from all known laboratories that had the Ames strain to reduce the number of suspect samples that could be reasonably considered as closely related to the evidentiary material. The bacteria carrying the genetic variants were present at 1% or less of the total concentration in the samples. With 8-12X coverage, which was standard for whole-genome analysis by shotgun sequencing, it would not have been possible to detect the variants with any reasonable degree of certainty. Today's massively parallel sequencing technologies, such as SOLiD™ (Applied Biosystems, Foster City, CA), Genome Analyzer and HiSeq (Illumina, San Diego, CA), 454 GS FLX (454 Life Sciences, Roche, Branford, CT) and other related technologies, offer rapid resequencing of whole bacterial genomes with much higher coverage [55–62] and at a significantly reduced cost per sample. These next (actually current) generation sequencing platforms would have been able to directly detect the low-level variants in the mixture. Indeed, there would have been no need for any development of a real-time PCR assay to specifically identify the four variants. By interrogating nearly every base of the genome, rare subpopulation polymorphisms (genetic variations) can be reliably discovered and detected in all samples, thus facilitating high-resolution strain diagnostics and increasing forensic attribution capabilities. In fact, low-level components of mixtures, such as those observed in the anthrax letter attack evidence, can be analyzed with high confidence. Suppose the four genetic variants were amplified by the PCR and each amplicon is approximately 200 base pairs in length, then each sample would be scanned at only these four sites, which constitute a total of 800 bases. Using the calculation reported by Cummings *et al.* [55], sequencing of these amplicons on the SOLiD™ system would yield a theoretical coverage depth of approximately 12.5 million, assuming a throughput of 10 GB (the throughput capability 2 years ago) per fragment run. Multiplexing (with barcoding to identify individual samples) capability enables 256 specimens to be analyzed simultaneously with a resulting coverage depth of approximately 50 000X (i.e., coverage = [10 billion nucleotide throughput]/[(256 individuals) (800 bases amplified)]). This depth of coverage allows for a high degree of confidence to detect variants present at less than 1 in 10 000 in a mixed sample. Thus, the potential of false negatives would drop dramatically compared with other technologies that were available in 2001–2003.

If another bioterrorism case were to occur, whole-genome sequencing of multiple isolates would be obtained with high accuracy within a matter of days, particularly for viable, culturable specimens. Because of the lower cost, combined with the exceedingly high coverage, large repositories could be completely sequenced, enabling interrogation of every base in the genome. With dedicated, efficient software for alignment and annotation, sequencing of whole genomes can now be used as a diagnostic and analytical tool for forensic investigations, rather than just as a research tool.

Since nucleic acid-based assays, and even whole-genome sequencing, are unlikely to achieve identification to the level of individualization, chemical and physical analyses of microbial forensic evidence may increase the power of attribution. While it is not within the scope of this chapter, it is important to appreciate when and where such technologies might be applied. These types of signatures can only be obtained from crimes where weaponized material or a delivery device is found; they have little use in the analysis of an isolate derived from the victims or a sample that is subsequently cultured. These technologies tend to focus on signatures of the processes of sample growth and production, processing for stability and delivery, geolocation, and time of production. The results of such analyses may provide information on how, when, and/or where microorganisms were grown and processed. Analyses can range from stable isotope ratios for geolocation or determination of potential sources of nutrients that are used to grow the material, to scanning electron microscopy coupled with energy dispersive X-ray microanalysis to determine the elemental composition of single cells or spores, to mass spectroscopic methods for the detection and characterization of toxins [35, 63–66].

Lastly, traditional forensic evidence such as fingerprints, hair, shoe prints, documents, and so on, can provide insight about the perpetrator. For example, a fingerprint found on a flask can be individualizing and may be a key in identifying an individual who had access to materials involved in the handling or production of the bioweapon.

Interpretation of Microbial Forensic Results

Interpretation of results in a forensic analysis often entails a comparison of an evidence sample(s) and a reference sample(s). There are three general categories of interpretation: inclusion (or association), exclusion, and inconclusive. An inclusion is stated when the pattern or profile from the two compared samples is sufficiently similar so that they potentially could have originated from the same source. For a microbial forensic investigation, this may be a pattern or profile from two compared samples, which can indicate that they have a recent common ancestor or that one sample is possibly related by lineage. Since direct transfer of evidence is an unlikely scenario in many microbial forensics investigations, perhaps the better term for microbial forensic evidence would be "association" (see below). An exclusion is rendered when the pattern or profile is sufficiently dissimilar such that the two samples could not have originated from the same source. Exclusions for most situations are rather straightforward for human DNA comparisons. However, for microbial forensic comparisons, scant diversity data, unknown endemicity, and unknown history and treatment of the bioweapon can make an interpretation of exclusion more difficult. An inconclusive interpretation is rendered when there are insufficient data to provide a conclusive interpretation.

When the interpretation favors an association, it is desirable to attach significance or weight to these results. But statistical inferences depend on the relative information content of the genetic site(s), detected by the method(s) employed and extant supporting data. Currently, there are few established statistical interpretation guidelines for microbial forensics data. The approaches are being developed. In a number of situations, the approach for applying significance will be strictly case dependent. The interpretation of the presence or absence of the four variants in the 1077 repository samples, compared with that in the letters and the RMR1029 flask, was not a typical population genetics-based analysis solely determining how rare the variants were in the Ames strain. Instead, the question could easily have been whether the probability of observing a mixture of subpopulations was more supported if the variants arose *de novo* in one sample preparation than if they arose from the combination of several culture samples.

For the interpretation of genetic results, the statistical framework is likely to be grounded on the use of lineage-based models. These models assess the degree of similarity/dissimilarity of the evidence with other evidence and/or reference samples under the hypothesis that a particular sample(s) belong(s) to one group or lineage versus not being related to the samples [48, 49]. Genotype similarity may need to be translated into evolutionary distance, which would then provide an inference about the most recent common ancestor of the compared samples or an inference on their lineage relationship. General and specific genome site stability studies, near-neighbor analyses, and diversity studies will enhance capabilities to quantitatively assess the significance of lineage-based comparisons [48, 49]. To be effective, horizontal transfer, gene conversion, and recombination also would have to be considered, as these mechanisms can confuse lineage relationships between phylogenetically distinct types [67–70] (hylogenetics is the study of evolutionary relationships among organisms or groups of organisms). At a minimum, the genetic systems will have to be defined well and the stability of the markers understood. Most importantly, when any interpretation of the significance of a comparison is performed, either quantitatively or qualitatively, care must be taken such that any information rendered is evaluated within the limits of the assay. Particular care must be taken to ensure that the evaluation, and therefore the importance of any conclusion, is not overstated.

Databases and their composition play an essential role in a microbial forensics investigation. Databases and accompanying software house information on the various microorganisms, diversity, recipes, sequence data, and so on, and could also provide bioinformatic tools to facilitate interpretation and statistical assessments about the strength of forensic evidence. Data banks can be archives and/or repositories of relevant microorganisms for research, development, and validation purposes or to facilitate investigations. Quality and accessibility are requirements for any database.

For microbial forensics, considerations of size and composition of databases depend on both contemporary and evolutionary diversities of the pathogens, their strains (even isolates), and their near-neighbors. Adequate sampling is an almost impossible task to define as is achieving an understanding of microbial diversity for most microorganisms (the anthrax letter attacks may be an exception because all known isolates were directly related to a single sample and

a rather comprehensive collection of known samples was achieved). As a consequence of sampling deficiencies, microbial databases can never be claimed to be exhaustive or comprehensive and may not reflect the diversity of the microorganism in the area where the crime occurred or the laboratory that produced the sample resides [49].

Inferences about the observation of a strain that has not been previously observed in an area might be considered strong evidence; however, because of unknown endemicity the inference may be overstated if the strain existed in the area but had yet to be observed. There is a need to understand the distribution and epidemiology of the microorganisms, and an example of how one might obtain such data is described by Williamson *et al.* [71]. Tick-borne diseases in the United States are typically surveyed in areas where disease outbreaks occur, that is, known endemic areas which are of value for public health planning, preventative measures, response to disease outbreak, and inferences on whether an outbreak is natural or a suspected biocrime/bioterrorism event. Areas with high rate of occurrence of diseases, such as Lyme disease, ehrlichiosis, and rickettsioses/spotted fever(s), have provided substantial amount of survey data for the causative agents (*Borrelia, Ehrlichia,* and *Rickettsia,* respectively). The data enhance the ability to recognize usual and, therefore, unusual patterns of occurrence. However, natural distribution and genetic variation of these microorganisms are rarely studied outside the foci of human disease. As a result, data are not widely available concerning the full range of tick-borne agents and their potential relationship to both new and characterized illnesses in the United States. A recent study of tick-borne disease in Texas by Williamson *et al.* [71] reported the frequency and identity of bacterial agents in ticks that parasitized humans, which were then submitted to the Texas Department of State Health Services for analysis. The survey data, of places where the incidence of human disease related to tick bites was low, revealed associations of bacterial agents and potential vectors that have not been reported previously. Spotted fever group *Rickettsia* spp. (SFGR) were the most common microorganisms detected. Genetic material from SFGR was identified in the lone star tick (*Amblyomma americanum*), the cayenne tick (*Amblyomma cajennense*), the American dog tick (*Dermacentor variabilis*), the black-legged deer tick (*Ixodes scapularis*), and the brown dog tick (*Rhipicephalus sanguineus*). DNA sequences consistent with those of *Borrelia* spp. were derived from *A. americanum, A. cajennense, D. variabilis,* and *I. scapularis* ticks. Genetic data consistent with those from *Ehrlichia* spp. were observed in *A. americanum, A. cajennense,* and *A. maculatum* ticks. The presence of these microorganisms in such broad geographic range and distribution of tick species, not characteristically thought to serve as vectors for these microorganisms, is informative both from a public health perspective and for laying a baseline for attribution inferences of bioterrorism attack. If an estimation of the distribution of these microorganisms were made solely on the public health case data, the distribution and, hence, diversity would not be assessed correctly. Similarly, if only the incidence of human infection were used as a predictor, it would not likely lead to the assumption of the presence of many of the microorganisms found by the survey, nor would the diversity of genetic profiles generated from those microorganism be considered.

Although the above tick-borne study was intended to be used in a public health setting, the data are valuable for establishing a baseline for understanding epidemiological considerations, especially, in relation to any instance where an unusual number of disease cases might come to the attention of the local public health infrastructure. The ability to quickly determine whether a disease outbreak is naturally occurring requires a clear understanding of what normally occurs in the surrounding environment. Detailed knowledge of the causative agents, their distribution, and the relationship to potential vectors is extremely valuable information when entering any type of epidemiological or microbial forensic investigation. Such data can help investigations attempting to establish whether the agent in question was intentionally introduced or is "out of context". Without the knowledge of what occurs naturally, relative to the location in which it was originally isolated/discovered, attempts to assess if the incident is out of place or of significance may prove inconclusive at best. This lack of endemic data clearly had an impact on the indecision on how to respond to some partial positive DNA results for *Francisella tularensis* from samples derived by routine monitoring of the mall in Washington, DC in 2005 (for more information on this case, see [72]).

Given what is described herein, one might get the impression that microbial forensics is in its infancy and that, for example, genetic inferences will be too limiting to be of any value in an investigation.

While scant data are a limiting factor, all is not lost. There are a number of examples of investigations that have yielded valuable insight into elucidation of the etiology of disease even many years after the event or that have effectively provided direction. Even historical studies are now able to use microbial forensic tools to investigate past events. Although not the result of a bioterrorist attack, the major Black Death epidemics in Europe (sixth and fourteenth centuries) caused substantial morbidity and mortality. There have been some questions about the etiologic agent of these pandemics. Haensch *et al.* [73] were able to obtain bacterial DNA from human skeletal remains, and by typing 17 SNPs and the *glpD, pla, caf1, rpoB,* and *napA* genes, combined with epidemiologic data, they demonstrated that *Yersinia pestis* was the causative agent of the mass fatalities from the plague. In addition, they showed that the strains causing the plague were unrelated to either *Medievalis* or *Orientalis* biovars (physiological and/or biochemical variants of the same species or strain). Hundreds of years after the events, microbial evidence can still yield results of what occurred during these devastating plagues. These same tools can be applied to bioterrorist attacks that may occur in the future.

Another example of utility is genetic investigations involving the human immunodeficiency virus type 1 (HIV-1) that elucidate microbial forensics relationships. HIV is a rapidly evolving RNA virus [74–76], and thus it is unlikely that even two recently related samples will have exactly the same RNA sequence. (RNA, or ribonucleic acid, is a genetic molecule that comprises the genome of some types of viruses.) Therefore, questions as to what constitutes an association (or the degree of dissimilarity) must be considered. Tools, such as phylogenetic analysis, already exist [77, 78] and are used in supporting or refuting relationships of isolates that have an alleged recent common ancestry with those that do not, with specific regard to the inherent variation in a sample (population) derived from a victim, alleged donor, and control samples. Dr Richard J. Schmidt was accused (and eventually convicted) of second degree attempted murder of his paramour Janice Trahan by injection with HIV [79]. He was accused of preparing a mixture of blood from two of his patients, one infected with HIV and one infected with hepatitis C, and injecting the mixture into Janice Trahan under the guise of it being vitamin B12. Trahan subsequently tested positive for HIV, and sometime thereafter, it was determined that she also suffered from hepatitis C. A microbial forensics/epidemiologic investigation began. The investigation involved epidemiologic factors such as lifestyle, occupation, and past health records. Blood was collected from the alleged HIV positive patient (the original donor of the blood used to infect Trahan), Trahan, and control samples (HIV positive individuals in the vicinity where the patient and victim reside – about 30 local control samples and two database samples). Sequence data were generated from two genes (*gp*120 and *RT*) from HIV isolates from all the samples and subsequent phylogenetic analyses demonstrated a clustering of sequence types from the patient and victim. These results supported the hypothesis that the HIV variants from the original HIV positive patient and Trahan were closely related and more closely related than all control samples obtained [79]. Dr Schmidt is currently serving a 50-year sentence. It should be noted that this particular analysis could not identify the direction of infection (i.e., who infected whom) because of the length of time between infection and diagnosis.

Conclusion

Microbial forensics combines advanced technology with traditional forensic and epidemiologic practices for attribution purposes, initially to determine the source of a bioweapon and ultimately to assist in determining the perpetrator(s) of the bioattack. The consequences of actions from results obtained from a microbial forensics investigation are serious. People's lives and liberty can impinge on the results, governments may take retaliatory action based on the findings, and the public can gain some sense of security from identification of the perpetrator(s). Because of the impact of microbial forensic evidence, scientists should remain ever vigilant and strive to use the best tools available, ensure that high quality assurance and quality control practices are in place, and be extremely cognizant that it is essential to understand the limitations of any analysis, so that the strength of the evidentiary results is not overstated.

References

[1] Bush, L.M., Abrams, B.H., Beall, A. & Johnson, C.C. (2001). Index case of fatal inhalational anthrax due to bioterrorism in the United States, *New England Journal of Medicine* **345**, 1607–1610.

[2] Hsu, V.P., Lukacs, S.L., Handzel, T., Hayslett, J., Harper, S., Hales, T., Semenova, V.A., Romero-Steiner, S., Elie, C., Quinn, C.P., Khabbaz, R., Khan, A.S., Martin, G., Eisold, J., Schuchat, A. & Hajjeh, R.A. (2002). Opening a *Bacillus anthracis*-containing envelope, Capitol Hill, Washington, D.C.: the public health response, *Emerging Infectious Diseases* **8**, 1039–1043.

[3] Jernigan, J.A., Stephens, D.S., Ashford, D.A., Omenaca, C., Topiel, M.S., Galbraith, M., Tapper, M., Fisk, T.L., Zaki, S., Popovic, T., Meyer, R.F., Quinn, C.P., Harper, S.A., Fridkin, S.K., Sejvar, J.J., Shepard, C.W., McConnell, M., Guarner, J., Shieh, W.J., Malecki, J.M., Gerberding, J.L., Hughes, J.M. & Perkins, B.A. (2001). Bioterrorism-related inhalational anthrax: the first 10 cases reported in the United States, *Emerging Infectious Diseases* **7**, 933–944.

[4] Keim, P., Budowle, B. & Ravel, J. (2011). Microbial forensic investigation of the anthrax-letter attacks, in *Microbial Forensics*, 2nd Edition, B. Budowle, S.E. Schutzer, R. Breeze, P.S. Keim & S.A. Morse, eds, Academic Press, Amsterdam, pp. 15–25.

[5] Popovic, T. & Glass, M. (2004). Laboratory aspects of bioterrorism-related anthrax – from identification to molecular subtyping to microbial forensics, *Croatian Medical Journal* **44**, 336–341.

[6] Traeger, M. S., Wiersma, S. T., Rosenstein, N. E., Malecki, J. M., Shepard, C. W., Raghunathan, P. L., Pillai, S. P., Popovic, T., Quinn, C. P., Meyer, R. F., Zaki, S. R., Kumar, S., Bruce, S. M., Sejvar, J. J., Dull, P. M., Tierney, B. C., Jones, J. D. & Perkins, B. A. (2002). First case of bioterrorism-related inhalational anthrax in the United States, Palm Beach County, Florida, 2001, *Emerging Infectious Diseases* **8**, 1029–1034.

[7] Breeze, R.G., Budowle, B. & Schutzer, S. (eds.) (2005). *Microbial Forensics*, Academic Press, Amsterdam.

[8] Budowle, B., Schutzer, S.E., Breeze, R., Keim, P.S. & Morse, S.A. (eds.) (2011). *Microbial Forensics*, 2nd Edition, Academic Press, Amsterdam.

[9] Budowle, B., Murch, R.S. & Chakraborty, R. (2005). Microbial forensics: the next forensic challenge, *International Journal of Legal Medicine* **119**, 317–330.

[10] Budowle, B., Schutzer, S.E., Einseln, A., Kelley, L.C., Walsh, A.C., Smith, J.A.L., Marrone, B.L., Robertson, J. & Campos, J. (2003). Building microbial forensics as a response to bioterrorism, *Science* **301**, 1852–1853.

[11] Budowle, B., Schutzer, S.E., Ascher, M.S., Atlas, R.M., Burans, J.P., Chakraborty, R., Dunn, J.J., Fraser, C.M., Franz, D.R., Leighton, T.J., Morse, S.A., Murch, R.S., Ravel, J., Rock, D.L., Slezak, T.R., Velsko, S.P., Walsh, A.C. & Walters, R.A. (2005). Towards a system of microbial forensics: from sample collection to interpretation of evidence, *Applied and Environmental Microbiology* **71**, 2209–2213.

[12] Budowle, B., Schutzer, S.E., Burans, J.P., Beecher, D.J., Cebula, T.A., Chakraborty, R., Cobb, W.T., Fletcher, J., Hale, M.L., Harris, R.B., Heitkamp, M.A., Keller, F.P., Kuske, C., LeClerc, J.E., Marrone, B.L., McKenna, T.S., Morse, S.A., Rodriguez, L.L., Valentine, N.B. &

Yadev, J. (2006). Quality sample collection, handling, and preservation for an effective microbial forensics program, *Applied and Environmental Microbiology* **72**(10), 6431–6438.

[13] Morse, S.A. & Khan, A.S. (2005). Epidemiologic investigation for public health, biodefense, and forensic microbiology, in *Microbial Forensics*, R. Breeze, B. Budowle & S. Schutzer, eds, Academic Press, Amsterdam, pp. 157–171.

[14] Morse, S. A. & Budowle, B. (2006). Microbial forensics-application to bioterrorism preparedness and response, *Infectious Disease Clinics of North America* **20**, 455–473.

[15] Butler, J. C., Cohen, M.L., Friedman, C.R., Scripp, R.M. & Watz, C.G. (2002). Collaboration between public health and law enforcement: new paradigms and partnerships for bioterrorism planning and response, *Emerging Infectious Disease* **8**, 1152–1156.

[16] Treadwell, T.E., Koo, D., Kuker, K. & Kahn, A.S. (2003). Epidemiologic clues to bioterrorism, *Public Health Reports* **118**, 92–98.

[17] Christopher, G.W., Cieslak, T.J., Pavlin, J.A. & Eitzen, E.M. (1997). Biological warfare: a historical perspective, *JAMA* **278**, 412–417.

[18] http://www.aarc.org/resources/biological/history.asp. Accessed 2011.

[19] Keim, P., Smith, K.L., Keys, C., Takahashi, H., Kurata, T. & Kaufmann, A. (2001). Molecular investigation of the Aum Shinrikyo anthrax release in Kameido, Japan, *Journal of Clinical Microbiology* **39**, 4566–4567.

[20] Robertson, A.G. & Robertson, L.J. (1995). From asps to allegations: biological warfare in history, *Military Medicine* **160**, 369–373.

[21] Carus, S.W. (2006). *Bioterrorism and Biocrimes: The Illicit Use of Biological Agents Since 1900*, Fredonia Books, The Netherlands.

[22] Bügl, H., Danner, J.P., Molinari, R.J., Mulligan, J., Roth, D.A., Wagner, R., Budowle, B., Scripp, R.M., Smith, J.A.L., Steele, S.J., Church, G. & Endy, D. (2007). A practical perspective on DNA synthesis and biological security, *Nature Biotechnology* **25**(6), 627–629.

[23] Cello, J., Paul, A.V. & Wimmer, E. (2002). Chemical synthesis of poliovirus cDNA: generation of infectious virus in the absence of natural template, *Science* **297**, 1016–1018.

[24] Soll, S.J., Neil, S.J. & Bieniasz, P.D. (2010). Identification of a receptor for an extinct virus, *Proceedings of the National Academy of Sciences of the United States of America* **107**(45), 19496–19501. DOI:10.1073/pnas.1012344107

[25] Cottam, E.M., Haydon, D.T., Paton, D.J., Gloster, J., Wilesmith, J.W., Ferris, N.P., Hutchings, G.H. & King, D.P. (2006). Molecular epidemiology of the foot-and-mouth disease virus outbreak in the United Kingdom in 2001, *Journal of Virology* **80**, 11274–11282.

[26] Ferguson, N.M., Donnelly, C.A. & Anderson, R.M. (2001). Transmission intensity and impact of control policies on the foot and mouth epidemic in Great Britain, *Nature* **413**(6855), 542–548.

[27] Thompson, D., Muriel, P., Russell, D., Osborne, P., Bromley, A., Rowland, M., Creigh-Tyte, S. & Brown, C. (2002). Economic costs of the foot and mouth disease outbreak in the United Kingdom in 2001, *Revue Scientifique et Technique* **21**(3), 675–687.

[28] Grigg, B. (1989). *The Cyanide Scare; A Tale of Two Grapes*, U.S. Government Printing Office. http://findarticles.com/p/articles/mi_m1370/is_n6_v23/ai_7755859/print

[29] Neher, N.J. (1999). The need for a coordinated response to food terrorism. The Wisconsin experience, *Annals of the New York Academy of Sciences* **894**, 181–183.

[30] Bailey, B.A., Apel-Birkhold, P.C., Akingbe, O.O., Ryan, J.L., O'Neill, N.R. & Anderson, J.D. (2000). Nep1 Protein from Fusarium oxysporum enhances biological control of opium poppy by *Pleospora papaveracea*, *Phytopathology* **90**(8), 812–818.

[31] Hebbar, K.P., Lumsden, R.D., Lewis, J.A., Poch, S.M. & Bailey, B.A. (1998). *Weed Science* **46**, 501–507.

[32] Arnon, S.S., Schechter, R., Inglesby, T.V., Henderson, D.A., Bartlett, J.G., Ascher, M.S., Eitzen, E., Fine, A.D., Hayer, J., Layton, M., Lillibridge, S., Osterholm, M.T., O'Toole, T., Parker, G., Perl, T.M., Russell, P.K., Swerdlow, D.L. & Tonat, K. (2002). Botulinum toxin as a biological weapon, in *Bioterrorism – Guidelines for Medical and Public Health Management*, D.A. Henderson, T.V. Inglesby & T. OToole, eds, American Medical Association Press, Chicago, pp. 141–165.

[33] CDC website http://www.bt.cdc.gov/agent/agentlist-category.asp. Accessed 2011.

[34] Gill, M.D. (1982). Bacterial toxins: a table of lethal amounts, *Microbiological Reviews* **46**, 86–94.

[35] Marks, J.D. (2011). Forensic aspects of biologic toxins. in *Microbial Forensics*, 2nd Edition, B. Budowle, S.E. Schutzer, R. Breeze, P.S. Keim & S.A. Morse, eds, Academic Press, Amsterdam, pp. 327–353.

[36] Olsnes, S. & Kozlov, J.V. (2001). Ricin, *Toxicon* **39**, 1723–1728.

[37] Knight, B. (1979). Ricin – a potent homicidal poison, *British Medical Journal* **1**(6159), 350–351.

[38] Mayor, S. (2003). UK doctors warned after ricin poison found in police raid, *British Medical Journal* **326**(7381), 126.

[39] Peters, R. P., van Agtmael, M. A., Danner, S. A., Savelkoul, P. H. & Vandenbroucke-Grauls, C.M. (2004). New developments in the diagnosis of bloodstream infections, *The Lancet* **4**, 751–760.

[40] Amann, R.I., Ludwig, W. & Schleifer, K.H. (1995). Phylogenetic identification and *in situ* detection of individual microbial cells without cultivation, *Microbiological Reviews* **59**, 143–169.

[41] Anderson, I.C. & Cairney, J.W.G. (2004). Diversity and ecology of soil fungal communities: increased understanding through the application of molecular techniques, *Environmental Microbiology* **6**, 769–779.

[42] Bridge, P. & Spooner, B. (2001). Soil fungi: diversity and detection, *Plant Soil* **232**, 147–154.

[43] Harayama, S., Kasai, Y. & Hara, A. (2004). Microbial communities in oil-contaminated seawater, *Current Opinion in Biotechnology* **15**, 205–214.

[44] Ranjard, L., Poly, F. & Nazaret, S. (2000). Monitoring complex bacterial communities using culture-independent molecular techniques: application to soil environment, *Research in Microbiology* **151**, 167–177.

[45] Torsvik, V., Goksoyr, J. & Daae, F.L. (1990). High diversity in DNA of soil bacteria, *Applied and Environmental Microbiology* **56**, 782–787.

[46] Zak, J.C. & Visser, S. (1996). An appraisal of soil fungal biodiversity: the crossroads between taxonomic and functional biodiversity, *Biodiversity and Conservation* **5**, 169–183.

[47] Budowle, B. (2004). Genetics and attribution issues that confront the microbial forensics field, *Forensic Science International* **146**(Suppl), S185–S188.

[48] Budowle, B. & Chakraborty, R. (2004). Genetic considerations for interpreting molecular microbial forensic evidence, in *Progress in Forensic Genetics 10*, C. Doutremepuich & N. Morling, eds, Elsevier, Amsterdam, pp. 56–58.

[49] Chakraborty, R. & Budowle, B. (2011). Population genetic considerations in statistical interpretation of microbial forensic data in comparison with the human DNA forensic standard, in *Microbial Forensics*, 2nd Edition, B. Budowle, S.E. Schutzer, R. Breeze, P.S. Keim & S.A. Morse, eds, Academic Press, Amsterdam, pp. 561–580.

[50] Keim, P., Price, L.B., Klevytska, A.M., Smith, K.L., Schupp, J.M., Okinaka, R., Jackson, P.J. & Hugh-Jones, M.E. (2000). Multiple-locus variable-number tandem repeat analysis reveals genetic relationships within *Bacillus anthracis*, *Journal of Bacteriology* **182**, 2928–2936.

[51] Keim, P., Van Ert, M.N., Pearson, T., Vogler, A.J., Huynh, L.Y. & Wagner, D.M. (2004). Anthrax molecular epidemiology and forensics: using the appropriate marker for different evolutionary scales, *Infection, Genetics and Evolution* **4**, 205–213.

[52] Pearson, T., Busch, J.D., Ravel, J., Read, T.D., Rhoton, S.D., U'Ren, J.M., Simonson, T.S., Kachur, S.M., Leadem, R.R., Cardon, M.L., Van Ert, M.N., Huynh, L.Y., Fraser, C.M. & Keim, P. (2004). Phylogenetic discovery bias in *Bacillus anthracis* using single-nucleotide polymorphisms from whole-genome sequencing, *Proceedings of the National Academy of Sciences of the United States of America* **101**(37), 13536–13541.

[53] Budowle, B., Johnson, M.D., Fraser, C.M., Leighton, T.J., Murch, R.S. & Chakraborty, R. (2005). Genetic analysis and attribution of microbial forensics evidence, *Critical Reviews in Microbiology* **31**(4), 233–254.

[54] Read, T.D., Salzberg, S.L., Pop, M., Shumway, M., Umayam, L., Jiang, L., Holtzapple, E., Busch, J.D., Smith, K.L., Schupp, J.M., Solomon, D., Keim, P. & Fraser, C.M. (2002). Comparative genome sequencing for discovery of novel polymorphisms in *Bacillus anthracis*, *Science* **296**, 2028–2033.

[55] Cummings, C.A., Bormann-Chung, C.A., Fang, R., Barker, M., Brzoska, P., Williamson, P.C., Beaudry, J., Matthews, M., Schupp, J., Wagner, D.M., Birdsell, D., Vogler, A.J., Furtado, M.R., Keim, P. & Budowle, B. (2010). Accurate, rapid, and high-throughput detection of strain-specific polymorphisms in *Bacillus anthracis* and *Yersinia pestis* by next-generation sequencing, *BMC Investigative Genetics* **1**, 5.

[56] Holt, K.E., Parkhill, J., Mazzoni, C.J., Roumagnac, P., Weill, F.X., Goodhead, I., Rance, R., Baker, S., Maskell, D.J., Wain, J., Dolecek, C., Achtman, M. & Dougan, G. (2008). High-throughput sequencing provides insights into genome variation and evolution in Salmonella Typhi, *Nature Genetics* **40**, 987–993.

[57] Travers, K.J., Chin, C.S., Rank, D.R., Eid, J.S. & Turner, S.W. (2010). A flexible and efficient template format for circular consensus sequencing and SNP detection, *Nucleic Acids Research* **38**(15), e159.

[58] Margulies, M., Egholm, M., Altman, W.E., Attiya, S., Bader, J.S., Bemben, L.A., Berka, J., Braverman, M.S., Chen, Y.J., Chen, Z., Dewell, S.B., Du, L., Fierro, J.M., Gomes, X.V., Godwin, B.C., He, W., Helgesen, S., Ho, C.H., Irzyk, G.P., Jando, S.C., Alenquer, M.L., Jarvie, T.P., Jirage, K.B., Kim, J.B., Knight, J.R., Lanza, J.R., Leamon, J.H., Lefkowitz, S.M., Lei, M., Li, J., Lohman, K.L., Lu, H., Makhijani, V.B., McDade, K.E., McKenna, M.P., Myers, E.W., Nickerson, E., Nobile, J.R., Plant, R., Puc, B.P., Ronan, M.T., Roth, G.T., Sarkis, G.J., Simons, J.F., Simpson, J.W., Srinivasan, M., Tartaro, K.R., Tomasz, A., Vogt, K.A., Volkmer, G.A., Wang, S.H., Wang, Y., Weiner, M.P., Yu, P., Begley, R.F. & Rothberg, J.M. (2005). Genome sequencing in micro-fabricated high-density picolitre reactors, *Nature* **437**, 376–380.

[59] Oh, J.D., Kling-Bäckhed, H., Giannakis, M., Xu, J., Fulton, R.S., Fulton, L.A., Cordum, H.S., Wang, C., Elliott, G., Edwards, J., Mardis, E.R., Engstrand, L.G. & Gordon, J.I. (2006). The complete genome sequence of a chronic atrophic gastritis *Helicobacter pylori* strain: evolution during disease progression, *Proceedings of the National Academy of Sciences of the United States of America* **103**, 9999–10004.

[60] Quail, M.A., Kozarewa, I., Smith, F., Scally, A., Stephens, P.J., Durbin, R., Swerdlow, H. & Turner, D.J. (2008). A large genome center's improvements to the Illumina sequencing system, *Nature Methods* **5**, 1005–1010.

[61] Wheeler, D.A., Srinivasan, M., Egholm, M., Shen, Y., Chen, L., McGuire, A., He, W., Chen, Y.J., Makhijani, V., Roth, G.T., Gomes, X., Tartaro, K., Niazi, F., Turcotte, C.L., Irzyk, G.P., Lupski, J.R., Chinault, C., Song, X.Z., Liu, Y., Yuan, Y., Nazareth, L., Qin, X., Muzny, D.M., Margulies, M., Weinstock, G.M., Gibbs, R.A. & Rothberg, J.M. (2008). The complete genome of an individual by massively parallel DNA sequencing, *Nature* **452**, 872–876.

[62] Wicker, T., Schlagenhauf, E., Graner, A., Close, T.J., Keller, B. & Stein, N. (2006). 454 sequencing put to the test using the complex genome of barley, *BMC Genomics* **7**, 275.

[63] Kreuzer-Martin, H.W., Chesson, L.A., Lott, M.J., Dorigan, J.V. & Ehleringer, J.R. (2004). Stable isotope ratios as a tool in microbial forensics – Part 1. Microbial isotopic composition as a function of growth medium, *Journal of Forensic Sciences* **49**(5), 954–960.

[64] Kreuzer-Martin, H.W., Chesson, L.A., Lott, M.J., Dorigan, J.V. & Ehleringer, J.R. (2004). Stable isotope ratios as a tool in microbial forensics – Part 2. Isotopic variation among different growth media as a tool for sourcing origins of bacterial cells or spores, *Journal of Forensic Sciences* **49**(5), 961–967.

[65] Kreuzer-Martin, H.W., Chesson, L.A., Lott, M.J. & Ehleringer, J.R. (2005). Stable isotope ratios as a tool in microbial forensics – Part 3. Effect of culturing on agar-containing media, *Journal of Forensic Sciences* **50**(6), 1372–1379.

[66] Velsko, S.P. (2011). Non-biological measurements on biological agents, in *Microbial Forensics*, 2nd Edition, B. Budowle, S.E. Schutzer, R. Breeze, P.S. Keim. & S.A. Morse, eds, Academic Press, Amsterdam, pp. 509–525.

[67] Horner-Devine, M.C., Lage, M., Hughes, J.B. & Bohannan, B.J. (2004). A taxa-area relationship for bacteria, *Nature* **432**, 750–753.

[68] Posada, D. & Crandall, K.A. (2002). The effect of recombination on the accuracy of phylogeny estimation, *Journal of Molecular Evolution* **54**, 396–402.

[69] Schierup, M.H. & Hein, J. (2000). Consequences of recombination on traditional phylogenetic analysis, *Genetics* **156**, 879–891.

[70] Vetsigian, K. & Goldenfeld, N. (2005). Global divergence of microbial genome sequences mediated by propagating fronts, *Proceedings of the National Academy of Sciences of the United States of America* **17**, 7332–7337.

[71] Williamson, P.C., Billingsley, P.M., Teltow, G.J., Seals, J.P., Turnbough, M.A. & Atkinson, S.F. (2010). *Borrelia, Ehrlichia*, and *Rickettsia spp.* in ticks removed from persons, Texas, USA, *Journal of Emerging Infectious Diseases* **16**(3), 441–446.

[72] CDC Health Advisory, Presence of low levels of Francisella tularensis in the Washington D.C. area, Distributed via Health Alert Network, Friday, September 30,

2005;19:37 EDT (7:37 PM EDT). http://www2a.cdc.gov/HAN/ArchiveSys/ViewMsgV.asp?AlertNum=00238

[73] Haensch, S., Bianucci, R., Signoli, M., Rajerison, M., Schultz, M., Kacki, S., Vermunt, M., Weston, D.A., Hurst, D., Achtman, M., Carniel, E. & Bramanti, B. (2010). Distinct clones of *Yersinia pestis* caused the black death, *PLoS Pathogens* **6**(10), ii: e1001134.

[74] Li, W.H., Tanimura, M. & Sharp, P.M. (1988). Rates and dates of divergence between AIDS virus nucleotide sequences, *Molecular Biology and Evolution* **5**, 313–330.

[75] O'Neil, P.K., Sun, G., Yu, H., Ron, Y., Dougherty, J.P. & Preston, B.D. (2002). Mutational analysis of HIV-1 long terminal repeats to explore the relative contribution of reverse transcriptase and RNA polymerase II to viral mutagenesis, *The Journal of Biological Chemistry* **277**, 38053–38061.

[76] Preston, B.D., Poiesz, B.J. & Loeb, L.A. (1988). Fidelity of HIV-1 reverse transcriptase, *Science* **242**, 1168–1171.

[77] Ou, C.Y., Ciesielski, C.A., Myers, G., Bandea, C.I., Luo, C.C., Korber, B.T., Mullins, J.I., Schochetman, G., Berkelman, R.L., Economou, A.N., Witte, J.J., Furman, L.J., Satten, G.A., MacInnes, K.A., Curran, J.W. & Jaffe, H.W. (1992). Molecular epidemiology of HIV transmission in a dental practice, *Science* **256**, 1165–1171.

[78] Robbins, K.E., Weidle, P.J., Brown, T.M., Saekhou, A.M., Coles, B., Holmberg, S.D., Folks, T.M. & Kalish, M.L. (2002). Molecular analysis in support of an investigation of a cluster of HIV-1-infected women, *AIDS Research and Human Retroviruses* **18**, 1157–1161.

[79] Metzker, M.L., Mindell, D.P., Liu, X., Ptak, R.G., Gibbs, R.A. & Hillis, D.M. (2002). Molecular evidence of HIV-1 transmission in a criminal case, *Proceedings of the National Academy of Sciences of the United States of America* **99**, 14292–14297.

Further Reading

Schaldach, C.M., Bench, G., DeYoreo, J.J., Esposito, T., Fergenson, D.P. & Ferreira, J. (2005). Non-DNA methods for biological signatures, in *Microbial Forensics*, R.G. Breeze, B. Budowle & S.E. Schutzer, eds, Elsevier Academic Press, San Diego, pp. 251–294.

Chapter 31
Wildlife Crime

Lucy M.I. Webster

Science and Advice for Scottish Agriculture, Edinburgh, UK

Introduction

Wildlife crime encompasses a huge range of offences where the victim is not a human but a plant, animal, or even a natural habitat. Examples can be varied: from the killing of a wild African rhinoceros for its horn, to the removal and sale of bluebell (*Hyacinthoides non-scripta*) bulbs from British woodlands. While the specific laws relating to wildlife crime vary greatly from country to country, they exist to protect rare species and habitats from exploitation and to prevent inhumane or unlawful treatment of more common species.

Public consciousness of wildlife crime has grown over the past 20 years as iconic species such as the tiger continues to be put under pressure from illegal exploitation and becomes increasingly rare in spite of huge conservation efforts.

From an enforcement perspective, it is now recognized that organized criminal gangs are heavily involved in the illegal wildlife trade as they perceive it as a lucrative source of income with low risk of detection [1]. As a result, police forces require more and more sophisticated detection techniques to tackle these highly motivated criminals, and the evidence produced must be robust to judicial scrutiny. As with any other crime, many specialist forensic analyses can now be applied in wildlife crime investigations [2, 3]. One of the key methods is the analysis of nonhuman DNA evidence.

DNA can be thought of as a database of coded information that all organisms carry around with them in their cells. Parts of animals and plants (e.g., feathers, hair, leaves, and roots) will also contain cellular material, from which the DNA can be extracted and queried for specific details that are useful for wildlife crime investigations.

In the following sections, the methods used to address common queries for DNA analysis in wildlife crime investigations are described with real case studies to illustrate the application of techniques.

Species Identification

One of the most common questions asked by wildlife crime investigators is "What species is this?". This most often arises when animal or plant parts are recovered by enforcement at some point in the supply chain, and the laws relating to trade are species-specific. In order to establish whether an offence has been committed the identification of the species is necessary.

Within each organism's DNA, there are regions that show very low variation between individuals from the same species but are more variable when the same region is compared among species. These regions provide a DNA sequence – sometimes called a *DNA barcode* [4] – which can be used to identify which species the part of an animal or plant has come from when other methods are not possible or practical. The DNA sequence is produced by first extracting the DNA from the evidence, amplifying the region of interest, and then adding fluorescent dyes to each individual nucleotide in the DNA sequence by a process known as *Sanger sequencing* (a good description of this method can be found in [5]). These fluorescently labeled products can then be "read" in order using a capillary DNA sequencer, recognizing a string of nucleotide bases (A, C, G, and T depending on dye attached), which form the DNA sequence for data analysis. By generating a DNA sequence from the

A Guide to Forensic DNA Profiling
Edited by Allan Jamieson and Scott Bader
© 2016 Crown Copyright
© 2016 John Wiley & Sons, Ltd in the rest of the world
ISBN: 9781118751527
Also published in EFS (online edition)
DOI: 10.1002/9780470061589.fsa1085

evidence and comparing it with a validated reference database, species identification is possible from a wide range of evidence types (e.g., blood, feathers, hair, leaves, and wood chips).

For animals, the regions usually used for species identification are the mitochondrial genes cytochrome B and cytochrome oxidase I. Each of these genes has been validated for use in species identification in a forensic context [6, 7], and a variety of tests have been published in the scientific literature based on these regions (reviewed in [4]).

In wildlife crime investigations, the species identification test applied to evidence can be applicable to a wide range of animal species [6, 8–10], but in some cases, a more specific test is required, for example, where DNA from multiple species may be present (see Case Study 1). These tests can also be applied in a wider context to identify fraud in our food chain (see Case Study 2).

Case Study 1: Egg Collecting

Egg collecting was a hobby made popular in Victorian times, and involves the taking of wild bird eggs from their nests and preserving the empty shell for display. However, this hobby can have a catastrophic effect on rare bird populations and was made illegal in the United Kingdom in 1954. In spite of this law change, persistent offenders repeatedly build up large collections.

One such offender was arrested in Scotland in 2011. Local residents had reported a man acting suspiciously around bird breeding sites. Wildlife crime officers were aware that the suspect had previous convictions for egg collecting and they recovered blown eggs and a set of implements thought to be an egg-blowing kit from his belongings. Officers wished to establish whether he had taken wild bird eggs and blown them using this kit – a separate offence from simply possessing blown eggs.

Swab samples were taken from various locations on the kit but standard tests gave a mixed DNA sequence, suggesting contributions from multiple bird species preventing any specific identification. The laboratory was given the names of five species the suspect may have targeted – including the Manx shearwater, a species of European conservation concern.

Species-specific tests were then designed to selectively amplify DNA from these five species. These tests were applied to the DNA extracts obtained from the kit, yielding positive results for three species – including the Manx shearwater. The suspect was prosecuted for several offences, including the taking of wild bird eggs. He received a 6-month custodial sentence and a lifetime ban on entering Scotland during the bird-breeding season.
Wildlife DNA Forensics unit, SASA, Edinburgh, UK

Species identification by DNA sequencing is, however, not always straightforward. In an ideal world, the same region would be used for all animal or plant species but this will not always give us the resolution we need for species identification [11]. For many plant species, a combination of two genes may be required for species-level identification and the ideal combination of genes for this may be different depending on which group of plants the species belongs [12]. Further complications include historic hybridization events [13], and the presence of multiple variants of the DNA barcoding region within a single organism [14]. An understanding of the strength of any DNA test for species identification, in addition to the use of a verified database for comparison, is imperative for such results to be used as evidence for wildlife crime investigations.

Case Study 2: Widespread Seafood Fraud Revealed Using DNA-Based Species Identification

In 2004, National Oceanic and Atmospheric Administration (NOAA) Special Agents in the United States suspected that certain companies and individuals were involved in seafood substitution and mislabeling schemes on a massive scale. In the following years, NOAA forensic scientists analyzed hundreds of samples from import shipments labeled as "wild-caught grouper" and "sole" and used genetic sequence analysis in the laboratory to reveal that the product was actually from *Pangasius hypophthalmus,* a farm-raised species of Asian catfish. This species is much less valuable than its advertised counterpart, making it difficult for law-abiding fishermen to compete and impossible for consumers to know what species they were purchasing. In more than a dozen cases, individuals and companies either pleaded or were found guilty in court of numerous mislabeling and fraud charges and sentenced to a combination of multiyear prison terms, probation, asset forfeitures, and/or monetary penalties in the millions (USD). Seafood substitution has escaped detection for decades, but the application of genetic technologies to such challenges has expanded the ability of law enforcement to pursue these substitution schemes.

Marine Forensics Program, NOAA, Charleston, USA

DNA Profiling

This type of analysis exploits regions of DNA that are variable between individuals of the *same* species. Provided these variations are quantifiable, and inherited in the expected manner from parent to offspring, DNA profiling can be used to address several issues.

In most cases, the regions of DNA used for profiling are *short tandem repeats* (STRs) – the same type of marker applied in human DNA profiling [15]. However, because STRs are often specific to a particular species, the methodology must be validated for purpose prior to use in criminal casework for each species.

Individual Identification

It is common for investigators to request an assessment of two samples recovered from different locations to see if they came from the same individual animal or plant (see Case Study 3). If one sample was found in the possession of a suspect, and another from a crime scene, it is necessary to demonstrate that two samples match with high statistical probability and are therefore are likely to be from the same individual. This requires not only thoroughly validated DNA profiling methods, but also background information on the genetics of the animal or plant population that the samples came from. This background information provides the details necessary to calculate the statistical probability that the samples could have matched by chance [16]. Where this value is very low, for example, a one-in-ten-million probability that the samples match by chance, this gives weight to the argument that the samples are from the same individual.

Specimen Origin

For many rare species, legislation regarding their protected status is dependent on its population of origin. For instance, different laws or regulations may apply to captive vs. wild populations, and indeed for some species, certain wild populations are protected, whereas others are not. An example of this is for ostriches, which are not threatened globally, but the fragile populations in some countries are protected from trade [17].

Captive populations of endangered species exist for many reasons, but often it is when the animal in question is valuable either in the pet trade (e.g., tortoises and birds of prey), or if products from the animal or plant are prized commodities (e.g., caviar producing sturgeon and vanilla producing orchids). The question can then arise – when a product is recovered in trade – is it from a captive population, an unprotected wild population, or a protected wild population?

Case Study 3: Individual Identification Matches Samples from Eagle Remains

Bald and golden eagles are two of the largest raptors in the United States, and both are revered in native cultures. Possession of bald eagle feathers or parts is restricted to official members of native tribes, and sale of eagle feathers or parts is prohibited. As a result, a black market exists for eagle feathers and parts, which fuels illegal exploitation of both species. Morphological identification is the primary method used to determine species origin of eagle feathers. DNA-based species identification techniques are useful for determining origin of items, which cannot be identified to species with traditional morphological techniques, such as blood or downy feathers. DNA profiling techniques are essential when feathers and parts removed from eagles need to be matched back to a carcass or other parts.

DNA tests for species identification were applied to a case in which multiple eagle carcasses were exhumed from banks along the Missouri River in the central United States, and eagle feathers and body parts (beaks, feet, and talons) were confiscated from several suspects. DNA samples taken from the decomposing buried birds, and the confiscated feathers and body parts were identified as bald eagle.

Individual identification analyses were conducted on each of the evidence items to determine if any of the feathers or body parts originated from the same individual, or from any of the exhumed bald eagle carcasses. DNA tests revealed that three sets of feathers and body parts originated from three different eagles, and each could be matched to three of the exhumed carcasses. The remaining feathers, body parts, and seven carcasses were shown to have originated from an additional 10 individual bald eagles. The suspects were charged with several wildlife offences relating to bald and golden eagles.

US Fish and Wildlife Service Forensics Laboratory, Ashland, USA

Official documentation should clarify these origins but if this is not present, or suspicious for other reasons, analysis of DNA profiling data can be used to determine the answer.

Parentage analysis requires DNA from the parents of the individual animal in question, and to establish if the DNA from the offspring is consistent with the parents' (see Case Study 4).

Case Study 4: Goshawk Parentage Analysis: Captive or Wild?

Falconry is a popular pastime, and captive birds of prey can be worth large sums of money for sporting and breeding purposes. In many countries it is now illegal to take birds of prey from the wild for use in falconry, to protect their natural populations. The legally required registration documents held for captive birds of prey in the United Kingdom will include unique identifiers of the bird (e.g., leg ring or microchip) and the identity of its parents. Falsification of these registration documents can occur if birds have been illegally taken from the wild.

In one such case, an owner requested new registration documentation as his female goshawk had lost her leg ring. However, an investigation was launched when the female bird was examined and found to be missing a registered microchip as well as her leg ring. DNA samples were taken from this female, her mate, and one of their registered offspring who was with a different owner, having been sold several years before.

Parentage analysis on DNA profiles from these three birds revealed that the female could not have been the mother of the offspring. It was believed that the registered female had died, and the owner had taken a wild goshawk to take her place for breeding purposes.

TRACE Wildlife Forensics Network, Edinburgh, UK

Geographic assignment, potentially used when only specific populations have legal protection, relies on established differences in DNA profile data among different populations (such as wild and captive) of the species in question. By comparing the DNA profile with a database of captive and wild populations, it can be possible to assign the specimen as having originated from one of these with a clear level of statistical confidence.

Limits of Detection

The different tests described here require different amounts of material in order to work. For species identification, the regions used for DNA barcoding are found in multiple copies within a cell. This means that this test can be successful with trace amounts of biological material – as little as a few cells. For DNA profiling, however, more starting material will be required to work effectively as the DNA regions targeted may only be present in one copy per cell – or even not present at all in the case of mammalian red blood cells. By way of an example, while a species identification test is likely to be successful from a single hair, a DNA profile is much less likely to succeed. Different starting material will also influence the likelihood of success. Skin and muscle tissue from animals is preferential to bone and hair, and DNA analysis from feces is not recommended.

While the amount and type of starting material is important, the way DNA evidence has been found and the length of time it has been exposed to environmental degradation will also impact on the success of different tests. Factors that influence the quality of DNA evidence are discussed elsewhere in relation to human DNA [18], but these will also be applicable in wildlife DNA forensic testing.

Emerging Techniques

Identification of species can be problematic if the evidence recovered is a mixture of several species and the likely contributors are unknown, making species-specific tests impossible (e.g., unlabeled Traditional Asian Medicine). While new methodologies in DNA sequencing now enable mixed samples to be analyzed and for the different species components to be isolated and identified, these methods have not been formally validated for use in wildlife forensics at the time of writing (2013). However, given the potential extra information that could be gleaned from each sample using these techniques it is likely that they will be validated and put to use in the not-too-distant future.

While STR markers are the standard for many DNA profiling tests, they experience several issues that, in practice, can make them problematic. Specifically, the development of new STR markers is time consuming, and validation for forensic use is lengthy and they can be problematic to transfer between laboratories. An alternative method for profiling uses multiple markers known as *single nucleotide polymorphisms* (SNPs), which are single base variations in DNA sequence. While more SNP than STR markers would be necessary to generate profiles with sufficient statistical power for individual identification, the simpler process of identifying SNP markers, validating them for forensic use, and transferring between labs mean they are likely to supersede STR markers for DNA profiling in wildlife forensics.

Standards

The high quality standards achieved for forensic analysis of human DNA is the benchmark wildlife DNA forensic analysis must meet [19]. Validating the methods to this level of quality assurance, such that the described tests are available for most species, will, however, take time given the number of species to cover. There are 30 000 species listed on the Convention for International Trade in Endangered Species of Flora and Fauna (CITES) alone (http://www.cites.org/eng/disc/species.php), and many more could be involved in aspects of wildlife crime, which do not involve endangered species.

The Society for Wildlife Forensic Sciences (SWFS) was established in 2009 and has produced a white paper of standards and guidelines for DNA analysis via the working group for wildlife forensic sciences (SWGWILD). A certification scheme based on these standards was launched in 2013, to encourage the highest standards among wildlife forensic laboratories across the world (http://www.wildlifeforensicscience.org/swgwild).

Acknowledgments

I would like to thank Trey Knott (NOAA, USA), Mary Burnham-Curtis (US Fish and Wildlife Service Forensics Laboratory), and Ross McEwing (TRACE Wildlife Forensics Network) for contributing case studies used in this article.

References

[1] Zimmerman, M.E. (2003). The black market for wildlife: combating transnational organized crime in the illegal wildlife trade, *Vanderbilt Journal of Transnational Law* **36**(5), 1657–1690.

[2] Goddard, K. (2009). Wildlife, in *Wiley Encyclopedia of Forensic Science*, John Wiley & Sons Ltd, Chichester, UK. pp. 1–6.

[3] Huffman, J.E. & Wallace, J.R. (eds) (2012). *Wildlife Forensics: Methods and Applications*, Wiley-Blackwell, Chichester, UK.

[4] Kress, W.J. & Erickson, D.L. (2012). DNA barcodes: methods and protocols, in *Methods in Molecular Biology*, Humana Press, New York, USA, pp. 3–8 Vol. 858.

[5] Men, A.E., Wilson, P., Siemering, K. & Forrest, S. (2008). Sanger DNA sequencing, in *Next-Generation Genome Sequencing: Towards Personalized Medicine*, Wiley-Blackwell, Weinheim, Germany, pp. 3–11.

[6] Dawnay, N., Ogden, R., McEwing, R., Carvalho, G.R. & Thorpe, R.S. (2007). Validation of the barcoding gene COI for use in forensic genetic species identification, *Forensic Science International* **173**(1), 1–6.

[7] Branicki, W., Kupiec, T. & Pawlowski, R. (2003). Validation of cytochrome b sequence analysis as a method of species identification, *Journal of Forensic Sciences* **48**(1), 83–7.

[8] Verma, S.K. & Singh, L. (2002). Novel universal primers establish identity of an enormous number of animal species for forensic application, *Molecular Ecology Notes* **3**(1), 28–31.

[9] Ivanova, N.V., Zemlak, T.S., Hanner, R. & Hebert, P.D.N. (2007). Universal primer cocktails for fish DNA barcoding, *Molecular Ecology Notes* **7**(4), 544–548.

[10] Hebert, P.D.N., Stoeckle, M.Y., Zemlak, T.S. & Francis, C.M. (2004). Identification of birds through DNA barcodes, *PLoS Biology* **2**(10), e312.

[11] Vences, M., Thomas, M., Bonett, R.M. & Vieites, D.R. (2005). Deciphering amphibian diversity through DNA barcoding: chances and challenges, *Philosophical Transactions of the Royal Society of London. Series B, Biological Sciences* **360**(1462), 1859–68.

[12] Hollingsworth, P.M., Graham, S.W. & Little, D.P. (2011). Choosing and using a plant DNA barcode, *PloS One* **6**(5), e19254.

[13] Ludwig, A. (2008). Identification of acipenseriformes species in trade, *Journal of Applied Ichthyology* **24**(Suppl. 1), 2–19.

[14] Ribeiro Leite, L.A. (2012). Mitochondrial pseudogenes in insect DNA barcoding: differing points of view on the same issue, *Biota Neotropica* **12**(3), 301–308.

[15] Bright, J.-A. (2009). Short tandem repeats, in *Wiley Encyclopedia of Forensic Science*, John Wiley & Sons Ltd, Chichester, UK.

[16] Weir, B.S. (2012). Statistics for wildlife forensic DNA, in *Wildlife Forensics: Methods and Applications*, Wiley-Blackwell, Chichester, UK, pp. 237–252.

[17] UNEP-WCMC (2013). UNEP-WCMC Species Database: CITES-Listed Species.

[18] Gilder, J.R. (2009). DNA: degraded samples, in *Wiley Encyclopedia of Forensic Science*, John Wiley & Sons Ltd, Chichester, UK.

[19] Moore, M.K. & Kornfield, I.L. (2012). Best practices in wildlife forensic DNA, in *Wildlife Forensics: Methods and Applications*, Wiley-Blackwell, Chichester, UK, pp. 201–231.

Related Articles

Degraded Samples

Related Articles in EFS Online

Short Tandem Repeats

Wildlife

PART D
Court

Chapter 32
DNA Databases – The Significance of Unique Hits and the Database Controversy

Ronald Meester

VU University Amsterdam, Amsterdam, The Netherlands

Introduction and the Controversy

Suppose we have a DNA profile found at the scene of a crime and also suppose that there are good reasons to believe that the profile comes from (one of) the criminal(s). If we select an individual with this DNA profile, then this individual may become a suspect in the case. There are, however, different ways to select an individual with the DNA profile found at the scene of the crime, and in this article, we are concerned with the evidential value of the match for various selection procedures. More precisely, we will distinguish between two different situations.

1. There is a person already identified as a suspect before the DNA profile came up. It so happens that the profile matches with this suspect.
2. We run the profile through a database of DNA profiles, and it so happens that there is a unique hit. The person corresponding to this becomes a suspect in the case.

In which of the two situations is the DNA evidence against the suspect larger? Is there a number that correctly reflects the "evidential value" of a unique hit in a database search? These simple questions have inspired a significant number of papers in the statistical forensic literature [1–11], and in this article, we try to explain why this question has been so controversial and how the controversy can be resolved.

There are at least two conflicting intuitive ideas concerning the strength of the database case versus the cold case.

These conflicting ideas can be summarized in a few lines, and they provide a good starting point for the discussion. Let us refer to the first of the two situations as the *cold case* and to the second as the *database case*.

View 1: One can argue that the evidential value of a database hit is much *larger* than in the cold case. Indeed, having a unique hit in a database simply means that all the other persons in the database are innocent. Therefore, we have the same information as in the cold case, plus the extra information that many other people are innocent. Clearly, this increases the weight of the evidence against the suspect. For support of View 1, see e.g., [1, 5] and [4].

View 2: On the other hand, one can argue that, in the database case, the evidential value of the hit is much *smaller* than in the cold case. If the frequency of the DNA profile is, say, 1 in a million and the database consists of, say, 1 million profiles, then it is quite reasonable to expect a match just by pure chance. If we assume that all persons in the database are innocent, then still there is a probability of about 0.63 that there will be a match. Therefore, a match in the database does not say very much, and the evidential value of a database match therefore is probably small. Here are the words of a proponent of this view (quote from [6] as an answer to criticism on an earlier article [10]):

> What to recommend in a case in which, after finding exactly one match in a database of size 630.000 […]. The random match probability with 5 analyzed STR loci is in the magnitude of 1 in 600.000. It is in our view inconceivable to assume, in such a situation, that the evidential value due

A Guide to Forensic DNA Profiling
Edited by Allan Jamieson and Scott Bader
© 2016 John Wiley & Sons, Ltd. ISBN: 9781118751527
Also published in EFS (online edition)
DOI: 10.1002/9780470061589.fsa1036

to the database is higher than without a database search. Rather, it seems that the contrary is of significance.

Which of the two views is correct? In order to address this question we have to be more precise about what we mean by "evidential value". A reasonable and standard way to quantify the evidential value is via a so-called likelihood ratio. The procedure leading to such a likelihood ratio is as follows. We set up two competing hypotheses; in our case, the first hypothesis is "The suspect left the DNA stain" and the competing hypothesis is "The suspect did not leave the DNA stain". Often, the first hypothesis is called H_p where the "p" stands for "prosecutor", and the second hypothesis is called H_d where the "d" stands for "defense". We next compare the probability of seeing the evidence under both hypotheses by computing the ratio

$$\frac{\text{the probability of the evidence given } H_p}{\text{the probability of the evidence given } H_d}. \quad (1)$$

This ratio is called the likelihood ratio. If this number is high, it implies strong evidence against the suspect because the probability of seeing the evidence is much higher when he/she is guilty than when he/she is innocent.

It seems, therefore, that we would be able to make a choice between the two views above by simply computing the likelihood ratios corresponding to the above two cases. Let me now sketch how this can be done, starting with the cold case.

The basic assumption is that DNA profiles of different people are independent and that for any profile there is a probability p that a given person has this profile. A smaller p simply means that the profile occurs less frequently. Clearly, the independence assumption is not met in reality because of, for instance, family relations, but it is well worth the effort to see what conclusion we can draw from a somewhat simplified situation.

Suppose the DNA profile found at the scene of the crime has a frequency p and suppose the suspect is guilty. The probability to observe the evidence in that case is simply 1 (or 100%, but we prefer probabilities to be numbers between 0 and 1). On the other hand, if the person is not guilty, the probability of seeing the evidence is p; indeed if the suspect is not guilty, then some unknown person has committed the crime, and the probability that he/she has this profile is just p. This

means that in the cold case, the likelihood ratio LR_c (the "c" stands for "cold") is equal to

$$LR_c = \frac{1}{p}, \quad (2)$$

and this makes intuitive sense: when the profile is very rare this implies a very small p and therefore a very high likelihood ratio.

Next we would like to perform a similar computation, with the same set of hypotheses in the database case, but this is slightly more complicated. It turns out that the likelihood ratio LR_d (the "d" stands for "database") in this situation can only be computed if we have more information, namely, the size N of the total population in question and the size n of the database. Given these two numbers, the likelihood ratio turns out to be equal to

$$LR_d = \frac{1}{p} \times \frac{N-1}{N-n}; \quad (3)$$

we explain this number in the Appendix. This number is larger than LR_c, giving support to View 1.

One may wonder what else there is to discuss. However, the situation is not at all that simple, for the following reason. It is fairly obvious in statistical matters that it is "not allowed" to use a data set first to find a reasonable hypothesis and then use the same dataset again to test this hypothesis. Indeed, one can tailor a hypothesis around a dataset, but then the very same dataset should not be used for testing this hypothesis. And yet, this is precisely what happens in the database problem. *After* looking at the data, that is, after we have found that there is a unique match in the database, we set up the hypothesis that the unique matching person is the criminal. Clearly, we have tailored the hypothesis around the data. It is, therefore, reasonable to say that one is simply not allowed to do this, and therefore, the above-mentioned hypotheses H_p and H_d leading to equation (4) should not be used when a suspect has been found through a database search.

Considerations of this type led the authors of the second National Research Council (NRCII) [9] to the conclusion that the likelihood ratio LR_d in the database case should be divided by the size of the database, as a correction for the effect that we described; this correction goes by the name "the *np*-rule". Stockmarr [11] took this point even further, providing a formal basis for the suggestion in NRCII. He suggested using the hypothesis "The database contains the criminal" versus "The database does not contain the criminal" instead of H_p and H_d, respectively; these hypotheses clearly do not depend on the data. Furthermore, *after* observing the data (that is, after observing the DNA profile at the scene of the crime and, in addition, a unique match in the database), this new set of hypotheses is completely equivalent to the old set. After having observed that there is a unique match, the statement that the database contains the criminal is the same as saying that the unique matching person is the criminal.

The obvious next question is what the likelihood ratio (we call it LR_s where the "s" stands for "Stockmarr") for this new set of hypotheses is. In this case, the computation is quite simple. Under the assumption that the database contains the criminal, the probability to have a unique match is just $(1 - p)^{n-1}$ since all the other persons in the database should not have the profile. If the database does not contain the criminal, then the probability that a given person in the database matches uniquely is given by $p(1 - p)^{n-1}$, and since there are n persons in the database, the total probability of a unique match is $np(1 - p)^{n-1}$. It follows that the likelihood ratio LR_s is equal to

$$LR_s = \frac{(1 - p)^{n-1}}{np(1 - p)^{n-1}} = \frac{1}{np}, \quad (4)$$

explaining the name "np-rule", confirming the advice of the NRCII, and supporting View 2, since the division by n leads to a much smaller likelihood ratio than in the cold case.

In a way, it is not surprising that LR_d and LR_s are different: after all, they refer to different sets of hypothesis so why should they be the same? It has been remarked by many authors that Stockmarr simply addresses the wrong question, since it is certainly not the database that is on trial (see, for instance, *Databases*, which partially overlaps with this contribution.)

Nevertheless, there is a problem. Recall the fact that the two sets of hypotheses are *equivalent* after seeing the evidence. So we have two sets of hypothesis, equivalent after seeing the evidence, and yet giving rise to different likelihood ratios, equations (3) and (4). Hence this raises doubts to the reasonableness of the method via likelihood ratios itself since it appears that the value of the likelihood ratio might depend on the particular way we phrase the hypotheses. However, there are

many other situations in which various natural sets of hypotheses can be set up, leading to different likelihood ratios; see e.g., [7] for some examples.

This is the essence of the database controversy. In the next section, I discuss a way to resolve the problems, at least from a mathematical point of view, by concentrating on another quantity, namely the posterior odds.

Posterior Odds

The controversy that we have described is based on the idea that a forensic expert can and should only report a likelihood ratio. Confronted with forensic evidence, a judge or lawyer will ask a forensic expert about the evidential value of the evidence: "What does this mean and how strong is the evidence?". The likelihood ratio is a quantity that can (in principle) be computed by a forensic expert or statistician, explaining the popularity of this number.

However, it should be equally clear that the likelihood is not of immediate interest *in itself*. After all, the judge is in the first place interested in the probability (whatever meaning one wants to assign to this word) that a suspect is in fact the criminal. Hence, the judge is in the first place interested in

$$\frac{\text{the probability that the suspect is guilty given the evidence}}{\text{the probability that the suspect is not guilty given the evidence}}, \quad (5)$$

and this really is something different from the likelihood ratio in equation 1. The quantity in equation (5) is called the posterior odds, since it describes the relation between the probability of guilt and the probability of not being guilty, *after* seeing the evidence. The posterior odds should be compared to the *prior odds*, which describes the same ratio but this time *before* seeing the evidence.

There is a simple relation between the likelihood ratio in equation (1), the posterior odds in equation (5), and the prior odds. Basic probability, in particular Bayes' rule, tells us that

Posterior odds = Likelihood ratio × Prior odds; (6)

We give more details on this in the Appendix. The likelihood ratio can hence be seen as only "updating" the odds after seeing the DNA evidence. As mentioned above, the likelihood ratio can be provided by a forensic expert, but the prior odds have nothing to do with the DNA evidence; after all, the prior odds are computed *before* seeing the DNA evidence. Therefore, the prior odds are for the judge to evaluate or estimate. The interpretation of what "probability" means in this context is debatable, but whatever interpretation is used, equation (6) will hold.

Seen this way, it becomes clear that the final posterior odds, that is, the final evaluation of the probability of guilt, is a *joint effort* of both the judge and the expert – one needs input from both in order to arrive at the meaningful quantity called the posterior odds.

Can we compute the posterior odds? Well, we can compute them if we have information about the prior odds, and this is not an easy matter since they may depend on the individual considerations of a judge or lawyer. However, we can see what so-called uniform priors will lead to, for all three situations described above. A uniform prior means that a priori, all persons in the relevant population have equal probability to be the criminal.

The cold case. The (uniform) prior probability that a given person is the criminal is $1/N$, with N the size of the population. The prior probability that the person is not the criminal is $(N - 1)/N$. This leads to prior odds of

$$\frac{1/N}{(N-1)/N} = \frac{1}{N-1}.$$

Hence the posterior odds are

$$\text{LR}_c \times \frac{1}{N-1} = \frac{1}{p(N-1)}. \tag{7}$$

This makes sense intuitively: when the population gets larger, the evidence gets weaker as it should.

View 1. The prior odds are the same as in the cold case, namely, $1/(N-1)$. Hence, the posterior odds are

$$\text{LR}_d \times \frac{1}{N-1} = \frac{1}{p(N-n)}. \tag{8}$$

View 2. According to the defenders of this view, the relevant hypotheses are phrased in terms of the probability that the database contains the criminal. The prior odds for the corresponding set of hypotheses are different now. The prior probability that the database contains the criminal is n/N, and the prior probability that the database does not contain the criminal is equal to $(N - n)/N$. Hence the prior odds are

$$\frac{n/N}{(N-n)/N} = \frac{n}{N-n}.$$

It follows that the posterior odds are

$$\text{LR}_s \times \frac{n}{N-n} = \frac{1}{p(N-n)}, \tag{9}$$

the *same* posterior odds as in the computation corresponding to View 1.

What can we conclude from all this? First of all, it is important to note that the posterior odds in equations (8) and (9) are the same. As far as the probability that the suspect is in fact the criminal is concerned, it is irrelevant which of the two views one adopts. In fact, it is not difficult to see that posterior odds will always be the same as soon as two sets of hypotheses are equivalent after seeing the evidence, see e.g., [3] and [7], and to some extent, this solves the controversy, at least from a purely mathematical point of view. It suggests that the quantity of interest is not the likelihood ratio in itself, but the posterior odds that are obtained by multiplying the likelihood ratio with the prior odds.

The question as to which number correctly expresses the evidential value of a unique database match is, therefore, not a very well-defined question. If we adopt the hypotheses that the uniquely matching person is guilty versus not guilty, then the evidential value (the likelihood ratio) is high, but in the final posterior odds this is compensated by very low prior odds. If we choose the second set of hypotheses, namely, the database contains the criminal versus its complement, then the evidential value (the likelihood ratio) is much smaller, but this is reasonable since we start with much higher prior odds.

When a forensic expert reports a likelihood ratio, it is important that a judge or lawyer knows which hypotheses were used and that in order to evaluate the strength of the case, they should be aware of the fact that a likelihood ratio in itself is not immediately relevant. In order to compute posterior odds, the (possibly very low) prior odds should be taken into account. In other words, even when the evidential value of a match is (very) high, this number has to be interpreted in the full context of all facts and circumstances. If the circumstances lead to low prior odds, for instance, via witness statements or otherwise, then the case as a whole may not be that strong, even taking into account the DNA evidence.

How Do Courts Deal with the Issue?

It is fairly obvious that the above discussion is somewhat difficult to explain to nonmathematicians like legal representatives. How do courts deal with the issue? Here, the situation is not so clear. There are many examples in the literature that testify to the idea that many courts do not avoid the so-called prosecutor's fallacy, which means that they do not know how to distinguish between the probability of the evidence given a hypothesis on one hand and the probability of a hypothesis given the evidence on the other. In many cases, this leads to the idea that the evidence is much stronger than it actually is.

Sometimes the legal system makes it impossible to do justice to the statistics, for instance, in systems where the jury is not allowed to know how the suspect has been selected. In particular, the jury is not allowed to know whether or not the suspect was found via a database search. It is evident that, in such a situation, the statistical issues cannot be dealt with in any reasonable way.

On the other hand, there are not many cases in which a DNA profile is the only connection between suspect and crime. I have found only one recent case in The Netherlands in which there was a matching DNA profile and *nothing* else; the suspect in this case was not convicted. One of the reasons that suspects are not convicted despite DNA evidence is that hypotheses are often phrased on the activity level ("How did the DNA get there?") rather than at the source level ("Is the DNA from suspect?"). In other words, the bare presence of DNA that could possibly be from the suspect is not automatically seen as decisive evidence. In light of the discussion above, this is quite reasonable since we could very well be in a situation with extremely small prior odds.

The NFI (Netherlands Forensic Institute) has formulated the following warning when reporting likelihood ratios of database matches (my translation):

> As the number of DNA profiles increases, the probability of a match with a person other than the donor increases. The DNA profile of this person matches 'by chance'. One should be especially aware of this possibility in case of mixed profiles and incomplete

profiles – indeed in these case the scientific evidential value is smaller than in case of a complete profile. In order to assess the possibility that the match is by accident, it is important to decide whether or not there are other reasons to link this person with the crime.

It is, in my opinion, highly debatable whether or not this warning is a reasonable summary of the difficulties involved, since the warning does not provide any practical hints as how to deal with likelihood ratios provided by the forensic expert. In particular, it remains rather vague as how to assess, use, and interpret the prior odds, which fall outside the provenance of the forensic or statistical expert.

Some Final Remarks and Conclusion

Returning to the original question as to whether a unique database hit is stronger or weaker than a cold case, we simply note that the posterior odds in the cold case are $1/p(N-1)$ (this is just equation (7)), whereas in the database case, the posterior odds are given by $1/p(N-n)$, irrespective of the view one adopts (this is just equations (8) or (9)). Of course, these odds were computed under the assumption of uniform priors, but nevertheless, they indicate that in principle, the database case constitutes a stronger case against the suspect, since the posterior odds are higher than in the cold case. So after all, the effect that other persons are excluded as the criminal outweighs the effect that a unique match is possibly based on bad luck, and in that sense it is fair to say that the intuition behind View 1 is correct.

It appears from equations (8) and (9) that a larger database, that is, a larger n, leads to higher posterior odds, suggesting that a larger database is "better". However, this is partially misleading, since we have performed our calculations based on the *assumption* that there is a unique hit. When the database gets larger, it is possible that the probability of a unique hit itself gets smaller so that the effectiveness of the database in fact goes down, see e.g., [8] for a discussion on this effect.

Recent research on this topic focuses on at least two different issues. First, there has been some effort in the use of Bayesian networks, see e.g., [2]. These networks are very suitable for demystifying and clarifying probabilistic effects. By designing a network involving all input parameters and relations in the model, it becomes very transparent how certain assumptions affect the probability of certain hypotheses. Careful considerations of Bayesian networks reinforce the fact that the mathematics of the situation is not the problem, but the interpretation and skillful use is.

Second, recently there has also been some attention to a generalization of database search called "familial searching". This is the search for *relatives* of a criminal rather than the criminal itself; see e.g., [8] and references therein. The statistical problems encountered in the database controversy play an even bigger role in familial searching, and the issue of evidential value plays a crucial role here as well. In addition, several search strategies are possible, and this complicates the situation considerably.

Appendix

The Formula for LR_d in equation (3)

Suppose that the suspect is guilty. What is the probability of the observed evidence, that is, the probability of a unique hit with the suspect? In this situation, a unique hit occurs exactly when all the other people in the database do *not* have the profile. The probability of this is $(1 - p)^{n-1}$ (assuming independence between the profiles of different people. This is reasonable in many cases but certainly not among members of the same family).

If the suspect is not guilty, then a unique match with the suspect can occur only when the true criminal is not in the database. The probability of this is $(N - n)/(N - 1)$, since we know already by assumption that the suspect is not the criminal. If the true criminal is not in the database, the probability that there is a unique match with the suspect is $p(1 - p)^{n-1}$, the p coming from the probability that the suspect should match and the $(1 - p)^{n-1}$ accounting for the event that all other persons in the database should not match. It then follows that the likelihood ratio is

$$\frac{(1-p)^{n-1}}{(N - n)/(N - 1)p(1 - p)^{n-1}} = \frac{1}{p} \times \frac{N - 1}{N - n}.$$

Explanation of equation (6)

The equality in equation (6) follows from the following basic calculation. We write A for the event that a

certain hypothesis is true and A^c for its complement. The evidence is denoted by E. The posterior odds are then

$$\frac{P(A|E)}{P(A^c|E)}$$

and these can be reformulated as

$$\frac{P(A|E)}{P(A^c|E)} = \frac{P(A \cap E)/P(E)}{P(A^c \cap E)/P(E)}$$

$$= \frac{P(A \cap E)}{P(A^c \cap E)} = \frac{P(E|A) \times P(A)}{P(E|A^c) \times P(A^c)}$$

$$= \frac{P(E|A)}{P(A^c|E)} \times \frac{P(A)}{P(A^c)}$$

$$= \text{likelihood ratio} \times \text{prior odds}.$$

References

[1] Balding, D.J. & Donnely, P. (1996). Evaluating DNA profile evidence when the suspect is identified through a database search, *Journal of Forensic Sciences* **41**, 603–607.

[2] Biedermann, A., Gittelson, S. & Taroni, F. (2011). Recent misconceptions about the 'database search problem': a probabilistic analysis using Bayesian networks, *Forensic Science International*, DOI: 10.1016/j.forsciint.2011. 05.013

[3] Dawid, A.P. (2001). Comment on Stockmarr's "Likelihood ratios for evaluating DNA evidence when the suspect is found through a database search", *Biometrics* **57**, 976–978.

[4] Dawid, A.P. & Mortera, J. (1996). Coherent analysis of forensic identification evidence, *Journal of the Royal Statistical Society: Series B*, 425–443.

[5] Donelly, P. & Friedman, R.D. (1999). DNA database searches and the legal consumption of scientific evidence, *Michigan Law Review* **97**, 931–984.

[6] Fimmers, R. *et al.* (2011). Reply of the letter of Taroni *et al.* to the editor with reference to "Recommendations of the German Stain Commission regarding the statistical evaluation of matches following searches in the national DNA database", *Rechtsmedizin* **12**, 57–60.

[7] Meester, R. & Sjerps, M. (2011). The evidential value in the DNA database search controversy and the two-stain problem, *Biometrics* **59**, 727–732.

[8] Meester, R. & Slooten, K. (2011). Forensic identification: the Island Problem and its generalisations, *Satistica Neerlandica* **65**, 202–237.

[9] National Research Council (1996). *The Evaluation of Forensic DNA Evidence*, Report, National Research Council, Washington D.C.: National Academy Press.

[10] Schneider, P.M. *et al.* (2010). Recommendations of the German Stain Commission regarding the statistical evaluation of matches following searches in the national DNA database, *Rechtsmedizin* **20**, 111–115.

[11] Stockmarr, A. (1999). Likelihood ratios for evaluating DNA evidence when the suspect is found through a database search, *Biometrics* **55**, 671–677.

Related Articles

DNA Databases and Evidentiary Issues

Chapter 33
DNA Databases and Evidentiary Issues

Simon J. Walsh[1] and John S. Buckleton[2]

[1]*Australian Federal Police, Canberra, ACT, Australia*
[2]*Institute of Environmental Science and Research Ltd., Auckland, New Zealand*

Introduction

DNA profiling and the compilation and use of forensic DNA databases are most often discussed with reference to the operational impact, the effect on intelligence-led models for forensic and policing practice, and the broader justice system ramifications such as the catalysis of legislative change, the increased socio-legal debate, and emergent aspects of jurisprudence. In this entry, the focus is refined to cover specific evidentiary issues associated with the use of DNA databases. The specific issues raised by the use of familial searches will not be treated here (see [1, 2] for the statistical issues and [3, 4] for some ethical considerations). The approach of familial speculative searches consists in searching a full profile left on a crime scene in the DNA database. No full match is returned, but a partial correspondence (on relatives sharing more of their DNA than unrelated persons, this partial match could indicate that the crime stain was left by a close relative of the person with whom the partial match was found) is obtained.

The collation into databases of DNA profiles taken from persons convicted of, or otherwise connected to, crimes has been a focal point of development efforts in the field of forensic biology for at least the past decade. The scale of database growth and use is now considerable, particularly in populous Western democracies. Databases in the United Kingdom, the United States, and Europe alone now house over 10 million profiles, and their use has resulted in almost 1 million intelligence links (Table 1).

Along with the increase in the volume of cases brought about by the introduction of DNA databases, there has also been an alteration to the types of crimes and evidence submitted for biological analysis. Initially, DNA profiling was applied primarily to serious crimes, whereas, in recent times, it has contributed to the investigation of a far broader spectrum of crimes, most notably extending to include vast numbers of property crimes [5]. An important aside to the broadened role that DNA evidence now plays in the criminal justice system, thanks largely to the introduction of DNA databases, has been the need for forensic scientists and administrators to operate in what is a more public environment with arguably greater levels of awareness and accountability.

While the investigative changes and rewards have been substantial, progress in the area of DNA databasing has also brought some measure of controversy. Much of the controversy is not associated with the investigative use of databases but rather with the areas where they intersect with evidentiary or other predominantly legal issues. For example, the enactment of specific legislation to allow broad-scale collection and storage of DNA samples from offenders, arrestees, and, in some cases, citizens otherwise associated with crimes has naturally brought comment on associated legal and ethical concerns [6]. There have been specific issues to consider in the courts also. Although the legislative regimes have assisted in easing troublesome issues in areas such as informed consent, they have brought challenges on interpretation that range from procedural issues to constitutionality. Approaches to evidence interpretation are also required to adapt to this changed environment so as to provide a framework to assist in the communication of outcomes across the interface of the forensic and legal sectors, most often in the

A Guide to Forensic DNA Profiling
Edited by Allan Jamieson and Scott Bader
© 2016 John Wiley & Sons, Ltd. ISBN: 9781118751527
Also published in EFS (online edition)
DOI: 10.1002/9780470061589.fsa126

Table 1 Summary of the size and effectiveness of major DNA database programs

Database	Combined	United Kingdom	Europe	United States
Date	–	Jan 2007	Jan 2007	July 2007
Total profiles	10 498 199	4 103 509	1 444 916	4 949 774
Offender profiles	9 729 432	3 790 551	1 173 451	4 765 430
Crime profiles	768 767	312 958	271 465	184 344
Investigations aided	969 428	762 280	154 282	52 866

form of expert evidence in criminal proceedings. As with other parts of the process, there have been specific issues in forensic statistics that have emerged through the use of DNA databases. The critical issues include (i) a refocusing on the likelihood of adventitious matches between profiles and robustness of interpretation models and (ii) controversy around the appropriate approach for reporting a DNA match statistic in cases where the suspect was identified by a database search.

Adventitious Matches

As the discriminating power of DNA multiplexes has increased, the reasonable question that has arisen is, *when can a DNA profile match be considered proof that two DNA samples have come from the same source?* The FBI announced a policy on this in November 1997 [7] and others have supported the appeal of such a position [8]. While not declaring "uniqueness", the FBI policy encourages the use of the term "source attribution", which is intended to describe the situation where "to a high degree of scientific certainty" the source of the stain can be assigned to a particular individual [9]. This policy suggested that a match probability of less than $p = 3.9 \times 10^{-11}$ will confer a 99% confidence that the evidentiary profile is "unique" in a population of equivalent size to the United States (or $N = 260$ million). While the simplicity is appealing, this move was controversial and has been criticized for its subjectivity [10] and the fact that the estimates were based on assumptions of independence at the population level [11]. We have previously stated our philosophical concern about scientists taking decisions such as these out of the hands of the courts [12].

While there is some effort in the advocacy of this approach to stress that source attribution applies only within the context defined by the case, and does not extend, for example, to the entire human population

[13], there remain many risks with this approach. The semantics of the distinction provided describe an intent that is similar to categorization, that is, the only acceptable proposition out of a defined set of alternatives, or, one of a kind. However, the effect of the approach aligns more with individualization, itself implying the one – the only. This misapprehension is obvious in the reflections on the policy from areas of the legal community. The American Prosecutors' Research Institute announced the policy by saying; "… Jurors may be spared technical and often confusing explanations of population genetics and statistics because DNA examiners will be able to testify to a matching DNA profile without qualifying the match with complicated mathematical probabilities. Furthermore, now that the FBI policy has paved the way for definitive identifications of an individual as the source of an evidentiary DNA sample, other laboratories conducting DNA analysis may soon implement similar policies" [14]. In *Young v State of Maryland*, the appellate court concluded (at 56–57) "when the random match probability (RMP) is sufficiently miniscule, the DNA profile may be deemed unique. In such circumstances, testimony of a match is admissible without accompanying statistics. In place of the statistics, the expert may inform the jury of the meaning of the match by identifying the person whose profile matched the profile of the DNA evidence as the source of that evidence" [15]. It is incongruent to speak of uniqueness in the context of the handful of people associated with a case, and not anticipate misunderstanding.

While it is the vanishingly small random match probabilities (RMP) that are derived from direct matches between 10 and 15 locus short tandem repeat (STR) profiles that have encouraged approaches such as the assignment of source attribution, the collation of large-scale DNA databases has refocused this issue somewhat. If a database of individuals is of size

Table 2   Crude demonstration of expected number of adventitious matches in databases of varying sizes

DB size	Number of comparisons	Expected number of matches	
		RMP = 1×10^{-9}	RMP = 3.9×10^{-11}
1	0	0	0
10	45	0	0
100	4950	0	0
1000	499 500	0	0
10 000	49 995 000	0	0
100 000	4 999 950 000	5	0
1 000 000	499 999 500 000	500	19
4 765 430[a]	11 354 659 159 735	11 355	443
10 000 000	49 999 995 000 000	50 000	1950

[a]Size of combined offender DNA index system (CODIS) offender database (July 2007)

N, with C entries on the crime stain database, this implies that there are $N(N - 1)/2$ pairs of individual profiles, $C(C - 1)/2$ pairs of crime profiles (involved in the crime-to-crime matching process), and NC person-to-crime comparisons during the matching of the two databases to each other. These numbers are not always on peoples' minds, and it is interesting to see how quickly they become large. With their increasing size comes the increasing likelihood of adventitious database matches [16].[a] In Table 2, we have estimated the number of matches expected in databases of various sizes (N) for a profile with an RMP of 1×10^{-9} or 3.9×10^{-11} (the FBI source attribution threshold).

For the purpose of this illustration there is no population substructure in the theoretical database, nor has there been any consideration given to the presence of relatives. The difference between this simple predictive model and an actual database is that a proportion of crime profiles are partial or derived from mixtures, implying that they do not have all loci scored. Such samples will have a higher RMP than full profiles and would be expected to match more frequently with other samples. Of course, there will be related people on the database and, for these people, the match probability will be larger than the match probability between unrelated people. These related people will increase the number of person-to-person matches but these are not considered as adventitious hits. The extent of relatedness in "offender" databases could be high. Likewise, there will be crime samples originating from people who are related to persons on the database. This increases the number of adventitious matches. A substructure is also present at the population level.

Accommodating these factors in predictive statistical models is a difficult task, largely because of the structure of databases and the fact that the match probabilities between two people, or between people and crime samples, are not constant. This matter has been tackled previously by Buckleton *et al.* [17] and is also addressed by Triggs and Buckleton [16]. Even without such models, it is possible to get the flavor of anticipated results (as illustrated in Table 2) and to understand clearly that adventitious matches between people on the database are expected to occur. Likewise, adventitious matches between crime samples and people are also expected. This is more likely in circumstances involving partial profiles on the database or from crime samples.

The likely event of adventitious matches seems counterintuitive for those unaccustomed to the mathematics, and we imagine it could confuse or alarm the general public. Perhaps for this reason, the issue has recently emerged in court as part of evidence questioning the validity of DNA match statistics. On occasions, these issues have been raised on the basis of observed results from databases of forensic DNA profiles. For example, reports exist in the literature relating to parentage- [18] and kinship [19, 20]-testing experiences that describe observed levels of matching or allele sharing that appear high in the context of associated DNA match statistics. There have also been anecdotal reports of coincidental matches at nine or more STR loci. All of these observations have involved comparisons with a database of some kind. One of the more noted recent examples was initiated following the observation of a single incident of an adventitious match within the Arizona State DNA Identification System (SDIS) [21]. A full search of the Arizona DNA offender database identified 144 partial matches; 122 nine-locus, 20 ten-locus, 1 eleven-locus, and 1 twelve-locus match (both of the latter two involved full siblings). At the time of the search, the database contained 65 493 profiles with an average RMP estimated to be less than 4.5×10^{-10} [22]. This finding caused alarm and led to legal requests for both State and Federal databases to be handed over in their entirety to independent researchers to undertake a full evaluation of the extent of allele and profile sharing [23]. There are many problems with using databases in this manner, mostly relating to what has to be done when a match is observed. Matching profiles may be the same person sampled twice under the same, similar, or different names, or they may originate from twins, close relatives, or unrelated people. Investigating this requires a considerable multiagency effort. The only advisable scientific safeguard is confirmation at additional STR or single nucleotide polymorphism (SNP) loci.

Some of the alarm surrounding the Arizona matches undoubtedly arose from misinterpretation of the data. As mentioned earlier, what is often overlooked in these circumstances is, first, that the critical information is the total number of comparisons involved, and, secondly, how the observed number of matches compares with that expected from the statistical models underpinning estimates of the RMP. This comparison has been made by Birus et al. [24] who gives the expected figures for 9- and 10-locus matches respectively as 100 and 3, using a model that assumes no relatedness in the database. While the observed number of matches exceeds the number predicted by this simplistic model, one can see that the number of observations is not as alarmingly high as one may have intuitively thought them to be.

One of the limitations of forensic statistical approaches, and one for which they are often criticized, is the inability to empirically validate the estimates produced, and thereby, the models that underpin them. This is compounded by the fact that the numbers themselves are so large (or small) that they raise justifiable concerns about the level of accuracy. As the examples above show, large DNA databases are a pool of empirical data that, despite the limitations mentioned earlier, can provide some

realistic basis by which theoretical estimates could be evaluated.

Weir [25] first addressed this issue using combined Australian profile data (~15 000 nine-locus profiles) and focussing not only on the fully matching profiles but also on those that partially match (for example, a profile where eight loci fully match and one allele or no alleles of the last locus match). The breakthrough made by Weir was to observe that the partially matching profiles do not suffer from the disadvantage that they may be the same person. Curran et al. [26] have recently extended this approach to include corrections in expected estimates for the common relationships, siblings, cousins, and parent/child, as well as unrelated persons. A variety of large datasets were utilized comprising diverse population groups (such as Caucasian, New Zealand Maori, and Australian Aborigine). The comparison of observed and expected numbers of partially matching profiles shows that, when subpopulation effects and relatedness are accounted for, the existing statistical models give an excellent fit to empirical observations.

From this aspect of databases, some interesting observations have emerged. The assembly of large databases of DNA profiles has brought the issue of adventitious sharing of DNA into sharp focus, which in turn raises questions about policies such as source attribution. Associated with DNA, there remains a significant issue around the expectation of the uninitiated. Most of the general public see DNA as a unique identifier and are befuddled when adventitious matches occur. These misappropriated expectations are easily exploitable by anyone wishing to denigrate the basis of the DNA match statistics, as, at first blush, the facts appear to contradict the model. Ironically, where the DNA databases themselves have generated this confusion, they also provide a resource for resolving long-held ambiguity about the validity of statistical estimates. In fact, the scientific analysis of these data that has so far been undertaken [25, 26] provides perhaps the strongest direct evidence yet as to the robustness of forensic DNA interpretation models.

Estimation of DNA Match Statistics after a Database Search

The strength of the DNA evidence resulting from an intelligence database match is often presented without any mention that the hit was obtained from a database. It is usually not in the suspect's interest to let a jury know that he or she has a sample on the DNA database. The question of whether searching a database for a match affects the strength of the evidence has been discussed extensively and forcefully in the literature. Unfortunately, there is much confused writing, and it would be very difficult for a court to make a reasoned decision based on a simple assessment of literature recommendations.

The issue was first countenanced in the first National Research Council (NRC [27]) report, which suggested that the loci used in the matching process should not be used in assessing the weight of evidence (124):

> The distinction between finding a match between an evidence sample and a suspect sample and finding a match between an evidence sample and one of many entries in a DNA profile databank is important. The chance of finding a match in the second case is considerably higher … The initial match should be used as probable cause to obtain a blood sample from the suspect, but only the statistical frequency associated with the additional loci should be presented at trial.

The second NRC report (NRC II [28]; Recommendation 5.1, pp. 133–135) recommended that an adjustment be applied by multiplying the RMP by the number of people on the database. Using an example of an intelligence database of 100 000 and a multiplex with an RMP of 1×10^{-6} would result in an adjusted database match probability of 0.1 being reported to the court. This approach is often referred to as the Np rule.[b] The conservativeness of this recommendation becomes extreme as the size of the database increases. For example, if the database were to hold the profiles of the entire world, and there was only one matching individual, logically this would provide an irrefutable association, yet, should Np be employed, the discriminating power of the match would be reduced by a factor of 6 billion.

In addition to the two NRC reports, [29–32] have also suggested that the match probability be multiplied by the number of people on the database. Lempert [33] suggests multiplying by the size of the suspect population and not the database. Morton [34] suggests confirmatory markers or the use of the Np approach. The DNA Advisory Board [13] highlights the question as being *especially important*, and favors the approach of [30], which it describes as being *more comprehensible* and *always conservative*.

The general consensus among noted authors in the field is that the evidence is slightly stronger after a database search and hence no correction is required [16, 35–47].

For a considerable portion of its history, the use of forensic DNA evidence in court fought to gain general acceptance. Having achieved a stage where its general suitability was less contentious, DNA evidence has at times struggled due to the difficulty the courts endured in interpreting its technicality. The present debate that is taking place around whether an adjusted (Np) or an unadjusted match statistic (p) should be presented impinges on both these fronts. Differences of opinion run the risk of being perceived as a lack of general acceptance across the expert community, and the technicalities of the issue could easily overwhelm lay court participants.

In the recent trial, [48] DNA evidence was excluded at trial under [49] due to the *raging debate* in the scientific literature on the issue of database match statistics. This was seen to indicate a lack of *general acceptance* in the scientific community and thereby preclude admissibility. This ruling was overturned on appeal. The appeal court ruling goes to some lengths to describe the issue. It cites three key approaches that could be used to estimate DNA statistics in the circumstance of a DNA database search that has resulted in a suspect's identification and subsequent trial. These were termed the *rarity statistic*,[c] which estimates how rare a profile is in a given society, the *database match probability*, which estimates the probability of a chance match from a particular database (calculated by Np), and the *Balding and Donnelly approach*, which gives a full consideration of the evidence in context (based on [38]). The Appeal court held as follows:

> there is no controversy … as to the accuracy of the various formulas … each approach accurately answers the question it seeks to address … Instead, the arguments raised by each of the proponents simply state that their formulation is most probative, not more correct … Thus the debate is one of relevancy, not methodology … and as such there is no basis to exclude the evidence in this case … What is and is not relevant is not appropriately decided by scientists and statisticians … determining what is and is not relevant is a hallmark responsibility of the

trial judge and that responsibility is not appropriately delegated to parties outside the court.

While the ruling in *Jenkins* is appreciative of the issues, it does not greatly assist as it gives equal legitimacy to all approaches. In fact, the debate occurring among scientists *is* on this quintessentially legal issue, as it hinges not upon the mathematics *per se* but on which statistic or statistics will help the jury appreciate the fact of a DNA match. To this end, another US appeal court ruling was more direct [50]. In dismissing the fact that the appellate was first identified as a possible suspect based on a database search as something that *simply does not matter* (at p. 15), the court also stated that "Jenkins does not convince us that the probability of obtaining a cold hit from a search of the CODIS database matters." (at p. 20).

The relevant question that must be assessed is, "Is the defendant the source of the DNA recovered from the crime scene?" For the purpose of an example, let us say that the questioned sample is a semen stain located on intimate swabs from a complainant in a sexual assault. The jury may embrace the proposition advanced by the prosecution (referred to as Hp) that the defendant is the source of the DNA on the swabs. Alternatively, it may embrace another proposition, possibly advanced by defense counsel (referred to as Hd). In general terms, this is that the defendant is not the source of the DNA on the swabs, but rather it has originated from an unrelated person who just happens to share the same profile as the defendant. Evidence that informs the jury as to the plausibility of this alternative proposition is therefore relevant.

If the defendant is selected for reasons that have nothing to do with his DNA profile, and no one else is tested, the chance of the match under the coincidence hypothesis is the RMP, p. However, if the defendant was selected following a database search (i.e., he was not the only person considered), this requires additional analysis. The frequentist argument is that, because a match following a search is much less surprising than a confirmation match following on from other evidence of association, Hd is much more plausible than p would suggest. Np indicates how probative the match is with respect to the hypothesis that the database contains the source of the crime scene DNA as opposed to the alternative hypothesis that the crime scene DNA came from someone not represented in the database. In other words, it estimates

how often searches of database's that do not include the true source generate an adventitious hit. But, as Kaye succinctly states [51]:

the database is not on trial. Only the defendant is. The DB match is only relevant to the extent that it affects the probability that the defendant – not the database – is the source. Thus, it appears that asking how probable a search of a particular database is to generate a false cold hit is the wrong question. The jury ought to be thinking about how probable the cold hit on the defendants profile would be when the specific defendant is, and is not, the source of the crime scene DNA. The likelihood ratio formed with these probabilities is the appropriate measure of the probative value of the DB match. This LR is more complex than the figure pertaining to the simple confirmation case. It includes not only the fact that the defendant matches but also the fact that everyone else in the database has been excluded. It can be shown that when this additional information is incorporated in the LR, the resulting number can be no greater than $1/p$. Consequently, introducing p as the indicator of probative value is not prejudicial. It understates the incriminatory power of the DNA evidence . . . .

We have previously summarized the mathematical argument [16] and reprise that proof here. For a population of size N, we index the suspect as person 1 and the remaining members of the population as $2 \ldots N$. The first $1 \ldots M$ of these are on the database. We call the hypothesis that person i is the source of the DNA: H_i. Because the suspect is indexed person 1, the hypothesis that the suspect is, in fact, the source of the DNA is H_1. The remaining hypotheses, $H_2, \ldots, H_N$ are those hypotheses where the true offender is one of the $N - 1$ "other" people from the population. Before we examine the evidence, each person has some probability of being the offender $\Pr(H_i) = \Pi_i$. The suspect is on the database and has been genotyped and we call his genotype G_s. The crime sample from the swabs has been typed and found to have the genetic profile G_c. The search of the database reveals that $G_c = G_s$ and that there are no other profiles on the database match (this latter requirement is unnecessary and a generalization is easy). We now know that the $2 \ldots M$ people on the database, other than the suspect, do not match. The remaining $M + 1, \ldots, N$ members of the population have genotypes $G_{M+1} \ldots G_N$, which are unknown to us. We require the probability $\Pr(H_1 | G_c, G_1 \ldots G_M)$.[d]

$\Pr(H_1|G_c, G_1 \dots G_M)$

$$= \frac{\Pr(G_c|H_1, G_1 \dots G_M)\Pr(H_1|G_1 \dots G_M)}{\sum\limits_{i=1}^{N} \Pr(G_c|H_i, G_1 \dots G_M)\Pr(H_i|G_1 \dots G_M)}$$

$$= \frac{\Pr(G_c|H_1, G_1 \dots G_M)\Pr(H_1|G_1 \dots G_M)}{\left(\begin{array}{l} \Pr(G_c|H_1, G_1 \dots G_M)\Pr(H_1|G_1 \dots G_M) \\ + \sum\limits_{i=2}^{M} \Pr(G_c|H_i, G_1 \dots G_M)\Pr(H_i|G_1 \dots G_M) \\ + \sum\limits_{i=M+1}^{N} \Pr(G_c|H_i, G_1 \dots G_M)\Pr(H_i|G_1 \dots G_M) \end{array} \right)} \quad (1)$$

In the equation above, we have split the denominator into the suspect, the other people on the database, and those other people in the population who are not on the database. Further, we assume $\Pr(G_c|H_1, G_1 \dots G_M) = 1$. This assumption, in words, is that the crime sample should match the suspect if it did indeed come from him. This gives

$\Pr(H_1|G_c, G_1 \dots G_M)$

$$= \frac{\Pr(H_1|G_1 \dots G_M)}{\left(\begin{array}{l} \Pr(H_1|G_1 \dots G_M) \\ + \sum\limits_{i=2}^{M} \Pr(G_c|H_i, G_1 \dots G_M)\Pr(H_i|G_1 \dots G_M) \\ + \sum\limits_{i=M+1}^{N} \Pr(G_c|H_i, G_1 \dots G_M)\Pr(H_i|G_1 \dots G_M) \end{array} \right)} \quad (2)$$

Because we know that the $2 \dots M$ "other" people on the database do not match $\Pr(G_c|H_i, G_1, \dots G_M) = 0$ for $i = 2$ to M. This gives

$\Pr(H_1|G_c, G_1 \dots G_M)$

$$= \frac{\Pr(H_1|G_1 \dots G_M)}{\Pr(H_1|G_1 \dots G_M) + \sum\limits_{i=M+1}^{N} \Pr(G_c|H_i, G_1 \dots G_M)}$$

$\Pr(H_i|G_1 \dots G_M) \quad (3)$

Under most conditions, we assume that the nonmatching people do not change our view of the match probability. However, making this assumption and assuming that the genotypes do not affect the

prior gives

$\Pr(H_1|G_c, G_1)$

$$= \frac{\Pr(H_1)}{\Pr(H_1) + \sum\limits_{i=M+1}^{N} \Pr(G_c|H_i, G_1)\,\Pr(H_i)} \quad (4)$$

We compare this with the equivalent probability for the same match without a database search

$\Pr(H_1|G_c, G_1)$

$$= \frac{\Pr(H_1)}{\Pr(H_1) + \sum\limits_{i=2}^{M} \Pr(G_c|H_i, G_1)\,\Pr(H_i) + \sum\limits_{i=M+1}^{M} \Pr(G_c|H_i, G_1)\,\Pr(H_i)} \quad (5)$$

Under any set of priors, equation (4) gives a larger value for the posterior probability than equation (5) since the denominator is larger in equation (4). Hence, reporting the approach leading to equation (5) is always conservative. In other words, the "no correction" approach is always conservative. Up to this point, we have not made any really contentious assumptions (although we accept Balding and Donnelly's argument that the search also informs the match probability). If we now assume that every person has the same prior chance of being the true offender (this assumption is quite contentious) and we write $\Pr(G_c|H_i, G_1)$ as p in equation (4), we obtain

$$\Pr(H_1|G_c, G_1) = \frac{1}{1 + (N - M - 1)\mathrm{P}m} \quad (6)$$

as compared to

$$\Pr(H_1|G_c, G_1) = \frac{1}{1 + (N - 1)\mathrm{P}m} \quad (7)$$

Again, equation (6) gives a larger posterior probability than equation (7). The mathematical solution leads to the conclusion that the evidence is stronger after a database search and reporting the standard match statistics is always conservative. Another simple explanation of this proof is given [39].

In summary, there is consensus on certain issues in this area. Estimating Np and p seeks to answer different questions and that one is not intended to substitute the other. There is no support for the original NRC recommendation. The weight of scientific opinion is against the use of Np, and this is supportable by mathematical proof and logic. The issue itself has not received extensive coverage in the scientific literature since the initial dispute in the late 1990s. This is not to say, however, that the debate is exhausted. It is only in the past 12–18 months that significant legal challenges have emerged in this area – which is indicative of the slower rate of technology adoption in the legal system. Duly considering issues such as these is a matter for science, and this particular issue has been researched and critiqued at the time of DNA database emergence. But the fruits of this process are only now being absorbed into jurisprudence. In addition, this is happening in such a way that the duration, extent, and weight of the scientific debate is diminished. While this is frustrating to us, it also serves as a tacit reminder of the need for prompt, robust investigation of scientific issues, and suitable disclosure through publication. It also reinforces the folly in assuming that knowledge or practice that is the scientific norm will be perceived as such by the courts, and that in the least any assessment of the fact will occur along different lines, and often for different reasons.

Conclusion

Despite DNA databases having established themselves in a practical sense, there remain some peculiarities regarding the integration of outcomes from DNA databases into evidence. The one peculiarity that has precipitated issues in court in the United States and Australia has been the occurrence or anticipated occurrence of adventitious matches. It has been shown in this article that adventitious matches occur at a rate that we can approximately predict. Most risk accrues from partial profiles and people on the database who have close relatives offending. This risk can be best ameliorated by adding discriminating power either to the database samples or at the confirmation phase, or by using all available trace evidence in addition. However, there is also a more subliminal risk associated with adventitious matches, which occurs through a lack of awareness of the likelihood of their occurrence and the subsequent influence this can bring to bear on public confidence regarding evidence interpretation models.

A residual debate is also going on regarding the correct method to interpret a database hit. The mathematics is very difficult to explain to a lay person and would certainly be difficult to explain in court. A simple census of informed opinion would show that some commentators hold an opinion favoring each side of the correction or no correction debate; however, most seem on the "no correction side".

End Notes

[a] Adventitious matches refer to genuine links provided through the DNA database where an individual could not have been involved in a given case but who shares a common DNA profile with the crime scene sample purely through coincidence.

[b] Where N_p indicates that the random match probability p is multiplied by the size of the database, N.

[c] Referred to throughout this section as the RMP.

[d] That is, the probability that the suspect is the source of the DNA, given the genotype of the crime profile and the remaining genotypes on the database.

References

[1] Storvik, G. & Egeland, T. (2007). The DNA database search controversy revisited: bridging the Bayesian-frequentist gap, *Biometrics* **63**(3), 922–925.

[2] United States v. Jenkins, No. F320-00 (D.C. Super. Ct., Apr. 5, 2005). rev'd, 887 A.2d 1013, 1017 (D.C. 2005).

[3] Frye v. United States, 54 AppDC 46, 293Fed 1013 (1923).

[4] People v. Johnson, 43 Cal.Rptr.3d 587 (Ct. App. 2006).

[5] Curran, J.M. (2005). An introduction to Bayesian credible intervals for sampling errors in DNA profiles, *Law, Probability and Risk*. **4**(1/2), 115–126.

[6] Faigman, D.L., Kaye D.H., Saks, M.J. & Sanders, J. (2007). *Modern Scientific Evidence: The Law and Science of Expert Testimony*, West Thompson, Egan.

[7] Curran, J.M. & Buckleton, J.S. (2008). Effectiveness of familial searches, *Science & Justice* **84**, 164–167.

[8] Greely, H.T., Riordan, D.P., Garrison, N.A. & Mountain, J.L. (2006). Family ties: the use of DNA offender databases to catch offenders' kin, *Journal of Law, Medicine and Ethics* **34**(2), 248–262.

[9] Haimes, E. (2006). Social and ethical issues in the use of familial searching in forensic investigations: insights from family and kinship studies, *Journal of Law, Medicine and Ethics* **34**(2), 263–276.

[10] Walsh, S.J. (2007). Current and future trends in forensic molecular biology, in *Molecular Forensics*, R. Rapely &

D. Whitehouse, eds, John Wiley & Sons, London, pp. 1–20.

[11] Nuffield Council on Bioethics (2007). The forensic use of bioinformation: ethical issues, http://www. nuffieldbioethics.org/go/ourwork/bioinformationuse/ publication_441.html

[12] Holden, C. (1997). DNA fingerprinting comes of age, *Science* **278**, 1407.

[13] Devlin, K. (2007). Scientific heat about cold hits, http://www.stanford.edu/~kdevlin/papers.html

[14] Budowle, B., Chakraborty, R., Carmody, G. & Monson, K.L. (2000). Source attribution of a forensic DNA profile, *Forensic Science Communications* **2**(3), http://www.fbi.gov/hq/lab/fsc/current/index.htm

[15] Inman, K. & Rudin, N. (2001). *Principles and Practice of Criminalistics: The Profession of Forensic Science*, CRC Press, Boca Raton.

[16] Weir, B.S. (2001). DNA match and profile probabilities: comment on Budowle *et al.* (2000) and Fung and Hu (2000), *Forensic Science Communications* **3**(1), http://www.fbi.gov/hq/lab/fsc/current/index.htm

[17] Buckleton, J.S., Walsh, S.J. & Harbison, S.A. (2001). The fallacy of independence testing and the use of the product rule, *Science & Justice* **41**, 81–84.

[18] DAB (2000). Statistical and population genetics issues affecting the evaluation of the frequency of occurrence of DNA profiles calculated from pertinent population database(s), *Forensic Science Communications*, **2**(3), http://www.fbi.gov/hq/lab/fsc/current/index.htm

[19] Hart, A. (1998). New FBI policy revolutionizes DNA court testimony, *Silent Witness* **4**(1), http://www.ndaa. org/publications/newsletters/silent_witness_volume_4_ number_1_1998.html; http://www.fbi.gov/hq/lab/fsc/ current/index.htm

[20] *Young v State of Maryland*. Appellate Court (2005).

[21] Walsh, S.J. & Buckleton, J.S. (2005). DNA intelligence databases, in *Forensic DNA Evidence Interpretation*, J.S. Buckleton, C.M. Triggs & S.J. Walsh, eds, CRC Press, Boca Raton, pp. 439–469.

[22] Weir, B.S. (2004). Matching and partially-matching DNA profiles, *Journal of Forensic Sciences* **49**(5), 1009–1014.

[23] Poetsch, M., Ludcke, C., Repenning, A., Fischer, L., Malyusz, V., Simeoni, E., Lignitz, E., Oehmichen, M. & von Wurmb-Schwark, N. (2006). The problem of single parent/child paternity analysis – practical results involving 336 children and 348 unrelated men, *Forensic Science International* **159**, 98–103.

[24] Birus, I., Marcikic, M., Lauc, D., Dzijan, S. & Lauc, G. (2003). How high should paternity index be for reliable identification of war victims by DNA typing, *Croatian Medical Journal* **44**, 322–326.

[25] Gornik, I., Marcikic, M., Kubat, M., Primorac, D. & Lauc, D. (2002). The identification of war victims by reverse paternity is associated with significant risks of false inclusion, *International Journal of Legal Medicine* **116**, 255–257.

[26] Troyer, K., Gilboy, T. & Koeneman, B. (2001). A nine locus match between two apparently unrelated individuals using AmpFlSTR® Profiler Plus™ and Cofiler™, *Proceedings of 12th International Symposium on Forensic Human Identification*, Nashville, www.promega.com/geneticidproc/ussymp12proc/ abstracts.htm (accessed 12 May 2007).

[27] Brenner, C.H. (2007). Arizona DNA database matches, http://dna-view.com/ArizonaMatch.htm (accessed 22 Apr 2007).

[28] Budowle, B., Planz, J.V., Chakraborty, R., Callaghan, T.F. & Eisenberg, A.J. (2006). Clarification of statistical issues related to the operation of CODIS, *Proceedings of 17th International Symposium on Human Identification*, Nashville, September 2006.

[29] Myers, S.P. (2006). Felon-to-felon STR partial profile matches in the Arizona database: don't panic! *Proceedings of California Association of Criminalists and the Forensic Science Society Spring Seminar – DNA Workshop*, Concord, 9 May 2006.

[30] Weir, B.S. (2004). Matching and partially matching profiles, *Journal of Forensic Sciences* **49**(5), 1009–1014.

[31] Curran, J.M., Walsh, S.J. & Buckleton, J. (2007). Empirical testing of estimated DNA frequencies, *Forensic Science International: Genetics* **1**(3–4), 267–272.

[32] National Research Council (1992). *Report: DNA Technology in Forensic Science*, National Academy Press, Washington, DC.

[33] National Research Council (1996). *Report: The Evaluation of Forensic DNA Evidence*, United States National Academy of Sciences, Washington, DC.

[34] Devlin, B. (1993). The evidentiary value of a DNA database search, *Biometrics* **56**, 1276.

[35] Stockmarr, A. (1999). Likelihood ratios for evaluating DNA evidence when the suspect is found through a database search, *Biometrics* **55**, 671–677.

[36] Stockmarr, A. (2000). The choice of hypotheses in the evaluation of DNA profile evidence, in *Statistical Science in the Courtroom*, J.L. Gastwirth, ed, Springer-Verlag, New York, pp. 143–159.

[37] Stockmarr, A. (2001). Author's reply, *Biometrics* **57**(3), 978–980.

[38] Lempert, R. (1997). After the DNA wars: skirmishing with NRC II, *Jurimetrics* **37**, 439–468.

[39] Morton, N.E. (1997). The forensic DNA endgame, *Jurimetrics* **37**, 477–494.

[40] Aitken, C.G.G. & Taroni, F. (2004). *Statistics and the Evaluation of Evidence for Forensic Scientists*, 2nd Edition, John Wiley & Sons, Chichester.

[41] Balding, D.J. & Donnelly, P. (1995). Inference in forensic identification, *Journal of the Royal Statistical Society of America* **158**(1), 21–53.

[42] Balding, D.J. & Donnelly, P. (1995). Evaluating DNA profile evidence when the suspect is identified through a database search, *Journal of Forensic Sciences* **41**(4), 603–607.

[43] Balding, D.J., Donnelly, P. & Nichols, R.A. (1994). Some causes for concern about DNA profiles – comment, *Statistical Science* **9**(2), 248–251.

[44] Berry, D.A. (1994). Comment of Roeder, K. (1994) DNA fingerprinting: a review of the controversy, *Statistical Science* **9**(2), 252–255.

[45] Dawid, A.P. (2001). Comment on Stockmarr's "likelihood ratios for evaluating DNA evidence when the suspect is found through a database search", *Biometrics* **57**(3), 976–980.

[46] Donnelly, P. & Friedman, R.D. (1999). DNA database searches and the legal consumption of scientific evidence, *Michigan Law Review* **97**(4), 931–984.

[47] Evett, I.W. & Weir, B.S. (1998). *Interpreting DNA Evidence*, Sinauer Associates, Sunderland.

[48] Evett, I.W., Foreman, L.A. & Weir, B.S. (2000). Letter to the Editor of Biometrics – reply to Stockmarr, *Biometrics* **56**, 1274–1277.

[49] Finkelstein, M.O. & Levin, B. (2001). *Statistics for Lawyers*, Springer-Verlag, New York.

[50] Meester, R. & Sjerps, M. (2003). The evidential value in the DNA database search controversy and the two-stain problem, *Biometrics* **59**(3), 727–732.

[51] Taroni, F., Biedermann, A., Garbolino, P. & Aitken, C.G.G. (2004). A general approach to Bayesian networks for the interpretation of evidence, *Forensic Science International* **139**(1), 5–16.

Related Articles

Databases

DNA: An Overview

Chapter 34
Communicating Probabilistic Forensic Evidence in Court

Jonathan J. Koehler

Northwestern University School of Law, Chicago, IL, USA

When a forensic scientist testifies about an evidentiary "match" in a trial, there is usually much discussion about his or her qualifications, methods, and conclusions. These are important matters. However, an issue that receives far less attention is the *wording* that the forensic scientist uses to describe that match. This is an important omission because laboratory research shows that even very subtle modifications of the forensic scientist's words can be the difference between a guilty verdict and an acquittal in a close case [1].

The first section of this article examines the different ways that a forensic science match may be characterized at trial. The emphasis is on quantitative characterizations for several reasons. First, the 2009 National Academy of Sciences report on the forensic sciences has expressly called on forensic science researchers to develop a well-grounded probabilistic framework for describing forensic science matches [2]. Second, a probabilistic framework is more likely to convey information about the probative value of a match than more qualitative characterizations. The importance of error rates is also noted in the first section and various common but erroneous match characterizations are identified. The second section examines how jurors view and use probabilistic forensic science evidence. This section shows that jurors struggle to understand probability evidence and that their judgments are heavily influenced by the particular ways in which this evidence is communicated. The third section is a brief concluding section. This section counsels forensic scientists to take care to avoid mischaracterizing the

strength of match evidence and to be up front with fact finders about the assumptions that lie behind the probabilities that they offer.

Characterizations of a Match

Many forensic scientists are accustomed to testifying that, in their expert opinion, a particular item of physical evidence came from a particular source. In some cases, forensic scientists offer probabilistic claims based on their experience [2]. Such testimony, if believed, could be dispositive in a host of criminal cases. For example, if a forensic scientist testifies that the ransom note was written by Mr. Smith, or that there is a 99% chance that the bite marks on the victim's wrist was created by Mr. Smith's upper incisors, fact finders will probably believe that Mr. Smith was involved in the crime. However, such source identifications and subjective probability estimates are generally inappropriate.[a] Instead, forensic scientists may offer qualitative or – where data are available – quantitative descriptions.

Qualitative Descriptions

When a forensic scientist cannot find any distinguishing characteristics between an evidentiary marking and a potential source, he may describe the correspondence as an "association", a "consistency", or an "inclusion". These words are synonyms and they do not by themselves provide any indication of evidentiary strength. The term *match* is more controversial because, for some, it connotes a degree of correspondence between the evidentiary marking and potential source that implies that this marking

A Guide to Forensic DNA Profiling
Edited by Allan Jamieson and Scott Bader
© 2016 John Wiley & Sons, Ltd. ISBN: 9781118751527
Also published in EFS (online edition)
DOI: 10.1002/9780470061589.fsa125.pub2

could *only* have been made by that potential source. But the term *match* logically connotes nothing more than that the measured features in two samples share some degree of correspondence [3]. It is important for the forensic scientist to explain the meaning of the observed correspondence in a way that jurors and other legal actors understand what it does and does not mean.

When a forensic scientist does not find an association between a marking and a potential source, the relationship is commonly classified as an exclusion (e.g., "this hammer is excluded as a potential source of this indentation"). If the forensic scientist is unable to determine whether particular characteristics are or are not shared between a marking and a potential source, he/she may describe the correspondence as inconclusive.

Quantitative Descriptions

Qualitative descriptions of a match may be misunderstood. For example, some fact finders may not realize that an impression that is "consistent with" a particular shoe may also be consistent with other shoes. In order to give fact finders a better sense of the probative value of a match, witnesses should provide information about how rare the identifiable characteristics are in the potential source population.[b]

Exclusion Probability. The exclusion probability conveys more information about the probative value of a match. The exclusion probability is the proportion of potential sources (i.e., people or objects) in a reference population[c] that can be excluded as a source of the forensic science marking. Alternatively, one may think of the exclusion probability as the chance that a randomly selected member of the reference population will not match the forensic science marking. Like all the probabilities, exclusion probabilities range from 0 to 1. Larger exclusion probabilities reflect greater probative value than smaller exclusion probabilities because large values indicate that matches are less likely to be the result of mere chance. In most forensic science work, exclusion probabilities are relatively high (98%, 99.86%, etc.).

Inclusion Probabilities: 1 − Exclusion Probability = RMP = Frequency. The inclusion probability (or profile frequency) is, simply, one minus the exclusion probability. The inclusion probability identifies

the proportion within the potential source population that might be the source of a marking. In DNA typing, the inclusion probability is commonly described as the random match probability (RMP). The RMP identifies the frequency of a genetic profile in a reference population. Alternatively, the RMP is the probability that a randomly selected person in a population would happen to match the genetic profile of the forensic science evidence. Lower RMPs (i.e., low-inclusion probabilities) indicate that the match is unlikely to be coincidental.

It is important to bear in mind that *exclusion and inclusion probabilities do not, by themselves, capture the probative value of a match report*. They do not, for example, account for the possibility of error, fraud, or misinterpretation. If any of these possibilities are orders of magnitude more likely than the chance of a coincidental match, then the chance of these events, rather than the probabilities described earlier, controls the probative value of a reported match. This point is elaborated in the section titled "Error Rates Matter".

Likelihood Ratios. Many scholars and scientific authorities have argued that likelihood ratios are an appropriate way of describing the value of forensic science matches [2, 4–11]. A likelihood ratio is the ratio of the probability that an item of evidence E would arise if hypothesis H was true to the probability that this same item of evidence would arise if alternative hypothesis $\overline{H}$ was true. In symbols,[d]

$$LR = \frac{P(E|H)}{P(E|\overline{H})} \qquad (1)$$

In theory, larger likelihood ratios values convey stronger evidentiary matches than smaller ones.

Despite their theoretical appeal, likelihood ratios often suffer from several significant practical shortcomings. First, there is no such thing as "the" likelihood ratio [6–8, 12, 13]. The value of a likelihood ratio depends critically on the choices one makes for describing the hypothesis H [14] Meester and Sjerps [12] give an example where there are two evidentiary stains (one on a pillow and the other on a sheet) and the suspect matches the pillow stain. The likelihood ratio in this example depends crucially on whether hypothesis H is "the suspect is one of the crime stain donors", or "the suspect is the donor of the pil low stain". Even in simpler one-stain situations, the value of the likelihood ratio will depend on which of the several hypotheses are used. For example, Koehler [8] showed that the hypotheses "Simpson is the source of the blood", "Simpson had contact with the crime scene", and "Simpson is guilty of the crime" would produce different likelihood ratio values.

Error Rates Matter

The statistical characterizations of matching evidence discussed earlier are legitimate ways to describe forensic science evidence. However, each characterization is predicated on assumptions. Failure to reveal those assumptions in written reports or testimony is unscientific and potentially misleading.

In the previous section, it is noted that most forensic likelihood ratios implicitly assume a laboratory error rate of zero. Similarly, exclusion probabilities, RMPs, and their equivalent representations generally do not take account of the possibility of that a reported match may not be a true match. This is important because one cannot represent the probative value of a reported forensic science match without taking the error rate into account. Indeed, the false-positive error rate may be so important that the probative value of a match report is controlled almost entirely by this number rather than by the RMP [9, 15–18]. This mathematical point has not been disputed. What is more controversial, however, is how one goes about estimating the chance that a particular analyst committed a false-positive error in a particular instance.[e]

One of the most vexing aspects of any discussion of forensic science error rates is that, although everyone knows that errors sometimes occur, no one really knows the rate of error in ordinary case work. This knowledge gap exists because there is rarely any ground truth against which to compare a criminalist's opinion. Some researchers have argued that proficiency test data can provide an indication of the rates at which errors occur. According to these data, error rates in the forensic sciences are sometimes surprisingly high [19].

However, a number of forensic scientist counter that these estimated error rates should not be introduced at trials [20–22].

One argument is that error rates computed from historical data overstate the risk of present error because they do not take into account the corrective steps that laboratories and analysts take to ensure that those errors do not happen again. A second

argument is that general error rates do not take into account the procedures used in a specific case to guard against the possibility of error. A third argument is that proficiency test data are misleading because the tests were usually not designed to measure error rates. These three arguments contain elements of truth, but they do not support the claim that data-based error rate estimates are *irrelevant*. Instead, these arguments suggest that historical error rates *alone* may not provide a reliable estimate of the chance of an error in a particular case.

Regarding the first argument, if factors that produced false-positive errors were corrected, then we would expect to see dramatic declines in the rate of errors across forensic science subfields each year. However, such evidence is lacking.

The second argument is an instance of the base rate fallacy ([23], for discussions in the forensic science context, see Refs [19, 24, 25]). The probability of error in a particular case requires an assessment of both the prior probability that the error will occur and the individuating features of the particular case. Because the general error rate informs the prior probability, it is *enormously relevant* to an estimate of the chance of error in a particular case. This point is neglected by those who say that "only case-specific rates of undetected errors are relevant" (Kloosterman *et al.*, 2014, p. 83). Of course, no one would suggest that the specific and unusual measures that laboratories or analysts take in case work to reduce the risk of error should be ignored. Where such data exist, they should be used to modify general error rate estimates [8]. However, care must be taken to ensure that these more specific considerations are not used selectively, and that they are, in fact, distinctive and diagnostic. After all, nearly every laboratory and analyst follows a detailed protocol designed to reduce the risk of error, and the success of these protocols is largely reflected in the general error rate estimates.

The third argument against estimated error rates is too broad. The question about whether proficiency test data inform us about error rates in practice does not turn simply on whether the tests were specifically designed to measure those error rates. A closer examination of the features of the proficiency tests in question is required. For example, if there is reason to believe that performance on the tests will be better than performance in case work (which might be true if the tests use relatively easy samples, or if the test participants are better trained than those who conduct case work), then the proficiency test data can inform us about lower bound error rates.

Erroneous Characterizations

In recent years, forensic scientists have come under fire for exaggerating the strength of the evidence they provide at trial [2, 26, 27]. In light of the underlying probative force of forensic evidence, it may seem surprising that some forensic scientists make unjustifiable claims about the strength of their evidence. However, some exaggerations appear to spring more from ignorance of the statistical character of forensic science evidence than from an intentional desire to mislead jurors. The later paragraphs discuss a series of faulty characterizations of forensic science evidence that tend to exaggerate the strength of reported matches is identified.

Individualization Exaggerations. Forensic scientists often claim object individualization as both a goal and an achievement [28]. That is, they commonly claim to have identified the one and only possible source of a marking to the exclusion of all other possible sources in the world. However, there is little scientific basis for such claims [2, 27, 29]. As a rule, source certainty statements are inappropriate and only obfuscate the probabilistic nature of the forensic science enterprise.

Prosecutor's Fallacy. The so-called prosecutor's fallacy [30] is the most well-known erroneous match characterization. The prosecutor's fallacy is committed when one *equates the RMP with the probability that a matching defendant is not guilty.* Suppose, for example, that a witness testifies that a defendant's DNA profile matches the DNA profile found on a knife that was used to kill someone, and the frequency with which that profile occurs in a relevant population is 1 in 1 000 000. If that witness (or anyone else) testifies that this means that there is only 1 chance in 1 000 000 that the defendant is not the person who committed the murder, then the witness has committed the prosecutor's fallacy. It is a fallacy to characterize the 1 in 1 000 000 match frequency this way because probabilities of guilt and innocence require consideration of *all* evidence, including prior odds of guilt or innocence.[f] Thus, if the defendant produced credible evidence that he

or she was nowhere near the crime scene when the murder occurred, then this bit of information should also be given weight by a trier of fact when assessing the chance that the defendant committed the murder. If RMPs alone could reveal probabilities of innocence or guilt, there would be no need to consider alibis, eyewitness testimony, or evidence implicating other suspects.

Source Probability Error. Perhaps, the most common error is the source probability error [31–34]. This error occurs when one *equates the RMP with the probability that a matching defendant is not the source of the forensic evidence.* Referring to the example in the Prosecutor's Fallacy section below, a witness who testifies that the 1 in 1 000 000 RMP means that there is only one chance in 1 000 000 that the defendant is not the source of the DNA on the knife has committed the source probability error. Just as one cannot identify the probability of guilt or innocence without detailed consideration of the nonforensic evidence, one cannot identify the probability that a potential person or object is the source of a stain or marking based on forensic science evidence alone. One also needs to know, for example, how many others could have been the source of the forensic evidence *before* the discovery that the suspect matches. This fact may come as a surprise to forensic scientists who routinely provide source probability estimates in court and are aware of others who do the same. However, the pervasiveness of the source probability error does not make it any less fallacious than its more easily recognizable cousin, the prosecutor's fallacy.

P (Another Match) Error. The P (another match) error also finds its way into the courtroom with a disturbing degree of regularity (see [31, 33]). This error occurs when one equates the RMP with the probability that there exists another person who matches the defendant's DNA profile. But a moment's reflection reveals why these two probabilities are not identical. If the RMP = 1 in 1 000 000, then about 300 people in a country the size of the United States (300 000 000) would match. Consequently, one could not obtain an RMP of 1 in 1 000 000 and conclude that the chances are just 1 in 1 000 000 that there exists another person who would match. Indeed, it is a near certainty that *many* other people match this profile!

The Numerical Conversion Error. Finally, the numerical conversion error occurs when experts describe the significance of the RMP in terms of the number of people who would have to be tested before one should expect another match to occur [31]. This computation is straightforward, though the answer is a bit surprising. For an RMP of 1 in 1 000 000, the number of people who would need to be tested before another match is expected is not 1 000 000; it is 693, 147.[g]

Most of the errors identified earlier tend to exaggerate rather than minimize the strength of statistical forensic science evidence. Such exaggeration, though, is hardly necessary because statistical forensic science evidence can be quite compelling when presented accurately.

How Do Jurors Think About and Use Match Statistics?

Even when a forensic scientist studiously avoids exaggerating or otherwise mischaracterizing the strength of an evidentiary match, there is still a danger that jurors will misunderstand the technical evidence they hear. Some misunderstandings arise because jurors have preconceived ideas about the strength of match evidence or because they oversimplify the evidence in an effort to understand it. Strictly speaking, such misunderstandings are not the fault of the forensic scientist. However, forensic scientists should know something about the psychology of how people process statistical evidence. Such knowledge could help forensic scientists prepare written reports and testify in ways that help jurors appreciate the probative value of the evidence.

The Mock Jury Study

How can we know how much jurors value forensic science evidence? After all, cases that involve scientific evidence are usually complex affairs, and it may be impossible to determine posttrial exactly how jurors valued any particular item of evidence. Verdicts provide only a very gross measure of how impressed jurors were with the totality of evidence in a case. Posttrial interviews with individual jurors may provide additional insight, although research shows that people have limited insight into factors that affect their judgments and choices [35].

A better method for assessing how jurors use statistical evidence is the mock jury study. Mock jury studies are controlled behavioral experiments that test causal relationships between predictor variables (e.g., different types of jury instructions) and outcome variables (e.g., jurors' verdicts). In the typical experiment, jury-eligible subjects assume the role of jurors and watch a videotape (or read a description) of a trial or part of a trial. Jurors are randomly assigned to groups that differ only in terms of the predictor variables of interest. For example, one version of the videotaped trial might include testimony from an expert who commits the prosecutor's fallacy, whereas another version might not. A well-run mock jury study enables researchers to isolate the direction and magnitude of various influences on jurors' judgments and verdicts.

The obvious and central disadvantage of the mock jury study is its artificiality. Mock jury studies often use students rather than real jurors, use written case summaries rather than videotaped or live testimony, or collect verdicts from individuals rather than from juries that have deliberated to unanimity. It is only natural to question the usefulness of data derived from such research.

Nevertheless, there is good reason to believe that mock jury studies provide a window into the minds of actual jurors. Bornstein [36] reviewed dozens of mock jury studies and concluded that "[There is] strong evidence that factors at trial affect students and non-students in the same way" [p. 80]. Bornstein [36] also reported that it makes little difference whether mock jury studies employ written summaries, transcripts, audiotape, or videotape: "[R]esearch on the trial medium tends not to find many differences." (p. 82, 84). A few scholars have noted that the matter may be more complicated if variables such as mock jury population and stimulus materials interact with the experimental variables of interest in a study [37]. Furthermore, it is possible that some of the conclusions reached in laboratory studies may not hold when the stakes are real. But as Hastie [38] has observed, "there are so many converging results concerning juror behavior from laboratories and from surveys of actual jurors that most of the conclusions from the studies reported are surely accurate descriptions of juror behavior in real trials." (p. 28). In short, although mock jury studies are imperfect representations of actual trials, they may provide insight into how jurors think and respond at trial.

The Results of Behavioral Experiments

Defense Attorney Fallacy. Thompson and Schumann [30] coined the phrase "the defense attorney fallacy" to describe the erroneous belief that non-unique match evidence is not probative. For example, suppose that a partial DNA profile from an evidentiary sample occurs with a frequency of 1 in 1000 and that the suspect population includes 30 000 adult males in a city. In this scenario, the defense attorney fallacy would occur if one argued that a DNA match on a particular suspect is worthless because approximately 30 adult males in the city would match. This argument is fallacious because it fails to distinguish between probative evidence and dispositive evidence. Non-unique evidence may be highly probative if the size of the inclusion group is small relative to that of the exclusion group. In our example, the partial DNA match is highly probative because 99.9% of people who were not the source would have been excluded, yet the defendant happens to be a member of the very small group of non-excluded people. Holding aside error rate considerations, the discovery of this match means that a juror should believe that the defendant is now about 1000 times more likely to be the source of the DNA evidence than he was before the discovery of the match.

Several studies have shown that significant minorities of jurors are susceptible to this fallacy [30, 39], particularly when it is explicitly offered as an argument by a defense attorney. Hans and coworkers [40] found that fully 40% of mock jurors agreed with the statement "The mtDNA evidence in this case is completely irrelevant because a substantial number of other people could also be the source of the hairs." (p. 17). Similarly, Thompson and Newman [34] found that approximately half of mock jurors indicated that the following statement about DNA or shoeprint evidence was correct: "The (DNA/shoeprint) evidence has little value for proving Brian Kelly is guilty because a lot of other (people besides Kelly/shoes besides Kelly's) could have left the (DNA/shoeprint)."

Conditional Probability Confusion. Mock jury studies have also demonstrated that jurors are prone to inverting conditional probabilities [41]. These inversion errors can lead to source probability errors and prosecutor's fallacies. In Bayesian terms, inversion errors sometimes lead jurors to confuse likelihood ratio components with posterior odds components.

Koehler [7] showed that mock jurors do not distinguish between likelihood ratio statements (e.g., "It is approximately 1000 times more likely we would see this DNA match if the defendant is the source of the semen than if the defendant is not the source of the semen") and posterior odds ratio statements (e.g., "Given that we see this DNA match, it is approximately 1000 times more likely that the defendant is the source of the semen than that he is not the source of the semen"). This finding supports other research that shows that people verbally confuse likelihood ratios with posteriors in nonlegal contexts [42, 43], and that expert witnesses frequently describe likelihood ratios as posterior probabilities [31].

The confusion between likelihood ratios and posteriors in the forensic context is important because it creates the mistaken impression that match evidence alone can identify the probability that a suspect committed a crime or is the source of trace evidence [44]. Consider, for example, expert testimony in a paternity case in which a genetics expert testifies that it is 100 times more likely that we would see this pair of genetic markers if the putative father was actually the father of the child than if he were not the father. In the language of probability, this statement could be written as P(Genetic Evidence | Father)/P(Genetic Evidence | Not Father). This is a likelihood ratio and, in this case, the likelihood ratio increases the posterior odds that the putative father is the father of the child in question 100-fold relative to what it was before the presentation of this genetic evidence. However, there is a substantial risk that a juror or other person who hears this evidence might mistakenly think that the expert has said (or means) that it is 100 times more likely that the putative father is actually the father of the child in light of this evidence relative to the chance that he is not the father. In other words, the jurors might think that the expert has provided the posterior odds ratio P(Father | Genetic Evidence)/P(Not Father | Genetic Evidence) rather than the likelihood ratio P(Genetic Evidence | Father)/P(Genetic Evidence | Not Father).

In light of the linguistically subtle differences between likelihoods and posteriors, it is hard to guard against this particular conditional probability confusion. In June 1995, Court TV commentator Dan Abrams noted that likelihood ratios were discussed so frequently during various legal motions and arguments in the O. J. Simpson criminal trial that it was important to explain to the viewing public what exactly a likelihood ratio is. Abrams then committed an inversion error when he explained that a likelihood ratio refers to how likely one hypothesis is true vs. how likely a competing hypothesis is true.

Failure to Appreciate the Role of Error Rates. Jurors have a hard time understanding how to combine error rates with RMPs. This is a serious problem because, as noted earlier, the probative value of a reported match is determined almost exclusively by the false-positive error rate in cases where the RMP is very small [9, 15–18]. Koehler *et al.* [15] were the first to examine how mock jurors intuitively combined error rates and RMPs. They found that jurors simply ignored error rates (e.g., 1 in 1000 and 2 in 100) when the RMP was very small (e.g., 1 in 1 000 000 000). Schklar and Diamond [45] (hypothesis 2) found that jurors who received separate estimates for the RMP and error rate were significantly more likely to return a guilty verdict than were jurors who received a single statistic that properly aggregated these two statistics for them. Instruction on how to combine the RMP and error rate had little impact [39, 45]. This result suggests that it is no simple matter to get jurors to appreciate the role that error rates play in the interpretation of match reports. Some recent work focuses on incorporating the risk of false positive and false negative testing errors into quantitative measures of the probative value of match evidence [46].

Reasoning by Exemplars. People tend to overweight low-probability events [47]. This phenomenon partially explains why people buy insurance and lottery tickets even though both purchases have negative expected values. RMPs are almost always low-probability events and sometimes they are extremely low-probability events. One might therefore expect that jurors will tend to assign too much weight to the remote possibility of a coincidental match and thereby underweight a reported DNA match. Research generally supports this position. Most studies that have looked at this issue find that jurors attach less weight to statistical match evidence than the evidence would seem to deserve (for reviews, see [40, 41]). However, caution is needed here. Although people tend to overweight low-probability events, *extremely* low-probability events may be *underweighted* if people view those probabilities as negligible.

Research shows that the weight that jurors assign to very low RMPs depends critically on how those probabilities are presented. When RMPs are presented in ways that make it easy for jurors to imagine others who might match the profile, then a reported DNA match seems less impressive and jurors give less weight to the match evidence. But when RMPs are presented in ways that make it hard to think about others who might match, jurors give significantly more weight to the match evidence.

In one study [1], jurors who were told "The probability that Mr. Clinton would match the semen stain if he were not its source is 0.1%", assigned higher probabilities to the hypothesis that Mr. Clinton was the source of the stain than did jurors who were told "1 in 1000 people in Washington, DC, who are not the source would also match the semen stain". Although the RMP is identical in the two cases, the latter description makes it easier to imagine examples of others who would also match. These imagined examples weaken the perceived strength of the match evidence. In another study [48], jurors who heard a DNA RMP described as "0.1 in 100" were more likely to believe that the person who matched the evidence was its source than were jurors who heard this same RMP described as "2 in 2000". Whereas the fractional numerator in the former format conveys a sense that others are unlikely to match, the latter format encourages people to think about a second matchee.

How Should a Forensic Scientist Communicate Match Statistics?

This article examined the various ways in which forensic scientists characterize a forensic science match and how jurors are likely to interpret match statistics. Whereas some ways of characterizing a match are more informative than the others from a strictly mathematical standpoint, it is unclear whether untrained lay jurors understand the meaning of those characterizations. So what should forensic scientists do?

They should begin by educating themselves about the foundational principles of probability and statistics. Science, after all, is a probabilistic enterprise and scientists speak the language of statistics. Forensic scientists should pay particular attention to Bayes theorem (odds form) in their studies. Once they understand the difference between prior probabilities, likelihood ratios, and posterior odds ratios, the forensic scientists will be less likely to commit many of the statistical misstatements discussed in the first section. They will understand why they should abandon traditional source identity claims in favor of carefully worded probabilistic claims. And they will be able to explain to jurors why his science does not enable him to identify the probability that this bullet came from this gun or that this toolmark was produced by this hammer.[h]

They will also be in a better position to correct and explain the misstatements implicit in the questions that attorneys and judges ask of them. For example, when an attorney attempts to confirm a 1 in 1 000 000 RMP by asking "In other words, you're saying that there is only one chance in a million that the blood could be of anyone other than the defendant's, correct?" the forensic scientist should not agree. Instead, he/she should explain why this statement mischaracterizes the RMP. In the context of rapid-fire courtroom exchanges, this may be a challenge. But the forensic scientist, like any scientist, is duty-bound to correct misstatements of his conclusions and to educate those who use his data to make important decisions.

In addition to avoiding and correcting misstatements, forensic scientists should disclose all relevant assumptions. For example, they should note that the RMP requires assumption of independence across characteristics, and that most of the forensic probabilities implicitly assume a zero error rate.

Forensic scientists should also be sensitive to the underlying psychology associated with how people think about statistical evidence, in general, and very small probabilities in particular. After all, the primary purpose of forensic science testimony is to convey probative information to the legal fact finder. If that information is conveyed in ways that make it hard for the trier of fact to understand, then adjustments are needed. One possibility is to place some of the burden on jurors by suggesting that they receive training to help them understand scientific and statistical evidence [50]. However, the practical realities are such that, for now, those who offer technical testimony must find simple and clear ways to explain their evidence, erring on the side of caution and conservatism.

An undesirable side effect of scientific conservatism is that recipients of the scientific message may give insufficient weight to the message. Scientific evidence that is accompanied by cautions about what the evidence does not represent, and cautions about the assumptions and limits of the accompanying statistics may discourage some fact finders from attaching sufficient weight to the evidence. In the case of forensic match evidence, jurors may be disappointed to learn, for example, that a handwriting match does not necessarily mean that the matchee authored the questioned document. When jurors realize that the match merely places the matchee in a small group of people who might have authored the document, they may see the evidence as weak or irrelevant because the forensic scientist was not able to individualize the handwriting. Indeed, as noted earlier, 40% of mock jurors in one recent study said they believed that statistical mtDNA evidence was "completely irrelevant" because more than one person could match [40]. Such results indicate that jurors need substantial help understanding how to value forensic science evidence. Assuming that jurors remain untrained, forensic scientists will need to provide that help. On the one hand, they must identify critical assumptions and avoid overstating their conclusions. On the other hand, they must teach jurors that a reported match can be powerful evidence of identity even when uniqueness and error-free methods cannot be assumed. In the end, forensic scientists should be truthful, candid, clear, helpful and, above all else, scientific.

End Notes

[a.] A source identification may be appropriate in rare cases in which all the potential sources of a marking are available for examination and only one of those potential sources matches the target marking.

[b.] The phrase *potential source population is used here* in much the same way as others use "suspect population" in cases that include human genetic material. The former phrase applies to a broader array of forensic cases (e.g., cases involving toolmarks) and does not attempt to make the forensic scientist the arbiter of which possible human sources should and should not be included in the groups of potential perpetrators. After all, some people may be members of the source population (e.g., they might be the source of the blood), but they might not be members of the suspect population if, for example, they were in prison at the time the crime at issue occurred.

c. Ideally, the reference population should be the potential source population. In practice, data for this population may be hard to construct. If so, then convenient alternatives such as the general population or an ethnic grouping within the general population are commonly used. The extent to which these alternative reference groups are adequate varies from case to case.

d. If the evidence E is described as "a true match", then there is no place for considerations of error in the likelihood ratio because E equates the *report* of a match with a true match. For this reason, it is more appropriate to describe E as "a reported match".

e. Discussions of "errors" in forensic science sometimes get bogged down by concerns about what exactly is meant by an error. For purposes of this paper, the words "error" and "error rate" are used as synonyms for false-positive error and false-positive error rate, respectively. A false-positive error arises when an analyst affirmatively claims that two markings match when, in fact, they do not share a common source.

f. In Bayesian terms,

$$\frac{P(\text{suspect is guilty}|\text{evidence})}{P(\text{suspect is not guilty}|\text{evidence})}$$

$$= \frac{P(\text{suspect is guilty})}{P(\text{suspect is not guilty})}$$

$$\times \frac{P(\text{evidence}|\text{suspect is guilty})}{P(\text{evidence}|\text{suspect is not guilty})}$$

Even if we simplify this formula by assuming that $P(\text{evidence}|\text{suspect is not guilty}) = \text{RMP}$, we may not conclude that $\text{RMP} = P(\text{suspect is not guilty}|\text{evidence})$ The latter conditional probability also depends on the prior probability that the suspect is guilty (i.e., the probability that the suspect is guilty based on nonforensic considerations).

g. In order to estimate the number of people who would need to be tested before there would be more than a 50% chance to find a match on a profile common to one in X people, one must compute the smallest N that makes this equation true: $(1 - 1/X)N < 0.50$. For computational simplicity, one may solve for N, where $N = [\ln(0.50)]/[\ln(1 - 1/X)]$.

h. These are posterior probabilities and therefore inaccessible to the forensic scientist absent an estimate of the prior probabilities. Estimates of prior probabilities are matters for the legal fact finder rather than the expert witness [49].

References

[1] Koehler, J.J. (2001). When are people persuaded by DNA match statistics? *Law and Human Behavior* **25**, 493–513.

[2] National Academy of Sciences, National Research Council & Committee on Identifying the Needs of the Forensic Science Community (2009). *Strengthening Forensic Science in the United States: A Path Forward*, National Academies Press, Washington, DC.

[3] Expert Working Group on Human Factors in Latent Print Analysis (2012). *Latent Print Examination and Human Factors: Improving the Practice through a Systems Approach*, U.S. Department of Commerce, National Institute of Standards and Technology.

[4] National Research Council & Committee on DNA Forensic Science (1996). *The Evaluation of Forensic DNA Evidence*, National Academy Press, Washington, DC.

[5] Evett, I.W. & Weir, B.S. (1998). *Interpreting DNA Evidence*, Sinauer, Sunderland.

[6] Dawid, A.P. (2004). Which likelihood ratio? (Comment on: why the effect of prior odds should accompany the likelihood ratio when reporting DNA evidence), *Law, Probability and Risk* **3**, 65–71.

[7] Koehler, J.J. (1996). On conveying the probative value of DNA evidence: frequencies, likelihood ratios and error rates, *University of Colorado Law Review* **67**, 859–886.

[8] Koehler, J.J. (1997). Why DNA likelihood ratios should account for error (even when a National Research Council report says they should not), *Jurimetrics Journal* **37**, 425–437.

[9] Scurich, N. & John, R.S. (2013). Mock jurors' use of error rates in DNA database trawls, *Law & Human Behavior* **37**, 424–431.

[10] Morrison, G.S. (2011). The likelihood-ratio framework and forensic evidence in court: A response to R v T, *International Journal of Evidence and Proof* **15**, 1–29.

[11] Tang, Y. & Srihari, S.N. (2014). Likelihood ratio estimation in forensic identification using similarity and rarity, *Pattern Recognition* **47**, 945–958.

[12] Meester, R. & Sjerps, M. (2004). Why the effect of prior odds should accompany the likelihood ratio when reporting DNA evidence, *Law, Probability and Risk* **3**, 51–62.

[13] Koehler, J.J. (2011). If the shoe fits, they might acquit: the value of shoeprint testimony, *Journal of Empirical Legal Studies.* **8**, 21–48.

[14] Fenton, N. (2014). Assessing evidence and testing appropriate hypotheses, *Science and Justice* **54**, 502–504.

[15] Koehler, J.J., Chia, A. & Lindsey, J.S. (1995). The random match probability (RMP) in DNA evidence: irrelevant and prejudicial? *Jurimetrics Journal* **35**, 201–219.

[16] Lempert, R. (1991). Some caveats concerning DNA as criminal identification evidence: with thanks to the Reverend Bayes, *Cardozo Law Review* **13**, 303–341.

[17] Koehler, J.J. (2013). Proficiency tests to estimate error rates in the forensic sciences, *Law, Probability & Risk* **12**, 89–98.

[18] Thompson, W.C., Taroni, F. & Aitken, C.G.G. (2003). How the probability of a false positive affects the value of DNA evidence, *Journal of Forensic Science* **48**, 47–54.

[19] Saks, M.J. & Koehler, J.J. (2005). The coming paradigm shift in forensic identification science, *Science* **309**, 892–895.

[20] Christensen, A., Crowder, C., Ousley, S. & Houck, M. (2014). Error and its meaning in forensic science, *Journal of Forensic Sciences* **59**, 123–126.

[21] Budowle, B., Bottrell, M.C., Bunch, S.G., Fram, R., Harrison, D., Meagher, S., Oien, C.T., Peterson, P.E., Seiger, D.P., Smith, M.B., Smrz, M.A., Soltis, G.L. & Stacey, R.B. (2009). A perspective on errors, bias, and interpretation in the forensic sciences and direction for continuing advancement, *Journal of Forensic Sciences* **54**, 798–809.

[22] Kloosterman, A., Sjerps, M. & Quak, A. (2014). Error rates in forensic DNA analysis: definition, numbers, impact and communication, *Forensic Science International: Genetics* **12**, 77–85.

[23] Kahneman, D. & Tversky, A. (1973). On the psychology of prediction, *Psychological Review* **80**, 237–251.

[24] Koehler, J.J. (2008). Fingerprint error rates and proficiency tests: what they are and why they matter, *Hastings Law Journal* **59**, 1077–1098.

[25] Koehler, J.J. (2013). Proficiency tests to estimate error rates in the forensic sciences, *Law, Probability & Risk* **12**, 89–98.

[26] Hsu, S.S. (April 18, 2015). FBI admits flaws in hair analysis over decades. *The Washington Post*. http://www.washingtonpost.com/local/crime/fbi-overstated-forensic-hair-matches-in-nearly-all-criminal-trials-for-decades/2015/04/18/39c8d8c6-e515-11e4-b510-962fcfabc310_story.html

[27] Saks, M.J. & Koehler, J.J. (2008). The individualization fallacy in forensic science evidence, *Vanderbilt Law Review* **61**, 199–219.

[28] Osterburg, J.W. (1969). The evaluation of physical evidence in criminalistics: subjective or objective process? *Journal of Criminal Law and Criminology* **60**, 97–101.

[29] Cole, S.A. (2014). Individualization is dead, long live individualization! Reforms of reporting practices for fingerprint analysis in the United States, *Law, Probability and Risk* **13**, 117–150.

[30] Thompson, W.C. & Schumann, E.L. (1987). Interpretation of statistical evidence in criminal trials: the Prosecutor's Fallacy and the Defense Attorney's Fallacy, *Law and Human Behavior* **11**, 167–187.

[31] Koehler, J.J. (1993). Error and exaggeration in the presentation of DNA evidence, *Jurimetrics Journal* **34**, 21–39.

[32] Aitken, C.G.G. & Taroni, F. (2004). *Statistics and the Evaluation of Evidence for Forensic Scientists*, 2nd Edition, John Wiley and Sons Ltd, West Sussex, England, pp. 81–2.

[33] Fenton, N. & Neil, M. (2011). Avoiding probabilistic reasoning fallacies in legal practice using Bayesian networks, *Australian Journal of Legal Philosophy* **36**, 114–150.

[34] Thompson, W.C. & Newman, E.J. (2015). Lay understanding of forensic statistics: evaluation of random match probabilities, likelihood ratios, and verbal equivalents, *Law & Human Behavior* **39**, 332–349.

[35] Nisbett, R. & Wilson, T. (1977). Telling more than we know: verbal reports on mental processes, *Psychological Review* **84**, 231–257.

[36] Bornstein, B.H. (1999). The ecological validity of jury simulations: is the jury still out? *Law and Human Behavior* **23**, 75–91.

[37] Wiener, R.L., Krauss, D.A. & Lieberman, J.D. (2011). Mock Jury Research: Where Do We Go from Here? *Behavioral Sciences and the Law* **29**, 467–479.

[38] Hastie, R. (1994). Introduction, in *Inside the Juror: The Psychology of Juror Decision Making*, R. Hastie, ed, Cambridge University Press, Cambridge, pp. 3–41.

[39] Nance, D.A. & Morris, S.B. (2005). Juror understanding of DNA evidence: an empirical assessment presentation formats for trace evidence with a relatively small random match probability, *Journal of Legal Studies* **34**, 395–444.

[40] Kaye, D.H., Hans, V.P., Dann, B.M., Farley, E. & Albertson, S. (2007). Statistics in the jury box: Haw jurors respond to mitochondrial DNA match probabilities, *Journal of Empirical Legal Studies* **4**, 797–834.

[41] Kaye, D.H. & Koehler, J.J. (1991). Can jurors understand probabilistic evidence? *Journal of the Royal Statistical Society Series A* **154**(1), 75–81.

[42] Wolfe, C.R. (1995). Information seeking on Bayesian conditional probability problems: a fuzzy-trace theory account, *Journal of Behavioral Decision Making* **8**, 85–108.

[43] Scurich, N. & John, R.S. (2012). Prescriptive approaches to communicating the risk of violence in actuarial risk assessment, *Psychology, Public Policy, and Law* **18**, 50–78.

[44] Evett, I.W. (1995). Avoiding the transposed conditional, *Science & Justice* **35**, 127–131.

[45] Schklar, J. & Diamond, S. (1999). Juror reactions to DNA evidence: errors and expectancies, *Law and Human Behavior* **23**, 159–184.

[46] Fenton, N., Neil, M. & Hsu, A. (2014). Calculating and understanding the value of any type of match evidence when there are potential testing errors, *Artificial Intelligence Law* **22**, 1–28.

[47] Kahneman, D. & Tversky, A. (1982). The psychology of preferences, *Scientific American* **146**, 160–173.

[48] Koehler, J.J. & Macchi, L. (2004). Thinking about low-probability events: an exemplar cuing theory, *Psychological Science* **15**, 540–546.

[49] Wagenaar, W.A. (1988). The proper seat: a Bayesian discussion of the position of expert witnesses, *Law and Human Behavior* **12**, 499–510.

[50] Koehler, J.J. (2006). Train our jurors, in *Heuristics and The Law, Dahlem Workshop Report 94*, G. Gigerenzer & C. Engel, eds, The MIT Press, Cambridge.

Related Articles

Cross-Examination of Experts

Direct Examination of Experts

DNA

Ethical Rules of Expert Behavior

Issues in Forensic DNA

Legal Issues with Forensic DNA in the USA

Quantitation

Report Writing for Courts

Verbal Scales: A Legal Perspective

Chapter 35
Report Writing for Courts

Rhonda M. Wheate

The Forensic Institute, Glasgow, UK

Introduction

Expert witnesses occupy a unique position within legal proceedings, different from other witnesses, in that experts are permitted to offer evidence not only of facts, but of their *opinions*. This arises from their special role of assisting the judge (and jury, if there is one) in areas relevant to the matter under consideration *and* outside the expertise of ordinary folk [1].

Another important distinction between lay and expert witnesses is that the former are generally confined to giving evidence of facts within their own direct knowledge. In contrast, expert witnesses are, because of their expertise and skill in an area of specialized knowledge, permitted to give evidence based on facts known or reported by others in their field, for example, via peer-reviewed publications [2]. This is particularly relevant in experts' written reports, which may be based at least partially on work performed by others (such as laboratory technicians) and based on facts determined by others (such as technical specifications provided by laboratory equipment suppliers).

It is important to note that their privileged position does not allow experts to usurp the role of the fact finder (be that the judge or jury, if there is one). For although experts' opinions may in practice appear to come very close to doing so, the role of the expert is never to determine the guilt of the accused [3].

Thus, experts bear a heavy responsibility concomitant with the privilege of offering opinions as to the conclusions that may be drawn from the results of their work. Part of this responsibility includes the duty to give evidence *for the court*, not necessarily for the party retaining the expert. In many jurisdictions, this is spelled out explicitly in legislation or subordinate legislation: For example, the *Civil Procedure Rules* in England and Wales state, "It is the duty of an expert to help the court on the matters within his expertise. This duty overrides any obligation to the person from whom he has received instructions or by whom he is paid".[a] It is an issue widely discussed in case law too, for example: "It has been accepted in Scotland for some time that an expert witness owes a duty to the court. It has become established practice for an expert to state in his report that he is aware of and has complied with that duty." [4]. It is this duty that must be at the forefront of an expert's mind when writing a report for the court.

Concurrent with this responsibility and duty, experts in some jurisdictions enjoy immunity from suit for the contents of their written reports and oral evidence. In Scotland, for example, this immunity may even extend to joint statements made by multiple experts for multiple parties in civil suits [5]. In contrast, experts in England and Wales are afforded no immunity for the content of their written reports and oral evidence – aggrieved parties may sue the experts if the written report amounts to serious professional misconduct, and have successfully done so [6].

Given the gravity of the task and the potential for expert evidence to significantly impact upon the outcome of the legal proceedings, there arise several important steps for an expert to take when contemplating on writing a report for the court:

1. When a case file or exhibits are presented to an expert for analysis, first the expert must identify what sort of analysis or assessment needs to be done, in their expert opinion. Although working within a single discipline may provide an expert with case after case of similar evidence, it is

A Guide to Forensic DNA Profiling
Edited by Allan Jamieson and Scott Bader
© 2016 John Wiley & Sons, Ltd. ISBN: 9781118751527
Also published in EFS (online edition)
DOI: 10.1002/9780470061589.fsa031.pub2

important for the administration of justice in every individual case to consciously analyze what needs to be done *in this case*.

2. The expert must identify *why* they think that sort of analysis or assessment needs to be done in this case. This is not a rhetorical question, as lawyers, jurors, and judges who do not share the expert's specialized knowledge will not be familiar with why a particular technique or method of assessment was chosen or rejected in this case. For example, a forensic biologist may decide not to conduct low copy number (LCN) DNA testing on a set of crime scene samples. If a DNA profile has not been obtained using standard techniques, the decision not to use an LCN may seem to be illogical and incomprehensible to the investigators, lawyers, jurors, or the judges. It is imperative that the expert in this scenario is conscious not only of why they chose to use standard DNA profiling methods, but equally of why they did not use LCN testing (e.g., because sufficient precautions were not taken to avoid contamination at the scene and of the samples) [7]. This necessarily requires specialized knowledge of the technique, method, examination, or assessment, and a conscious evaluation by the expert of the appropriateness, validity, reliability, and limitations of the options available to them in the circumstances of the individual case.

3. Which techniques, examinations, or assessments were, in fact, carried out? This may differ from what the expert anticipated in steps 1 and 2. The report must reflect what was actually done, rather than any sort of idealized version of what the methods/techniques should have been and the results should have shown. If the results indicated that further or different examination/assessment needed to be conducted, the expert must be able to identify why this was or was not done, and what the results (or lack of results) mean. The report must reflect the work that was done and the results that were obtained, including the negative results. The latter is particularly important when the expert has been retained by the prosecution in a criminal trial. The duty of the prosecution to examine all of the evidence relating to the alleged crime – including evidence that exonerates the accused – extends to disclosing *negative* results to the defense.

4. In writing the report, the expert should be conscious of each of the previous steps. Sufficient details must be given in the report so that an interested lay audience is capable of comprehending the results and assessing the reliability and significance of the examination and/or assessment.

Legal Requirements of an Expert Report

Although the details vary depending on the jurisdiction,[b] expert reports usually require consideration of some or all of the elements set out below.[c] In common law countries, these arise both from legislation and from case law[d]; in some instances, it has been case law that precipitated changes to legislation. For instance, in England and Wales, the *Civil Procedure Rules* and *Criminal Procedure Rules* model the guidelines for expert witnesses set out in the *Ikarian Reefer* case.[e]

1. The expert must be independent. As discussed above, the primary duty of an expert is to the court. This means that the evidence given by the expert should not vary on the basis of the side paying the expert's fee. That is not to say that the form and content of the expert's report cannot vary. Naturally, each side to a legal dispute would ask different questions of the same expert and it is entirely permissible for an expert's report to focus on answering the questions asked by the side that retained them.[f] Furthermore, the expert is not necessarily required to volunteer every possible avenue of investigation or piece of information that has not specifically been asked of him, however, the expert is under a duty to volunteer information if a failure to do so would amount to leaving the court with a misleading impression of the expert's opinion on the issue [8].

What is additionally important is that if the expert was asked the *same* question by both parties, the expert's answer should be the same. Experts should consult with the lawyer who retained them to ensure that they are addressing the issues required by the retainer, and that they are not addressing matters that are not issues in the case and do not need to be included in the report.

Experts should also consider what might be asked of them in examination-in-chief and especially in cross-examination, where they should be prepared to explain how the theories they have based their opinions on have been developed, tested, measured, and found valid and reliable [9]. In particular, are they prepared to remain within the bounds of the statements contained in their written report, or do they expect to give evidence beyond what they have written? If the answer is the latter, the expert should consider why they have not contained this additional information in their written report. This is important, particularly where the expert has been retained by the prosecution, as the prosecution is obliged to disclose their case to the defense before the commencement of the criminal trial. If the report does not contain all of the information the expert considers important, or contains expressions of opinion in weaker/stronger terms than the expert would be prepared to give in oral evidence, this may be an issue in terms of appropriate disclosure.

2. The expert should not act as an advocate. If the specialized knowledge of the expert supports the case of the side, which called him/her, then the expert is entitled to assist the court with this knowledge. It is not necessary, desirable, or permissible, however, for an expert to have any vested interest in seeking to support one side or the other in a legal dispute. Neither the expert's report nor the oral testimony should move beyond their objective opinion[g] and into the territory of advocacy.

3. The expert must define[h] and remain within his/her area of expertise. "An expert should make it clear when a question or issue falls outside his expertise and when he is not able to reach a definite opinion, for example, because he has insufficient information".[i] There are two important principles in this statement.

First, an expert must be able to clearly identify, to themselves and to the court, their area of expertise. Judges and juries rely on expert witnesses to provide assistance in areas in which the judge/jury does not have specialized knowledge. It is important for expert evidence to be based on a recognized and developed academic discipline [10], and for experts to stay within their area of expertise,[j] both when writing their report and giving evidence in court.

Second, expert opinions and conclusions must be scientifically justifiable.[k] The nature of the discipline or a lack of available information may make it scientifically impossible for the expert to reach a definite opinion. This is sufficient and important information for the judge or jury, but the bases and limits of the evidence must be made clear.[l] There may be a valid and wide-ranging variety of opinions among experts in the field.[m] This does not invalidate the particular opinion of the author of the report, however, the range of opinions must be acknowledged by them. It is legally, scientifically, and morally imperative therefore that expert witnesses do not fabricate knowledge, omnipotence, or certainty that they do not have.

In addition, it is necessary to identify in writing any other persons who assisted in the examinations or assessments recorded in the report. This usually includes a reference to other experts, laboratory staff, etc., who have handled/tested/participated in the testing of exhibits. This safeguards the expert who may not have handled the exhibits or samples at every step of the forensic process, but who has been asked to write a report setting out the work that has been carried out and their expert opinion of the results.

4. The expert must state the facts and assumptions that underlie his/her opinion. This is an important tool, which seeks to enable judges and juries to assess the expert's opinion [11]. For example, under the *Civil Procedure Rules* in England and Wales, the expert's report must state the substance of all material instructions, whether written or oral, on the basis of which the report was written.[n] In addition, if the expert is relying on professional literature as a source of facts or assumptions in their report, this should be made clear [12]. It is not necessary to provide a thesis explaining the basis of the discipline; however, the expert must be a specialist in the relevant field [13], or a closely related field [14], and, particularly if the methods used are at the cutting edge of science, the expert should refer the court directly to relevant published literature. Despite their expertise, expert witnesses are not the final word on technical, scientific, or medical questions in a legal dispute [15]. The judge or jury must ultimately decide whether or not they accept the opinion of the expert, and to do this they must know the facts and assumptions that created the basis of the expert's opinions [16].

When writing a report, an expert should also make clear the distinction between facts and opinions.

Although the expert is allowed to give evidence of both (unlike ordinary witnesses, who are not generally allowed to offer opinions), the judge or jury needs to know which aspects of the expert's report are accepted facts and which are the opinions of the particular witness.

5. The expert must consider all material facts. In order for the expert opinion to be useful to the judge or jury, the expert must consider not only the facts that support the case theory of the side that retained them but also all of the material facts. Case law amply demonstrates instances of individuals deciding that particular pieces of information are not relevant to the case at hand, when, in fact, if each of those individual pieces of information was disclosed, a significant picture could emerge. This was the case in *R v. Ward*, where seemingly innocuous individual decisions by police officers, prosecutors, counsel, and others combined to remove a significant body of evidence from the trial, resulting in a successful appeal by the accused. "Taken by itself, [the omitted statement] may well have been thought to have no bearing on the question of the appellant's responsibility for the offences with which she was charged, but when compared with the other [evidence that was withheld], its relevance to the crucial problem of discovering the truth or falseness of the appellant's various statements becomes apparent" [17].

6. If, in the course of their participation in legal proceedings, the expert changes their mind or significantly modifies the opinion expressed in their written report, this should be communicated to the party retaining them, and, if necessary, communicated to the court.[o] In the early stages of proceedings, for instance, in the information-gathering phase before a trial proper, it is particularly important that the written report accurately reflects the view of the expert. The lawyer retaining the expert may be proceeding with a particular case theory or mode of building their case, which rests on what they think the expert will be able to assist them with in the court. Thus, it is imperative that the expert is utterly forthcoming with their legal retainer at all times.

7. Other requirements and considerations: Most jurisdictions provide guidance[p] or specify other requirements for expert reports,[q] which may include a list of the expert's qualifications and experience, their accreditation by relevant professional bodies, membership of professional institutions, career history, a list of prior court testimony, a list of documents or exhibits used to prepare the report, any limitations or qualifications of the report, and compensation received for the expert's opinion.[r] Experts are advised to consult the lawyer who retained them to ensure that such requirements are met for the jurisdictions in which they have been asked to write the report. Other considerations such as the length and format of the report vary widely and should be clarified on a case-to-case basis. In all jurisdictions, it is helpful if the expert report is written using plain language, and that jargon and abbreviations are used only when necessary and are defined in the report. Draft reports should be marked as such; these may be subject to discovery in some jurisdictions (*see Discovery of Expert Findings*).

Overall, experts are reminded that everything in a report is examinable in court. It does not serve justice, or the reputation of the expert, or that of their profession, if written reports prepared for legal proceedings contain statements of fact or opinion that are not true, or that stretch beyond the expertise of the expert or the state of play in their field. Expert reports should be accurate, comprehensive, balanced, and transparent, in order to fulfill the privileged role afforded to expert witnesses in legal proceedings.

Acknowledgments

The author would like to acknowledge the invaluable guidance and editorial assistance given by Professor Allan Jamieson toward the production of this article.

End Notes

[a.] Civil Procedure Rules 1998 (England and Wales) Rule 35.3. The Criminal Procedure Rules 2014 (England and Wales) contain an equivalent provision at Rule 33.2.

[b.] It is noted that the US Department of Justice and the National Institute of Justice (Office of Justice Programs) have, under "The DNA Initiative", funded the National Forensic Science Technology Centre to develop Guidelines for Forensic Experts along similar lines to the points set out in this article. The US Guide can be found at swgfast.org "Law 101: Legal Guide for the Forensic Expert".

c. The legal requirements of expert reports in the United States of America are set out in Discovery in the United States: Civil Cases and Discovery in the United States: Criminal Cases.

d. See Forensic Science Regulator *Legal Obligations* FSR-I-400 (2012) for an overview of the obligations placed on expert witnesses in the criminal justice system in England and Wales.

e. National Justice Compania Naviera SA *v* Prudential Life Assurance Co Ltd (the *'Ikarian Reefer'* case) (No 1) (1995). 1 Lloyd's Rep 455 per Cresswell J. Although an English case, the *Ikarian Reefer* has been approved many times in other jurisdictions, e.g., Elf Caledonian Limited v London Bridge Engineering Limited (*'Piper Alpha'*) OHCS 2 September 1997, unreported, at 224; and McTear v Imperial Tobacco Ltd [2005] CSOH 69.

f. See Lord Carloway's judgment in Amy White-head's Legal Representative v Graeme John Douglas and Another [2006] CSOH 178, which although focusing on oral evidence, may be applied to written reports too.

g. Criminal Procedure Rules 2014 (England and Wales) Rule 33.2.

h. Criminal Procedure Rules 2014 (England and Wales) Rule 33.2.

i. Civil Procedure Rules (UK) "Experts and Assessors" Practice Direction 1.5. Also Criminal Procedure Rules 2014 (England and Wales) Rule 33.2.

j. Criminal Procedure Rules 2014 (England and Wales) Rule 33.2.

k. Law Commission *Report on Expert Evidence in Criminal proceedings in England and Wales* (Law Com No 325) (2011) Schedule 1 Part 1; see also Young v HM Advocate 2014 SLT 21 (HCJ) at 54 per Lord Menzies.

l. Law Commission *Report on Expert Evidence in Criminal proceedings in England and Wales* (Law Com No 325) (2011) Schedule 1 Part 1; see also Young v HM Advocate 2014 SLT 21 (HCJ) at 54 per Lord Menzies.

m. Law Commission *Report on Expert Evidence in Criminal proceedings in England and Wales* (Law Com No 325) (2011) Schedule 1 Part 1.

n. Civil Procedure Rules (UK) Rule 35.10.

o. National Justice Compania Naviera SA *v* Prudential Life Assurance Co Ltd (the *'Ikarian Reefer'* case) (No 1) (1995). 1 Lloyd's Rep 455 per Cresswell J. Also Criminal Procedure Rules 2014 (England and Wales) Rule 33.2.

p. See, for instance, the "Code of Practice: Expert Witnesses Engaged by Solicitors" by the Law Society of Scotland http://www.expertwitnessscotland.info/-codepract.htm

q. See Criminal Procedure Rules 2014 (England and Wales) Rule 33.4 for a comprehensive list of these sorts of required inclusions.

r. Even if not required in the written report, testimony as to compensation paid to or forgone by the witness may be raised as an issue during oral testimony. See McTear v Imperial Tobacco Ltd [2005] CSOH 69 at [5.18] per Lord Nimmo Smith.

References

[1] See, for example, Gage v HM Advocate (No 1), HCJCA 40, 2012 SCCR 161 (2011).

[2] R v Adadom, 1 WLR 126 at 129 per Lord Justice Kerr (1983).

[3] Davie v Edinburgh Magistrates, SC 34 at 40 per Lord Cooper (1953).

[4] BSA International SA v Irvine, CSOH 77; 2009 S.L.T. 1180 per Lord Glennie (2009).

[5] Watson v McEwan, 7 F (HL) 109 (1905).

[6] Jones v Kaney, UKSC 13, in a landmark decision, held by a majority of 5-2 (2011).

[7] R v Hoey,. NICC 49 (20 December 2007) per Weir J (2007).

[8] BSA International SA v Irvine, CSOH 77; 2009 S.L.T. 1180 (2009).

[9] Young v HM Advocate, SLT 21 (HCJ) at 54 per Lord Menzies (2014).

[10] Young v HM Advocate, SLT 21 (HCJ) at 54 per Lord Menzies (2014).

[11] Dingley v The Chief Constable, Strathclyde Police, SC 548, 2000 SC (HL) 77 at 604 (1998) per Lord Prosser: "…the fact that a particular view was or is held by someone of great distinction, whether he is a witness or not, does not seem to me to give any particular weight to his view, if the reasons for his coming to that view are unexplained, or unconvincing. As with judicial or other opinions, what carries weight is the reasoning, not the conclusion."

[12] Main v Andrew Wormald Ltd, SLT 141 at 142 per Lord Justice-Clerk (Lord Ross) (1988).

[13] Main v Andrew Wormald Ltd, SLT 141 at 143 per Lord McDonald (1988).

[14] Main v Andrew Wormald Ltd, SLT 141 at 142 per Lord Justice-Clerk (Lord Ross) (1988).

[15] McTear v Imperial Tobacco Ltd, CSOH 69 at [5.16] per
      Lord Nimmo Smith (2005).
[16] John Pierce v HM Advocate, SCLR 783 1981.
[17] R v Ward, 1 WLR 619 (1993).

Related Articles in EFS Online

Discovery: Depositions

Discovery: Discovery Motions

Discovery of Expert Findings in the United States: Federal Civil Cases

Discovery in the United States: Criminal Cases

Chapter 36
Discovery of Expert Findings

Rhonda M. Wheate

The Forensic Institute, Glasgow, UK

Introduction

Discovery (also termed *disclosure* in some jurisdictions) is a pretrial process by which a party to a legal action seeks to gain access to documents or other evidence held by, or for, another party. The aim of discovery is to ensure that there is a fair, transparent, and consistent process for informing the respondents to legal proceedings (i.e., the defense in criminal trials and the respondent in civil proceedings) about relevant material sought to be relied upon by the instigator of legal proceedings (i.e., the prosecution in criminal trial and the claimant in civil proceedings). Discovery also allows the parties to find evidence, confirm evidence, identify issues, identify areas of agreement, identify material that the instigator of proceedings will not be relying upon in the legal proceedings, and to avoid surprise evidence (trial by ambush). In some matters, disclosure is automatic, and parties are entitled to access. In other matters, a case has to be made for disclosure, and the matter is determined by a judicial officer. The requirements are highly jurisdiction specific.

In forensic science, discovery is not necessarily limited to the formal expert report that is prepared for use in court.[a] Discovery of "material" generally includes disclosure of primary records contained in the case file, any pertinent materials recovered or generated during the testing or examination, any secondary records such as batch records, standardization and calibration records, audio and video tapes, computer records, and survey information.[b]

Thus, discovery is intended to enable a party to ascertain the underlying method and results that created the opinion and conclusions reported in the expert's statement. In addition, discovery may be necessary to determine the significance of items not seized, examined, tested, or reported in the expert's statement. "Unused material," in this context, is that material which is not identified within the expert's report(s) or statement(s)[b] but which may still be relevant, particularly to opposing parties. Discovery is also a means of investigating the validation and accreditation of methods, the training and competence of analysts, and contamination issues. The additional materials sought through the process of discovery may be contained in briefing papers, internal reports, staff training and performance assessments, laboratory records, case files, submission forms, labels, electronic data, apparatus printouts, calculations, notes, drafts, and correspondence. Not all of this information is automatically disclosed in all jurisdictions, and in some instances, a court order may be required for discovery of particular material. In some jurisdictions of the United States, for instance, discovery of the electronic data underlying DNA profiling evidence may require the party seeking disclosure to obtain a court order, though many of the obligations of disclosure in the United States occur informally [1].

Expert witnesses in most jurisdictions have a formal duty to keep accurate, up-to-date, and thorough records of all dealings that relate to the matters set out in their reports for court. For example, the Code set out by the Forensic Regulator of the United Kingdom requires that "full records shall be kept of work done and the results obtained."[c] This provides a basis for discovery by opposing parties, about the foundations of the expert's opinions and report.

A Guide to Forensic DNA Profiling
Edited by Allan Jamieson and Scott Bader
© 2016 John Wiley & Sons, Ltd. ISBN: 9781118751527
Also published in EFS (online edition)
DOI: 10.1002/9780470061589.fsa011.pub2

Discovery in Common and Civil Law Systems

Formal processes of discovery are mainly a feature of *common law* jurisdictions (e.g., the United States, the United Kingdom, Canada, and Australia), which use an adversarial legal process. Under common law principles, "the law" is sourced not only from legislation but also from precedents laid down by judges in equivalent or higher courts (*stare decisis*). In this system, the parties (rather than the judge) largely control the direction of the matter, the nature of the investigations, the list of witnesses, and the extent to which discovery of information is sought and pursued.

Conversely, legal systems based on Roman and/or Germanic legal traditions (e.g., in France, Germany, Spain, and Italy) center upon codified laws. In these systems, legal decisions are based on legislative codes rather than on precedents from other courts (although judicial decisions may, in practice, be persuasive). Judges play a more active role in investigating incidents and determining how procedural matters are handled. Discovery in this context is usually fully expected,[d] actively controlled,[e] and openly investigated by the judge, rather than by the parties. The emphasis in this system is on the substance of the material sought for the investigation, rather than on the form of the discovery procedures.

In Germany, for example, discovery is governed by the *Code of Criminal Procedure (StPO)*[f] and the *Code of Civil Procedure (ZPO)*.[g] Judges are duty-bound to investigate the charges against the accused, by finding and examining whatever material will assist in determining the truth, and by appointing and directing experts as required. Formal procedures of discovery and considerations of rules of evidence are of minor importance in this model, compared with their importance in common law systems.

In 1989, Italy attempted a large-scale legislative reform to change the existing inquisitorial system to an "accusatorial" model (a combination of inquisitorial and adversarial features). This may have had some impact on the procedural criminal law relating to discovery; however, frequent subsequent legislative revisions largely seem to have returned to an inquisitorial, judge-led investigation of all relevant material held by expert witnesses for both the prosecution and defense.[h]

Criminal and Civil Law Procedures

Even in a discussion of "discovery of expert findings," a distinction must also be drawn between *criminal* and *civil* matters. While the former is usually the prosecution of an individual by the state (e.g., a murder trial), the latter is usually the action of an individual against another individual (e.g., a negligence claim by a patient against a doctor).

Discovery in Criminal Matters

In criminal matters, in most jurisdictions, there is a constitution-level standard of protection for the accused. For example, *Article 6* of the *European Convention on Human Rights (ECHR)*[i] – *The Right to a Fair Trial* impliedly enables the accused in a criminal matter to have access to the evidence against him, including the expert evidence. Most of the laws of discovery in criminal proceedings focus on broad and automatic disclosure by the prosecution to the defense. This reflects the inherent imbalance of power between the state and the individual and seeks to bring an equality of arms to the criminal trial [2].

In Scotland, for instance, the ECHR requirements are given more detail in local legislation[j] which places upon the prosecution a duty, in perpetuity, to provide to the defense all *material* information including that which[k]:

(a) would materially weaken or undermine the evidence that is likely to be led by the prosecutor in the proceedings against the accused,
(b) would materially strengthen the accused's case, or
(c) is likely to form part of the evidence to be led by the prosecutor in the proceedings against the accused.

This "materiality test"[l] includes forensic material which the prosecution (and by extension, the experts retained by the prosecution) are aware of that might assist the defense, for example, by undermining or casting reasonable doubt upon the prosecution case [3].

Note that the "materiality test" does *not* require the prosecution in Scotland to disclose everything. Neutral information or information that would be damaging to the defense but which does not form part of the prosecution case does *not* need to be disclosed and does not need to be brought to the attention of the court (as it is considered to be "of no evidential significance" to any party) [4].

The duty of the prosecution to disclose the above material in Scotland does *not* depend on the defense making an application or request for disclosure [5]; however, in practice, defense experts may be provided with a copy of the prosecution expert's written report and little more.[m] Thus, in order to ascertain what material was available for testing by the prosecution expert and to verify the testing that was performed by them (including checking that the methods were appropriate, the tests properly performed, the results correctly derived, and the opinion reliably inferred from the result), defense experts in Scotland attend the prosecution laboratory to "precognose" the prosecution expert.[n] This approach has been endorsed by the courts [6].

Overall, it is noted that "[i]n most other jurisdictions, including England and Wales, there is disclosure of the Crown's case which virtually removes the need for independent investigation by the Defence. The practice of precognition-taking costs the [Scottish] taxpayer between £20 million and £27 million per year."[o]

In contrast to Scotland, in England and Wales it is a fundamental feature of the criminal trial that the defendant should know the case against him or her. Thus, "disclosure is at the very heart of the criminal process in England and Wales" [7].

In England and Wales, the Criminal Procedure Rules 2014 Part 33[p] requires that:

> (3) A party who wants to introduce expert evidence otherwise than as admitted fact must –

> (d) if another party so requires, give that party a copy of, or a reasonable opportunity to inspect –

> (i) a record of any examination, measurement, test or experiment on which the expert's findings and opinion are based, or that were carried out in the course of reaching those findings and opinion, and
> (ii) anything on which any such examination, measurement, test or experiment was carried out.

Although the Rules confer responsibility for disclosure onto the prosecution and the police, rather than directly onto the expert witness, it is imperative that expert witnesses enable the prosecution and police to comply with their obligations under the law.[q] Therefore, for most expert witnesses called by the prosecution, the range of material required for discovery is wide and the obligation is ongoing.[r]

Under the common law and under the Criminal Procedure Rules in England and Wales, the defense does not share the obligations of voluntary discovery imposed upon the prosecution – indeed, defense experts "are not obliged to reveal a previous report they have made" [8] or any previous "adverse judicial criticism" they or their reports may have attracted [8]. Under the Criminal Procedure Rules, however, it is noted that the court has explicit case management powers that enable it to require a significant amount of disclosure and cooperation between experts. In this process, previous reports or criticisms may become apparent in the course of case management hearings and/or cross-examination, and a failure by the defense expert to disclose them earlier may reflect poorly on the credibility and trustworthiness of that witness.[s]

While the legislation in England and Wales has evolved,[t] discovery is also governed by guidance[u] and case law, where full disclosure has been termed a *golden rule* of the criminal trial [9]. Cases such as R v Ward [10], R v Davis [11], and R v H&C [12] have firmly established that a duty of disclosure exists irrespective of any request by the defense; it extends to *all* material matters that affect the scientific case relied upon by the prosecution; and, that the duty is ongoing. *Ward* placed a clear obligation on expert witnesses who have carried out or know of experiments or tests which tend to cast doubt upon the opinion being expressed, to bring records of those tests to the attention of the instructing solicitor [10].

Failure by prosecution experts to disclose material (either to the prosecution or the defense[v]) may result in a delayed prosecution, or cessation of the prosecution altogether, a successful appeal by the defense (i.e., a finding that a conviction is unsafe), censure of the expert, or the inability to use expert evidence that was not properly disclosed.[w]

In the United Kingdom, primary disclosure by expert witnesses is usually initiated by the prosecution serving the expert's report on the defense.[w] If the defense, or defense-retained experts, require further material from the prosecution, arrangements are made through the prosecution legal team.

In contrast, in France, the *Code of Criminal Procedure* enables investigating judges to control the disclosure of "available information helpful for the discovery of the truth," a list of expert witnesses, timely disclosure of expert reports, and so on.[x] Broad provisions go on to provide that a judicial police officer may order any person, public, or private establishment or organization, likely to possess "any documents relevant to the inquiry in progress," including those produced from a computer or data-processing system, to provide them with these documents. Failure to comply as quickly as possible can result in a fine or criminal sanction.[y]

Discovery in Civil Matters

For discovery in civil actions, rules are usually set out in legislation and regulations. Arguments ordinarily arise as to the extent of the disclosure sought and the likely burden imposed on the party from whom disclosure is sought.

Disclosure in civil matters in England and Wales is governed by the Civil Procedure Rules (*CPR*).[z] One of the objectives of the *CPR* is to ensure that parties are on an equal footing.[aa] This harks back to the "equivalence of arms" theory, which posits that both parties in a legal action are entitled to know what weapons are held by the opposing side and to have the opportunity to arm themselves accordingly. The *CPR* defines "document" broadly, as meaning "anything in which information of any description is recorded."[ab] Disclosure is required of any document relied upon by a party, and documents that support or adversely affect a party's case or another party's case.[ac] The duty of disclosure is ongoing in civil matters; it continues until proceedings are concluded.[ad] A party who fails to disclose or permit inspection of documents may not rely on that document in the proceedings.[ae]

Civil procedure in Germany is governed by the *Code of Civil Procedure (ZPO)*,[af] which specifies procedures from prehearing stages to the decision. Parties and witnesses can be sworn to tell the truth, with perjury or false statements being classified as criminal offences. Evidence is adduced in a number of forms, including site inspection, witness testimony (expert and lay), private or public documents, and evidence from the parties. As in criminal disclosure procedures, the evidence-taking procedures in civil matters are controlled by the judge.[ag]

Conclusion

The rules of discovery are particular to each jurisdiction, though the underlying necessity of the accused

(in criminal matters) or the respondent (in civil proceedings) knowing the case against them remains the same in all jurisdictions. The extent to which parties in common law jurisdictions have to apply for or actively seek discovery, and the ease with which they are able to obtain material (used or unused in the action against them) from their opposition, depends on not only statutory provisions but also government-ministry or department-level guidelines, local case law, and local practice. In civil law jurisdictions, where judicial discretion and power is more encompassing, discovery of all relevant material is a matter for the presiding judicial officer.

Acknowledgments

The author would like to acknowledge the invaluable guidance and editorial assistance given by Professor Allan Jamieson toward the production of this article.

End Notes

a. See Forensic Science Regulator *Legal Obligations* FSR-I-400 (2012) Part 6 for an overview of the Disclosure and Preservation obligations placed on expert witnesses in the criminal justice system in England and Wales.

b. The Forensic Science Regulator "Codes of Practice and Conduct for Forensic Science Providers and Practitioners in the criminal Justice System," Version 2.0 August 2014 at 25.4.2.

c. The Forensic Science Regulator "Codes of Practice and Conduct for Forensic Science Providers and Practitioners in the criminal Justice System," Version 2.0 August 2014 at 25.1.4.

d. The Criminal Code of the Kingdom of Spain, at Article 460, for instance, states "Should the witness, expert or interpreter, without substantially misconstruing the truth, alter it with hesitation, inexactness or by silencing relevant facts or data known to him, he shall be punished with the penalty of a fine from six to twelve months and, when appropriate, suspension from public employment and office, profession or trade, of six months to three years."

e. Criminal Procedure Code of the French Republic Section 9: The Expert.

f. German Code of Criminal Procedure (StPO) Chapter VII Experts and Inspection.

g. Code of Civil Procedure (ZPO) Title 8 Evidence Provided by Experts, which contains clauses such as: "s404a(1) The court is to direct the expert in terms of his activities and may issue instructions as concerns their nature and scope" and "s407a(4) Should the court so demand, the expert is to surrender or communicate the files and any other documents he has used to prepare his report, as well as any results of his investigations, doing so without undue delay. Should he fail to comply with this obligation, the court shall order that such files, documents, and results be surrendered."

h. The Criminal Procedure Code of the Republic of Italy provides that the public prosecutor is responsible at first instance for investigating alleged crimes, including appointing experts to carry out examinations (Article 219). If the matter moves beyond this initial investigation and a preliminary hearing before a judge, a trial is conducted during which all evidence, including the expert evidence, is re-examined.

i. Adopted in 1950 under the auspices of the Council of Europe, to which all European states (except Belarus, Kazakhstan, and the Holy See) have acceded.

j. Criminal Justice and Licensing (Scotland) Act 2010 Part 6: Disclosure. At s166 pf the Act it is noted that this legislation replaces any equivalent common law rules about disclosure in Scotland in so far as they are covered by or inconsistent with the statute.

k. Criminal Justice and Licensing (Scotland) Act 2010 s 121(3).

l. In England and Wales it is referred to as the "Disclosure test."

m. The "Disclosure Manual – Prosecution Policy Guidance," Crown Office and Procurator Fiscal Service, Dec 2014 Part 6.9 Forensic Files (http://www.copfs. gov.uk/publications/prosecution-policy-and-guidance) states at Part 6.9.4: There is no obligation on the Crown to obtain from the Forensic Laboratory and thereafter disclose to the defence, the written recordings of their workings which relate to the examination carried out and form the basis of the report which is then prepared and revealed to the Crown. And at 6.9.5: These items will form the contents of a forensic case file. There is no routine obligation to reveal such information or to provide the contents of the forensic case file to the police or Crown unless it contains relevant information which has not been included within the joint report or associated witness statement(s). And at 6.9.6: There may occasionally be the need for limited, supervised access to forensic notes during defence precognitions or defence examinations to allow a defence expert with sufficient knowledge and skill to interpret such notes in order to assess them for materiality. Followed by 6.9.7: Forensic scientists will not provide the defence with copies of material from the file or allow the case files or any part of them to be removed or copied unless on the directly [sic] instruction of the prosecutor.

n. Precognition is a practice used in Scotland to take a factual statement from a witness prior to civil or criminal proceedings. The statement itself is not admissible as evidence (McNeilie v H.M.A. 1929 J.C. 51 per Lord Justice-General Clyde); rather, the purpose of the precognition is to give the precognoser some indication of what the witness might say in court. Precognitions are often undertaken by trainee lawyers or special precognition officers (many of whom are former police officers) employed by legal firms. (The Work of Precognition Agents in Criminal Cases, David J. Christie Susan R. Moody University of Dundee The Scottish Executive Central Research Unit 1999.) Precognition has not traditionally been part of the skill set of a forensic scientist, but the recent policies of the Scottish Police Authority Forensic Services and Scottish Crown Office and Procurator Fiscal's Service now require it. Defence experts in Scotland must formulate questions about the contents of the prosecution expert's case file, case notes, testing, methods, results and opinions, purely on the basis of the expert's official report. If necessary they are able to return more than once to the prosecution laboratory (or to the court, seeking an order for commission and diligence) to ask additional questions based on what has been disclosed so far.

o. The Work of Precognition Agents in Criminal Cases David J. Christie Susan R. Moody University of Dundee The Scottish Executive Central Research Unit 1999.

p. Largely replacing rules about disclosure previously found in the Criminal Procedure and Investigations Act (CPIA) 1996 and the Criminal Justice Act (CJA) 2003.

q. Crown Prosecution Service: Prosecution Policy and Guidance: Legal Guidance: Disclosure Manual (at http://www.cps.gov.uk/legal/d_to_g/disclosure_manual).

r. Guidance Booklet for Experts: Disclosure: Expert's Evidence, Case Management and Unused Material Crown Prosecution Service, May 2010.

http://www.cps.gov.uk/legal/d_to_g/disclosure_
manual/annex_k_disclosure_manual/

[s.] Forensic Science Regulator (UK) Legal Obligations FSR-I-400 (2012) Part 6.

[t.] The obligations in relation to unused material and disclosure are determined by the date on which the investigation began. Where the investigation began before 1 April 1997, the common law disclosure rules will apply. Investigators and prosecutors should refer to the 2000 Guidelines, the 1997 Code of Practice and the Joint Operational Instructions 2002. Where the investigation began on or after 1 April 1997 but before 4 April 2005, then the unamended Criminal Procedure and Investigations Act will apply, and investigators and prosecutors should refer to the above editions of the Code of Practice and the Joint Operational Instructions. Where the investigation began on or after 4 April 2005, then the Criminal Procedure and Investigations Act 1996, as amended by the Criminal Justice Act 2003, applies. Investigators and prosecutors should therefore refer to the 2005 editions of the Code of Practice, and this edition of the Disclosure Manual (formerly the Joint Operational Instructions). All judicial interpretations of the Criminal Procedure and Investigations Act 1996 and Code of Practice from time to time will continue to apply, (e.g., R v H and C (2004) UKHL 3). See http://www.cps.gov.uk/legal/d_to_g/disclosure_
manual/disclosure_manual_chapter_1/.

[u.] See "Attorney General's Guidelines on Disclosure" at http://www.cps.gov.uk/legal/a_to_c/attorney_
generals_guidelines_on_disclosure/.

[v.] Crown Prosecution Service: Prosecution Policy and Guidance: Legal Guidance: Disclosure Manual (at http://www.cps.gov.uk/legal/d_to_g/disclosure_
manual/disclosure_manual_foreword/) which states: the scheme set out in the Criminal Procedure and Investigations Act 1996 (the CPIA 1996) as amended by the Criminal Justice Act 2003 and the revised Code of Practice issued under it (the Code of Practice) is designed to ensure that there is a fair system for the disclosure of unused material, which: assists the defence in the timely preparation and presentation of its case; does not overburden the parties; and enables the court to focus on all the important issues in the trial. This endeavour is supported by compliance with the requirements of the current version of the Consolidated Criminal Procedure Rules. The operational instructions contained in this manual are designed to provide a practical guide to disclosure principles and procedures, building on the framework of the CPIA 1996, the Code of Practice and the Attorney General's Guidelines.

[w.] Guidance Booklet for Experts: Disclosure: Expert's Evidence, Case Management and Unused Material Crown Prosecution Service, May 2010. http://www.cps.gov.uk/legal/d_to_g/disclosure_
manual/annex_k_disclosure_manual/.

[x.] Code of Criminal Procedure (France) Article 60–2.

[y.] Code of Criminal Procedure (France) Article 60–1.

[z.] Civil Procedure Rules (UK) Part 31: Disclosure and Inspection of Documents.

[aa] Civil Procedure Rules (UK) Part 1: Overriding Objective.

[ab] Civil Procedure Rules (UK) Part 31: 31.4.

[ac] Civil Procedure Rules (UK) Part 31: 31.6.

[ad] Civil Procedure Rules (UK) Part 31: 31.11.

[ae] Civil Procedure Rules (UK) Part 31: 31.21.

[af] Code of Civil Procedure (ZPO) Title 8 Evidence Provided by Experts.

[ag] The practise in Germany is representative of similar regimes for civil disclosure in other civil law states including France, Italy, and Spain.

References

[1] Moenssens, A. (2009). Discovery in the United States: criminal cases, in *Wiley Encyclopedia of Forensic Science*, Wiley-VCH, Weinheim.

[2] Sinclair v Her Majesty's Advocate, SCCR 446 per Lord Hope (2005).

[3] McDonald v HM advocate [AC], SCCR 154 at para 50 (2008).

[4] R v H&C, AC 1324 (2004).

[5] McDonald v HM Advocate [AC], SCCR 154 at para 55 and also Sinclair v Her Majesty's Advocate (2005). SCCR 446 or 2005 SC (PC) 28 at para 53 (2008).

[6] HM Advocate v Robert Leiper Graham, Lord uist, unreported. 23 August (2011).

[7] Niblett, J. (1997). *Disclosure in Criminal Proceedings*, Blackstone, London.

[8] R v Henderson and Ors, EWCA Crim 1269 at 211 (2010).

[9] R v H and Others, 2 WLR 335 at 14–17 (2004).

[10] R v Ward, 1 WLR 619 (1993).

[11] R v Davis (1993) 1 WLR 613, which refined the procedural implications of R v Ward (1993) 1 WLR 619 and was, in effect, sanctioned by ss 3(6), 7(5), 14(2), 15(2), and 21(2) of the Criminal Procedure and Investigations Act 1996, by the Crown Court (Criminal Procedure and Investigations Act 1996) (Disclosure) Rules 1997

(SI 1997/698) and by the Magistrates' Courts (Criminal Procedure and Investigations Act 1996) (Disclosure) Rules 1997 (SI 1997/703).

[12] R v H&C (2004) UKHL 3 in which it was held, at [14], that "[f]airness ordinarily requires that any material held by the prosecution which weakens its case or strengthens that of the defendant, if not relied on as part of its formal case against the defendant, should be disclosed to the defence. Bitter experience has shown that miscarriages of justice may occur where such material is withheld from disclosure. The golden rule is that full disclosure of such material should be made."

Related Articles in EFS Online

Discovery: Depositions

Discovery: Discovery Motions

Discovery of Expert Findings in the United States: Federal Civil Cases

Discovery in the United States: Criminal Cases

Chapter 37
Ethical Rules of Expert Behavior

Andre A. Moenssens[1,2]

[1]University of Missouri at Kansas City, Kansas City, MO, USA
[2]University of Richmond, Richmond, VA, USA

Introduction

DNA experts involved in criminal casework generally operate within a forensic rather than a medical or bioscience environment. The general ethics and codes of practice applying to them are therefore those encountered by the forensic community, although not always. There are no ethical codes of practice designed specifically for DNA analysts or experts. Indeed forensic DNA experts may or may not be members of several organizations that have codes of practice, or none. All forensic practitioners must nevertheless be compliant with the legal requirements for expert witnesses within their jurisdiction. Regardless of whether there is a legal requirement to adhere to a Code of Practice it may be expected that a court would consider these absent any other means by which to judge an expert's performance and behavior in the event of litigation being pursued against an expert. This discussion therefore encompasses the wider forensic community.

It is universally understood that, in the practice of their professions, forensic scientists are required to refrain from unethical practices. But what is "unethical" is often difficult to determine. By what standard is the ethical nature of one's conduct to be measured? The first source of information of what is considered unacceptable professional behavior is usually to be found in the Code of Ethics of the professional association to which one belongs. Most forensic membership groups maintain a Code of Ethics.[a] As many scientists belong to more than one society, the person's conduct may be governed by several different codes of ethics that may not necessarily look similar. All of them, however, make engaging in ethical conduct a requirement of belonging to the association and provide sanctions for violating the professional standards of conduct.

In addition to defining unprofessional conduct, codes of ethics also typically contain procedural mechanisms whereby purported unethical conduct is to be investigated and, if appropriate, sanctioned. Such sanctions can run the gamut from a mere reprimand to expulsion from membership in the organization. This may, at times, be accompanied with loss of license, accreditation, or board certification. Because the law in common law countries tends to view membership in a professional association as a valuable property right, the mechanisms whereby a person is stripped of that right must comport with procedural safeguards against abusive and otherwise improper exercise of the power to sanction. Because of the great variety of mechanisms this article will not concern itself with the "due process" aspects of procedures that seek to enforce the ethical injunctions imposed upon an association's membership. This article is confined to a general overview of what conduct may be regarded unethical.

The conflicts between the codes of various groups are at times *de minimis*, but one must nevertheless remain sensitive to the fact that wide differences in approach to ethics can exist. Some experts who also must possess a license to practice their profession granted by governmental authorities in some countries – i.e., medical doctors, dentists, psychiatrists, and psychologists, and so on – may see their licenses jeopardized if found to have been sanctioned for unethical professional behavior.

Update based on original article by Andre Moenssens, Wiley Encyclopedia of Forensic Science © 2009, John Wiley & Sons, Ltd.

A Guide to Forensic DNA Profiling
Edited by Allan Jamieson and Scott Bader
© 2016 John Wiley & Sons, Ltd. ISBN: 9781118751527
Also published in EFS (online edition)
DOI: 10.1002/9780470061589.fsa017.pub2

Professionals may also belong to specialty boards with different ethical codes, such as that of the generalist group,[b] as well as the codes of ethics promulgated by specialty boards. The same is true of the members of virtually every specialty group within the forensic sciences.

Finally, it should be remembered that, in addition to the sanctions that can be imposed by a professional society upon its own members, there is a "common law" of ethical conduct as well. Violating these common law prohibitions against unethical conduct – usually involving professional conduct that includes deception, fraud, overreaching, perjury, or behavior merely considered to be dishonest or inequitable whereby either the public or society in general is injured – as by engaging in "negligent" professional conduct – may expose an expert to civil legal sequellae in damage actions and potential criminal liability for perjury or fraud. These are sanctions professional societies cannot impose. Even the expert witness who does not belong to an organization that has a mandatory code of conduct may be subject to such legal actions. Potential liability of this sort falls within the area of "professional malpractice" for either intentional or unintentional (negligent) conduct – tortious conduct – as defined by applicable law.

Defining Ethics

The existing ethics provisions in forensic science vary greatly in how the terms "ethics" or "unethical conduct" are defined. Indeed, many organizations do not use the word at all but describe codes of practice. Some list specific prohibitions, others frame ethical principles in terms of aspirations. How these rules will be applied in specific fact settings is not always clear with words such as "appropriate" or "relevant" leaving some scope for different interpretations to be placed on actions. Outside of the legal profession, most professional societies do not publish compilations of ethics complaints that were decided by its boards. In addition, while general ethical principles may be listed, how ethics codes have been applied in illustrative cases may remain obscure to the general membership.

In general, the professional codes of conduct devote much more space to outlining the procedure to be followed when an accusation of questionable ethics

has been made, than to the definition of ethics itself. Perhaps, that is understandable because notions of fair play and clear advance notice of what conduct is complained of require provisions that outline the process of *enforcing* codes in more elaborate terms. The notion of "due process" that pervades the forensic sciences because of its close connection to civil and criminal litigation of necessity requires it to exemplify fairness in the application of its rules of conduct to its members.

Defining Prohibited Conduct

The definition of what constitutes unacceptable expert behavior is stated, in some ethics codes, only in general terms. Other codes go into great detail about the type of conduct that it requires of its members. Perhaps, the majority of codes of conduct define ethics in terms of prohibitions. An example of the broad general approach is that of the American Academy of Forensic Sciences (AAFS), which contains just four general prohibitions:

(a)   Every member … shall refrain from exercising professional or personal conduct adverse to the best interests and purposes of the Academy. The objectives stated in the Preamble to these By-Laws include: promoting education for and research in the forensic sciences, encourage the study, improving the practice, elevating the standards and advancing the cause of the forensic sciences;

(b)   No member or affiliate … shall materially misrepresent his or her education, training, experience, area of expertise, or membership status within the Academy.

(c)   No member or affiliate … shall materially misrepresent data or scientific principles upon which his or her conclusion or professional opinion is based;

(d)   No member or affiliate … shall issue public statements that appear to represent the position of the Academy without specific authority first obtained from the Board of Directors.[c]

Items b and c are expressed in some form or another in most codes.

It is understandable that required conduct provisions of a society such as the AAFS, which gathers under its umbrella members who are engaged in a wide variety of different disciplines, be fairly general. It is impossible to describe specific instances of prohibited conduct when the organization contains a broad spectrum of specialties, each of which may also be subject to ethics codes within its own specialty.

An example of a code of professional conduct that is more explicit in terms of prohibited professional behavior are the American Board of Criminalistics (ABC) Rules of Professional Conduct which, in Article IV.5.d of the bylaws, enumerate 18 specific mandatory rules of behavior that its members "shall" obey. Unlike the AAFS Code, it enjoins members to report to its Board any violation of the rules by another applicant or Diplomate.[d] The ABC Rules place a great emphasis on impartiality and integrity when dealing with evidence, and prohibit members from using "techniques and methods that are known to be inaccurate and/or unreliable." Considering that users of a technique will invariably advocate its reliability, there may nevertheless be an important segment within a profession that frowns upon use of some methods of analysis, which they consider lack reliability. A number of such controversies exist within the area of DNA profiling. One wonders how controversies on those issues can ever be effectively resolved.

Defining Ethical "Aspirations"

Rather than defining the prohibited conduct, the approach within some disciplines is to define appropriate professional conduct in terms of the aspirations toward which its members should strive. The Chartered Society of Forensic Sciences in the United Kingdom (formerly The Forensic Science Society) is an example. Its three-part Code of Conduct states that members have a duty to:

… conduct themselves honourably in the practice of their profession

promote to the utmost of their power the interests of the Society * * *

have special regard at all times to the public interest and to the maintenance of the highest standards or competence and integrity * * *

only undertake any forensic activity commensurate with and in the field within which they are registered or accredited by the Society.[e]

Some groups eschew categorizing any specific instances of unprofessional conduct or the categorization of "standards" of behavior. An example of such a group is the American Psychological Association (APA), which describes the "Ethical Principles of Psychologists and Code of Conduct" into five rather wordy aspirations, wherein a full paragraph of text each is devoted to: beneficence and nonmalficence; fidelity and responsibility; integrity; justice; and respect for people's rights and dignity. The APA Code then elaborates on these aspirations in more than a dozen pages of ethical standards stated in broad, generalized concepts.[f]

While flexibility in terms of expected professional aspirations are the norm in the behavioral sciences, similar approaches are also considered in some organizations that deal with physical or comparative sciences. The International Association for Identification (IAI) Code of Ethics is not worded in terms of prohibited conduct but is, instead, worded in the form of a personal pledge of good behavior that its members publicly affirm. Its true "code" of prohibited conduct then follows as "Standards of Professional Conduct."[g]

The importance of a thorough familiarity with a profession's ethics rules is particularly crucial because potential legal sequellae may follow from proven unethical conduct. When legal actions for damages are brought against forensic scientists based on either negligent or willful conduct, or when a prosecution for criminal conduct is initiated, whether the activity that is the subject of the complaint is considered "ethical" or in accord with "professional standards" may well be taken by courts as depending on what conduct the applicable professional society expects of its members.

Fact Settings Presenting Potential Ethical Problems

Fact settings in professional practice that may involve ethical problems fall within certain categories. While clear authority for each fact setting may be difficult to provide, the experience of persons serving on ethics committees may serve as a guide.

A first type, and perhaps the most frequent complaint lodged against experts is in regard to inaccuracies in the way they represent their training, education, and experience. Misrepresentation of this sort may occur in statements made in a public forum (in speeches, on websites, in correspondence), or in drafting curriculum vitae that are disseminated to potential clients and courts. If the inaccuracies simply amount to exaggeration that can be justified as "puffing," the perceived inaccuracy will not necessarily be considered an unethical practice. More often, the assertions are made in support of establishing the expert's competence and qualifications in depositions or in court testimony. If the misrepresentation is deemed significant and occurs at a time the expert is giving sworn information to a court, whether in a deposition or testimony, the expert may also be subject to criminal prosecution for perjury, or in damages in a civil suit by parties injured or aggrieved as a result of willful misstatement of one's background and experience.[h]

Examples of misstatements that are normally considered material and significant would be to assert having received credentials (diplomas, academic degrees, board certifications, and honors) that were not in fact obtained. In this same category fall claims of membership or of a category of membership status for which the expert has not been admitted or qualified.

A second category of ethical complaints, and one that is more fraught with enforcement difficulties, encompasses assertions that a person was incompetent when he engaged in a certain examination. In many disciplines, there it may be disputed whether a particular method leads to reliable or repeatable results. When a method is fairly novel, there exists a danger in prematurely using an unproven method as the basis for expert opinions in court. Influential people in a discipline may assert the method was not properly validated and that, consequently, reliance on test results produced by such methods is evidence of incompetency. Because of the difficulty of defining "competency," some associations refrain from entertaining complaints based on incompetency altogether, especially if the organization has fairly rigorous standards for admission to membership and the person complained of has met these criteria.

Lack of established reliability or inability to establish method validation has become a more frequently litigated issue in courts as a result of court decisions and other legal provisions that place restrictions on opinion testimony based on unreliable processes or technologies.[i]

A third category of potential problems has to do with fraud and deceit in such areas as misrepresenting data examined, results obtained, or in testifying to conclusions that are not supported by the examinations conducted. While fraud and deceit typically connote willful conduct, in this same category may be placed certain acts of omission – allegations that a person did

not use a recommended or standard methods, which the profession recognizes as valid and routine for a specific purpose.

Finally, there exists a category of potential ethical conflicts that do not fall within the above-mentioned categories, such as those arising from conflicts of interest or violation of confidentiality rules. Alleged unethical conduct in these areas often depends on existing law on conflicts of interest and confidentiality in the jurisdiction where the conduct arose.

Sanctions against Experts for Unethical Conduct

Most, but not all, ethics codes provide for a gamut of potential consequences that befall a member found to have violated its ethical provisions. The sanctions range from measures that may be seen by the public as a simple "slap on the wrist," such as a reprimand (whether oral or in writing), to the more serious ones that encompass public censure, suspension of membership for a stated period of time, or expulsion. Where applicable, the most severe sentence of expulsion may also be accompanied by a revocation of credentials or professional certifications.

The imposition of severe sentences against professionals such as membership suspension or expulsion can be imposed only if a procedural code exists that affords due process to the accused member. Due process typically requires notice of the specific charges brought, presentation of evidence at a hearing at which the accused is permitted to attend, confront the charges against him, and present evidence to rebut them. It also typically requires the complaining association to carry the burden of proving that the violation occurred, though the quantum of proof is by no means uniform.

In some codes, the quantum of required proof of unprofessional conduct must be "beyond a reasonable doubt," though more typically ethics provisions require that unprofessional conduct be established by either the greater weight of the evidence or, at most, by clear and convincing evidence. Some ethics codes permit the member against whom the complaint is filed to be assisted by legal counsel at the hearing. Some codes also make provisions for a right to appeal an ethics board decision to the entire membership of the organization.

Because the imposition of a severe sanction may impair the ability of the member to engage in his profession, especially when an expulsion also has the effect of revoking the member's certification, courts whose power was thereafter invoked by the expelled member have insisted that the procedure whereby the expulsion was effectuated comported with due process of law. In deciding such lawsuits, when the procedural aspects of the ethics codes were found to satisfy notions of fairness and fair play, courts tend to be deferential to the professional society's factual determination of unprofessional conduct.

Conclusion

If professional societies intend to retain the power to sanction conduct of their members that is deemed unethical, the rules of professional conduct must be described with particular care to provide adequate notice to its members of the type of conduct that is deemed unacceptable. The process by which violations of the codes of professional conduct are to be enforced must also comport with basic notions of fair play and due process.

End Notes

a. For a sample of the codes prescribing the required ethical provisions for its members of just a few of the dozens of professional societies in forensic sciences not specifically mentioned in this article, see, e.g.:

International Association for Identification, https://theiai.org/about/code_of_ethics.pdf

International Association of Forensic Criminologists: http://www.profiling.org/abp_conduct.html

Piette, Michael J., "Codes of Professional Ethics for Forensic Economists: Problems and Prospects," [1991], Jl. Forensic Economics 4(3), 269–276.

Australian and New Zealand Forensic Science Society, http://anzfss.org/wp-content/uploads/2012/05/ANZFSS-Code-of-Professional-Practice-Final.pdf

Forensic Consultants Association, http://sdfca.org

Northwest Association of Forensic Scientists, http://www.nwfs.org/Documents/Code%20of%20Ethics.pdf

Forensic Science Regulator (England & Wales) - https://www.gov.uk/government/uploads/system/uploads/attachment_data/file/351197/The_FSR_Codes_of_Practice_and_Conduct_-_v2_August_2014.pdf

b. For example, medical examiners will belong to generalist country-wide, state or local medical societies, such as the American Medical Association (AMA), and further be subject the professional rules of conduct of the National Association of Medical Examiners (NAME), the American Board of Forensic Pathology, and the Pathology-Biology Section of the American Academy of Forensic Sciences.

c. The Code of Ethics and Conduct is contained in Article II of the group's Bylaws, Sec 201. Directory of Members and Affiliates, American Academy of Forensic Sciences, p. 284. It will be noted that subsection a. appears to be a catch-all provision that may be difficult to enforce for lack of specificity. Both subsections b. and c. deal with misrepresentations, but the addition of the word "material" may also make it difficult to know in advance when a misrepresentation might not rise to the level of materiality.

d. http://www.criminalistics.org and http://www.criminalistics.com/page/rules-of-professional-conduct

e. http://www.forensic-science-society.org.uk

f. http://www.apa.org/ethics/code/principles.pdf

g. www.theiai.org/about/code_of_ethics. Code of Ethics and Standards of Professional Conduct, International Identification of Identification. Resolution 2011–15.

h. A different, but related, form of "unethical" conduct of this nature exists experts, in their student days, are shown to have resorted to falsification of data, plagiarism, or other fraudulent practices in academic pursuits. When these practices are discovered years later, experts may suffer the added consequence of seeing their earned credentials revoked for fraud. See, Johnston, R.G. & Oswald, J.D., "Academic Dishonesty: Revoking Academic Credentials," 32 J. Marshall L. Rev. 67 (1998).

i. See, in this regard, the influential court decisions in Daubert v. Merrell Dow Pharmaceuticals and in Kumho Tire v. Carmichael [514]. In the UK, in R v Hoey ([2007] NICC 49), the judge made specific comments on the extent of the validation conducted by the prosecution experts in relation to Low Copy Number DNA testing at paras 62–64.

Chapter 38
Verbal Scales: A Legal Perspective

Tony Ward

University of Hull, Hull, UK

This article concerns the admissibility of testimony in criminal trials in which forensic scientists attempt to convey the probative value of their findings by means of a "verbal scale" of degrees of support for a certain hypothesis. It is concerned primarily with the law of England and Wales but also draws on case law and commentaries from Scotland, Australia, and New Zealand.

Three principles are relevant to the admissibility of such evidence, although the second and third are particular aspects of the first and fundamental principle: that expert evidence is admissible only if it is both relevant and "helpful" [1]. "Helpful" is a broad term which gives the courts wide discretion to balance the benefit to the jury of hearing the information the expert can provide against the risk that it may mislead or confuse the jury or render their task unnecessarily complex.

The second principle can be called – after its classic enunciation in a leading Scottish case [2] – the *Davie* principle. It specifies *how* experts are expected to help the jury, namely by furnishing a basis on which the jury can independently assess the weight of the expert's evidence in the context of the other evidence in the case. Whether verbal scales are sufficiently helpful in this respect to warrant the admission of evidence in this form is, arguably, the crux of the legal issue.

The third principle, which has recently taken on new prominence in English law, is that expert evidence must be "sufficiently reliable to be admitted". The Law Commission, in its report on expert evidence in criminal trials [3], recommended that this should be a new statutory test of admissibility, and proposed a definition of "sufficient reliability" together with a set of

statutory guidelines to assist judges in applying it. The proposed legislation was not enacted but the guidelines have been incorporated, substantially unchanged, in the *Criminal Practice Direction* [4]. As the Practice Direction indicates (para. 33A.1), these guidelines are to be applied in determining whether evidence meets the common-law criteria of relevance and helpfulness, and whether the individual expert is competent to give such evidence. "Sufficiently reliable to be admitted", then, means sufficiently reliable to be relevant and helpful and to establish that the expert is competent.

Helpfulness

Whether verbal scales are "helpful" is not a straightforward question, as can be seen by comparing the Court of Appeal judgments in *R v Atkins* [5] and *R v T (footwear mark evidence)* [6] – probably the most controversial English decisions of the present century on expert evidence in criminal trials. In *Atkins*, the Court upheld the admission of evidence from a medical artist that a comparison of a surveillance camera image with a photograph of one of the defendants lent something between "support and strong support" (the second and third levels of a five-point verbal scale) to the hypothesis that the defendant rather than another person was the man in the photograph. In *T*, the Court held that a statement of "moderate scientific support" was inadmissible, both because the calculations on which it was based had not been disclosed, and because the basis of those calculations was insufficiently reliable to justify admitting the evidence.

In *Atkins* [5] the Court of Appeal explained why it considered the use of a scale to be helpful:

> An expert who spends years studying this kind of comparison can properly form a judgment as to the significance of what he has found in any particular

A Guide to Forensic DNA Profiling
Edited by Allan Jamieson and Scott Bader
© 2016 John Wiley & Sons, Ltd. ISBN: 9781118751527
Also published in EFS (online edition)
DOI: 10.1002/9780470061589.fsa1145

case. It is a judgment based on his experience. A jury is entitled to be informed of his assessment. The alternative, of simply leaving the jury to make up its own mind about the similarities and dissimilarities, with no assistance at all about their significance, would be to give the jury raw material with no means of evaluating it. It would be as likely to result in over-valuation of the evidence as under-valuation. (para. 23.)

In *T* [6], however, the Court of Appeal clearly did not find the use of the verbal scale helpful. The phrase "moderate scientific support" was characterized as "opaque", and the use of the word "scientific" was criticized for giving an undue "impression … of precision and objectivity" (paras. 73, 96).

These two decisions are not necessarily inconsistent. The contrast between them may simply indicate that whether an opinion expressed by means of a verbal scale is admissible is a fact-sensitive decision that has to be taken in the context of the expert's proposed evidence as a whole. The reasons why the use of the scale in *Atkins* was more acceptable than its use in *T* may become clearer when we consider the *Davie* principle and the question of reliability.

The *Davie* principle

In the much-quoted words of Lord Cooper:

> Expert witnesses … cannot usurp the functions of the jury or Judge sitting as a jury…. Their duty is to furnish the Judge or jury with the necessary scientific criteria for testing the accuracy of their conclusions, so as to enable the Judge or jury to form their own independent judgment by the application of these criteria to the facts proved in evidence. …. In particular the bare *ipse dixit* of a scientist, however eminent, upon the issue in controversy, will normally carry little weight, for it cannot be tested by cross-examination nor independently appraised, and the parties have invoked the decision of a judicial tribunal and not an oracular pronouncement by an expert ([2], p. 40).

The use of the word "scientific" may have been appropriate on the facts of *Davie*, which involved rather simple science and a trial judge who appeared quite capable of understanding and evaluating it, but it will be unrealistic in many cases to expect a jury to apply "scientific criteria" independently. What is essential is that the jury be provided with the information it needs in order to make an independent judgment of the significance of the scientific evidence in the context of the other evidence in the case. The principle that the expert must "keep faith with and preserve the essential independence of the jury's role" by giving evidence in terms that helps the jury reach an independent view rather than telling them what their view ought to be, was strongly reaffirmed (under New Zealand law) by the Privy Council in the recent case of *Pora v The Queen* [7].

Although Lord Cooper's remarks, in the context of a civil case tried by judge alone, were phrased in terms of weight rather than admissibility, when taken together with the *Turner* helpfulness principle – which forms part of Scots as well as English law [8] – they imply that the "bare *ipse dixit* of a scientist" is unhelpful and therefore inadmissible. In *R v Tang* [9], the New South Wales Court of Criminal Appeal applied the *Davie* principle, as paraphrased by Heydon J in the leading New South Wales case of *Makita v Sprowles* [10], to the evidence of an anthropologist who used a verbal scale to report the results of a "body mapping" exercise. She claimed to have applied a "rigorous protocol" but refused to give details as she was in the process of trying to patent it. Her evidence on this point was treated as inadmissible "*ipse dixit*".

The English Court of Appeal in *Atkins* did not consider that the "facial mapping" expert's use of a scale in that case was open to the same objections as that of the "body mapping" expert in *Tang*. Edmond *et al.* [11], however, argue in effect that the evidence in *Atkins* also amounted to *ipse dixit*, because the expert could give no scientific explanation of how he translated the similarities he observed between the two photographs into a judgment of the degree of support they provided for an identification. In response to this, it could be argued that it is unrealistic to expect experts to able to provide a full verbal explanation of their judgments, which depend to a great extent on "tacit knowledge" gained by prolonged experience [12, p. 199]. But if the jury is to rely on the expert's tacit knowledge it must have evidence that such knowledge is reliable. This could be provided by telling the jury the results of proficiency tests undertaken by the expert, who could testify in some such terms as: "I'm not as confident as I would be to make an identification in a proficiency test where I was correct in 95% of cases, but the images are similar enough that I would regard them as providing moderate support for an identification".

In *R v T* [6], unlike *Atkins*, the expert did have a method of deciding at what level of the verbal scale to pitch his evidence. In accordance with the methodology of Case Assessment and Interpretation (*see* **Communicating Probabilistic Forensic Evidence in Court**), it involved estimating a likelihood ratio between the hypothesis that the defendant's shoes made the mark in question and the hypothesis that some other shoe made the mark. Likelihood ratios were arranged in a logarithmic scale corresponding to different verbal expressions: >1–10 to "weak or limited support", 10–100 to "moderate support", 100–1000 to "moderately strong support" and so on (para. 31). Having calculated a ratio of "~100", (para. 37), the expert plumped conservatively for the expression "moderate degree of scientific support" (para. 41). He failed, however, to disclose these calculations in his report. Not only did this leave his conclusion as bare *ipse dixit*, it led to his being cross-examined on the basis of data that was much more favorable to the prosecution than that which the expert had actually used.

If the Court of Appeal had contented itself with quashing the conviction on the basis of this "elementary and catastrophic failure of transparency" [13, p. 349], the decision might have been relatively uncontroversial. Thomas LJ went further, however, by saying that if the expert *had* disclosed the calculations underlying his statement, this would also have been unacceptable because it would have created "a verisimilitude of mathematical probability" in circumstances where the limitations of the available data meant that only a rough estimate of probability was possible. Consequently, there was not a "sufficiently reliable basis for an expert to be able express an opinion based on the use of a mathematical formula" ([6], para. 86).

There appear to be two objections to the use of verbal scales to express judgments based on estimated likelihood ratios. One is that by, in effect, telling the jury the weight of his own evidence, the expert may "conceal the element of judgment on which [the likelihood ratio] entirely depends" [14], and thus fail in the duty set out in *Davie* [2] to provide the jury with the information needed to make an independent judgment of the weight of the evidence. The other is that in cases such as *T* [6] where the frequency of some features has to be estimated, and where there is a choice of available databases (statistics of shoes sold or of shoes belonging to suspects and forensically examined) that will give different likelihood ratios, any calculation of

a likelihood ratio will be insufficiently reliable to be admitted. The first objection seems relatively easy to meet by telling the jury "in deciding which point on the scale is appropriate I made some statistical calculations but the figures on which I based those calculations involve a large element of subjective judgment based on my experience". The crucial issue is when, if ever, the use of a verbal scale will pass the test of reliability.

"Sufficiently Reliable to be Admitted"

In reaching decisions about reliability, criminal judges in England and Wales now have the benefit of guidance provided by the *Criminal Practice Direction*, part 33A [4]. This guidance in closely based on that set out in the Law Commission's report on expert evidence [3]. The ultimate test of "sufficient reliability", however, is not the statutory one proposed by the Law Commission, but rather whether the evidence is sufficiently reliable to pass the common-law tests of relevance, helpfulness, and competence. Where there is a complete lack of evidence that the expert's judgment has a reliable basis, it will be irrelevant, and a failure to show that the individual expert was competent to apply a reliable method may also lead to inadmissibility; but in most cases the question is likely to be whether the criteria set out in the Practice Direction [4] are met to a sufficient extent to render the evidence helpful to the jury.

The first three factors set out in the Practice Direction [3] at 33A.5 appear particularly relevant to the use of verbal scales:

(a) the extent and quality of the data on which the expert's opinion is based, and the validity of the methods by which they were obtained; (b) if the expert's opinion relies on an inference from any findings, whether the opinion properly explains how safe or unsafe the inference is (whether by reference to statistical significance or in other appropriate terms); (c) if the expert's opinion relies on the results of the use of any method (for instance, a test, measurement or survey), whether the opinion takes proper account of matters, such as the degree of precision or margin of uncertainty, affecting the accuracy or reliability of those results . . . .

Regarding factor (a), the contrasting judgments in *Atkins* [5] and *T* [6] point to a paradoxical conclusion. Apparently, where the expert's opinion is based on virtually no data other than personal experience, as in *Atkins*, it may be sufficiently reliable to be admitted. Where, on the other hand, there is some data available but the likelihood ratio obtained from such data depends to some extent on matters of judgment, including the choice of an appropriate reference class, any conclusion based on such data may be *in*sufficiently reliable, as in *T*.

This apparent paradox is not as odd as it may at first appear, if "sufficient reliability" is understood in a way informed by the *Davie* principle, as meaning that the jury has a sufficient basis to reach an informed decision as to how far to rely on the evidence [15]. In *T* ([6], para. 94), Thomas LJ (now Lord Thomas CJ, the author of the amended Practice Direction), appears to have taken the view that the evidence in *Atkins* was sufficiently reliable because, as Hughes LJ pointed out in the *Atkins* judgment (para. 23), the lack of a database would inevitably be exposed in cross-examination (if not explained in chief, which seems more consistent with the expert's duty to assist the Court). The jury would therefore understand that the reliability of the evidence was a matter of the reliance they were willing to place on the subjective judgment of an experienced expert. In *T*, on the other hand, the extent and quality of the data were deemed insufficient to justify the kind of reliance that might be placed on evidence clothed in a "verisimilitude of mathematical probability".

Similarly, the cases of *Thomas* [16] and *Dlugosz* [17] indicate that a "sliding scale" should not be used to give an opinion about mixed DNA profiles which do not admit of statistical analysis. It nevertheless appears that some forensic scientists do use a verbal scale when writing reports in cases of this kind. [18] The author has seen one such report (not, in the event, relied on by the prosecution) which refers to mixed DNA profiles as providing "at least strong" or "at least moderate" support for the defendant's DNA being on two different items. By "at least", the author of the report appears to mean that had it been possible to undertake statistical analysis, it *might* have resulted in a likelihood ratio corresponding to a higher point on the verbal scale. Such speculation about hypothetical likelihood ratios appears unhelpful in the extreme.

Turning to factor (b), we must ask whether the use of a verbal scale "properly explains" how safe is an expert's inference from certain findings, such as perceived similarities between footwear marks or facial images. It seems highly questionable whether the kind of verbal scale in current use can pass this test. Empirical research (discussed in **DNA in the UK Courts**) suggests that these scales only very imperfectly convey to potential juries the degree of probability they are intended to express [19, 20]. This is hardly surprising, particularly where the scale is used as a nonmathematical way of conveying likelihood ratios, because it is hard to see how anyone could have more than the vaguest idea of what the scale is meant to convey without understanding that it is based on a logarithmic scale of likelihood ratios – and yet the need to understand these concepts is precisely what the use of the scale aims to avoid.

As Jeremy Gans [21] has forcefully argued with reference to DNA evidence, the verbal scale can be highly misleading if one does not understand that what it expresses is the likelihood ratio of the evidence, not the posterior probability of the relevant hypothesis. "Strong support" for a proposition is, as Gans puts it, in reality "laughably weak" if all it means is that the defendant is one of several thousand possible sources of whatever has been tested ([21] p. 534). This can hardly be considered a "proper explanation" of the safety or otherwise of inferring identity from the expert's findings. On the contrary, it is an explanation that is distinctly "unhelpful", particularly when a clearer alternative is available. That alternative, as Ligertwood and Edmond [22] suggest, is to give an estimate of the number of people (in the world or in the vicinity of the crime scene) who could be the source of the item of evidence in question. Where only a very rough "guesstimate" is possible, it should be clearly presented as such; and, where applicable, the expert should make the kind of point that the Court of Appeal made in *T*:

> A particular shoe might be very common in one area because a retailer has bought a large number or because the price is discounted or because of fashion or choice by a group of people in that area. There is no way in which the effect of these factors has presently been statistically measured . . . . (para. 82).

This line of argument does not establish that *every* use of the verbal scale will fall so far short of a proper explanation as to be inadmissible. The question is not whether the verbal scale in isolation constitutes a proper explanation of the safety of the inference, but whether the opinion as a whole does so. From what we are told in the *Atkins* judgment ([5], paras. 7–8) about the "facial mapping" expert's evidence to the jury, it seems that he did explain in some detail the factors that could make it unsafe to infer identity from the similarity between the images – and did so in chief, rather than waiting for concessions to be extracted from him in cross-examination. Had the Practice Direction been in force at the time, the Court might have concluded that the evidence as a whole did provide a proper explanation. The jury should have been able to grasp the essential point, namely that while the similarities between images could not be relied on in isolation to identify one of the defendants, they were something to weigh together with the very considerable circumstantial evidence in deciding whether guilt was proved to the criminal standard. By contrast, the expert in *T* completely failed to explain how he reached the inference he did, and the uncertainties involved in that process.

Similarly, with respect to factor (c), it could be argued that in *Atkins* the evidence as a whole took "proper account of matters, such as the degree of precision or margin of uncertainty, affecting the accuracy or reliability" of the results of "facial mapping". The argument against this view is that while the expert *acknowledged* the limited degree of precision in his methods, there was nothing to indicate how he had *taken it into account* in his use of the verbal scale [11]. The Practice Direction, had it been in force at the time of *Atkins*, would have given the defence a ground to argue that the verbal scale was insufficiently reliable to be admitted, even if the "facial mapping" evidence was otherwise admissible. The defence might have urged that the jury should simply have been told the nine reasons they were in fact given why the type of comparison undertaken could be unreliable, together with the fact that there were, nevertheless, marked similarities between the images which were more likely to be found if the images were of the same person than if they were not – though how much more likely, given the current state of knowledge, it was impossible to say.

Responding to the *R v T* judgment [6], a distinguished group of forensic scientists signed an editorial defending the "logical principles of evidence evaluation" embodied in the Bayesian use of verbal scales [23]. Martire *et al.* [24], however, concluded in 2014,

"The claim made in the 2011 position statement [in [23]] that verbal formulations of likelihood ratios are the most appropriate basis for communicating with decision-makers looks increasingly questionable, as does the broader ideal of the Bayesian juror."

The "range of opinion" rule

It is also important to note, particularly with reference to any future case similar to *Atkins*, that criticism of expert evidence from other experts in the same field – such as Glenn Porter, one of the co-authors of Edmond *et al.*'s critique [11] – itself alters the terms in which such evidence can properly be given in England and Wales. So, more broadly, does the critical academic literature on the use of verbal scales. This is because r. 33.4(f) of the Criminal Procedure Rules 2014 requires that an expert's report must:

where there is a range of opinion on the matters dealt with in the report –
(i) summarise the range of opinion, and
(ii) give reasons for the expert's own opinion . . . .

To comply with this Rule, any use of a verbal scale should be prefaced with a suitable "health warning", perhaps along the following lines (the details will vary with the type of evidence):

I acknowledge that the use of this type of verbal scale is controversial. Some people think that it is a valuable way of explaining that all forensic science evidence can do is to make a certain hypothesis more or less probable. It can provide 'support' for one party's view of the facts, but it cannot offer certainty. In using a verbal scale I am trying to make that point without using statistics in a way that could be confusing. Other people argue that such a verbal scale is potentially misleading. Whatever point on the scale I select, the form of words I use could be interpreted in very different ways by different people. It may be understood as either a stronger or a weaker statement than I intend it to be. The use of the scale can also be criticised because we do not as yet have a rigorous method in my field of taking the various possibilities of error into account in deciding which point on the scale to use. Nevertheless, I take the view that this is the best way of conveying to the jury my own sense of the strength of the scientific evidence, which I accept is largely a subjective judgment based on my experience.

Whether an opinion qualified in this way will be helpful to the jury will then be for the judge to decide.

References

[1]   R *v* Turner (1975). QB 834.
[2]   Davie *v* Magistrates of Edinburgh (1953). SC 34.

[3] Commission, L. (2011). *Expert Evidence in Criminal Proceedings in England and Wales (LC No. 325)*, The Stationery Office, London.

[4] *Practice Direction (Criminal Proceedings: Various Changes)* (2014). EWCA Crim 1569.

[5] R v Atkins (2009). EWCA Crim 1876.

[6] R v T (footwear mark evidence) (2010). EWCA Crim 1876.

[7] Pora v The Queen (2015). UKPC 9.

[8] HM Advocate v Grimmond (2000). SLT 508.

[9] R v Tang (2006). NSWCCA 167.

[10] Makita (Australia) Pty Ltd v Sprowles (2001). NSWCA 305.

[11] Edmond, G., Kemp, R., Porter, G., Hamer, D., Burton, M., Biber, K. & San Roque, M. (2010). *Atkins* v *The Emperor*: the 'cautious' use of unreliable 'expert' opinion, *International Journal of Evidence and Proof* **14**(2), 146–166.

[12] Dreyfus, H.L. & Dreyfus, S. (1986). *Mind Over Machine: The Power of Human Intuition and Expertise in the Era of the Computer*, Free Press, New York.

[13] Redmayne, M., Roberts, P., Aitken, C. & Jackson, G. (2011). Forensic science evidence in question, *Criminal Law Review* **2011**, 347–356.

[14] R v Adams (1996). Cr App R 467.

[15] Ward, T. (2015). 'A new and more rigorous approach' to expert evidence in England and Wales?, *International Journal of Evidence and Proof* **19**(4) (forthcoming).

[16] R v Thomas (2011). EWCA Crim 1295.

[17] R v Dlugosz (2013). EWCA Crim 2.

[18] Jamieson, A. (2015). Personal communication.

[19] Mullen, C., Spence, D., Moxey, L. & Jamieson, A. (2014). Perception problems of the verbal scale, *Science and Justice* **54**, 154–158.

[20] Martire, K.A. & Watkins, I. (2015). Perception problems of the verbal scale: A reanalysis and application of a membership function approach, *Science and Justice* http://dx.doi.org/10.1016/j.scijus.2015.01.002

[21] Gans, J. (2011). A tale of two High Court forensic cases, *Sydney Law Review* **33**, 515–543.

[22] Ligertwood, A. & Edmond, G. (2012). Expressing evaluative forensic science opinions in a court of law, *Law, Probability and Risk* **11**, 289–302.

[23] Martire, K.A., Kemp, R.I., Sayle, M. & Newell, B.R. (2011). Expressing evaluative opinions: a position statement, *Science and Justice* **51**(2011), 1–2.

[24] Martire, K.A., Kemp, R.I., Sayle, M. & Newell, B.R. (2014). On the interpretation of likelihood ratios in forensic science evidence: Presentation formats and the weak evidence effect, *Forensic Science International* **240**, 61–68.

Chapter 39
Direct Examination of Experts

Andre A. Moenssens[1,2]

[1]*University of Missouri at Kansas City, Kansas City, MO, USA*
[2]*University of Richmond, Richmond, VA, USA*

Nature, Purpose, and Scope

When an expert witness is summoned to give testimony at a judicial proceeding, he is normally not permitted to get on the witness stand and simply tell the court what he knows. Instead, testimony is elicited in the form of questions posed by the litigant, to which inquiries the witness gives answers. This process is called *direct examination*. The prohibition against testifying in the narrative is to allow the opposing side to interpose objections to certain questions if they call for inappropriate or inadmissible answers under the rules of evidence. As with all trial proceedings, rules may vary from jurisdiction to jurisdiction. We discuss those that are most prevalently used in the adversary system.

Questions asked on direct examination must tend to assist the fact finder in understanding the fact and the issues of the case. Information that is irrelevant, incompetent, or immaterial to the issues in the case, cannot be elicited. There may also be countervailing policies that restrict potentially helpful information from being introduced. Thus, information about certain privileged matters may be restricted, as would information that tends to inflame the jury and has been determined to be more prejudicial than probative. The purpose of these restrictions on use of information is to protect the fairness of the judicial process and prevent decisions from being based on conjecture or on evidence of doubtful or limited probative worth.

In addition to restrictions on the content of information sought to be elicited, there are also evidentiary restrictions on the manner in which a question is phrased. These are called *objections* to the form of the question. Eliciting information may not be done on direct examination by asking leading questions. A leading question is one which suggests what the answer ought to be, for example, the question, "and then you identified the defendant as the perpetrator"?

There are, however, a number of exceptions to the prohibition against the use of leading questions. Leading questions can be used in the beginning of a direct examination to orient the witness to the subject matter about which questions are about to be posed. That information is only deemed to be preliminary and therefore not crucial. In many jurisdictions, questions about the qualifications of an expert may also be posed in a leading form. Lawyers are also permitted to ask leading questions when the witness has trouble understanding what is happening: witnesses who are old, feeble, young, or forgetful. Further, the rule against using leading questions is always relaxed or overlooked when questioning is addressed to a hostile witness, or to the adversary person in a civil dispute, or to someone who is closely associated with the adverse party. These witnesses may not freely supply the information that is sought to be elicited.

It also is always appropriate to use leading questions on cross-examination. Indeed, most cross-examiners will ask leading questions because it is the only way they retain some measure of control in seeking to avoid nonresponsive or volunteered statements.

There is one form of a leading question that is always improper, even when asked on cross-examination. It is the asking of questions that are misleading, argumentative, or compound – meaning two questions in one. A typical example of such a compound, argumentative, and improper question of a witness who has been confronted with a prior inconsistent statement would be: were you lying then or are you lying now?

A Guide to Forensic DNA Profiling
Edited by Allan Jamieson and Scott Bader
© 2016 John Wiley & Sons, Ltd. ISBN: 9781118751527
Also published in EFS (online edition)
DOI: 10.1002/9780470061589.fsa010

In jurisdictions where rules of evidence still closely approximate the common law, there may be other rules that affect the form of questioning experts. Examples involve when a witness who is testifying orally may use a writing to assist in remembering information. Lawyers who call the expert, typically explain the manner in which present recollection may be refreshed by use of a writing that is not in evidence, or when and how past recollection recorded can be proved.

Expert Witnesses and Opinion Evidence

Some lay witnesses may offer opinion evidence about facts which the witness has observed. Thus a lay witness may be permitted to testify, for example, "I saw the defendant cross the street and, in my opinion, he was drunk." Lay witnesses are hardly ever permitted to offer an opinion that goes to the ultimate issue to be decided. This would be whether negligence existed in a tort case, or an opinion on the guilt of innocence of an accused in a criminal case. Even if such an opinion were to be rationale based on perception, it is deemed not to be helpful to the fact finder.

What sets experts apart from ordinary fact witnesses is that an expert can not only testify to facts personally known or observed, or to data collected and examined, but will also be allowed a far greater latitude in expressing opinions based on the data collected, as long as the opinions are likely to be helpful to the fact finder. In jurisdictions, where a common law prohibition against "ultimate issue testimony" still exists, expert witnesses are most frequently exempted from that restriction. Thus, under Federal Rules of Evidence in the United States, and in those jurisdictions that have similar provisions, expert opinion evidence is not inadmissible, except for a few narrow exceptions, merely because the opinions embrace the ultimate issue to be decided.

Eliciting the Testimony of the Expert on Direct Examination

The law considers a witness to be an expert if he is shown to be qualified by knowledge, skill, experience, training, or education in a particular profession or occupation. While formal education is not required of experts, and a person can become an expert merely by having gained experience and skill in a particular task,

there may be additional qualifications that courts exact for some professionals. Medical doctors, and other highly credentialed researchers and specialists, will be normally permitted to qualify only when they have obtained the required official certification or licensure that may be needed for practicing in their fields or the formal education required by the rules of their professions.

Thus, before a witness is permitted to offer opinion testimony as an expert, it must be shown that the witness is qualified in the discipline in which he proposes to offer testimony. It is the judge who initially makes the decision whether a witness has the necessary qualifications to be an expert. That process follows five distinct but fairly routine steps, consisting of (i) showing that the witness qualifies according to law to give opinion testimony; (ii) how the witness became involved in the case; (iii) how the witness conducted an examination or collected data; (iv) what conclusions were drawn from the findings; and (v) the probative meaning of the conclusions.

1. **Qualifying Process**
    The initial process of qualifying the witness is designed to enable the judge to rule that the proffered witness is permitted to give opinion evidence during the direct examination. This process elicits the following information:

    (a) personal information about the witness, his employment history, and current position;
    (b) formal education, training, and possession of current licensure or certification, if required;
    (c) additional continuing education activities and attendance at professional symposia;
    (d) membership in professional societies, and participation in society activities or leadership functions (officers, committees, etc.);
    (e) specialized training beyond that which is obtained in colleges and universities;
    (f) writings, publications, lecturing, and teaching;
    (g) extent of the witness's experience in dealing with the specific tasks or examinations that are particularly applicable to the case before the court;
    (h) how examinations of the type relevant to the case are conducted and what results may be expected; and
    (i) prior testimony in similar cases.

After this information has been elicited, in some jurisdictions, the direct examiner moves that the witness be permitted to qualify as an expert. At this point, the opposing attorney may request permission to *voir dire* the witness. Such questioning, if permitted, will be limited to a cross-examination on the witness's qualifications. After the *voir dire*, the court will decide whether the witness is qualified to offer opinion testimony.

2. **The Witness's Involvement in the Case**
In a fairly perfunctory manner, questions will next elicit when and how the expert became involved with the case at bar, and through what process evidence was obtained for examination. This stage is important in maintaining an unbroken chain of custody of any physical evidence that may be available.

3. **The Expert's Examination**
Questioning next focuses on the actual examination, wherein the witness will not only be asked to explain what was done but also to establish that each and every step of the recommended or required examination protocol was followed. This is true also of a description of the analysis, comparison, evaluation, and verification process. In discussing the methods used in the analysis, the expert must also be mindful of other methods that were not performed, and the reasons why a certain process was preferred or selected. The witness may likely be cross-examined on any methods that were available but not utilized.

4. **The Results of the Examination**
An expert's appearance in court would be meaningless unless he had arrived at a conclusion. This is the part of the direct examination where the ultimate opinion of the expert will be elicited. Most courts require that the opinion be provided to the court with a reasonable degree of professional certainty. Opinions that are merely guesses, or cannot be substantiated with the data, are normally not admissible since they are deemed to be based on conjecture and speculation.

For that reason, it is important for the expert to be able to justify the basis for his opinion in a cogent, understandable manner.

5. **The Importance of the Opinion in the Context of the Disputed Issues**
The direct examination testimony will conclude with an assessment of the value of the opinion in relation to the issues, which the fact finder must decide. This varies greatly depending not only on the discipline involved but also on the quantum of evidence that was available for examination. Some forensic disciplines engaged in impression comparisons, profess to express their findings as "matches" or "individualizations." Others merely state that a certain conclusion is likely, possible, improbable, or similar characterizations of the probative impact of the evidence.

Modern courts dealing with highly sophisticated crime laboratory techniques may want to know whether the methodology used is accepted as a standard of the profession. Of equal importance may be whether it has been widely publicized in the literature and subjected to peer review, and whether error rates have been established.

All of these facets of the examination will also be extremely important for the cross-examination of the evidence, which is ready to commence when the direct examiner hands over the witness for questioning by the opposing attorney.

Related Articles

Cross-Examination of Experts

Related Articles in EFS Online

In Limine **Motions and Hearings**

Ultimate Issue Evidence by Experts

Chapter 40
Cross-Examination of Experts

Andre A. Moenssens[1,2]

[1]*University of Missouri at Kansas City, Kansas City, MO, USA*
[2]*University of Richmond, Richmond, VA, USA*

Nature, Purpose, and Scope

When a witness, whether lay or expert, has been called by a party to a law suit to give sworn testimony in a court or court-related procedure, and that witness has been subjected to questions by the party who called him on direct examination (*see Direct Examination of Experts*), the opposing party has thereafter an opportunity to ask questions of that same witness. This stage of the trial process is called the *cross-examination*. During the direct examination, the cross-examiner would have listened very carefully to the answers given by the expert, who must be prepared to be challenged on all the answers that he or she had given. The properly prepared witness would also have discussed, with the direct examiner, any areas in his testimony that are open for possible challenge.

Cross-examination is permitted so that the veracity and accuracy of the witness' testimony can be questioned and challenged where appropriate. In the context of testimony by experts, the litigant may seek to explore potential weaknesses in the expert's qualifications, question the appropriateness and accuracy of the methods of examination used, explore potential insufficiency and inaccuracy of the data obtained, and throw doubt on the credibility of the conclusions drawn from the data. In this article, only issues relating to the above are discussed.

Additionally, witnesses may be cross-examined on issues unrelated to job performance but relating only to credibility or honesty of the experts. These issues are typically referred to as *matters impeaching the credibility of the expert* and are discussed separately.

Not all possible avenues are explored on cross-examination in each case. Prior to commencing the cross-examination, a litigant will typically evaluate which approach is most likely to result in information useful to him, and forgo other possible avenues of exploration. Some cross-examiners are extremely skilled and conduct searching cross-examinations that, in important cases, may take many hours, even days, to complete. Others may, for whatever reason, be more perfunctory. Effective cross-examination skills are believed to be an art and are highly individual to each trial attorney.

The form, duration, and manner of cross-examination of experts may differ from jurisdiction to jurisdiction. Local procedure dictates, to a large extent, how cross-examination is to be conducted.

In the adversary system, the person against whom a witness has testified has an absolute right to subject the witness to cross-examination. In criminal cases, if the right of cross-examination is abridged, the direct testimony of the witness cannot stand and must be stricken from the record.

The right of cross-examination is not without limits. Local statutes, court rules, custom, or common law may dictate the extent, duration, and scope of such questioning.

It must be noted that the right of cross-examination extends to court-related procedures only. This includes not only actual trials but also such pretrial proceedings of a judicial nature as are depositions, pretrial hearings, and even some posttrial hearings.

The style of advocates conducting a cross-examination differs also according to the personal attributes of the advocates, the credentials of the witness, and even the locale where the trial occurs. In the United Kingdom, Canada, and other adversary system jurisdictions, the tone tends to be less adversarial and strident as may be seen in many American courtrooms. When called to give testimony

A Guide to Forensic DNA Profiling
Edited by Allan Jamieson and Scott Bader
© 2016 John Wiley & Sons, Ltd. ISBN: 9781118751527
Also published in EFS (online edition)
DOI: 10.1002/9780470061589.fsa007

as a court-appointed expert – a process that while widely permitted by law is invoked seldom – both sides to the dispute are permitted to cross-examine the witness.

In civil law systems, the right of cross-examination serves a more limited function. When the examining magistrate questions witnesses while compiling the file that would make up the *dossier* upon which the decision to prosecute would be made, such questioning of witnesses by the magistrate may not allow for cross-examining the witnesses by an attorney for an accused, assuming that a potential accused has already been identified. Local practices may vary in this regard.

Cross-Examination – Some Additional Concepts

Preliminarily, a litigant who has the right to cross-examine an expert witness must decide whether it is strategically wise to do so. Secondarily, recognizing that answers given by an opposing party's witness cannot always be anticipated with confidence, the structuring of an effective cross-examination requires skillful preparation on the part of the interrogator. If a cross-examination is not carefully prepared, the questioning may well have the undesired result of strengthening, rather than weakening, an opponent's case. Along with books about brilliant cross-examinations resulting in true reversals of fortune, there are also many examples to be found, where inept cross-examinations simply permitted the expert to repeat answers that were already given on direct examination.

Thus, as a matter of tactics and in recognition of the imponderables of asking questions to which the attorney may not know the answer, lawyers are ordinarily taught that if an opposing witness has not damaged the client's case on direct, little is to be gained by cross-examining the witness at all, unless an opportunity exists to elicit evidence from the witness that has not yet been brought out and may be helpful in clarifying or supporting the opponent's position.

Generally, all testimony must be relevant to the disputed issues before the court. During cross-examination, that means the questions posed are limited to matters discussed during direct examination. Most courts, however, do not impose strict limitations on the scope of cross-examination and will permit questioning on any issues that are raised, either expressly or implicitly, by the direct examiner or by the issues before the court. In addition, impeachment regarding matters that pertain to the witness' honesty and credibility are always appropriate within the limits of the law.

Cross-Examining the Qualifications of the Witness

In adversary system jurisdictions, after a witness has been found qualified to give opinion evidence as an expert following direct examination, it is still permissible to cross-examine an opponent's expert as to his qualifications, because the extent of the expert's education and experience as a witness affects the weight and credibility of his opinion.

Litigants have many opportunities to explore the extent of an expert's knowledge-base and experience. There are professional societies who maintain the curriculum vitae of their members or have, at the least, registers that show whether a person is a member, has obtained certain certifications and distinctions, or has been subject to ethics complaints and/or sanctions. In addition, much information about the extent of an expert's knowledge is currently available on the Internet from a great variety of sources. This includes not only professional sources but also contact information about attorneys who have opposed the same expert in other cases. These lawyers may be willing to furnish transcripts of earlier testimony that appear to contradict what an expert is stating in the current case.

It becomes important for the meticulous expert to constantly review the standard texts, protocols, and tenets of his profession, so as to be properly prepared to answer challenges on every aspect of his professional experience. It is often said among forensic scientists that they can never stop learning and must not only "keep up" with the latest advances in their field but they must also constantly review what the accepted wisdom of the past was. Nothing in the expert's professional field is immune from challenge on cross-examination.

Attempts seeking to exclude an expert witness's testimony can be made prior to trial by the filing of a motion *in limine*. Such a motion may be based on the lack of appropriate qualifications of the proffered witness, weaknesses in the training of the witness, or other factors that may disqualify the expert from giving opinion evidence about a specific issue – such as professed unreliability of a technique espoused. Even if the pretrial motion to exclude the expert's testimony is unsuccessful and the witness is allowed to testify, the same questions posed to the expert prior to trial in support of exclusion may again be made on cross-examination during the trial. These questions remain relevant to the credibility of the expert – an issue the jury must evaluate.

Any expert witness who (i) possesses appropriate qualifications for a profession, (ii) has the needed experience, (iii) has performed a professional examination following approved protocols, (iv) has accurately obtained certain results, (v) has drawn conclusions from these observations that are readily recognized as valid in the profession, and (vi) has properly reviewed all data before taking the witness stand has little to fear from cross-examination. The important admonition to the expert is to always state the truth, not deceive expressly or by omission, and to follow standards of the profession.

Cross-Examining with Contrary Opinions Expressed in the Expert's Professional Literature

In most jurisdictions, challenging an expert's testimony on cross-examination on the basis of professional literature or textbooks in the expert's discipline is subject to evidentiary limitations. This is true particularly in adversary system jurisdictions where stringent rules against the use of hearsay evidence may remain. Views expressed by authors of published materials who are not present in court are often believed to be hearsay because they represent assertions of persons who are not subject for cross-examination.

However, when such views by acknowledged authorities in the field are brought in only for the purpose of contradicting the testifying expert's views, the questions may be appropriate because they are offered, not for the truth of the published views, but to reflect on whether the witness on the stand is believable. The cross-examiner simply attempts to show, by this method, that there are distinguished authorities in the profession who hold views differing from those of the testifying expert.

Despite such evidence not being "hearsay", the use of treatises and professional literature is subject to some limitations. They can be used to impeach an expert only if the text or treatise is first recognized as "authoritative" through the testimony of an expert. In limited situations, such treatises or publications may indeed themselves become positive proof of the truth of their content.

There are two different rules concerning the use of written authorities on cross-examination to impeach or discredit an expert. The first rule allows cross-examining an expert on a published statement only if the expert has relied on the written authority. A less restrictive rule also permits cross-examination on the basis of published professional literature if the expert admits that the particular publication is a recognized authority, even though the expert did not rely on it in reaching an opinion. If an expert being cross-examined refuses to recognize a particular publication as authoritative, such fact may be established by another expert, or even by judicial notice.

In most jurisdictions that permit the admission in evidence of a published treatise or periodical, the publication itself is not admissible as substantive evidence if its excerpts are used solely for impeachment purposes. Excerpts that call in doubt the expert's conclusions may be read to the jury, but the publication itself is not received in evidence. The rationale for that limitation on evidentiary use is that while the reading of the author's text may be justified as an exception to the rule against hearsay, it should not be permitted to assume additional dignity by being taken to the jury room during deliberations because there was no cross-examination of its author.

Redirect and Re-Cross-Examination

In most jurisdictions, after an expert has been cross-examined, the litigant who called the witness has an opportunity to conduct a redirect examination. This process is often referred to as *rehabilitating the witness*. It consists of asking explanations about answers given during cross-examination that appear to have damaged the witness's credibility. Redirect is limited only to matters raised during cross-examination.

When the process of redirect examination has been concluded, the challenging litigant may have a further opportunity, subject only to limitations imposed by court rules or the judge's discretion, to further cross-examine the expert on answers given during redirect examination. In some jurisdictions, i.e., Canada, re-cross-examination is either prohibited entirely, or subject to stringent limitations.

Related Articles

Direct Examination of Experts

Related Articles in EFS Online

Adversary Systems of Justice

Civil Law Systems of Justice

Discovery: Depositions

Hearsay Evidence

In Limine Motions and Hearings

Judicial Notice of Scientific Principles and Facts

Learned Treatises as Evidence

Ultimate Issue Evidence by Experts

Chapter 41
DNA in the UK Courts

Rhonda M. Wheate

The Forensic Institute, Glasgow, UK

Introduction

This article refers primarily to criminal proceedings, as the use of DNA-profiling evidence in the criminal courts has been more extensive and complex than the DNA evidence generally used in civil proceedings (primarily, paternity testing) in the United Kingdom (UK). Note that the United Kingdom includes England, Wales, Northern Ireland, and Scotland.

Since the introduction of DNA-profiling techniques to forensic casework in the United Kingdom in 1987, the development of DNA profiling to improve sensitivity and specificity (discriminatory power) and the growth of national DNA databases have combined to make DNA-profiling evidence ubiquitous in the UK courts. Further, "DNA typing is now universally recognized as the standard against which many other forensic individualization techniques are judged. DNA enjoys this pre-eminent position because of its reliability and the fact that, absent fraud or an error in labeling or handling, the probabilities of a false positive are quantifiable and often miniscule."[a]

A key feature of DNA-profiling evidence, which has distinguished it from other forensic disciplines, has been the availability of statistical measures of the significance of DNA results.

[N]o forensic methods other than nuclear DNA analysis has been rigorously shown to have the capacity to consistently and with a high degree of certainty support conclusions about "individualisation" (more commonly known as "matching" of an unknown item of evidence to a specific known source.[b]

A Guide to Forensic DNA Profiling
Edited by Allan Jamieson and Scott Bader
© 2016 John Wiley & Sons, Ltd. ISBN: 9781118751527
Also published in EFS (online edition)
DOI: 10.1002/9780470061589.fsa1132

Thus, DNA evidence has been lauded as a gold standard in court because the frequency of DNA types in the population is measurable; the results of DNA-profiling techniques were highly reproducible; and the forensic significance of any "match" between two profiles could be calculated by reference to the population data. More recently, however, jurisprudence from the United Kingdom indicates that the courts are willing to admit DNA-profiling results into evidence without statistics and without the level of reproducibility, reliability, and transparency for which DNA evidence has been lauded in the past. This article traces the trajectory of DNA evidence in the UK courts from its statistical origins, to its most recent manifestation based on the "experience" of the expert witness.[c]

Admissibility

In 1987 in the United Kingdom, DNA evidence was first used in a criminal investigation of seemingly connected rape and murder cases, which had occurred in 1983 and 1986. The DNA results were able to suggest a single source for the semen found at both crime scenes, and to exclude a suspect from the investigation [1].

Over the following decade DNA profiling continued to be used for investigative purposes, but became increasingly useful for evidentiary purposes in court proceedings. In this context, DNA analysis is admitted into evidence in UK courts as "expert evidence", on the basis of three legal requirements [2]: Whether there is a body of knowledge or experience that is sufficiently organized or recognized to be accepted as reliable, whether the study and experience of that knowledge would give a witness' opinion, the authority that an opinion from a lay person would lack; and whether the witness in question possesses the requisite skill and knowledge. It has been held that

> [i]f these conditions are met the evidence of the witness is in law admissible, although the weight to be attached to his opinion must of course be assessed by the tribunal of fact. [3]

This had been expressed by other courts in a similar manner, when referring to all types of expert evidence [4] – Is the subject matter an organized body of knowledge so specialized that a lay person would require the assistance of an expert in order to form a sound judgment on it? Does the witness have sufficient expertise on the matter that they may render an opinion of value on it to the court? [5]. Thus, all expert witnesses in the United Kingdom, including DNA experts, are entitled to give an opinion on their evidence, unlike ordinary (lay) witnesses, who may give evidence only of facts [6]. As noted by Steyn LJ in R v Clarke [1995],

> it would be wrong to deny to the law of evidence the advances to be gained from new techniques and new advances in science, [7]

and this has been particularly true in relation to DNA cases [8].

By the time of *Doheny and Adams* in 1997, the Court of Appeal for England and Wales set out the requirements for DNA evidence specifically, including the limitations on what a DNA expert witness may say. Phillips LJ stated [9] –

> When the scientist gives evidence it is important that he should not overstep the line which separates his province from that of the jury.
> He will properly explain to the jury the nature of the match ('the matching DNA characteristics') between the DNA in the crime stain and the DNA in the blood sample taken from the defendant. He will properly, on the basis of empirical statistical data, give the jury the random occurrence ratio – the frequency with which the matching DNA characteristics are likely to be found in the population at large. Provided that he has the necessary data, and the statistical expertise, it may be appropriate for him then to say how many people with the matching characteristics are likely to be found in the United Kingdom – or perhaps in a more limited relevant subgroup, such as, for instance, the Caucasian sexually active males in the Manchester area.
> This will often be the limit of the evidence, which he can properly and usefully give. It will then be

for the jury to decide, having regard to all the relevant evidence, whether they are sure that it was the defendant who left the crime stain, or whether it is possible that it was left by some one else with the same matching DNA characteristics.
> The scientist should not be asked his opinion on the likelihood that it was the defendant who left the crime stain, nor when giving evidence should he use terminology which may lead the jury to believe that he is expressing such an opinion.

At this stage, DNA evidence with statistical data about the significance of the profile in relation to the frequency of DNA types in the population was the norm, and the courts did not see any need for an enhanced US style "Frye" or "Daubert" admissibility test for expert evidence in the United Kingdom. That is, the United Kingdom does not require DNA evidence to pass the tests of "general acceptance" (*Frye, Daubert*), falsifiability (*Daubert*), known error rate (*Daubert*), or peer-review (*Daubert*) required in many states of the United States under *Frye, Daubert,* and the Federal Rules of Evidence. Nor, in the United Kingdom, is the trial judge required to act as a "gate-keeper" who rules evidence inadmissible for failing the enhanced tests, rather than admitting the evidence and permitting the jury to determine whether or not the evidence should be given any weight.

> The better, and now more widely accepted, view [in the UK] is that so long as the field is sufficiently well established to pass the ordinary tests of relevance and reliability, then no enhanced test of admissibility should be applied, but the weight of the evidence should be established by the same adversarial forensic techniques applicable elsewhere. [10]

Thus, the UK courts have traditionally been content to admit DNA (and other expert evidence) under a fairly low threshold, and then to rely on cross-examination and judicial directions to the jury [11] to test not only the weight of the evidence, but also to some degree its very reliability [12].

This has raised some concern as to the reliability and validity of forensic science tendered to UK courts as evidence. For instance, the House of Commons Science and Technology Committee[d] noted in 2005 that:

> The absence of an agreed protocol for the validation of scientific techniques prior to their being admitted in court is entirely unsatisfactory. Judges

are not well placed to determine scientific validity without input from scientists. We recommend that one of the first tasks of the Forensic Science Advisory Council be to develop a "gate-keeping" test for expert evidence. This should be done in partnership with judges, scientists, and other key players in the criminal justice system, and should build on the US Daubert test.

To date no *Daubert*-style test has been enacted in legislation[e] and once expert evidence is held admissible in a UK court proceeding, it remains the role of the jury (or judge, if there is no jury) to determine the reliability, validity, and weight of the evidence [13]. Very heavy reliance is still placed on the ability of cross-examination to expose deficiencies in expert evidence [14] and judicial directions to cure any other defects [15].

Where judges have deviated from the principles set out above (as did the trial judge in *Broughton,* who stated that the test that a judge should apply was merely "whether there appeared to be a risk that the evidence might be unreliable so that it would potentially mislead the jury rather than help them") [16], they have sometimes been corrected upon appeal.

Statistics and DNA Profiles

The way in which the courts have dealt with DNA evidence has also been affected by significant developments in DNA-profiling techniques and analysis since the evidence was first introduced. This was recognized by the court in *R v Bates (2006),* which noted that

> the techniques now in use, although in substance the same as those described in [*Doheny and Adams*], involve an extension and refinement of those that were in use in 1990 when that case was being prepared for trial … The process currently employed is known as 'SGM Plus', but no doubt as time goes on the techniques we describe will be further extended and refined and this summary will become out of date in its turn. [17]

In 2006, *Bates* also extended the jurisprudence of *Doheny* [18] by examining mixed and partial (*see Degraded Samples*) DNA profiles. In relation to the latter, and the absence of complete statistics owing to missing peaks, the court could

> see no reason why partial profile DNA evidence should not be admissible provided that the jury are

made aware of its inherent limitations and are given a sufficient explanation to enable them to evaluate it. [19]

In particular,

> [t]he fact that they could not assess with any statistical accuracy the chances that there might have been a "missing" allele which exculpated the appellant did not prevent them from making proper use of the evidence for what it could establish,

provided sufficient judicial direction were given to the jury at the end of the trial [20].

It is important to understand that this judgement was specifically dealing with an issue that would emerge in the coming years; the evaluation of the significance of alleles of the defendant that were NOT seen in the DNA profile. The Court specifically dismissed an attempt by the defense to place an evidential value on the "voids", a situation that was later, perhaps unwittingly, reversed.

In the meantime, other forensic disciplines were exploring how they might introduce more consistency and transparency to their work by adopting statistics, databases, and the mathematical methods used in DNA profiling. For instance, in *R v T (2010)*, evidence was given of a developing body of published work in footwear analysis, which attempted (as far as possible) to use databases, statistics, and calculations of likelihood ratios like those found in DNA evidence, to improve the quality of footwear analysis in criminal prosecutions. The Court of Appeal noted that

> no case was drawn to [their] attention which suggests that a mathematical formula is appropriate where it has no proper statistical basis [21],

and the Court was especially keen to be assured that the basis of the statistics was sound:

> [In relation to statistics adduced for footwear mark evidence] … An approach based on mathematical calculations is only as good as the reliability of the data used. [22]

Once again it was noted that DNA was a gold standard in the sense that

> It is important to appreciate that the data on footwear distribution and use is quite unlike DNA. A person's

DNA does not change and a *solid statistical base* has been developed which enable [sic] accurate figures [in DNA evidence] to be produced [23].

In 2010, the Court of Appeal in *Broughton* re-examined the issue of statistics and DNA evidence and asserted the importance of the former. In *Broughton*, the trial judge directed the jury that if they did not accept the Crown expert's opinion about the components of the DNA evidence, then the expert's DNA statistics would also be "destroyed" and the jury should "exercise caution" because they were not themselves experts in statistics. The Court of Appeal corrected this erroneous view and asserted that juries should never be left to "fill in" a statistical void – If they did not accept the Crown expert's view on statistics and they were not provided with any alternative view, they should be directed to acquit, as there was no basis on which they could assess the match probabilities themselves [24].

In *Walsh (2011)*, however,

the samples from which the DNA had been extracted … whilst sufficient to enable the analysis to be carried out, was [sic] nevertheless insufficient in quantity to permit any statistical calculation to be carried out,

Thus, the expert gave evidence that the DNA components "could have been contributed" by the defendant, but did not give any statistical evaluation of this statement [25]. The Court in *Walsh* applied *Bates (2006), Atkins (2009), Reed (2009) R v T (2010)* to conclude that

provided the scientific basis for the expression of an opinion is sufficiently reliable to permit the opinion to be admitted, the absence of a statistical calculation to demonstrate the implications of that opinion of itself does not justify the exclusion of evidence which is otherwise admissible [26]

and that the interpretation of what the witness meant by "could have been contributed" was a matter for the jury to figure out.

This line of authority was again followed in *R v Martin (2012)*, in which the Court of Appeal held that

[n]on-statistical opinion evidence can be admissible whether or not this is referable to any informal scale of probability if relevant and reliable. In appropriate

cases it may be necessary to warn the jury not to attempt to carry out any statistical analysis of their own [27].

The position was now that even when the scientist was incapable of measuring the weight of evidence, the jury were entitled, regardless of *Broughton*, to draw their own conclusion. The court had apparently adopted principles from disciplines, which lacked the scientific underpinning that had elevated DNA evidence, to bring it back into line with those others that had for decades relied on experience rather than robust and reliable scientific studies. This problem had been identified in the NAS report;

The bottom line is simple: In a number of forensic science disciplines, forensic science professionals have yet to establish either the validity of their approach or the accuracy of their conclusions, and the courts have been utterly ineffective in addressing this problem.[f]

Statistics, Experience, and Expertise

DNA has long been held as a gold standard in forensic science and expert evidence, because of the quantifiable nature of the sample material and the amenability of the significance of DNA results to statistical analysis. It is also necessary, however, to take into consideration the courts' views on other kinds of forensic evidence, and the impact this jurisprudence has come to exert on DNA evidence itself.

In *Atkins (2009)*, in relation to facial mapping evidence, the court stated [28]: "We agree that the fact that a conclusion is not based upon a statistical database recording the incidence of the features compared as they appear in the population at large needs to be made crystal clear to the jury. However, we do not agree that the absence of such a database means that no opinion can be expressed by the witness beyond rehearsing his examination of the photographs. An expert who spends years studying this kind of comparison can properly form a judgment as to the significance of what he has found in any particular case. *It is a judgment based on his experience.* A jury is entitled to be informed of his assessment. The alternative, of simply leaving the jury to make up its own mind about the similarities and dissimilarities, with no assistance at all about their significance, would be to give the jury raw material with no means of evaluating it. It would be as likely to result in over-valuation of the evidence as under-valuation. It would be more, not less, likely to result in an unsafe conclusion than providing the jury with the expert's opinion, properly debated through cross-examination and, if not shared by another expert, countered by contrary evidence."

In this way, the "experience" of an expert witness appears to suffice in the United Kingdom, where the evidence itself may be lacking because it is not suitable for statistical analysis [29], scientific knowledge is incomplete [30], there is no way of telling which of several possibilities is more likely [31], or simply because the fact finders (be they jury or judge) require assistance.

The UK Criminal Court of Appeal has expressed approval of experts who are

> punctilious in underlining the danger of a scientist expressing views beyond that expert's competence. [The expert in question] rightly emphasised the dangers that can arise when a scientist expresses views beyond the narrow scientific point on which the expert is asked to opine. There is, we accept, always a danger that if an expert expresses one part of his scientific evidence with confidence, and also expresses other views, those other views can, unless care is taken, be given a verisimilitude of certainty by association. [32]

The Court has gone on to differentiate between the experience of experts from different jurisdictions[g]; and has been particularly discerning about whether the experience is based on examining crime scenes [33] and "practical experience" [34]; "limited to the examination of DNA ... in the laboratory" [35]; or based on scholarship [34] and "papers and discussions with other scientists" [36], with a premium being placed on the evidence of experts, who have worked in the field. Once again, the Court of Appeal has emphasized that if the experience of an expert is in doubt, the correct procedure for dealing with this is to admit their opinion into evidence and thence rely on cross-examination to determine its weight:

> A court in determining whether there is a sufficiently reliable scientific basis for expert evidence to be given and a jury in evaluating evidence will be entitled to take into account the experience of experts and, if their experience is challenged, to test that. If the evidence upon which they rely for the basis of their experience is challenged, then that can be evaluated by cross-examination. [37]

The obvious difficulty that arises if an expert relies on experience, including unpublished data, to form their opinion, is how that opinion is fairly to be evaluated (and, if necessary, challenged) by the opposing party. The Court of Appeal at present does not appear to have a practical solution to this paradox and has stated that where

> the experience and evidence upon which [the prosecution expert] relies is not publicly available and was not available to [the defence expert] . . . . the real problem was that [the defence expert] was a scholar not a person who had experience of this form of science [38]

and

> if one tries to question science purely by reference to published papers and without the practical day-to-day experience upon which others have reached a judgment, that attack is likely to fail, as it did in this case. [38]

Thus, on the basis of *Weller*, experts who do not work for a front-line forensic provider in the United Kingdom do not appear to be welcome as experts in legal proceedings:

> We do hope that the courts will not be troubled in future by attempts to rely on published work by people who have no practical experience in the field and therefore cannot contradict or bring any useful evidence to bear on issues that are not always contained in scientific journals. There are plenty of really experienced experts who are available and it is to those that the courts look for assistance in cases of this kind. [38]

Low Template DNA (LTDNA) Evidence

An important feature of the adversarial legal system in the United Kingdom is that unless expert evidence is challenged by the opposing party, it may pass unnoticed into legal proceedings, being admitted into evidence time and again, unobtrusively gaining legal legitimacy because it has been used in multiple cases (i.e., it has become precedent). It has been noted by the Court of Appeal that

> unless the admissibility is challenged, the judge will admit that evidence. That is the only pragmatic way in which it is possible to conduct trials, as sufficient safeguards are provided by [the Criminal Procedure Rules as to what an expert must include in his/her report] [39]

This was particularly evident in relation to a DNA technique originally referred to as *low copy number (LCN) DNA profiling*, and now also known as *low template DNA (LTDNA) evidence*. This technique was developed by the Forensic Science Service (the prosecution) in the United Kingdom and is used to examine trace amounts of DNA, in quantities which standard DNA-profiling methods are not able to analyze.

LTDNA evidence appears to have been used by the prosecution in the UK criminal justice system since 1999,[h] however, it was not until 2007, when Sean Hoey was prosecuted in the Crown Court of Northern Ireland for a series of bombings, which had taken place over 1998–1999, that the technique was seriously scrutinized [40].

Given the time lapse between the crimes and the analysis in the *Hoey* case, and the fact that contaminants in trace samples could significantly compromise the integrity of the results, the reliability of the LCN DNA profiling was subject to close scrutiny. In this case, Weir J held that

> it is for the prosecution to establish the integrity and freedom from possible contamination of each item throughout the entirety of the period between seizure and any examination relied upon. [The defence] contend, and I accept the contention, that the court must be satisfied by the prosecution witnesses and supporting documents that all dealings with each relevant exhibit have been satisfactorily accounted for from the moment of its seizure until the moment when any evidential sample relied upon by the prosecution is taken from it and that by a method and in conditions that are shown to have been reliable. This means that each person who has dealt with the item in the intervening period must be ascertainable and be able to demonstrate by reference to some proper system of bagging, labelling, and recording that the item has been preserved at every stage free from the suspicion of interference or contamination. For this purpose they must be able to demonstrate how and when and under what conditions and with what object and by what means and in whose presence he or she examined the item. Only if all these requirements have been satisfactorily vouched can a tribunal have confidence in the reliability of any forensic findings said to have been derived from any examination of the item. [41]

In addition to problems with contamination, Weir J identified "concern about the present state of the validation of the science and methodology associated with LCN DNA and, in consequence, its reliability as an evidential tool." [42] Given that it appears the prosecution had been adducing LCN DNA evidence in criminal trials in the United Kingdom for almost a decade already, the issues raised by Weir J prompted a review by the Crown Prosecution Service in 2008, which held that

> the CPS has not seen anything to suggest that any current problems exist with LCN. Accordingly we conclude that LCN DNA analysis provided by the FSS (Forensic Science) should remain available as potentially admissible evidence.[i]

This was followed by a review conducted for the Forensic Science Regulator of the United Kingdom [43], which also concluded that "It appears that it is the position of the FSS and UKAS that the technique of LCN is fit for purpose and we would wish to support this view."[j] The reviewers did note, however, that "The LTDNA/LCN DNA technique conversely has yet to be implemented widely by the international forensic science community",[k] and that

> [a]ny new methods of analysis used by a forensic science provider that will result in the presentation of evidence to the courts must be validated using appropriate and sound internationally recognised scientific principles. The details of such validation, including copies of raw data, should be lodged with the forensic science regulator *before* it is introduced into service.[l]

In any case, the appeal of *Reed & Reed* in 2010 cemented the legal view on the validity of the LCN method: "[A] challenge to the validity of the method of analyzing Low Template DNA by the LCN process should no longer be permitted at trials where the quantity of DNA analyzed is above the stochastic threshold of 100–200 pg in the absence of new scientific evidence." [44]

Following *Reed,* the appeal of *Broughton* in 2010 clarified that even where evidence was obtained from DNA samples below the stochastic threshold of 100 pg, it may still be admissible in legal proceedings [45], notwithstanding the allelic dropout, drop-in, stutter, and inhibition effects noted in the Review conducted by the Forensic Regulator.[m] This was confirmed in *R v C* [46], where the Court of Appeal held that "[t]he sole question was whether, despite the low quantity, a reliable profile could be produced" [47].

This jurisprudence was extended by the case of *R v Thomas (2011)* in which the Court of Appeal had to consider LCN DNA evidence in which the results were unsuitable to any kind of statistical evaluation whatsoever [48]. In these circumstances, the Court was called upon to adjudicate between the prosecution view that the results "provided support" for the appellant's blood being on the gun, and the defense expert's view that the results "could not exclude" the appellant as a contributor to the DNA on the gun [49]. The prosecution relied in part on unpublished "simulation experiments" mentioned in the footnotes of a Forensic Science Service manual which said only that "[u]npublished simulation experiments have shown that it is rare to observe all twenty alleles by chance" [50]. The prosecution witness had not conducted, witnessed, or seen details of the experiments, nor were the details provided when requested by the defense [51]. In *Thomas*, the judge at first instance referred to *Weller (2010)*, in support of the finding that unpublished papers and the experience of experts can provide a sufficiently reliable basis for expert evidence [52]. This was upheld on appeal, despite the Appeal Court noting that

> [t]he difficulty about the simulation experiments in this case is not that they were unpublished but that Miss Cornelius seems to have known virtually nothing about them beyond the bare statement in the FSS manual that "Unpublished simulation experiments have shown that it is rare to observe all twenty alleles by chance". Taken by itself, that would provide an extremely thin basis for Miss Cornelius's statement of opinion about the significance of the DNA results; and there is the added concern that, in the absence of any further information about the simulation experiments, the defence expert had no way of assessing their significance. [53]

In oral evidence, the prosecution DNA expert in *Thomas* explained that she relied on her 12 years experience as a forensic science, rather than any statistical evaluation, for her finding that the DNA results "provided support" for the appellant having handled the gun, and she was not able to provide any further indication of the degree of support the results provided. The Court of Appeal found this to be "a troubling feature" [54] of her evidence and noted that the expert was not even using a sliding scale such as that used in facial mapping evidence, where expressions of support are arranged in a hierarchy and can be compared [55].

Nevertheless, the evidence was admitted at trial and upheld on appeal [56]. Thus, UK courts appear now to accept DNA-profiling evidence without statistics and the admission of this material into evidence appears to be based on the "experience" of the expert.

The acceptance by the courts of evidence absent a robust statistical calculation had now led some experts to offer subjective opinions on the evidential weight of some DNA profiles. Those opinions have been accepted when unchallenged, although there have been successful challenges to their admissibility inasmuch as the prosecution have withdrawn the evidence rather than await the outcome of a *voire dire*.

Transfer and Persistence of DNA

In *Reed*, it was also held that

> in cases where a reliable DNA profile has been obtained ... but the type of cellular material from which it has been obtained is unknown ... an expert can in many cases, in addition to giving evidence of the profile match and match probability, give evidence enumerating the possibilities as to how the DNA has been transferred to the object from which the DNA profile has been obtained. [57]

Furthermore, provided the summary given by the judge to the jury sufficiently addresses the limitations of DNA evidence in relation to transfer and persistence, evidence that suggests how particular DNA might have arrived at the location in which it was found will generally be admissible [58].

In addition, the Court of Appeal will accept evidence as to the weight which should be given to opinions about transfer and persistence, even where these opinions are based only on experience and not on peer-reviewed publications or validated techniques. As explained in *Weller (2010)*, the Court of appeal

> had [the Crown expert's] evidence of his experience as a scientist in the day-to-day work that he conducts as a scientist looking at DNA. His evidence was that he had built up himself and in discussions through colleagues details about the ease or difficulty in which DNA was transferred in the huge variety of circumstances that one sees in day-to-day life. For example, he referred to the many attempts he had made to obtain DNA from hair. *None of this was published, but his conclusions were not in doubt.* The problem, it seems to us, that [the defence expert]

faced was that he simply did not have that practical day-to-day experience of work that necessarily is unpublished, but from which it is possible to draw scientific conclusions. [59]

Ironically, DNA transfer is possibly one area of scientific research where the greater the number of research papers, the more complex and apparently contradictory the evidence is becoming. A review of the published literature in 2013 concluded;

The published work to date establishes:

(a) The possibility, but not the probability, of DNA transfer.

(b) It is not possible to use the amount of DNA recovered from a surface to assess whether the DNA was deposited there by a single touch or by regular use.

(c) It is not possible to use the amount of DNA recovered from an item of interest to inform whether the DNA was deposited by direct contact or indirect transfer.

(d) There is no strong correlation between a full or partial profile and the amount of DNA template (at suboptimal amounts of DNA)

(e) The quality of a DNA profile cannot be used to establish whether the DNA recovered came from the last handler.

(f) The number of factors, and the relative effect of those factors, involved in the transfer of DNA is unknown.

(g) The initial amount of DNA deposited, and any activity likely to reduce the number of cells or DNA-containing material from donor surfaces (e.g., hand), and the time since those activities, is a key factor in determining the amount of DNA recovered. [60]

Recent Jurisprudence

A recent case bringing together many of the issues outlined above is *R v Dlugosz and Others (2013)*. Here,

[a]ll three appeals proceeded on the basis that the DNA evidence was given without any of the experts being able to provide a random match probability, essentially because it was not possible to attribute particular alleles to any contributor. It was a further feature of each case, as is common in Low Template DNA cases, that it was not possible to tell when the DNA was deposited or how it had been deposited (whether by primary, secondary or tertiary transfer) or the origin of the DNA, such as skin or fluid. [61]

The experts in these cases were not "prepared to give evidence using the sliding scale of expressions used

in other areas of expert evidence such as handwriting, fibers, glass fragments, footwear patterns or 'facial mapping'", but were prepared to defend various evaluative opinions (such as "rarely", "lends no support", "somewhat unusual", "lends powerful support") [62]. For instance, one prosecution expert concluded from his analysis of a mixed and partial LTDNA profile that "the results were *more likely to be consistent with* [the victim's] account than [the defendant's] account, but he could not express a view on the strength of the support as no statistical evaluation could be carried out." This evidence was admitted and was upheld on appeal as both relevant and not prejudicial or confusing [63].

The Court of Appeal concluded that "Evaluative evidence" is admissible and "an expert is not bound to express an evaluative opinion by reference to the hierarchy; he can use other phrases" [64]. The Court accepted that such results are variable and that there is no objective standard, but held that even though

[a]n evaluative opinion would necessarily in such cases be subjective ... that does not mean that it should not be admitted provided that there is a reliable scientific basis for it [65].

The Court found that provided a court is satisfied that there is a sufficiently reliable scientific basis for the evidence to be admitted, the opposing views about the correct choice of evaluative descriptor is a matter to be tested before the jury [66]. Furthermore, while the Court could

appreciate that juries could attach a false weight to DNA evidence where statistical evidence cannot be given.. [S]uch a risk is no reason for excluding the evidence, providing that the nature of the evaluative opinion is clearly explained to the jury and it is made clear to them that the opinion is an evaluative one based on experience and not on statistics [67].

One part of the evidence that was ruled inadmissible in the trial at first instance in *Dlugosz*, and not overturned on appeal, was the software program that the Crown contended *could* provide a statistical evaluation of the profiles. The trial judge ruled this evidence inadmissible, accepting the submission made on behalf of the defendant that

"the work had not been sufficiently assessed and peer reviewed so that it could be considered to have a sufficient scientific basis to be regarded as part of a body of knowledge and experience recognised as reliable" [68]. The trial judge had "little doubt that in due course the validity of his software program would be accepted, but there had not by the time of the trial been sufficient assessment and review" [68].

Thus, the overall effect of *Dlugosz's* case appears to be that attempts to statistically evaluate DNA evidence need to have been fully validated and founded on a sufficient scientific basis in order to be held reliable and therefore admissible. Where this objective, scientifically evaluated and validated information is not available, the court will permit experts in England and Wales to express their opinions using "Evaluative" phrases that need not be part of an organized or objective hierarchy, and cannot be assigned any particular strength, so long as the court is satisfied that there is some sort of "reliable scientific basis" for the opinion.

Scotland – Different Jurisdiction, Different Standard?

The most recent Scottish case combining many of these issues is *HMA v Sinclair,* which dealt with partial, mixed profiles obtained from LCN DNA analysis conducted over 20 years after the crimes were committed. In addition to the LCN technique, the prosecution laboratory also used [69]: Crimelite (a filtered light source that screens for fluorescent material); Extended acid phosphatase (AP) testing (i.e., extending the time limit for semen screening); Sperm elution (improving the separation of sperm from cellular material); Minifiler (to obtain profiles from weak and degraded samples); Enhanced DNA (further amplification to increase the sensitivity); and LikeLTD software (stats software for LCN profiles of mixtures – which the court found

"is considerably more sophisticated and allows a calculation which also takes into account the fact that there are bands present in the profile of the respondent which are not present in the partial profile identified." [70]) The court held that the effect of all of this new evidence was "to transform the significance of the findings from neutral to having evidential significance supportive of an inference of violence" [70],

which was the basis for allowing a fresh prosecution, ultimately leading to a conviction.

The court in Sinclair made additional observations about material from the Crown laboratory that was not admissible, namely, results that are not able to be interpreted with any accuracy – This included DNA evidence for which neither a match probability nor a likelihood ratio could be calculated. The court stated

It was not appropriate to rely on results which are below the criteria normally applied for investigative purposes. It is not normal practice to include or report on samples which cannot be subjected to statistical evaluation… [A Scottish Police Forensic Scientist], gave evidence that she would not normally include in her report a result which could be given neither a match probability nor a likelihood ratio. This is a matter bearing on the admissibility of the evidence, not simply its weight. This is evidence which cannot be interpreted by any scientist with any accuracy. [71]

This appears to contradict the ruling in R v Dlugosz and immediately separate the approach of Scottish and English courts.

Overall

Overall, despite the fact that DNA evidence has long been held up as a gold standard to which other forensic disciplines should aspire, the very features that made it seemingly impeachable (reproducibility, quantifiability, basis in measurements, mathematics, and statistics) have been eroded in the case law and replaced with a loose reliance on unpublished data, undefined descriptors (such as "moderate support") and the supposed expertise of (primarily prosecution) witnesses. This has enabled the admission of evidence based on partial profiles, mixed profiles, degraded samples, and low quantities of DNA for consideration by juries. This pragmatic approach is in sharp distinction to the moves being made in other forensic disciplines toward more formal, measurable, reproducible, and objective methods of providing forensic science for the courts.

In the United Kingdom, great emphasis is placed on the fact that DNA evidence is not the totality of the evidence likely to be heard in legal proceedings: As set out in *Reed*

… if the DNA evidence stood alone, you could not convict on it on any count. But it does not stand alone and you will consider its value carefully and use it as part of the evidence when you consider each count individually in the case as a whole. [72]

When deciding upon the admissibility and weight of both standard and low template DNA-profiling evidence, the courts have been consistent in the assertion that "the significance of DNA evidence depends to a large extent upon other evidence in the case" [73]. Therefore, DNA evidence in its various forms (with statistics, without statistics, based on published material or unpublished material, and the expert's experience) should be admitted into evidence as "the jury should be entitled to assess the DNA evidence against the background of the other evidence in the case" [73].

Where a witness' credentials as an expert are not in dispute, and his/her opinions are not so overtly unreliable or so lacking in foundation as to make them inadmissible or to compel their exclusion in the interests of fairness, they will be admitted into evidence. It is considered of potentially greater assistance to the jury to have this sort of evidence than to be denied it altogether [74]. The accepted course in the UK courts is that the evidence be adduced and then tested in cross-examination, so that its limitations and its weight could be assessed by the jury [14]. This applies even in cases where the DNA evidence is not suitable for statistical analysis, where it has been held that "evaluative opinions" are admissible,

> provided it is made clear to the jury the very limited basis upon which an evaluation can be made without a statistical database, a jury can be assisted in its consideration of the evidence by an expression of an evaluative opinion by the experts. [75]

End Notes

a. Strengthening Forensic Science in the United States: A Path Forward (2009), *National Academy of Sciences USA,* at p. 130.
b. Strengthening Forensic Science in the United States: A Path Forward (2009), *National Academy of Sciences USA,* at p. XX.
c. The Report "Legal Obligations", Forensic Science Regulator (UK), FSR-I-400 (2012) gives an overview of some of the caselaw and principles outlined in this article, up until 2012.
d. House of Commons Science and Technology Committee, "Forensic Science on Trial" Report (29 March 2005) at [55].

e. Despite the recommendations of the Law Commission of England and Wales in "Expert Evidence in Criminal Proceedings in England and Wales", Law Commission of England and Wales, Report No. 325, 2011, calling for a statutory test of admissibility for expert evidence. The government has instead chosen to amend the Criminal Procedure Rules, Part 33 of which deals with Expert Evidence, the duty of the expert, the content of the expert's report, disclosure of expert evidence, and the court's power to direct that evidence be given by a single joint expert.
f. Strengthening Forensic Science in the United States: A Path Forward (2009), *National Academy of Sciences USA,* at pp. 1–14.
g. "We have also taken into account the fact that his experience is of a different jurisdiction where the scientist who gives evidence may have a narrower type of expertise and the scope of evidence an expert can give may not be the same as the scope in this jurisdiction" in R v Reed, Reed and Garmson [2009]. *EWCA Crim* 2698; [2010] 1 *Cr App R* 23 at [103]. See also HMA v Sinclair [2014]. *HCJAC* 131 at [121].
h. Caddy *et al.* [43] at 7.2.
i. Crown Prosecution Service, "Review of the use of Low Copy Number DNA analysis in current cases: CPS statement", 14 January 2008.
j. Caddy *et al.* [43] at 7.3.
k. Caddy *et al.* [43] at 7.3.
l. Caddy *et al.* [43] at 14. (*Emphasis added*)
m. Caddy *et al.* [43], as referred to in R v Broughton [2010]. EWCA Crim 549 at [33–38].

References

[1] Gill, P. & Werrett, D.J. (1987). Exclusion of a man charged with murder by DNA fingerprinting, *Forensic Science International* 35, 145–148.
[2] R v Robb (1991) 93 Cr App R 161 at 165, per Bingham LJ; R v Bonython (1984). 38 SAAR 45, as approved in R v Reed, Reed and Garmson (2009). EWCA Crim 2698; (2010) 1 Cr App R 23 at [111].
[3] R v Robb, 93 Cr App R 161 at 165, per Bingham LJ (1991).
[4] See R v Clarke, 2 Cr App R 425 (1995); R v Gilfoyle (No 2), 2 Cr App R 57 (2001); R v Dallagher, EWCA Crim 1903 (2002); 1 Cr App R 12 (2003); Luttrell, EWCA Crim 1344 (2004); 2 Cr App R 31 and in Scotland Davie v Edinburgh Magistrates 1953 SC 34 (2004).
[5] R v Bonython (1984), South Australian Supreme Court Reports 45 at 46, per King CJ. Although this is an Australian case, it has been cited with approval in UK

cases (see The Ardent (1997) 2 Lloyd's Rep 547 at 597 etc).

[6]   R v Atkins and Atkins, EWCA Crim 1876 (2009); 1 Cr App R 8 at [9] (2010).

[7]   R v Clarke, 2 Cr App R 425 at 429 (1995).

[8]   Clarke cited with approval in R v Reed, Reed and Garmson, EWCA Crim 2698 (2009); 1 Cr App R 23 at [111] (2010).

[9]   R v Doheny and Adams, 1 Cr App R 369 at 374D, per Phillips LJ (1997).

[10]   R v Dallagher, EWCA Crim 1903 (2002); 1 Cr App R 12 at 29 (2003), citing Cross and Tapper on Evidence (9th ed, 1999), LexisNexis UK at 523.

[11]   R v Luttrell, EWCA Crim 1344 (2004); 2 Cr App R 31 (2004), see especially [32]–[36].

[12]   R v Luttrell, EWCA Crim 1344 (2004); 2 Cr App R 31 at [36] (2004).

[13]   See, for example, Thomas Ross Young v HM Advocate, HCJAC 145 at [54]–[55] (2013).

[14]   R v Thomas, EWCA Crim 1295 at [39] (2011).

[15]   R v Thomas, EWCA Crim 1295 at [44] (2011).

[16]   Cited in R v Broughton, EWCA Crim 549 at [10] and overruled at [32] (2010).

[17]   R v Bates,. EWCA Crim 1395 at [10] (2006). See R v Reed, Reed and Garmson, EWCA Crim 2698 (2009); 1 Cr App R 23 at Part II: The Science of the Analysis of DNA and Low Template DNA, which provides just such an update (2010).

[18]   R v Doheny and Adams, 1 Cr App R 369 (1997).

[19]   R v Bates, EWCA Crim 1395 at [30] (2006).

[20]   R v Bates, EWCA Crim 1395 at [31] (2006).

[21]   R v T, EWCA Crim 2439 at [78] (2010).

[22]   R v T, EWCA Crim 2439 at [80] (2010).

[23]   R v T, EWCA Crim 2439 at [83] (2010).

[24]   R v Broughton, EWCA Crim 549 at [48–49] (2010).

[25]   R v Walsh, NICC 32 at [8] (2011).

[26]   R v Walsh, NICC 32 at [13] (2011).

[27]   R v Martin, NICA 7 at [31] (2012).

[28]   R v Atkins and Atkins, EWCA Crim 1876 (2009); 1 Cr App R 8 at [23] (2010).

[29]   R v Atkins and Atkins, EWCA Crim 1876 (2009); 1 Cr App R 8 (2010).

[30]   R v Reed, Reed and Garmson, EWCA Crim 2698 (2009); 1 Cr App R 23 at [133] (2010).

[31]   R v Reed, Reed and Garmson, EWCA Crim 2698 (2009); 1 Cr App R 23 at [120–127] (2010); R v Weller, EWCA Crim 1085 at [19–20] (2010).

[32]   R v Reed, Reed and Garmson, EWCA Crim 2698 (2009); 1 Cr App R 23 at [102] (2010).

[33]   See, for instance, the court's description of a suitably experienced witness in R v Reed, Reed and Garmson, EWCA Crim 2698 (2009); 1 Cr App R 23 at [126] (2010).

[34]   R v Weller, EWCA Crim 1085 at [26–27] (2010).

[35]   R v Reed, Reed and Garmson, EWCA Crim 2698 (2009); 1 Cr App R 23 at [103] (2010).

[36]   R v Reed, Reed and Garmson, EWCA Crim 2698 (2009); 1 Cr App R 23 at [106] (2010).

[37]   R v Weller, EWCA Crim 1085 at [48] (2010).

[38]   R v Weller, EWCA Crim 1085 at [49] (2010).

[39]   R v Reed, Reed and Garmson, EWCA Crim 2698 (2009); 1 Cr App R 23 at [113] (2010).

[40]   R v Hoey, NICC 49 (20 December 2007) (2007).

[41]   R v Hoey, NICC 49 (20 December 2007) at [46] (2007).

[42]   R v Hoey, NICC 49 (20 December 2007) at [64] (2007).

[43]   Caddy, B., Taylor, G. & Linacre, A. (2008). *A Review of the Science of Low Template DNA Analysis*, Forensic Science Regulator (UK), The Stationary Officer, London.

[44]   See R v Reed, Reed and Garmson, EWCA Crim 2698 (2009); 1 Cr App R 23 at [74] (2010).

[45]   R v Broughton, EWCA Crim 549 at [31] (2010).

[46]   R v C, EWCA Crim 2578 (2010).

[47]   R v C, EWCA Crim 2578 at [26] (2010).

[48]   R v Thomas, EWCA Crim 1295 at [4] (2011).

[49]   R v Thomas, EWCA Crim 1295 at [14–15] (2011).

[50]   R v Thomas, EWCA Crim 1295 at [15] (2011).

[51]   R v Thomas, EWCA Crim 1295 at [26] (2011).

[52]   R v Thomas, EWCA Crim 1295 at [38] (2011).

[53]   R v Thomas, EWCA Crim 1295 at [35] (2011).

[54]   The Court of Appeal in R v Thomas (2011). EWCA Crim 1295 at [36] was quoting directly from R v Atkins and Atkins (2009). EWCA Crim 1876; 1 Cr App R 8 at [23] (2010).

[56]   As was similar "experience-based" evidence in R v Dlugosz and Others, EWCA Crim 2 – see [44–46] (2013).

[57]   R v Reed, Reed and Garmson, EWCA Crim 2698 (2009); 1 Cr App R 23 at [78] and [119–127] (2010). See also R v Wootton & Ors (2012). NICC 1 for a recent Northern Irish example of this.

[58]   R v Reed, Reed and Garmson, EWCA Crim 2698 (2009); 1 Cr App R 23 at [211] (2010).

[59]   R v Weller, EWCA Crim 1085 at [41–49] (2010).

[60]   Meakin, G. & Jamieson, A. (2013). DNA transfer: review and implications for casework, *Forensic Science International: Genetics* 7, 434–443.

[61]   R v Dlugosz and Others, EWCA Crim 2 at [4] (2013).

[62]   R v Dlugosz and Others, EWCA Crim 2 at [5] (2013).

[63]   R v Dlugosz and Others, EWCA Crim 2 at [77] and [80] (2013).

[64]   R v Dlugosz and Others, EWCA Crim 2 at [10–14] (2013).

[65]   R v Dlugosz and Others, EWCA Crim 2 at [26] (2013).

[66]   R v Dlugosz and Others, EWCA Crim 2 at [11] (2013).

[67]   R v Dlugosz and Others, EWCA Crim 2 at [53] (2013).

[68]   R v Dlugosz and Others, EWCA Crim 2 at [100] (2013).

[69]   HMA v Sinclair, HCJAC 131 at [36] (2014).

[70]   HMA v Sinclair, HCJAC 131 at [78] (2014).

[71]   HMA v Sinclair, HCJAC 131 at [89] (2014).

[72]   R v Reed, Reed and Garmson, EWCA Crim 2698 (2009); 1 Cr App R 23 at [213] (2010), citing the judge's charge to the jury in Garmson's trial at first instance.

[73]   R v Thomas, EWCA Crim 1295 at [27] (2011).

[74]   In R v Dlugosz and Others, EWCA Crim 2 at [60] (2013) it was held that the view of the DNA experts that finding all of an individual's alleles in a mixed LCN

sample was either "rare" or "somewhat unusual", was of real assistance to the jury, and as such the evidence was admitted.

[75]   R v Dlugosz and Others, EWCA Crim 2 at [24] (2013).

Related Articles

Degraded Samples

DNA

DNA: An Overview

DNA Databases and Evidentiary Issues

DNA Databases – The Significance of Unique Hits and the Database Controversy

Sources of DNA

Quantitation

Related Articles in EFS Online

Daubert v. Merrell Dow Pharmaceuticals

Expert Opinion: United States

Federal Rule of Evidence 702

Frye v. United States

General Acceptance Test for Novel Expert Evidence

Interpretation: Low Template DNA

Low Copy Number DNA

Low Template DNA Analysis and Interpretation

Mixture Interpretation: DNA

Chapter 42
Legal Issues with Forensic DNA in the USA

Christopher A. Flood

Federal Defenders of New York, Inc., New York, NY, USA

Forensic DNA has achieved some great things within the American criminal justice system. Touted as a "truth machine",[a] it has helped solve cold cases and given closure to many victims of crime. Perhaps most importantly, DNA has exonerated the innocent. DNA technology has been a major tool in the efforts to correct some of the many mistakes we have made, and helped bring wrongful convictions to light. Since its inception in 1992, the Innocence Project has freed at least 173 people with the help of some form of DNA technology.[b] For the innocent, the power of DNA is at its zenith, as its greatest strength is to exclude.[c] DNA's capability to identify or *include* suspects has also been profound,[d] if contested, since its introduction as courtroom evidence in the mid-1980s.[e] The initial "DNA Wars" have largely passed as almost every jurisdiction now routinely allows DNA evidence in criminal cases.[f] Even respected critics of the technique agree that, when such evidence is measured conservatively, the probative value of DNA is remarkable.[g]

However, perhaps the time has come to question how far this technology, and the useful inferences, can be pushed. The DNA chemistry that enables profiling was first developed in the clinical rather than forensic setting, helping it adopt a more scientific base than any other forensic tool.[h] DNA was described as the "gold standard" in the forensic field.[i] The attendant prestige of the technology helped spark a reassessment of the value of finality in criminal justice, and compelled access to testing for the accused.[j] But market forces and political grandstanding have distorted this early promise. These developments have both diminished DNA's probative value and threatened to relegate forensic DNA to the same status as the questionable techniques it once outshined.

Specifically, there are three distinct ways that commercial and political forces are distorting the promise of forensic DNA. The first is that there has been a focus on the creation of databases. The expanding set of people required by law to submit DNA samples has created a very large set of "known" samples as compared to the number of actual evidence samples processed by labs for upload into state and federal databases. The utility of this mix for legitimate law enforcement purposes is in serious question. The sponsors of the enabling legislation campaign on their political "achievement".

For huge databases to function, the data must be standardized. The FBI's CODIS (combined DNA index system) database incorporates data from hundreds of labs around the country.[k] The enormous technical challenge this entails has meant backlogs,[l] and imposing a centralized set of standards.[m] Recently, private corporations have begun marketing custom forensic DNA databases of limited size and scope that are not intended to ever connect with CODIS. More than simply a private lab conducting testing, private data management is a paradigm shift that may threaten DNA's utility as a tool for justice.

The second way that the status of forensic DNA has been threatened is that the industry has focused on increasing the sensitivity of methods rather than improving the accuracy (risking reliability) or the quality control of the powerful systems that are already in place. The emergence of highly sensitive low copy number (LCN) DNA testing[n] has pushed the threshold limits of the amount of DNA necessary to produce a DNA profile. At the same time, the technique is highly susceptible to contamination, produces unpredictable

A Guide to Forensic DNA Profiling
Edited by Allan Jamieson and Scott Bader
© 2016 John Wiley & Sons, Ltd. ISBN: 9781118751527
Also published in EFS (online edition)
DOI: 10.1002/9780470061589.fsa1133

stochastic effects that challenge accurate interpretation, and undermines the meaning of reliable statistical correlations. Meanwhile, scientific peer review of forensic DNA work is hardly comparable to the rigorous testing of examiner conclusions.[o] Yet, as will be explored using the specific case example of *United States v. Johnny Morgan*,[p] New York City's Office of the Chief Medical Examiner (OCME) routinely conducts LCN testing in criminal casework despite this questionable technique.

And the third way forensic DNA has been challenged is that the industry has become increasingly closed to outside scrutiny. The natural advantages enjoyed by the prosecution over the defense are multiplied in this crucial area. The government not only decides whether and what to test but also directs funding to the forensic DNA industry, and elects what if any standards are meaningful. For example, lab quality assurance and quality control (hereinafter QA/QC) standards that helped define the oversight regime integrated into CODIS have gone unenforced.[q] And even where oversight is exercised, in the case of the OCME, it is arguable whether it is taken seriously at all.[r] While secrecy and unfair tactical advantage have no place when it comes to the fair administration of justice, they appear to be common in the highly technical world of forensic science. Blue ribbon attempts to address the problem have been met with friction, leading to the recent brief resignation of respected federal judge Jed Rakoff from the National Commission on Forensic Science over prosecutorial discovery practices.[s]

Corporate resistance to basic disclosure obligations have marked the path of forensic DNA's development, most recently with the creation of "expert" systems for mixture interpretation and subsequent refusal to reveal source codes.[t] These practices echo the worst practices of "trial by ambush", long discredited as unfair. DNA was expected to help bring about a new era of clarity and truthfulness to the criminal justice system.

Grand solutions are elusive, but the responsibility for setting DNA straight lies with the community of defenders whose historic role in protecting the rights of the accused now assumes greater importance than ever. Although resources will have to be provided to ensure that defenders can perform this function, an adequate defense remains the most effective means to challenge, highlight, and expose the flaws with current practices.

The history of American justice is strewn with examples of serious abuses committed in the course of "the often competitive enterprise of ferreting out crime".[u] DNA once helped fix these abuses, but its amazing precision has not led to a more fair or accurate justice system. The problem is not with our tools; it is with the users.

Building the Database Empire

With the advent of DNA evidence as a truth-finding device, a market was also born. Demand increased with awareness and acceptance of the evidence in courtrooms. With each cold hit, each exoneration, forensic DNA has grown less novel, and more presumptively accurate. Benefitting from this broad acceptance, the DNA industry has shaped public policy, as in the very choice of the 13 locus PCR/STR (polymerase chain reaction/short tandem repeat) profile becoming defined as the "industry standard".[v] Commercial crime labs wasted no time in taking advantage of the obvious marketing opportunity in selling "certain" results.[w]

This kind of certainty also has obvious political appeal. Efforts to compel people to submit their biological material for testing and upload into state and national databases have continuously broadened. While at first only people convicted of a certain class of sex offenses were required to submit samples, that group expanded to include people convicted of violent felonies, then all convicted felons, and then many misdemeanors.[x] Today, in many states, the government can compel people to submit a sample of biological material for DNA testing simply for being *arrested*. The Supreme Court endorsed this practice in *Maryland v. King*,[y] though the decision has since been roundly criticized.[z]

The political appeal of including a greater proportion of society in CODIS is based on a specious logic – that more known profiles in the database will increase public safety. But, short of including everybody (a practical impossibility),[aa] the inclusion of an ever-expanding class of people in CODIS has little empirical justification.[ab] Research suggests that uploading *evidence* samples are far more valuable to solving crime than uploading known samples – particularly those of arrestees.[ac] As the United States packs more and more of its suspect population into CODIS, our yield of database hits does not keep pace with the United Kingdom, a nation that adds a greater proportion of evidence samples to its database and sees a corresponding greater number of case hits.[ad]

CODIS is already enormous, boasting over 11 million profiles[ae] (an unknown number of which may be duplicates or otherwise erroneous). Every new evidence sample that is compared against this large set is surprisingly likely to produce a hit.[af] Because many evidence samples are of lower quality and do not always yield a full 13-locus profile, the chances of generating a hit in the database increases (because with fewer loci examined, there will be more people who are a chance match), producing an investigative lead.[ag] Yet, DNA work that is going through labs and into established databases is *heavily* weighted toward known samples, rather than more valuable evidence samples.[ah]

The political expediency of such statutes for their drafters certainly cannot be doubted. DNA is perceived as an effective crime fighting tool, and being "tough on crime" is a time-tested political weapon. But the irony is that these efforts are intrinsically self-defeating. Setting aside the intrusiveness, indignity, and risk of false inclusion that attends placement of one's profile in a DNA databank,[ai] we have slowed down valuable casework. Backlogs are a fact of life in forensic labs.[aj] The evidence suggests, however, that work on more challenging evidence samples is affected by backlogs more than is the relatively standardized process of testing known profiles.[ak]

This trend is likely to continue. In the wake of *King*, more statutes calling for mandatory testing and upload of DNA profiles are likely to become law.[al] Continuing backlogs are a predictable consequence. The public safety message feels good, even if it makes little empirical sense and is costly. In the words of one leading scholar, "Americans want security, and we are willing to give up some privacy to get it, especially the privacy of others".[am]

Opting Out – Private Databases

With backlogs has come pressure to find alternative solutions.[an] The free market has a long history of filling gaps in public services. Though some once thought it ethically questionable, private forensic labs have always taken overflow work from state labs.[ao] A striking new development, however, is the private housing of DNA data. The marketers promise the ability to develop one's *own* database.[ap] Even if it were not self-apparent that a "hit" from a private database is of uncertain probative value, the marketing materials avoid the word "evidence", opting instead for the looser "investigative leads".[aq] The focus is not on reliability, but speed and local control.

The very existence of these databanks tends to circumvent the centralized quality control built into CODIS, however weakly implemented. The focus is not on uniform standards any more than it is on solving cold cases in another jurisdiction or discovering an evidentiary link that undoes a wrongful conviction. The private database is made to satisfy the demands of the lone law enforcement officer, and may give him his "own" data free from the encumbrance of evidentiary standards, protocols, or any other encumbrances that accompany participation with CODIS.

There is serious risk that *any* database will be misused, especially where those whose profiles are included in it disproportionately come from minority communities.[ar] Practically nothing is known of the composition of these databanks. Existing outside of the CODIS framework, the only mechanism available for oversight is a challenge that a "hit" was a sufficient "investigative lead" to justify a subsequent arrest, search, or seizure. To date, no such hearing has been reported.

It is perhaps too big a project to nationalize *anything* in America, whatever the purpose.[as] To implement a system of DNA casework requires acceptance from local law enforcement officers who have had to obey centrally defined rules and endure long wait times. While our national history of resistance by local law enforcement to federal authority seemed to be of another era[at] – or at least until recently[au] – the benefits of DNA evidence seemed to make an obvious case for CODIS. Private databases speak to a frustration with the inefficiencies of this system.

CODIS is a highly secretive and closed system, and not easily searchable by the defense.[av] If CODIS made more information available, potentially we would avoid more wrongful convictions, and assist more of the wrongfully convicted. Also, theoretically, CODIS is a vehicle for promulgating uniformly high QA/QC lab standards. However, governance of CODIS has involved knowing neglect of enforcement of standards.[aw] If such standards were seriously enforced, CODIS could be an engine for national improvement.

Whether private data signals the high water mark of coordinated national efforts like CODIS and a descent into good-enough-for-my-county standards or will be a short-lived and potentially dangerous phenomenon remains to be seen.

The emergence of private databases also raises important questions about privacy, about suspicion, and about what statistics apply in the event of a "hit". These questions may have been too big to face head-on under a monolithic single database regime. But in a post-CODIS world, these questions take on new urgency.

Focusing on Sensitivity over Accuracy

History could have alone foreshadowed that we would stretch even DNA's capacity. The "tipping-point technology" was called LCN but now frequently referred to as low template or high sensitivity testing. The hallmark of this testing is that the same sample will produce more or less different results from the same sample because of the sampling effects (called stochastic) of such low numbers of DNA molecules. The problem, and the danger, emerged from the methods used to interpret such variable results. But these dangers were specifically predicted, and largely unheeded, by one of forensic DNA's strongest proponents. Starting in 2001, Bruce Budowle, then a senior scientist at the FBI Crime Laboratory, conveyed concern with stretching PCR/STR techniques in pursuit of greater sensitivity.[ax] Other commentators warned of the dangers of widespread, and increasingly accepted, use of such samples.[ay] The caution was that pushing the methods too far gave rise to unacceptable likelihoods of serious error.

Increased sensitivity sounds like a laudable and cost-free goal, like adding a higher power lens to a telescope. In truth, however, heightened sensitivity creates a set of tough interpretive problems.[az] LCN drives PCR/STR technology in ways that it was not designed to perform. Even with ideal levels of biological material, the PCR/STR system is susceptible to contamination which can complicate the analysis, generate inaccurate profiles, and skew later statistical interpretations. With LCN, however, there is so little source material being put into the PCR process that these risks are seriously increased.

Add to this the reality that no lab can control what happens at the scene, how the evidence is collected, or how evidence is stored before it reaches the lab. When testing for trace levels of biological material, the risk of cross-contamination – and false inclusion – is grave. In the United Kingdom, cross-contamination with subsequent DNA results have led criminal suspicion to befall those unfortunate enough to have been tended to by the same ambulance crew who later collected crime scene evidence[ba] and even one who worked in the factory manufacturing swabs.[bb]

But results from LCN tests (and indeed many crimestains even with "standard" methods) are not always clear, and mistakes in interpretation can lead to false inclusion. High-sensitivity LCN testing usually produces mixed DNA profiles, which, even with optimum amounts of DNA, present devilish interpretive problems of their own[bc] but which are particularly difficult to parse in the high-sensitivity context. High-sensitivity LCN tests are prone to unpredictable and irreproducible stochastic effects – the appearance and disappearance of alleles, as well as peak height imbalance, and enhanced stutter – all of which undermine accurate and reliable interpretation of results. Assigning fair statistical values to an LCN "match" is truly challenging.

An Example: *The NYOCME and US v Johnny Morgan*[bd]

The quest for results that helped push the limits of DNA technology[be] was writ large in New York City, where the OCME performs the forensic lab work for one of the world's largest criminal court systems. The OCME greatly expanded its PCR/STR capacity after receiving generous grants to eliminate – largely via subcontracting to private labs – what at the time were significant forensic backlogs in sex assault cases,[bf] and to help identify remains from the World Trade Center site.[bg]

The OCME built significant in-house PCR/STR capacity and addressed its forensic casework backlog. The lab retained this expanded capacity and began in the mid-2000s to utilize it in a broad category of cases. While other jurisdictions were enduring long delays for DNA results in the most serious cases, the New York courts began to see DNA evidence produced in property crimes. DNA evidence is now commonplace in New York gun possession cases.[bh]

At the same time, the OCME became the first state lab in which LCN testing was routinely conducted. Despite this unique status, it appears that no court weighed in on the admissibility of LCN evidence for several years. The only reported decision, *People v. Megnath*, came from a Queens trial court that admitted LCN evidence after a truncated *Frye* hearing.[bi] Although *Megnath* has been repeatedly cited for the proposition that LCN evidence is accepted in New York courts,[bj] the opinion is not well-supported. It avoids the heart of the technical issues that differentiate LCN, and instead likens the technique to a simple evolution of PCR/STR. Recent criticism of *Megnath* likens the court's comparison of LCN to STR/PCR to "reasoning that if a recipe works by cooking the dish for 30 min at 300°, it will work equally well cooking it for 15 min at 600°".[bk]

For the first time in several years, in 2013, a series of challenges in state and federal court were brought against the use of the OCME's LCN test results in criminal trials. A telling example of the intensity of the ensuing conflict is the case of *United States v. Johnny Morgan*.

US v. Johnny Morgan

Johnny Morgan was accused of firing a gun, but did not have a gun on him when he was arrested. The NYPD (New York City Police Department) found a pistol on the sidewalk near where Mr. Morgan had been stopped. The arresting officer took possession of the gun, as well as a number of Mr. Morgan's personal items, placed them together, and brought them all back to the precinct house.[bl]

The OCME conducted LCN testing on swabs from the gun, which in accordance with their standards, is done in triplicate. Each assay produced a widely variant mixed profile. All four stochastic effects prevalent in LCN testing were present in the evidence. The examiner resolved the three different profiles into a single-source Male Donor A profile and calculated a statistical value for that profile, which was consistent with Johnny Morgan's known profile – a "match". Mr. Morgan was charged in federal court.

This evidence was excluded from Mr. Morgan's first trial for discovery issues, and jury could not reach a verdict. The government elected to subject Mr. Morgan to a second trial and gave notice that it intended to introduce the LCN evidence. The defense moved to exclude the LCN evidence as unreliable under the *Daubert* standard prevailing in federal court.

Shifting Standards

The risks inherent in LCN testing call for strict adherence to conservative protocols. In Mr. Morgan's case,

however, the OCME appears to have ignored them. The sample tested in Johnny Morgan's case was only 14.15 pg – (or trillionths of a gram 10 to the −12). This is the equivalent biological mass of only a few cells.

The OCME had never sought accreditation to conduct such low-level LCN testing. The New York State Commission on Forensic Science develops standards and accredits forensic labs in New York State.[bm] The DNA Subcommittee evaluates the specific methods of forensic labs throughout the state and submits a binding recommendation to "the Commission". To obtain approval of its LCN testing program, the leadership of the OCME repeatedly and clearly represented that the lab would not conduct LCN case testing below 20 pg.[bn] To date, despite the Commission's mandate for "approval of forensic laboratories for the performance of specific forensic methodologies", neither the DNA Subcommittee nor the Commission has ever reviewed the OCME's testing of such small sample sizes. That the OCME still conducted such testing in Mr. Morgan's case speaks volumes about the limitations of regulatory oversight.

The evidence in Mr. Morgan's case produced a mixed sample including a contested number of potential contributors. At two loci, the presence of additional alleles signaled the possibility of as many as five potential contributors. The parties took opposing positions as to the interpretation of the evidence. The defense contended that the presence of additional alleles indicated additional contributors to the mixture. The OCME claimed that the additional alleles were evidence of stochastic allelic drop-in, and drop-out, in the triplicate runs. The government, for its part, defended the OCME's call, taking the somewhat odd position that the aberrant random appearance of false alleles made the OCME's conclusions more reliable.

The effect of this debate on the statistics should have been meaningful.[bo] But the OCME appears to have disregarded the number of contributors anyway to determine that there was a partial profile of a major contributor to the mixture, consistent with Mr. Morgan. Presumably utilizing the random match probability (RMP) to calculate these odds, the OCME reported that the "most likely profile of Male Donor A is expected to be found in approximately 1 in 1.43 million people".[bp]

The lab had no objective experience against which to base this call. The OCME's smallest validation studies for mixed LCN samples were on 25 pg samples from buccal swabs not evidence swabs, but that did not deter this interpretation.[bq] The result was not reliable enough to preserve in a databank. Leaving aside CODIS, once called, Male Donor A's profile could not be entered into the OCME's *own internal database* because the OCME's protocols prohibit entering LCN DNA profiles deduced from mixed samples "because of the uncertainty" of those profiles.[br]

One key reason for this uncertainty in LCN mixture interpretation is the problem with "peak heights".[bs] The main tool used to discern major and minor contributors to a mixture is the amount of biological material in the PCR product, roughly represented by the height of a "peak" at a given locus. A complication arises with LCN testing with the commonly observed stochastic effect of "peak height imbalance", or the nonreproducible wide variation in the size of heterozygous peaks from samples originating from the same source.

In the sample in *Morgan*, the OCME concluded that stochastic effects were present. Only where those effects buttressed the prosecution theory, however, were they incorporated. The government's case against multiple contributors to the mixture was based on the stochastic effects of allelic drop-out and allelic drop-in. But on the same evidence, where those effects supported the defense theory – to ignore peak height imbalance in isolating Male Donor A – stochastic effects were discounted. It is very hard to square this interpretation with good forensic science. The changing rulebook depending on who asks the question is almost Kafkaesque, and harkens to the worst kind of shamanistic interpretative subjectivity of discredited forensic methods.

It is not difficult, however, to see the crude forms of examiner bias at play in Mr. Morgan's case even at the once highly regarded OCME as in so many other less prestigious labs.[bt] For example, it is impossible to understand the biological significance of the lab notes that the "case at the moment is circumstantial", "the gun was not taken off his body" or especially that "the defendant has been arrested 75xs before".[bu] This is not science, or even good police work. With so much uncertainty – a mixed sample of such a miniscule sample size, testing beyond the limits of the lab's validation studies, with observed variation in the results (the stochastic effect typifying such samples) – common sense would call for conservative interpretations. The OCME appears to have done the opposite,

making every effort to use the most damning statistics available.

The court admitted the LCN evidence and Mr. Morgan was convicted at his second trial.

Legal Controversy and Implications

The case presents a number of curious contradictions, beginning with the United States Department of Justice taking a litigation position in opposition to the scientific standards set by its own enforcement arm, the FBI Laboratory. While the FBI and CODIS will not accept the LCN casework results[bv] in *US v. Morgan,* the government vigorously fought to take advantage of the OCME's different and more permissive standards. The evidence was not reliable enough to enter into CODIS, yet strong enough for a criminal trial. Where one can look to find a principle beyond "might makes right" is not here answered.

The OCME proved itself to be willing in the *Morgan* case to push to the furthest edge of interpretation, subject to biasing, reading through past allelic drop-in, drop-out, stutter, and peak height imbalance, and breezing past the absence of validation studies into the dangerous terrain of mixed samples in order to employ the most damning statistics available.

The federal courts and the permissive *Daubert* standard did not have a shining moment. Although a hearing was held, the court's ruling was issued orally on the final day of testimony.[bw] Given the number of issues that had been fairly joined, and the historic role of the federal courts in protecting the rights of the accused, at minimum, a written ruling would have given guidance to future litigants.

Encouragingly, a recent state court decision excluding OCME LCN evidence in a challenge brought by New York public defenders has kept pressure on the lab to reform its practices.[bx] Although the New York State courts employ a different legal test for admissibility of scientific and technical evidence, questioning the general acceptance rather than the reliability of a technique, this result provides a glimmer of optimism for those who do not accept the reliability of these LTDNA techniques. Ironically, in public statements responding to this ruling, prosecutors have objected on behalf of the innocent assisted by LCN testing. While it is difficult to reconcile the court's exclusion of LCN evidence from a criminal trial with a prosecutor's consideration of LCN testing results when electing to dismiss a case on behalf of a wrongfully convicted person, the erosion of standards evident in the *Morgan* case is a *far* more troubling development for the innocent. Given the contortions that OCME appears to have gone through to help convict Johnny Morgan, it is not hard to imagine a lab with biases against a wrongfully convicted person using every interpretive method *against* the innocent. It is a very short hop from *Morgan* to a false inclusion-by-failure-to-exclude.

Pushing DNA past the stochastic threshold in the name of sensitivity, LCN takes us leagues away from DNA's core reliability to a realm where nearly *all* is subjective interpretation. The defendant's DNA is not present? Allelic drop-out puts him back in. Another contributor is in the mixture? Allelic drop-in removes them. The difference between these loose standards and palm reading or astrology is hard to discern. The most troubling aspect of it all is that, because of LCN's origins in more reliable forms of DNA, it may be accepted by courts, practitioners, and juries alike as simply "DNA evidence".

Closing Off DNA from Defense Scrutiny

The battle waged in *Morgan* would not be possible were it not for the persistent efforts of the defense team to secure discovery. Such scrutiny is increasingly rare, and has always been the exception. Though their proponents may want them to be taken as gospel, forensic DNA test results are not objective "truth machines". Subjectivity enters into the process at several steps. Yet many labs issue reports that reveal only the lab technician's final conclusions, concealing the areas where a technician exercised judgment in a particular case. If such a report were the whole of discovery provided to the defense, then even cross-examination of the lab technician who conducted the testing[by] would be of little value. This kind of sandbagging is neither accidental nor unique.

Much of criminal justice is characterized by secrecy. When the object is to win, neither side is eager to open their files for the other's inspection. And while there are certainly legitimate justifications for not sharing certain aspects of law enforcement's operations, the information control around forensic DNA has become almost cynical. For example, none of the government's initial disclosures in *Morgan* noted that the case even involved LCN testing. Neither the

OCME's Laboratory Report[bz] nor the government's expert notice[ca] made mention of this highly significant fact.

Economic incentives also distort legitimate systemic needs. Corporate secrecy has been used to prevent defense scrutiny of a range of issues from basic chemistry to analytical software.[cb] This secrecy highly favors the prosecution, by virtue of the fact that they are the proponent of the evidence but also wield tremendous influence in the field.

Whatever genius in its design, the adversarial system is deeply flawed in its function. Unfairness is deeply woven into the way we process criminal cases. We have dubious policing inputs,[cc] overloaded and underfunded court systems,[cd] and extreme punishment regimes[ce] that leverage settlements in lieu of trials.[cf] Our nation's cultural, racial, and economic history plays out every day in criminal courtrooms across every region of the country. Race plays a disproportionate role in policing, prosecuting, and punishment.[cg] Economic class plays a similarly determinative role. Well over 85% of defendants in state and federal courts each year are too poor to afford to hire their own lawyer.[ch]

The *only* resource available to the vast majority of people charged with crimes in our country is appointed counsel. Our staggering ability to produce wrongful convictions demonstrates that the mere presence of counsel alone does not ensure fairness or accuracy. Appointed counsel in America has historically been under-resourced, overloaded, and undervalued. The result is a huge shift in power toward the police and prosecution, a breakdown of historic due process protections, and a failure of basic rationality in the system. The painful truth is that for most people accused of a crime, fairness is simply out of reach because we have never taken delivery of defense services to the indigent seriously. For those with practical experience in our courts, the maxim is obvious that "it is better to be rich and guilty than poor and innocent".[ci] Inadequate discovery in DNA cases cannot be separated from this phenomenon.

For public defenders and appointed counsel who represent the vast majority of people charged with crimes, DNA evidence presents a serious challenge. To the uninitiated, the bewildering technical complexity of DNA systems is confusing and intimidating. The proponents of DNA evidence claim levels of certainty far beyond normal human experience. Considering the extreme stakes defendants often face, defenders already denied adequate time to treat each matter with a truly fitting level of care and attention can feel overwhelmed in the face of this evidence. Even for those practicing in larger public defender offices, technical resources are rarely sufficient. Few defender offices have the resources to train and staff a specialized unit to handle forensic DNA cases. Forensic DNA evidence has always threatened to overwhelm the capacity of an indigent defense system already stretched to its limit by crushing caseloads. In this austere environment, less discovery equates with more difficulties for the defense in unpacking the government's accusations. With unabating caseloads, an executive summary of a DNA "match" may be treated as close enough for the culpable.

And yet, DNA forensics is, at its core, an interpretive technique, open to critique and dispute. Human error and bias is inevitable.[cj] Scholars still tend to disagree over the proper method of evaluating DNA evidence.[ck] The admissibility and weight of DNA evidence can be challenged on a number of grounds.[cl] But as with many other forensic tools, the legal community is too quick to forget the subjectivity inherent in forensic analysis, and has granted DNA profiling wholesale, empirical acceptance, resulting in a "self-sustaining rationale" that "do[es] away with the need [for scientists] to re-examine their assumptions to discern a basis in scientific principles".[cm]

A system designed to predominantly support prosecution-side research and development only exacerbates this problem.[cn] The mere verbiage connected to successful DNA profiling, that is, the "match", is a microcosm of this problem: the insistence on and expectation of perfect accuracy silences dispute.[co]

To do so requires fair disclosure, and it requires trained counsel. Forensic DNA remains an area of highly specialized knowledge that requires extensive training and experience for lawyers to obtain professional competency. Few are able to dedicate sufficient time to such study. The result is a lack of adversarial systemic functioning and loss of oversight of the forensic industry at precisely a time when the field is experiencing the dramatic changes discussed above.

Standards governing the necessary precision for a match or the soundness of a methodology have, over time, theoretically become built into law governing the reliability of evidence.[cp] But the technical complexity of methods inevitably makes judicial scrutiny less likely.[cq] With few functioning checks, we have to question whether trusting forensic scientists to define the

bounds of these legal standards is a sound program. We should be especially wary of accepting laboratory practices despite judicial reluctance, because fewer later judges will want to revisit the issue, and will proceed to accept the methodology as if it had the necessary close scrutiny from the outset.[cr] Even more dangerous is when flimsy evidence is cloaked in the garb of certainty.[cs] In the face of even the lowest quality LCN evidence, the *Morgan* jury convicted.

Denying close scrutiny of such evidence on account of high probabilities flies in the face of constitutional standard of certainty required in criminal cases.[ct]

But even before the question of whether the quantum of certainty we have in certain evidence is sufficient, our mere acceptance of the science (and all of the subjectivity it accommodates) should give us pause. Weighing the minimal oversight of labs,[cu] the profit and political motives addressed above,[cv] with the tremendous stakes of cases in which DNA evidence is often proffered,[cw] it should alarm us that forensic labs have nearly unfettered discretion to decide what goes into their conclusions.[cx]

The ramifications are greatest in the courthouses where DNA evidence is implemented.[cy] The legal profession, the judiciary, and risk-averse defendants have not been far behind in accepting whatever putative DNA link a government lab claims to find in many criminal cases. Persuaded of the power of such evidence, defense attorneys may not seek to challenge a "match", judges may deny scarce funding to an indigent defendant for reanalysis of a sample, and, perhaps worst of all, defendants may be intimidated into acquiescing in the face of such seemingly certain evidence.[cz] Whether the DNA evidence would in fact withstand close scrutiny remains unknown, and its momentum grows.

Our criminal justice community has seen scientific evidence misused before.[da] Perhaps we have preconceived notions that DNA evidence is "qualitatively different from other evidence because of its presumed scientific rigor and accuracy".[db] We certainly live in a culture that has mystified DNA forensics as talismans of objectivity and certainty. Whatever our reasons, we decline to challenge the evidence as much as we could.

Conclusion

If we can understand anything about the current trends in DNA forensics, it is that they cannot be isolated from the justice system within which they emerge. The crisis within that system directly implicates the progress of DNA forensics. Relentless policing policies keep court dockets crowded and crime labs stocked with new work in offender known samples.

We cannot expect a legislative solution to reverse this trend. As has been discussed, political motives to appear tough on crime and the appeal of adding more known profiles to state and national databases has already led to misguided legislative efforts. Rolling back on them seems highly unlikely.

Help from the executive branch is not soon forthcoming. As line-level prosecutors continue to exact convictions with LCN DNA, whether by plea or after trial, they are not likely to be restrained from using it without a fight.

The judiciary cannot act on its own, and is traditionally reluctant to strike reliable evidence without a strong record to support suppression or exclusion. Only by making such a record can any one defendant or one community hope to challenge the practices of a DNA forensic lab. To be able to fix forensic DNA, we have to address the crisis in indigent defense.

In the modern age, an adequate defense must encompass a full understanding of the techniques and science behind DNA. But it also means less technical, more lawyerly concerns like full discovery, adequate access to evidence and time to prepare. In short, the defense must have equality of arms with law enforcement when it comes to DNA forensics, including equivalent access to perform necessary database searches.

DNA alone has not solved the crisis in the US criminal justice system, nor will any technological fix ever address what fundamentally is a complex cultural problem. But to avoid losing DNA to the very corruptive influences that it once promised to overcome, strong efforts must be undertaken now.

End Notes

a. *See* Naftali Bendavid, *U.S. Targets DNA Backlog*, Chi. Trib., August 2, 2001, at 10 (quoting John Ashcroft, at a DOJ news conference to announce new funding for president's DNA initiatives, as praising DNA as "nothing less than the 'truth machine' of law enforcement, ensuring justice by identifying the guilty and exonerating the innocent").

b. *DNA Exoneree Case Profiles*, Innocence Project, http://www.innocenceproject.org/know/ (last visited January 27, 2015).

c. *See* Erin Murphy, *supra* note, at 731 n.33. (The power of DNA evidence to exclude a suspect has never been in serious dispute.)

d. *See* Brandon L. Garrett, *DNA and Due Process*, 78 Fordham L. Rev. 2919, 2950 (2010) (noting that while partial or degraded DNA samples may contain enough information to *exclude* a person, the same evidence *may* not be sufficient to *include* a person); 4 David H. Kaye and George Sensabaugh, Modern Scientific Evidence § 31:49 (2014–2015 ed.).

e. Patrick Haines, *Embracing the DNA Fingerprint Act*, 5 J. Telecomm. & High Tech. L. 629, 632 (2007) (summarizing the history of early DNA use in courtrooms).

f. Patrick Haines, *supra* note at 632; Richard Lempert, *After the DNA Wars: Skirmishing with Nrc II*, 37 Jurimetrics J. 439 (1997).

g. Paul C. Giannelli, *supra* note at 381; *see also* J. Herbie DiFonzo and Ruth C. Stern, *Devil in A White Coat: The Temptation of Forensic Evidence in the Age of CSI*, 41 New Eng. L. Rev. 503, 529 (2007) ("Good science can, and should, be persuasive. DNA testing, when performed properly, is 'the most remarkable forensic tool we have ever had.'" (quoting Margaret A. Berger, *The Impact of DNA Exonerations on the Criminal Justice System*, 34 J.L. Med. & Ethics 320, 322 (2006))).

h. *See* National Academy of Sciences, *Strengthening Forensic Science in the United States: A Path Forward* (2009), 41 (contrasting the degree of scrutiny and trust applied to DNA against methods that came out of forensic disciplines).

i. *See, e.g.*, *United States v. Bentham*, 414 F. Supp. 2d 472, 473 (S.D.N.Y. 2006) (Rakoff, J.) ("Even the 'gold standard' of forensic testing, DNA tests, may, because of human error, prove fallible." (citing Paul C. Gianelli, *Crime Labs Need Improvement*, Issues in Sci. & Tech. (Fall 2003)).

j. *See, e.g.*, Innocence Protection Act, P.L. 108–405, October 30, 2004, 118 Stat. 2260, codified at 18 U.S.C. § 3600A.

k. *See* Combined DNA Index System Operational and Laboratory Vulnerabilities, U.S. Department of Justice (May, 2006), http://www.justice.gov/oig/reports/FBI/a0632/final.pdf (background on CODIS).

l. *See, e.g.*, Christopher H. Asplen, Integrating DNA Technology into the Criminal Justice System, 83

Judicature 144, 146 (1999) (discussing the backlogs resulting from the volume of samples and insufficient state laboratory capacity).

m. 42 U.S.C. § 14132(b)(1–2).

n. Low copy number testing (hereinafter referred to as "LCN") is also known as "Trace DNA", "high sensitivity" DNA testing, "low template" or "touch" DNA.

o. *See, e.g.*, Erin Murphy, *The New Forensics: Criminal Justice, False Certainty, and the Second Generation of Scientific Evidence*, 95 Cal. L. Rev. 721, 746 (2007) ("'Peer review' in forensic science approximates self-congratulation." (citations omitted)).

p. *United States v. Morgan*, No. 12-CR-223 VM, 2014 WL 5317508 (S.D.N.Y. October 3, 2014).

q. *See* Brief of 14 Scholars of Forensic Evidence as *Amicus Curiae* Supporting Respondent at 32, Maryland v. King, 133 S. Ct. 1958 (2013) (No. 12-207) (discussing the importance of audits and quality control and the failure of the Department of Justice to enforce such enacted standards) (hereinafter Forensic Scholars Amicus); Erin Murphy, *The New Forensics: Criminal Justice, False Certainty, and the Second Generation of Scientific Evidence*, 95 Cal. L. Rev. 721, 785–786 (2007) (suggesting need for greater reliance upon accreditation and oversight of accredited laboratories), cited in *Williams v. Illinois*, 132 S. Ct. 2221, 2250 (2012) (Breyer, J., concurring).

r. *See infra* notes (discussion of *United States v. Morgan*).

s. *See* Spencer S. Hsu, *Judge Rakoff returns to forensic panel after Justice Department backs off decision*, Wash. Post (January 30, 2015), http://www.washingtonpost.com/local/crime/in-reversal-doj-lets-forensic-panel-suggest-trial-rule-changes-after-us-judge-protests/2015/01/30/2f031d9e-a89c-11e4-a2b2-776095f393b2_story.html.

t. *See, e.g.*, *People v. Superior Court (Chubbs)*, No. B258569, 2015 WL 139069, at *1 (Cal. Ct. App. January 9, 2015) (granting writ of mandate to overturn lower court ruling compelling disclosure of TrueAllele DNA analysis source code on Confrontation Clause grounds).

u. *Johnson v. United States*, 333 U.S. 10, 14 (1948).

v. *See* H.R. Rep. No. 106-900(1), at 27 (2000) *reprinted in* 2000 U.S.C.C.A.N. 2323 (codified at 42 U.S.C. §§ 13701–14223 (2012)) (noting that national methodological standards regarding junk DNA have shaped the legal rule because it does "not reveal information relating to any medical condition or other trait.").

w. *See* James Herbie DiFonzo, *In Praise of Statutes of Limitations in Sex Offense Cases*, 41 Hous. L. Rev. 1205, 1262 (2004) ("The business of DNA typing markets itself as a seller of certainty." (citing Michael J. Saks, *Merlin and Solomon: Lessons from the Law's Formative Encounters with Forensic Identification Science*, 49 Hastings L.J. 1069, 1092 n. 106 (1998))).

x. *See* Solomon Moore, *F.B.I. and States Vastly Expand DNA Databases*, New York Times, April 18, 2009, A1, http://www.nytimes.com/2009/04/19/us/19DNA.html?_r=0 (describing the expansion of DNA laws); Elizabeth E. Joh, *Maryland v. King: Policing and Genetic Privacy*, 11 Ohio St. J. Crim. L. 281, 289 (2013) (same).

y. 133 S. Ct. 1958 (2013).

z. *See, e.g.*, Andrea Roth, *Maryland v. King and the Wonderful, Horrible DNA Revolution in Law Enforcement*, 11 Ohio St. J. Crim. L. 295 (2013).

aa. Roth, *Maryland v. King and the Wonderful, Horrible DNA Revolution in Law Enforcement*, *supra* note at 297.

ab. Forensic Scholars Amicus, *supra* note at 4–6.

ac. Forensic Scholars Amicus, *supra* note at 4–6.

ad. Forensic Scholars Amicus, *supra* note at 5–6.

ae. *CODIS–NDIS Statistics*, Federal Bureau of Investigation, http://www.fbi.gov/about-us/lab/biometric-analysis/codis/ndis-statistics (last accessed January 21, 2015).

af. Andrea Roth, *Safety in Numbers? Deciding When DNA Alone Is Enough to Convict*, 85 N.Y.U. L. Rev. 1130, 1140 and n. 43 (2010).

ag. *Id.*

ah. Andrea M. Burch, Matthew R. Durose, and Kelly A. Walsh, Census of Publicly Funded Forensic Crime Laboratories, Dep't of Just. Bureau of Just. Stats. 4 (2009), http://bjs.ojp.usdoj.gov/content/pub/pdf/cpffcl09.pdf (hereinafter 2009 Census).

ai. *Compare* Roth, *supra* note at 297 (concluding the "best policy choice" to avoid racial inequities and harness DNA's power is to expand DNA databases to include the entire population), *with supra* note (discussing the adverse effects of database expansion falling disproportionately on certain racial communities).

aj. Kevin J. Strom and Matthew J. Hickman, *Unanalyzed Evidence in Law Enforcement Agencies: A National Examination of Forensic Processing in*

Policing Departments, 9 Criminology & Pub. Pol'y 381, 382 (2010).

ak. 2009 Census, *supra* note at 4–5.

al. *See* Elizabeth E. Joh, *Maryland v. King: Policing and Genetic Privacy*, 11 Ohio St. J. Crim. L. 281, 289 (2013). (King does little to limit states from expanding the scope of their arrestee profiles to all arrestees, regardless of the severity of the offense.); see also Associated Press, *Virginia Would Expand This List of Offenses Requiring DNA*, ABC News (February 7, 2015, 10:45 A.M.), http://abcnews .go.com/US/wireStory/virginia-expand-list-offenses-requiring-dna-28797910 (discussing proposed expansion of DNA sampling to misdemeanors such as trespass).

am. Andrea Roth, *Maryland v. King and the Wonderful, Horrible DNA Revolution in Law Enforcement*, 11 Ohio St. J. Crim. L. 295 (2013).

an. *See* Joseph L. Peterson and Anna S. Leggett, *The Evolution of Forensic Science: Progress Amid the Pitfalls*, 36 Stetson L. Rev. 621, 647 (2007). (There is also greater public acceptance of forensic techniques, but along with it, greater pressure to perform at a high level.); *see also* National Academy of Sciences, *supra* note at 60 (noting the tendency of an increase in case-work capacity to increase pressure to complete cases quickly and get a certain result, and "extend opinions beyond the scientific method" (citation omitted)).

ao. Seeing this as another manifestation of the "problem of information transfer from the scientific community to the legal community", Louis J. Elsas II, *A Clinical Approach to Legal and Ethical Problems in Human Genetics*, 39 Emory L.J. 811, 852 (1990), many in the criminal justice system at first questioned the reliability of tests conducted for profit and sought protections against privateering. Paul C. Giannelli, *The DNA Story: An Alternative View*, 88 J. Crim. L. & Criminology 380, 412 (1997) ("More significant, there was an unquestioned need for standards to guarantee the reliability of DNA testing, particularly testing done by the commercial laboratories run for profit ...." (quoting Harlan Levy, *And The Blood Cried Out: A Prosecutor's Spellbinding Account of the Power of DNA* 52 (1996)); Louis J. Elsas II, *supra* note at 852 (1990). ([T]he scientific community must develop guidelines for proficiency testing and quality control of commercial laboratories offering DNA analysis on a fee-for-service basis. Currently, as companies develop DNA methods for profit, there is little legal, moral, or scientific control of the use and technical competence of test results.)

ap. Bode Technology, *Increase Your Investigative Leads Using the Power of DNA*, http://www.bodetech .com/wp-content/uploads/2012/11/BodeHITS-072712 -web.pdf).

aq. Id.

ar. Tania Simoncelli, *Dangerous Excursions: The Case Against Expanding Forensic DNA Databases to Innocent Persons*, 34 J.L. Med. & Ethics 390, 394 (2006); Christian B. Sundquist, *Genetics, Race and Substantive Due Process*, 20 Wash. & Lee J. Civil Rts. & Soc. Just. 341, 380 (2014) (noting the "dire implications for racial justice" of the expansion of DNA databases, due to the "risk of false incrimination ... fall[ing] disproportionately" on certain communities comprising the databases (quoting Osagie K. Obasogie, *Playing the Gene Card? A Report on Race and Human Biotechnology*, Ctr. for Genetics & Soc'y (2009) (internal quotation marks omitted))).

as. *See, e.g.*, David Orentlicher, *Rights to Healthcare in the United States: Inherently Unstable*, 38 Am. J.L. & Med. 326 (2012) (discussing the inherent difficulties imposed by American system of governance on a national healthcare system).

at. *See, e.g.*, Gilbert King, *Devil in the Grove: Thurgood Marshall, the Groveland Boys, and the Dawn of a New America* (2012) (discussing the Groveland Boys scandal); Harvey Fireside, *The "Mississippi Burning" Civil Rights Murder Conspiracy Trial: A Headline Court Case* (2002) (discussing the Mississippi civil rights murders).

au. David Neiwart, *Indiana Sheriff with Antigovernment Views Creates Stir by Traveling to Bundy Ranch*, Southern Poverty Law Center (May 7, 2014, 12:05 P.M.), http://www.splcenter.org/blog/2014/05/07/ indiana-sheriff-with-antigovernment-views-creates-stir-by-traveling-to-bundy-ranch/ (local resistance to federal government in Nevada).

av. 42 U.S.C. § 14135 (limiting the ability to conduct DNA analysis to the government); *see also* Lina Alexandra Hogan, *Fourth Amendment-Guilt by Relation: If Your Brother Is Convicted of A Crime, You Too May Do Time*, 30 W. New Eng. L. Rev. 543, 576 and n. 265 (2008) (noting that CODIS is limited to governmental use).

aw. *See* Forensic Scholars Amicus, *supra* note at 32 (discussing DOJ's refusal to conduct oversight of laboratory misconduct and negligence).

ax. "Because of the successes encountered with STR typing, it was inevitable that some individuals would endeavor to type samples containing very minute amounts of DNA .... When few copies of DNA template are present, stochastic amplification may occur, resulting in either a substantial imbalance of two alleles at a given heterozygous locus or allelic drop out." B. Budowle *et al.*, *Low Copy Number – Consideration and Caution*, Proceedings of 12th International Symposium on Human Identification (2001) (http://www.promega.com/~/media/files/resources/conference%20proceedings/ishi%2012/oral%20 presentations/budowle.pdf?la=en), quoted in William C. Thompson, *et al.*, *Forensic DNA Statistics: Still Controversial In Some Cases*, Champion, December 2012, at 14; *see also United States v. McCluskey*, 954 F. Supp. 2d 1224, 1277 (D.N.M. 2013) ("LCN testing carries a greater potential for error due to difficulties in analysis and interpretation caused by four stochastic effects: allele drop-in, allele drop-out, stutter, and heterozygote peak height imbalance." (citing John M. Butler, *Fundamentals of Forensic DNA Typing* 331 (2010))); *id.* (LCN testing often yields "unreliable and nonreproducible results because of the significant increase in stochastic effects").

ay. Simon A. Cole and Michael Lynch, *The Social and Legal Construction of Suspects*, 2 Ann. Rev. L. & Soc. Sci. 39, 43–44 (2006).

az. *See generally* Peter Gill, *Misleading DNA Evidence* (2014).

ba. Andrea Roth, *Maryland v. King and the Wonderful, Horrible DNA Revolution in Law Enforcement*, *supra* note at 302.

bb. Peter Gill, *supra* note at 32.

bc. Forensic Scholars Amicus, *supra* note at 26–27.

bd. Declaration of interest; Ms Rita Glavin, coauthor of this article, was Counsel for Johnny Morgan. Professor Allan Jamieson, Coeditor of this volume, was the defence DNA expert.

be. Bruce Budowle, *Low Copy Number Typing Still Lacks Robustness and Reliability* (2010), http://www.promega.com/resources/profiles-in-dna/low-copy-number-typing-still-lacks-robustness-and-reliability/ ("Due to the success of DNA typing, the envelope of the technology is being pushed to type ever smaller amounts of DNA....").

bf. *See, e.g., People v. Brown*, 918 N.E.2d 927, 929 (N.Y. 2009) (discussing the additional funding received and used to address the backlog via subcontracting with commercial laboratories).

bg. *See* Eric Lipton, *At Limits of Science, 9/11 ID Effort Come to End*, N.Y. Times, April 3, 2005, Section I, Page 29.

bh. *See, e.g., People v. Beam*, 912 N.Y.S.2d 263 (N.Y. App. Div. 2nd Dep't. 2010) (appeal regarding admission of DNA evidence after conviction for criminal possession of a weapon); *see also* Joseph Blozis, *Using DNA to Fight Property Crime*, Evidence Magazine (October 2012), http://www.evidence magazine.com/index.php?option=com_content&task =view&id=1031 (discussing the expanding universe of crimes in which DNA is used in New York, including weapon possession).

bi. *People v. Megnath*, 898 N.Y.S.2d 408, 414 (Queens Cty. Sup. Ct. 2010).

bj. *E.g., United States v. McCluskey*, 954 F. Supp. 2d at 1277; *People v. Styles*, 975 N.Y.S.2d 369 (Kings Cty. Sup. Ct. 2013).

bk. David L. Faigman *et al.*, Modern Scientific Evidence § 31:32 (2014–2015 ed.).

bl. Defendant Johnny Morgan's Memorandum of Law In Support of His Motion to Exclude Evidence of Low Copy Number DNA Test Results and Request for a *Daubert* Hearing at 4, *United States v. Morgan*, No. 12 Cr. 223 (S.D.N.Y. December 23, 2013), 2013 WL 9850382.

bm. N.Y. Executive Law §§ 995-a to -b.

bn. Declaration of Rita M. Glavin in Further Support of Johnny Morgan's Motion on New Information at Exhibit 3, *United States v. Morgan*, No. 12 Cr 223 (S.D.N.Y. February 23, 2014), ECF No. 104 (December 6 2005 meeting minutes).

bo. Although the court record is not clear, it appears that the interpretation guidelines used by the OCME did not correspond with the FBI's standards as set forth in http://www.fbi.gov/about-us/lab/biometric-analysis/codis/swgdam-interpretation-guidelines. For a mixed sample, the Combined Probability of Exclusion, or CPE, should have been reported, which would take into account the number of potential contributors to the mixture.

bp. Defendant Johnny Morgan's Memorandum of Law In Support of His Motion to Exclude Evidence of Low Copy Number DNA Test Results and Request for a *Daubert* Hearing at Exhibit A, United States v. Morgan, No. 12 Cr. 223 (S.D.N.Y. December 23, 2013), ECF No. 68-1 at 4 (OCME Laboratory Report).

bq. *See* Transcript of *Daubert* Hearing at 190–191, 193–194, *United States v. Morgan*, No. 12 Cr. 223 (S.D.N.Y. February 18, 2014), ECF No. 91 at 37–38,

40–41 (testimony of Dr. O'Connor); *id.* at Ex. 5 (OCME LCN Validation Study).

[br.] Defendant Johnny Morgan's Memorandum of Law In Support of His Motion to Exclude Evidence of Low Copy Number DNA Test Results and Request for a *Daubert* Hearing at Exhibit C, United States v. Morgan, No. 12 Cr. 223 (S.D.N.Y. December 23, 2013), ECF No. 68-2 at 11 (OCME Forensic Biology Evidence and Case Management Manual).

[bs.] Electropherograms reveal concentrations of PCR product as "peaks" on the *X*-axis of a chart.

[bt.] Like most labs, OCME has had its share of scandals, most recently with an examiner who falsified records. *See* Joseph Goldstein, *Report Details the Extent of a Crime Lab Technician's Errors in Handling Evidence*, N.Y. Times, December 5, 2013, A30, http://www.nytimes.com/2013/12/05/nyregion/report-details-the-extent-of-a-crime-lab-technicians-errors-in-handling-evidence.html.

[bu.] Defendant Johnny Morgan's Memorandum of Law In Support of His Motion to Exclude Evidence of Low Copy Number DNA Test Results and Request for a *Daubert* Hearing at Exhibit A, *United States v. Morgan*, No. 12 Cr. 223 (S.D.N.Y. December 23, 2013), ECF No. 68-1 at 26 (OCME Lab Records in *Morgan*).

[bv.] "No ... DNA records developed using Low Template or Low Copy DNA Analysis shall be submitted to NDIS." National DNA Index System (NDIS) Operational Procedures Manual, Federal Bureau of Investigation Laboratory 35 (January 1, 2015), http://www.fbi.gov/about-us/lab/biometric-analysis/codis/ndis-procedures-manual. (Rule 4.2.1.10).

[bw.] *See* Transcript of *Daubert* Hearing at 297, *United States v. Morgan*, No. 12 Cr. 223 (S.D.N.Y. February 18, 2014), ECF No. 93 at 57 (ruling from bench denying defendant's motion).

[bx.] Shayna Jacobs, *Judge tosses out two types of DNA evidence used regularly in criminal cases*, N.Y. Daily News, January 5, 2015, http://www.nydailynews.com/new-york/nyc-crime/judge-tosses-types-dna-testing-article-1.2065795.

[by.] *Bullcoming v. New Mexico*, 131 S. Ct. 2705, 2710 (2011).

[bz.] *See*, Defendant Johnny Morgan's Memorandum of Law In Support of His Motion to Exclude Evidence of Low Copy Number DNA Test Results and Request for a *Daubert* Hearing at Exhibit A, *United States v. Morgan*, No. 12 Cr. 223 (S.D.N.Y. December 23,

2013), ECF No. 68-1 at 3–6 of 27 (OCME Laboratory Report in *Morgan*).

[ca.] *See* Affidavit of Rita M. Glavin in Support of Defendant Johnny Morgan's Motion to Compel the Production of Documents, *United States v. Morgan*, No. 12 Cr. 223 (S.D.N.Y. December 23, 2013), ECF No. 137 at 2.

[cb.] Jennifer N. Mellon, *Manufacturing Convictions: Why Defendants are Entitled to the Data Underlying Forensic DNA Kits*, 51 Duke L.J. 1097, 1099 (2001) (discussing lab efforts to shield primer sequences from discovery); *People v. Superior Court (Chubbs)*, No. B258569, 2015 WL 139069, at *9 (Cal. Ct. App. January 9, 2015) (granting writ of mandate denying access to TrueAllele source code as protected trade secret).

[cc.] *See, e.g., Floyd v. City of New York*, 959 F. Supp. 2d 540 (S.D.N.Y. 2013), *appeal dismissed* (September 25, 2013).

[cd.] *E.g., State v. Peart*, 621 So. 2d 780, 789, 791 (La. 1993) (finding New Orleans' indigent defense system so overloaded and underfunded that it adopted a rebuttable presumption of ineffective assistance); *see also* Thomas Giovanni and Roopal Patel, *Gideon at 50: Three Reforms to Revive the Right to Counsel*, Brennan Center for Justice, at 4, available at http://www.brennancenter.org/sites/default/files/publications/Gideon_Report_040913.pdf (discussing the overburdened nature of public defense offices throughout the country).

[ce.] *See, e.g.,* La. Rev. Stat. Ann. § 15:529.1 (providing for potential life imprisonment for third felony conviction under Louisiana's Uniform Controlled Substances Act); *id.* § 40:966 (criminalizing distribution of Schedule I substances under Louisiana's Uniform Controlled Substances Act with a minimum of ten years imprisonment); *id.* § 40:964 (listing marijuana as a Schedule I substance).

[cf.] David Patton, *Federal Public Defense in an Age of Inquisition*, 122 Yale L.J. 2578, 2581–2582 (2013).

[cg.] American Civil Liberties Union Foundation, *The War on Marijuana in Black and White*, 4, 47, 66–67 (2013), https://www.aclu.org/files/assets/aclu-thewaronmarijuana-rel2.pdf.

[ch.] Caroline Wolf Harlow, Ph.D., *Bureau of Justice Statistics Special Report: Defense Counsel in Criminal Cases*, Dep't of Just. Bureau Of Just. Stats. 1 (2000), http://www.bjs.gov/content/pub/pdf/dccc.pdf (placing federal numbers at 85%); Rita A. Fry, *Gideon at Forty: The Promise Comes With a Price Tag*, 24 NLADA's

Cornerstone 4 (Winter 2002–2003), available at http://www.nlada.org/DMS/Documents/1043772615. 53/Gideon%20at%2040%20-%20The%20Promise% 20Comes%20With%20a%20Price%20Tag.doc (estimating state numbers at 80–90%).

[ci.] Bryan Stevenson, Address at TED, *We need to talk about an injustice* (March 2012) (transcript available at http://www.ted.com/talks/bryan_stevenson_we_need_ to_talk_about_an_injustice/transcript?language=en).

[cj.] National Academy of Sciences, *supra* note at 47; J. Herbie DiFonzo, *The Crimes of Crime Labs*, 34 Hofstra L. Rev. 1, 7–8 (2005); Erin Murphy, *supra* note at 721 (asserting that the guaranteed certainty and reliability of the vast majority of DNA evidence does "not necessarily render [it] less susceptible to misuse").

[ck.] *See* Allan Jamieson, *supra* note at 1046. (Although many of the technical difficulties in producing DNA profiles have been overcome, the correct approach to interpretation and evaluation of DNA profiles is still very much a matter for debate.).

[cl.] Joel D. Lieberman *et al.*, *Gold Versus Platinum: Do Jurors Recognize the Superiority and Limitations of DNA Evidence Compared to Other Types of Forensic Evidence?*, 14 Psychol. Pub. Pol'y & L. 27, 31 (2008) (listing as potential challenges "deficiencies in lab proficiency testing, contamination, lack of written protocols, lab accreditation, reliability of the technique, quality control/assurances, chain of custody, and temperature-regulation variances").

[cm.] J. Herbie DiFonzo and Ruth C. Stern, *supra* note at 524.

[cn.] *See* Erin Murphy, *supra* note at 747–748 ("[S]tructural barriers impede the development of robust 'defense-oriented' forensic research and practices. Although defense testing does and can occur, there is generally no centralized market to drive the development of institutional 'defense-side' forensic testing or research facilities. Without such institutions, defense attorneys must rely either on the benevolence of government laboratory analysts, or find independent analysts, who are often simply retired government technicians." (citations omitted)).

[co.] National Academy of Sciences, *supra* note at 47.

[cp.] Allan Jamieson, *The Philosophy of Forensic Scientific Identification*, 59 Hastings L.J. 1031, 1038 (2008).

[cq.] Erin Murphy, *supra* note at 768.

[cr.] Erin Murphy, *supra* note at 768.

[cs.] *See generally* J. Herbie DiFonzo and Ruth C. Stern, *supra* note (protesting the glamorization of forensic science in television and film for its reinforcing jurors' mistaken beliefs in the infallibility of forensic evidence); *see also* Tania Simoncelli, *supra* note at 393 (discussing the "imprimatur of certainty" attached to DNA creating certain perverse incentives, such as planting DNA evidence, or investigators overlooking other important evidence); *Panel Two: Criminal Law and DNA Science: Balancing Societal Interests and Civil Liberties*, 51 Am. U. L. Rev. 401, 417 (2002) (comments of William Moffitt). ([W]hat we are essentially being sold is the notion that we can have a degree of certainty... When you learn that forensic science is not done by neutral parties and you also learn that the poorest of people, the people who cannot hire an independent group to do the science, have to rely on law enforcement for their science, you become extremely concerned. What this means and how this operates or should operate in a system that presumes the innocence – not the guilt – of a defendant is disturbing.)

[ct.] Erin Murphy, *supra* note at 774–775.

[cu.] *See generally* National Academy of Sciences, *supra* note at 193–215 (identifying the problem of a lack of oversight of forensic labs and making recommendations relating thereto).

[cv.] *See supra* note (discussing profit motives of labs).

[cw.] *See, e.g.*, Josh Bowers, *Punishing the Innocent*, 156 U. Pa. L. Rev. 1117, 1179 n. 62 (2008) (referring to the cases in which DNA challenges usually occur as "very high-stakes").

[cx.] *See* Kimberly A. Wah, *A New Investigative Lead: Familial Searching As an Effective Crime-Fighting Tool*, 29 Whittier L. Rev. 909, 928 (2008) (noting, as an example, that, in Virginia, the "vague" standard that authorizes familial searching is simply whatever Virginia forensic laboratories choose to adopt).

[cy.] National Academy of Sciences, *supra* note at 185.

[cz.] James Herbie DiFonzo, *supra* note at 1262–1263.

[da.] *See* Paul C. Giannelli, *supra* note at 410 (citing as examples paraffin test results, voiceprint evidence, and hypnotically-refreshed testimony); *Panel Two: Criminal Law and DNA Science: Balancing Societal Interests and Civil Liberties*, *supra* note at 419 (suggesting that we can easily look to other similar twentieth-century examples of panaceas to demonstrate that "[DNA] is [not a] panacea that will cure whatever ails us in this society").

[db.] Joel D. Lieberman *et al.*, *supra* note at 32.

Chapter 43
Issues in Forensic DNA

Allan Jamieson
The Forensic Institute, Glasgow, UK

Introduction

No scientific technology has had the impact on the investigation and prosecution of crimes against the person as DNA profiling. In most forensic sciences, the task is to establish whether two items could have had the same origin, such as paint, glass, fibers, or a body fluid such as saliva or semen. The way that this is achieved is usually by comparing what has been recovered from the crime scene with another sample that is usually recovered from a suspect. For example, glass may be recovered from a broken window and compared with glass fragments found on a suspect. If the samples are thought to match, then the significance of the match can be assessed by considering the rarity of the type of glass.

To make a good technique for providing evidence, it is useful to be able to work with a small amount of material and the match can be used to differentiate between members of the wider population. These are described scientifically as the sensitivity and specificity of the technique.

Developments in DNA technology have increased the specificity and sensitivity well beyond the original application that required a visible amount of body fluid (e.g., blood, semen, and saliva). Using population data, the DNA analyst can now obtain a profile from cellular material left at crime scenes (or anywhere else) that is invisible to the naked eye and establish the probability of finding the particular combination of DNA in another randomly selected person as less than one in several billion. This may have prompted

the National Academy of Sciences[a] to state (as is often quoted);

> With the exception of nuclear DNA analysis, however, no forensic method has been rigorously shown to have the capacity to consistently, and with a high degree of certainty, demonstrate a connection between evidence and a specific individual or source. …
> Thus, DNA analysis – originally developed in research laboratories in the context of life sciences research – has received heightened scrutiny and funding support. That, combined with its well-defined precision and accuracy, has set the bar higher for other forensic science methodologies, because it has provided a tool with a higher degree of reliability and relevance than any other forensic technique.

While some forensic practices were arguable in their ability to declare a match, two DNA profiles either matched or they did not. Even if two things matched, the forensic significance was established by how rare the match was. However, the sensitivity and specificity of the technology is being pushed to limits that are now, as then, being challenged. Profiling smaller and smaller amounts of recovered cellular material produces new problems in the interpretation of profiles.

These are added to the problem created by mixtures of DNA. A mixture is a profile comprising of DNA from more than one person. Simply put, if we create a profile with components (called *alleles*, described later) ABCD and we know that each person has contributed two alleles, then although there are only two *actual* contributors, the *possible* contributors are AB, AC, AD, BC, BD, and CD. We have created six suspect profiles from the mixture, although there are only two true contributors.

A Guide to Forensic DNA Profiling
Edited by Allan Jamieson and Scott Bader
© 2016 John Wiley & Sons, Ltd. ISBN: 9781118751527

There are various methods claimed to interpret the evidential significance of a mixed DNA profile, and the debate about which is best continues [1–3]. But, even as that scientific debate persists about the best way to interpret DNA mixtures, two developments have followed efforts to extract more evidence from ever-smaller amounts of DNA.

One of these is low copy number (LCN) or low template DNA analysis that continues to be challenged in courts around the world. When such small amounts of DNA are involved, different runs of the same sample produce different results [4]. One complication of low template profiles is the occurrence of the voids previously disparaged by the Appeal Court of England & Wales (*R v. Bates* [5]). Although the challenge in England & Wales was effectively extinguished in *R v. Reed & Reed* [6], challenges continue in courts internationally to the reliability of such profiles[b], [7–10]. I have commented elsewhere on the apparent difficulties in Courts' comprehension of the issues in LCN cases.[c]

The second development is the introduction of statistical methods to deal with these voids (among other things) so complex that they can only produce results using "expert systems" [11–14]. These are claimed to calculate the probability of evidence that hasn't been seen.

Initially, the Court of Criminal Appeal for England and Wales set out how DNA evidence was to be adduced; a statistical calculation that must be set out in clear terms (*Doheny & Adams*) [15]. This was followed in other cases with a clear direction that nothing could or should be inferred from voids in profiles where for a variety of reasons a DNA type is not seen in a particular area of the profile (*Bates* and *R v. Broughton* [16]); in simple terms, what you don't see in a profile can't count as evidence against someone.[d]

Interpretation of Mixtures

We lose about 30,000–40,000 skin cells an hour. In a year, each person sheds about 8 lbs of cells. It is therefore unsurprising that many samples recovered from crime scenes and objects have DNA from more than one person. These mixtures of DNA create a new difficulty in interpretation; given that there are many possible ways to create any mixture, how should the mixture be interpreted to evaluate what the evidence provides for the court. Matters are further complicated by;

- Different amounts of DNA being contributed by different contributors
- The same allele being contributed by more than one contributor (allele sharing)
- Degradation of the DNA of one or more contributors causing alleles to be missing or being present in smaller amounts

Interpretation of a profile requires the analyst to consider and assess the entire profile, but in coming to almost any opinion, it would have been necessary to make some assumptions about, for example, the number of contributors.

These considerations apply mostly to "good quality" DNA available in sufficient amounts to be easily detected by the kit. Not all DNA found at a crime scene is of good quality, or quantity. This can affect the interpretation of the resultant profiles.

Issues

Mixture Interpretation

Figure 1 provides a simple illustration of the problem created even by simple mixtures. The crimestain sample is represented by the four circles with letters in the center of the figure showing the four alleles (ABCD). We assume that there are two contributors to the crimestain. Because the alleles of each "suspect" are present in the crimestain, they can all be considered potential contributors to the profile. There are two other heterozygous types that could also be considered contributors meaning that this mixture creates six suspect profiles (we are ignoring homozygote possibilities on the assumption that this is a two-person mixture). Without further information, each of the six suspects is equally likely to be an actual contributor.

Extrapolating this single locus example to the 10-locus SGM+ kit generates over 60 million heterozygous profiles, and the 15-locus kit generates over 470 billion "suspect" profiles, all of which would be considered possible contributors to the mixture if they were associated with an individual, which of course most of them will not be – but there is no way of knowing which.

Different approaches have been proposed to deal with this problem.[e]

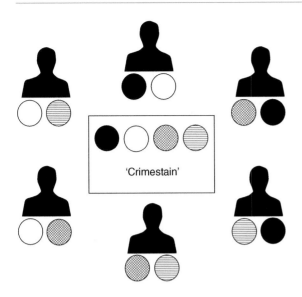

Figure 1 Illustration of the mixture problem – six "suspect profiles" from only two actual contributors

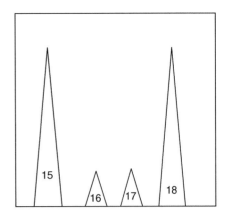

Figure 2 CPI illustration

Random Match Probability and the Combined Probability of Inclusion (CPI)

The random match probability (RMP) is used traditionally for single-source profiles and is conceptually probably the easiest to understand. The significance of the evidence is determined by the probability that another person has the same profile as, or alleles that are present in, the crime scene profile. Even when all of the loci do not produce results because of degradation or other reasons, the absence of those simply reduces the strength of the evidence. The result is called a *partial profile*. An assumption as to the number of contributors is still required.

Of course the same question can be asked of a mixture of alleles. If there are four alleles present, then the question can be framed as, "what is the probability of anyone in the population being a potential contributor to this profile?" Using the frequencies of the observed alleles, this can be calculated. That figure is called the *combined probability of inclusion* (CPI). The CPI does not require any assumption about the number of contributors.

However, a problem does arise in that, in its simplest form, the CPI does not take account of information that could rule out some genotypes, such as information from the peak heights observed in the analysis. For example, in Figure 2, if the peak heights are ignored and we assume two contributors, then all combinations of the alleles 15, 16, 17, and 18 are possible (i.e., 15 16, 15 17, 15 18, 16 17, 16 18, and 17 18).

However, if we take the peak heights into consideration and we again assume that there are only two contributors, then the genotypes 15 16, 15 17, 16 18, and 17 18 are excluded as possibilities.

The reason that we exclude a tall peak and small peak as being from the same person is because, if they came from the same person, they would have approximately equal heights because each allele would produce about the same amount of DNA. This is one way of assessing whether a locus has DNA from more than one person. The concept is termed *heterozygous balance*.

When peak height is used to exclude possible genotypes, the process is called *restricted*. So the "restricted CPI", having fewer possible genotypes, will produce a different statistic to the "unrestricted CPI" and will usually have less evidential value regarding the presence of a particular "suspect" genotype.

Likelihood Ratio

The likelihood ratio (LR) is a relatively simple concept. In the case of forensic evidence, including DNA profiles, it is the ratio of two probabilities:

$$
LR = \frac{\left(\begin{array}{c}\text{the probability of the evidence}\\ \text{given the prosecution hypothesis}\end{array}\right)}{\left(\begin{array}{c}\text{the probability of the evidence}\\ \text{given the defence hypothesis}\end{array}\right)}
$$

The notation is $p(E)$ for the probability of the evidence. "Given" is represented by a vertical bar "|", the "prosecution hypothesis" as H_p, and the defense hypothesis as H_d. Hence, the LR $= p(E|H_p)/p(E|H_d)$; *the hypotheses are assumed*.

The evidence (E) is the DNA profile. The probability calculations, therefore, assume a prosecution hypothesis (usually that a suspect's DNA is part of the profile) and a defense hypothesis (usually that the suspect's DNA is not part of the profile).

There has been a plethora of publications promoting the use of the LR as one of the methods of evaluating forensic scientific evidence [17–19], and some promoting it as the only one (It is logical and it is coherent. Furthermore, it is the only logical and coherent approach to forensic science interpretation. There are no others [20]). Current practice in assessing the LR for DNA evidence for single source profiles is to consider the prosecution proposition as the suspect's profile(s) is the source of the evidence while the defense hypothesis is assumed to be that the source is someone other than *s*. The probability of finding the suspect(s) profile *if* the suspect is the source is 1. The probability of the evidence arising according to the defense hypothesis is the frequency of the profile in the relevant population, usually termed the *RMP*. The RMP for a 10-locus profiling kit is generally lower than 1 in 1 billion.

The RMP enables an estimate of the number of people in a population that could be expected to have the observed profile. This is frequently done to provide a jury with some understanding of the weight of evidence. It answers the questions, "what is the chance of finding the same profile at random from someone else?", and, if the number in a population is known, "how many other people could have produced the same result?"

Mixtures of DNA from more than one person are frequently encountered in forensic work. The situation for evaluating mixtures is not quite so straightforward. Now the prosecution hypothesis becomes

1. *s* and an unknown person are the contributors

The defense hypothesis is generally assumed by the prosecution expert, and usually of the form,

2. two unknown persons are the contributors

Herein lies the problem with the claim that the LR is the "only" way of evaluating evidence in a forensic setting: it provides only the weight of evidence against the specific defendant without reference to other people who would also have an LR greater than 1 (i.e., prosecution hypothesis more likely than defense hypothesis) [21]. In effect, the LR is a sophisticated version of the disparaged "consistent with" statement [22]: the LR merely states that the evidence is consistent with the hypothesis, with an ascribed measure of the apparent "weight of evidence". It is accepted even by proponents of the LR approach that there is no "true" LR and no way of assessing whether an LR is even of the right order of magnitude [11,23].

Adherence to the "gospel" of the LR can create problems in Court. For example, in the case of Manoharan [24] in New Zealand, the judgment of the Appeal Court states,

> As mentioned, [the scientist] expressed her findings in terms of a likelihood ratio, namely that the likelihood of obtaining the DNA results obtained was at least 20 times more likely if this DNA originated from Mr Manoharan rather than from someone else unrelated to him and selected at random from the general New Zealand population. ...
> [50] In cross-examination [the scientist] resisted any attempt to express the findings in any other way including resisting endorsing the proposition that many other New Zealanders would contain the same four identified alleles in their DNA profile. Her justification for maintaining such a strong stand was that the likelihood ratio approach is recognised in peer-reviewed literature as being a robust and reliable approach.
> [51] We appreciate and respect the need for scientists to be precise. However in the trial context, it is also important that the evidence be presented in a way that is easily understood by laypeople. That is especially so having regard to what is often termed "the CSI effect" of DNA evidence on juries.
> [52] In this case the DNA evidence was not strong and there was a real risk that unless it was expressed in a way that made its limitations readily apparent to a layperson, the jury would attribute a weight to it that was not warranted.
> [53] In our view, as an expert witness whose role is to assist the court, [the scientist] should have unreservedly assented to the proposition that was put to her. We also know of no reason why the jury could not also have been told that another way of saying essentially the same thing was that it is likely that 200,000 other New Zealanders share the profile found. We agree with Mr Stevenson that laypeople are likely to find that formulation more understandable than a likelihood ratio.

This case also reminds us that even single source profiles can exhibit stochastic effects.

Although there are many (often many tens of millions) profiles that can be generated from a crimestain DNA mixture, and therefore could all be considered potential contributors to the crimestain, the LR evaluates the evidence using only the suspect as the known assumed contributor. In my opinion, this is potentially highly misleading to a court.

Put simply, if one defense hypothesis is simply to change any or all of the alleles in the profile of *s* with those within the crimestain but not belonging to *s* and suggest that any of these profiles is the true contributor, then it is likely that there will be millions of profiles that have LR's greater than 1. Many of these are almost certain to have an LR greater than the suspect [20].

Combining this with the fact that even true contributors may have an LR less than 1 and/or less than *s*, how is the court to assess the LR?

Another problem that arises with the use of the LR is the creation of false positives, by which I mean noncontributors who produce an LR greater than 1. Some claim that there is no such thing as a false positive using the LR as the result is simply what it is – an LR. However, it is clear that any statement that the evidence is "more likely if Mr X and an unknown are a contributor rather than two unknowns" is likely to incriminate Mr X if that is the evidence led to a court. Perhaps an LR greater than 1 is, therefore, better described as an incriminating result rather than a false positive, and those LRs greater than 1 that occur for noncontributors better described as "falsely (or wrongly) incriminating".

The difficulty created by the occurrence of wrongly incriminating profiles is frequently dealt with by proponents of the LR in order to test the general principle that use of an LR does not get things wrong: by taking a random selection of profiles from a database and comparing them to a profile of a mixture [20], it is then claimed that a small or zero number of profiles showing an LR less than 1 in such "experiments" demonstrate the validity of the process. However, this does not really answer the question of how many people could be accidentally included in the list of suspects for a particular mixture in a casework profile as it does not calculate the LRs for possible contributors who have DNA components *actually present in the mixture*.

The LR as routinely presented to a court does not provide any indication of

1. how many other people may be considered potential contributors to the profile,
2. the LR for any or all of those potential contributors, or
3. the values of the numerator and denominator.

In LCN or LTDNA, the problem is that some alleles may not be observed at all, or are uncertain because they have only been observed once [25]. Some authors, therefore, created models that attempted to provide the probability of the evidence by estimating the probability that these alleles were actually there even though not seen in the analysis. These calculations had also to take account of the probability that they were indeed spurious alleles and were what was termed *drop-in*.

Some models include consideration of peak height [26] (for standard profiles) [27, 28] while others ignore peak height [4, 11]. Ignoring peak height may be acceptable given the wide variation in peak heights when only low amounts of DNA are present; drop-out of an allele in one analysis while it is present in another is an extreme form of this peak height variation. Some models, therefore, ignore peak height and consider only whether an allele is present regardless of any information that peak height may contribute to the assessment.

A further difference among models is how the probability of drop-out or drop-in is calculated. Some use empirical data derived from laboratory experiments [29] while others use estimates or simply insert values that maximize the parameter under each hypothesis [11].

There are, therefore, a number of variations on the general theme regarding the use of the LR in the interpretation of mixtures. There is no general agreement on whether the LR or CPI or any other statistic is the best approach in legal decision making.

Low Template DNA Analysis and Interpretation

The LTDNA or LCN process is a procedure that uses the "standard" manufactured DNA profiling kit and one or more of several methods to increase the sensitivity of the kit to enable the profiling of smaller amounts of DNA. Most achieve this principally by increasing the number of amplification cycles, but this may be coupled with various "clean-up" procedures. The main features of the method were set out in two papers published in 2000 and 2001

[25, 30] (referring to LCN with the SGM+kit) and various authors thereafter [29]. Since then, it has been argued, in a kind of "argument of the beard"[f] way, that the features of low template DNA may be present in other samples and that there is a continuum from high template to low template samples with no distinct stochastic threshold, although attempts have been made to better define the threshold and its meaning [31].

However it is defined (and the presence of increased stochastic effects seems to be the generally accepted version), a number of difficulties were apparent from the use of the low template technique. The technique is claimed to be so sensitive that it will identify single alleles that are in fact a contaminant not associated with the sample under test. These single alleles are called *drop-in*. Because these drop-in alleles should be rare events, the technique requires two runs to reduce or eliminate the possibility that such contamination will not be counted as "true" alleles. The process, therefore, requires at least two runs, although theoretically there is no reason why low template analysis and interpretation cannot be conducted on a single run. Some laboratories use a "consensus profile", created by including any allele that is observed at least twice, regardless of the number of runs. Two runs are most common in practice, but three can be found frequently in casework.

The development of techniques of amplification and interpretation of very low amounts of DNA, which continues, has been accompanied by frequent confusing changes in definitions and terminology that have created problems in the scientific and legal debate. The debate on the reliability and acceptability of low template DNA profiling continues with recent papers by Budowle *et al.* [32,33], Caragine *et al.* [28], and recent Appeal Court judgments in the United Kingdom [6], the United States [7,8] and New Zealand [9] as well as State and Federal Court judgments in the United States. Despite the volume of literature offered to support the forensic application of low template DNA technologies, the proponents have failed to convince a number of scientists, including the FBI, that this is a reliable application for criminal casework. Success or failure in court is not vindication or rejection of the reliability of any science; that decision is for the scientific community.

Most judgments on the admissibility of low template DNA methods appear to follow a well-trodden path where low template DNA analysis and the use of software programs have been successfully presented as being based on reliable science. This has been achieved by asserting that all of the components of the challenged process have been used for a long time and are therefore generally accepted. The *Rodriguez* judgment in New York states,

> On the basis of the totality of the evidence, the Court finds that FST rests firmly upon two pillars, Polymerase Chain Reaction-Short Tandem Repeat (PCR-STR) DNA analysis and the likelihood ratio or LR. Both have long been generally accepted by forensic scientists as reliable …
> Key to the Court's finding that the FST evidence passes the Frye test, is the fact that the program is firmly rooted in PCR-STR DNA testing. Also of importance is that likelihood ratios accommodating allelic drop-out and drop-in, the primary analytic feature of FST, are generally accepted as reliable within the community of forensic scientists.

I disagree with the inclusion of "accommodating allelic drop-out and drop-in" as being generally accepted; there is no general agreement as to how or if this has been achieved.

What appears to have been excluded from the Court's consideration is that reliable science, and in particular analytical methods, operate within set parameters. Beyond those parameters, the science may not be reliable. The proponents of LTDNA procedures, rather than having to demonstrate the reliable application of science to the specific process of low template DNA analysis, appear to have succeeded in convincing some courts of the acceptability of a more restricted argument that the general science is used elsewhere and so must be acceptable when combined.

Until 2015, I was aware of only one judgment [*Espinho*] that has recognized the flaw in the proponents' argument. In that judgment, the Court correctly states,

> Dr. Staub's testimony, which is sort of, in conforming with the people, is we're dealing with a accepted testing method, and all we have is a smaller sample, and he sort of suggests that we need not worry about the fact that it's a smaller sample because it's the same testing procedure and everything else, only smaller.
> But I don't think the general scientific community views it that way, at least not yet. Certainly, we all understand the laws of physics apply from things, entire solar systems down to a grain of sand, but once

you get to the atomic level, all of a sudden all the rules change and the laws of physics don't apply, and we have to start employing guesswork.

So simply getting smaller is not inconsequential, because at some point we will get small enough to where the results are unreliable. I don't know where that point is. 100 picograms may be well within the range of reliability, and with time, the scientific community may reach that conclusion. Or 50 picograms or 6 picograms or, you know, whatever the number is, if the proper procedures are followed, but I don't think there's acceptance in the scientific community as to what those procedures are because there's just not enough time, not enough analysis.

To cite two simplified analogies:

- one would not expect a family car to be able to corner at high speed like a racing car despite the underlying "science" of cars and driving being the same;
- an airplane wing will perform very well above the stall speed, below which point it simply stops flying.

In a recent (2015) written judgment in a New York State case,[g] after a *Frye* hearing, the judge ruled the LCN technique used by Office of the Chief Medical Examiner (OCME) and their statistical software program (FST) inadmissible as they failed to reach the standard of general acceptability in the scientific community. I was involved as a defense expert in that case. It is likely that the decision will, or should, lead to a closer scrutiny of the process used by OCME.

So, extending a known technology beyond its limits does not mean that reliability is maintained. Indeed, the SWGDAM standard requires those limitations to be established for DNA analysis.

Despite the judgment in *Rodriguez* (and others) citing many authorities including the FBI (which has explicitly rejected low template technology in criminal casework following their own experimentation[h]), the salient point remains that none of these authorities has actually examined in detail the source validation data claimed to underpin their method. In every case in which I have been involved, the laboratory has refused to voluntarily disclose the validation data upon which they depend to support their claim of reliability for their testing protocol (e.g., FSS Ltd, UK; ESR Ltd, New Zealand; OCME, USA). In my opinion, disclosure of all validation data should be a requirement

of accreditation[i], which each laboratory has claimed ensures their results are reliable.

Expert Systems (Probabilistic Genotyping Software)

The increased complexity of the statistical models used to interpret mixtures has reached the point where paper calculation is impossible or impractical. A number of software programs have been developed that claim to perform these calculations (e.g., LikeLTD, STRMix, LoComotioN, TrueAllele, and LabRetriever). Proponents of the statistical models and computer programs that perform the calculations claim to take account of drop-in and drop-out. Some do this using empirical data derived from laboratory experiments, others do not rely on empirical data. Some use the data available from the DNA profiling process including peak heights and some do not. Although some of the models may be sound, there is no currently generally accepted method for validating such programs, knowing whether the calculated LR is accurate, and the data to support the calculations is frequently unavailable.

In June 2015, SWGDAM published guidelines[j] for the validation of such software. These state,

> Probabilistic genotyping does not utilize a stochastic threshold. Instead, it incorporates a probability of alleles dropping out or in. In making use of more genotyping information when performing statistical calculations and evaluating potential DNA contributors …

The guidelines do not say how the "probability of alleles dropping out or in" should be assessed, although they do require such probabilities to be established. There are a number of difficulties in establishing many of the parameters discussed in the guidelines, and time will tell whether they provide any useful yardstick for assessing the reliability of any software. However, some major difficulties can be readily identified.

For example, although the guideline introduction identifies the specific sample types for which such software is intended, including "complex mixtures", it also states (under the section on assessing accuracy),

> 3.2.6.1. These studies should include the comparison of the results produced by the probabilistic

genotyping software to manual calculations, or results produced with an alternate software program or application, to aid in assessing accuracy of results generated by the probabilistic genotyping system. Calculations of some profiles (e.g., complex mixtures), however, may not be replicable outside of the probabilistic genotyping system.

It is accepted by proponents of the LR approach that there is no "true" LR and no way of assessing whether an LR is even of the right order of magnitude [11,22]. Given that accuracy is the proximity of a result to a true value, it is difficult to see how this claim can be reconciled with the published statement that, "many different LRs can be proposed, each with some justification" [11]. If we do not know the true value, accuracy cannot be assessed.

Other work is under way to suggest validation guidelines and some authors have created their own validation suggestions. In my opinion, it is difficult to see how the term validation can be applied to such systems when the accuracy of the answers (i.e., the "true" result) is unknown and to a great extent unknowable. There is no established truthful LR in the way that one can prepare and test a known amount of alcohol, DNA, or other analyte in a conventional validation process.

Examination of the numerator and denominator of the LR can reveal interesting features. In a recent case involving a low template profile, the numerator and denominator of the LR (derived using LikeLTD) were disclosed on request as 10^{-48} and 10^{-55}; the LR was reported as "over 40 million". In the same case, even though the profile showed a clear single major allele that was in the profile of the defendant, the calculated LR was less than 1 for that locus and therefore was to be considered more likely under the defense hypothesis than the prosecution hypothesis.

One of the papers upon which LikeLTD's calculations are based states,

> We show that some current approaches to interpretation, such as ignoring a discrepant locus or reporting a "Random Man Not Excluded" (RMNE) probability, can be systematically unfair to defendants, sometimes extremely so. We also show that the LR can depend strongly on the assumed value for the drop-out probability, and there is typically no approximation that is useful for all values. …
> We agree with [5] that there does not yet exist a fully satisfactory analysis of DNA profiles obtained from

LTDNA samples, and so approximations and simplifying assumptions are required. However we are concerned that some approximations and assumptions being used in courts have not been adequately justified. …
> Other novel aspects developed here involve drop-out at homozygote alleles, and uncertainty about whether a peak is allelic or stutter or masking. …
> Computing an LR requires a probability model to describe the real-world processes underlying an LTDNA profile. However, LTDNA profiling is complex, and there are many plausible probability models, and hence many different LRs can be proposed, each with some justification. Inevitably, fully realistic models of all sources of variation are unachievable, and approximations must be made and assessed [22]. [my emphasis]

It is therefore correctly acknowledged that

1. this is a novel approach,
2. it is one of several,
3. there are many possible results from this process, and
4. no realistic model is available.

Despite these limitations, results from such programs have almost always been admitted in courts when insufficiently challenged.

Some authors claim that convergence of, or at least broadly similar, results from the same data when re-evaluated by the same software support the validity and reliability of the results. This may be so, assuming that there is no inherent bias in the basic method.

DNA Transfer

As the improving technology of profiling allowed smaller amounts of material to be profiled, it became possible to obtain profiles from material invisible to the naked eye. Further, it became impossible to identify the source of the material as coming from a specific body fluid (e.g., blood, semen, saliva, and skin). A consequence of this was that inevitable questions arose as to where the material had originated and how it came to be in a specific place.

Despite years of research and numerous publications, a review in 2013 [34] concluded,

> The published work to date establishes:
>
> (a) The possibility, but not the probability, of DNA transfer.

(b) It is not possible to use the amount of DNA recovered from a surface to assess whether the DNA was deposited there by a single touch or by regular use.

(c) It is not possible to use the amount of DNA recovered from an item of interest to inform whether the DNA was deposited by direct contact or indirect transfer.

(d) There is no strong correlation between a full or partial profile and the amount of DNA template (at sub-optimal amounts of DNA).

(e) The quality of a DNA profile cannot be used to establish whether the DNA recovered came from the last handler.

(f) The number of factors, and the relative effect of those factors, involved in the transfer of DNA is unknown.

(g) The initial amount of DNA deposited, and any activity likely to reduce the number of cells or DNA-containing material from donor surfaces (e.g. hand), and the time since those activities, is a key factor in determining the amount of DNA recovered.

This has not prevented experts in some cases from attempting to convince that one mechanism is more likely than another when there is no other support for that view than their "casework experience".

Experience

Although scientific criticism of several court judgments involving the admissibility (or acceptability) of experience, and the neglect of published scientific work, have been well documented[k,l] [35], the courts and some experts continue to accept experience as somehow validating their opinion. Indeed, in the United Kingdom, some experts even include the court judgment(s) in their reports to warrant their subjective opinion.

Using experience, or "counting alleles", when no statistical evaluation of a DNA profile is possible has been recently endorsed by the Court of Criminal Appeal of England and Wales. There have been several scientific responses to that judgment, including,

> The ruling assumes that a scientist who has quantitatively evaluated a large number of mixtures cases will have the knowledge to assign a reliable qualitative opinion of weight of evidence in a case that is too complex for a quantitative assessment.
> However, there is no scientific basis for this belief – no scientific literature provides a reliable methodology, scientists are not trained to make

such assessments and there is no body of standards to support them. Casework experience is not a substitute.
> The true composition of the DNA result in any given case cannot be known so it does not provide a reliable control for learning purposes.[i]

Similarly with DNA transfer, the Court of Criminal Appeal has endorsed the admissibility of evidence based on experience despite the acknowledged lack of sufficient reliable science. Indeed, in one case, the unpublished data created by the prosecution laboratory supported the defense more than the prosecution and yet still lost to experience.[m] That court also created a dangerous environment for scientific evidence when it stated,

> we do hope that the courts will not be troubled in future by attempts to rely on published work by people who have no practical experience in the field and therefore cannot contradict or bring any useful evidence to bear on issues that are not always contained in scientific journals. There are plenty of really experienced experts who are available and it is to those that the courts look for assistance in cases of this kind [36].

Setting aside the court's misunderstanding of "practical experience", this view appears to misapprehend the entire scientific method that is based on the publication of controlled and peer-reviewed work that can then be tested by the scientific community. No scientist performs all of the experiments required to support his or her opinion. In fact, most do not perform any of the experiments other than the case-specific analyses. Every scientist depends entirely on published scientific work, or the laboratory validation, to underpin his or her opinion.

The scientific responses to the Court in *Weller* were dismissive:

> Recent legal cases in the UK may have potentially begun to move us into what is an uncomfortable arena, where suggestions that years of practical experience are more important to the courts than sound science. ...
> Relying exclusively on personal knowledge and experience, I would suggest, is not enough and experts must have an understanding of the uncertainties associated with the evolution of a particular fact upon which they may rely.
> "We believe that the courts should be more troubled by 'really experienced experts' (what counts a really

experienced?) than by attempts to rely on actual data".[k]

Following publication of the review of the research on DNA transfer, Champod states,

In my view, what is critical, when it comes to offer expert opinions (in the present discussion regarding DNA transfer), is striking the appropriate balance between structured documented data (published or not) and unfettered personal opinion. Should these opinions be based *in extenso* on experience? My answer is clearly negative. I believe that experience constitutes a poor substitute to a systematic and structured acquisition of data [37].

The scientific perspective is therefore different to the Court's seeming "anything is better than nothing" approach:

A jury is entitled to be informed of his assessment. The alternative, of simply leaving the jury to make up its own mind about the similarities and dissimilarities, with no assistance at all about their significance, would be to give the jury raw material with no means of evaluating it. It would be as likely to result in over-valuation of the evidence as undervaluation. It would be more, not less, likely to result in an unsafe conclusion than providing the jury with the expert's opinion, properly debated through cross-examination and, if not shared by another expert, countered by contrary evidence [38].

While showing a touching, if erroneous, view of the reliability of cross-examination to inform a jury about arcane science, it is difficult to see, if the expert's view has nothing more than experience to support it, how the jury are any better equipped to judge that experience than they are to judge the underpinning science. As Faigman has pointed out (quoted in Rudin and Inman[k]),

Many witnesses have learned to invoke experience as a means of circumventing the responsibility of supporting an opinion with hard facts. For the witness, it eases cross-examination. But it also removes the scientific basis for the opinion.

The Courts have not dealt with the wider problem, and indeed increasingly appear to overtly accept "case experience" over the gold standard of science – published research.

Conclusion

The 2009 NAS report stated,

For a variety of reasons – including the rules governing the admissibility of forensic evidence, the applicable standards governing appellate review of trial court decisions, the limitations of the adversary process, and the common lack of scientific expertise among judges and lawyers who must try to comprehend and evaluate forensic evidence – the legal system is ill-equipped to correct the problems of the forensic science community. In short, judicial review, by itself, is not the answer.[a]

Those reasons are easily demonstrable, and yet remain as a barrier to the effective use of DNA evidence in courts.

The reliability of forensic science is being increasingly questioned by the wider scientific community. The criticism is focused on the lack of underpinning science yet this is the area which, in my opinion, the courts have consistently failed to appreciate how science works, or simply to ignore science and rely on the claimed experience of the scientist.

The need for a more objective analysis of the evidence should not encourage acceptance of any technique simply because it makes the claim of objectivity, especially if part of the technique involves subjective decisions about what to include or exclude from the assessment (e.g., the input to many software programs).

So, the three main controversies in laboratory forensic DNA profiling and evaluation are

1. How to reliably interpret and ascribe a significance or weight of evidence to mixtures from two or more people.
2. Whether samples exhibiting stochastic effects are capable of reliable interpretation, in particular using probabilistic genotyping software.
3. Whether it is possible to reliably assess mechanisms of DNA transfer using the profile information.

The increasing complexity of many DNA profiles being encountered and used in criminal cases exposes the limitations of the science and the scientist. It should not be forgotten that there remains a core of reliable, useful DNA analysis, interpretation, and evaluation being performed in laboratories every day.

While courts may expect and occasionally demand an immediate unconditional certain answer, scientists must remind them that science, and in particular forensic DNA profiling, is rarely certain. Attempts to push the technology have inevitably been the cause of considerable scientific debate that remains unsettled. That debate should and will continue.

End Notes

a. Strengthening Forensic Science in the United States: A Path Forward Committee on Identifying the Needs of the Forensic Sciences Community; Committee on Applied and Theoretical Statistics, National Research Council.

b. US v McCluskey Cr. No. 10-2734 JCH (New Mexico).

c. http://www.theforensicinstitute.com/news-articles/views-and-opinions/confusion-in-court-with-ltdna

d. For a UK lawyer's perspective on these issues, the paper by Bentley and Lownds (Archbold Review, Issue 1 February 15, pp. 6–9, 2011) is informative.

e. Good descriptions of these and other DNA matters can be found at http://swgdam.org/docs.html.

f. For example, see http://mason.gmu.edu/~cmcgloth/portfolio/fallacies/argumentbeard.html.

g. People v. Jaquan Collins and Andrew Peaks.

h. A point endorsed in written testimony by Tina Delgado of the FBI DNA laboratory in 2011 in the case of US v Jeffrey McDonald and oral testimony on 10 November 2014 in US v Johnny Morgan.

i. Evett, I. Pope, S. The science of mixed results. Law Society Gazette at http://www.lawgazette.co.uk/law/practice-points/science-of-mixed-results/5036961.fullarticle.

j. SWGDAM, Guidelines for the Validation of Probabilistic Genotyping Systems (2015) available at http://swgdam.org/SWGDAM%20Guidelines%20for%20the%20Validation%20of%20Probabilistic%20Genotyping%20Systems_APPROVED%200615 2015.pdf.

k. Rudin, N. & Inman, K. The CACNews, 4th Quarter 2010.

l. Jamieson A., Meakin, G. "Experience is the name that everyone gives to their mistakes". Barrister Magazine at http://www.barristermagazine.com/archive-articles/issue-45/experience-is-the-name-that-every one-gives-to-their-mistakes.html.

m. Bader, S. 'Publish or perish, but meanwhile study what's out there'. Barrister Magazine, available at http://www.barristermagazine.com/barrister/index.php?id=536.

References

[1] Budowle, B., Onorato, A.J., Callaghan, P.F., Manna, A.D., Gross, A.M., Guerrieri, R.A., Luttman, J.C. & McClure, D.L. (2009). Mixture interpretation: defining the relevant features for guidelines for the assessment of mixed DNA profiles in forensic casework, *Journal of Forensic Science* **54**(3), 1–12.

[2] Gill, P. & Buckleton, J. (2010). Commentary on: mixture interpretation: defining the relevant features for guidelines for the assessment of mixed DNA profiles in forensic casework, *Journal of Forensic Science* **55**(1), 265–268.

[3] Budowle, B., Chakraborty, R. & van Daal, A. (2010). Authors' response, *Journal of Forensic Science* **55**(1), 269–272.

[4] Gill, P. (2001). Application of low copy number DNA profiling, *Croatian Medical Journal* **42**(3), 229–232.

[5] R v Bates, EWCA Crim 1395 (2006).

[6] R v Reed & Reed and Garmson, EWCA Crim 2698 (2009).

[7] People v Espino, NA076620 (2009).

[8] People v Megnath, NY Slip Op 20037 [27 Misc 3d 405] (2010).

[9] R v Wallace, NZCA 46 (CA590/2007) (2010).

[10] People v Collins & Peaks Supreme Court of the State of New York, County of Kings: Part 26 Indictment No. 8077/2010. (2014).

[11] Gill, P., Kirkham, A. & Curran, J. (2007). LoComatioN: A software tool for the analysis of low copy number DNA profiles, *Forensic Science International* **166**, 128–138.

[12] Balding, D. (2013). Evaluation of mixed-source, low-template DNA profiles in forensic science, *PNAS* **110**(30), 12241–12246.

[13] Perlin, M.W., Legler, M.M., Spencer, C.E., Smith, J.L., Allan, W.P., Belrose, J.L. & Duceman, B.W. (2011). Validating TrueAllele DNA mixture interpretation, *Journal of Forensic Science* **56**(6), 1430–1447.

[14] Benschop, C.C.G. & Sijen, T. (2014). LoCIM-tool: an expert's assistant for inferring the major contributor's alleles in mixed consensus DNA profiles, *Forensic Science International: Genetics* **11**, 154–165.

[15] R v Doheny and Adams 1 Crim App R 369 (1997).

[16] R v Broughton EWCA Crim 549 (2010).

[17] Gill, P., Brenner, C.H., Buckleton, J.S., Carracedo, A., Krawczak, M., Mayr, W.R., Morling, N., Prinz, M., Schneider, P.M. & Weir, B.S. (2006). DNA commission of the International Society of Forensic Genetics: recommendations on the interpretation of mixtures, *Forensic Science International* **160**, 90–101.

[18] Gill, P., Curran, J., Neumann, C., Kirkham, A., Clayton, T., Whitaker, J. & Lambert, J. (2008). Interpretation of

complex DNA profiles using empirical models and a method to measure their robustness, *Forensic Science International: Genetics* **2**, 91–103.

[19] Gill, P., Gusmao, L., Haned, H., Mayr, W.R., Morling, N., Parson, W., Prieto, L., Prinz, M., Schneider, H., Schneider, P.M. & Weir, B.S. (2012). DNA commission of the International Society of Forensic Genetics: Recommendations on the evaluation of STR typing results that may include drop-out and/or drop-in using probabilistic methods, *Forensic Science International: Genetics* **6**, 679–688.

[20] Berger, C.E.H., Buckleton, J., Champod, C., Evett, I.W. & Jackson, G.W. (2011). Response to Faigman et al, *Science and Justice* **51**, 215.

[21] Dørum, G., Bleka, O., Peter Gill, P., Haned, H., Snipen, L., Sæbø, S. & Egeland, T. (2014). Exact computation of the distribution of likelihood ratios with forensic applications, *Forensic Science International: Genetics* **9**, 93–101.

[22] Macfarlane, B.A. (2012). Wrongful convictions: is it proper for the crown to root around, looking for miscarriages of justice?, *Manitoba Law Journal* **36**(1), 1–36.

[23] Balding, D. & Buckleton, J. (2009). Interpreting low template DNA profiles, *Forensic Science International: Genetics* **4**, 1–10.

[24] Manoharan v R, NZCA 237, CA5/2013 (2015).

[25] Gill, P., Whitaker, J., Flaxman, C., Brown, N. & Buckleton, J. (2000). An investigation of the rigor of interpretation rules for STRs derived from less than 100 pg of DNA, *Forensic Science International* **112**, 17–40.

[26] Cowell, R.G., Lauritzen, S.L. & Mortera, J. (2007). Identification and separation of DNA mixtures using peak area information, *Forensic Science International* **166**, 28–34.

[27] Puch-Solis, R. (2014). A dropin peak height model, *Forensic Science International: Genetics* **11**, 80–84.

[28] Puch-Solis, R., Rodgers, L., Mazumder, A., Pope, S., Evett, I., Curran, J. & Balding, D. (2013). Evaluating forensic DNA profiles using peak heights, allowing for multiple donors, allelic dropout and stutters, *Forensic Science International: Genetics* **7**, 555–563.

[29] Caragine, T., Mikulasovich, R., Tamariz, J., Bajda, E., Sebestyen, J., Baum, H. & Prinz, M. (2009). Validation of testing and interpretation protocols for low template DNA samples using AmpFlSTR® Identifiler®, *Croatian Medical Journal* **50**, 250–67.

[30] Whitaker, J.P., Cotton, E.A. & Gill, P. (2001). A comparison of characteristics of profiles produced with the SGM Plus multiplex system for both standard and Low Copy Number (LCN) STR DNA analysis, *Forensic Science International* **123**, 215–223.

[31] Gill, P., Puch-Solis, R. & Curran, J. (2009). The low-template-DNA (stochastic) threshold – Its determination relative to risk analysis for national DNA databases, *Forensic Science International: Genetics* **3**, 104–111.

[32] Budowle, B., Eisenberg, A.J. & van Daal, A. (2009). Validity of low copy number typing and applications to forensic science, *Croatian Medical Journal* **50**, 207–17.

[33] Budowle, B., Eisenberg, A.J. & van Daal, A. (2009). Low copy number typing has yet to achieve "general acceptance", *Forensic Science International: Genetics* **2**, 551–2.

[34] Meakin, G. & Jamieson, A. (2013). DNA transfer: review and implications for casework, *Forensic Science International: Genetics* **7**, 434–443.

[35] Editorial (2010). *Science and Justice* **50**, 111–112.

[36] R v Weller, EWCA Crim 1085 (2010).

[37] Champod, C. (2013). DNA transfer: informed judgment or mere guesswork?, *Frontiers in Genetics* **4**, Article 300.

[38] R v Atkins & Anor, EWCA Crim 1876 (para.23) (2009).

Chapter 44
Future Technologies and Challenges

Allan Jamieson

The Forensic Institute, Glasgow, UK

Given that it was only in the late 1990s that DNA forensic profiling technology became a reality, it is a very short history upon which to base predictions of the future. The influence of this technology goes beyond each case. "From crime scene to court" is the traditional domain of forensic science. With DNA profiling comes ethical, societal, and political matters such as familial searching and the creation of databases that may or may not be better informed by the basic science of creating a profile. The reach of the science is well beyond science.

Predictions are based on more or less current information but many predictions will also depend on progress in a number of areas. For example, would the ability to process crimestains at the scene be affordable and afforded by law enforcement or governments? It is impossible to neatly compartmentalize the issues in DNA profiling. Whether crime scene processing is possible will depend on whether the laboratory technology is transferrable and uses the same outputs (e.g., CODIS loci) and the ability to remotely access databases in the search for suspects. If the scene analysis also encompass automated software for the deconvolution of complex mixtures, it is likely to produce a large number of suspect profiles. With larger databases, this could lead to more erroneous "hits" as police chase the immediate "lead" generated at the scene, and ultimately a loss of confidence in the system.

The areas considered here are

1. The crime scene (collection)
2. Laboratory analysis (production of the profile)
3. Interpretation (assessment of the potential contributor(s))
4. Evaluation (what the presence of DNA means)
5. Court (presentation)

Crime Scene

There are two main evidence types found at a crime scene: movable (e.g., cigarette ends and weapons) and immovable (e.g., blood on walls). Of course, with a will and a way (and the finance), the immovable may move! Movable items are conveyed to some other place for the removal of possible cellular material, usually by swabbing or taping. In some instances, the removal is performed at a police station or similar places, whereas in others this is conducted at the same laboratory where the profiling will be performed. Removal of possible cellular material is done on-site for immovable items.

Ultimately, the removed material is provided to the laboratory for analysis. This involves the extraction and amplification of the DNA and the production of the profile. A combination of circumstances such as transportation and laboratory backlogs usually means that the time to produce a profile and therefore act on any information arising from it takes longer than the current shortest time to produce a profile from a sample (about an hour). Such delays can produce negative media coverage for the agencies involved[a]. In the United States, the problem was, and is, so prevalent that the DNA Backlog Reduction Program[b] was created in 2011 (having merged with Convicted Offender and/or Arrestee Backlog Reduction Funding). The fact that the Program still exists and spent over $74 million in 2013 (the last year for which figures were available as at June 2015) suggests that the problem still exists. However, this spending compares with over $390 million in 2004.

A Guide to Forensic DNA Profiling
Edited by Allan Jamieson and Scott Bader
© 2016 John Wiley & Sons, Ltd. ISBN: 9781118751527

So, fast reliable profiling that would reduce pressure on the laboratory and enable investigators to receive and act on any information arising from the profiling would seem to be a desirable end. It should also be noted that the same technology could also enable profiling of a suspect to take place at a police station or even by patrol officers in vehicles, again producing faster data for the law enforcement agencies.

One such system from the United Kingdom achieved significant media coverage in 2011; "A new device that can identify suspects from DNA left at the scene of a crime in under an hour is set to transform the way police track down criminals"[c]. The system, developed by LGC Forensics and called RapiDNA, represented "a multi-million pound investment" [1]. The system was developed to become two products ParaDNA Intelligence Test and ParaDNA Screening Test. These are described in scientific papers in 2015

> the ParaDNA Screening System identifies the presence of DNA on a variety of evidence items including blood, saliva and touch DNA items. [2]
> The ParaDNA Intelligence Test system amplifies D3S1358, D8S119, D16S539, D18S1358 and TH01 STR loci and the gender typing locus amelogenin. [3]

Although not a complete profile when compared to currently used systems within the United Kingdom and elsewhere, the system shows promise of fulfilling its claim to be a screening or intelligence application. Many crimestains are mixtures. It is not immediately obvious how the system, or any other current system, provides any assistance from a mixed sample without some means of deconvoluting the profile.

Another system, which has been subject to perhaps exaggerated claims in its commercial promotion, is the RapidHit system [4]. This study claims,

> the RapidHIT system is ready for customer "system" or internal validation (underway or completed by early adopters of the system), and adoption as part of the routine workflow for forensic laboratories.

It should be noted that the current gap between the best lab time and actuality are because of backlogs, either too many samples or too few resources. Widespread adoption of on-site testing may simply move the problem closer to the source of the sample. Agencies may wish giving more consideration to addressing in-lab times rather than developing

on-site technology (the Rapid HIT machine costs $250 000 – and each cartridge costs between $150 and $300 for a test[d]).

Several problems remain to be solved before any such system will perform the current role of the laboratory. As yet, the forecast uptake by police forces is yet to materialize, but time will tell whether these, or other systems using similar or novel technology, will meet the perceived need. Some of the problems in taking this type of technology to market have been published by the developers [5].

Laboratory Analysis

Short Tandem Repeats (STRs)

Short tandem repeats (STRs) are currently the most ubiquitous targets for forensic DNA profiling technology and are likely to remain so for some time because they form the basis for every national DNA database and consequently the systems for exchanging information between and among international law enforcement agencies. The Interpol Web site states,

> We advocate international technical standards and systems in order to enhance the opportunities for successful cross-border collaboration. For example:
>
> • The DNA Gateway is developed to its internationally recognized standard to facilitate the electronic transfer of DNA data between INTERPOL and its member countries.
> • The Gateway is also compatible with the EU Pruem DNA Data Exchange Network, and for selected international export of DNA profiles for countries using CODIS (the FBI-designed DNA matching software).
> • The G8 DNA Search Request Network uses INTERPOL's I-24/7 system and DNA standards to communicate profiles among G8 countries.[e]

Development of STR technology, for whatever reason, has been in two main areas:

1. Improving sensitivity
2. Improving specificity

Improving sensitivity involves reducing the amount of DNA necessary to produce a profile. The first DNA profiling technology (restriction fragment length polymorphism – RFLP) required visible amounts of material such as a blood spot or semen stain. Amounts in the microgram range (10^{-6} g) were required, one thousand times greater than the standard technique now requires and a hundred thousand times more than required for low template work. That original technology is very different to the current STR technology based on the polymerase chain reaction (PCR). The STRs are stretches of DNA with a small number (up to 20*-something) of identical repeating units arranged one after the other like the carriages of a train. To visualize these, it is necessary with the current technology to multiply or amplify each of these STRs using the PCR process. The PCR process exploits DNA's ability to replicate itself to produce billions of copies of the relevant STRs. These different lengths of DNA are then separated by electrophoresis to produce the electrophoretogram or electropherogram (EPG) from which the DNA profile is inferred.

Almost all DNA profiling conducted by law enforcement agencies is achieved using commercial profiling kits and equipment. The most popular current kits were designed to amplify between about 0.5 and 1.5 ng (10^{-9} g or 0.000000001 g) of DNA. This design limit is compromised in some mixed samples wherein there may be, say, 0.9 ng (900 pg, 1 pg = 10^{-12} g) of the DNA from one person and 100 pg of DNA from another. While one contributor's amount (the "major" contributor) is within the design limit, the lower contributor (or "minor" contributor) is below the design limit.

Some samples are also degraded. This means that there is more intact DNA at some loci than at others. Some loci may therefore be within the design limit, whereas others are not.

So, while theoretically, and now practically [6], it is possible to produce a reliable DNA profile from a single cell, for forensic samples, achieving this goal has created considerable controversy. This is because there are a number of factors, such as degradation and mixed samples, that thwart the ability of the kits to produce repeatable results with some samples with very low amounts of DNA (i.e., those with DNA components with amounts lower than the recommended inputs to the analyses). This has led to the development of strategies to overcome these limitations.

These strategies involve either or both of

1. Improving the sensitivity of the analysis
2. Development of interpretation protocols to account for the variable results

Improvements in sensitivity have been claimed using increased numbers of amplification cycles and processes to improve the effectiveness of the electrophoresis process by either "cleaning up" the sample or increasing the amount of sample input to the electrophoresis.

The use of increased amplification cycles for forensic samples is generally credited to the developers of the low copy number (LCN) technique, which was first published in 2000, although several others had already used increased cycle number to improve the sensitivity of the PCR process. Several problems were encountered with the increased amplification cycle number approach including the detection of alleles that were not in the known sample (called *allelic drop-in*) and the absence of alleles that were in the known sample (called *allelic drop-out*). Other effects included increased stutter and extreme peak height imbalance between allelic peaks that should have been similar in height (the extreme expression of which is allelic drop-out).

These so-called stochastic or random effects were not resolved by improving the physical processes of extraction, amplification, or separation, but instead novel methods of interpreting the results were proposed. The interpretation of LCN or low template samples is discussed later.

Given that we can produce a profile from a single cell, it would appear that we have therefore reached the sensitivity limit in the amount that can be extracted from forensic DNA samples using current STRs as the nature of the samples (i.e., mixed and possibly degraded) and the environment (e.g., possible existence of "free" DNA contaminating samples).

In terms of increasing the specificity of profiling perhaps the most obvious route is simply to increase the number of loci analyzed. This is indeed a route that has been followed by all of the major kit manufacturers. From the original "Quad" of four loci, two of which (vWA and THO1) survived the 1995 development followed to six loci (Second Generation Multiplex or SGM system colloquially called the *hex and sex* system), and then to the 10-locus SGM+ kit (plus Amelogenin sex locus) used in the United Kingdom from 1999 until recently (some labs still use the SGM+ kit). The recently introduced "standard" set of loci for the United Kingdom (called *DNA17* in order to encompass several alternative commercially available kits) analyzes 16 autosomal loci plus the Amelogenin locus simultaneously. In the United States, 15 and more loci are routinely analyzed. The US CODIS database uses 13 loci. The only hurdle to be overcome with the approach of increasing the number of loci is that we have only 23 chromosomes. Therefore, if more than 23 loci are involved, then at least two of them must be on the same chromosome and the possibility of linkage has to be considered. Linkage increases the probability of inheriting an allele at one locus along with an allele from the linked locus on the same chromosome and thereby complicates the statistics.

Single Nucleotide Polymorphisms (SNPs, Frequently Called "Snips")

The degradation of DNA is related to the length of the DNA involved. Despite the inherent robustness of the DNA molecule, the longer the stretch of DNA being considered is, the more is chance of it being chopped by physical or chemical means. The problem, and a proposed solution, is expressed succinctly in one of the first papers to describe the forensic use of the alternative SNP process:

> The current method of DNA profiling used for the National DNA Database1 (AMPFISTR1 SGM plus™) exploits the polymorphic nature of short tandem repeat (STR) sequences to discriminate between both related and unrelated individuals [1]. The technique is highly discriminating but is limited by the size of the DNA fragments produced for detection (ranging from 100–360 bases in length). As DNA becomes degraded, the higher molecular weight STR loci fail to amplify [2] giving a "partial" DNA profile that has a lower discrimination power.
> We have developed a multiplex system using bi-allelic SNPs, selected from The SNP Consortium database. By designing closer to the single polymorphic base, the likelihood of obtaining a result when STRs fail is increased. The discrimination power of SNPs increases with the number of loci multiplexed. There are many different assays available for SNP genotyping, although these are generally used when there is ample DNA available, something not often encountered with forensic DNA profiling. To achieve a large stable multiplex we have used the Amplification Refractory Mutation System (ARMS) combined with Universal reporter primers (URP) in a two-phase PCR reaction, to amplify DNA fragments ranging from 57 to 146 base pairs in length. [7]

In other words, the authors use shorter DNA lengths as targets for the PCR process, thereby improving the chance of finding an allele that has not been disrupted and rendered therefore invisible to the PCR chemistry.

The results when compared to "standard" profiling for such degraded samples were impressive:

> Saliva stains degraded for 147 days generated an 81% complete SNP profile whilst short tandem repeats (STRs) were only 18% complete; similarly blood degraded for 243 days produced full SNP profiles but only 9% with STRs.

A year later, the European DNA Profiling Group (EDNAP), following an interlaboratory exercise, concluded in 2006:

> The results of the collaborative exercise were surprisingly good and demonstrate that SNP typing with SBE, capillary electrophoresis and multicolour detection methods can be developed for forensic genetics.

Although several problems had emerged during the exercise, including

- difficulty in standardizing the signal strength
- SNaPshot kit adding nucleotides
- sensitivity varied between laboratories
- discrepancies in SNP types reported (although this was considered to be caused by poor sample quality, insufficient experience, suboptimal equipment, and technical problems due to the lack of standardization of the kit)

The development of SNPs continued with some improvements as exemplified in the work of Børsting *et al.* in 2013 [8]:

> The sensitised *SNPforID* assay with 100 SBE [single base extension] cycles in combination with the AmpFISTR SEfiler Plus Master Mix made it possible to type all the degraded crime case samples in this study. A minimum of 41 SNPs were typed and the match probabilities ranged from 1.1×10^{-15} to 7.9×10^{-23} for the single source samples. In comparison, four of the samples could not be typed with the commercial STR kits and the match probabilities were higher than 10^{-7} for six other samples. This confirmed the conclusions from previous studies that SNPs and indels [base insertions or deletions] may be the preferred markers for typing of highly degraded DNA.

The SNPforID set of SNPs was developed in 2006 by a consortium of laboratories [9]. Despite this promise and over 10 years of development in the forensic context, there are few signs to date of any significant uptake of the use of SNPs by law enforcement.

Possible reasons may be the heavy investment already made in STR technologies, increased difficulty of interpreting mixtures using SNPs, and the higher amount of material generally required. Also, at least one of the problems associated with previous STR kits for which the use of SNPs was intended, that of loss of sensitivity due to degradation, has been somewhat alleviated in the new STR kits. The amplicon lengths of several of the loci have been shortened so as to enable PCR amplification from shorter template DNA.

SNPs have been used in ancestry tracing (e.g., by the SNP for ID Consortium) [10] and in phenotyping, but several problems have been identified including [11]

- existing investment in STRs
- cost
- poor performance for mixtures
- dropout at low amounts of DNA

> Next-generation sequencing (NGS), also known as massively parallel sequencing, provides the opportunity to collect information from numerous STRs and SNPs simultaneously. [40]

WGA

The first paper on whole genome amplification (WGA) shows clearly why the technique was of major interest to researchers in forensic genetics:

> The sensitivity of the polymerase chain reaction is great enough to allow the analysis of DNA in a single cell. … In all these cases the single cell can be analyzed only once and independent confirmation of the genotype of any one cell is impossible. We have developed a method to circumvent this limitation. Multiple copies of the DNA sequences present in a single cell are made by an in vitro method that we call primer-extension preamplification (PEP). Multiple rounds of extension with the Taq DNA polymerase and a random mixture of 15-base oligonucleotides as primers produce multiple copies of the DNA sequences originally present in the sample. It is estimated that at least 78% of the genomic sequences in a single human haploid cell can be copied no less than 30 times. As a result, only a small aliquot of the amplified sample

has to be used to analyze any one gene and material remains for additional analyses. Our method not only extends the possible applications of single cell studies but also has implications for the analysis of any small DNA sample.[12]

The original WGA method (PCR) was augmented by a different approach in 2002 [13] called *multiple displacement amplification* (MDA). Initial interest and hope in WGA as a forensic technique have faded as the practical problems with the technique emerged.

> A promising new WGA method, mIPEP, has been developed that appears to be suitable for the types of samples encountered in forensic genetics and may permit the recovery of DNA proWles from otherwise intractable samples.
> Specifically, low copy number DNA samples, including fingerprints and environmentally induced degraded DNA, appear to be suitable substrates for this technique. [14]
> The methods did amplify DNA, but performed poorly on forensically relevant samples; the maximum amplicon size was reduced, and MDA often resulted in extraneous bands following polymerase chain reaction. Taken together, WGA appears to be of limited forensic utility unless the samples are of a very high quality. [15]
> Seven WGA methods were compared in terms of their possible application for degraded and nondegraded DNA analysis in forensic genetics. The best results for nondegraded DNA were obtained with GenomiPhi and PEP methods. MDAbased GenomiPhi technique is one of the most often used methods in forensic genetics; however, it requires good quality template which reduces its usefulness in this field.
> The best results for degraded DNA (200 bp) were obtained with GenomePlex which successfully amplified even severely degraded DNA (100 bp), enabling correct typing of not only Y-SNP loci (100–150 bp) but also mtDNA (~400 bp). Although none of the analyzed methods gave fully satisfactory results, some of them may be very useful in analysis of LCN or degraded DNA in forensic genetics, especially after application of some improvements (sample pooling and replicate DNA typing). [16]

As yet, there is no indication of a significant interest in pursuing WGA technologies as a replacement for STR approaches, although it may be that the advantages for low template amounts may lead to the development of niche products in some laboratories.

Mitochondrial DNA (mtDNA)

Mitochondria (s. mitochondrion) are contained within every cell. Mitochondria contain their own separate DNA (mtDNA), which has a different structure from the nuclear DNA that we have been discussing so far. Each cell has many mitochondria, in the range of hundreds to 2000, and therefore potentially more "targets" for DNA profiling. However, the advantage of those multitudes of mitochondria is compromised from a forensic perspective by the fact that the mtDNA is inherited solely via the maternal route. This is because at fertilization, when the sperm and egg come together, the new embryonic cells contain only mitochondria from the egg. Therefore, all children of the same mother have the same mtDNA, as does the mother's mother and all of the female children's children. The ability of mtDNA profiles to discriminate among individuals is thereby reduced.

This statistical drawback is further complicated by the fact that mutations are more frequent in the tested mtDNA regions than the very low rate in nuclear STR loci. Additionally, there is a low, but increasing, number of databases that can provide the necessary frequency data to enable the significance of a match to be calculated. Mixtures present an even more difficult problem in mtDNA analysis interpretation than in nuclear DNA interpretation, although there is at least one proposal for how to approach this problem [17].

> Technical issues regarding mtDNA typing were not discussed here but we are aware of the many complications that could complicate the statistical interpretation of real cases. For instance, background noise in sequencing electropherograms could be a hamper mtDNA mixture interpretation. Also, it is not possible to distinguish between two aggressors belonging to the sample matrilineage, given that they share the same mtDNA profile.

The advantage of mtDNA is that the numbers available lead to higher sensitivity of testing in practical terms of the number of cells required to produce a profile, and the generally better survival of mtDNA in some sample types (e.g., bone). The ubiquitous nature of mitochondria also increases the risk of contamination in casework.

Additionally, mtDNA is the only type of DNA found in some sample types (e.g., hair without roots). However, the discrimination power of mtDNA analysis is limited compared to that of STR analysis.

The future of forensic mtDNA formed part of a recent paper which concluded [18]

> The most significant challenge for mtDNA analysis remains the high cost and low throughput for evidentiary samples. …
> The system is robust when a sample contains good-quality abundant DNA, but also works well for difficult samples when all possible extra steps for recovering a profile are applied. …
> Postextraction improvements in PCR amplification and sequencing, or the introduction of new methods that do not require abundant template for detection of variation at the level of fine discrimination, are desirable. …
> Significant growth of forensic mtDNA databases to serve as foundations for population statistics continues to be a priority. …
> There is need for a statistical method that appropriately weights a failure to exclude when a forensic case contains both questioned and known samples with the same site heteroplasmy. …
> Using appropriate computer algorithms, overlapping amplicons, and phylogenetic contexts, mixture deconvolution may for the first time become routine, expanding the pool of samples with degraded and insufficient nuclear DNA for mitochondrial DNA analysis.

Next Generation Sequencing (NGS)

Next generation sequencing (NGS), sometimes referred to as "massive parallel sequencing" because it is performing several different techniques simultaneously, has recently been extensively reviewed [19]. The potential benefits of NGS are described in the abstract of the review,

> More information may be obtained from unique samples in a single experiment by analyzing combinations of markers (STRs, SNPs, insertion/deletions, mRNA) that cannot be analyzed simultaneously with the standard PCR-CE methods used today. The true variation in core forensic STR loci has been uncovered, and previously unknown STR alleles have been discovered. The detailed sequence information may aid mixture interpretation and will increase the statistical weight of the evidence.

The term is applied to a collection of technologies including those already described (and should probably become redundant as the "next" generation will surely come along in the same way that after "first generation" multiplexes came "second generation multiplex" (SGM)). As described in the review,

> some platforms were referred to as second generation sequencers and the single-molecule sequencer sometimes referred to as third generation sequencers or the next–next generation sequencers

One application where NGS appears to have produced results previously thought to be practically impossible is in the genetic differentiation of twins [20].

Interpretation

There are a number of ways to report the evidential significance of DNA profiles in forensic casework. There is little useful debate regarding the interpretation of single source DNA profiles, although there is sometimes a dogged resistance to recognizing the validity and utility of alternative approaches.

The current state of play insofar as the interpretation of DNA mixtures has been expressed in several papers;

> We have over the past few years developed great technological capabilities that in some ways have outpaced our ability to appropriately interpret evidence results obtained. We have emphasized methods for enhanced sensitivity while not working equally hard to improve our understanding of possible genotypes that may compose the evidence results (i.e. the specificity of results). Thus, for forensic DNA typing to move forward responsibly we must improve the framework and consistency of DNA evidence interpretation. [21]
> Both commercial companies and forensic laboratories have initiated the process, however, the current software solutions are not sufficiently advanced and more work and collaboration between the companies and the forensic community is necessary. [18]

Assuming that STRs remain the targets for analysis and we have reached the limit of detection for DNA molecules, then the most important developments in forensic DNA profiling in the future are likely to be in the interpretation and evaluation of DNA profiles. I am using here the definitions of interpretation and evaluation proposed previously [22] whereby interpretation is the decision as to what alleles are present within the profile (and consequently inferences such as the number of contributors) and evaluation is what

the interpretation means in the context of the case (e.g., the identity of possible contributors and how the DNA came to be where it was found).

The use of more loci in DNA profiling kits has improved the specificity of the results of the statistical evaluation of profiles. However, the detection of increasingly complex single and mixed profiles has complicated the already difficult task of assessing the significance or weight of evidence for these complex profiles. Even for obvious mixtures with no stochastic issues such as drop-out or drop-in, there is no general agreement as to the best method to use in the assessment of the weight of evidence for such profiles. The debate regarding the interpretation and evaluation of mixtures affected by stochastic variation and perhaps featuring the integration of the results from several profiling attempts to the same sample is more complex and has at times been heated. These debates are described in other articles herein.

In considering the future, it does seem that what is termed *probabilistic genotyping* of one form or another will be developed. Although there are a number of software programs available currently, these have had a rough and patchy ride in court, some accepted in some courts and not in others (*see* **Issues in Forensic DNA**). None has achieved general acceptance and each uses a different approach (some significantly different, e.g., the use or nonuse of peak height information). Guidelines for validation have only recently (June 2015) been issued by SWGDAM [23] and even then appear to be vague to say the least.

Many current systems depend on the manual input of the alleles, and in some the peak heights (e.g., STRMix[f] – a commercial product), to the software system. Others use the data from the analytical instrument as input to the software (e.g., TrueAllele[g] another commercial product that also has a number of published papers describing the broad approach). Some software performs a single calculation using empirically derived data to deal with stochastic effects (e.g., FST – used by the Office of the Chief Medical Examiner in New York, USA; the approach is published [24]), whereas others perform many thousands of iterations to derive these parameters using statistically derived values (e.g., LikeLTD, published [25] and freely available from the author[h]).

So, while there is as yet no generally accepted method of mixture interpretation or approach to dealing with stochastic effects, it is nevertheless reasonable to speculate that the integration of the raw data generated by the analytical equipment will provide the input to a software program that will calculate the statistical weight of evidence. None of the currently available components would appear to be ready for that task just yet.

As Butler said in 2015,

> Because sensitive DNA detection technology has the potential to outpace reliable interpretation, the forensic DNA community needs to be vigilant in efforts to appropriately interpret challenging evidence without pushing too far. [20]

This echoes my own sentiment expressed in 2008 [26],

> Failure to use DNA properly will almost certainly result in unintentional but significant damage that could threaten its more restricted but beneficial use.

Evaluation

Familial

Slooten and Meester in this volume in their discussion on familial searching state,

> It has been shown that a familial search on a mixture using 15 loci in many cases, especially the forensically relevant ones, has true and false positive rates comparable to those obtained from a single source profile using 10 loci. This last type of search is routinely done, but the former is not; we conclude that from a statistical point of view, there is no reason to discard mixtures as being too little informative.

It is that last conclusion that elicits speculation about the future.

A single-source profile is a single entity to compare for possible allele sharing with profiles in a database. But even a "simple" mixture produces millions of complete profiles that can be considered contributors, even more if partial profiles are to be added as the index search profile looking for possible relatives. We have worked on cases where the mixtures generated billions of potential contributor profiles. It is inevitable that such numbers, coupled with increasing numbers of profiles stored in databases, will produce false "hits" to profiles on the database that will distract investigators chasing spurious "leads" and causing distress to anyone caught up innocently in the investigation.

It has been said that,

> While familial searching is unlikely to be conducted on a national level in the USA, it has produced some successes in the UK through aiding identification of 41 perpetrators in 188 police investigations. Genetic privacy concerns are often raised in opposition to familial searching, and so the future of this technique is probably limited due to practical and privacy issues. [27]

The decision as to whether this is acceptable is of course a political and not a scientific one, but should at least be properly informed by the science.

Phenotyping

All of the DNA techniques that have been described herein have been invisible traits that do not assist an investigator to identify a suspect other than perhaps by use of a database already containing the profile of the suspect. We have therefore been discussing the genotype of the individual. That is, the alleles are present at a genetic locus. Most of the loci that we have so far been discussing are also noncoding or associated with a gene. That is, they have no product that can be detected such as other loci that may contain the gene for insulin, hemoglobin, amylase, or the thousands of other proteins that are the output of the body's DNA.

Although a locus within an individual may contain different alleles from each parent at the same locus, the visible output of the locus may be indistinguishable from those where both alleles are identical. Geneticists therefore use the term "genotype" to describe the actual alleles at a locus, whereas the term "phenotype" is used to describe how the alleles are expressed at that locus. For example, if a person inherits the allele for cystic fibrosis (CF) from both parents, he or she will have the disease; CF is both his or her genotype and phenotype. However, if they inherit the CF allele from only one parent, then they will be heterozygous (i.e., one CF and one non-CF allele) but will not show any sign of the disease. Their phenotype is therefore normal, even though their genotype contains the disease gene.

Many characteristics that make a person recognizable are dependent on the alleles present at specific loci within the genome. The most obvious phenotype is gender. A female is normally clearly different from a male. However, from a forensic perspective, that genotype is detected routinely using the current profiling technology. Although the environment, such as nutrition and exercise, may influence many of these, the genotype may provide the basis for knowledge of the phenotype for some characteristics, thereby enabling investigators to have a description of some visible features of the suspect. Obvious examples are hair color, height, build, eye color, and other visible traits. In the literature on forensic phenotyping, these have been termed *externally visible characteristics* (EVC). Some of these are affected more or less by environmental factors, which complicates any findings.

The connection between genes and appearance has created the notion that these phenotypic characters could be derived from the DNA from crimestains and used to predict the appearance of the source of the stain [28]. This particular form of forensic genetics is in its infancy. In 2015, it was reported [29] that the only practical examples of forensic phenotyping (described by the authors as forensic DNA phenotyping or FDP, which of course could equally be applied to forensic DNA *profiling*) so far are eye color, skin pigmentation [30], and hair color [31].

When considering the ideal forensic identification system, the immutability of the target feature (e.g., fingerprint and DNA profile) has been considered an important virtue of the strategy. It is obvious, even to proponents of forensic phenotyping, that all of the extremely limited results so far have been obtained using easily alterable features such as hair color. Even eye color can be disguised by the use of contact lenses, and skin tone can be affected by tanning (natural or artificial). Despite the review [26] citing 100 publications, results to date are simply not encouraging and the obvious ability of people to change their appearance for many of these traits will be known to criminals who have adapted their ways as each identification technology is introduced (e.g., wearing gloves to avoid leaving fingerprints), thereby presenting a very human obstacle to the utility of phenotyping.

Kayser [26] responds to this aspect by saying,

> Additionally, perpetrators would need to get their feigned appearance registered in police documentations. ID cards, drivers licenses, passports etc. all have portrait images, passports in some countries have height and eye color records; all this documented appearance information in principle could be used, together with DNA-predicted appearance from evidence material, for investigative purposes.

Even allowing that the ethical and legal issues with such a trawl had been overcome, the accuracy of the identification would have to be very close to 100% to avoid the false positive rate creating an impractical number of "hits". There were 14 million US passports issued in 2014[i]. A false positive rate of 0.01% would return 14,000 people and, given that the criminal may not have a passport, be a 100% false positive return in that case. There are over 210 million drivers licensed in the United States. A similar false positive rate provides over 200 000 "hits".

Phenotyping suffers other problems in a forensic context. Many crimestains from which the DNA would be recovered are mixtures and therefore without reliable methods of deconvoluting the mixture the technology is inapplicable. The current methods also require relatively large amounts of material.

Given the very limited circumstances in which phenotyping could apply, the influence of the environment on most visible characteristics, the ability of a perpetrator to circumvent the result by disguise, the likely cost of applying the technology, and the extremely accurate predictions required, it is unlikely that the proponents will receive the desired necessary funding for this particular technology.

DNA Transfer

Generally, there are two matters to be assessed from forensic DNA profiles: who did it come from and how did it get there. The current status of DNA transfer is dealt with elsewhere but what does the future hold for this topic?

The history of DNA transfer studies can be summarized in the quote attributed to Albert Einstein, "The more I learn, the more I realize how much I don't know".

The increase in sensitivity of profiling technology, combined with the propensity of individuals to shed cells almost constantly and everywhere, has led to the detection of cellular material that has nothing to do with a crime. There is also the unfortunate fact (so far as law enforcement is concerned) that it is also frequently possible to touch an item and leave no detectable DNA. The consequence of these is that the finding or not of DNA may or may not be relevant to a crime.

A general article in 2009,[j] commenting on the state of play regarding DNA transfer, said

Since so many of the available journal articles present conflicting information, more work is needed to see how likely it is to both transfer and detect DNA in a secondary or even a tertiary fashion, especially considering the sensitivity of modern forensic DNA analysis.

That theme is reflected in almost every published research article since. In 2013, a review [32] concluded that the published work considered to date established the possibility, but not the probability, of DNA transfer. That remains the case today and it is difficult to see, considering the range of possible circumstances found in casework and the inherently unknowable aspects of many, the circumstances where those probabilities can be reliably developed other than bespoke (and expensive) experiments designed to test a specific scenario in a case.

"Blue Sky" Thinking

Most difficulties in forensic DNA profiling arise from mixtures of DNA from mostly unknown contributors. The current techniques of mixture analysis demand a complex statistical approach, even though it may not be clear which statistic is most appropriate or even what it means to a Court. An apparently insurmountable problem is that when the DNA from the cells in a mixture are released from the cell, there is no reliable way of telling which allele came from which cell and therefore which could be linked with another to form a profile. If the cells could be separated *before* the profiling process, then the profile could be attributed unequivocally to a particular cell. This would also enable an unequivocal assessment of the number of contributors to the mixture.

This separation of individual cells could be facilitated by exploiting cell surface markers[k] which vary among people. Even if some people share markers, the chance of them occurring together in a crime stain may be relatively low. Some of these markers can be used to identify particular cell types. This may be an advantage in some cases where the tissue source provides important case-related information.

It has been possible for some time to obtain a profile from a single cell, although there are obviously some circumstances where that may not be possible (e.g., degraded cells). There are a number of ways in which individual cells or types of cell can be separated. Laser

microdissection[l] (LMD), for example, allows the isolation of single cells, and fluorescence activated cell sorting[m] may form the basis of other approaches. LMD has already been used in criminal cases to separate sperm cells [33].

Of course, although these technologies exist, to implement them in their current state for individual samples in forensic casework would be prohibitively expensive. Nevertheless, there is no reason in principle why the process cannot be fully or partially automated with a consequent return in better, less ambiguous, and more informative results from crimestain samples.

Pragmatically, the situation is probably better and more succinctly summarized by Butler in 2015,

> As noted almost 7 years ago by the Research and Development Working Group of the National Commission on the Future of DNA Evidence, STRs will probably be the markers of choice for the foreseeable future because of their widespread use in national DNA databases. We will likely see evolutionary progression in typing technology, more rapid amplification methods, additional STR kits containing new loci, and computer programs that will enable fast evaluation of STR typing data. Through continued advances, STR typing technologies may become miniaturized and integrated with other parts of the process, such as DNA extraction and amplification. [20]

Things will get better *mutatis mutandis*. Probably.

End Notes

[a.] Any internet search using "DNA lab delays" as a search term will produce media stories of problems, such as other crimes being committed as a consequence of failing to identify a perpetrator from a sample already held.

[b.] http://www.nij.gov/topics/forensics/lab-operations/evidence-backlogs/pages/backlog-reduction-program.aspx. Accessed 27 June 2015.

[c.] http://www.telegraph.co.uk/news/science/science-news/8584014/New-DNA-profiling-technology-could-tell-police-who-suspects-are-in-under-an-hour.html#disqus_thread

[d.] http://www.forensicmag.com/articles/2015/05/first-ever-rapid-dna-profile-uploaded-ndis?et_cid=4557550&et_rid=611016341&location=top

[e.] http://www.interpol.int/INTERPOL-expertise/Forensics/DNA. Accessed 27 June 2015.

f. http://strmix.esr.cri.nz

g. http://www.cybgen.com/systems/casework.shtml

h. http://cran.r-project.org/web/packages/likeLTD/index.html

i. http://travel.state.gov/content/passports/english/passports/statistics.html

j. http://www.lawofficer.com/articles/2009/01/transfer-theory-forensic-dna-a.html

k. https://www.qiagen.com/gb/products/genes%20and%20pathways/complete%20biology%20list/cell%20surface%20markers

l. https://en.wikipedia.org/wiki/Laser_capture_microdissection

m. https://en.wikipedia.org/wiki/Flow_cytometry#Fluorescence-activated_cell_sorting_.28FACS.29

References

[1] The Forensic Science Service (2013) Seventh Report of Session 2010-12, **1**. Great Britain: Parliament: House of Commons: Science and Technology Committee

[2] Dawnay, N., Stafford-Allen, B., Moore, D., Blackman, S., Rendell, P., Hanson, E.K., Ballantyne, J., Kallifatidis, B., Mendel, J., Mills, D.K., Nagy, R. & Wells, S. (2014). Developmental Validation of the ParaDNA® Screening System - A presumptive test for the detection of DNA on forensic evidence items, *Forensic Science International: Genetics* **11**, 73–79.

[3] Ball, G., Dawnay, N., Stafford-Allen, B., Panasiuk, M., Rendell, P., Blackman, S., Duxbury, N. & Wells, S. (2015). Concordance study between the ParaDNA® Intelligence Test, a rapid DNA profiling assay, and a conventional STR typing kit (AmpFlSTR® SGM Plus®), *Forensic Science International: Genetics* **16**, 48–51.

[4] Hennessy, L.K., Franklin, H., Li, Y., Buscaino, J., Chear, J., Gass, J., Mehendale, N., Williams, S., Jovanovich, S., Harris, D., Elliott, K. & Nielsen, W. (2013). Developmental validation studies on the RapidHIT™ Human DNA Identification System, *Forensic Science International: Genetics* Supplement Series **4**, e7–e8.

[5] Dawnay, N., Ahmed, R. & Naif, S. (2014). The ParaDNA® Screening System - a case study in bringing forensic R&D to market, *Science and Justice* **54**(6), 481–486.

[6] Findlay, I., Taylor, A., Quirke, A., Frazier, R. & Urquhart, A. (1997). DNA fingerprinting from single cells, *Nature* **389**, 555–556.

[7] Dixon, L.A., Murray, C.M., Archer, E.J., Dobbins, A.E., Koumi, P. & Gill, P. (2005). Validation of a 21-locus autosomal SNP multiplex for forensic identification purposes, *Forensic Science International* **154**, 62–77.

[8] Børsting, C., Mogensen, H.S. & Morling, N. (2013). Forensic genetic SNP typing of low-template DNA and highly degraded DNA from crime case samples, *Forensic Science International: Genetics* **7**, 345–352.

[9] Sanchez, J.J., Phillips, C., Borsting, C., Balogh, K., Bogus, M., Fondevila, M., Harrison, C.D., Musgrave-Brown, E., Salas, A., Syndercombe-Court, D., Schneider, P.M., Carracedo, A. & Morling, N. (2006). A multiplex assay with 52 single nucleotide polymorphisms for human identification, *Electrophoresis* **27**, 1713–1724.

[10] Phillips, C., Salas, A., Sánchez, J.J., Fondevila, M., Gómez-Tato, A., Álvarez-Dios, J., Calaza, M., Casares de Cal, M., Ballard, D., Lareu, M.V., & Carracedo, A. (2007). Inferring ancestral origin using a single multiplex assay of ancestry-informative marker SNPs, *Forensic Science International, Genetics* **1**, 273–280.

[11] Balding, D. (2005). *Weight of evidence for DNA profiles*, John Wiley & Sons ISBN 0-470-86764-7.

[12] Zhang, L., Cui, X., Schmitt, K., Hubert, R., Navidit, W. & Arnheim, N. (1992). Whole genome amplification from a single cell: Implications for genetic analysis, *PNAS* **89**, 5847–5851.

[13] Dean, F.B., Hosono, S., Fang, L., Wu, X., Faruqi, A.F., Bray-Ward, P., Sun, Z., Zong, Q., Du, Y., Du, J., Driscoll, M., Song, W., Kingsmore, S.F., Egholm, M. & Lasken, R.S. (2002). Comprehensive human genome amplification using multiple displacement amplification, *PNAS* **99**, 5261–5266.

[14] Ballantyne, J. & Hanson, E.K. (2005). Whole genome amplification strategy for forensic genetic analysis using single or few cell equivalents of genomic DNA, *Analytical Biochemistry* **346**, 246–257.

[15] Barber, A.L. & Foran, R. (2006). The utility of whole genome amplification for typing compromised forensic samples, *Journal of Forensic Science* **51**(6), 1344–1349.

[16] Maciejewska, A., Jakubowska, J. & Pawłowski, R. (2013). Whole genome amplification of degraded and nondegraded DNA for forensic purposes, *International Journal of Legal Medicine* **127**, 309–319.

[17] Egeland, T. & Salas, A. (2011). A statistical framework for the interpretation of mtDNA mixtures: forensic and medical applications, *PLoS One* http://journals.plos.org/plosone/article?id=10.1371/journal.pone.0026723

[18] Melton, T., Holland, C. & Holland, M. (2012). Forensic mitochondrial DNA analysis: current practice and future potential, *Forensic Science Review* **24**, 101–122.

[19] Børsting, C. & Morling, N. (2015). Next generation sequencing and its applications in forensic genetics, *Forensic Science International: Genetics* 10.1016/j.fsigen.2015.02.002 (In press at the time of writing, July 2015).

[20] Weber-Lehmann, J., Schilling, E., Gradl, G., Richter, D.C., Wiehler, J. & Rolf, B. (2014). Finding the needle in the haystack: Differentiating "identical" twins in paternity testing and forensics by ultra-deep next generation Sequencing, *Forensic Science International: Genetics* **9**, 42–46.

[21] Butler, J.M. (2007). Short tandem repeat typing technologies used in human identity testing, *BioTechniques* **43**, Sii–Sv. http://www.biotechniques.com/multimedia/archive/00003/BTN_A_000112582_O_3268a.pdf available at

[22] Jamieson, A. (2008). The philosophy of forensic scientific identification, *Hastings Law Journal* **59**(5), 1031–1046.

[23] SWGDAM (2015). Available at Guidelines for the Validation of Probabilistic Genotyping Systems. http://swgdam.org/SWGDAM%20Guidelines%20for%20the%20Validation%20of%20Probabilistic%20Genotyping%20Systems_APPROVED%2006152015.pdf

[24] Mitchell, A.A., Tamariz, J., O'Connell, K., Ducasse, N., Budimlija, Z., Prinz, M. & Caragine, T. (2012). Validation of a DNA mixture statistics tool incorporating allelic drop-out and drop-in, *Forensic Science International: Genetics* **6**(6), 749–761.

[25] Balding, D.J. (2013). Evaluation of mixed-source, low-template DNA profiles in forensic science, *PNAS* **110**(30), 12241–12246.

[26] Jamieson, A. (2008) Mixed results. The Guardian, 28 February 2008. Available at http://www.theguardian.com/commentisfree/2008/feb/28/ukcrime.forensicscience

[27] Butler, J.M. (2015). The future of forensic DNA analysis, *Philosophical Transactions of the Royal Society B: Biological Sciences* **370**, 20140252. available at http://dx.doi.org/10.1098/rstb.2014.0252

[28] Kayser, M. & Schneider, P.M. (2009). DNA-based prediction of human externally visible characteristics in forensics: motivations, scientific challenges, and ethical considerations, *Forensic Science International: Genetics* **3**, 154–161.

[29] Kayser, M. (2015). Forensic DNA Phenotyping: Predicting human appearance from crime scene material for investigative purposes, *Forensic Science International: Genetics* **18**, 33–48.

[30] Valenzuela, R.K., Henderson, M.S., Monica, H.W., Garrison, N.A., Kelch, J.T., Cohen-Barak, O.C., Erickson, D.T., Meaney, F.J., Walsh, J.B., Cheng, K.C., Ito, S., Wakamatsu, K., Frudakis, T., Thomas, M. & Brilliant, M.H. (2010). Predicting phenotype from genotype: normal pigmentation, *Journal of Forensic Science* **55**, 315–322.

[31] Walsh, S., Liu, F., Wollstein, A., Kovatsi, L., Ralf, A., Kosiniak-Kamysz, A., Branicki, W. & Kayser, M. (2013). The HIrisPlex system for simultaneous prediction of hair and eye colour from DNA, *Forensic Science International: Genetics* **7**, 98–115.

[32] Meakin, G. & Jamieson, A. (2013). DNA transfer: Review and implications for casework, *Forensic Science International: Genetics* **7**, 434–443.

[33] Elliott, K., Hill, D.S., Lambert, C., Burroughes, T.R. & Gill, P. (2003). Use of laser microdissection greatly improves the recovery of DNA from sperm on microscope slides, *Forensic Science International* **137**, 28–36.

Index

Printed and bound by CPI Group (UK) Ltd, Croydon, CR0 4YY

16/04/2025

14658389-0002